# CURRENT PSYCHOTHERAPIES

SEVENTH EDITION

**Editors**

*Raymond J. Corsini*
*Danny Wedding*

THOMSON
BROOKS/COLE

Australia • Canada • Mexico • Singapore • Spain
United Kingdom • United States

# THOMSON

## BROOKS/COLE

Executive Editor: Lisa Gebo
Senior Acquisitions Editor: Marquita Flemming
Assistant Editor: Shelley Gesicki
Editorial Assistant: Amy Lam
Technology Project Manager: Barry Connoly
Marketing Manager: Caroline Concilla
Marketing Assistant: Mary Ho
Advertising Project Manager: Tami Strang
Project Manager, Editorial Production:
   Katy German

Art Director: Vernon Boes
Print/Media Buyer: Doreen Suruki
Permissions Editor: Kiely Sexton
Compositor: G&S Book Services
Photo Researcher: Sue C. Howard
Copy Editor: Heather Forkos
Cover Designer: Jeanne Calabrese
Cover Image: Getty Images
Printer: Transcontinental

Printed in Canada
1 2 3 4 5 6 7 08 07 06 05 04

For more information about our products,
contact us at:
**Thomson Learning Academic Resource Center
1-800-423-0563**

For permission to use material from this text,
contact us by:
**Phone:** 1-800-730-2214   **Fax:** 1-800-730-2215
**Web:** http://www.thomsonrights.com

Library of Congress Control Number: 2003116138

SE: ISBN 0-534-63850-3

IE: ISBN 0-534-63856-2

**Brooks/Cole—Thomson Learning**
**10 Davis Drive**
**Belmont, CA 94002**
**USA**

**Asia**
Thomson Learning
5 Shenton Way #01-01
UIC Building
Singapore 068808

**Australia/New Zealand**
Thomson Learning
102 Dodds Street
Southbank, Victoria 3006
Australia

**Canada**
Nelson
1120 Birchmount Road
Toronto, Ontario M1K 5G4
Canada

**Europe/Middle East/Africa**
Thomson Learning
High Holborn House
50/51 Bedford Row
London WC1R 4LR
United Kingdom

**Latin America**
Thomson Learning
Seneca, 53
Colonia Polanco
11560 Mexico D.F.
Mexico

**Spain/Portugal**
Paraninfo
Calle Magallanes, 25
28015 Madrid, Spain

# CONTENTS

# CONTRIBUTORS

Jacob A. Arlow, MD
Clinical Professor of Psychiatry,
New York University College of Medicine,
New York, New York

Aaron T. Beck, MD
University Professor of Psychiatry,
University of Pennsylvania,
Philadelphia, Pennsylvania

Adam Blatner, MD
Retired Physician,
Formerly University of Louisville,
Louisville, Kentucky

Raymond J. Corsini, PhD
Affiliate, Graduate Faculty,
University of Hawaii, Honolulu, Hawaii

Claire Douglas, PhD
Private Practice, Malibu, California

Albert Ellis, PhD
President, Albert Ellis Institute,
New York, New York

Herbert Goldenberg, PhD
Emeritus Professor,
California State University,
Los Angeles, California

Irene Goldenberg, EdD
Professor of Psychiatry,
University of California–Los Angeles,
Los Angeles, California

Lynne Jacobs, PhD
Private Practice,
Pacific Gestalt Institute,
Los Angeles, California

Arnold A. Lazarus, PhD
Distinguished Professor Emeritus,
Graduate School of Applied
and Professional Psychology,
Rutgers University,
Piscataway, New Jersey

Alvin R. Mahrer, PhD
School of Psychology,
University of Ottawa, Ottawa, Canada

Rollo May, PhD
Deceased

Harold H. Mosak, PhD
Distinguished Service Professor
of Clinical Psychology,
Adler School of Professional Psychology,
Chicago, Illinois

Nathaniel J. Raskin, PhD
Emeritus Professor of Psychiatry
and Behavioral Sciences,
Northwestern University Medical School
Chicago, Illinois

Carl R. Rogers, PhD
Deceased

Danny Wedding, PhD, MPH
Director,
Missouri Institute of Mental Health,
St. Louis, Missouri

Marjorie Weishaar, PhD
Clinical Associate Professor
of Psychiatry and Human Behavior,
Brown University School of Medicine,
Providence, Rhode Island

G. Terence Wilson, PhD
Oscar K. Buros Professor of Psychology,
Rutgers University,
Piscataway, New Jersey

Irvin Yalom, MD
Emeritus Professor of Psychiatry
and Behavioral Sciences,
Stanford University School of Medicine,
Stanford, California

Gary Yontef, PhD
Private Practice,
Pacific Gestalt Institute,
Santa Monica, California

# ACKNOWLEDGMENTS

Every text is shaped and refined by the comments of those readers who have discussed its content and form. This book is no different, and we have benefited from the suggestions of literally hundreds of our students, colleagues, and friends. We have been particularly vigilant about getting feedback from those professors who use *Current Psychotherapies* as a text, and their comments help shape each new edition.

Kathryn Moon of the Chicago Counseling and Psychotherapy Center assisted Nathaniel Raskin in the revision of his chapter on Person-Centered Therapy. Professor Frank Dumont, McGill University, provided invaluable assistance in preparing this edition, and we are deeply grateful for his insight, advice, and multiple contributions.

The following individuals also helped plan the seventh edition, and we genuinely appreciate their contributions.

Marty Amerikaner
*Marshall University*

Martin Antony
*McMaster University*

Allan Barclay
*St. Louis University*

Larry Beutler
*Pacific Graduate School of Psychology*

Mary Ann Boyd
*Southern Illinois University–Edwardsville*

Vicki Eichhorn
*University of Missouri–Columbia*

Ken Freedland
*Washington University*

James Hennessy
*Fordham University*

Mary Johnson
*University of Missouri–Columbia*

Jessica Kohout
*American Psychological Association*

Joseph Labarbera
*Vanderbilt University*

Anthony Marsella
*University of Hawaii*

Mary Martini
*University of Hawaii*

Donald Meichenbaum
*University of Waterloo*

Jill Meyer
*University of Missouri–Columbia*

Richard Nelson-Jones
*Chiang Mai University, Thailand*

Kathryn Norsworthy
*Rollins College*

Chris Pearce
*University of Missouri–Columbia*

Kenneth Pope
*Private Practice, Los Angeles*

Sarah Prud'homme
*University of Ottawa*

Casey Reever
*American Psychological Association*

Michael Ross
*St. Louis University*

Sara Serot
*St. Louis*

Michael Stevens
*Illinois State University*

Sombat Tapanya
*Chiang Mai University, Thailand*

Diane Willis
*Oklahoma University*

Wang Xumei
*China Medical University*

# PREFACE

For this edition, chapters of the previous edition have been reviewed by the authors and a number of minor changes have been made to bring the book up to date. We also provide two new chapters.

## PSYCHODRAMA

I believe psychodrama belongs in every therapist's armamentarium because, after the interview, it is potentially the most important tool of the therapist. It can be used to great effect to complement any of the other systems in this book, or it can stand alone. Dr. Adam Blatner, the doyen of psychodrama, ably expounds the value of this system in both individual and group psychotherapy.

In 50 years of experience as a psychotherapist, there were many occasions when I felt trapped, unable to move, unsure of what to do—and psychodrama came to my rescue. Let me share a simple example. A wife confided in therapy that her husband had struck her for "no reason at all," and had rushed out of the house in anger. She was still angry because he had struck her. I suggested that we role-play the situation. She told me she wanted to use their car that day, but I (acting as her husband) told her that the car needed to be repaired and that I-he had promised to bring it to a shop that day. Our discussion heated up and progressed from a discussion to an argument. Eventually, my client got into the spirit of the psychodrama and started a series of attacks on my (her husband's) family and me (her husband), displaying violence that I would never have expected from her. Luckily, we got all of it on audiotape. I gave the tape to her, and the next week she said she could not believe what she had said to me. She stated that she had apologized to her husband and that he had forgiven her. She, in turn, had forgiven him for hitting her.

Consequently, I suggest that all psychotherapists consider psychodrama as a procedure they can use to enrich and expand their practice. I personally never had any formal training in this system, but eventually became the president of the American Society of Group Psychotherapy and Psychodrama, edited several books about psychodrama, and have taught this system to hundreds of other therapists. I believe any competent psychotherapist should be able to use psychodrama to good effect after reading this book and one or more of the other books Dr. Blatner recommends and getting some supervised experience.

## EXPERIENTIAL PSYCHOTHERAPY

The other new chapter in this book is called Experiential Psychotherapy. However, as Dr. Alvin Mahrer states, there are a number of systems, all different, that are referred to as "experiential psychotherapy." In the process of editing the *Handbook of Innovative Therapy,* in which some 70 systems are analyzed, I searched for the ideal system of psychotherapy. When I read Mahrer's contribution, I was amazed by the audacity of experiential psychotherapy, which in many ways turns the world upside down. For example, clients who participate in classical psychoanalysis lie down on a couch and the therapist listens and makes notes. Alfred Adler and his clients sat upright and faced each other, and most other therapists follow the same procedure. In psychodrama, people may interact with other clients or the therapist either standing up or sitting down. However, Mahrer's system is strikingly innovative in that the client and the therapist lie down on separate couches, next to each other, facing the same way. Both clients and therapists often have their eyes closed. They must be in a soundproof room, because both the client and the therapist can shout, scream, and do with their body whatever they wish. The goal of therapy is to reach a climactic moment of strong feeling leading to peace and understanding, with change expected in every session.

A version of experiential therapy was discussed in the first edition of this book in a chapter written by Dr. Eugene Gendlin. That version and this one have one thing in common: They are both difficult to understand. Dr. Wedding, Dr. Frank Dumont (our consultant), and I have wrestled with Mahrer's language to try to clearly explain this complex system to the reader. I believe it would be best for many readers to begin with the case example first in order to understand this unique system. To my knowledge no one has studied psychotherapy's origins in philosophy or science as well as Mahrer has. He has truly broken new ground.

I have always believed that the best psychotherapy method would be a treatment that achieved desired results quickly. A major flaw in many conventional therapies is their expectation that change requires lengthy treatment. One of the reasons I have always advocated psychodrama (when it is properly used) is that it simultaneously involves actions and words and—most importantly—strong emotions. However, Mahrer's experiential psychotherapy goes even further than psychodrama in achieving beneficial effects quickly.

All therapists should consider learning this approach. It is not just another method; in fact, I consider it as revolutionary as was Freud's 100 years ago and Carl Rogers's 50 years ago. Experiential psychotherapy is a revolutionary concept that must be tried to be appreciated.

*Raymond Corsini*

# 1 INTRODUCTION

*Raymond J. Corsini*

Psychotherapy cannot be defined with any precision. A definition might go as follows:

> Psychotherapy is a formal process of interaction between two parties, each party usually consisting of one person but with the possibility that there may be two or more people in each party, for the purpose of amelioration of distress in one of the two parties relative to any or all of the following areas of disability or malfunction: cognitive functions (disorders of thinking), affective functions (suffering or emotional discomforts), or behavioral functions (inadequacy of behavior), with the therapist having some theory of personality's origins, development, maintenance and change along with some method of treatment logically related to the theory and professional and legal approval to act as a therapist.

The definition may appear rather comprehensive. Nevertheless, some modes of therapy will not fit it.

Would the system of psychotherapy that Sigmund Freud underwent, about which Karen Horney (1942) wrote a book, and which Theodore Reik (1948) claimed to be the best of all therapies fit this definition? The system is *self-therapy*. In self-therapy there is only one party; there is no formality and no professional or legal approval, and yet it certainly is therapy.

If we examine various theories and procedures in psychotherapy, we find a bewildering set of ideas and behaviors. There have been systems of therapy that had no therapist (Schmidhoffer, 1952); systems in which the therapist says and does nothing (Bion, 1948); systems in which patients are asked to scream or to strike out (Bach & Goldberg, 1975; Janov, 1970); methods in which the therapist makes fun of the patient, treating him or her with apparent disrespect (Farrelly & Brasma, 1974), and methods that treat the patient or client with utmost respect (Losoncy, 1981); methods in which patients are treated as children (Painter & Vernon, 1981); methods that stress religion (Lair & Lair, 1973; van Kaam, 1976); and methods that are conglomerates of a wide variety of procedures (Gazda, 2001; Shostrom & Montgomery, 1978).

What one authority considers to be psychotherapy may be completely different from how other authorities see the process.

Counseling and psychotherapy are the same qualitatively; they differ only quantitatively. There is nothing that a psychotherapist does that a counselor does not do.

No definition can be made that will include all psychotherapies and exclude all counseling methods. Various attempts to separate the psychotherapies and exclude all counseling methods have failed. The concept that psychotherapy goes into depth, while counseling does not, is gainsaid by procedures such as behavior modification that operate at the level of symptom removal (Wolpe, 1958). Behavior modifiers could hardly be called counselors, because they do not counsel. Also, when we have a term such as *nondirective counseling,* we have a semantic absurdity.

## COUNSELING AND PSYCHOTHERAPY

The terms *counseling* and *psychotherapy* probably seem interchangeable to many people, but they tend to have different meanings for people in the helping professions. Generally, counseling is understood by helping professionals to be a relatively short process, often occurring in one session and rarely comprising more than five sessions, whereas psychotherapy usually runs for many sessions and can even continue for years. Counseling is usually seen as problem-oriented, while psychotherapy is person-oriented. The actual processes that occur in counseling and psychotherapy are identical, but they do differ relative to the time spent.

Essentially, counseling stresses the giving of information, advice, and orders by someone considered to be an expert in a particular area of human behavior, while psychotherapy is a process of helping people discover why they think, feel, and act in unsatisfactory ways. A counselor is primarily a teacher, while a psychotherapist is essentially a detective.

A simple example will help illustrate the difference between counseling and psychotherapy. Say that a married couple comes to a professional helper (a psychiatrist, psychologist, social worker, nurse practitioner, etc.) for help in their marriage. The helper puts on her counseling hat, listens as they tell their stories, asks questions, and finally gives information, advice, and "orders" (that is to say, she may insist that the couple must follow her suggestions if they are to achieve their goals). After all, if they came to her for counseling, they must be prepared to make suggested changes.

Let us assume the counselor gives the couple the following information: Many marriages are unhappy because of little things, but if a couple can communicate their dissatisfactions to each other and agree by means of a mutual contract to change their behavior, the marriage may change from being unhappy to happy. She then advises them to establish a new contract within their marriage. Let us assume the couple agrees to establish a mutual contract. The husband states that he wants his wife to stop smoking, and the wife wants her husband to put away his clothes and belongings rather than scattering them all over the house (two common complaints in marriages).

Consequently, the helper, working as a counselor, helps the couple establish a contract relative to the wife's smoking and the husband's sloppiness in the house.

Now, let us assume that both partners live up to their agreements and that thereby marital harmony is established. The counseling has been successful.

Now let us assume a different scenario. The couple returns to report that they are still unhappy. The wife has stopped smoking, but the husband is still leaving his possessions all over the house. As the result of further discussions, the helper suggests that the husband may need psychotherapy to try to discover why, even though he has agreed to stop this behavior, he continues it. Say that the husband accepts the suggestion and decides to have psychotherapy.

The professional now puts on her psychotherapy hat. From now on, she no longer views herself as an expert on marriage who can give information, advice, and orders but instead sees herself as a facilitator, helping the husband to understand himself in general, and specifically to find out why he was not able to keep to his agreement to be neat in the house.

The helper may give no information, advice, or orders, but may act in any of a variety of unusual ways. For example, if she is a follower of Carl Rogers she will not ask or answer questions, and she will be unwilling to give advice or suggestions. In this book we discuss a dozen ways of thinking and acting in therapy. The helper may have her own eclectic theory, and her methods of operating may be quite diverse.

Let us say that the therapy is successful, that the reason for the husband's resistance is uncovered, and that a favorable change in his behavior then occurs and the marriage is happy.

Successful therapy may result regardless of theory and the method used. But what is important to recognize here is that in acting as a psychotherapist the helper did not presume to be an expert on marriage but rather served as a kind of detective relative to the husband's inability or unwillingness to conform to his own agreement. The helper as the therapist was a partner or collaborator with the husband to achieve a new state of being. Consequently, counselors are generally people who have considerable knowledge and expertise in specific areas of behavior. There are marriage and family counselors, educational and vocational counselors, counselors for people who abuse substances such as alcohol, and counselors for people who are handicapped in particular ways or have special problems such as chronic or contagious illnesses. Counselors depend on their specialized knowledge and their common sense. On the other hand, psychotherapists are generalists who tend to hold any of a variety of unusual theories or combinations of theories and who may use one or more procedures to try to achieve desired results.

## PATIENT OR CLIENT

In the first four editions of this book, in the Adlerian chapter, Dr. Harold Mosak used the term *patient;* in the fifth edition he changed this term to *client.* Some of our authors use one or the other of the two terms, and some use both.

Psychotherapists who come out of a medical orientation tend to see those they work with as patients, while those who come from other orientations tend to see them as clients. So, it is possible for two therapists to see the same person at the same time in multiple therapy, with one viewing that person as a patient and the other therapist seeing that same person as a client.

Neither term is really satisfactory. *Patient* implies illness, and *client* implies a business relationship. Someday, someone may coin a term that more exactly describes the role of the person who is undergoing psychotherapy. Meanwhile, in this book, each author uses whatever term he or she feels most comfortable with.

All modes of trying to help people improve themselves via symbolic methods can be called *psychotherapy,* just as all methods to help improve psychological functioning through medications, surgery, electric shock, and other somatic procedures may be called *psychiatry.* Consequently, the interview, role-playing, projective techniques, and the like that we shall take up in this book can be considered procedures in counseling or psychotherapy, but it is best, in my judgment, to call them all processes of psychotherapy. Therefore, when Carl Rogers repeats what you have said, using his own terminology (as he did with me when I was in therapy with him), *this is psychotherapy;* when Rudolph Dreikurs, an Adlerian, points out basic life-style errors (as he did for me when I was in therapy with him), *this is psychotherapy;* when Albert Ellis contradicts your point of view (as he often has with me), *this is psychotherapy;* and when J. L. Moreno has people play different roles in front of a group (as I did when working with him) then *this is psychotherapy.*

A number of years ago, in Paris, I met with a French colleague, Dr. Anne Schutzenberger, and during the course of our conversation I mentioned psychotherapy. "Ah," she said, *"Psychothérapie comme ça—ou comme ça?"* (Psychotherapy like this—or like this?) At the first *ça* she put the palms of her hands about an inch apart, and at the second *ça* she moved her hands out as far as she could, with the palms still facing each other. She was asking me whether I had a narrow conception of psychotherapy or a wide one. We can do the same thing with the hands vertically and ask about the depth of psychotherapy. Essentially, depth is a function of time spent in therapy rather than a matter of technique, and two people with the same theory and technique will vary with respect to depth, depending primarily on the time spent with the client. (I call the subjects of psychotherapy *clients* if I see them in a private office and *patients* if they are in a hospital or institution.)

## AN UNUSUAL EXAMPLE OF PSYCHOTHERAPY

About 50 years ago, when I was working as a psychologist at Auburn Prison in New York, I participated in what I believe was the most successful and elegant psychotherapy I have ever done. One day an inmate, who had made an appointment, came into my office. He was a fairly attractive man in his early 30s. I pointed to a chair, he sat down, and I waited to find out what he wanted. The conversation went something like this (P = Prisoner; C = Corsini):

P: I am leaving on parole Thursday.
C: Yes?
P: I did not want to leave until I thanked you for what you had done for me.
C: What was that?
P: When I left your office about two years ago, I felt like I was walking on air. When I went into the prison yard, everything looked different, even the air smelled different. I was a new person. Instead of going over to the group I usually hung out with—they were a bunch of thieves—I went over to another group of square Johns [prison jargon for noncriminal types]. I changed from a cushy job in the kitchen to the machine shop, where I could learn a trade. I started going to the prison high school and I now have a high school diploma. I took a correspondence course in drafting and I have a drafting job when I leave Thursday. I started back to church even though I had given up my religion many years ago. I started writing to my family and they have come up to see me and they remember you in their prayers. I now have hope. I know who and what I am. I know I will succeed in life. I plan to go to college. You have freed me. I used to think you bug doctors [prison slang for psychologists and psychiatrists] were for the birds, but now I know better. Thanks for changing my life.

I listened to this tale in wonderment, because to the best of my knowledge I had never spoken with him. I looked at his folder and the only notation there was that I had given him an IQ test about two years before.

"Are you sure it was me?" I finally said. "I am not a psychotherapist, and I have no memory of ever having spoken to you. What you are reporting is the sort of personality and behavior change that takes many years to accomplish—and I certainly haven't done anything of the kind."

"It was you, all right," he replied with great conviction, "and I will never forget what you said to me. It changed my life."

"What was that?" I asked.

"You told me I had a high IQ," he replied.

With one sentence of five words I had (inadvertently) changed this person's life.

Let us try to understand this event. If you are clever enough to understand why this man changed so drastically as a result of hearing these five words "You have a high IQ," my guess is that you have the capacity to be a good therapist.

I asked him why this sentence about his IQ had such a profound effect, and I learned that up to the time that he heard these five words he had always thought of himself as "stupid" and "crazy"—terms that had been applied to him many times by his family, teachers, and friends. In school, he had always gotten poor grades, which confirmed his belief in his mental subnormality. His friends did not approve of the way he thought and called him crazy. And so he was convinced that he was both an ament (low intelligence) and a dement (insane). But when I said, "You have a high IQ," he had an "aha!" experience that explained everything. In a flash, he understood why he could solve crossword puzzles better than any of his friends. He now knew why he read long novels rather than comic books, why he preferred to play chess rather than checkers, why he liked symphonies rather than jazz. With great and sudden intensity he realized through my five words that he was really normal and bright and not crazy or stupid. He had experienced an *abreaction* that ordinarily would take months. No wonder he had felt as if he were walking on air when he left my office two years before!

His interpretation of my five words generated a complete change of self-concept—and consequently a change in both his behavior and his feelings about himself and others.

In short, I had performed psychotherapy in a completely innocent and informal way. Even though what happened in no way accords to the definition given earlier, even though there was no agreement between us, no theory, no intention of changing him—the five-word comment had a most pronounced effect, and so it *was* psychotherapy.

Conversely, I have had two clients who, after more than 10 years of psychotherapy, made little progress as far as I could tell.

## COMPARISONS OF THEORIES

Karl Popper (1968), the philosopher of science who wrote *Conjectures and Refutations,* makes the astute observation that Marxists, Freudians, and Adlerians are all able to find evidence of the validity of their theories in any aspect of human behavior. In *Conjectures and Refutations* he states:

> During the summer of 1919 . . . I began to feel more and more dissatisfied with these theories . . . and I began to feel dubious about their claim to scientific status. . . . Why are they so different from Newton's theory and especially from the theory of relativity? . . . It was not my doubting the truth of these theories which bothered me . . . what worried me was . . . that these . . . theories, though posing as sciences, had in fact more in common with primitive myths than with science: that they resembled astrology more than astronomy. (p. 34)

Popper goes on to say that he at the time had no reason to believe that Einstein's theory was correct, but Eddington's observation that light did not travel in a straight line but was bent by the sun due to gravitational attraction gave proof of the incorrectness of previous theories (such as Newton's) and so established Einstein's theory as superior to Newton's theory. Popper concluded: (1) it is easy to find confirmation of the validity of theories, (2) confirmation should only be considered if it results from a risky prediction, (3) the more a theory "forbids," the better it is, (4) a theory that is not possibly refutable is a poor theory, (5) genuine tests of theories are attempts to refute them, and (6) the only good evidence is negative evidence—in other words, an unsuccessful attempt to refute a particular theory.

Unfortunately, if we accept Popper's contention that the scientific status of any theory rests on its potential for falsification, no theory of psychotherapy qualifies as scientific.

## MODES OF PSYCHOTHERAPY

All psychotherapies are methods of learning. All psychotherapies are intended to change people: to make them think differently (cognition), to make them feel differently (affection), and to make them act differently (behavior). Psychotherapy is learning: it may be learning something new or relearning something one has forgotten; it may be learning how to learn or it may be unlearning; paradoxically, it may even be learning what one already knows.

### Cognition

There are two general ways we learn: directly by experience, or indirectly by symbols.

To give a simple example: A child about three years old sees the toast shooting up from a toaster and goes to touch the shiny gadget. The child has no idea that the toaster is hot. Now, how can the child learn that a toaster can be hot and can hurt? One way would be for the child to touch the toaster, thus learning by direct experience. Another way is by symbols (words), by being told: "When we use the toaster, it gets hot, and if you touch it you will be burned."

In both cases, the child learns—in one case, actively (through experience) and in another case, passively (through information).

Some therapists tend to use "active" methods, and their clients essentially learn on their own, while some therapists tend to make their clients passive learners. Two strongly contrasting learning styles are represented by the methodologies of Carl Rogers and Albert Ellis. In psychoanalysis, both modes occur. For example, while free associating, the patient may be said to be learning actively. Let us show this by a hypothetical example:

> Patient: "And I really think my mother liked my brother more than she liked me. I can't understand why. I tried so hard to win her affection, but somehow I never was able to make her really like me. But recently when I spoke about this with my brother, he told me he always thought that I was Mother's favorite. How could this be? Could I have misinterpreted my mother? He thought I was the favorite and I thought he was. Who was? Maybe no one? Maybe Mamma liked us both equally, or as equally as possible. How did we come to have opposite conclusions? I think we are just both pessimists, that's what it is! I am sure of it, both of us misinterpreted Mother."

This is an example of someone talking to himself, conducting a self-analysis, engaged in active learning.

An example of passive learning follows:

> Client:   I had the funniest dream. I was being chased by a rooster, and I was running for my life, and I knew if I got to Lokonner Bay that I would be safe.

Therapist:    How do you spell that?

C:   I don't know. It is pronounced LOKONNER BAY.

T:   And you don't know any such place?

C:   No.

T:   Can you figure out what Lokonner means?

C:   I have been thinking all day about it. It makes no sense to me.

T:   Should I tell you what I think it means?

C:   Please. I have absolutely no idea.

T:   Well, dreams are all symbols. The rooster that is chasing you is a symbol of the male sexual organ, so you are running away from sex. But you believe you will be safe if you can get to Lokonner Bay.

C:   But what does Lokonner Bay mean? I have never heard of such a place.

T:   Lokonner is probably a contraction for "Love, honor, and obey." What you are saying in your dream is this: Some man is pressuring you to have sex and you want him to marry you. You are afraid to have sex, but if you can get him to marry you (love, honor, and obey), you will be safe.

The examples illustrate two general ways of learning in psychotherapy: actively through self-analysis and passively through being helped to understand the meaning of a dream.

## Behavior

Learning can also occur through action. For example, during World War I, Ernst Simmel was a German army psychiatrist, concerned with curing German soldiers who were suffering from what was then called shell shock (Simmel, 1949). Believing that their condition was caused by repressed hatred of their officers, he gave these men bayoneted rifles and had them attack straw-filled dummies dressed as German officers.

The modality of treatment was physical action, what Eugene Landy (1994) calls disjunctive therapy. Plain physical exercise is believed to be psychotherapeutic by some people. Action is used in a number of psychotherapies.

One argument for body therapies is the assertion that there is no mind. If we can affect the body, that is all that is needed: the body learns, the body is real, all else is an illusion. A contrary argument for body therapies is that the mind does exist, that conditions of the body affect the mind, and that if we work from the outside in, by changing the body we can change the mind. An example might be plastic surgery. Changing someone's looks can affect how that person views himself or herself.

Other examples of physical behavior as psychotherapy would include complex physical activities, such as role-playing, or doing therapeutic "homework," that is, doing under direction things one would not ordinarily do, such as asking for a date or looking for a job. As in the case of cognitive therapies, behavioral work in therapy can range from active to passive. In examining the various systems in this book, the reader may want to consider how much physical behavior is called for in the particular therapy.

## Affection

A third modality in psychotherapy is affection, known more popularly as emotions or feelings. The therapist may believe that this modality will be most effective with a particular client or patient, and so will do things to stir up the person: to raise the individual's emotional state through attempts to make him or her fearful, anxious, angry, hopeful, and so on. We cannot really work directly with the emotions and must reach them indirectly through the intellect or the body.

Emotions are an important part of human psychology. However, we cannot manipulate emotions in the sense that we can manipulate thinking or behaving. Some systems of psychotherapy are intended to reduce or negate emotions, seeing them as hindering the therapeutic process. Adlerian psychotherapy, for example, is essentially a cognitive therapy, and Adlerians usually see emotions as sabotaging efforts in the therapeutic process. However, in psychodrama, for example, both the words that the therapist will employ and the behavior directed by the other actors are intended to generate strong emotions.

Some people see emotions as epiphenomena accompanying but not affecting therapeutic change, others see emotions as powerful agents leading to change, and still others see emotions as evidence of change. The whole issue of the relationship of emotions to psychotherapy is unsettled. The reader would do well to attempt to see the place of emotions in the various systems described.

All therapies are essentially combinations of all three of these modalities. While some are rather pure in that they attempt to deal only with the body, the intellect, or the emotions, elements of each apply in most cases. Thus, for example, in rational emotive behavior therapy, even though rational thinking is utilized for the most part in dealing with the patient, the therapist may give the client direct orders to do certain things (homework). In cognitive therapy, emotionally upsetting situations will develop.

A therapist may think that improvement is a function of one element, but the curative process may actually be something else. It may not be a message that generates a change, but rather the interpretation that the client gives to it. Were exactly the same treatment to be done by a robot, it might not have any beneficial psychological effect. Change may well result from the interpretation, "Someone cares for me enough to do this to me."

One final common pathway for all therapies is a new way of seeing life, a reevaluation of self and others. If so, then all therapies are essentially cognitive. Still another way of considering psychotherapy is to see it as a process of "selling"—of trying to help a person to accept a new view of self and of others. From this point of view, the psychotherapist is a persuader or a facilitator attempting to change opinions.

A clear-cut example of persuasion would be attempting to do psychotherapy with someone with a fixed paranoid delusion. A more common example is dealing with a person with incapacitating feelings of inferiority by trying "to sell him" on the notion that he is really OK. Another common example would be dealing with someone with mistaken ideas about marriage or parenting. In all these cases, the therapist is, in a real sense, a salesperson attempting to sell new ideas, new concepts, and new behaviors.

## MECHANISMS OF PSYCHOTHERAPY

One of the most exciting meetings I ever attended included a major presentation by Carl Rogers on the necessary and sufficient conditions for psychotherapy. It was a most logical and impressive speech and it deeply affected me. However, the next speaker was Albert Ellis, who had been asked to comment on Rogers's paper. Ellis stated that in 25 years of clinical experience he had had many successful cases, but none of Rogers's criteria seemed to him to be either necessary or sufficient.

There was not then and there is not now any consensus about what constitutes the basis for change in psychotherapy. Each contributor to this volume uses a section titled *Mechanisms of Psychotherapy* to discuss what makes psychotherapy work. However, I have my own ideas that I would like to share with readers at this point.

Some 50 years ago, with a psychiatrist colleague, Dr. Bina Rosenberg, I searched through more than 300 articles to identify the critical elements necessary for changing people (Corsini & Rosenberg, 1955). We found 220 statements such as "People change when they think that others believe in them" and "The realization that they are not alone makes the difference." We eliminated redundant items, performed a "clinical factor analysis," and identified nine factors.

## Cognitive Factors

*Universalization.* Clients improve when they realize that they are not alone, that others have similar problems, and that human suffering is universal.

*Insight.* Growth occurs as clients increasingly come to understand themselves and others and gain different perspectives on their own motives and behaviors.

*Modeling.* People benefit from watching other people. A client may model himself or herself on the therapist.

## Affective Factors

*Acceptance.* This factor reflects the sense of getting unconditional positive regard, especially from the therapist.

*Altruism.* Change can result from the recognition that one is the recipient of the love and care of the therapist or other members of the group or from being the one who provides love and care to others as well as feeling he or she is helping others.

*Transference.* This factor identifies the emotional bond that occurs between the therapist and the client or between clients in a group setting.

## Behavioral Factors

*Reality testing.* Change becomes possible when clients experiment with new behaviors in the safety of the therapy hour, receiving support and feedback from the therapist and other group members.

*Ventilation.* This factor encompasses those statements attesting to the value of "blowing off steam" through shouting, crying, or displaying anger in a context in which one can still feel accepted.

*Interaction.* Clients improve when they are able to openly admit to the group that there is something wrong with themselves or their behavior.

I believe these nine factors encapsulate the basic mechanisms of therapeutic change. Close examination of this model reveals that the cognitive factors imply "Know yourself," the affective factors tell us "Love your neighbor," and the behavioral factors essentially suggest "Do good works." Perhaps there is nothing new under the sun, for this is what philosophers have told us for millennia: Know thyself, love thy neighbor, and do good works.

# THE CURRENT SITUATION IN PSYCHOTHERAPY

Corsini (2001) listed 250 different systems of psychotherapy, but currently there are probably more than 400 such systems. Just as there are some religions that are well known and well accepted, so too, some psychotherapies are well known and well accepted. And just as there are religions viewed as unorthodox and absurd, there are systems of psychotherapy that exist on the fringe of traditional approaches.

I was originally trained as a Rogerian therapist (which I believe is probably the best way for a would-be therapist to start training—and for some people, the best way to remain). After 10 years' experience with this mode of therapy, I applied for a job at a prestigious institute, and while being interviewed I was asked how I dealt with the problem of transference. I think I could not have shocked my learned colleagues more had I slapped them on the face when I replied, "To the best of my knowledge, none of my clients ever formed a transference relationship with me." They held their mouths open, staring first at me and then at each other, unable to believe what they had heard me say. For this particular group, transference was a necessary factor in psychotherapy, and for someone who claimed to be a psychotherapist to deny transference was unthinkable.

In psychotherapy, ideological enclaves are found. Some enclaves consist of people who believe that they have the right, the final, the complete, and the only answer—and that all other systems are incomplete, tentative, weak, or simply mistaken.

People within these enclaves (known as schools of therapy) tend to communicate mostly with others they meet at conventions. They read each other's writings, and they tend over time to develop specialized vocabularies. They reinforce one another by recounting their successes with the former clients of therapists of different persuasions, "proving" to one another the superiority of their way of thinking and acting. As time goes on, within any particular method of psychotherapy, alternative positions tend to develop, schismatic groups begin to form, and then these groups are either expelled from the original enclave or take off on their own. This has happened many times in the case of people originally trained as Freudian psychoanalysts.

I believe this situation is changing and these ideological boundaries are becoming more permeable. Garfield and Bergin state: "A decisive shift in opinion has quietly occurred; and it has created an irreversible change in professional attitudes about psychotherapy and behavior change. The new view is that the long-term dominance of the major theories is over and that an eclectic position has taken precedence" (1994, p. 7).

I would go even further and state that all good therapists are eclectic. This does not mean that they do not follow a particular theory or use specific methods associated with particular approaches to therapy; it does mean that technique and method are always secondary to the clinician's sense of what is the right thing to do with a given client at a given moment in time, irrespective of theory. Put more simply, psychotherapy remains an art. So if formal eclecticism is on the rise, this is all to the good: It shows the maturing of psychotherapy.

Why then, a book such as this? In order to be effectively eclectic, one needs to know as many different theories and systems as possible, from which one can develop a personal theory, a personal system, and an integrated approach. Initially, the neophyte therapist is best served by operating as strictly as possible within the limits of a given system, with close supervision by a skilled practitioner of that system. Later, with experience, one can begin to develop one's own individual style of therapy.

## The Whohowwhom Factor

I have come to believe that what counts in psychotherapy is who does it and how and to whom it is done: the *whohowwhom* factor. This belief developed from my experiences in a small group practice in which all the therapists had the same basic theoretical and operational concepts. We consulted on each other's cases, worked together in cotherapy, met weekly to discuss cases we were handling, and came to know each other quite well over the six-year period that I was with this group of Adlerians. However, although we all shared the same theoretical position and generally operated in the same manner, any new clients who came to our clinic were likely to get different kinds of therapy due to the *whohowwhom* factor. One therapist liked to tell stories to make various points. Another liked to ask Socratic questions. Still another would frequently interrupt to demonstrate errors in the client's thinking and behavior. One played the role of the loving father, while another was quite sarcastic. Some were friendly, while others were distant. Some saw clients as equals, while others saw clients as students who needed to be taught more effective ways to operate. So even in this particular group with a shared theory and methodology, there were wide variations in therapy practice and style. The senior therapist, who had trained the others, was in a good position to decide which new client was to go to which therapist. For example, he tended to assign me difficult adult clients but no adolescents.

Sometimes the *how* variable will be of less importance than the match between *who* and *whom,* because differences in actual technique may be relatively small for some systems. However, at times an apparently circumscribed method, such as the person-centered approach, may achieve superior results for some people when other more complex methods will fail. I am reminded of the fable of the cat and the fox. The fox bragged about how he had so many ways of escaping from dogs. The cat had only one: to climb a tree. Both the cat and the fox were chased by dogs. The cat went up the tree and remained there until the dogs went away. The fox used all his tricks but eventually was caught. So too, sometimes something simple is superior to something complex, and even in psychotherapy, less can be more.

## Research

Many people in the recent history of psychotherapy have wondered about the effectiveness of counseling and psychotherapy. At one time, Dr. Wedding wanted to include a section in every chapter of this book examining relevant research findings for each system, but practically every contributor was against the idea. Nonetheless, the sentiment expressed by Strupp and Bergin (1969, p. 20) is very much on people's minds:

> The problem of psychotherapy research in its most general terms should be reformulated as a standard scientific question: What specific therapeutic interventions produce specific changes in specific patients under specific conditions?

Perhaps the best and most complete answer to the issue of such research was given by C. H. Patterson (1987, p. 247):

> Before this model (relative to research) could be implemented we would need (1) a taxonomy of client problems or psychological disorders . . . ; (2) a taxonomy of client personalities; (3) a taxonomy of therapeutic techniques . . . ; (4) a taxonomy of therapists; and (5) a taxonomy of circumstances. . . . If we did have such systems of classification, the practical problems would be insurmountable. Assuming five classes of variables, each with ten classifications, . . . a research design would require $10 \times 10 \times 10 \times 10 \times 10$ or 100,000 cells. . . . So, I conclude we don't need complex multivariate analyses and should abandon any attempt to do the crucial, perfect study of psychotherapy. It simply is not possible.

It is difficult for me or anyone else brought up with nomothetic approaches, imbued with Edward Lee Thorndike's concept that anything that exists can be measured, to accept this pessimistic point of view, but I contend that Patterson, who has studied this issue intensively and written widely on the problems of research in counseling and psychotherapy, is essentially correct.

Psychotherapy is an art based on science, and as is true for any art, there can be no simple measures of so complex an activity.

# CORRECTION OF A HISTORICAL ERROR

In many historical accounts found in textbooks, an essentially incorrect view of the early years of psychotherapy is recounted. The story given generally goes as follows: In the beginning Sigmund Freud started a brand new system of psychotherapy called psychoanalysis. A number of other people learned about it and became his students. In later years, for a variety of reasons, they decided to separate from him and went on to start their own systems of thought.

In reality, numerous people preceded Freud, doing psychotherapy in a variety of ways. We may start with the Swiss physician Paul Dubois (1848–1918), one of the first psychotherapists in the modern sense of the term, because his method of treating psychotics was to talk with them in a reasonable manner. Still another person to be considered is Pierre Janet (1859–1947), referred to by Ellenberger as "the first person to found a new system of dynamic psychiatry aimed at replacing those of the nineteenth century" (1970, p. 331). Janet, at about the time that Sigmund Freud began his work, was the best-known and most respected psychotherapist of his time.

There was a great deal of interest and activity in psychotherapy prior to Freud, and there were already the conflicts, schisms, claims, and jealousies that were also to be found later. The whole history of psychotherapy is replete with personality clashes and other signs of struggles for superiority.

In 1902, Sigmund Freud invited several colleagues to meet with him to discuss personality theory. The group was later to be called the Wednesday Psychological Society. Some of the members were independent thinkers, each with his own position; Freud, the oldest, the best known, and the most published, was the host. It is important to understand that some members of this group were *psycho-analysts* and not *psychoanalysts.* Hyphenated, this word meant that these people were interested in the analysis of the psyche; spelled as one word it meant that they were followers of Sigmund Freud.

Three members of this Wednesday night group are the subjects of the next three chapters: Sigmund Freud, Alfred Adler, and Carl Jung. From the beginning, these three moved in quite different directions. Freud was a mechanistic, deterministic thinker who developed a system of psychology with essentially biological/hydraulic elements: a system of stresses and strains, conflicts and tensions, with a dynamic interaction between biological instinctive drives and social demands. Adler was essentially a common-sense thinker with a shrewd understanding of people's motivations. Jung was an internalized person, mystical, religious, creative.

Freud was the ideal German scientist, a keen student of minutiae, a pedant; Adler was a man of the people, socially oriented and concerned; Jung was an introverted, distant but friendly person. Their theories of personality and their psychotherapeutic systems can be seen as direct extensions of their manifest personalities.

Since the deaths of Freud in 1939, Adler in 1937, and Jung in 1961, the theories of the latter two have remained more or less constant. On the other hand, the theory of Freud has divided into a number of different approaches, some quite different from Freud's original thinking. There are now a variety of psychoanalytic groups with varying orientations. To make a religious analogy, psychoanalysis may be likened to Christianity; in both, various groups use the same ultimate authority (in one case, the Bible; in the other, Freud's papers) but have different interpretations of these basic writings.

During the period from 1910 to about 1939, these big three dominated psychotherapy in Europe and the United States. However, a number of other points of view existed at that time, most of which have either disappeared or have been incorporated into eclectic thinking, including the theories of such people as Pierre Janet, Jules Déjèrine, Trigant Burrow, Alfred Korzybski, Otto Rank, and Wilhelm Reich. However, a number of theories and methodologies considered to be deviations from pure Freudian psychoanalysis, such as the therapies of Harry Stack Sullivan, Karen Horney, and Theodore Reik, are still very much alive.

Since 1940, when Carl Rogers gave his historic Psi Chi paper in Minnesota, a considerable number of alternative systems of psychotherapy have begun. It is difficult to establish the dates of their beginnings because there is generally a considerable lapse of time between when a system starts and when publications about it first appear. But it might not be too far off to say that from about 1900 to 1939 there were three major points of view and about a dozen minor ones in psychotherapy and that during the next 60 years there were a dozen major points of view (including the original three) and perhaps two dozen others of consequence.

This situation leads to the speculation that as time goes on there may continue to be an expanding universe of major and minor systems of psychotherapy. If psychotherapy is essentially a matter of philosophy, then ultimately there will be multiple systems; if it is essentially a matter of science, then ultimately there will be one eclectic system.

## PSYCHOTHERAPY AND PSYCHOTHERAPIST

There appears to be a concordance between the personality of a psychotherapy innovator and the system he or she has developed. In an article titled "Freud, Rogers and Moreno" (Corsini, 1956), I made a comparison between the manifest personalities of these three men and their systems of psychotherapy. I never met Freud, but there is a good deal of biographical information about him, and there seems to be no question that his personality and his method of psychoanalysis were congruent. Freud was a rather shy person, uncomfortable with people, a pedantic, bookish type, an intellectual. His methodology—having people lie down, with him sitting behind them and out of sight while he listened intently to what they said—fits exactly his manifest personality. The system and the man seem identical.

I got to know Carl Rogers quite well. As a graduate student at the University of Chicago (1953–55), I was in contact with him both as a client and as a student. In later years I met him on many occasions socially and at professional meetings. Rogers, whether in his social life, as a teacher, or as a therapist, was exactly the same. He and his system were identical.

I also got to know J. L. Moreno, the founder of psychodrama, quite well. I listened to him lecture many times, I was often on the psychodrama stage with him, and we had a social relationship. There was no question at all about the congruence of Moreno's unique personality and his methodology. Again, the system and the man were identical.

What is the implication of these similarities for the reader? I believe that if one is to go into the fields of counseling and psychotherapy, then the best theory and methodology to use must be one's own. The reader will not be either successful or happy using a method not suited to his or her own personality. The really successful therapist adopts or develops a theory and methodology congruent with his or her own personality. (See Corsini, 1991, and Dumont & Corsini, 2000, for examples.)

In reading these accounts, in addition to attempting to determine which school of psychotherapy seems most sensible, the reader should also attempt to find one that fits his or her philosophy of life, one that seems most right in terms of its theory, and one with a method of operation that appears most appealing in use.

A final value of this book lies in the greater self-understanding that may be gained by close reading. This book about psychotherapies may be psychotherapeutic for the reader. Close reading vertically (chapter by chapter) and then horizontally (section by section) may well lead to personal growth as well as better understanding of current psychotherapies.

# REFERENCES

Bach, G. R., & Goldberg, H. (1975). *Creative aggression.* Garden City, NY: Doubleday.

Bion, J. (Ed.). (1948). *Therapeutic social clubs.* London: Lewis.

Corsini, R. J. (1956). Freud, Rogers and Moreno. *Group Psychotherapy, 9,* 274–281.

Corsini, R. J. (1968). Counseling and psychotherapy. In E. F. Borgotta & W. W. Lambert (Eds.), *Handbook of personality theory and research.* Chicago: Rand McNally.

Corsini, R. J. (1991). *Five therapists and one client.* Itasca, IL: F. E. Peacock.

Corsini, R. J. (Ed.). (2001). *Handbook of innovative therapy* (2nd ed.). New York: Wiley.

Corsini, R. J., & Rosenberg, B. (1955). Mechanisms of group psychotherapy. *Journal of Abnormal and Social Psychology, 51,* 406–411.

Dumont, F., & Corsini, R. J. (2000). *Six therapists and one client.* New York: Springer.

Ellenberger, H. (1970). *The discovery of the unconscious.* New York: Basic Books.

Farrelly, F., & Brasma, J. (1974). *Provocative therapy.* Cupertino, CA: Meta.

Garfield, S. L., & Bergin, A. E. (1994). Introduction and historical overview. In A. E. Bergin & S. L. Garfield, *Handbook of psychotherapy and behavior change.* New York: Wiley.

Gazda, G. M. (2001). Life skills training. In R. J. Corsini (Ed.), *Handbook of innovative therapy* (pp. 354–359). New York: Wiley.

Horney, K. (1942). *Self-analysis.* New York: Norton.

Janov, A. (1970). *The primal scream.* New York: Vintage Books.

Lair, J., & Lair, J. C. (1973). *Hey, God, what should I do now?* New York: Doubleday.

Landy, E. E. (1994). Disjunctive therapies. In R. J. Corsini, *Encyclopedia of psychology* (2nd ed, pp. 426–429). New York: Wiley.

Losoncy, L. (1981). *Encouragement therapy.* Englewood Cliffs, NJ: Prentice-Hall.

Painter, G., & Vernon, S. (1981). Primary relationship therapy. In R. J. Corsini (Ed.), *Handbook of innovative psychotherapies.* New York: Wiley.

Patterson, C. H. (1987). Comments. *Person-Centered Review, 1,* 246–248.

Popper, K. R. (1968). *Conjectures and refutations.* Oxford: Oxford University Press.

Reik, T. (1948). *Listening with the third ear.* New York: Farrar and Strauss.

Schmidhoffer, E. (1952). Mechanical group therapy. *Science, 115,* 120–123.

Shostrom, E. L., & Montgomery, D. (1978). *Healing love.* Nashville: Abington.

Simmel, E. (1949). War neuroses. In S. Lorand (Ed.), *Psychoanalysis today* (pp. 227–248). New York: International Universities Press.

Strupp, H. H., & Bergin, A. E. (1969). Some empirical and conceptual bases for coordinated research in psychotherapy. *International Journal of Psychiatry, 1,* 18–90.

van Kaam, A. (1976). *The dynamics of spiritual self-direction.* Denville, NY: Dimension Books.

Wolpe, J. (1958). *Psychotherapy by reciprocal inhibition.* Stanford, CA: Stanford University Press.

Sigmund Freud, 1856–1939

# 2    PSYCHOANALYSIS

*Jacob A. Arlow*

## OVERVIEW

*Psychoanalysis* is a system of psychology derived from the discoveries of Sigmund Freud. Originally used for treating hysteria, psychoanalysis is now used to treat many other psychological difficulties, and it is the foundation for a general theory of psychology. Knowledge derived from the treatment of individual patients has led to insights into art, religion, social organization, child development, and education. In addition, by elucidating the influence of unconscious forces on the physiology of the body, psychoanalysis has made it possible to understand and treat many psychosomatic illnesses.

### Basic Concepts

There are many different theories of pathogenesis and psychotherapy from the psychoanalytic point of view, yet most psychoanalysts subscribe to several basic concepts. These may be summarized under the headings of determinism, dynamics, topography, and genetics. *Determinism* encompasses the idea that psychological events are causally related to each other and to the individual's past. In short, the elements that occur in consciousness are not random and unrelated. The concept of *dynamics* attests to the notion of the interplay of forces in the mind, forces acting in unison or in opposition and ultimately finding expression in a form representing a compromise of the participating elements. *Topography* concerns the relation of individual psychic elements to consciousness, a sort of layering of mental contents according to

15

the criterion of accessibility to awareness. The *genetic* principle recognizes the prevailing and enduring influence of the past upon current mental activity. It recognizes the extent to which the past is embedded in the present and shapes current thoughts, behavior, and feelings.

The principles just mentioned serve as the basis for the investigative and therapeutic tool of psychoanalysis, namely, the psychoanalytic situation. While analysts today differ widely on their theories of pathogenesis and their modes of therapeutic technique, what they share in common is the use of the psychoanalytic situation, which consists of the following: The patient assumes a recumbent position on a couch, facing away from the analyst, and is asked to report, without criticism as far as possible, the thoughts that come to his or her mind. The basic premise of this arrangement is that the dynamic pressure of the patient's conflicts will bring to the surface derivative manifestations of the patient's unconscious conflicts. These are the basic elements that enter into the organization of the psychoanalytic situation. There are other factors that will be elaborated upon in the section on therapy. Under these standard conditions, the flow of the patient's thoughts is considered free association, representing the moment-to-moment fluctuations of the interplay of the forces in conflict, which led Ernst Kris (1950) to say that psychoanalysis may be defined as human nature seen from the vantage point of conflict, and Brenner (1982) to define psychoanalysis in terms of a psychology of conflict and compromise formation. These principles of conflict and compromise formation are applicable not only to the elucidation of pathogenesis and the foundation for psychotherapy; they have also been applied to the understanding of art, religion, social organization, character and personality formation, and to all aspects of mental life.

In a classic article, Waelder (1962) elucidated the various levels of psychoanalytic doctrine and their relationship not only to therapy, but also to the philosophy of science. He pointed out that there are various levels of relevance of the data obtained within the psychoanalytic situation. At the basic level, the analyst is in a position to learn many facts about the patient that other people may not get to know. Among these are certain facts of conscious life that people are not eager to reveal to others and about which they frequently are not interested in telling the truth or the whole truth. The analyst and the patient may explore material that individuals usually do not think about, but which comes to their minds in the peculiar climate created by the psychoanalytic situation. More than that, as will be discussed later, the configuration in which material appears reveals a meaning not deducible from the manifestly conscious elements alone. This level of experience Waelder called the level of *clinical observation*. To this may be added that data are then made the subject of interpretation regarding their interconnections and their relationships with other behavioral content, i.e., the level of *clinical interpretation*. From all the accumulated data and their interrelationships, certain interpretations and generalizations become possible, which lead to a level of *clinical generalization*. Among such pooled observations may be the structure of symptoms, the genesis of certain character types, the effect of certain family constellations, and the impact of important affective life experiences. On the basis of this clinical experience and interpretation of phenomena, certain formulations of a theoretical nature, either implicit in the material or extracted from it, may lead to general clinical theories encompassing and integrating the observations. Waelder called this the level of *clinical theory*.

Beyond this level there are certain concepts used by some, but not all, psychoanalysts; these are broader and more abstract concepts that go beyond inferences drawn from clinical observation. They may include concepts borrowed from physics, biology, or other disciplines. This approach was very important to Freud. It includes such concepts as psychic energy, cathexis, and biological instincts. Since these concepts go beyond psychology, Freud referred to them as *metapsychology*. They were important to him because he wanted to base his theorizing as much as possible on concepts derived from the physical sciences. Currently, metapsychological concepts have fallen out of favor in psycho-analytic discussions of theory. Even Freud (1915b) said that metapsychological hypotheses are "not the bottom, but the top of the whole structure [of science] and they can be replaced and discarded without damaging it" (p. 77).

Finally, Waelder pointed out that Freud, like other thinkers, had his own philosophy, which was in the main a philosophy of positivism and of faith in the possibility of human betterment through reason. In this spirit, Freud had much to say about the role of war, religion, social structure, and political organization in the course of human affairs but, strictly speaking, this had no direct relation to psychoanalysis as a theory of the mind or as the basis for a system of therapy.

Freud (1911) believed there were a number of general principles of human behavior. Foremost among these was the *pleasure principle,* namely, the idea that human psychology is governed by a tendency to seek pleasure and avoid pain. Such responses derive from the biological inheritance of human beings and must have been of evolutionary significance in the struggle of the species to survive. The earliest experiences of pleasure and pain play a crucial role in shaping each individual's psychological structure, and the importance of these experiences is intensified in the case of a human infant because, in contrast to animals, the child has a much longer period of biological dependence upon adults. Without the parents' care and solicitude, the infant cannot survive. This fact of biology eventuates in an early and abiding attachment to others with all the possible consequences, good and bad, for the psychological development and well-being of the individual. It helps explain why the vicissitudes of the early years of life are so significant in shaping the mind of every individual.

## Other Systems

Psychoanalysis has influenced many forms of modern psychotherapy. According to Rangell (1973), most forms of psychotherapy now widely practiced are based on some element or other of psychoanalytic theory or technique. This variety of practice does not imply that such forms of therapy are invalid or ineffective. Quite the contrary. While some psychoanalysts, like Fenichel (1945), believe that there are many ways to treat neurosis but only one way to understand it, that is, through psychoanalysis, it would be a mistake to think that psychoanalysts believe their method to be the only worthwhile form of treatment. There are many situations where a nonanalytic treatment is preferable to an analytic one. For many forms of mental illness, in fact, psychoanalysis is inadvisable or contraindicated.

Historically, the line of descent of *Jungian analysis* and *Adlerian therapy* from psychoanalysis is clear (Freud, 1914a). Both Carl Jung and Alfred Adler broke with Freud early in the history of the psychoanalytic movement. Jung had serious differences with Freud's theory of the drives. He placed less emphasis on maturational and developmental processes and emphasized instead the significance of culturally determined, unconsciously transmitted symbolic representations of the principal themes of human existence. Behind the transformations of individual experience, Jung saw the constant recurrence of mythic themes common to all humanity. His concept of the transmission of unconscious fantasies through a collective unconscious has been criticized as being too mystical. However, Jung's views of the collective unconscious come close to the Freudian concept of primitive universal fantasies; analysts now regard these only as vehicles for derivatives of the instinctual drives rather than original determinants of behavior, culturally and biologically transmitted. They are secondary rather than primary factors in shaping personality. Some of Jung's concepts are particularly useful in elucidating the more regressed manifestations seen in schizophrenic patients (Jung, 1909).

Adler (Ansbacher & Ansbacher, 1956) believed that Freud underestimated the role of social and political pressures in shaping personality. Undoubtedly there is considerable validity to this criticism, since analysts originally concentrated primarily on the transformation of the derivatives of the energy of the sexual drive, the *libido*. To Adler, the cause of conflicts was determined by factors such as inferiority over social status, sexual role, inadequate physical endowment, sexual weakness, and discrimination. Many of these concepts presaged later psychoanalytic contributions concerning the role of self-esteem, particularly in relation to the so-called narcissistic personality disorders.

Recent years have seen the burgeoning of many forms of therapy in which the central aspect of the treatment consists of self-expression, releasing emotion, overcoming inhibitions, and articulating in speech and behavior the fantasies or impulses previously suppressed. The *encounter movement* (Burton, 1969; Schultz, 1967) represented one such school; *primal scream therapy* represented another. These forms of treatment were exaggerations and caricatures of the principle of emotional catharsis that Freud advanced in his early studies of hysteria (Freud, 1895). At that time, he thought that discharge of pent-up emotion could have a beneficial therapeutic effect. Subsequent experience with the treatment of neurotic patients, however, convinced Freud that this method was of limited usefulness and, in the long run, ineffectual.

In the expressive forms of treatment, the group experience plays an enormous role in mitigating anxiety. Expressing in the presence of others what is ordinarily inexpressible can go far in ameliorating a sense of guilt. The burden of guilt, furthermore, is lightened by the knowledge that other members of the group admit to the same or similar feelings and impulses. Everyone's guilt is no one's guilt (Sachs, 1942). The effect of such treatment, however, depends to a large extent on the continuity of contact with the group experience. Since no essential insight or psychological restructuring has taken place, the tendency for relapse once the group experience is discontinued is strong. Furthermore, there are cases in which the individual perceives the temptation and the opportunity to express forbidden impulses as so overwhelming a danger that he or she is unable to cope and may suffer a psychotic break.

Mitigating the influence of conscience on the total psychological equilibrium seems to be the essential feature of the *Rational Emotive Behavior Therapy* of Albert Ellis (1994). Ellis attempts to get the patient to change his or her values, particularly in regard to sexuality, helping relieve the patient of irrational guilt that may have inhibited many aspects of life and behavior. When this treatment is effective, it can be understood in terms of the patient's having identified with the therapist's personality and values. The therapist comes to serve as an auxiliary conscience that may replace or alter the patient's patterns of judgment, self-evaluation, and ideal aspirations. This is similar to what one observes in cases where individuals are "cured" of their difficulties through religious conversion, usually as the result of an attachment to some charismatic religious or political figure (Freud, 1921).

As part of the psychoanalytic situation, the analyst listens patiently, sympathetically, uncritically, and receptively. This aspect of psychoanalytic technique forms the core of the nondirective listening of Carl R. Rogers (1951). In other forms of treatment, sympathetic listening may be combined with counseling, with the therapist trying to guide the patient in a rational manner through the real and imaginary pitfalls of living. Otto Fenichel (1945) pointed out that verbalization of vaguely felt anxieties may bring relief because the individual can face concretized, verbalized ideas better than unclear, emotional sensations. Transference also plays a role. The fact that a therapist spends time and shows interest and sympathy reawakens memories of previous situations in which the patient was helped by friends or relatives.

All the foregoing forms of therapy make use of one or more of the fundamental features of psychoanalytic therapy, namely, a setting in which the patient can express thoughts and feelings spontaneously and freely to an uncritical, receptive observer; the achievement of insight through interpretation; and finally, and perhaps most important, an awareness of the power of the transference relationship.

Other forms of therapy, such as *reality therapy* (Glasser, 1967) and *behavior therapy* (Wolpe, 1958), illustrate the principles just mentioned. Essentially, the therapist is unconsciously cast in the role of a model or the transference instrument in an effort either to deny or to project the effects of internal conflicts. The therapist unconsciously joins the patient in a pattern of playing out some derivative of the patient's childhood fantasies. Accordingly, such forms of therapy play into patients' tendency to act out expressions of unconscious conflicts.

## HISTORY

### Precursors

Psychoanalysis, as originated by Sigmund Freud (1856–1939), represented an integration of the major European intellectual movements of his time. This was a period of unprecedented advance in the physical and biological sciences. The crucial issue of the day was Darwin's theory of evolution. Originally, Freud had intended to pursue a career as a biological research scientist and, in keeping with his goal, he became affiliated with the Physiological Institute in Vienna, headed by Ernst Brücke. Brücke was a follower of Helmholtz and part of the group of biologists who attempted to explain biological phenomena solely in terms of physics and chemistry (Berenfeld, 1944). It is not surprising, therefore, that models borrowed from physics and chemistry, as well as the theory of evolution, recur regularly throughout Freud's writings, particularly in his early psychological works.

Freud came to psychoanalysis by way of neurology. During his formative years, great strides were being made in neurophysiology and neuropathology. Freud himself contributed to the advancement of science with original work on the evolution of the elements of the central nervous system, aphasia, cerebral palsy, and the physiological functions of cocaine. In *The Interpretation of Dreams,* Freud (1901) offered a model of the human mind based on the physiology of the reflex arc.

This was also the time when psychology separated from philosophy and began to emerge as an independent science. Freud was interested in both fields. He knew the works of the "association" school of psychologists (J. F. Herbart, Alexander von Humboldt, and Wilhelm Wundt), and he had been impressed by the way Gustav Fechner (Freud, 1894) applied concepts of physics to problems of psychological research. Ernest Jones (1953) has suggested that the idea of using free association as a therapeutic technique may be traced to the influence of Herbart. In the mid-nineteenth century, there was great interest in states of split consciousness (Zilboorg & Henry, 1941). The French neuropsychiatrists had taken the lead in studying conditions such as somnambulism, multiple personalities, fugue states, and hysteria. Hypnotism was one of the principal methods used in studying these conditions. The leading figures in this field of investigation were Jean Charcot, Pierre Janet, Hippolyte Bernheim, and Ambrose Liebault. Freud worked with several of them and was particularly influenced by Charcot.

### Beginnings

Many accounts of the history of psychoanalysis fail to do justice to the fact that Freud was constantly revising his theories and practice as new and challenging findings came to his attention. In the section that follows, special emphasis will be placed on the correlation between Freud's empirical findings and the consequent reformulations of his theories. Several of his writings serve as nodal points in the history of the evolution of his theories:

1. *Studies on Hysteria*
2. *The Interpretation of Dreams*
3. *Three Essays on Sexuality*
4. *On Narcissism*
5. The metapsychology papers
6. *Beyond the Pleasure Principle* (the Dual Instinct Theory)
7. *The Ego and the Id* (the Structural Theory)

## Studies on Hysteria (1895)

The early history of psychoanalysis begins with hypnotism. Josef Breuer, a prominent Viennese physician, whose acquaintance Freud made in Brücke's laboratory, told Freud of his experience using hypnosis to treat a hysterical woman. When he placed the patient in a hypnotic trance and made her relate what was oppressing her mind at the moment, she would frequently tell of some highly affective fantasy or event in her life. When this experience was repeated with a discharge of emotion appropriate to the nature of the event, the patient would be relieved of her symptoms. While awake, however, the patient was completely unaware of the "traumatic" event or of its connection with her disability. The report made a deep impression upon Freud, and it was partly in pursuit of the therapeutic potential of hypnosis that he undertook studies first with Charcot in Paris and later with Bernheim and Liebault at Nancy, France. Charcot used hypnosis to reproduce the symptoms of hysteria. The school at Nancy went even further, using hypnosis to cure the symptoms of hysteria. When he returned to Vienna, Freud used Breuer's procedures on other patients and was able to confirm the validity of Breuer's findings. The two then established a working relationship, which culminated in *Studies on Hysteria*. In this joint work, Breuer and Freud (1895) argued that the symptoms of hysteria result from an undischarged quantity of emotion, affect, or excitation connected with a painful memory. Normally such memories are not pathogenic because the quantity of emotion associated with them is either discharged in conscious psychological reactions (*abreacted*) or is gradually integrated by assimilation with associated mental operations. In hysteria, however, these reactions do not take place because the painful memories have been split off from their connection with the rest of the mind. They are in a state of repression and they may be said to be unconscious. Freud and Breuer noted that recalling the traumatic events alone was not sufficient to effect a cure. Discharge of an appropriate amount of excitation or emotion was necessary. The task of treatment, they concluded, was to achieve *catharsis* of the undischarged affect connected with the painful traumatic experience. The concept of a repressed trauma was fundamental in Freud's conceptualization of hysteria, which led him, in an aphoristic way, to say that hysterics suffer mainly from reminiscences.

Breuer and Freud differed on how the painful memories in hysteria had been rendered unconscious. Breuer's explanation was a "physiological" one, in keeping with theories of psychoneuroses current at that time. The memory of the traumatic event, he suggested, was split off from the rest of the mind because the event had taken place while the patient was in a hypnotic state. In contrast, Freud favored a psychological theory. The traumatic events were forgotten or excluded from consciousness precisely because the individual sought to defend himself or herself from the painful emotions that accompany recollection of repressed memories. That the mind tends to pursue pleasure and to avoid pain became one of the basic principles of Freud's subsequent psychological theory. In keeping with this principle, it was the defensive resistance of the mind to recollection that eventuated the repression. Breuer refused to continue this line of research, but Freud continued to work independently. For Freud, the therapeutic task represented the need to overcome resistances in order to undo the effect of repression. Hypnosis proved far from effective in this respect. Not all patients were hypnotizable, and many others did not seem to go into a trance deep enough to produce significant results. Freud then employed suggestion, placing his hand upon the patients' foreheads and insisting that they attempt to recall the repressed traumatic event. Not surprisingly, patients obliged by offering accounts of events in keeping with Freud's expectations. Unfortunately, the memories they recalled were false and unreliable.

At this point, Freud developed a suitable substitute for hypnosis and suggestion. He recalled an experiment he had witnessed while working with Bernheim. In his *Autobiographical Study* (1925, p. 8), Freud described the incident in these words:

> When the subject awoke from the state of somnambulism, he seemed to have lost all memory of what had happened while he was in that state, but Bernheim maintained that the memory was present all the same; and if he insisted upon the subject remembering, if he asseverated that the subject knew it all and had only to say it, and if at the same time he laid his hand on the subject's forehead, then the forgotten memories began to return, hesitatingly at first, but eventually in a flood and with complete clarity.

Accordingly, Freud abandoned hypnosis in favor of a new technique, the technique of forced associations, of recollection carried out at the insistent demand of the therapist, which later developed into the technique of "free" associations.

This technical innovation coincided with another interest that pervaded Freud's thoughts at the time. He had found that two elements were characteristic of the forgotten traumatic events to which he had been able to trace the hysterical symptoms. In the first place, the incidents invariably proved to be sexual in nature. Second, in searching for the pathogenic situations in which the repression of sexuality had set in, Freud was carried further and further back into the patient's life, reaching ultimately into the earliest years of childhood, i.e., before the age of puberty, the time when sexuality was supposed to begin. It is highly probable that, in addition to the other factors already mentioned, the "error" of the seduction theory of the etiology of hysteria may in part be ascribed to the strong component of suggestion that characterized Freud's technique of forced association. In any event, the early crucial sexual experiences of childhood were shrouded in what Freud called "infantile amnesia," and his emphasis in therapy and investigation now shifted from the cathartic effect of abreaction to the task of undoing infantile amnesia. Because at the time it was generally believed that children before the age of puberty had no sexual drives, Freud concluded that the patients he observed had all been seduced by an older person. In his further investigation, Freud came to realize that this was not always true. Freud had unknowingly come upon the data that were to serve as the basis for the discovery of childhood sexuality.

*abreaction* [handwritten margin note]

## The Interpretation of Dreams (1900)

The second phase of Freud's discoveries concerned a solution to the riddle of the dream. The idea that dreams could be understood occurred to Freud when he observed how regularly they appeared in the associations of his neurotic patients. *Dreams* and *symptoms,* he came to realize, had a similar structure. Both were end products of a compromise between two sets of conflicting forces in the mind—between unconscious childhood sexual wishes seeking discharge and the repressive activity of the rest of the mind. In effecting this compromise, an inner censor disguised and distorted the representation of the unconscious sexual wishes from childhood. This process makes dreams and symptoms unintelligible. The wishes that entered into the formation of dreams were connected with the pleasurable sensations that children get from the mouth, anus, skin, and genitals, and resembled the various forms of overt sexual activity often associated with fetishes, exhibitionism, and the other examples of sexual deviance that are labeled as *paraphilias* in the *Diagnostic and Statistical Manual* (DSM-IV) of the American Psychiatric Association.

*The Interpretation of Dreams* was a partial record of Freud's own self-analysis. In it Freud first described the *Oedipus complex,* an unconscious sexual desire in a child, especially a male child, for the parent of the opposite sex, usually accompanied by hostility to the parent of the same sex. The Oedipus complex is perhaps the most striking of Freud's many ideas. In the concluding chapter of this work, Freud attempted to elaborate a theory of the human mind that would encompass dreaming, psychopathology, and normal functioning. The central principle of this theory is that mental life represents an unrelenting conflict between the conscious and unconscious parts of the mind. The unconscious parts of the mind contain the biological, instinctual sexual drives, impulsively pressing for discharge. Opposed to these elements are forces that are conscious or readily available to consciousness, functioning at a logical, realistic, and adaptive level. Because the fundamental principle of this conceptualization of mental functioning concerned the depth or "layer" of an idea in relationship to consciousness, this theory was called the *topographic theory*. According to this theory, the mind could be divided into three systems: *consciousness,* resulting from perception of outer stimuli as well as inner mental functioning; the *preconscious,* consisting of those mental contents accessible to awareness once attention is directed towards them; and finally the *unconscious,* comprising the primitive, instinctual wishes. At that time Freud considered these wishes to be significantly, if not exclusively, sexual in nature.

The concepts developed in *The Interpretation of Dreams*—unconscious conflict, infantile sexuality, and the Oedipus complex—enabled Freud to attain new insights into the psychology of religion, art, character formation, mythology, and literature. These ideas were published in *The Psychopathology of Everyday Life* (1901), *Jokes and Their Relationship to the Unconscious* (1905a), *Three Essays on Sexuality* (1905b), and *Totem and Taboo* (1913).

Having convinced himself that the origin of psychoneurotic symptoms was sexual in nature, Freud began to investigate the manifold variations of the sexual impulse. In keeping with his dedication to explaining phenomena in terms of physics and chemistry, he developed a metapsychological theory about the nature of the sexual drive. As early as 1894, he developed the concept that "among the psychic functions, there is something that should be differentiated (an amount of affect, the sum of excitation), having all the attributes of a quantity—although we possess no means of measuring it—a something which is capable of increase, decrease, displacement and discharge and which extends itself over the memory traces of an idea like an electric current over the surface of the body. . . . It is provisionally justified by its utility in coordinating and explaining a great variety of psychical states" (1894, p. 61). Freud called this investment of emotional energy *cathexis*.

Having been convinced of the etiological significance of the sexual drive in psychoneurosis, Freud turned his attention to the origin, development, and aberrations of the sexual drive in the course of human development. He reasoned that sexuality was present at birth and that it followed a biologically predetermined pattern of maturation vested in the zones and functioning of the body. Until the final stamp of one's constitution was imprinted in the later years of puberty, sexuality was capable of the widest developmental variations as a result of environmental influence. For Freud, sexuality became a unifying concept that could describe the symptoms of neurosis, perversion, the sex life of the adult and the development of the child, the impulses of the dream and the fantasies of literature. Above all, sexuality was a force capable of "increase, decrease, displacement and discharge." It answered in all respects Freud's requirement for a more precise energizing force in mental activity.

The transition to the *libido theory* was a quick and natural step. In keeping with his dualistic approach, Freud now conceived of mental activity as representative of two sets of drives: libidinal drives seeking gratification and ultimately related to the preservation of the species, opposed by the ego drive, seeking to preserve the existence of the individual by curbing, when necessary, dangerous (antisocial) sexual wishes. The operation of the libidinal drives was for the most part unconscious. The self-preservative drives were conscious, intellectually controlled, and regulated by the adaptive requirements of the individual.

Taking as his point of departure the similarity between the manifest sexual activity encountered in the paraphilias and the sexual interest and activities of children, Freud proposed a maturational and developmental sequence of the sexual drives. Each component of the sexual drive was related to the biological development and needs of the individual. The earliest phase, extending from birth to about the middle of the second year, was dominated by nutritive needs. The source of the drive was in the *oral* zone. The aim was to incorporate into the body what was needed for survival. The object was the food, e.g., mother's milk, that satisfied the need. Gratification of these instinctual needs was accompanied by pleasure. The next phase developed out of the experiences related to the activities of the *anal* zone. The aim here was to achieve pleasure by retaining or expelling the contents of the body. A clearer concept of the "other" develops at this time, the person who becomes a secondary object of the instinctual drive. Somewhat later (ages 3½ to 6), the child enters the *phallic* phase in which the genitals become the dominant source of pleasure. By this time, complex fantasies have begun to form in the mind of the child. These fantasies often are related to power, attachment, or a wish for sexual union with important adult figures in the child's life.

These early psychosexual phases, Freud felt, were followed by a period of relative latency. From the age of six to the onset of puberty, sexual tension abates. Under the influence of the biological changes of puberty, a period of turbulence and readjustment sets in, which culminates in the achievement, when successful, of adequate mastery of sexual drives, leading to adaptation, sexual and moral identity, and attachment to significant others.

## On Narcissism (1914)

The next phase in the development of Freud's concepts focused on his investigation into the psychology of the psychoses, group formation, and love—for one's self, one's children, and significant others. This phase represented a shift in Freud's metapsychological theory. What became the major quality of mental life was the relative investment of libidinal energy in mental representations of the self as opposed to mental representations of others. In Freud's metapsychology, psychoses could be understood as the consequence of an overwhelmingly excessive investment of libidinal cathexis in self-representations, leading to a major disturbance in the interaction between the individual and his or her world. Furthermore, some individuals led lives dominated by the pursuit of self-esteem and grandiosity. These same factors also seemed to operate in the relationship of an individual to the person with whom he or she was in love. The beloved was aggrandized and endowed with superlative qualities, and separation from the beloved was seen as a catastrophic blow to self-esteem. And finally, of course, Freud noted the extreme affection people have for their children; he believed these feelings represented a displacement of self-love.

## The Metapsychology Papers (1915)

From his clinical observations, Freud came to recognize certain inconsistencies in his topographical model of the mind, and he increasingly appreciated the important role in mental life played by unconscious fantasies. He noted that there were other unconscious thoughts that were, in fact, anti-instinctual and self-punitive; clearly a strict qualitative differentiation of mental phenomena according to a single criterion of accessibility to consciousness was no longer tenable. In several papers, notably *Repression* (1915a) and *The Unconscious* (1915b), Freud tried to synthesize his psychological concepts under the heading *metapsychology*. By this term he meant describing a mental process in all of its aspects—dynamic, topographic, and economic. The papers written during this period represent a transitional phase in Freud's thinking before he embarked upon a major revision of his theory.

## Beyond the Pleasure Principle (1920)

The role of aggression in mental life convinced Freud that he had to revise his theory of drives. He observed how self-directed aggression operated in depression, masochism, and, generally, in the many ways people punish themselves. Individuals wrecked by success, persons who commit crimes out of a sense of guilt in the hope of being punished, and patients in therapy who respond negatively to the insight they achieve belong to this category. In 1920, in his essay *Beyond the Pleasure Principle,* Freud extended his dualistic concept by putting forward the notion of two instincts, libido and aggression, both derived in turn from broader, all-pervading biological principles—an instinct of love (*Eros*) and an instinct toward death and self-destruction (*Thanatos*). While many psychoanalysts were ready to accept the role of aggression as an independent drive, they were uneasy with the metapsychological concept of a basic biological instinct towards death and self-destruction, a drive that Freud called Thanatos as a counterbalance to libido and eros. In recent years, the concept of Thanatos has practically disappeared from the psychoanalytic lexicon.

## The Ego and the Id (1923)

Having recognized that in the course of psychic conflict, conscience may operate at conscious and/or unconscious levels, and having perceived that even the methods by which the mind protects itself from anxiety may be unconscious, Freud reformulated his theory in terms of a structural organization of the mind. Mental functions were grouped according to the role they played in conflict. Freud named the three major subdivisions of the psychic apparatus the ego, the id, and the superego. The *ego* comprises a group of functions that orient the individual toward the external world. It also serves as a mediator between one's external and internal worlds. In effect, it executes drives and correlates these demands with a proper regard for conscience and the world of reality. The *id* represents the organization of the sum total of the instinctual pressures on the mind, basically the sexual and aggressive impulses. The *superego* is a split-off portion of the ego, a residue of the early history of the individual's moral training and a precipitate of the most important childhood identifications and ideal aspirations. Under ordinary circumstances, there is no sharp demarcation among these three major components of the mind. Intrapsychic conflict, however, highlights the differences and demarcations between them.

One of the major functions of the ego is to protect the mind from internal dangers, and from the threat of a breakthrough into consciousness of unacceptable conflict-laden impulses. The difference between mental health and mental illness depends upon how well the ego can succeed in this responsibility. In his monograph *Inhibitions, Symptoms and Anxiety* (1926), Freud detailed that the key to the problem is the appearance of the unpleasant affective state of anxiety, perhaps the most common symptom of neurosis. Anxiety serves as a warning signal, alerting the ego to the danger of overwhelming anxiety or panic that may supervene if a repressed, unconscious wish emerges into consciousness. Once warned, the ego may utilize any of a wide array of defenses. This new view had far-reaching implications for both the theory and practice of psychoanalysis.

## Current Status

It is almost impossible to grasp the extent to which psychoanalysis has changed since the death of Freud in 1939. The earlier defections by Adler and Jung have already been noted, but a serious split began within psychoanalysis even during Freud's lifetime. This grew out of the teaching and the influence of Melanie Klein in London, which eventuated in the so-called English school of psychoanalysis. Klein emphasized the importance of primitive fantasies of loss (the *depressive position*) and persecution (the *paranoid position*) in the pathogenesis of mental illness. Melanie Klein's influence is preeminent in England, many parts of Europe, and South America.

When Nazi persecution forced many of the outstanding European analysts to migrate to this country, the United States became, for a time, the world center of psychoanalysis. The leading figures in this movement were Heinz Hartmann, Ernst Kris, and Rudolph Loewenstein. These three collaborators (1946, 1949) tried to establish psychoanalysis as a general psychology. They did so by extending Hartmann's concepts of the adaptive function of the ego (Hartmann, 1939) and clarifying fundamental working hypotheses concerning the drives and the development of the psychic apparatus (Hartmann & Kris, 1945). Hartmann, in particular, emphasized the role of the transformation of the basic instinctual drives in a set of metapsychological propositions which in large measure have been abandoned in recent years. Closely related to the work of Hartmann, Kris, and Loewenstein were the complementary efforts of Anna Freud (1936, 1951), derived from studies of long-term child development. Her book, *The Ego and the Mechanisms of Defense* (1936), became a classic.

For a while, issues concerning the development of the sense of self and personal identity were most prominent in the psychoanalytic literature. These centered around the works of D. W. Winnicott (1953) and John Bowlby (1958) in England and Edith Jacobson (1954) and Margaret Mahler (Mahler, Pine, & Bergman, 1975) in the United States. All of these studies underlined the importance of the child's early attachment to the mother and the emergence of the self as an independent entity. While Mahler emphasized the emergence of a sense of self through a process of separation and individuation, Winnicott emphasized the continuing influence of the psychological experience of the young child at a stage where the distinction between self and object is not yet clearly defined, and where representations of the external world for a period of time constitute a stage that Winnicott called the stage of the *transitional object*. Subsequent psychological experience, demonstrating the role of the transitional object, plays an important part in Winnicott's psychoanalytic concepts.

The notion that psychoanalysis represented a monolithic structure of thought was never true, and it is even less true today. In fact, there are so many differing, competing theories concerning the causes and treatment of mental illness that Wallerstein (1988) spoke of the need to recognize many psychoanalyses instead of just one. Some authors have emphasized the importance of interpersonal relationships (Sullivan, 1953) and the role of identification and the transformations of the personality during the life cycle (Erikson, 1968). Karen Horney (1940) and Erich Fromm (1955) have stressed the social, political, and cultural factors in the development of the individual. A separate school of analysis known as *self psychology* has coalesced around the writings of Heinz Kohut

(1971) and Arnold Goldberg (1998), while Otto Kernberg (1968) sees psychoanalysis from the vantage point of the persistence of early object relationships. In addition, the nature of psychoanalysis as science is a subject of debate, with such analysts as Arlow and Brenner (1988) and Rangell (1963) maintaining that it is part of natural science, while Schafer (1976) and Gill (1987) maintain that it is a hermeneutic science or perhaps a form of linguistics.

Perhaps the most significant and consequential differences within the field today concern the nature of the analyst's technique in the treatment situation. The issue is often drawn in terms of whether analysis is a one-person or a two-person psychology. What is meant by this proposition is whether the treatment involves understanding the mental reactions of the patient exclusively, or whether it constitutes an examination of the interaction between two individuals under very special circumstances. At issue is the question of to what extent the analyst reveals and discusses with the patient his or her (i.e., the analyst's) personal feelings and thoughts as a fundamental aspect of treatment. This new approach, designated *intersubjectivity,* demands a considerable degree of self-revelation on the part of the therapist.

Much has changed in the organizational structure of psychoanalysis in recent years. While the American Psychoanalytic Association remains the largest and most prestigious of psychoanalytic societies in the United States, consisting of more than 3,300 members and comprising 42 affiliate societies and centers for the professional training of psychoanalysts, the participation and contribution of analytically trained social workers and psychologists has grown enormously. The latter have their own societies and training institutes, are recognized by the International Psychoanalytic Association, and are accepted into membership in that organization. In addition, the training institutes affiliated with the American Psychoanalytic Association are increasingly accepting members from other professions and disciplines, e.g., art history, economics, literature.

Recent years have witnessed a burgeoning of the psychoanalytic literature. In addition to the longstanding major publications in the field, such as the *American Psychoanalytic Association Journal,* the *International Journal of Psychoanalysis,* the *Psychoanalytic Quarterly,* the *Psychoanalytic Study of the Child,* the *Psychoanalytic Review,* and *Psychiatry,* many new journals have appeared, such as the *International Psychoanalytic Review,* the *Chicago Annual of Psychoanalysis,* the *International Journal of Psychoanalytic Psychotherapy, Psychoanalysis and Contemporary Science,* and *Psychological Issues.*

The 24-volume *Standard Edition of the Complete Works of Sigmund Freud* is the basic source for theory and instruction in psychoanalysis. In 1945 Fenichel wrote *The Psychoanalytic Theory of Neurosis,* the closest approximation to a textbook in psychoanalysis. Unfortunately, this valuable source book has not been brought up to date. The three-volume biography of Freud by Ernest Jones (1953) contains a comprehensive overview of Freud's contributions.

# PERSONALITY

## Theory of Personality

The psychoanalytic theory of personality is based on a number of fundamental principles. First and foremost is *determinism.* Psychoanalytic theory assumes that mental events are not random, haphazard, accidental, and unrelated phenomena. Thoughts, feelings, and impulses are events in a chain of causally related phenomena. They result from experiences in the life of the individual. Through appropriate methods of investigation, the connection between current mental experience and past events can be established. Many of these connections are unconscious.

The second principle is the *topographic* viewpoint. Every mental element is judged according to its accessibility to consciousness. The process by which certain mental contents are barred from consciousness is called *repression,* an active effort to keep certain thoughts out of awareness to avoid pain or unpleasantness. Psychoanalytic investigation of normal and pathological phenomena has demonstrated the important role unconscious forces play in the behavior of the individual. Some of the most important decisions in one's life may be determined by unconscious motives.

The third basic approach is the *dynamic* viewpoint. This pertains to the interaction of libidinal and aggressive impulses. Because of their biological roots, these impulses have been loosely and inaccurately referred to as *instincts.* The correct term in psychoanalytic theory, translated from the German *Treib,* is *drives.* Because the term *instinct* is used so widely, *instinct* and *drive* will be used interchangeably in the rest of this chapter.

It is important to distinguish drives in humans from instinctive behavior in animals. *Instinct* in animals is a stereotyped response, usually with clear survival value, evoked by specific stimuli in particular settings. As used in psychoanalysis, *drive* is a state of central excitation in response to stimuli. This sense of central excitation impels the mind to activity, with the ultimate aim of bringing about a cessation of tension and a sense of gratification. Drives in humans are capable of a wide variety of complex transformations. Drive theory in psychoanalysis accounts for the psychological findings gathered in the clinical setting. Biology supports many of the formulations regarding the libidinal drive. This is not so in the case of the aggressive drive, a concept founded almost exclusively on psychological data (Brenner, 1971).

The fourth approach to personality theory, called the *genetic* viewpoint, traces the origins of later conflicts, character traits, neurotic symptoms, and psychological structure to the crucial events and wishes of childhood and the fantasies they generated. The genetic approach is not a theory; it is an empirical finding confirmed in every psychoanalysis. In effect, it states that in many ways we never get over our childhood. We do not have a complete answer to the question of why we fail to do so. One factor undoubtedly resides in the long period of biological dependence characteristic of the human infant. There seems to be a broad tendency in the higher forms of life for our earliest experiences to have a persistent and crucial effect on later development. Freud's observations about the crucial role of events in early childhood in shaping later behavior have been confirmed by ethologists in their studies of other forms of life (Lorenz, 1952; Tinbergern, 1951).

Personality evolves out of the interaction between inherent biological factors and the vicissitudes of experience. For any individual, given a typical environment, one may anticipate a more or less predictable sequence of events constituting the steps in the maturation of drives and the other components of the psychic apparatus. Whatever happens to the individual—illness, accidents, deprivation, abuse, seduction, abandonment—will alter the native endowment and influence the ultimate personality structure.

The terminology used for describing the development of the drives originally applied only to the libidinal drives. Freud conceptualized them first and did not postulate an independent aggressive drive until later. The early phases of the libidinal drives are quite distinct and clearly relate to specific zones of the body. The somatic substrate of aggression is not defined as clearly.

In keeping with the genetic principle of psychoanalysis, during treatment one attempts to trace both the normal and pathological psychological formations through their developmental origins in the early phases of psychosexual development. Accordingly, the investigative inquiry concentrates on the vicissitudes of experience during the early developmental phases, taking into account genetic endowment. The psychological apparatus consistently evolves during childhood and eventually is transformed into the adult personality structure. Traditionally it has been customary to separate the early phases of development in keeping with the instinctual drives dominant at the period, but it must be borne in mind that object concepts and relationships and the concomitant mechanisms of adaptation are shaped *pari passu.*

## Variety of Concepts

### Oral Phase

The earliest phase of development has been labeled the *oral phase.* This phase extends from birth to approximately 18 months. The chief source of libidinal gratification during the oral phase centers around feeding and the organs connected with that function—mouth, lips, and tongue—together with feelings of security that result from being held and comforted. Gratification of oral needs in the form of satiety brings about a state of freedom from tension and induces sleep. Accordingly, many disturbances of sleep have been connected with unconscious fantasies involving oral wishes (Lewin, 1946, 1949). During this phase, the basic orientation seems to be to take in what is pleasurable and to expel what is unpleasant. One of the earliest analysts, Abraham (1924), observed that people whose oral needs were excessively frustrated turned out to be pessimists, while those whose oral desires had been gratified tended to be more optimistic. In later psychological developments, unconscious fantasies and wishes concerning biting and devouring, chopping objects into bits, and swallowing both friendly and unfriendly, desirable and undesirable, pleasurable and unpleasurable objects may play an important role, especially in conditions such as depression or elation. While these tendencies of the oral drive dominate the earliest months of life, they do not disappear in the course of development, even though they may be superseded at times by the emergence of subsequent drive manifestations (Arlow, 1963).

### Anal Phase

Between the ages of 18 months and three years, the main source of pleasure and libidinal gratification comes from retaining and passing feces. The fundamental instinctual orientation concerns what is to be retained and is therefore valuable, and what is to be expelled and ultimately seen as worthless. During the *anal phase,* interest in the body processes—in smelling, touching, and playing with feces—is paramount. Regarded for a while as an extruded portion of one's self, the feces are considered a particularly valuable and highly prized possession. The disgust displayed by those who train the child and the shame the child is made to feel may contribute to a lowered sense of self-esteem. In reaction, the child may respond by stubborn assertiveness, contrary rebelliousness, and the determination to be in control. Through *reaction formation* the child may overcome the impulse to soil by becoming meticulously clean, excessively punctual, and quite parsimonious in handling possessions (Freud, 1917). Although the aggressive components of the anal drive are easily recognized, their clinical manifestations are diverse. They seem to play an especially important role in the dynamics of the obsessive-compulsive neurosis and in cases of paranoia.

### Phallic Phase

After the third year, the main area of libidinal gratification shifts to the genitals. For both boys and girls, the penis becomes the principal object of interest in the *phallic phase.* At this time the clitoris, embryologically an analogue of the penis, begins to be appreciated for the pleasurable sensations evoked by stimulation. Some awareness of the pleasure potential of the vagina is present at this phase in many little girls (Greenacre, 1967). Also prominent in the phallic phase are exhibitionistic and voyeuristic wishes.

By the time children reach the phallic phase, their psychology is very complex and their basic orientation is subtle and complicated. Although children remain basically self-centered, their relations with others in the environment take on a rich texture. They love and want to possess those who give them pleasure; they hate and want to annihilate those who stand in their way and frustrate them. They become curious about sexual differences and the origin of life, and in a primitive, childlike way they fashion their own answers to these important questions. They want to love and be loved, to be admired and to emulate those they admire. They may overidealize themselves or share a sense of power by feeling at one with those they idealize. During this time, children may entertain intensely hostile wishes and develop fantasies in which the penis serves as an instrument for aggression. This gives rise to intense fears of retaliation, usually directed against the penis. It is also the era of the discovery of the anatomical distinction between the sexes, a phase from which the fear of female genitalia and envy of male genitalia originate.

Three salient features in the development of drives must be mentioned here. First is the concept of *autoerotism*. When gratification of a particular instinctual urge is not forthcoming, it is always possible for children to gratify themselves by stimulating the appropriate zones of their bodies, combining such activities with appropriate fantasies. This evolves into the more common forms of childhood masturbation. Second, as the individual passes from one libidinal phase to another, the interest in the gratification of the preceding phase is not completely surrendered. It is only partially superseded by the succeeding libidinal gratification. When there is a particularly strong and persistent attachment to libidinal gratification from a particular object of infancy, one speaks of *fixation*. Fixations are usually unconscious and often serve as a focus for symptom formation later in life. A third feature of libidinal development is the potentiality for *regression*, the reactivation of or the return to an earlier mode of libidinal gratification.

Regressive reactivation of earlier modes of mental functioning is common and not necessarily pathological. Usually the regression reactivates some childhood libidinal and aggressive impulses that had been involved in the process of fixation.

For each of these phases of development, there is a characteristic danger. During the oral phase, the greatest danger is that the mother will not be available. This is usually referred to as the danger of *loss of the* (need-satisfying) *object*. During the anal phase, after the concept of the mother as an independent entity has crystallized, *losing the mother's love* constitutes the danger. Typical of the phallic phase is fear of retaliation or punishment for forbidden sexual and aggressive wishes. The kind of punishment usually imagined by both boys and girls takes the form of injury to the body, specifically to the genitals. For this reason, the danger characteristic of the phallic phase is referred to as the *fear of castration*. Later in life, after external prohibitions and threats of punishment have been internalized into the personality in the form of the superego, *fear of conscience* takes its place among the danger situations. Each one of these situations evokes anxiety as a signal alerting the ego to set in motion various mental maneuvers to eliminate or minimize the danger. Anna Freud (1936) called these maneuvers the *mechanisms of defense* because they protect the rest of the personality from the unpleasant affect of anxiety.

The combined influence on the mind of the libidinal and aggressive wishes constitutes the *id*. The other components of the mind are the *ego* and the *superego*. It will be possible to present only a few observations on the development of these psychological structures. The earliest psychological experience of the infant is most likely one of global sensory impingement (Spitz, 1955). The infant makes no differentiation between self and the rest of the world, between what is in the body and what is outside of it. The inherent capacities to perceive, to move, and, later, to speak mature gradually. The concept of the self as an independent entity develops over a period of two to three years (Jacobson, 1954; Mahler et al., 1975). There is evidence that for a certain period during the first year of life, the child is unable to distinguish between himself and the person who cares for him. An object in the external world, such as a blanket or a toy, may be experienced at times as being part of the self and at other times as part of the external world (Winnicott, 1953).

At first the instinctual drives center mainly on the self—a state called *narcissism.* As other people come to be appreciated as sources of sustenance, protection, and gratification, some of the energy of the libidinal drive is vested in mental representations of others. Technically, these others are referred to as *love objects,* or *objects* for short. At its core, the human personality retains a considerable complement of childish self-centeredness. The capacity to need others, to love, to want to please, and to want to become like others is one of the most significant indicators of psychological maturity. In addition to constitutional factors, the quality of experience with others during the early years is decisive in shaping the all-important capacity to love and identify with others. Disturbances in this process because of traumatic experiences or poor interpersonal relations contribute to the severe forms of pathology known as narcissistic character disorders, borderline states, and psychoses.

Needing, wanting, and identifying with valued persons are fraught with the dangers of frustration, disappointment, and, inevitably, conflict. The imperious wishes of childhood can never be gratified in full. Inexorably, relations with important objects come to involve a mixture of love and hatred. Such feelings come to a climactic crisis with the oedipal longings of the phallic phase. Between the ages of three and six the child develops intense erotic longings for the parent of the opposite sex and a hostile competitive orientation toward the parent of the same sex. Circumstances may induce enormous variations in this basic pattern, including a total inversion of the choice of sexual object. It is the responsibility of the ego to deal with these conflicts. Under favorable circumstances, oedipal wishes are given up or repressed, and they become unconscious. They are, however, not totally obliterated but continue in the form of unconscious fantasies. Disguised versions of these fantasies may persist in consciousness as the familiar daydreams of childhood. They continue to exert an important influence on nearly every aspect of mental life: on the forms and objects of adult sexuality; on creative, artistic, vocational, and other sublimated activity; on character formation; and on whatever neurotic symptoms the individual may later develop (Arlow, 1969; Brenner, 1973).

Under favorable circumstances, the child relinquishes most of the hostile and neurotic impulses of the Oedipus complex and identifies with the parent of the same sex, especially with his or her moral standards and prohibitions. This is the matrix of the moral part of the personality called the superego. This agency observes the self and judges its thoughts and actions in terms of what it considers right and wrong. It may prescribe punishment, reparation, or repentance for wrong-doing or may reward the self with heightened esteem and affection for virtuous thought and action. The superego is the seed of the conscience and the source of guilt. Under certain conditions, its functioning may be as impulsive and demanding as any primitive instinctual wish of the id. This is particularly true in states of depression.

The ubiquitous nature of the wishes and conflicts of the oedipal phase has been noted not only by psychoanalysts, but also sociologists, anthropologists, historians, and mythologists. When one thinks of it, this fact is not surprising. In every society or culture, no matter how advanced or primitive the environment, no matter where in the world he or she is, the child between the ages of three and six is faced with overwhelming existential dilemmas. Why is he or she small and powerless while others are big and strong? Where did he or she come from? Who belongs to whom and why? Why are the sexes different? What happens to people when they die? How does one explain the way the body works? Who sleeps with whom? The child attempts to answer these questions using the limited resources of his or her understanding—a mixture of observation, magic, fantasy, wishful thinking, and the poorly digested, half-understood explanations offered by grownups. It is from this matrix of confusion, wishful thinking, and conflict that the persistent unconscious fantasies of the mind are formed, as well as universal mythological themes common to all cultures (Arlow, 1969).

It would be an oversimplification to think of the development of the moral conscience as a direct consequence of the so-called resolution of the Oedipus complex. In fact, moral development begins much earlier, gradually and imperceptibly, based on the early prohibitions and encouragement experienced at the hands of grownups, and, perhaps even more importantly, by the capacity to form compassionate identification with other persons, a kind of negative restatement of the golden rule. By imagining the pain the child could inflict upon another and identifying with the object of his aggression, the child begins to develop control, out of which the moral imperative develops (Arlow, 1989).

There can be no doubt that Freud's concept of female psychosexual development was *phallocentric.* As a result, his views on the subject were unquestionably one-sided and reductionistic. During the past three decades, from clinical and developmental studies contributed in the main by female scholars, it has become clear that the evolution of female sexual identity and its concomitant influence on character formation and sexual function is much more complex than in the male and more complicated than had been appreciated by psychoanalysts following Freud's position. Awareness of the form and function of the female genitals begins much earlier in the young child than had hitherto been suspected and is conceptualized in a much richer and more complicated fashion than the simple feelings of inferiority and penis envy that were central in Freud's views.

## Latency Period

With the passing of the Oedipus complex and the consolidation of the superego, a relatively quiescent phase ensues, called the *latency period.* Children now can be socialized and can direct their interests to the larger world, where the process of education becomes a more formalized experience. This state prevails until the onset of puberty and adolescence. The transformations that take place during this period are crucial in establishing the adult identity. As a result of the physiological and psychological changes involved in assuming the adult role, the conflicts of childhood are evoked anew. Variations of fantasies that originally served as vehicles for the drives during childhood become the conscious concomitants of adolescent masturbation. Guilt over masturbation derives primarily from unconscious wishes that find substitute expression in the masturbation fantasies. During adolescence, a second attempt is made to master the conflicts arising from childhood wishes. Through the successful resolution of these conflicts, individuals consolidate their identity about their sexual role, assume more responsibility, and choose a profession.

Conflicts stemming from some earlier phase of life are part of normal human development. Uncontrolled expression of certain instinctual impulses could have calamitous consequences for the individual. Free expression of drives represents a major confrontation with one's morality and could, under certain circumstances, provoke a severe superego response in the form of guilt or self-punishment. It falls upon the ego to mediate the demands made upon it by the id and the superego with due consideration for the needs of reality. All of mental life represents a tenuously stable equilibrium between the pressures of the id, the superego, and reality. Presumably, the most effective way to deal with a conflict would be to bar the impulse permanently from consciousness. When this occurs, one may speak of successful *repression*. However, this is most unusual. By their very nature, unconscious wishes remain dynamic and from time to time threaten to overcome the repression instituted to constrain them. Such intrusion may precipitate panic attacks or anxiety. Under such circumstances, the ego undertakes fresh measures to ward off feelings of anxiety. If successful repression cannot be maintained, various compromises have to be effected by calling into play the different mechanisms of defense.

Unsuccessful resolution of intrapsychic conflicts eventuates in neurotic illness and neurotic character traits, inhibitions, paraphilias, and patterns of behavior of a neurotic or self-defeating nature. In fact, intrapsychic conflicts are never truly resolved. Instead, more adaptive compromises between impulses, guilt, and defense are worked out, resulting in a more adaptive and stable personality structure.

# PSYCHOTHERAPY

## Theory of Psychotherapy

The principles and techniques of psychoanalysis as therapy are based upon the psychoanalytic theory of neurosis. As the theory of neurosis changed, so did therapy. Originally, Freud felt that neurotic symptoms were the result of pent-up, undischarged emotional tension connected with the repressed memory of a traumatic childhood sexual experience. At first, he used hypnosis to bring about emotional *catharsis* and *abreaction* of the trauma. Because many of his patients could not be hypnotized, he dropped hypnosis in favor of forced suggestion, a technique of recollection fostered by the insistent demanding pressure of the therapist. Among other things, this technique produced artifacts in the form of sexual fantasies about childhood, which the patient offered the therapist as if they were recollections of actual events. Taking advantage of his new operational concepts of the dynamic unconscious and the principle of strict psychic determinism, Freud reduced the element of suggestion to a minimum by a new technical procedure in which he asked his patients to report freely and without criticism whatever came into their minds. Thus, the technique of *free association* evolved.

During the period when the topographic model of the psychic apparatus was paramount in Freud's mind (1900–1923), the principal technical goal was to make conscious the contents of the unconscious. The patient's productions were interpreted according to principles very similar to those described in *The Interpretation of Dreams*. The most striking discovery Freud made during this period was the existence of *transference*, the attitude the patient develops toward the analyst which represents a repetition of the individual's fantasy wishes concerning objects of the past, foisted onto the analyst. In addition, the discovery that the anti-instinctual forces of the mind, such as the defense mechanisms, guilt, and self-punishment, could operate at an unconscious level contributed to the elaboration of the structural theory. The structural theory pointed to the need to analyze the functioning of the defense mechanisms and the self-punitive trends. Elucidating the nature of the unconscious danger and the quality of the anxiety attendant upon its appearance have since become central elements of analytic technique.

In later years, in an attempt to apply psychoanalytic therapy to cases that were refractory to treatment, newer techniques were suggested. Franz Alexander (1932) felt that because most patients had been traumatized by parental mismanagement during childhood, it was necessary for the analyst to arrange a "corrective emotional experience" to counteract the effects of the original trauma. A more recent elaboration of these ideas has been proposed by E. R. Zetzel (1970) and Ralph Greenson (1967), who emphasized particular measures required to instill confidence and create a proper alliance between therapist and patient. Some analysts, influenced by Melanie Klein, see in the analyst's emotional reaction a mirror of what the patient is experiencing consciously or unconsciously (Racker, 1953; Weigert, 1970).

Recent years have seen the development of major innovations and changes in the psychoanalytic theory of pathology and treatment. The teachings of Kohut have become the basis for a school known as *self psychology*. According to this approach, the regulation of self-esteem and the vicissitudes of what is called the "self state" are the primary factors in pathology and in many ways dictate the analyst's approach to the treatment of the patient. Very early dissonance in a mother/child interaction creates the basis for narcissistic vulnerability, the untoward effects of which have to be ameliorated during treatment. Another major development may be seen in theories concerning *object relations*. These theories, as well as those of Kohut, developed out of experience with so-called borderline and narcissistic personality disorders. A preeminent spokesman for the object relations school is Kernberg, who emphasizes in his writings how the relations with the earliest significant objects in the individual's life leave a residue of internalized relationship concepts that may continue throughout the individual's life.

## Onset of Neurosis

The conflicts of childhood are of critical importance in the genesis of neurotic disorders. By far the most common and most significant conflicts involve the wishes of the oedipal phase. All children have conflicts, and most children develop some kind of childhood neurosis. Usually *childhood neurosis* assumes the form of general apprehensiveness, nightmares, phobias, tics, mannerisms, or ritualistic practices. Most primary behavior disorders of children represent disguised forms of neurosis from which the element of manifest fear has disappeared. Phobia is probably the most frequent symptom of childhood neurosis. In most cases, with the passage of the oedipal phase, the disturbances caused by instinctual conflicts have been sufficiently ameliorated to permit the child to progress normally. In some cases, a childhood neurosis continues with relatively little change into adult life.

Neuroses develop in adults when the balance between the pressures of the drives and the defensive forces of the ego is upset. There are three typical situations in which this may occur.

1. An individual may be unable to cope with the additional psychological burden of normal development. The unconscious significance of becoming an adult and undertaking the competitive and aggressive challenges of maturity may prove too much for the individual to handle.

2. Disappointment, defeat, loss of love, physical illness, or some other consequence of the human condition may lead an individual to turn away from current reality and unconsciously seek gratification in the world of fantasy. This usually involves a reactivation (regression) of the fantasy wishes of the oedipal phase. As these wishes are regressively reactivated, the conflicts and anxieties of childhood are revived and the process of symptom formation begins. The fantasy wishes that are regressively reactivated are the ones that earlier had been the subject of fixation.

3. By a combination of circumstances, an individual may find himself or herself in adult life in a situation that corresponds in its essential features to some trauma or conflict-laden fantasy. Current reality is then misperceived in terms of the childhood conflict, and the individual responds as he or she did in childhood, by forming symptoms.

## Process of Psychotherapy

The standard technical procedure of psychoanalysis for studying the functioning of the mind is known as the *psychoanalytic situation*. The patient is asked to lie down on the couch, looking away from the analyst. The patient is asked to express in words whatever thoughts, images, or feelings come to mind, and to express these elements without distortion, censorship, suppression, or prejudgment concerning the significance or insignificance of any particular idea. Seated behind the couch, the analyst listens in an uncritical, nonjudgmental fashion, maintaining an attitude of benign curiosity. The analyst's values and judgments are strictly excluded from the therapeutic interaction.

From time to time the analyst interrupts the patient's associations. In doing so, he or she momentarily interferes with the patient's role as passive reporter and makes the patient observe and reflect upon the significance and possible connections among such associations. The analyst's interventions momentarily change the patient's role from passive reporter to active observer and, at times, interpreter. The principle of free association is somewhat modified in connection with the interpretation of dreams. In this instance, the analyst may ask the patient to share whatever comes to mind in connection with specific images from the dream.

The practical conditions of the treatment are strictly regulated. A fixed schedule of fees and appointments is maintained. Any attempt by the patient to deviate from the basic understanding of the analytic situation calls for investigation and analysis. Changes in the basic conditions of the treatment are inadvisable and when necessary are effected by mutual consent between the patient and the analyst after the problem has been analyzed.

The patient's thoughts and associations should come primarily from persistent dynamic internal pressure of drives organized in unconscious fantasies. Thoughts and associations should not represent responses to external manipulation, exhortation, stimulation, or education. This is what is uniquely psychoanalytic in the therapeutic interaction. Under the conditions of the analytic situation, the influence of inner mental forces can be more easily and clearly observed than in more usual situations. It becomes possible for the material formerly suppressed or repressed to be verbalized and examined through derivative substitutive manifestations. This presupposes the strictest adherence to professional principles on the part of the analyst. Everything must be done in the interest of advancing the patient's insight through the process of analysis.

There is no greater responsibility in the analytic situation than the strict preservation of the patient's confidentiality. Communication of any material of the analysis to any source is contrary to the spirit of the analytic situation, even when the patient believes a breach of confidentiality is in his or her own best interests.

Psychoanalysis involves a commitment to change through critical self-examination. To maintain continuity of the analytic process, at least four sessions a week are indicated. Each session lasts at least 45 minutes. The course of treatment may run for several years. Undertaking psychoanalytic treatment involves considerable sacrifice in time, effort, and money. These are not conditions into which one should enter lightly.

The psychoanalytic situation has been structured in this manner with the intention of making it possible to accomplish the goal of psychoanalytic therapy, namely, to help the patient achieve a more adaptive compromise between conflicting forces through understanding the nature of the conflicts and dealing with them in a more mature and rational manner. Because the analytic situation is relatively uncontaminated by the intrusion of ordinary interpersonal relationships, the interaction of the three components of the mind—the ego, the id, and the superego—may be studied in a more objective way, making it possible to demonstrate to the patient what parts of thought and behavior are determined by inner wishes, conflicts, and fantasies and what parts represent a mature response to objective reality. The objective, helpful, therapeutic demeanor of the analyst in time becomes a model for the patient's own approach to his or her productions in the sessions.

## Mechanisms of Psychotherapy

Classically the treatment process has been subdivided into four phases, but this is more of a teaching artifact than a universal summary of psychotherapeutic experience. Retrospectively, in the closing phases of treatment, one may recognize a broad division of the experience into the following phases:

1. The opening phase
2. Development of transference
3. Working through
4. Resolution of transference

### The Opening Phase

Psychoanalytic observation begins with the first contact. Everything the patient says and does is noted for possible significance and use later in the treatment. The initial set of interviews is part of the opening phase. During these interviews, the nature of the patient's current difficulty is ascertained and a decision is reached concerning whether analysis is indicated. To determine this, it is necessary for the analyst to learn as much as possible about the patient; for example, his or her current life situation and difficulties, what the patient has accomplished, how the patient relates to others, and the history of his or her family background and childhood development. Formalized history taking, following a prescribed outline, is discouraged. Priorities in the subjects to be discussed should be left to the patient. Much is learned from how the patient approaches the practical task of making his or her problems known to the therapist and how he or she responds to the delineation of the analytic contract. The understanding of the analytical situation must be clearly defined at the outset and the respective responsibilities of both parties explicitly stated.

After a few sessions of face-to-face interviews, the second part of the opening phase begins when the patient moves to the couch. No two patients begin treatment in the same way. Some find it difficult to lie on the couch and say whatever comes to mind; others take readily to this new set of conditions. Everything the patient says and does—the position assumed on the couch, the clothes worn, characteristic phrases, what the patient chooses to present as the opening statement of the session, and punctuality—offers clues to unconscious mental processes.

During the opening phase, the analyst learns more about the patient's history and development. The analyst begins to understand in broad outline the nature of the patient's unconscious conflicts and has an opportunity to study the characteristic ways in which the patient resists revealing himself or becoming aware of repudiated thoughts and feelings. Gradually the analyst is able to detect a continuous thread of themes that follow relatively uniform sequences and repeat themselves in a variety of meaningful configurations. These productions can be understood in terms of persistent, unconscious fantasies representing wishes from childhood, dynamically active in the patient's current life in disguised and distorted ways. In the early phases, the analyst deals almost exclusively with the superficial aspects of the patient's material. The analyst tries to demonstrate to the patient significant correlations in the material presented but focuses primarily on those elements that are readily accessible to consciousness and not too close to the patient's basic conflicts. In ordinary cases, the initial phase of treatment lasts from three to six months.

## Development of Transference

The next two phases of treatment—transference and working through—constitute the major portion of the therapeutic work and actually overlap. At a certain stage in the treatment, when it appears the patient is just about ready to relate his or her current difficulties to unconscious conflicts from childhood, concerning wishes over some important person or persons in his life, a new and interesting phenomenon emerges. Emotionally, the analyst assumes major significance in the life of the patient. The patient's perceptions of and demands upon the analyst become inappropriate. The professional relationship becomes distorted as the patient tries to introduce personal instead of professional considerations into every interaction.

Understanding transference was one of Freud's greatest discoveries. He perceived that in the transference, the patient was unconsciously reenacting a latter-day version of forgotten childhood memories and repressed unconscious fantasies. *Transference,* therefore, could be understood as a form of memory in which repetition in action replaces recollection of events. It is not unusual for the transference to begin even before the patient sees the analyst for the first time. The prospect of being in treatment for the purpose of examining the depth of one's psychological experience may intensify the pressure exerted by unconscious wishes and conflicts so the potential patient begins to feel or act out derivatives of these conflicts from the time of the first contact with the analyst either on the telephone or in person.

Analysis of the transference is one of the cornerstones of psychoanalytic technique. It helps the patient distinguish fantasy from reality, past from present, and it makes real to the patient the force of the persistent, unconscious fantasy wishes of childhood. Analysis of transference helps the patient understand how one misperceives, misinterprets, and relates to the present in terms of the past. In place of the automatic, uncontrolled, stereotyped ways through which the patient unconsciously responds to unconscious fantasies, the patient is able to evaluate the unrealistic nature of the impulses and anxieties and to make appropriate decisions on a mature and realistic level. In this way, analysis helps the patient achieve a major realignment in the dynamic equilibrium between impulse and conflict that ultimately leads to a satisfactory resolution of the conflict.

## Working Through

This phase of the treatment coincides with and continues the analysis of transference. One or two experiences of insight into the nature of one's conflicts are not sufficient to bring about change. Analysis of the transference has to be continued many times and in many different ways. The patient's insight into problems by way of the transference is constantly deepened and consolidated by *working through,* a process that consists of repetition, elaboration, and amplification. Working through acts as a kind of catalyst between analysis of transference and overcoming of the amnesia concerning crucial childhood experiences (Greenacre, 1956). Usually the experience of successful analysis of a transference phenomenon is followed by the emergence into memory of some important event or fantasy from the patient's past, i.e., analysis of the transference facilitates recall. Recall in turn illuminates the nature of the transference. This reciprocal interplay between understanding the transference and recollecting the past consolidates the patient's insight into conflicts and strengthens his or her conviction concerning the interpretive reconstruction made in the course of treatment. It would be a mistake to believe that in the course of treatment the actual emergence of a repressed, forgotten, traumatic memory of childhood regularly takes place. Perhaps the more common situation is for many strands of evidence to coalesce into an inescapable conclusion that a certain event did actually occur and had specific psychological consequences that have persisted throughout the patient's life.

## Resolution of Transference

The resolution of transference is the termination phase of treatment. When the patient and the analyst are satisfied that the major goals of the analysis have been accomplished and the transference is well understood, a date is set for ending treatment. Technically, the analyst's aim is to resolve the patient's unconscious neurotic attachment. There are a number of striking features typical of this phase of treatment. Most characteristic and dramatic is a sudden and intense aggravation of the very symptoms for which the patient sought treatment. It seems as if all the analytic work has been done in vain. Upon further analysis, this turn of events can be understood as a last-ditch effort on the part of the patient to convince the analyst that the patient is not yet ready to leave treatment and that treatment should continue indefinitely. There are many motives for this unconscious attitude. In part, the patient is unwilling to surrender so gratifying and helpful a relationship. In part, it constitutes a continuation of some passive, dependent orientation from childhood. But most of all, it represents a last-chance endeavor to get the analyst to fulfill the very unconscious, infantile fantasy wishes that were the source of the patient's conflicts to begin with. In addition, it often happens that some important conflict, previously concealed, makes itself manifest in the closing phase of treatment.

During the termination phase of treatment repressed memories often emerge that confirm or elaborate the reconstructions and interpretations made earlier in the treatment. It is as if the patient presents new insight or findings to the analyst as a parting gift of gratitude. Unconsciously, it often has the significance of presenting the analyst with a child, a gift of new life, as a form of thanks for the new life that analysis has made possible for the patient.

Finally, during the closing phase of treatment, the patient may reveal a hitherto concealed group of wishes amounting to a desire to be magically transformed into some omnipotent or omniscient figure, a striving kept secret throughout the analysis but a wish that the patient had quietly hoped would be fulfilled by the time the treatment was over. It is important during this phase to analyze all the fantasies the patient has about how things will be after the analysis is over (Schmideberg, 1938). If one fails to deal with all the problems mentioned above, the possibilities of relapse remain high.

# APPLICATIONS

## Problems

From the description of psychoanalysis as therapy, it should be clear that any potential patient must be able to fulfill certain objective as well as personal requirements. Essentially, patients must be strongly motivated to overcome their difficulties by honest self-scrutiny. Because it is difficult at the beginning to predict how long treatment will last, individuals must be in a position to commit the time necessary to carry the analysis through to successful termination. In addition, patients must accept the discipline of the conditions proposed by the psychoanalytic contract. The psychoanalytic dialogue is an unusual form of communication, inevitably entailing frustration of transference wishes. Patients must be able to accept such frustration and to express thoughts and feelings in words rather than action. Impulsive, willful, self-centered, and highly narcissistic individuals may not be able to accommodate themselves to such structures. People who are basically dishonest, psychopathic, or pathological liars obviously will not be equal to the task of complete and unrelenting self-revelation. Furthermore, because cooperation with the analyst in an enterprise of self-exploration requires some degree of objectivity and reality testing—functions that are severely impaired in the psychoses—psychoanalysis can rarely be used in the treatment of psychotic conditions.

Because psychoanalysis is a time-consuming, expensive, and arduous form of treatment, it is not indicated for minor difficulties. Genuine suffering and pain are the most reliable allies of the analytic process. Through insight, psychoanalysis hopes to enable the patient to overcome inner conflicts. This can be helpful only insofar as such insights can be put to constructive use in altering one's life situation. If the person's objective situation is so bad that there is nothing one can do about it, psychoanalysis will be of no avail. This can be seen, for example, where the analyst recognizes how the story the patient presents reflects a lifelong struggle against the psychological consequences of severe congenital deformity or crippling disease early in childhood. No psychological insight can compensate for the injustices of life.

Because so much of psychoanalytic technique depends on analysis of the transference, psychoanalysis is best suited for conditions in which transference attachments tend to be strong. This is especially true in the classical psychoneurotic entities—hysteria, anxiety disorders, obsessive-compulsive disorders, and all conditions in which anxiety is a primary symptom. In actual practice, the symptomatologies of these disorders tend to overlap. The diagnostic label attached to a particular condition usually reflects the major defense mechanism characteristically used to ward off anxiety. In hysteria, for example, through a process called *conversion,* the energy of a sexual wish that the ego was unable to repress successfully may be transformed into alterations of body functions, such as paralysis, absence of sensation, and abnormal sensations. An unconscious fantasy of sucking on a penis or swallowing it may manifest itself consciously in the feeling that there is an abnormal lump in the throat that cannot be swallowed—classical *globus hystericus.* Symptoms such as these unconsciously and simultaneously gratify the wish and the need for punishment.

*Phobias* are anxiety disorders in which the patient wards off anxiety by treating some external object or situation as the representative of an unconscious impulse. In one form of *agoraphobia,* for example, a patient may become anxious whenever she goes out on the street because the street represents a place where it is possible to realize her unconscious wish to be a prostitute. The mechanism of defense is a double one. The internal (sexual) danger is projected onto the street, an external situation. By avoiding the external object, the patient controls an internal danger. The mechanisms of defense represent a combination of projection and avoidance.

Sexual difficulties and depression are ordinarily quite amenable to psychoanalytic treatment. More generalized patterns of behavior that interfere with the patient's conscious goals for happiness and success can be traced to unconscious conflicts and treated psychoanalytically. Some men, for example, repeatedly fall in love with and marry the same kind of woman, although they know from previous experience that the marriage will end disastrously. Similarly, certain women seem incapable of choosing men other than those who will hurt, abuse, and humiliate them. Other people unconsciously arrange their lives so any success is followed by an even greater failure. These are problems that can be successfully treated by psychoanalysis (Reich, 1973).

In recent years, many patients seeking psychoanalytic treatment seem to be suffering from masochistic character disorders or from narcissistic neuroses. Into this latter category fall those paradoxical combinations of low self-esteem and heightened grandiosity. Mood swings, depression, tendencies toward drug dependence, compulsive strivings for recognition and success, and patterns of promiscuous sexual behavior are common clinical problems. Such patients often complain of inner emptiness, lack of goals, hypochondriasis, and an inability to make lasting attachments or love relationships. Because of new contributions to the technical management of these problems, the prognosis for their treatment by psychoanalysis seems much better today than in previous years.

A number of conditions may be helped by psychoanalysis under especially favorable conditions. Among these are some cases of drug addiction, paraphilias, borderline personalities, and, on rare occasions, psychoses. Pioneering work applying psychoanalytic principles, if not the complete technique, to the treatment of psychotics has been done by Paul Federn (1952), Frieda Fromm-Reichmann (1950), H. Rosenfeld (1954), and H. F. Searles (1965).

## Evaluation

Unfortunately, no adequate study exists evaluating the results of psychoanalytic therapy. In a general way, this is true of almost all forms of psychotherapy. There are just too many variables to be taken into account to make it possible to establish a controlled, statistically valid study of the outcome of the therapy. Several attempts have been made in this direction, beginning with Otto Fenichel (1930), including studies by Fred Feldman (1968), H. J. Eysenck (1965), Julian Meltzoff and Melvin Kornreich (1970), R. S. Wallerstein and N. J. Smelser (1969), and A. Z. Pfeffer (1963). None of the findings of these studies has proven definitive or irrefutable. By and large, the number of "cures" that result from psychoanalysis range from 30 to 60 percent, depending on the studies and the criteria employed.

In any individual case, evaluation of the outcome of treatment has to be judged in a global fashion. Comparisons are made between the situation at the beginning of treatment and the conditions of the patient's life and symptoms at termination. The patient may have been cured of more conditions than he or she initially complained about, and previously unforeseen possibilities of self-fulfillment may have been realized. On the other hand, unrecognized complicating difficulties and unforeseen events may have changed the total configuration of the patient's life. In the face of objective reality, the claims of psychoanalysis must be modest. At best, psychoanalysis tries to help the patient effect the best possible solution that circumstances will allow. It seeks to achieve the most stable equilibrium possible between various conflicting forces. How well that equilibrium is sustained will also depend on how favorably life treats the patient during and after treatment. Freud himself was quite modest about the therapeutic claims of psychoanalysis (Freud, 1937). The validity of what psychoanalysis has discovered concerning human nature and the functioning of the human mind are not necessarily related to the effectiveness of psychoanalysis as treatment. Nonetheless, the fact remains that when properly applied to the appropriate condition, psychoanalysis remains one of the most effective modes of therapy yet devised.

## Treatment

Freud compared writing about psychoanalysis to explaining the game of chess. It is easy to formulate the rules of the game, to describe the opening phases, and to discuss what has to be done to bring a chess game to a close. What happens in between is subject to infinite variation. The same is true of psychoanalysis. The analytic contract, the opening phase, and the tasks of termination can be described definitively. The analysis of the transference and the process of working through consist of countless bits of analytic work. Rudolf Loewenstein (1958) approached the problem by distinguishing between tactical and strategic goals in psychoanalytic technique. *Tactical goals* involve analysis of the immediate presenting material in terms of some conflict, usually involving the analyst. The *strategic goal* is to elucidate the nature of the unconscious childhood fantasy and to demonstrate the many ways in which it affects the patient's current life.

How this appears in actual practice may be demonstrated in the following illustration. The patient was a middle-aged businessman whose marriage had been marked by repeated strife and quarrels. His sexual potency had been tenuous. At times he suffered from premature ejaculation. At the beginning of one session, he began to complain about having to return to treatment after a long holiday weekend. He said, "I'm not so sure I'm glad to be back in treatment even though I didn't enjoy my visit to my parents. I feel I just have to be free." He then continued with a description of his visit home, which he said had been depressing. His mother was bossy, aggressive, manipulative, as always. He felt sorry for his father. At least in the summertime, the father could retreat to the garden and work with the flowers, but the mother watched over him like a hawk. "She has such a sharp tongue and a cruel mouth. Each time I see my father he seems to be getting smaller and smaller; pretty soon he will disappear and there will be nothing left of him. She does that to people. I always feel that she is hovering over me ready to swoop down on me. She has me intimidated just like my wife."

The patient continued, "I was furious this morning. When I came to get my car, I found that someone had parked in a way that hemmed it in. It took a long time and lots of work to get my car out. I was very anxious and perspiration was pouring down the back of my neck.

"I feel restrained by the city. I need the open fresh air; I have to stretch my legs. I'm sorry I gave up the house I had in the country. I have to get away from this city. I really can't afford to buy another house now, but at least I'll feel better if I look for one.

"If only business were better, I could maneuver more easily. I hate the feeling of being stuck in an office from nine until five. My friend Bob had the right idea—he arranged for early retirement. Now he's free to come and go as he pleases. He travels, he has no boss, no board of directors to answer to. I love my work but it imposes too many restrictions on me. I can't help it, I'm ambitious. What can I do?"

At this point, the therapist called to the patient's attention the fact that throughout the material, in many different ways, the patient was describing how he feared confinement, that he had a sense of being trapped.

The patient responded, "I do get symptoms of claustrophobia from time to time. They're mild, just a slight anxiety. I begin to feel perspiration at the back of my neck. It happens when the elevator stops between floors or when a train gets stuck between stations. I begin to worry about how I'll get out."

The fact that he suffered from claustrophobia was a new finding in the analysis. The analyst noted to himself that the patient felt claustrophobic about the analysis. The conditions of the analytic situation imposed by the analyst were experienced by the patient as confining. In addition, the analyst noted, again to himself, these ideas were coupled with the idea of being threatened and controlled by his mother.

The patient continued, "You know, I have the same feeling about starting an affair with Mrs. X. She wants to and I guess I want to also. Getting involved is easy. It's getting uninvolved that concerns me. How do you get out of an affair once you're in it?"

In this material, the patient associates being trapped in a confined space with being trapped in the analysis and with being trapped in an affair with a woman.

The patient continued, "I'm really chicken. It's a wonder I was ever able to have relations at all or get married. No wonder I didn't have intercourse until I was in my twenties. My mother was always after me, 'Be careful about getting involved with girls; they'll get you in trouble. They'll be after you for your money. If you have sex with them, you can pick up a disease. Be careful when you go to public toilets; you can get an infection, etc.' She made it all sound dangerous. You can get hurt from this, you can get hurt from that. It reminds me of the time I saw two dogs having intercourse. They were stuck together and couldn't separate—the male dog was yelping and screaming in pain. I don't even know how old I was then, maybe five or six or perhaps seven, but I was definitely a child and I was frightened."

At this point, the analyst is able to tell the patient that his fear of being trapped in an enclosed space is the conscious derivative of an unconscious fantasy in which he imagines that if he enters the woman's body with his penis, it will get stuck; he will not be able to extricate it; he may lose it. The criteria used in making this interpretation are clear; they consist of the sequential arrangement of the material, the contiguity of related themes, the repetition of the same or analogous themes, and the convergence of the different elements into one common hypothesis that encompasses all the data, namely, an unconscious fantasy of danger to the penis once it enters a woman's body. This is the immediate tactical goal that can be achieved on the basis of material available up to this time. It constitutes an important step toward the strategic goal which in this case, on the basis of material previously revealed but not yet interpreted, concerns a childhood conflict, an unconscious fantasy of having relations with his mother and a concomitant fear, growing out of the threatening nature of her personality, that in any attempt to enter her she would swoop down upon him. In this case, there was a threat of danger associated with these wishes, namely, a fantasy that within the woman's body there lurked a representation of the rival father who would destroy the little boy or his penis as it entered the enclosure of the mother's body. In making the patient aware of the persistent effects of these unconscious childhood conflicts, the patient would get some insight into the causes of his impotence and his stormy relations with women, particularly his wife, as well as his inhibited personal and professional interactions with men. To this patient, having to keep a definite set of appointments with the analyst, having his car hemmed in between two other cars, being responsible to authorities, and getting stuck in elevators or in trains were all experienced as dangerous situations that evoked anxiety. Consciously, he experienced restrictions by rules and confinement within certain spaces. Unconsciously, he was thinking in terms of experiencing his penis inextricably trapped inside a woman's body.

This is the essence of the neurotic process—persistent unconscious fantasies of childhood serve to create a mental set that results in selective and idiosyncratic interpretations of events.

The material of a single analytic session is by no means always so dramatic. Yet one must be careful not to prejudge the significance and possible ramifications of any event or session, no matter how trivial it may appear at first. A seemingly insignificant interaction between the patient and the analyst may lead to very important discoveries illuminating the origins and the meaning of the neurosis. For the most part, however, the major portion of the analytic work is directed toward understanding the patient's defenses and overcoming resistances. It is not always easy to distinguish between mechanisms of defense and resistances. Typically, the *mechanisms of defense* are repetitive, stereotyped, automatic means used by the ego to ward off anxiety. *A resistance* is any one of a wide range of phenomena distracting the patient from pursuing the requirements of the analytic situation.

It may seem strange that a patient who has made so serious a commitment to self-understanding should not follow the course of action in treatment that is intended to bring relief. However, this is not at all unexpected. Because the mind characteristically turns away from or tries to repress unpleasant feelings and thoughts and because the neurotic process develops when it has been unable to accomplish this end successfully, it should come as no surprise that the endeavor to both fulfill and control forbidden impulses should continue into analytic experience. Herman Nunberg (1926) showed how the patient unconsciously brings into the analysis a wish to preserve intact the same infantile strivings that caused his difficulties in the first place.

The analysis of defenses and resistances is slow, piecemeal work. Nevertheless, much can be learned from it about how the patient's character was shaped in response to the critical events and relations of childhood. A particularly difficult resistance to overcome during treatment comes from the use of the mechanism known as *isolation.* This is the tendency for the patient to deal with his thoughts as if they were empty of feeling or unrelated to other ideas or to his behavior. A patient may begin a session by mentioning in two or three short sentences an incident that took place on his way to the session, as in the following example. The patient had passed a man on the street who suddenly, without cause or warning, extended his arm in such a way that he almost struck the patient. This reminded the patient of an incident some years earlier when he saw someone actually being hit in the same manner. On this occasion, as in the past, the patient, not a native New Yorker, shrugged the incident off with the reassuring judgment, "Well, that's New York for you. It's a good thing he didn't have a knife." All of this was stated in an even, flat, unemotional tone.

With no transition, the patient turned to matters of closer concern to him. He described at great length, and again in an even-tempered way, how his boss had criticized his work in front of his colleagues. Many of the criticisms, he felt, were unjustified, but mindful of his position, he had maintained a calm, respectful demeanor. Even when recounting the incident in the session, he showed little sign of anger. When this was called to his attention, he admitted that indeed he had been angry and was surprised that he had not transmitted that feeling to the therapist. At this point, the therapist made the connection for the patient between his opening report of a near-assault on the street and the experience with his boss. Actually, the patient had been saying, "There are dangerous people abroad. If one is not careful, they may strike you, even kill you. They have murderous impulses." The incident in the street served as a convenient locus onto which the patient projected his own murderous wishes to retaliate against the boss. He dealt with these impulses in an isolated way, making intellectual judgments about someone else's motives.

At this stage of the treatment, he could grasp only intellectually, by inference, the intensity of his vengeful wishes. Much could be learned from the analysis of this experience beyond illustrating how the patient manages to control and to suppress his feelings. The patient was particularly vulnerable to any assault on his pride; especially if such an incident occurred in public, it was experienced as extremely humiliating. Later in the analysis, it was possible to demonstrate the connection between these components of the patient's character and the feelings of defeat, insignificance, and humiliation he experienced during the oedipal phase while watching his parents having intercourse in the bedroom he shared with them.

It would be impossible to catalogue all the forms that resistance can take. Some of the more usual ones may be noted here. The most direct and unequivocal form of resistance occurs when the patient finds he has nothing to say. The patient may remain silent on the couch for minutes on end. Even a trivial lateness of a few minutes may carry some hidden meaning. Often a patient may miss sessions, "forget" them, or oversleep. He or she may be tardy in paying the bill for treatment, giving very realistic explanations to account for the tardiness. Sometimes patients will talk endlessly about trivial day-to-day events, revealing little or nothing that can be used to understand their problems. A patient may introduce a dream at the beginning of a session and make no reference to it for the rest of the analytic hour. On the other hand, the patient may fill the entire session with dreams, making it impossible to learn more than the facade of what had been recorded of the night's experience. Some patients report how they have become ardent advocates of psychoanalysis, proselytizing their friends and relatives, urging all of them to enter into treatment, at a time when they themselves are making little effort or progress in the analytic work.

The important principle governing all manifestations of resistance is that they must be analyzed like everything else that happens in the course of analysis. What must be understood is why the patient is behaving in a certain way at a particular moment. What is the motive behind his unconscious wish to break off the analytic work? What conflict is he trying to avoid? Exhortation, suggestion, encouragement, prohibitions—any of a number of educational procedures that in other forms of therapy may be introduced at such a time—must be carefully avoided in psychoanalysis. No matter how provocative, frustrating, or irritating the patient's behavior may be, the analyst never departs from the responsibility to make the patient understand his behavior. His attitude must remain at all times analytic.

How the analyst works can best be understood by examining three aspects of treatment: empathy, intuition, and introspection. An analyst must be capable of empathizing with his patient. *Empathy* is a form of "emotional knowing," the experiencing of another's feelings. It is a special mode of perceiving. It presupposes an ability on the analyst's part to identify with the patient and to share the patient's experience affectively as well as cognitively. The empathic process is central to the psychotherapeutic relationship and is also a basic element in all human interaction. It finds its highest social expression in the aesthetic experience of the artist as well as in religion and other group phenomena. It is based upon the dynamic effect of unconscious fantasies shared in common (Beres & Arlow, 1974). Two features characterize empathy. First, the identification with the patient is only transient. Second, the therapist preserves separateness from the object (the person being analyzed). The analyst's empathy makes it possible to receive and perceive both the conscious and unconscious processes operating in the patient.

It is impossible for the analyst at any one time to keep in the foreground of his or her thinking everything the patient has shared. How then does the analyst arrive at an understanding of the patient? This is done through *intuition.* The myriad data communicated by the patient are organized in the analyst's mind into meaningful configurations outside the scope of consciousness. What the analyst perceives as his or her understanding of the patient is actually the end product of a series of mental operations carried out unconsciously. The analyst becomes aware of this by the process of *introspection* when the interpretation comes to his or her mind in the form of a free association. Not everything that comes to the analyst's mind in the course of a session is necessarily the correct interpretation. If the analyst is working properly, it is usually some commentary on the patient's material. Analysts do not necessarily impart their introspective speculations to the patient immediately. The analyst evaluates these ideas in light of what has been learned from the patient, and the validity of the idea is judged in terms of contiguity, repetition, coherence, consistency, and convergence of theme. Intuition gives way to *cognitive elaboration.* In the long run, the validity of an interpretation is confirmed in several ways, primarily by the immediate dynamic effect that ensues, e.g., the immediate response of the patient in the form of additional confirmatory material, associations of comparable dynamic formulations, and, on occasion, the emergence of forgotten memories, repeating or substantiating the essence of the analytic interpretation. In effect, one observes how the analyst's intervention affects the equilibrium between impulse and defense.

In his original writings on technique, Freud urged the therapist to be as detached and objective as possible, like a surgeon at the operating table. He urged the analyst to reflect only what the patient had exposed—in other words, to function as a mirror to the patient's productions. Such affective detachment was, of course, an impossible ideal and, because of his compassion, Freud himself was a notorious violator of the precepts that he had laid down.

All analysts agree that, in addition to intellectual apprehension, the therapist's subjective experience is an important guide to understanding the nature of the patient's productions and the underlying conflicts. While listening to the patient, every analyst experiences a wide range of responses to what he or she has been hearing from a patient. The range of possible thoughts stimulated in the analyst's mind is boundless and can include feelings of sympathy or contempt, anger or compassion, condemnation or a wish to encourage, memories of his or her own life, affective reactions, anger, sexual arousal, and boredom.

One of the major challenges, perhaps the major one, concerning psychoanalytic technique consists of how to employ the analyst's personal thoughts and feelings to advance the therapeutic process. On this issue, there is a sharp division of opinion. Should the analyst talk only about how the patient's mind works? Or should one disclose the complementary psychic experience of the analyst, the interactive or intersubjective play between the two personalities, analyst and analysand? Theoretically, the debate is often posed in the form of a question: "Is analytic treatment a one-person or a two-person experience?" Among the outstanding contributors to the latter position are Gill (1987), Mitchell (1998), Mitchell and Greenberg (1983), Renik (1995), Hoffman (1994), Poland (1996), and Jacobs (1991). These authors represent what is perhaps the most significant and powerful trend concerning modern-day psychoanalytic technique. Under the heading of the interpersonal, interactive, or intersubjective point of view, those analysts who subscribe to these theories emphasize the important role that the actual personality and behavior of the analyst have on the course of therapy. The patient's perception of the analyst, they claim, is not all transference and such perception must be dealt with in the treatment situation, including the need for self-revelation on the part of the analyst.

An associated issue consists of defining the limits of what is known as *countertransference*. Just as the patient transfers onto the person of the analyst derivatives of his or her unconscious conflicts, so too may the analyst project onto the patient feelings and attitudes derived from the analyst's own persistent unconscious conflicts. Does this constitute an interference to the objective understanding of the patient and his or her difficulties, or does it represent a special way of knowing and understanding the patient through one's own inner emotional life? Ultimately it would seem that the question boils down to the degree to which the analyst's inner responsiveness to the patient facilitates or interferes with the fulfillment of his or her therapeutic task. A highly conflictual, i.e., neurotic, countertransference on the part of the analyst toward the patient can constitute a serious problem, interfering with the analyst's objectivity and sensitivity. When the analyst becomes aware of this difficulty, he or she will usually try to analyze the problem without outside help. If this effort is ineffective, the analyst may seek advice from a colleague. If the analyst cannot control countertransference responses, he or she may seek further analysis. In addition, the therapist may choose to discuss the issues honestly and frankly with the patient, and will arrange to transfer the patient to another therapist.

## CASE EXAMPLE

The course of an analysis proceeds unevenly, and it is impossible to capture in any condensed presentation the essence of the psychoanalytic experience. Seemingly fragmented material, arduously assembled over long periods and incompletely comprehended, suddenly may be brilliantly illuminated in a few dramatic sessions, when thousands of disparate threads organize themselves into a tapestry of meaning. A deeper understanding of the meaning of the origin of the patient's conflicts becomes possible during these periods and the insight thus gained enables the analyst to formulate the sequence and the level of the interventions to be communicated to the patient. Sessions like these demonstrate and clarify the methodology of analytic interpretation and show how inferences are drawn, tested, and used to guide the technical interventions of the analyst. The brief clinical fragment that follows will serve to demonstrate the principles just enunciated.

The patient was a 45-year-old male physician, married with two children, who sought treatment because of persistent but mild depression and a chronic feeling of hopelessness. He never expected things to go right and accordingly got very little satisfaction from what he had already managed to achieve in the course of his professional life. He was deeply pessimistic, never expecting anything really good to happen to him. He had tried analysis with a female therapist, but felt that nothing had come from it.

What follows is an unusually rich and revealing session that helped clarify his symptomatology and character structure. This session occurred during the second year of the patient's treatment.

The patient entered the consultation room, slightly stooped, with a tired and grim-looking expression on his face. He laid down on the couch and, in an exhausted tone, began as follows. "I had to get up early this morning and make my own breakfast. I was feeling kind of down and sad. It was dark outside, gray, cold. Everyone in the house was asleep in bed. I started to squeeze the oranges to get some orange juice. As I looked at the halved oranges, it seemed to me that they looked just like breasts. As I was squeezing them I thought of the fluid squirting out, of how thirsty I was, then of the different fluids which come in bottles. Then I thought of poison. At that moment I remembered that this was my sister's birthday. I thought: I have to get her something for her birthday. Maybe I'll get her a bottle of liquor or I'll get her Three Cross Scotch—no, three cross, that's the sign for poison. I mean Three Star Scotch. If I don't get her anything, she'll start squawking. From the time she was a kid I could hear her squawking. She was always squawking. I can't tell now what woke me up more during the night when I was a child, her crying or the fire engines across the street. After a while, I couldn't sleep at night either. I had problems going to bed. Every time I went into my bedroom I used to run and jump onto the bed. I was afraid that there were lions and tigers underneath the bed that would jump out and bite me. I don't know what this has to do with what we are talking about. (Pause)

"My sister was a sickly kid. It was no fun having her around. I was four and a half years old when she was born and because of her sickness, a congenital defect, my mother was always busy with her. When I was a year old, my mother left me in order to go back to school to finish her training as a dentist, but when she got finished with school, along came this kid sister. It seems that my mother was busy with her all the time. There's a story in the family—I don't know if it's true—that when my mother went back to school, she left me in the care of my grandmother. I was inconsolable. I cried all the time. I could not be comforted. I wouldn't eat. I kept tearing at my grandmother's breast. So one day— she probably didn't know what to do, she must have been desperate—anyway, according to the story, she took out her dry breast and let me suck on it. Whenever I think of that story, another memory comes to my mind, supposedly from the years when my mother was back at school. In this memory, I'm standing at the kitchen table. My grandmother was grinding meat for hamburger with a hand-mill that was attached to the end of the table. I used to stand where the meat was coming out and I would eat it raw. To this day I like steak tartare."

At this point, the observation was made by the analyst that, having felt abandoned by the mother when she left to go to school and having been displaced by the sister, the patient was overwhelmed by vengeful impulses to destroy the mother and the sister (and the ungiving breast) by attacking them with his teeth.

(After another pause) The patient responded, "I'm worried about my mother. I wonder how she is doing today. I'm going to have to call her when I leave this session. I spoke to her doctor yesterday. It seems that the cancer in her breast has spread pretty far. He is not sure how much time there is left. It makes me feel very guilty. I wonder if the injections that I gave her for the menopause had anything to do with bringing on the cancer. What they say is true. Doctors shouldn't treat members of their own family."

These thoughts were followed by a long silence. The patient was asked what had come to his mind.

"I was just thinking of those fire engines again. Just as luck would have it, when I was in treatment with Dr. G.—that lady didn't do a thing for me—her office was right across the street from a firehouse. Every time I would be in a session and getting somewhere—zoom, those fire engines would come streaming out. She never said a thing about it. At least she could have apologized. You know, she was pregnant during the time that I was in treatment with her and all the time I could hear her sewing, snipping behind the couch. She must have been making things for the baby she was expecting. She never did anything for me. Nobody ever does anything for me. I have to do everything for myself. As a matter of fact, I take better care of others than I was taken care of. I look after our two boys much better than my wife does. When they were young and I saw them playing near an open window, I would make sure to shut the window. Finally, to play safe, I got some metal protectors and barricaded the windows. I didn't want anybody falling out of the windows."

After another pause, the patient said, "I feel tired. I feel sleepy. I guess nothing will come from this treatment either. Nothing ever does."

Clearly this is a most dramatic and revealing session. What are the elements that made possible the emergence of this crucial material at this particular juncture? Most important of all is the element of context. On the day after he learned of his mother's worsening condition, the patient is feeling sorry for himself for having to make his own breakfast while everyone else is comfortably asleep in bed. It is his sister's birthday but he does not remember it, not until the hemispheric appearance of the sectioned orange reminds him of breasts, bottles, and poison. The concatenation of these events facilitates the emergence of derivatives of an unconscious fantasy to destroy the ungiving breasts of the mother and to feed the younger sister, not nourishment, but poison. It should be noted that this was not the first time that he was squeezing the fruit to get orange juice, but in *this* particular context the orange sections reminded him of breasts.

Immediately contiguous to the idea of destroying the frustrating breasts and the sister whose birth deprived him of food and mother's love, there appears a thought that is seemingly totally irrelevant, namely, the patient's childhood neurosis, a fear of wild animals that kill and devour. At this stage in the treatment, it would be premature to consider with the patient his childhood wish to kill and devour mother and sister, together with his fear of retaliation in kind. Note should also be made of the fact that, by a process of displacement onto wild animals, the patient's hostile wishes and fears concerning the mother and sister are kept from consciousness.

By projecting his wishes and fears onto the animals, the patient as a child protected himself, as well as mother and sister. The same purpose may be achieved in quite another way, through a mechanism of defense designated *reaction formation*. By a process of turning the hostile impulse into its opposite, the individual is spared conflicts that could lead to anxiety and guilt. In fact, an individual's personality could be enriched. This mechanism is illustrated in the patient's concern for the safety of his children. Rather than wanting to see these surrogate siblings fall to their death, the patient does his best to protect them from an ever-present danger that threatens young children. (Later in the treatment, material emerged from which it was possible to demonstrate to the patient that his concern for children falling out of a building was derived from an unconscious fantasy wish to extrude his expected sibling from her habitat in the mother's body.)

Although there were many determinants for the patient choosing the profession of medicine, the impulse to help and heal, rather than to damage and kill, was very significant.

One of the most important aspects of psychoanalytic treatment is dramatically portrayed in the material just cited. It will be noted that, at the point where the patient's thoughts turned to his mother's impending death and to the possibility that he may have contributed to it, he paused and then introduced material of a different nature. Instead of continuing the theme of his anger, hostility, and guilt toward his mother, the patient's attention now turned to his previous experience with a woman analyst who was pregnant and, in the patient's mind, neglected him. Finally, the patient concluded the session by stating that he did not expect the current male analyst to be any more helpful than the previous female analyst (and his mother) was. Clearly his thoughts and feelings involving his analysts represented a shift from the very painful conflicts concerning his mother and sister onto the more neutral figure of the analyst. This shift illustrates an important principle. It represents a defensive transfer of the conflict-laden impulses and thoughts concerning the important primary objects, in this case the mother and the sister, onto the female analyst and the child she was expecting, as well as onto his current male analyst. In many, if not in most cases, transference in the treatment situation serves the purpose of defense by shifting expression of conflictual wishes away from the primary object, in this case the mother, and onto the analyst.

A striking confirmation of the dynamics of the unconscious wishes in this patient appeared in the course of the analysis when his mother died. She died at home and was placed in a coffin in the living room. The patient had a fantasy that it would be impossible for the coffin to be borne down the narrow staircases of the apartment building and accordingly, he imagined a solution to the problem. He thought of chopping up her body, eating the pieces, coming down into the street and then regurgitating the fragments, which were then reconstituted as the corpse and placed in the coffin. This most bizarre fantasy constituted a striking derivative of severely regressive, primitive fantasies of oral vengeance.

To be sure, the conflicts that originated in connection with his feelings of abandonment and wishes for retaliation associated with his mother and his sister did not constitute the totality of the patient's psychological difficulties, but in one way or another, they influenced his subsequent psychological development. Hence, for example, when he entered the oedipal phase, his relationship toward the father was fraught with contradictory impulses that intensified the usual developmental difficulties typical of that period.

## SUMMARY

As a system of thought and a technique of dealing with mental illness, psychoanalysis has been developing and changing over the years. What seemed at first a monolithic theory is now being examined critically from many different points of view. Technical innovations and reformulations of theoretical concepts are appearing in ever-increasing numbers. In addition, the literature of psychoanalysis has expanded enormously and there are special volumes dedicated to psychoanalysis and sociology, anthropology, history, childhood, aesthetics, developmental psychology, religion, and biography.

Clinical investigation in the therapeutic setting according to the rules of the psychoanalytic situation remains the fundamental base of psychoanalytic knowledge and will clearly continue to be so in the future. After a heyday of popularity during the 1950s and early 1960s, psychoanalysis has been the subject of severe criticism and disaffection. Nonetheless, it has remained a continuing discipline with a growing number of practitioners and an increasing number of journals and books.

Two points have to be borne in mind about the position of psychoanalysis as therapy and as a system of thought. Not all forms of mental disturbance can or should be treated by psychoanalysis. Paradoxically, the demands of psychoanalysis require the cooperation of a patient with a fairly healthy ego who is well motivated to change and capable of facing himself or herself honestly. For properly selected patients, psychoanalysis can offer the promise of help in attaining the best possible solution that can be realized from overcoming inner conflicts. It does not pretend to create perfectly balanced superhumans, in harmony with themselves and the universe.

The second point to be emphasized is that the reliability of the conclusions of psychoanalytic investigation diminishes the further one gets away from the clinical base of the psychoanalytic situation. Whenever psychoanalytic knowledge and insights are applied outside the analytic situation, one must take into consideration the possibility of innumerable alternative hypotheses and influences.

Because of the changing nature of the psychopathology of our time, notably the great increase in patients suffering from narcissistic, neurotic, and character disorders, and from paraphilias and addictions, one can anticipate that psychoanalysis will produce new discoveries, fresh observations, original theoretical formulations, and innovative technical procedures.

## ANNOTATED BIBLIOGRAPHY

The following books are recommended for those who want to attain deeper knowledge of psychoanalysis as theory and practice:

Brenner, C. (1973). *An elementary textbook of psychoanalysis.* New York: International Universities Press. There is no better presentation of current psychoanalytic theory than this volume, *An Elementary Textbook of Psychoanalysis,* which has become a worldwide introduction to psychoanalysis. It is the most comprehensive, systematic, and intelligible presentation of the subject, a worthy companion piece to Anna Freud's *The Ego and the Mechanisms of Defense.* The theoretical development flows smoothly, logically, and cautiously. In addition to presenting the basic theory of psychoanalysis, the author describes the part played by unconscious forces in daily living and surveys the remarkable contribution of psychoanalysis to human knowledge. Current trends in the field are assessed, and problems still requiring exploration are examined.

Brenner, C. (1982). *The mind in conflict.* New York: International Universities Press. In *The Mind in Conflict,* Brenner extends his critique of structural theory, minimizing metapsychological considerations and emphasizing the concept of the functioning of the mind as representing a compromise between certain basic elements, namely, drive derivatives, guilt, defense against unpleasant affect, depression, or anxiety.

Freud, A. (1966). *The ego and the mechanisms of defense. The writings of Anna Freud* (Vol. 2). New York: International Universities Press. (Originally published in 1936.) Anna Freud has the finest and clearest writing style in psychoanalysis. *The Ego and the Mechanisms of Defense* is an established classic for its lucidity in portraying the theoretical implications of the structural theory and its application to problems of technique. In a relatively small volume, the author offers a definitive presentation of the psychoanalytic concept of conflict, the functioning of the anxiety signal, and the many ways in which the ego attempts to establish a stable homeostasis between impulse and defense. The sections on the origin of the superego, identity, and the transformations in adolescence present a clear picture of how the postoedipal child becomes an adult.

Freud, S. (1915–1917). *Introductory lectures on psychoanalysis.* London: Hogarth Press. These lectures make up Volumes 15 and 16 of *The Complete Psychological Works of Sigmund Freud.* The books are based upon a set of lectures Freud gave at the University of Vienna. His lectures are a model of lucidity, clarity, and organization. Introducing a new and complicated field of knowledge, Freud develops his thesis step by step, beginning with simple, acceptable, commonsense concepts, and advancing his argument consistently until the new and startling ideas that he was to place before his audience seemed like the inevitable and logical consequences of each individual's own reflection. *Introductory Lectures on Psychoanalysis* provide the easiest and most direct approach to the understanding of psychoanalysis.

Jones, E. (1953). *The life and work of Sigmund Freud.* New York: Basic Books. This three-volume biography of Freud is one of the great biographies of our time. It captures the intellectual and spiritual ambience of Freud's period in history. It is a remarkable portrayal of the personality and thought of a great thinker. In addition, this book contains an accurate and readable summary of almost all of Freud's important contributions. It traces the history and leading personalities of the psychoanalytic movement to Freud's death in 1939.

Mitchell, S. A., & Greenberg, J. (1983). *Object relations and psychoanalytic theory.* Cambridge: Harvard University Press. This book presents the reader with a point of view that departs from the most common psychoanalytic paradigm, the structural theory, in favor of a concept that emphasizes the persistent dynamic effects of the earliest interactions between the child and his or her environment, particularly the influence of the parents.

# CASE READINGS

Arlow, J. A. (1976). Communication and character: A clinical study of a man raised by deaf-mute parents. *Psychoanalytic Study of the Child, 31,* 139–163.

The adaptive capacities of the individual, even under difficult environmental circumstances, are illustrated in this well-documented case of a person raised by deaf-mute parents. In many respects, overcoming real hardships and conquering shame contributed to the character development of this person. In addition, one can observe how more than adequate mothering was possible on the part of a woman handicapped by deafness and educational deprivation.

Boyer, L. B. (1977). Working with a borderline patient. *The Psychoanalytic Quarterly, 46,* 389–420. [Reprinted in D. Wedding and R. J. Corsini (Eds.). (2005). *Case studies in psychotherapy* (4th ed.). Belmont, CA: Wadsworth.]

This is a teaching case that illustrates the application of psychoanalytic techniques in the treatment of a patient with a severe character disorder. Dr. Boyer describes his long relationship with this patient with considerable humor and sensitivity, and the case provides vivid examples of many of the issues discussed in the current chapter.

Freud, S. (1963). The rat man. In S. Freud, *Three case histories.* New York: Crowell-Collier. [Reprinted in D. Wedding and R. J. Corsini (Eds.). (1979). *Great cases in psychotherapy.* Itasca, IL: F. E. Peacock.]

The case of the "rat man" was a landmark in Freud's developing theory of psychoanalysis. In precise, clinical reporting, Freud outlined the role of the primary process, magical thinking, ambivalence, and anal fixation in the structure of an obsessive-compulsive neurosis. Although in his later writings Freud expanded his clinical theory and metapsychology, this case report represents a prime example of how Freud utilized clinical observation to elucidate new findings and to shed light on previously obscure problems.

Winnicott, D. W. (1972). Fragment of an analysis. In P. L. Giovacchini, *Tactics and technique in psychoanalytic therapy* (pp. 455–493). New York: Science House.

Winnicott's approach to psychoanalytic theory and practice represented an important turning point in psychoanalysis. This case report demonstrates his special approach to problems of pathogenesis and treatment, an approach which emphasizes the influence of interpersonal interactions and feelings. Winnicott's technical precepts have had a strong and lasting effect on psychoanalytic practice.

# REFERENCES

Abraham, K. (1924). The influence of oral eroticism on character formation. In *Selected papers of Karl Abraham, Vol. 1* (pp. 393–496). London: Hogarth Press.

Alexander, F. (1932). *The medical value of psychoanalysis.* New York: Norton.

Ansbacher, H., & Ansbacher, R. (Eds.). (1956). *The individual psychology of Alfred Adler.* New York: Basic Books.

Arlow, J. A. (1963). Conflict, regression and symptom formation. *International Journal of Psychoanalysis, 44,* 12–22.

Arlow, J. A. (1969). Unconscious fantasy and disturbances of conscious experience. *Psychoanalytic Quarterly, 38,* 28.

Arlow, J. A. (1989). Psychoanalysis and the quest for morality. In H. Blum, E. M. Weinshel, & F. Rodman (Eds.), *The psychoanalytic core: Essays in honor of Leo Rangell* (pp. 147–166). Madison, CT: International Universities Press.

Arlow, J. A., & Brenner, C. (1988). The future of psychoanalysis. *Psychoanalytic Quarterly, 57,* 1–14.

Berenfeld, S. (1944). Freud's earliest theories and the school of Helmholtz. *Psychoanalytic Quarterly, 13,* 341–362.

Beres, D., & Arlow, J. A. (1974). Fantasy and identification in empathy. *Psychoanalytic Quarterly, 43,* 4–25.

Bowlby, J. (1958). The nature of the child's ties to the mother. *International Journal of Psychoanalysis, 39,* 350–373.

Brenner, C. (1971). The psychoanalytic concept of aggression. *International Journal of Psychoanalysis, 52,* 137–144.

Brenner, C. (1973). *An elementary textbook of psychoanalysis.* New York: International Universities Press.

Brenner, C. (1982). *The mind in conflict.* New York: International Universities Press.

Breuer, J., & Freud, S. (1895).[1] *Studies on hysteria. Standard edition of the complete psychological works of Freud, Vol. 2.* London: Hogarth Press.

Burton, A. (Ed.). (1969). *Encounter.* San Francisco: Jossey-Bass.

Ellis, A. (1994). *Reason and emotion in psychotherapy revised.* Secaucus, NJ: Citadel.

Erikson, E. (1968). *Identity, youth and crisis.* New York: Norton.

Eysenck, H. J. (1965). The effects of psychotherapy. *International Journal of Psychiatry, 1,* 99–142.

[1]All references to Sigmund Freud are from James Strachey (Ed.). (1974). *Standard edition of the complete psychological works of Sigmund Freud.* London: Hogarth Press.

Federn, P. (1952). *Ego psychology and the psychoses.* New York: Basic Books.

Feldman, F. (1968). Results of psychoanalysis in clinic case assignments. *Journal of the American Psychoanalytic Association, 16,* 274–300.

Fenichel, O. (1930). *Zehn Jahre Berliner psychoanalytischer Institut.* Vienna: International Psychoanalytischer Verlag.

Fenichel, O. (1945). *The psychoanalytic theory of neurosis.* New York: Norton.

Freud, A. (1936). *The ego and the mechanisms of defense.* New York: International Universities Press.

Freud, A. (1951). Observations on child development. *Psychoanalytic Study of the Child, 6,* 18–30.

Freud, S. (1894). *The neuropsychoses of defense.* (Standard Edition, Vol. 3.)

Freud, S. (1895). *Studies on hysteria.* (Standard Edition, Vol. 2.)

Freud, S. (1900). *The interpretation of dreams.* (Standard Edition, Vol. 4.)

Freud, S. (1901). *The psychopathology of everyday life.* (Standard Edition, Vol. 6.)

Freud, S. (1905a). *Jokes and their relationship to the unconscious.* (Standard Edition, Vol. 8.)

Freud, S. (1905b). *Three essays on sexuality.* (Standard Edition, Vol. 7.)

Freud, S. (1911). *Formulations regarding the two principles of mental functioning.* (Standard Edition, Vol. 12.)

Freud, S. (1913). *Totem and taboo.* (Standard Edition, Vol. 13.)

Freud, S. (1914a). *The history of the psychoanalytic movement.* (Standard Edition, Vol. 14.)

Freud, S. (1914b). *On narcissism: An introduction.* (Standard Edition, Vol. 14.)

Freud, S. (1915a). *Repression.* (Standard Edition, Vol. 14.)

Freud, S. (1915b). *The unconscious.* (Standard Edition, Vol. 14.)

Freud, S. (1917). *On transformations of instinct as exemplified in anal eroticism.* (Standard Edition, Vol. 17.)

Freud, S. (1920). *Beyond the pleasure principle.* (Standard Edition, Vol. 18.)

Freud, S. (1921). *Group psychology and the analysis of the ego.* (Standard Edition, Vol. 18.)

Freud, S. (1923). *The ego and the id.* (Standard Edition, Vol. 19.)

Freud, S. (1925). *An autobiographical study.* (Standard Edition, Vol. 20.)

Freud, S. (1926). *Inhibitions, symptoms and anxiety.* (Standard Edition, Vol. 20.)

Freud, S. (1937). *Analysis terminable and interminable.* (Standard Edition, Vol. 23.)

Fromm, E. (1955). *The sane society.* New York: Holt, Rinehart and Winston.

Fromm-Reichmann, F. (1950). *Principles of intensive psychotherapy.* Chicago: University of Chicago Press.

Gill, M. N. (1987). The analyst as participant. *Psychoanalytic Inquiry, 7,* 249.

Glasser, W. (1967). *Reality therapy.* New York: Julian Press.

Goldberg, A. (1998). Self-psychology since Kohut. *Psychoanalytic Quarterly, 67,* 240–255.

Greenacre, P. (1956). Re-evaluation of the process of working through. *International Journal of Psychoanalysis, 37,* 439–444.

Greenacre, P. (1967). The influence of infantile trauma on genetic pattern. *Emotional Growth, 1,* 216–299.

Greenson, R. (1967). *The technique and practice of psychoanalysis.* New York: International Universities Press.

Hartmann, H. (1939). *Ego psychology and the problem of adaptation.* New York: International Universities Press.

Hartmann, H., & Kris, E. (1945). The genetic approach to psychoanalysis. *Psychoanalytic Study of the Child, 1,* 11–30.

Hartmann, H., Kris, E., & Loewenstein, R. N. (1946). Comments on the formation of psychic structure. *Psychoanalytic Study of the Child, 2,* 11–38.

Hartmann, H., Kris, E., & Loewenstein, R. N. (1949). Notes on the theory of aggression. *Psychoanalytic Study of the Child, 4,* 9–36.

Hoffman, I. Z. (1994). Dialectical thinking and therapeutic action in the psychoanalytic process. *Psychoanalytic Quarterly, 63,* 187–218.

Horney, K. (1940). *New ways in psychoanalysis.* New York: Norton.

Jacobs, T. J. (1991). *The use of the self. Countertransference in the analytic situation.* Madison, CT: International Universities Press.

Jacobson, E. (1954). The self and the object world: Vicissitudes of the infantile cathexes and their influence on ideational and affective development. *Psychoanalytic Study of the Child, 9,* 75–127.

Jones, E. (1953). *The life and work of Sigmund Freud.* New York: Basic Books.

Jung, C. (1909). *The psychology of dementia praecox.* New York: Nervous and Mental Disease.

Kernberg, O. (1968). The therapy of patients with borderline personality organization. *International Journal of Psychoanalysis, 49,* 600–619.

Kohut, H. (1971). The analysis of the self. *Monograph Series of the Psychoanalytic Study of the Child (No. 4).* New York: International Universities Press.

Kris, E. (1950). Preconscious mental processes. *Psychoanalytic Quarterly, 19,* 540–560.

Lewin, B. D. (1946). Sleep, the mouth and the dream screens. *Psychoanalytic Quarterly, 15,* 419–434.

Lewin, B. D. (1949). Mania and sleep. *Psychoanalytic Quarterly, 18,* 419–433.

Loewenstein, R. (1958). Remarks on some variations in psychoanalytic technique. *International Journal of Psychoanalysis, 39,* 202–210.

Lorenz, C. (1952). *King Solomon's ring.* New York: Crowell.

Mahler, M., Pine, F., & Bergman, A. (1975). *The psychological birth of the human infant.* New York: Basic Books.

Meltzoff, J., & Kornreich, M. (1970). *Research in psychotherapy.* New York: Atherton Press.

Mitchell, S. A. (1998). The analyst's knowledge and authority. *Psychoanalytic Quarterly, 67,* 1–31.

Mitchell, S. A., & Greenberg, J. (1983). *Object relations and psychoanalytic theory.* Cambridge: Harvard University Press.

Nunberg, H. (1926). The will to recovery. *International Journal of Psychoanalysis, 7,* 64–78.

Pfeffer, A. Z. (1963). The meaning of the analyst after analysis. A contribution to the theory of therapeutic results. *Journal of the American Psychoanalytic Association, 11,* 229–244.

Poland, W. S. (1996). *Melting the darkness.* Northvale, NJ: Jason Aronson.

Racker, E. (1953). A contribution to the problem of countertransference. *International Journal of Psychoanalysis, 34,* 313–324.

Rangell, L. (1963). Structural problems and intrapsychic conflict. *Psychoanalytic Study of the Child, 18,* 103–138.

Rangell, L. (1973). On the cacophony of human relations. *Psychoanalytic Quarterly, 42,* 325–348.

Reich, A. (1973). *Psychoanalytic contributions.* New York: International Universities Press.

Renik, O. (1995). The ideal of the anonymous analyst and the problem of self-disclosure. *Psychoanalytic Quarterly, 64,* 466–495.

Rogers, C. (1951). *Client-centered therapy.* New York: Houghton Mifflin.

Rosenfeld, H. (1954). Consideration concerning the psychoanalytic approach to acute and chronic schizophrenia. *International Journal of Psychoanalysis, 35,* 135–140.

Sachs, H. (1942). *The creative unconscious.* Cambridge, MA: Sci-Art Publishers.

Schafer, R. (1976). *A new language of psychoanalysis.* New Haven & London: Yale University Press.

Schmideberg, M. (1938). After the analysis. *Psychoanalytic Quarterly, 7,* 122–142.

Schultz, W. C. (1967). *Joy.* New York: Grove Press.

Searles, H. F. (1965). *Collected papers on schizophrenia and related subjects.* New York: International Universities Press.

Spitz, R. (1955). The primal cavity: A contribution to the genesis of perception and its role in psychoanalytic theory. *Psychoanalytic Study of the Child, 10,* 215–240.

Sullivan, H. S. (1953). *The interpersonal theory of psychiatry.* New York: Norton.

Tinbergern, N. (1951). *The study of instinct.* London: Oxford University Press.

Waelder, R. (1962). Review of psychoanalysis, scientific method and philosophy. *Journal of the American Psychoanalytic Association, 10,* 617–637.

Wallerstein, R. S. (1988). One psychoanalysis or many? *Psychoanalytic Quarterly, 55,* 414.

Wallerstein, R. S., & Smelser, N. J. (1969). Articulations and applications. *International Journal of Psychoanalysis, 50,* 693–710.

Weigert, E. (1970). *The courage to love.* New Haven: Yale University Press.

Winnicott, D. W. (1953). Transitional objects and transitional phenomena: A study of the first not-me possession. *International Journal of Psychoanalysis, 34,* 89–97.

Wolpe, J. (1958). *Psychotherapy by reciprocal inhibition.* Stanford, CA: Stanford University Press.

Zetzel, E. R. (1970). *The capacity for emotional growth: Theoretical and clinical contributions to psychoanalysis.* New York: International Universities Press.

Zilboorg, G., & Henry, G. W. (1941). *A history of medical psychology.* New York: Norton.

Alfred Adler, 1870–1937

# 3    ADLERIAN PSYCHOTHERAPY

*Harold H. Mosak*

## OVERVIEW

*Adlerian psychology* (Individual Psychology), developed by Alfred Adler, views the person holistically as a creative, responsible, "becoming" individual moving toward fictional goals within his or her phenomenal field. It holds that one's life-style is sometimes self-defeating because of inferiority feelings. The individual with "psychopathology" is discouraged rather than sick, and the therapeutic task is to encourage the person to activate his or her social interest and to develop a new life-style through relationship, analysis, and action methods.

### Basic Concepts

Adlerian psychology is predicated upon assumptions that differ in significant ways from the Freudian "womb" from which it emerged. Adler throughout his lifetime credited Freud with primacy in the development of a dynamic psychology. He consistently gave credit to Freud for explicating the purposefulness of symptoms and for discovering that dreams were meaningful. The influence of early childhood experiences in personality development constitutes still another point of agreement. Freud emphasized the role of psychosexual development and the Oedipus complex, and Adler focused upon the effects of children's perceptions of their family constellation and their struggle to find a place of significance within it.

Adlerian basic assumptions can be expressed as follows:

1.   All behavior occurs in a social context. Humans are born into an environment with which they must engage in reciprocal relations. The oft-quoted statement by the gestalt psychologist Kurt Lewin that "behavior is a function of person and environment" bears a striking parallel to Adler's contention that people cannot be studied in isolation.

2.   Individual Psychology (Adler's term) is an interpersonal psychology. How individuals interact with the others sharing "this crust of earth" (Adler, 1931/1958,[1] p. 6) is paramount. Transcending interpersonal transactions is the development of the feeling of being a part of a larger social whole that Adler (1964b) incorporated under the heading of *Gemeinschaftsgefühl,* or social interest.

3.   Adlerian psychology rejects reductionism in favor of holism. The Adlerian demotes part-functions from the central investigative focus in favor of studying the whole person and how he or she moves through life. This renders the polarities of *conscious* and *unconscious, mind* and *body, approach* and *avoidance, ambivalence* and *conflict* meaningless except as subjective experiences of the whole person. That is, people behave *as if* the conscious mind moves in one direction while the unconscious mind moves in another. From the external observer's viewpoint, all part-functions are subordinate functions of the individual's goals and style of life.

4.   *Conscious* and *unconscious* are both in the service of the individual, who uses them to further personal goals. Adler (1963a) treats *unconscious* as an adjective rather than a noun. That which is unconscious is the nonunderstood. Like Otto Rank, Adler felt that humans know more than they understand. *Conflict,* defined as intrapersonal by others, is defined as a "one step forward and one step backward movement," the net effect being to maintain the individual at a point "dead center." Although people experience themselves in the throes of a conflict, unable to move, in reality they *create* these antagonistic feelings, ideas, and values because they are unwilling to move in the direction of solving their problems (Mosak & LaFevre, 1976).

5.   Understanding the individual requires understanding his or her *cognitive organization* and life-style. The latter concept refers to the convictions individuals develop early in life to help them organize experience, to understand it, to predict it, and to control it. *Convictions* are conclusions derived from the individual's apperceptions, and they constitute a biased mode of apperception. Consequently, a *life-style* is neither right nor wrong, normal nor abnormal, but merely the "spectacles" through which people view themselves in relationship to the way in which they perceive life. Subjectivity rather than so-called objective evaluation becomes the major tool for understanding the person. As Adler wrote, "We must be able to see with his eyes and listen with his ears" (1931/1958, p. 72).

6.   Behavior may change throughout a person's life span in accordance with both the immediate demands of the situation and the long-range goals inherent in the life-style. The life-style remains relatively constant through life unless the convictions change through the mediation of psychotherapy. Although the definition of *psychotherapy* customarily refers to what transpires within a consulting room, a broader view of psychotherapy would include the fact that life in itself may often be psychotherapeutic.

7.   According to the Adlerian conception, people are not pushed by causes; that is, they are not determined by heredity and environment. "Both are giving only the frame and the influences which are answered by the individual in regard to the styled creative power"

---

[1] "1931/1958" indicates that the original date of publication was 1931, but the page number refers to the reprint published in 1958.

(Ansbacher & Ansbacher, 1956). People move toward self-selected goals that they feel will give them a place in the world, will provide them with security, and will preserve their self-esteem. Life is a dynamic striving. "The life of the human soul is not a 'being' but a 'becoming'" (Adler, 1963a, p. ix).

8. The central striving of human beings has been variously described as completion (Adler, 1931), perfection (Adler, 1964a), superiority (Adler, 1926), self-realization (Horney, 1951), self-actualization (Goldstein, 1939), competence (White, 1957), and mastery (Adler, 1926). Adler distinguishes among such strivings in terms of the direction a striving takes. If strivings are solely for the individual's greater glory, he considers them socially useless and, in extreme conditions, characteristic of mental problems. On the other hand, if the strivings are for the purpose of overcoming life's problems, the individual is engaged in the striving for self-realization, in contribution to humanity, and in making the world a better place to live.

9. Moving through life, the individual is confronted with alternatives. Because Adlerians are either nondeterminists or soft determinists, the conceptualization of humans as creative, choosing, self-determined decision makers permits them to choose the goals they want to pursue. Individuals may select socially useful goals or they may devote themselves to the useless side of life. They may choose to be task-oriented or they may, as does the neurotic, concern themselves with their own superiority.

10. The freedom to choose (McArthur, 1958) introduces the concepts of *value* and *meaning* into psychology. These were unpopular concepts at the time (1931) that Adler wrote *What Life Should Mean to You.* The greatest value for the Adlerian is *Gemeinschaftsgefühl,* or social interest (Ansbacher, 1968). Although Adler contends that it is an innate feature of human beings, at least as potential, acceptance of this criterion is not absolutely necessary. Mosak (1991) defines social interest as a construct rather than as an innate disposition. People possess the capacity for coexisting and interrelating with others. Indeed, the "iron logic of social living" (Adler, 1959) demands that we do so. Even in severe psychopathology, total extinction of social interest does not occur. Even people who are psychotic retain some commonality with "normal" people.

As Rabbi Akiva noted two millennia ago, "The greatest principle of living is to love one's neighbor as oneself." If we regard ourselves as fellow human beings with fellow feeling, we are socially contributive people interested in the common welfare and, by Adler's pragmatic definition of *normality,* mentally healthy (Dreikurs, 1969; Shoben, 1957).

If my feeling derives from my observation and conviction that life and people are hostile and I am inferior, I may divorce myself from the direct solution of life's problems and strive for personal superiority through overcompensation, wearing a mask, withdrawal, attempting only safe tasks where the outcome promises to be successful, and other devices for protecting my self-esteem. Adler said the neurotic in terms of movement displayed a "hesitating attitude" toward life (1964a). Also, the neurotic was described as a "yes-but" personality (Adler, 1934); at still other times, the neurotic was described as an "if only . . ." personality (Adler, 1964a): "If only I didn't have these symptoms, I'd . . ." The latter provided the rationale for "The Question," a device Adler used for differential diagnosis as well as for understanding the individual's task avoidance.

11. Because Adlerians are concerned with process, little diagnosis is done in terms of nomenclature. Differential diagnosis between functional and organic disorder does often present a problem. Because all behavior is purposeful, a *psychogenic* symptom will have a psychological or social purpose and an *organic* symptom will have a somatic purpose. An Adlerian would ask "The Question" (Adler, 1964a; Dreikurs, 1958, 1962), "If I had a magic wand or a magic pill that would eliminate your symptom immediately, what would be different in your life?" If the patient answers, "I'd go out more often socially" or "I'd write my book," the symptom would most likely be psychogenic. If the patient responds, "I wouldn't have this excruciating pain," the symptom would most likely be organic.

12. Life presents challenges in the form of life tasks. Adler named three of these explicitly but referred to two others without specifically naming them (Dreikurs & Mosak, 1966). The original three tasks were those of *society, work,* and *sex.* The first has already been alluded to. Because no person can claim self-sufficiency, we are all interdependent. Not only do we need social recognition, each of us also is dependent upon the labor of other people and they, in turn, are dependent upon our contribution. Work thus becomes essential for human survival. The cooperative individual assumes this role willingly. In the sexual realm, because two different sexes exist, we must also learn how to relate to that fact. We must define our sex roles, partly on the basis of cultural definitions and stereotypes, and train ourselves to relate to the *other,* not the *opposite,* sex. Other people, of either sex, do not represent the enemy. They are our fellows, with whom we must learn to cooperate.

Fourth (Dreikurs & Mosak, 1967) and fifth tasks (Mosak & Dreikurs, 1967) have been described. Although Adler alluded to the *spiritual,* he never specifically named it (Jahn & Adler, 1964). But each of us must deal with the problem of defining the nature of the universe, the existence and nature of God, and how to relate to these concepts. Finally, we must address the task of *coping with ourselves.* William James (1890) made the distinction between the self as subject and the self as object, and it is as imperative, for the sake of mental health, that good relations exist between the "I" and the "me" as between the "I" and other people. In this task we must also deal, subjectively and reductionistically on the part of the person, with the "good me" and the "bad me."

13. Because life constantly provides challenges, living demands courage (Neuer, 1936). Courage is not an *ability* one either possesses or lacks. Nor is courage synonymous with bravery, such as falling on a grenade to save one's buddies from injury or death. *Courage* refers to the *willingness* to engage in risk-taking behavior when one either does not know the consequences or when the consequences might be adverse. We are all *capable* of courageous behavior provided that we are *willing.* Our willingness will depend upon many variables, internal and external, such as our life-style convictions, our degree of social interest, the extent of risk as we appraise it, and whether we are task-oriented or prestige-oriented. Given that life offers few guarantees, all living requires risk taking. It would require very little courage to live if we were perfect, omniscient, or omnipotent. The question we must each answer is whether we have the courage to live despite the knowledge of our imperfections (Lazarsfeld, 1966).

14. Life has no intrinsic meaning. We give meaning to life, each of us in our own fashion. We declare it to be meaningful, meaningless, an absurdity, a prison sentence (cf., the adolescent's justification for doing as he pleases—"I didn't ask to be born"), a vale of tears, a preparation for the next world, and so on. Dreikurs (1957, 1971) maintained that the meaning of life resided in doing for others and in contributing to social life and social change. Viktor Frankl (1963) believed the meaning of life lay in love. The meaning we attribute to life will "determine" our behavior. We will behave *as if* life were really in accord with our perceptions, and, therefore, certain meanings will have greater practical utility than others. Optimists will live an optimistic life, take chances, and not be discouraged by failure and adversity. They will be able to distinguish between failing and being a failure. Pessimists will refuse to be engaged with life, refuse to try, sabotage their efforts if they do make an attempt, and, through their methods of operation, endeavor to confirm their preexisting pessimistic anticipations (Krausz, 1935).

## Other Systems

Students often have asked, "Do you Adlerians believe in sex too?" The question is not always asked facetiously. Freud accorded sex the status of the master motive in behavior. Adler merely categorized sex as one of several tasks the individual was required to solve.

Freud employed esoteric jargon and Adler favored common-sense language. One story has it that a psychiatrist took Adler to task after a lecture, denigrating his approach with the criticism, "You're only talking common sense," to which Adler replied, "I wish more psychiatrists did." We can place other differences between these two men in columnar form, as shown in Table 3.1.

A more extended comparison of Freud's and Adler's concepts of humankind may be found in articles by H. W. von Sassen (1967) and Otto Hinrichsen (1913).

## Adler and the Neo-Freudians

Adler once proclaimed that he was more concerned that his theories survived than that people remembered to associate his theories with his name. His wish apparently was granted. In discussing Adler's influence upon contemporary psychological theory and practice, Henri Ellenberger commented, "It would not be easy to find another author from which so much has been borrowed from all sides without acknowledgment than Adler" (1970, p. 645). However, many neo-Freudians have credited Adler with contributing to and influencing their work. In her last book, Karen Horney wrote of "neurotic ambition," "the need for perfection," and "the category of power." "All drives for glory have in common the reaching out for greater knowledge, wisdom, virtue or powers than are given to human beings; they all aim at the absolute, the unlimited, the infinite" (1951, pp. 34–35). Those familiar with Adler's writings on the neurotic's perfectionistic, godlike striving will immediately be struck with the similarity in viewpoint.

Horney (1951) rejected Freud's pessimism, "his disbelief in human goodness and human growth," in favor of the Adlerian view that a person could grow and could "become a decent human being."

Others have also remarked upon the resemblance between the theories of Horney and Adler; the reviewer of one Horney book wrote that Karen Horney had just written a new book by Alfred Adler (Farau, 1953).

Erich Fromm also expresses views similar to those of Adler. According to Fromm, people make choices. The attitude of the mother in child rearing is of paramount importance. Life fosters feelings of powerlessness and anxiety. Patrick Mullahy (1955) indicates that:

> The only adequate solution, according to Fromm, is a relationship with man and nature, chiefly by love and productive work, which strengthens the total personality, sustains the person in his sense of uniqueness, and at the same time gives him a feeling of belonging, a sense of unity and common destiny with mankind. (pp. 251–252)

Although Harry Stack Sullivan places greater emphasis upon developmental child psychology than does Adler, Sullivan's "person" moves through life in much the same manner as does Adler's. Thus, Sullivan (1954) speaks of the "security operation" of the individual, a direct translation of Adler's and Lene Credner's (1930) *Sicherungen*. His "good me" and "bad me" dichotomy, in expression if not in manner of development, is essentially the same as that described by Adlerians.

So many similarities between Adler and the neo-Freudians have been noted that Gardner Murphy concluded, "If this way of reasoning is correct, neurosis should be the general characteristic of man under industrialism, a point suspected by many Freudians and, in particular, by that branch of the Freudian school (Horney and her associates) that has learned most from Adler" (1947, p. 569). A summary of such resemblances appears in Heinz and Rowena Ansbacher's *Individual Psychology of Alfred Adler* (1956) as well as in an article by Walter James (1947). Fritz Wittels (1939) has proposed that the neo-Freudians should more properly be called "neo-Adlerians," and a study by Heinz Ansbacher (1952) suggests that many traditional Freudians would concur.

**TABLE 3.1  Comparison of Freud's and Adler's Concepts**

| Freud | Adler |
|---|---|
| 1. Objective | 1. Subjective |
| 2. Physiological substratum for theory | 2. A social psychology |
| 3. Emphasized causality | 3. Emphasized teleology |
| 4. Reductionistic. The individual was divided into "parts" that were antagonistic toward each other: e.g., id-ego-superego, Eros vs. Thanatos, conscious vs. unconscious. | 4. Holistic. The individual is indivisible. He or she is a unity, and all "parts" (memory, emotions, behavior) are in the service of the whole individual. |
| 5. The study of the individual centers about the intrapersonal, the intrapsychic. | 5. People can only be understood interpersonally and as social beings moving through and interacting with their environment. |
| 6. The establishment of intrapsychic harmony constitutes the ideal goal of psychotherapy. "Where id was, there shall ego be." | 6. The expansion of the individual, self-realization, and the enhancement of social interest represent the ideal goals for the individual. |
| 7. People are basically "bad." Civilization attempts to domesticate them, for which they pay a heavy price. Through therapy the instinctual demands may be sublimated but not eliminated. | 7. People are neither "good" nor "bad," but as creative, choosing human beings, they may choose to be "good" or "bad" or both, depending upon their life-styles and their appraisal of the immediate situation and its payoffs. Through the medium of therapy people can choose to actualize themselves. |
| 8. People are victims of both instinctual life and civilization. | 8. People, as choosers, can shape both their internal and external environments. Although they cannot always choose what will happen to them, they can always choose the posture they will adopt toward life's stimuli. |
| 9. Description of child development was postdictive and not based upon direct observation of children but upon the free associations of adults. | 9. Children were studied directly in families, schools, and family education centers. |
| 10. Emphasis on the Oedipus situation and its resolution. | 10. Emphasis upon the family constellation. |
| 11. People are enemies. Others are our competitors, and we must protect ourselves from them. Theodore Reik quotes Nestroy, "If chance brings two wolves together, . . . neither feels the least uneasy because the other is a wolf; two human beings, however, can never meet in the forest, but one must think: That fellow may be a robber" (Reik, 1948, p. 477). | 11. Other people are *mitmenschen,* fellow human beings. They are our equals, our collaborators, our cooperators in life. |
| 12. Women feel inferior because they envy men their penises. Women are inferior. Anatomy is destiny. | 12. Women feel inferior because in our cultural milieu women are undervalued. Men have privileges, rights, and preferred status, although in the current cultural ferment, their roles are being reevaluated. |
| 13. Neurosis has a sexual etiology. | 13. Neurosis is a failure of learning, a product of distorted perceptions. |
| 14. Neurosis is the price we pay for civilization. | 14. Neurosis is the price we pay for our lack of civilization. |

## Adler and Rogers

Although the therapies of Adler and Carl Rogers are diametrically opposed, their theories share many commonalities. Both are phenomenological, goal-directed, and holistic. Each views people as self-consistent, creative, and capable of change. To illustrate, Rogers (1951) postulates the following:

1. The organism reacts as an organized whole to the phenomenal field (p. 486).
2. The best vantage point for understanding behavior is from the internal frame of reference of the individual (p. 494).
3. The organism reacts to the field as it is experienced and perceived (pp. 484–845).
4. The organism has one basic tendency and striving—to actualize, maintain, and enhance the experiencing organism (p. 487).

Much of the early research on nondirective and person-centered therapy measured the discrepancy between *self-concept* and *self-ideal.* The Adlerian would describe the extent of discrepancy as a measure of inferiority feelings.

## Adler and Ellis

The theories of Adler and Ellis exhibit many points of convergence. Albert Ellis (1970, 1971) finds his rational-emotive psychology to parallel that of Adler. What Adler calls basic mistakes, Albert Ellis refers to as irrational beliefs or attitudes. Both accept the notion that emotions are actually a form of thinking and that people create or control their emotions by controlling their thinking. They agree that we are not victims of our emotions but their creators. In psychotherapy, they (1) adopt similar stances with respect to unconscious motivation, (2) confront patients with their irrational ideas (basic mistakes or internalized sentences), (3) counterpropagandize the patient, (4) insist upon action, and (5) constantly *encourage* patients to assume responsibility for the direction of their lives in more positive channels. The last phrase seems to reflect the major disagreement between Adler and Ellis, namely, what is "positive." Ellis argues:

> Where Adler writes, therefore, that "All my efforts are devoted towards increasing the social interest of the patient," the rational therapist would prefer to say, "Most of my efforts are devoted towards increasing the self-interest of the patient." He assumes that if the individual possesses rational self-interest he will, on both biological and logical grounds, almost invariably tend to have a high degree of social interest as well. (1957, p. 43)

## Adlerian and Cognitive Therapy

Adlerian and cognitive therapy share much in common, as Beck and Weishaar (2005) acknowledge. Both are phenomenological psychologies, and both are concerned with the way individuals view the world and themselves. Both emphasize the role of cognition in emotion and behavior (Beck & Weishaar, 2005; Dreikurs, 1951; Mosak, 1985). Each posits a set of cognitive structures (for the Adlerian it is the life-style; for the cognitive therapist, it is a schema). These cognitive structures *may be* (the cognitive therapist would say *are*) related to certain kinds of emotional behavior (Beck & Weishaar, 2005; Mosak, 1968). Beck and Weishaar speak of cognitive distortion and Adler of "basic mistakes." Beck and Weishaar's term is preferable, but both are describing processes that are essentially the same. The reader may wish to compare Beck's description of cognitive distortions (p. 247) and Mosak's description of "basic mistakes" (p. 71) in this volume.

Therapy in each system is a collaborative effort, both employing what Beck and Weishaar call "collaborative empiricism, Socratic dialogue, and guided discovery" (Beck & Weishaar, 2005).

The two therapies differ in significant ways. Cognitive therapy is not designed for personal growth, while Adlerians focus on personal growth even for the patient with psychopathology. Cognitive therapists narrow the types of psychopathology with which they will deal; Adlerians do not. For example, cognitive therapists do not obtain good results with people coping with psychosis (Beck & Weishaar, 2005), but Adlerians regularly treat these patients. As with Freudian analysis, a certain amount of intellectual and/or psychological sophistication on the part of the patient brings the best results from cognitive therapy. However, the Adlerian therapist has no such requirement and meets the patient's level of sophistication by speaking at the patient's level of intelligence and in the patient's idiom (Mosak & Shulman, 1963). In spite of these differences, cognitive therapy appears to be "variations on a theme by Adler," even though Beck reads better because of his use of the language of contemporary psychology rather than the archaic language of Adler and his contemporaries.

## Adler and Other Systems

The many points of convergence and divergence between Adler and several of the existentialist thinkers have been noted by many writers (Birnbaum, 1961; Farau, 1964; Frankl, 1970). Phyllis Bottome had written in 1939 that "Adler was the first founder of an existence psychology" (p. 199). Given that existential psychology is not a school but a viewpoint, it is difficult to make comparisons, but interested readers may discover for themselves in an editorial by Ansbacher (1959) the lines of continuity between Adler's ideas and existential thought.

The recognition of Adler as one of the earliest humanistic psychologists is clear. Ellis pays homage to Adler as "one of the first humanistic psychologists" (1970, p. 32). Abraham Maslow (1962, 1970) published five papers in Adlerian journals over a period of 35 years. As we have already observed, many of Adler's ideas have been incorporated by the humanistic psychologists with little awareness of Adler's contributions. "The model of man as a composite of part functions" that James Bugental (1963) questioned has been repudiated by Adlerians for more than half a century. Adlerian psychology is a value psychology (Adler wrote *What Life Should Mean to You* in 1931), as Viktor Frankl and Rollo May, among others, recognize in acknowledging their debt to Adler. Frankl wrote:

> What he [Adler] . . . achieved and accomplished was no less than a Copernican switch. . . . Beyond this, Alfred Adler may well be regarded as an existential thinker and as a forerunner of the existential-psychiatric movement. (1970, p. 38)

May expresses his debt as follows:

> I appreciate Adler more and more. . . . Adler's thoughts as I learned them in studying with him in Vienna in the summers of 1932 and 1933 led me indirectly into psychology, and were very influential in the later work in this country of Sullivan and William Alanson White, etc. (1970, p. 39)

Abraham Maslow wrote:

> For me Alfred Adler becomes more and more correct year by year. As the facts come in, they give stronger and stronger support to his image of man. I should say that in one respect especially the times have not yet caught up with him. I refer to his holistic emphasis. (1970, p. 39)

# HISTORY

## Precursors

Adler's insistence that people cannot be studied in isolation but only in their social context was previously expressed by Aristotle, who referred to the human being as a *zoon politikon,* a political animal (Adler, 1959). Adler exhibits his affinity with the philosophy of stoicism, as both Ellenberger (1970) and H. N. Simpson (1966) point out. Other commentators have noted the resemblance of Adler's writings to Kant's philosophy, especially with respect to the categorical imperative, private logic, and overcoming. Adler and Nietzsche have often been compared, and much has been made of their common usage of the concept of the *will to power* (Ansbacher, 1972; Crookshank, 1933). Adler spoke of it in terms of the normal strivings for competence, however, while Nietzsche's references to this concept involved what Adler would call the "useless side of life." Nietzsche stressed the *Übermensch* (superman) and Adler spoke of equality. Adler further stressed *social feeling,* a concept totally alien to the Nietzschian philosophy.

Throughout history, philosophers have struggled with the mind-body problem. Psychology experienced a renaissance when psychologists and psychiatrists began to apply themselves to the study of psychosomatic syndromes. Psychosomatic and somatopsychic hypotheses were advanced to explain how emotions could influence the production of symptoms and how bodily states might create emotional or mental illness. Adler rejected such divisions. Like Kurt Lewin (1935), he rejected categorization and dichotomies. Like Jan Smuts (1961), he was a holist, and *Individual Psychology* was not meant to describe the psychology of the individual. It referred rather to Adler's holistic stance, that a person could be understood only as a whole, an indivisible unity. To study people atomistically was to not capture fully the nature of humanity. For Adler, the question was neither "How does mind affect body?" nor "How does body affect mind?" but rather "How does the individual use body and mind in the pursuit of goals?" Although Adler's *Study of Organ Inferiority and Its Psychical Compensation* (1917) might seem to contradict such statements by expressing a causalistic viewpoint, this highly original theory was formulated when Adler was a member of the Freudian circle. Later Adler added the subjective factor:

> It might be suggested, therefore, that in order to find out where a child's interest lies, we need only to ascertain which organ is defective. But things do not work out quite so simply. The child does not experience the fact of organ inferiority in the way that an external observer sees it, but as modified by his own scheme of apperception. (1969)

Perhaps the greatest influence upon Adler was Hans Vaihinger's (1965) "philosophy of 'as if.'" According to Vaihinger, a fiction is "a mere piece of imagination" that deviates from reality but that is nevertheless utilitarian for the individual. Both the concept of the world and the concept of the self are subjective, that is, fictional, and therefore in error. *Truth* is "only the most expedient error, that is, the system of ideas which enables us to act and to deal with things most rapidly, neatly, and safely, and with the minimum of irrational elements" (p. 108).

Finally, Adler's psychology has a religious tone (Adler, 1958; Jahn & Adler, 1964; Mosak, 1987c). His placement of social interest at the pinnacle of his value theory is in the tradition of those religions that stress people's responsibility for each other. Indeed, Adler maintained that "Individual Psychology makes good religion if you are unfortunate enough not to have another" (Rasey, 1956, p. 254).

# Beginnings

Adler was born near Vienna on February 7, 1870, and he died while on a lecture tour in Aberdeen, Scotland, on May 27, 1937. After graduating from the University of Vienna in 1895, Adler entered private practice as an ophthalmologist in 1898. He later switched to general practice and then to neurology. During this period, Adler gave portents of his later social orientation by writing a book on the health of tailors (1898). In this respect, he may be regarded as the progenitor of industrial medicine and of community outreach.

In 1902, Adler, at Freud's invitation, joined in the latter's Wednesday evening discussion circle. Biographers agree that Adler wrote two defenses of Freud's theories that may have gained him the invitation. Although textbooks frequently refer to Adler as a student of Freud, Adler was actually a colleague (Ansbacher, 1962; Ellenberger, 1970; Federn, 1963; Maslow, 1962). Through the next decade, Adler had one foot in and one foot out of the Freudian circle. Although his *Study of Organ Inferiority* won Freud's unqualified endorsement, Adler's introduction of the aggression instinct in 1908 met with Freud's disapproval. Not until 1923, long after Adler had discarded instinct theory, did Freud incorporate the aggressive instinct into psychoanalysis (Sicher & Mosak, 1967), at which time Adler declared, "I enriched psychoanalysis by the aggressive drive. I gladly make them a present of it!" (Bottome, 1939, p. 63).

Adler's increasing divergence from Freud's viewpoint led to discomfort and disillusion in the Vienna Psychoanalytic Society. Adler criticized Freud's sexual stance; Freud condemned Adler's ego psychology. They disagreed on (1) the unity of neuroses, (2) penis envy (sexual) versus the masculine protest (social), (3) the defensive role of the ego in neuroses, and (4) the role of the unconscious. Freud did not think Adler had discovered anything new but had merely reinterpreted what psychoanalysis had already said. He believed that what Adler discovered was "trivial," and that it was "methodologically deplorable and condemns his whole work to sterility" (Colby, 1951). In 1911, after a series of meetings where these issues were discussed in an atmosphere of fencing, heckling, and vitriol (Brome, 1968), Adler resigned as president of the Vienna Society. Later that year, Freud forced the choice between Adler and himself. Several members of the circle expressed their sympathy for Adler by resigning and forming the Society for Free Psychoanalytic Research. The word "free" was meant to imply that this was still a psychoanalytic society, but it was free of Freud.

During the next decade, with the exception of the war period, Adler and his coworkers developed the social view of the neuroses. Their focus was primarily clinical, although as early as 1908 Adler (1914) had demonstrated an interest in children, families, and education. In 1922 Adler initiated what was perhaps the first community-outreach program, child-guidance centers within the community. These centers were located in public schools and were directed by psychologists who served without pay. The method, for which Adler drew much criticism, was that of public family education, a method still used in Adlerian family education centers. Twenty-eight such centers existed in Vienna until 1934, when an unfriendly government closed them. This form of center was transported to the United States by Rudolf Dreikurs and his students (Dreikurs, Corsini, Lowe, & Sonstegard, 1959). The success of these centers motivated the Vienna school authorities to invite several Adlerians to plan a school along Adlerian lines, and from this invitation emerged the school described in Oskar Spiel's *Discipline Without Punishment* (1962). The school emphasized encouragement, class discussions, democratic principles, and the responsibility of children for themselves and for each other—educational methods that are still in use today.

The social orientation of Adler's Individual Psychology inevitably led to interest in group methods and Adler's introduction of family therapy (1922). Dreikurs (1959) is credited with the first use of group psychotherapy in private practice.

Between World Wars I and II, Adlerian groups existed in 20 European countries and in the United States. In 1926 Adler was invited to the United States to lecture and until 1934, when fascism took hold in Austria, he divided his time between the United States, where he was on the medical faculty of the Long Island College of Medicine, and abroad. Two of his children, Alexandra and Kurt, practiced psychiatry in New York City. With the march of Nazism, many Adlerians were forced to flee their European homelands and made the United States the center of their activities. Today Individual Psychology societies exist in the United States, England, Canada, France, Denmark, Switzerland, Germany, Austria, the Netherlands, Greece, Italy, Israel, and Australia.

## Current Status

The resurgence of the Adlerian school after the dispersion from Europe was an uphill effort. Personal hardships of refugee Adlerians were compounded by the existing psychological climate in this country. The economic depression still prevailed. The Freudian school held a near monopoly, both in the treatment area and with respect to appointments in medical schools. Some Adlerians defected; others became crypto-Adlerians. However, others persevered in retaining their identity and their optimism. Local societies were founded, and 1952 saw the formation of the American Society of Adlerian Psychology (now the North American Society of Adlerian Psychology). Several journals appeared; the major American one is the *Journal of Individual Psychology,* formerly called *Individual Psychology,* which itself was the successor of the *Individual Psychology Bulletin,* of which Dreikurs was the editor for many years. The International Association of Individual Psychology also publishes the *Individual Psychology Newsletter.*

Training institutes that offer certificates in psychotherapy, counseling, and child guidance are found in New York; Chicago; Minneapolis; Berkeley, CA; San Francisco; St. Louis; Fort Wayne, IN; Vancouver; Montreal; and Toronto. Individual courses and programs of study are offered at many universities, such as Oregon, Arizona, West Virginia, Vermont, Governors State, Southern Illinois, and Georgia State. Master's degrees based on an Adlerian curriculum are offered by Bowie State College and by the Adler School of Professional Psychology in Chicago. The latter has been accredited to offer a doctoral program in clinical psychology.

Although Adlerian psychology was once dismissed as moribund, superficial (i.e., an "ego psychology"), and suitable mainly for children, it is today considered a viable psychology.

Today's Adlerian may operate as a traditional clinician but remains innovative. For example, Joshua Bierer was a pioneer in social psychiatry (Bierer & Evans, 1969) and a leader in the day-hospital movement (1951). Therapeutic social clubs have been in operation at the Alfred Adler Mental Hygiene Clinic in New York and at Saint Joseph Hospital in Chicago. Dreikurs originated multiple psychotherapy (1950), and he, Harold Mosak, and Bernard Shulman contributed to its development (1952a, 1952b, 1982). Rudolf Dreikurs, Asya Kadis, Helene Papanek, and Bernard Shulman have made extensive contributions to group therapy. Because they prefer the goal of prevention to that of healing, Adlerians function extensively in the area of education. Manford Sonstegard, Raymond Lowe, Bronia Grunwald, Oscar Christensen, Raymond Corsini, and Loren Grey are among those responsible for applying Adlerian principles in the schools. All of these have been students of Dreikurs, who transported the tradition from Vienna, and who himself made a great contribution in this area. In the Adlerian social tradition, Adlerians may be involved in community outreach programs or dedicating their efforts to the study of subjects such as drugs, aging, delinquency, religion, and poverty.

The contemporary Adlerian finds the growth model of personality infinitely more congenial than the sickness model. The Adlerian is not interested in curing sick individuals or a sick society, but in reeducating individuals and in reshaping society.

# PERSONALITY

## Theory of Personality

Adlerian psychology is a psychology of use rather than of possession. This assumption decreases the importance of the question, "How do heredity and environment shape the individual?" The functionalist, holistic Adlerian asks instead, "How does the individual use heredity and environment?" Since theirs is a psychology of use, Alderians find it improper to use such phrases as "He *has* social interest." People *display* social interest rather than possess it (Mosak, 1991).

For Adler, the *family constellation* constitutes the primary social environment. Every child searches for significance in this environment and competes for position within the family constellation. One sibling becomes the "best" child, another the "worst" one. Being favored, being one of the favored sex within the family, adopting the family values, or identifying or allying oneself with a parent or sibling may provide the grounds for the feeling of having a place. Handicaps, organ inferiorities, or being an orphan are other "position makers" for some children.

Of supreme importance is the child's position in the family constellation. Thus, it would appear that the first child usually is a conservative and the second is often a rebel. The baby is ordinarily either everyone's darling or one who stands on tiptoes to see above the preceding siblings. If these general characteristics possess any validity, at best they exist as statistical probabilities and not as defining traits. Considering the family constellation in terms of birth order or ordinal position creates the problem of characterizing, let us say, the fifth child in the family. Although the fifth child is often encountered in the therapy situation, he or she never receives any attention in the literature. Birth order, per se, also ignores the gender position of the child. The children in two-sibling families in which the possible configurations are boy-boy, girl-girl, boy-girl, and girl-boy do not possess similar characteristics based upon ordinal position alone (Shulman & Mosak, 1977).

The Adlerian prefers to study the family constellation in terms of the *psychological* position. A simple example illustrates this point of view. Take two siblings separated in age by 10 years. In birth order research, these would be treated as a first child and a second child. From the Adlerian point of view the psychological position of each would *most likely* be that of an only child with *perhaps* the older child functioning as an additional parent figure for the younger. The italicized terms *most likely* and *perhaps* are used expressly to indicate that: (1) Adlerians do not recognize a causalistic, one-to-one relationship between family position and sibling traits; and (2) whatever relationship exists can only be understood in context, that is, when one knows the family climate and the total configuration of factors in the family constellation. Adler, whenever he generalized or ventured a prediction, was fond of reminding his students, "Everything could also be quite different."

The search for significance and the consequent sibling competition reflect the values of the competitive society in which we live. We are encouraged to be first, to excel, to be popular, to be athletic, to be a "real" man, to "never say die," to recall that "practice makes perfect," and to "dream the impossible dream." Consequently, each child must stake out a piece of "territory" that includes the attributes or abilities that are hoped will give a feeling of worth. If through their evaluations of their own potency (abilities, courage, and confidence) children are convinced that they can achieve this place through useful endeavor, they will pursue "the useful side of life." Should children feel that they cannot attain the goal of having a "place" in this fashion, they will become discouraged and engage in disturbed or disturbing behavior in their efforts to find a place. For the Adlerian the "maladjusted" child is not a "sick" child. He or she is a "discouraged" child. Dreikurs (1948, 1949) classifies the goals of the discouraged child into four groups—attention getting, power seeking, revenge taking, and declaring deficiency or defeat. Dreikurs is speaking of immediate rather than long-range goals. These are the goals of children's "misbehavior," not of all children's behavior (Mosak & Mosak, 1975b).

In the process of becoming socialized human beings, children form conclusions on the basis of their subjective experiences. Because judgment and logical processes are not highly developed in young children, many of their growing convictions contain errors or only partial "truths." Nevertheless, they accept these conclusions about themselves and others *as if* they were true. They are subjective evaluations, biased apperceptions of themselves and of the world, rather than objective "reality." Thus, one can be truly inferior without feeling inferior. Conversely, one can feel inferior without being inferior.

The child creates a cognitive map or life-style that will assist "little me" in coping with the "big" world. The life-style includes the aspirations, the long-range goals, and a "statement" of the conditions, personal or social, that are requisite for the individual's "security." The latter are also fictions and are stated in therapy as "If only . . . , then I . . ." Mosak (1954) divided life-style convictions into four groups:

1. The *self-concept*—the convictions I have about who I am.
2. The *self-ideal* (Adler coined this phrase in 1912)—the convictions of what I should be or am obliged to be to have a place.
3. The *Weltbild,* or "picture of the world"—convictions about the not-self (world, people, nature, and so on) and what the world demands of me.
4. The *ethical convictions*—the personal "right-wrong" code.

When there is a discrepancy between self and ideal-self convictions ("I am short; I should be tall"), *inferiority feelings* ensue. Although an infinite variety of inferiority feelings exist, one that Adler discussed while he was still in the Freudian Society should be mentioned—an idea that eventually led to the rift between Adler and Freud. It assumes monumental importance in some circles today—the *masculine protest.* In a culture that places a premium on masculinity, some women feel inferior because they have not been accorded the prerogatives or privileges of men ("I am woman; I should be equal to man"). But men also suffered from the masculine protest because being a man is not sufficient to provide a "place" for some men ("I am a man, but I should be *a real* man"). Because Adler believed in the equality of the sexes, he could not accept these fictions (Mosak & Schneider, 1977).

Lack of congruence between convictions in the self-concept and those in the *Weltbild* ("I am weak and helpless; life is dangerous") also results in inferiority feelings. Discrepancies between self-concept and ethical convictions ("One should always tell the truth; I lie") lead to inferiority feelings in the moral realm. Thus, the guilt feeling is merely a variant of the inferiority feeling (Mosak, 1987b).

These variations of inferiority feelings in and of themselves are not "abnormal." It would be difficult to quarrel with Adler's observations that to live is to *feel* inferior. It is only when individuals act *as if* they were inferior, develop symptoms, or behave as "sick" that we see evidence of what in the medical model would be called *pathology* and what Adlerians call *discouragement* or the *inferiority complex.* To oversimplify, the *inferiority feeling* is universal and "normal," although it may leave us uncomfortable; the *inferiority complex* reflects the discouragement of a limited segment of our society and is usually "abnormal." The former may be masked or hidden from the view of others; the latter is an open demonstration of inadequacy, or "sickness."

Using their "maps," people facilitate their movements through life. This permits them to evaluate, understand, experience, predict, and control experience. Lawrence Frank writes in this connection:

> The personality process might be regarded as a sort of rubber stamp which the individual imposes upon every situation by which he gives it the configuration that he, as an individual, requires; in so doing he necessarily ignores or subordinates many aspects of the situation that for him are irrelevant and meaningless and selectively reacts to those aspects that are personally significant. (1939, p. 392)

Although the life-style is the instrument for coping with experience, it is very largely nonconscious. The life-style comprises the cognitive organization of the individual rather than the behavioral organization. As an illustration, the conviction "I require excitement" may lead to the vocational choices of actor, racing car driver, explorer, or to "acting out" behavior. Such a conviction may further lead to getting into jams or exciting situations, engaging in creative acts, or discovery.

Within the same life-style, one can behave usefully or uselessly. The above distinction permits Adlerians (e.g., Dreikurs, 1961; Nikelly, 1971a) to distinguish between *psychotherapy* and *counseling.* The former, they maintain, has as its aim the change of life-style; the latter has as its goal the change of behavior within the existing life-style.

Because the Adlerian literature discusses the life tasks of occupation, society, and love so extensively, these tasks of life will not be elaborated upon here, except for some brief comments. Lewis Way points out that "The problems they pose can never be solved once and for all, but demand from the individual a continuous and creative movement toward adaptation" (1962, pp. 179–180).

*Love,* as an emotion like other emotions, is cognitively based. People are not "victims" of their emotions. They create emotions to assist them in the attainment of their goals. Love is the conjunctive emotion we create when we want to move toward people.

Although the life tasks of love, occupation, and society demand solution, it is possible to avoid or postpone them if one can compensate in other areas. "Even successful persons fall into neurosis because they are not more successful" (Way, 1962, p. 206). The *neurotic symptom* is an expression of "I *can't* because I'm sick"; the person's movement betrays the "I *won't* because my self-esteem might get hurt" (Krausz, 1959, p. 112). Although neurotics' movements are consonant with their "private logic" (Nikelly, 1971b), they still cling to "common sense." They know what they should do or feel, but they "can't." Adler referred to them as "yes-but" personalities. Eric Berne (1964) has graphically described their interpersonal maneuvers in the "Why don't you—Yes, but" game. The genesis of neurosis lies in discouragement. People avoid and postpone or take circuitous routes to solutions so they can "save face." Even when they expect or arrange to fail, they try to salvage some self-esteem. Students, fearful of failing examinations, will refrain from studying. In the event they do fail, they merely have to hold that they were lazy or neglectful but not stupid.

The psychotic's goal of superiority is often loftier than that which can be achieved by mere humans. "Individual Psychology has shown that the goal of superiority can only be fixed at such attitudes when the individual has, by losing interest in others, also lost interest in his own reason and understanding . . . common sense has become useless to him" (Adler, 1964a, pp. 128–129). Adler used "common sense" in much the same manner that Sullivan spoke of "consensual validation." In the pseudo work area, the psychotic becomes superintendent of the mental hospital. In the pseudo social area, the hypomanic patient resembles the cheerful extrovert and the more acutely manic patient becomes a "name dropper" and "swallows up" people (Shulman, 1962). The paranoid patient pictures people as threatening and manifests a "search for glory," to use Karen Horney's (1951) phrase, by the persecutory delusion that *they* are conspiring to do something to *me.* The delusions of grandeur of the psychotic depressive patients ("I'm the *worst* sinner of all time") and of the schizophrenic who claims to be Christ are some other "solutions" to the pseudo spiritual tasks. The reifying hallucinations of talking with the devil fall in this category (Adler, 1963a; Mosak & Fletcher, 1973).

The *psychologically healthy* or *normal* individual has developed social interest and is willing to commit to life and the life tasks without evasion, excuse, or "side shows" (Wolfe, 1932). This person proceeds with confidence and optimism about meeting life's challenges. There is a sense of belonging and contributing, the "courage to be imperfect," and the serene knowledge that one can be acceptable to others, although imperfect. Above all, this person rejects the faulty values that culture projects and attempts to substitute for them values more consonant with the "ironclad logic of social living." Such a person does not exist, nor will psychotherapy produce such a person. Yet this is the Adlerian ideal, and because Adler's intent was to substitute small errors for larger errors, many of these goals can be approximated in psychotherapy. Many fortunate people have the courage (Adler, 1928) and social interest to do this for themselves without therapeutic assistance.

## Variety of Concepts

The simplicity of Adlerian vocabulary renders definition and interpretation generally unnecessary. Yet some differences of opinion and emphasis about Adlerian concepts remain unresolved. In terms of *life-style,* Adlerians disagree with respect to what it describes—behavioral or cognitive organization. *Social interest* (Bickhard & Ford, 1976; Crandall, 1981; Edgar, 1975; Kazan, 1978; Mosak, 1991) apparently is not a unitary concept but a cluster of feelings and behaviors (Ansbacher, 1968). Although social interest is often described as "innate," many Adlerians wonder what makes it so, given that it appears to be neither genetic nor constitutional. As one looks at the theories of Adler, Freud, and Jung, one is struck with the effort on the part of all three to "biologize" their theories. Perhaps it was the temper of the times. Perhaps it was because all three were physicians. Perhaps it resulted from the need to make their theories respectable during a period when psychoanalysis was held in low esteem. None of these theories would incur any great damage if "instincts," "social interest," and "racial unconscious" were treated as psychological constructs rather than as biological processes. Adler, having introduced the concept of *organ inferiority* with its consequent compensation, actually had proposed a biopsychological theory, but it must be recalled that this transpired during his "Freudian period." Later he substituted the *social inferiority feeling* for actual organ inferiority, and with the exception of one important article (Shulman & Klapman, 1968), Adlerians have published little on organ inferiority. Although people undoubtedly do compensate for organ inferiority, the latter is no longer the cornerstone of the Adlerian edifice.

Gardner Murphy (1947) took issue with Adler's use of compensation as the only defense mechanism. Literally, Adler's writings do read that way. On the other hand, if one reads more closely, compensation becomes an umbrella to cover all coping mechanisms. Thus, Adler speaks of safeguards, excuses, projection, the depreciation tendency, creating distance, and identification. Although a Freudian might view these as defense mechanisms, the Adlerian prefers to view them as problem-solving devices the person uses to protect self-esteem, reputation, and physical self. Because Adlerians do not accept the concept of *the* unconscious, such mechanisms as repression and sublimation become irrelevant. Adlerian theory has no room for instincts, drives, libido, and other alleged movers.

Because of their mutual emphasis on behavior (movement), Adlerian psychology and behavior-modification theory have been equated. This is an error. Adlerians, although interested in changing behavior, have as their major goal not behavior modification but *mo-*

*tivation* modification. Dreikurs writes: "We do not attempt primarily to change behavior patterns or remove symptoms. If a patient improves his behavior because he finds it profitable at the time, without changing his basic premises, then we do not consider that as a therapeutic success. We are trying to change goals, concepts, and notions" (1963, p. 79).

# PSYCHOTHERAPY

## Theory of Psychotherapy

All scientific schools of psychotherapy have their shares of successes and failures. A considerable number of therapies based upon nonscientific foundations probably result in equivalent levels of success. In any event, regardless of its validity or endurance, any theory must be implemented within the context of the therapist-patient relationship. As Fred Fiedler (1950) has shown, therapeutic success is a function of the expertness of the therapist rather than of the therapist's orientation.

Given that the underlying psychodynamic theory is not the crucial factor in therapy, perhaps it is the special techniques that contribute to therapeutic effectiveness. This would certainly seem to have been Rogers's early position before nondirective therapy became person-centered therapy. For the early nondirective school, the creation of a warm, permissive, nonjudgmental atmosphere; reflection of feeling; and avoidance of interpretation, advice, persuasion, and suggestion were paramount in the therapeutic situation.

The Freudian assigns central importance to transference, but behavior modification therapists ignore it. To many directive therapists, content and manner of interpretation are crucial. The Adlerian emphasizes interpretation of the patient's life-style and movement.

Criteria for "getting well" correspond to the particular therapeutic emphasis. Some therapists propose depth of therapy as the decisive factor. For most Adlerians, depth of therapy does not constitute a major concern. In this connection, therapy is neither deep nor superficial except as the patient experiences it as such.

If neither theory nor the use of prescribed techniques is decisive, is it the transference relationship that makes cure possible? Or the egalitarian relationship? Or the warm, permissive atmosphere with the nonjudgmental therapist accepting the patient as is? Because all of these relationships are involved in various forms of both effective and ineffective therapy, we must hypothesize either that therapeutic effectiveness is a matter of matching certain therapeutic relationships to certain patients or that all therapeutic relationships possess common factors. These factors—variations on the Christian virtues of faith, hope, and love—appear to be necessary, but not sufficient, conditions of effective therapy.

### Faith

D. Rosenthal and Jerome D. Frank (1956) discuss the implications of faith in the therapeutic process. Franz Alexander and Thomas French state:

> As a general rule, the patient who comes for help voluntarily has this confidence, this expectation that the therapist is both able and willing to help him, before he comes to treatment; if not, if the patient is forced into treatment, the therapist must build up this feeling of rapport before any therapeutic change can be effected. (1946, p. 173)

Many therapeutic mechanisms may enhance the patient's faith. A simple explanation clarifies matters for some patients, a complex interpretation for others. The therapist's own faith in him- or herself; the therapist's appearance of wisdom, strength, and assurance; and the therapist's willingness to listen without criticism may all be used by patients to strengthen their faith.

## Hope

Patients seek treatment with varying degrees of hope, running the gamut from complete hopelessness to hope for (and expectation of) everything, including a miracle. Because of the efficacy of the self-fulfilling prophecy, people *tend* to move in the direction of making their anticipations come true. Therefore, the therapist must keep the patient's hope elevated.

Because the Adlerian holds that the patient suffers from *discouragement,* a primary therapeutic technique lies in encouragement. Expression of faith in the patient, noncondemnation, and avoidance of being overly demanding may give the patient hope. The patient may also derive hope from feeling understood. Accordingly, the construction of therapy as a "we" experience where patients do not feel they stand alone, where they feel security in the strength and competency of their therapist, and where they feel some symptom alleviation may all prove helpful. They may also gain hope from attempting some course of action they feared or did not know was available to them. Humor assists in the retention of hope (Mosak, 1987a). Lewis Way comments, "Humor such as Adler possessed in such abundance is an invaluable asset, since, if one can occasionally joke, things cannot be so bad" (1962, p. 267). Each therapist has faith in his methods for encouraging and sustaining hope. They are put to the most severe test in patients who are depressed or suicidal.

## Love

In the broadest sense of love, the patient must feel that the therapist cares (Adler, 1963a, 1964a). The mere act of treating the patient may furnish such evidence by employing empathic listening, "working through" together, or having two therapists in multiple psychotherapy offering interest in the patient. Transfer of a patient to another therapist or from individual to group therapy may have a contrary effect unless it is "worked through."

However, the therapist must avoid pitfalls such as infantilizing, oversupporting, or becoming a victim of the patient when the patient accuses the therapist of not caring enough. In Adlerian group therapy, the group is conceptualized as a "reexperiencing of the family constellation" (Kadis, 1956). Thus, the therapist may be accused of playing favorites, of caring too much for one or too little for another patient.

The Adlerian theory of psychotherapy rests on the notion that psychotherapy is a cooperative educational enterprise involving one or more therapists and one or more patients. The goal of therapy is to develop the patient's social interest. To accomplish this, therapy involves changing faulty social values (Dreikurs, 1957). The subject matter of this course in reeducation is the patient—the life-style and the relationship to the life tasks. Learning the "basic mistakes" in the cognitive map, the patient has the opportunity to decide whether to continue in the old ways or move in other directions. "The consultee must under all circumstances get the conviction in relation to treatment that he is absolutely free. He can do, or not do, as he pleases" (Ansbacher & Ansbacher, 1956, p. 341). The patient can choose between self-interest and social interest. The educational process has the following goals:

1.  The fostering of social interest.
2.  The decrease of inferiority feelings, the overcoming of discouragement, and the recognition and utilization of one's resources.

3. Changes in the person's life-style, that is, perceptions and goals. The therapeutic goal, as has been mentioned, involves transforming big errors into little ones (as with automobiles, some need a "tune-up" and others require a "major overhaul").

4. Changing faulty motivation that underlies even acceptable behavior, or changing values.

5. Encouraging the individual to recognize equality among people (Dreikurs, 1971).

6. Helping the person to become a contributing human being.

"Students" who reach these educational objectives will feel a sense of belonging and display acceptance of themselves and others. They will feel that they can arrange, within life's limits, their own destinies. Such patients eventually come to feel encouraged, optimistic, confident, courageous, secure—and asymptomatic.


## Process of Psychotherapy

The process of psychotherapy, as practiced by Adlerians, has four aims: (1) establishing and maintaining a "good" relationship; (2) uncovering the dynamics of the patient, including life-style and goals, and assessing how they affect life movement; (3) interpretation culminating in insight; and (4) reorientation.


### The Relationship

A "good" therapeutic relationship is a friendly one between equals. Both the Adlerian therapist and the patient sit facing each other, their chairs at the same level. Many Adlerians prefer to work without a desk because distancing and separation may engender undesirable psychological sets. Having abandoned the medical model, the Adlerian looks with disfavor upon casting the doctor in the role of the actor (omnipotent, omniscient, and mysterious) and the patient in the role of the acted-upon. Therapy is structured to inform the patient that creative human beings play a role in creating their problems, that one is responsible (not in the sense of blame) for one's actions, and that one's problems are based upon faulty perceptions and inadequate or faulty learning, especially of faulty values (Dreikurs, 1957). If this is so, one can assume responsibility for change. What has not been learned can be learned. What has been learned "poorly" can be replaced by better learning. Faulty perception and values can be altered and modified. From the initiation of treatment, the patient's efforts to remain passive are discouraged. The patient has an active role in the therapy. Although assuming the role of student, the patient is still an active learner responsible for contributing to his or her own education.

Therapy requires cooperation, which means alignment of goals. Noncoincidence of goals may not permit the therapy to get off the ground, as, for example, when the patient denies the need for therapy. The initial interview(s) must not, therefore, omit the consideration of initial goals and expectations. The patient may wish to overpower the therapist or to make the therapist powerful and responsible. The therapist's goal must be to avoid these traps. The patient may want to relinquish symptoms but not underlying convictions, and may be looking for a miracle. In each case, at least a temporary agreement upon goals must be arrived at before the therapy can proceed. Way cautions:

> A refusal to be caught in this way [succumbing to the patient's appeals to the therapist's vanity or bids for sympathy] gives the patient little opportunity for developing serious resistances and transferences, and is indeed the doctor's only defence against a reversal of roles and against finding that he is being treated by the patient. The cure must always be a cooperation and never a fight. It is a hard test for the doctor's own balance and is likely to succeed only if he himself is free from neurosis. (1962, p. 265)

Adler (1963a) offers similar warnings against role reversal.

Because the problems of resistance and transference are defined in terms of patient-therapist goal discrepancies, throughout therapy the goals will diverge and the common task will consist of realigning the goals so patient and therapist move in the same direction.

The patient, in bringing a life-style to therapy, expects from the therapist the kind of response expected from all others. The patient may feel misunderstood, unfairly treated, or unloved and may anticipate that the therapist will behave accordingly. Often the patient unconsciously creates situations to invite the therapist to behave in this manner. For this reason, the therapist must be alert to what Adlerians call "scripts," and Eric Berne (1964) calls "games," and foil the patient's expectations. A patient, for example, will declare, "Have you ever seen a patient like me before?" to establish uniqueness and to challenge the therapist's competence. The therapist's response may be a straightforward, but not sarcastic, "Not since the last hour," followed by a discussion of uniqueness. Because assessment begins with the first moment of contact, the patient is generally given some interpretation, usually phrased as a guess, during the first interview. This gives the patient something to think about until the next interview. The therapist will soon find it possible to assess how the patient will respond to interpretation, to therapy, and to the therapist, and will gain some glimpse of the life-style framework. The therapist does not play the patient's game because at that game the patient is the professional, having played it successfully since childhood (although often in self-defeating fashion), whereas the therapist is a relative amateur. The therapist does not have to *win* the game but merely does not play it. Only one side wins in a tug-of-war. However, in this case, one side (the therapist) is uninterested in victories or defeats and merely does not pick up the end of the rope. This renders the "opponent's" game ineffective, and the two can proceed to play more productive, cooperative games (Mosak & Maniacci, 1998).

The whole relationship process increases the education of the patient. For some patients, it is their first experience of a good interpersonal relationship involving cooperation, mutual respect, and trust. Despite occasional bad feelings, the relationship can endure and survive. The patient learns that good and bad relationships do not merely happen—they are products of people's efforts—and that poor interpersonal relationships are products of misperceptions, inaccurate conclusions, and unwarranted anticipations incorporated in the life-style.

## Analysis

Investigation of a patient's dynamics is divided into two parts. The therapist, first, wants to understand the patient's life-style and, second, aims to understand how the life-style affects current function with respect to the life tasks. Not all suffering stems from the patient's life-style. Many patients with adequate life-styles develop problems or symptoms in the face of intolerable or extreme situations from which they cannot extricate themselves.

Analytic investigation begins with the first moment. The way a patient enters the room, posture, and choice of seating (especially important in family therapy) all provide important clues. What the patient says and how it is said expand the therapist's understanding, especially when the therapist interprets the patient's communications in interpersonal terms, or "scripts," rather than in descriptive terms. Thus, the Adlerian translates the descriptive statement, "I am confused" into the admonition, "Don't pin me down." "It's a habit," conveys the declaration, "And that's another thing you're not going to get me to change" (Mosak & Gushurst, 1971). The therapist assesses, follows up, and juxtaposes clues in patterns, accepting some hypotheses and rejecting others in an effort to understand the patient. As therapy progresses, the patient offers information one way or another, and the therapist pieces it together bit by bit like a jigsaw puzzle.

## The Life-Style Investigation

In formal assessment procedures, the patient's family constellation is explored. The therapist obtains glimpses of what position the child found in the family and how he or she went about finding a place within the family, in school, and among peers. The second portion of the assessment consists of interpreting the patient's early recollections. An *early recollection* occurs in the period before continuous memory and may be inaccurate or a complete fiction. It represents a single event ("One day I remember . . .") rather than a group of events ("We used to . . ."). Adlerians refer to the latter as *a report* rather than a recollection. Reports are important to the therapeutic assessment process. However, they are not interpreted the same way as early recollections (Shulman & Mosak, 1988). Recollections are treated as a projective technique (Mosak, 1958). If one understands the early recollections, one understands the patient's "Story of My Life" (Adler, 1931), because people selectively recollect incidents consonant with their life-styles. The following recollection of Adler (1947) may serve to illustrate the consonance between his earliest recollection and his later psychological views:

> One of my earliest recollections is of sitting on a bench, bandaged up on account of rickets, with my healthy elder brother sitting opposite me. He could run, jump, and move about quite effortlessly, while for me movement of any sort was a strain and an effort. Everyone went to great pains to help me, and my mother and father did all that was in their power to do. At the time of this recollection I must have been about two years old. (p. 9)

In a single recollection, Adler refers to organ inferiority, the inferiority feeling, the emphasis upon "my desire to move freely—to see all psychic manifestations in terms of movements" (p. 10), and social feeling (Mosak & Kopp, 1973).

The summary of early recollections, the story of the patient's life, permits the derivation of the patient's "basic mistakes." The life-style can be conceived as a personal mythology. The individual will behave *as if* the myths were true because, for him or her, they are true. So there are "truths" or partial "truths" in myths and there are myths we confuse with truth. The latter are *basic mistakes*.

Basic mistakes may be classified as follows:

1. *Overgeneralizations.* "People are hostile." "Life is dangerous."
2. *False or impossible goals of "security."* "One false step and you're dead." "I have to please everybody."
3. *Misperceptions of life and life's demands.* Typical convictions might be "Life never gives me any breaks" and "Life is so hard."
4. *Minimization or denial of one's worth.* "I'm stupid" and "I'm undeserving" or "I'm just a housewife."
5. *Faulty values.* "Be first even if you have to climb over others."

Finally, the therapist is interested in how the patient perceives his or her assets.

The following sample life-style summary is not intended to be a complete personality description, but it does offer patient and therapist initial hypotheses.

### Summary of Family Constellation

John is the younger of two children, the only boy. He grew up fatherless after age nine. His sister was so precocious that John became discouraged. Because he felt he would never become famous, he decided perhaps he could at least be notorious, and through negative behavior brought himself to the attention of others. He acquired the reputation of a "holy terror." He was going to do everything his way, and nobody was going to stop him. He followed the guiding lines of a strong, masculine father from whom he learned that the toughest man wins. Because notoriety came with doing the disapproved, John early became interested in and engaged in sex. This also reinforced his feelings of masculinity. Because both parents were handicapped and yet still "made it," John apparently decided that without any physical handicaps, the sky would be the limit for him.

### Summary of Early Recollections

"I run scared in life, and even when people tell me there's nothing to be scared of, I'm still scared. Women give men a hard time. They betray them, they punish them, and they interfere with what men want to do. A real man takes no crap from anybody. Somebody always interferes. I am not going to do what others want me to do. Others call that bad and want to punish me for it, but I don't see it that way. Doing what I want is merely part of being a man."

### "Basic Mistakes"

1. John exaggerates the significance of masculinity and equates it with doing what he pleases.
2. He is not on the same wavelength as women. They see his behavior as "bad"; he sees it as only "natural" for a man.
3. He is too ready to fight, many times just to preserve his sense of masculinity.
4. He perceives women as the enemy, even though he looks to them for comfort.
5. Victory is snatched from him at the last moment.

### Assets

1. He is a driver. When he puts his mind to things, he makes them work.
2. He engages in creative problem solving.
3. He knows how to get what he wants.
4. He knows how to ask a woman "nicely."

During the course of the treatment, other forms of analysis will occur. Because the therapist views the life-style as consistent, it will express itself in all of the patient's behavior—physical behavior, language and speech, fantasy productions, dreams, and interpersonal relationships, past and present. Because of this consistency, the patient may choose to express herself or himself in any or all of these media because they all express life-style. The therapist observes behavior, speech, and language closely during each interview. Sometimes the dialogue will center on the present, sometimes on the past, often on the future. Free association and chitchat, except when the latter serves a therapeutic purpose, are mostly discouraged. Although dream analysis is an integral part of psychotherapy, the patient who speaks only of dreams receives gentle dissuasion (Alexandra Adler, 1943). The analysis proceeds with an examination of the interplay between life-style and the life tasks—how the life-style affects the person's function and dysfunction vis-à-vis the life tasks.

## Dreams

Adler saw the dream as a problem-solving activity with a future orientation, in contrast to Freud's view that it was an attempt to solve an old problem. The *dream* is seen by Adlerians as a rehearsal of possible future courses of action. If we want to postpone action, we forget the dream. If we want to dissuade ourselves from some action, we frighten ourselves with a nightmare.

The dream, Adler said, was the "factory of emotions." In it we create moods that move us toward or away from the next day's activities. Commonly, people say, "I don't know why but I woke up in a lousy mood today." The day before Adler died, he told friends, "I woke smiling . . . so I knew my dreams were good although I had forgotten them" (Bottome, 1939, p. 240). Just as early recollections reflect long-range goals, the dream experiments with possible answers to immediate problems. In accord with the view of the individual's uniqueness, Adlerians reject the theory of fixed symbolism. One cannot understand a dream without knowing the dreamer, although Adler (1963b) and Erwin Wexberg (1929) do address themselves to some frequently encountered dream themes. Way admonishes:

> One is reminded again of two boys, instanced by Adler [1964a, p. 150], each of whom wished to be a horse, one because he would have to bear the responsibility for his family, the other to outstrip all the others. This should be a salutary warning against making dictionary interpretations. (1962, pp. 282–284)

The interpretation of the dream does not terminate with the analysis of the content but must include the purposive function. Dreams serve as weather vanes for treatment, bringing problems to the surface and pointing to the patient's movement. Dreikurs describes a patient who related recurrent dreams that were short and actionless, reflecting his lifestyle of figuring out "the best way of getting out of a problem, mostly without doing anything. . . . When his dreams started to move and become active he started to move in his life, too" (Dreikurs, 1944, p. 26).

## Reorientation

Reorientation in all therapies proceeds from persuading the patient, gently or forcefully, that change is in his or her best interest. The patient's present manner of living accords "safety" but not happiness. Because neither therapy nor life offers *guarantees,* one must risk some "safety" for the possibility of greater happiness and self-fulfillment. This dilemma is not easily solved. Like Hamlet, the patient wonders whether it is better to "bear those ills we have than fly to others that we know not of."

## Insight

Analytic psychotherapists frequently assign central importance to insight, upon the assumption that "basic change" cannot occur in its absence. The conviction that insight must precede behavioral change often results in extended treatment, in encouraging some patients to become "sicker" to avoid or postpone change, and in increasing their self-absorption rather than their self-awareness. Meanwhile, patients relieve themselves from the responsibility of living life until they have achieved insight.

A second assumption, treasured by therapists and patients alike, distinguishes between *intellectual* and *emotional* insight (Ellis, 1963; Papanek, 1959), a dualism the holistic Adlerian experiences difficulty in accepting. This and other dualisms, such as conscious versus unconscious, undeniably exist in the patient's subjective experience. But these antagonistic forces are creations of the patient that delay action. Simultaneously the patient can maintain a good conscience because he or she is the victim of conflicting forces or an emotional block. Solving problems is relegated to the future while the patient pursues insight. *Insight,* as the Adlerian defines it, is understanding translated into constructive action. It reflects the patient's understanding of the purposive nature of behavior and mistaken apperceptions as well as an understanding of the role both play in life movement. So-called intellectual insight merely reflects the patient's desire to play the game of therapy rather than the game of life.

## Interpretation

The Adlerian therapist facilitates insight mainly by interpretation of ordinary communications, dreams, fantasies, behavior, symptoms, the patient-therapist transactions, and the patient's interpersonal transactions. The emphasis in interpretation is on purpose rather than cause, on movement rather than description, on use rather than possession. Through interpretation, the therapist holds up a mirror for the patient.

The therapist relates past to present only to indicate the continuity of the maladaptive life-style, not to demonstrate a causal connection. The therapist may also use humor (Mosak, 1987a) or illustrate with fables (Pancner, 1978), anecdotes, and biography. Irony may prove effective, but it must be handled with care. The therapist may "spit in the patient's soup," a crude expression for exposing the patient's intentions in such a way as to make them unpalatable. The therapist may offer the interpretation directly or in the form of "Could it be that . . . ?" or may invite the patient to make interpretations. Although timing, exaggeration, understatement, and accuracy are technical concerns of any therapist, they are not emphasized by the Adlerian therapist, who does not view the patient as fragile.

## Other Verbal Techniques

Advice is often frowned upon by therapists. Hans Strupp relates, "It has been said that Freud, following his own recommendations, never gave advice to an analysand on the couch but did not stint with the commodity from the couch to the door" (1972, p. 40). Wexberg (1929/1970) frowned on giving advice to a patient, but the Adlerian therapist freely gives advice, as did Freud, taking care, however, not to encourage dependency. In practice, the therapist may merely outline the alternatives and let the patient make the decision. This invitation develops faith in self rather than faith in the therapist. On the other hand, the therapist may offer direct advice, taking care to encourage the patient's self-directiveness and willingness to stand alone.

Given that Adlerians consider the patient discouraged rather than sick, it is no surprise that they make extensive use of encouragement. Enhancing the patient's faith in self, "accentuating the positive and eliminating the negative," and keeping up the patient's hope all contribute to counteracting discouragement. The patient who "walks and falls" learns it is not fatal and can get up and walk again. Therapy also counteracts the patient's social values, thus altering his or her view of life and helping give meaning to it. Moralizing is avoided, although therapists must not deceive themselves into believing their system has no value orientation. The dialogue concerns "useful" and "useless," rather than "good" or "bad" behavior.

The therapist avoids rational argument and trying to "out-logic" the patient. These tactics are easily defeated by the patient who operates according to the rules of *psycho-logic* (private) logic rather than formal logic. Catharsis, abreaction, and confession may afford the patient relief by freeing him or her from carrying the burden of "unfinished business," but as has been noted (Alexander & French, 1946), these may also be a test of whether the patient can place trust in the therapist.

## Action Techniques

Adlerians regularly use role-playing, talking to an empty chair (Shoobs, 1964), the Midas technique (Shulman, 1962), the behind-the-back technique (Corsini, 1953), and other action procedures to assist the patient in reorientation. The extent of use is a function of the therapist's preference, training, and readiness to experiment with the novel.

## Mechanisms of Psychotherapy

### The Therapist as Model

The therapist represents values the patient may attempt to imitate. Adlerian therapists represent themselves as "being for real," fallible, able to laugh at themselves, caring—models for social interest. If the therapist can possess these characteristics, perhaps the patient can, too, and many patients emulate their therapists, whom they use as referents for normality (Mosak, 1967).

### Change

There comes a time in psychotherapy when analysis must be abandoned and the patient must be encouraged to move forward. Insight has to give way to decisive action.

Some of the techniques Adlerians use to elicit change are described below and by Mosak and Maniacci (1998). They are not panaceas, nor are they used indiscriminately. The creative therapist will improvise techniques to meet the needs of the therapeutic moment, and remember, above all, that people are more important than techniques and strategies. Losing sight of these cautions, the therapist is a technician who does all the "right" things but is never engaged in a human encounter with another human being.

### Acting "As If"

A common patient refrain in treatment is "If only I could . . ." (Adler, 1963a). Adlerian therapists often request that for the next week the patient act "as if." The patient may protest that it would only be an act and therefore phony. We explain that all acting is not phony pretense, that one can try on a role as one might try on a suit. It does not change the person wearing the suit, but sometimes with a handsome suit of clothes, one may feel differently and perhaps behave differently, thus becoming a different person.

### Task Setting

Adler (1964a) gave us the prototype for task setting in his treatment of depressives, writing:

> To return to the indirect method of treatment: I recommend it especially in melancholia. After establishing a sympathetic relation I give suggestions for a change of conduct in two stages. In the first stage my suggestion is "Only do what is agreeable to you." The patient usually answers, "Nothing is agreeable." "Then at least," I respond, "do not exert yourself to do what is disagreeable." The patient, who has usually been exhorted to do various uncongenial things to remedy this condition, finds a rather flattering novelty in my advice, and may improve in behavior. Later I insinuate the second rule of conduct, saying that "it is much more difficult and I do not know if you can follow it." After saying this I am silent, and look doubtfully at the patient. In this way I excite his curiosity and ensure his attention, and then proceed, "If you could follow this second rule you would be cured in fourteen days. It is helpful to consider from time to time how you can give another person pleasure. It would very soon enable you to sleep and would chase away all your sad thoughts. You would feel yourself to be useful and worthwhile."
>
> I receive various replies to my suggestion, but every patient thinks it is too difficult to act upon. If the answer is, "How can I give pleasure to others when I have none myself?" I relieve the prospect by saying, "Then you will need four weeks." The more transparent response, "Who gives *me* pleasure?" I counter with what is prob-

ably the strongest move in the game, by saying, "Perhaps you had better train your-self a little thus: Do not actually DO anything to please anyone else, but just think out how you COULD do it!" (pp. 25–26)

The tasks are relatively simple and are set at a level at which patients can sabotage the task, but they cannot fail and then scold the therapist.

The patient must understand that not the physician but life itself is inexorable. He must understand that ultimately [he will have] to transfer to practical life that which has been theoretically recognized. . . . But from the physician he hears no word of re-proach or of impatience, at most an occasional kindly, harmless, ironical remark. (p. 101)

A 50-year-old man who professed "genuine" intention to get married but simulta-neously avoided women was instructed to seek one meaningful contact with a woman (how to do so was up to him) every day. After raising many objections, he complained, "But it's so hard! I'll get so tired out I won't be able to function." The therapist good-humoredly relented and informed him, "Since God rested on the seventh day, I can't ask you to do more than God. So you need carry out the task only six days a week."

One form of task setting Adler introduced is called *antisuggestion* by Wexberg (1929) and *paradoxical intention* by Frankl (1963). This method, used nonclinically by Knight Dunlap (1933), was labeled *negative practice*. The symptomatic patient unwit-tingly reinforces symptoms by fighting them, by saying, "Why did this have to happen to *me*?" The insomniac keeps one eye open to observe whether the other is falling asleep and then wonders at the difficulty in falling asleep. To halt this fight, the patient is in-structed to intend and even increase that which he or she is fighting against.

## Creating Images

Adler was fond of describing patients with a simple phrase—for example, "the beggar as king." Other Adlerians give patients similar shorthand images that confirm the adage that "one picture is worth a thousand words." Remembering this image, the patient can re-member goals, and in later stages, can learn to use the image to laugh at self. One over-ambitious patient, labeled "Superman," one day began to unbutton his shirt. When the therapist made inquiry, the patient laughingly replied, "So you can see my blue shirt with the big 'S' on it." Another patient, fearing sexual impotence, concurred with the thera-pist's observation that he had never seen an impotent dog. The patient advanced as ex-planation, "The dog just does what he's supposed to do without worrying about whether he'll be able to perform." The therapist suggested that at his next attempt at sexual in-tercourse, before he made any advances, he should smile and say inwardly, "Bow wow." The following week he informed the members of his group, "I bow wowed."

## Catching Oneself

When patients understand personal goals and want to change, they are instructed to catch themselves "with their hand in the cookie jar." Patients may catch themselves in the midst of their old behavior but still feel incapable of doing anything about it at the moment. With additional practice, they learn to anticipate situations before their occurrence.

## The Push–Button Technique

This method, effective with people who feel they are victims of their disjunctive emo-tions, involves requesting patients to close their eyes, to re-create a pleasant incident from past experience, and to note the feeling that accompanies this image. Then they are asked to re-create an unpleasant incident of hurt, humiliation, failure, or anger and to note the accompanying feeling. Following this the patient re-creates the first scene again. The lesson Adlerians try to teach clients is that they can create whatever feeling they wish merely by deciding what they will think about. One is the creator, not the victim, of emotions. To be depressed, for example, requires *choosing* to be depressed. We try to impress the patient with their power for self-determination. This method, devised for clinical use by Mosak (1985), has been the subject of experimental investigation by Brewer (1976), who found it an effective technique in treating state depression.

### The "Aha" Experience

The patient who gains awareness in treatment and increases participation in life recurrently has "aha" or "eureka" experiences. With this greater understanding, the patient generates self-confidence and optimism, resulting in increased encouragement and willingness to confront life's problems with commitment, compassion, and empathy.

### Posttherapy

After therapy is over, the patient can implement newly acquired learning. Operationally, the goal of therapy may be defined as that of making the therapist superfluous. If therapist and patient have both done their jobs well, the goal will have been achieved.

## APPLICATIONS

### Problems

Although Adler, like the other *Nervenärzte* ("nerve doctors") of his era, conducted one-to-one psychotherapy, his own social outlook moved him out of the consulting room and into the community. Although he never relinquished his clinical interests, he concurrently was an educator and a social reformer. Joost Meerloo, a Freudian, eulogizes Adler with his confession:

> As a matter of fact, the whole body of psychoanalysis and psychiatry is imbued with Adler's ideas, although few want to acknowledge this fact. We are all plagiarists, though we hate to confess it. . . . The whole body of social psychiatry would have been impossible without Adler's pioneering zest. (1970, p. 40)

### Clinical

All the early pioneers in psychotherapy treated neurotics. Psychotics were considered not amenable to psychotherapy because they could not enter into a transference relationship. Adlerians, unencumbered by the concept of transference, treated psychotics regularly. Henri Ellenberger (1970, p. 618) suggests that "among the great pioneers of dynamic psychiatry, Janet and Adler are the only ones who had personal clinical experience with criminals, and Adler was the only one who wrote something on the subject from his direct experience." An Adlerian, Ernst Papanek (1971), of whom Claude Brown (1965) wrote so glowingly in his *Manchild in the Promised Land,* was director of Wiltwyck School (a reform school), and with Mosak set up a group therapy program at Cook County Jail in Chicago employing paraprofessionals as therapists (O'Reilly, Cizon, Flanagan, & Pflanczer, 1965). The growth model implicit in Adlerian theory has prompted Adlerians to see human problems in terms of people's realizing themselves and becoming fellow human beings. Much "treatment" then is of "normal" people with "normal" problems. A therapy that does not provide the client with a philosophy of life, whatever else it may accomplish in the way of symptom eradication or alleviation, behavior modification, or insight, is an incomplete therapy. Hence, the Adlerian is concerned with the client's problems of living and existence. Deficiency, suffering, and illness do not constitute the price of admission to Adlerian therapy. One may enter therapy to learn about oneself, to grow, and to actualize oneself.

## Social

Adler's interests were rather catholic. In the area of education, he believed in prevention rather than cure and founded family education centers. Dreikurs and his students (Dreikurs et al., 1959) have founded family education centers throughout the world. Off-shoots of these centers include hundreds of parent study groups (Soltz, 1967). In addition, professional therapists have used a variety of methods for teaching child-rearing practices (Allred, 1976; Beecher & Beecher, 1966; Corsini & Painter, 1975; Dreikurs, 1948; Dreikurs & Soltz, 1964; Painter & Corsini, 1989).

Adler himself wrote on social issues and problems such as crime, war, religion, group psychology, Bolshevism, leadership, and nationalism. Among contemporary Adlerians (Angers, 1960; Clark, 1965, 1967a, 1967b; Elam, 1969a, 1969b; Gottesfeld, 1966; Hemming, 1956; La Porte, 1966; Lombardi, 1969; Nikelly, 1971c) the "newer" social problems of protest, race, drugs, social conditions, and the "newer" views of religion (Mosak, 1987b) have been added to the Adlerians' previous interests.

## Evaluation

Until very recently, little research had emerged from the Adlerian group. As was the case with most European clinicians, European Adlerians were suspicious of research based upon statistical methods. A complicating factor was the *idiographic* (case method) approach upon which Adlerians relied. Even now statisticians have not developed appropriate sophisticated methods for idiographic studies. The research methods lent themselves well to studies of "causal" factors, but the Adlerian rejected causalism, feeling that causes can only be imputed (and therefore disputed) in retrospective fashion but that they contributed little to the understanding of humans.

The most often-cited studies involving Adlerian psychology were conducted by non-Adlerians. Fred Fiedler (1950) compared therapeutic relationships in psychoanalytic, nondirective, and Adlerian therapy. He found there was greater similarity between therapeutic relationships developed by experts of the three schools than between expert and less expert therapists within the same school. Crandall (1981) presented the first large-scale investigation of an Adlerian construct. Using his Social Interest Scale, Crandall found positive correlations between social interest and optimism about human nature, altruism, trustworthiness, being liked, and several measures of adjustment and well-being. Because of the number of ways social interest has been defined (Bickhard & Ford, 1976; Crandall, 1981; Edgar, 1975; Kazan, 1978; Mosak, 1991), his study represents a valuable contribution to the understanding of this concept.

A joint research study conducted by the (Rogerian) Counseling Center of the University of Chicago and the Alfred Adler Institute of Chicago examined the effects of time limits in psychotherapy (Shlien, Mosak, & Dreikurs, 1962). Patients of both groups of therapists were given 20 interviews, and the groups were compared with each other and with two control groups. The investigators reported changes in self-ideal correlations. These correlations improved significantly and, according to this measure, suggest that time-limited therapy "may be said to be not only *effective,* but also twice as *efficient* as time-unlimited therapy." Follow-up of these patients in both experimental groups indicated that the gains were retained one year later.

Much of the research in family constellation has also been done by non-Adlerians. Charles Miley (1969) and Lucille Forer (1977) have compiled bibliographies of this literature. The results reported are contradictory, probably because non-Adlerians treat birth order as a matter of ordinal position and Adlerians consider birth order in terms of psychological position (Mosak, 1972). Walter Toman (1970) recognized this distinction in his many studies of the family constellation.

Ansbacher (1946) and Mosak (1958) have also distinguished between Freudian and Adlerian approaches to the interpretation of early recollections. Robin Gushurst (1971) provides a manual for interpreting and scoring one class of recollections. His reliability studies demonstrate that judges can interpret early recollection data with high interjudge reliability. He also conducted three validity studies to investigate the hypothesis that life goals may be identified from early recollection data and found that he could do this with two of his three experimental groups. While Fiedler compared therapists of different orientations, Heine (1953) compared patients' reports of their experiences in Adlerian, Freudian, and Rogerian therapy. Taylor (1975) has written an excellent review of some early recollection validity studies.

Adlerian psychology would undoubtedly benefit from more research. With the shift in locus from Europe to the United States, with the accelerated growth of the Adlerian school in recent years, with the introduction of more American-trained Adlerians into academic settings, and with the development of new research strategies suitable for idiographic data, there is increasing integration of Adlerians into research activities. A summary of these activities appears in two articles by Watkins (1982, 1983).

## Treatment

One can hardly identify a mode of treatment in which some Adlerian is not engaged. From a historical viewpoint the initial Adlerian modality was one-to-one psychotherapy. Many Adlerians still regard individual psychotherapy as the treatment of choice. Adlerians have demonstrated willingness to undertake treatment with any who sought their services.

Dreikurs, Mosak, and Shulman (1952a, 1952b, 1982) introduced *multiple psychotherapy,* a format in which several therapists treat a single patient. It offers constant consultation between therapists, prevents the emotional attachment of a patient to a single therapist, and obviates or dissolves impasses. Countertransference reactions are minimized. Flexibility in the number of therapist roles and models is increased. Patients are more impressed or reassured when two therapists independently agree. The patient also may benefit from the experience of observing disagreement between therapists and learn that people can disagree without loss of face.

Multiple therapy creates an atmosphere that facilitates learning. Therapeutic impasses and problems of dependency are resolved more easily. These include the responsibility for self, therapist-transference reactions, and termination. In the event that therapist and patient do not hit it off, the patient does not become a therapeutic casualty and is merely transferred to the second therapist.

Dreikurs (1959) in the mid-1920s initiated group therapy in private practice. This application was a natural evolution from the Adlerian axiom that people's problems were always social problems. Group therapy finds considerable adherents among Adlerians. Some Adlerian therapists regard group therapy as the method of choice either on practical grounds (e.g., fees, large numbers of patients to be treated, etc.) or because they believe that human problems are most effectively handled in the group social situation. Others use group therapy as a preface to individual therapy or to taper patients off from intensive individual psychotherapy. A number of therapists combine individual and group psychotherapy in the conviction that this combination maximizes therapeutic effect (Papanek, 1954, 1956). Still other therapists visualize the group as assisting in the solution of certain selected problems or with certain types of populations. Cotherapist groups are very common among Adlerians.

An offshoot of group treatment is the therapeutic social club in a mental hospital as initiated by the British Adlerian, Joshua Bierer. Although these clubs possess superficial similarities to Abraham Low's recovery groups (Low, 1952) and to halfway houses in that all attempt to facilitate the patient's reentrance into society, the therapeutic social club emphasizes the "social" rather than the "therapeutic" aspects of life, taking the "healthy" rather than the "sick" model. Psychodrama has been used by Adlerians, sometimes as separate therapy, sometimes in conjunction with another therapeutic modality (Starr, 1977).

Marriage counseling has figured prominently in Adlerian activities. Adlerians defied the trend of the times and preferred to treat the couple as a unit rather than as separate individuals. To "treat" merely one mate may be compared to having only half the dialogue of a play. Seeing the couple together suggests that they have a joint relationship problem rather than individual problems and invites joint effort in the solution of these problems. The counselor can observe and describe their interaction (Mozdzierz & Lottman, 1973; Pew & Pew, 1972). Married couples group therapy (Deutsch, 1967) and married couples study groups constitute two more settings for conducting marriage counseling. Phillips and Corsini (1982) and Dinkmeyer and Carlson (1989) have written self-help books to be used by married people who may be experiencing trouble in their marriage.

In the early 1920s, Adler persuaded the Viennese school administration to establish child-guidance centers. The social group was the primary vehicle for treatment (Adler, 1963a; Alexandra Adler, 1951; Seidler & Zilahi, 1949). Dreikurs wrote several popular books and many articles (Dreikurs, 1948; Dreikurs & Grey, 1968; Dreikurs & Soltz, 1964) to disseminate this information to parents and teachers, and currently thousands of parents are enrolled in study groups where they obtain supplementary information on child rearing.

Adler's preventive methods in schools were adopted by educators and school counselors who used them in individual classes, schools, and in one instance in an entire school system (Mosak, 1971). The methods were originally applied in the Individual Psychological Experimental School in Vienna (Birnbaum, 1935; Spiel, 1962) and have been elaborated upon in this country (Corsini, 1977, 1979; Dinkmeyer & Dreikurs, 1963; Dreikurs, 1968, 1972; Dreikurs, Grunwald, & Pepper, 1982; Grunwald, 1954).

With respect to broader social problems, Dreikurs devoted the last part of his life to the problem of interindividual and intergroup conflict resolution. Much of this work was performed in Israel and has not been reported. Kenneth Clark, a former president of the American Psychological Association, has devoted much of his career to studying and providing recommendations for solutions for problems of African-Americans, as have Harry Elam (1969a, 1969b) and Jacqueline Brown (1976).

## The Setting

Adlerians function in every imaginable setting: the private-practice office, hospitals, day hospitals, jails, schools, and community programs. Offices do not need any special furnishings, but reflect either the therapist's aesthetic preferences or the condition of the institution's budget. No special equipment is used, except perhaps for special projects. Although voice recordings are a matter of individual choice, they are sometimes maintained as the patient's file.

In the initial interviews, the therapist generally obtains the following kinds of information (in addition to demographic information):

1. Was the patient self-referred?

2. Is the patient negative about treatment? If the patient is reluctant, "conversion" is necessary if therapy is to proceed.

3. What does the patient come for? Is it treatment to alleviate suffering? If so, suffering from what?

   Some new patients are "supermarket shoppers" who announce the number of therapists who have helped them already. Their secret goal is to be perfect. Unless such a patient's fictional goal is disclosed, today's therapist may be the latest of many therapists about whom the patient will be telling the next therapist.

4. What are the patient's expectations about treatment?

5. What are the patient's expectations about outcome? Perfection? Failure? A solution for a specific problem without any major personality alterations? Immediate cure?

6. What are the patient's goals in psychotherapy? We must distinguish between stated goals—to get well, to learn about self, to be a better spouse and parent, to gain a new philosophy of life—and nonverbalized goals—to remain sick, to punish others, to defeat the therapist and sabotage therapy, to maintain good intentions without changing.

The patient may also resist in order to depreciate or defeat the therapist because the patient lacks the courage to live on the useful side of life and fears that the therapist might nudge him or her in that direction. The intensification of such escape methods may become most pronounced during the termination phase of treatment, when the patient realizes he or she must soon face the realistic tasks of life without the therapist's support.

## Tests

Routine physical examinations are not required by Adlerians in view of the therapy's educational orientation. Nevertheless, many patients do have physiological problems, and Adlerians are trained to be sensitive to the presence of these problems. The therapist who suspects such problems will make referrals for physical examination.

Adlerians are divided on the issue of psychological testing. Most Adlerians avoid nosological diagnosis, except for nontherapeutic purposes such as filling out insurance forms. Labels are static descriptions and ignore the *movement* of the individual. They describe what the individual *has,* but not how he or she moves through life.

Regine Seidler placed more faith in projective testing than in so-called objective tests, maintaining that the latter are actually subjective tests because "the *subjective attitude* of each and every individual toward any given test necessarily renders the test nonobjective" (1967, p. 4). Objective tests were more useful to her as measures of test-taking attitude than of what the test was purportedly measuring.

Early recollections serve as a test for Adlerians, assisting them in the life-style assessment. Younger Adlerians employ many conventional tests and some unconventional ones for diagnostic purposes as well as in the treatment of the patient.

## The Therapist

The Adlerian therapist ideally is an authentically sharing, caring person. Helene and Ernst Papanek write: "The therapist participates actively. Without playing any sharply defined 'role,' he shows warmth toward and a genuine interest in the patient and encourages especially his desire for change and betterment. The relationship itself has a purpose: to help the patient help himself" (1961, p. 117).

Adlerian therapists remain free to have feelings and opinions and to express them. Such expression in a spontaneous way permits patients to view therapists as human beings. If therapists err, they err—but then the patient may learn the courage to be imperfect from this experience (Lazarsfeld, 1966). The experience may also facilitate therapy.

Therapists must not inject evaluation of their worth into the therapy; rather, they must do their therapeutic job without concern for prestige, not reveling in successes or becoming discouraged by failures. Otherwise, they may bounce like a rubber ball from therapy hour to therapy hour or perhaps even within the same hour. The therapist's worth does not depend upon external factors but rather on what lies within the self. The therapist is task-oriented rather than self-oriented.

Therapists reveal themselves as persons. The concept of the *anonymous therapist* is foreign to Adlerian psychology. Such a role would increase social distance between therapist and patient, interfering with the establishment of an egalitarian, human relationship. The "anonymous therapist" role was created to facilitate the establishment of a transference relationship, and because the Adlerian rejects the transference concept as Freud formulated it, the maintenance of such a posture is considered irrelevant, if not harmful, to the relationship. Dreikurs (1961) deplored the prevalent attitude among therapists of not coming too close to patients because it might affect the therapeutic relationship adversely. Shulman (Wexberg, 1929/1970, p. 88) defines the role of the therapist as that of "a helping friend." Self-revelation can occur only when therapists feel secure, at home with others, unafraid to be human and fallible, and thus unafraid of their patients' evaluations, criticism, or hostility (cf. Rogers's "congruence").

Is the Adlerian therapist judgmental? In a sense all therapists are judgmental in that therapy rests upon some value orientation: a belief that certain behavior is better than other behavior, that certain goals are better than other goals, that one organization of personality is superior to another form of organization. Given that two cardinal principles of the Adlerian intervention are caring and encouragement, a critical or judgmental stance is best avoided.

## Patient Problems

If the therapist does not like the patient, it raises problems for a therapist of any persuasion (Fromm-Reichman, 1949). Some therapists merely do not accept such patients. Still others feel they ought not to have or ought to overcome such negative feelings and accept the patient for treatment, leading to both participants' "suffering." It appears difficult to possess "unconditional positive regard" for a patient you dislike. Adlerians meet this situation in the same manner other therapists do.

Seduction problems are treated as any other patient problem. The secure therapist will not frighten, panic, or succumb. If the patient's activities nevertheless prevent the therapy from continuing, the patient may be referred to another therapist. Flattery problems are in some ways similar and have been discussed elsewhere (Berne, 1964; Mosak & Gushurst, 1971).

Suicide threats are always taken seriously (Ansbacher, 1961, 1969). Alfred Adler warned, however, that our goal is "to knock the weapon out of his hand" so the patient cannot make us vulnerable and intimidate us at will with his threats. As an example, he narrates, "A patient once asked me, smiling, 'Has anyone ever taken his life while being treated by you?' I answered him, 'Not yet, but I am prepared for this to happen at any time'" (Ansbacher & Ansbacher, 1956, pp. 338–339). Kurt Adler postulates "an underlying rage against people" in suicide threats and believes that this goal of vengefulness must be uncovered. He "knocks the weapon out of the patient's hand" as follows:

> Patients have tested me with the question of how would I feel if I were to read of their suicide in the newspaper. I answer that it is possible that some reporter hungry for news would pick up such an item from a police blotter. But, the next day, the paper will already be old, and only a dog perhaps may honor their suicide notice by lifting a leg over it in some corner. (1961, p. 66)

Alexandra Adler (1943), Lazarsfeld (1952), Pelzman (1952), Boldt (1994), and Zborowski (1997) discuss problems beyond the scope of this chapter.

# CASE EXAMPLE

## Background

The patient was a 53-year-old, Vienna-born man, in treatment almost continuously with Freudian psychoanalysts, both in the United States and abroad, since he was 17. With the advent of tranquilizers, he had transferred his allegiances to psychiatrists who treated him with a combination of drugs and psychotherapy and finally with drugs alone. When he entered Adlerian treatment, he was being maintained by his previous therapist on an opium derivative and Thorazine. He failed to tell his previous therapist of his decision to see us and also failed to inform us that he was still obtaining medication from his previous therapist.

The treatment process was atypical in the sense that the patient's "illness" hampered us from following our customary procedure. Having over the years become therapy-wise, he invested his creativity in efforts to run the therapy. Cooperative effort was virtually impossible. In conventional terms, the cotherapists, Drs. A and B, had their hands full dealing with the patient's resistances and "transference."

## Problem

When the patient entered treatment, he had taken to bed and spent almost all his time there because he felt too weak to get up. His wife had to be constantly at his side or he would panic. Once she was encouraged by a friend to attend the opera alone. The patient wished her a good time and then told her, "When you return, I shall be dead." His secretary was forced into conducting his successful business. Everyone was forced into "the emperor's service." The price he paid for this service was intense suffering in the form of depression, obsessive-compulsive behavior, phobic behavior, especially agoraphobia, divorce from the social world, somatic symptoms, and invalidism.

## Treatment

The patient was seen in multiple psychotherapy by Drs. A and B, but both therapists were not present at each interview. We dispensed with the life-style assessment because the patient had other immediate goals. It seemed to us from the patient's behavior that he probably had been raised as a pampered child and that he was using "illness" to tyrannize the world and to gain exemption from the life tasks. If these guesses were correct, we anticipated he would attempt to remain "sick," would resist giving up drugs, and would demand special attention from his therapists. As part of the treatment strategy, the therapists decided to wean him from medication, to give him no special attention, and not to be manipulated by him. Given that he had undergone analysis over a period of more than three decades, the therapists thought he could probably produce a better analysis of his problems than they could. For this reason, interpretation was kept at a minimum. The treatment plan envisaged a tactical and strategic, rather than interpretive, approach. Some excerpts from the early part of treatment are reproduced on the following pages.

### March 8

Dr. B wanted to collect life-style information but the patient immediately complained that he wanted to terminate. He said his previous therapist, Dr. C, had treated him differently. Therapist B was too impersonal. "You won't even give me your home phone number. You aren't impressed by my illness. Your treatment is well meaning but it won't help. Nothing helps. I'm going to go back to Dr. C and ask him to put me in the hospital. He gave me advice and you are so cruel by not telling me what to do."

*March 19*

Relatively calm. Compares B with Dr. C. Later compares B with A. Favors B over Dr. C because he respects former's strength. Favors B over A because he can succeed in ruffling latter but not former. Talk centers about his use of weakness to overpower others.

*March 22*

Telephones to say he must be hospitalized. Wife left him [untrue] and secretary left him [it turns out she went to lunch]. Would B come to his office to see him? B asks him to keep appointment in B's office. Patient races about office upset. "I'm sweating water and blood." When B remains calm, patient takes out bottle of Thorazine and threatens to take all. Next he climbs up on radiator, opens window (17th floor), jumps back, and says, "No, it's too high."

"You don't help me. Why can't I have an injection?" Then he informs B that B is a soothing influence. "I wish I could spend the whole day with you." B speaks softly to patient and patient speaks quietly. Patient asks for advice about what to do this weekend. B gives antisuggestion and tells him to try to worry as much as he can. He is surprised, and dismisses it as "bad advice."

*March 29*

B was sick on March 26, so patient saw A. "It was useless." No longer worried about state hospital. Thinks he will now wind up as bum because he got drunk last week. His secretary gave him notice but he hopes to keep her "by taking abuse. No one treats a boss like she treats me." Got out of bed and worked last week. Went out selling but "everyone rejected me." When B indicates that he seems to be better, he insists he's deteriorating. When B inquires how, he replies paradoxically, "I beat out my competitors this week."

*April 2*

Has habit of sticking finger down throat to induce vomiting. Threatens to do so when enters office today. B tells patient about the logical consequences of his act—he will have to mop up. Patient withdraws finger. "If you would leave me alone, I'd fall asleep so fast." B leaves him alone. Patient angrily declaims, "Why do you let me sleep?"

*April 9*

Too weak even to telephone therapist. If wife goes on vacation, he will kill himself. How can he survive with no one to tell him to eat, to go to bed, to get up? "All I do is vomit and sleep." B suggests that he tyrannizes his wife as he did his mother and sister. He opens window and inquires, "Shall I jump?" B recognizes this as an attempt to intimidate rather than a serious threat and responds, "Suit yourself." Patient closes window and accuses, "You don't care either." Asks whether he can see A next time and before receiving answer, says, "I don't want him anyway." Follows this with, "I want to go to the state hospital. Can you get me a private room?" At end of interview falls to knees and sobs, "Help me! Help me to be a human being."

*April 12*

Enters, falls to knees, encircles therapist's knees, whimpers, "Help me!" So depressed. If only he could end it all. B gives him Adler's suggestion to do one thing each day that would give someone pleasure. Patient admits behaving better. Stopped annoying secretary and let her go home early because of bad weather. Agitation stops.

*April 15*

Didn't do anything this weekend to give pleasure. However, he did play cards with wife. Took her for drive. Sex with wife for "first time in a long time." B gives encouragement and then repeats "pleasure" suggestion. He can't do it. Calm whole hour. Says his wife has told him to discontinue treatment. Upon inquiry, he says she didn't say exactly that but had said, "I leave it up to you."

*April 19*

Wants B to accompany him back to his office because he forgot something. Wants shorter hour this week and longer one next week. "Dr. C let me do that." When B declines, he complains, "Doctor, I don't know what to do with you anymore."

*April 23*

Wouldn't consider suicide. "Perhaps I have a masochistic desire to live." B suggests he must be angry with life. He responds that he wants to be an infant and have all his needs gratified. The world should be a big breast and he should be able to drink without having to suck [probably an interpretation he had received in psychoanalysis]. Yesterday he had fantasy of destroying the whole city.

This weekend he helped his wife work in the garden. He asks for suggestions for weekend. B and patient play "yes-but." B does so deliberately to point out game (cf. Berne's "Why don't you . . . ? Yes but" [1964]) to patient. Patient then volunteers possibility of clay modeling. B indicates this may be good choice in that patient can mold, manipulate, and "be violent."

*April 29*

Had birthday last week and resolved to turn over new leaf for new year but didn't. Cries, "Help me, help me." Depreciates B. "How much would you charge me to come to my summer home? I'm so sick, I vomited blood." When B tells him if he's that sick, hospitalization might be advisable, he smiles and says, "For money, you'd come out." B and patient speak of attitude toward B and attitude toward his father. Patient depreciates both, possibly because he could not dominate either.

*May 1*

Didn't think he could make it today because he was afraid to walk on street. Didn't sleep all night. So excited, so upset [he seems calm]. Perhaps he should be put in hospital, but then what will happen to his business?

"We could sit here forever and all you would tell me is to get clay. Why don't you give me medicine or advice?" B points out that the patient is much stronger than any medication, as evidenced by number of therapists and treatments he has defeated.

He says he is out of step with world. B repeats an earlier interpretation by A that the patient wants the world to conform to him and follows with statement about his desire to be omnipotent, a desire that makes him feel weak and simultaneously compensates for his feelings of weakness. He confirms with "All Chicago should stand still so I could have a holiday. The police should stop at gunpoint anyone who wants to go to work. But I don't want to. I don't want to do anything anymore. I want a paycheck but I don't want to work." B remarks on shift from "I can't" to "I don't want to." Patient admits and says, "I don't want to get well. Should I make another appointment?" B refers decision back to him. He makes appointment.

## May 6

"I'm at the end, dying with fear [enumerates symptoms]. Since five this morning I'm murdering ——— and ———. Such nice people and I'm murdering them and I'm elec- trocuted. And my secretary and wife can't stand it anymore. Take me to a state hospital. I don't want to go. Take me. I'm getting crazy and you don't help me. Help me, *Lieber Doktor!* I went to the ladies' room twice today to get my secretary and the girls com- plained to the building office. I'm not above the rules. I knew I violated them. My zipper was down again [he frequently "forgets"] and I just pulled it up before you came in to- day." B agrees that state hospital might be appropriate if he is becoming "crazier." "Then my wife will divorce me. It's terrible. They have bars there. I won't go. I'm not that bad yet. Why, last week I went out and made a big sale!" B suggests he "practice" his fears and obsessions.

## May 8

Seen by A and B, who did summary of his family constellation. It was done very tenta- tively because of the meager information elicited.

## May 13

Complains about symptoms. He had taken his wife to the movies but "was too upset to watch it." He had helped with the raking. Returns to symptoms and begging for Tho- razine. "How will I live without Thorazine?" B suggests they ought to talk about how to live. He yells, "With your quiet voice, you'll drive me crazy." B asks, "Would you like me to yell at you like your father did?" "I won't talk to you anymore."

"*Lieber Gott,* liberate me from the evil within me." Prays to everyone for help. B counters with, "Have you ever solicited your own help?" Patient replies, "I have no strength, I could *cry.* I could shout. I don't have strength. Let me vomit."

## May 15

Demands Thorazine or he will have heart attack. B requests a future autobiography. Re- sponds "I don't anticipate anything" and returns to Thorazine question. B points out his real achievement in staying off Thorazine. Patient mentions price in suffering. B points out that this makes it an even greater achievement. Patient accepts idea reluctantly. B points out that they are at cross-purposes because patient wants to continue suffering but have pills; B's goal is to have him stop his suffering. "I want pills." B offers clay. "Shit on your clay."

## May 20

Must have Thorazine. Has murderous and self-castrating fantasies. Tells A that A does not know anything about medicine. Dr. C did. Why don't we let him go back to Dr. C? A leaves room with patient following. After three to four minutes patient returns and complains, "You call this treatment?" Dr. A points out demand of patient to have own way. He is a little boy who wants to be big but doesn't think he can make it. He is a pam- pered tyrant. A also refers to patient's favorite childhood game of lying in bed with sister and playing "Emperor and Empress."

Patient points out innate badness in himself. A points out he creates it. Patient talks of hostility and murder. A interprets look on his face as taking pride in his bad behavior. Patient picks up letter opener, trembles, then grasps hand with other hand but continues

to tremble. A tells him that this is a spurious fight between good and evil, that he can decide how he will behave.

He kneaded clay a little while this weekend.

## May 22

Last weekend he mowed lawn, tried to read but "I'm nervous. I'm talking to you like a human being but I'm not really a human being." Raw throat. Fears might have throat cancer. Stopped sticking finger down throat to vomit as consequence. Discussion of previously expressed ideas of "like a human being." Fantasy of riding a boat through a storm. Fantasy of A being acclaimed by crowd and patient in fantasy asking B, "Are you used to A getting all the attention?"

Complains about wife and secretary, neither of whom will any longer permit tyrannization.

## June 3

Relates fantasy of being magician and performing unbelievable feats at the White House. He asked the President whether he was happily married and then produced the President's ring. Nice weekend. Made love to wife at his initiative. Grudgingly admits enjoying it.

## June 10

"Ignored my wife this week." Yet he took initiative and they had sex again. Both enjoyed it but he was afraid because he read in a magazine that sex is a drain on the heart. At work secretary is angry. After she checks things, he rechecks. Pledged to God today he wouldn't do it anymore. He'll only check one time more. Outlines several plans for improving business "but I don't have the strength." Wants to cut down to one interview per week because he doesn't get well and can't afford to pay. B suggests that perhaps he is improving if he wants to reduce the number of sessions. Patient rejects and agrees to two sessions weekly.

## June 24

Talks about fears. B tells him he will go on vacation next week. He accepts it calmly although he had previously claimed to be unendurably upset. Patient tells B that he has given up vomiting and masturbation, saying, "You have enormous influence on me." B encourages by saying patient made the decision by himself.

## Sept. 4

[Patient was not seen during August because he went on a "wonderful" vacation.] Stopped all medication except for occasional use of a mild tranquilizer his family physician prescribed. Able to read and concentrate again. Has surrendered his obsessive ruminations. He and his secretary get along without fighting although she doesn't like him. He is punctual at the office. He and wife get along well. He is more considerate of her. Both are sexually satisfied.

B and patient plan for treatment. Patient expresses reluctance, feeling that he has gone as far as he can. After all, one psychoanalyst said that he was hopeless and had recommended a lobotomy, so this was marked improvement. B agreed, telling patient that if he had considered the patient hopeless, he would not have undertaken treatment, nor would he now be recommending continuation. "What kind of treatment?" B tells him that no external agent (e.g., medicine, lobotomy) will do it, that his salvation will come from within, that he can choose to live life destructively (and self-destructively) or constructively. He proposes to come weekly for four weeks and then biweekly. B does not accept the offer.

## Sept. 17

Since yesterday his symptoms have returned. Heart palpitations.

## Sept. 25

Took wife to dinner last night. Very pleasant. Business is slow and his obligations are heavy but he is working. He has to exert effort not to backslide. B schedules double interview. Patient doesn't want to see A. It will upset him. He doesn't see any sense in seeing B either but since B insists. . . . Heart palpitations disappeared after last interview. Expresses realistic concerns today and has dropped usual frantic manner. Wants biweekly interviews. B wants weekly. Patient accepts without protest.

As therapy continued, the patient's discussion of symptoms was superseded by discussion of realistic concerns. Resistance waned. When he entered treatment, he perceived himself as a good person who behaved badly because he was "sick." During therapy, he saw through his pretenses and settled for being "a bad guy." However, once he understood his tyranny and was able to accept it, he had the opportunity to ask himself how he preferred to live his life—usefully or uselessly. Because the therapists used the monolithic approach (Alexander & French, 1946; Mosak & Shulman, 1963), after resolving the issue of his tyranny, therapy moved on to his other "basic mistakes," one at a time. The frequency of interviews was decreased and termination was by mutual agreement.

## Follow-Up

The patient improved, remaining off medication. When he devoted himself to his business, it prospered to the point where he could retire early. He moved to a university town, where he studied archaeology, the activity he liked best in life. His relationship with his wife improved and they traveled abroad. Because of the geographical distance between them, the therapists and the patient had no further contact.

## SUMMARY

Adlerian theory may be described as follows:

1.   Its approach is social, teleological, phenomenological, holistic, idiographic, and humanistic.

2.   Its underlying assumptions are (a) the individual is unique, (b) the individual is self-consistent, (c) the individual is responsible, (d) the person is creative, an actor, a chooser, and (e) people in a soft-deterministic way can direct their own behavior and control their destinies.

3.   Its personality theory takes as its central construct the life-style, a system of subjective convictions held by the individual that contains his or her self-view and world view. From these convictions, other convictions, methods of operation, and goals are derived. The person behaves *as if* these convictions were true and uses his life-style as a cognitive

map with which he explores, comprehends, prejudges, predicts, and controls the environment (the life tasks). Because the person cannot be understood *in vacuo* but only in his or her social context, the interaction between the individual and the individual's life tasks is indispensable for the purpose of fully comprehending that individual.

4.   "Psychopathology," "mental illness," and similar nomenclature are reifications and perpetuate the *nominal fallacy,* "the tendency to confuse naming with explaining" (Beach, 1955). The "psychopathological" individual is a discouraged person. Such people either have never developed or have lost their courage with respect to meeting the life tasks. With their pessimistic anticipations, they create "arrangements"—evasions, excuses, sideshows, symptoms—to protect their self-esteem, or they may "cop out" completely.

5.   Because people's difficulties emanate from faulty perceptions, learnings, values, and goals that have resulted in discouragement, therapy consists of an educative or reeducative endeavor in which two equals cooperatively tackle the educational task. Many of the traditional analytic methods have been retained, although they are understood, and sometimes used, differently by the Adlerian. The focus of therapy is the encouragement of the individual. The individual learns to have faith in self, to trust, and to love. The ultimate, *ideal* goal of psychotherapy is to release people's social interest so they may become fellow human beings, cooperators, and contributors to the creation of a better society. Such patients can be said to have actualized themselves. Because therapy is learning, everyone can change. On the entrance door of the Guidance Clinic for Juvenile Delinquency in Vienna was the inscription, "It is never too late" (Kramer, 1947).

Adlerian psychology has become a viable, flourishing system. Neglected for several decades, it has in recent years acquired respectability. Training institutes, professional societies, family-education centers, and study groups continue to proliferate. With Adlerians being trained in universities rather than solely in institutes, they are writing more and doing research. Non-Adlerians are also engaged in Adlerian research. The previously rare Adlerian dissertation has become more commonplace. Currently Adlerians are moving into society to renew their attention to the social issues Adler raised 70 years ago—poverty, war, conflict resolution, aggression, religion, substance abuse, and social cooperation. As Way apprises, "We shall need not only, as Adler says, more cooperative individuals, but a society better fitted to fulfill the needs of human beings" (1962, p. 360).

Complementing the Adlerians' endeavors are individuals and groups who have borrowed heavily from Adler, often without acknowledgment or awareness. Keith Sward, for example, reviewed Alexander and French's *Psychoanalytic Therapy* (1946), writing:

> The Chicago group would seem to be Adlerian through and through. . . . The Chicago Institute for Psychoanalysis is not alone in this seeming rediscovery of Rank and Adler. Psychiatry and psychology as a whole seem to be drifting in the same direction. Adler has come to life in other vigorous circles, notably in the publications of the "Horney" school. (1947, p. 601)

We observe glimpses of Adler in the Freudian ego-psychologists, neo-Freudians, existential systems, humanistic psychologies, person-centered theory, rational-emotive therapy, integrity therapy, transactional analysis, and reality therapy. This is not an augury of the eventual disappearance of Adlerian psychology through absorption into other schools of psychology, for, as the motto of the Rockford, Illinois, Teacher Development Center claims, "Education is like a flame. . . . You can give it away without diminishing the one from whom it came." As Joseph Wilder writes in his introduction to *Essays in Individual Psychology* (Adler & Deutsch, 1959), "Most observations and ideas of Alfred Adler have subtly and quietly permeated modern psychological thinking to such a degree that the proper question is not whether one is Adlerian but how much of an Adlerian one is" (p. xv).

# ANNOTATED BIBLIOGRAPHY

Ansbacher, H. L., & Ansbacher, R. (Eds.). (1964). *Individual psychology of Alfred Adler* (2nd ed.). New York: Harper Torchbooks.
An almost encyclopedic collection of Adler's writings, this volume displays both the great variety of topics that commanded his attention and the evolution of his thinking. Because of the nature of the construction of this book, it is imperative that the reader read the preface.

Manaster, G. J., & Corsini, R. J. (1982). *Individual psychology.* Itasca, IL: F. E. Peacock.
This is the first textbook of Adlerian psychology written in English by two students of Rudolf Dreikurs. Corsini was the former editor of the *Journal of Individual Psychology* and Manaster succeeded him. Written in a much simpler style than the Ansbacher and Ansbacher text (1956), this book covers more or less the same materials. Two features make it unique: It contains the single most complete Adlerian psychotherapy case summary published to date, and there is a section abstracting the more important research studies published in the field of Adlerian psychology.

Mosak, H. H., & Maniacci, M. (1998). *Tactics in counseling and psychotherapy.* Itasca, IL: F. E. Peacock.
The authors present a variety of tactics which may serve as interventions for both Adlerians and non-Adlerians. These tactics aim to answer such questions as "What do I do when my patient . . . ?" Various differential diagnosis, encouragement, confrontation, and countertactics are among the methods described and illustrated.

# CASE READINGS

Adler, A. (1929). *The case of Miss R. The interpretation of a life study.* New York: Greenberg.
Adler does an interlinear interpretation of the case study of a patient who in his time would have been labeled "psychoasthenic." The patient is also agoraphobic. Since Adler did not treat this patient, the course of therapy is unknown. However, we can observe how Adler constructs a life-style as well as his understanding of the patient's approach to the life tasks.

Adler, A. (1964). *The case of Mrs. A.: The diagnosis of a life style.* In H. L. Ansbacher & R. R. Ansbacher (Eds.), *Superiority and social interest* (pp. 159–190). Evanston, IL: Northwestern University Press (1969). Chicago: Alfred Adler Institute. Reprinted in D. Wedding & R. J. Corsini (Eds.) (1979). *Great cases in psychotherapy.* Itasca, IL: F. E. Peacock. (Original work published in 1931.)
This publication is similar to the one discussed above and interprets the case study of an obsessive-compulsive woman who fears that she will kill her children.

Ansbacher, H. L. (1966). Lee Harvey Oswald: An Adlerian interpretation. *Psychoanalytic Review, 53,* 379–390.
The psychodynamics of John F. Kennedy's assassin are presented from the Adlerian point of view.

Dreikurs, R. (1959). A record of family counseling sessions. In R. Dreikurs, R. Lowe, M. Sonstegard, & R. J. Corsini (Eds.), *Adlerian family counseling* (pp. 109–152). Eugene, OR: University of Oregon Press.
Two sessions of family counseling conducted by Rudolf Dreikurs and Stefanie Necheles are presented. The identified patient, a nine-year-old boy, is described by his parents as an angry child.

Frank, I. (1981). My flight toward a new life. *Journal of Individual Psychology, 37*(1), 15–30.
A young anorexic woman describes the course of her eating problem as well as the various treatments, Adlerian and non-Adlerian, which she underwent until the problem was resolved.

Manaster, G. J., & Corsini, R. J. (1982). *Individual Psychology.* Itasca, IL: F. E. Peacock.
Chapter 17 offers verbatim excerpts of a course of therapy of a man who in dualistic fashion perceives himself as conflicted, ambivalent, and self-contradictory.

Mosak, H. H. (1972). Life-style assessment: A demonstration based on family constellation. *Individual Psychology, 28,* 232–247.
A verbatim description of a life-style assessment done in public demonstration is presented. The subject is a teenage girl who feels that she is the sole "non-very" person in a "very" family.

Mosak, H. H., & Maniacci, M. (2005). The case of Roger. In D. Wedding & R. J. Corsini (Eds.), *Case studies in psychotherapy.* Belmont, CA: Wadsworth.
This case history was specifically written to complement the current chapter and it illustrates many of the methods, techniques, and principles of Adlerian psychotherapy. Careful reading of the case should help the student more fully appreciate how an Adlerian actually proceeds in therapy.

# REFERENCES

Adler, Alexandra (1943). Problems in psychotherapy. *American Journal of Individual Psychology, 3,* 1–5.

Adler, Alexandra (1951). Alfred Adler's viewpoint in child guidance. In E. Harms (Ed.), *Handbook of child guidance.* New York: Child Care Publications.

Adler, A. (1898). *Gesundheitsbuch für das Schneidergewerbe.* Berlin: C. Heymanns.

Adler, A. (1914). *Das Zärtlichkeitsbedürfnis des Kindes.* In A. Adler & C. Furtmüller (Eds.), *Heilen und Bilden.* München: Reinhardt.

Adler, A. (1917). *Study of organ inferiority and its psychical compensation.* New York: Nervous & Mental Disease Publishing Co.

Adler, A. (1922). *Erziehungsberatungsstellen.* In A. Adler & C. Furtmüller (Eds.), *Heilen und Bilden.* München: Reinhardt.

Adler, A. (1926/1972). *The neurotic constitution.* Freeport, NY: Books for Libraries Press.

Adler, A. (1928). On teaching courage. *Survey Graphic, 61,* 241–242.

Adler, A. (1929). Position in family influences lifestyle. *International Journal of Individual Psychology, 3,* 211–227.

Adler, A. (1931/1958). *What life should mean to you.* New York: Capricorn Books.

Adler, A. (1934). Lecture to the Medical Society of Individual Psychology, London. *Individual Psychology Pamphlets, 13,* 11–24.

Adler A. (1947). How I chose my career. *Individual Psychology Bulletin, 6,* 9–11.

Adler, A. (1959). *Understanding human nature.* New York: Premier Books.

Adler, A. (1963a). Contributions to the theory of hallucinations. In A. Adler, *The practice and theory of individual psychology* (pp. 51–58). Paterson, NJ: Littlefield, Adams.

Adler, A. (1963b). Dreams and dream interpretations. In A. Adler, *The practice and theory of individual psychology* (pp. 214–226). Paterson, NJ: Littlefield, Adams.

Adler, A. (1964a). *Problems of neurosis.* New York: Harper & Row.

Adler, A. (1964b). *Social interest: A challenge to mankind.* New York: Capricorn Books.

Adler, A. (1969). *The science of living.* New York: Doubleday Anchor Books.

Adler, K. A. (1961). Depression in the light of individual psychology. *Journal of Individual Psychology, 17,* 56–67.

Adler, K. A., & Deutsch, D. (Eds.) (1959). *Essays in individual psychology.* New York: Grove Press.

Alexander, F., & French, T. M. (1946). *Psychoanalytic therapy.* New York: Ronald Press.

Allred, G. H. (1976). *How to strengthen your marriage and family.* Provo, UT: Brigham Young University Press.

Angers, W. P. (1960). Clarifications toward the rapprochement between religion and psychology. *Journal of Individual Psychology, 16,* 73–76.

Ansbacher, H. L. (1946). Adler's place today in the psychology of memory. *Journal of Personality, 15,* 197–207.

Ansbacher, H. L. (1952). "Neo-Freudian" or "Neo-Adlerian"? *American Journal of Individual Psychology, 10,* 87–88. [Also in *American Psychologist* (1953), *8,* 165–166.]

Ansbacher, H. L. (1961). Suicide: Adlerian point of view. In N. L. Farberow & E. S. Schneidman (Eds.), *The cry for help.* New York: McGraw-Hill.

Ansbacher, H. L. (1962). Was Adler a disciple of Freud? A reply. *Journal of Individual Psychology, 18,* 126–135.

Ansbacher, H. L. (1968). The concept of social interest. *Journal of Individual Psychology, 24,* 131–141.

Ansbacher, H. L. (1969). Suicide as communication: Adler's concept and current applications. *Journal of Individual Psychology, 25,* 174–180.

Ansbacher, H. L. (1972). Adler's "striving for power," in relation to Nietzsche. *Journal of Individual Psychology, 28,* 12–24.

Ansbacher, H. L., & Ansbacher, R. (Eds.). (1956). *The individual psychology of Alfred Adler.* New York: Basic Books.

Beach, F. A. (1955). The descent of instinct. *Psychological Review, 62,* 401–410.

Beck, A. T., & Weishaar, M. E. (2005). Cognitive therapy. In R. J. Corsini & D. Wedding (Eds.), *Current psychotherapies* (pp. 238–268). Belmont, CA: Wadsworth.

Beecher, W., & Beecher, M. (1966). *Parents on the run.* New York: Agora Press.

Berne, E. (1964). *Games people play.* New York: Grove Press.

Bickhard, M. H., & Ford, B. L. (1976). Adler's concept of social interest. *Journal of Individual Psychology, 32,* 27–49.

Bierer, J. (1951). *The day hospital, an experiment in social psychiatry and synthoanalytic psychotherapy.* London: H. K. Lewis.

Bierer, J., & Evans, R. I. (1969). *Innovations in social psychiatry.* London: Avenue Publishing.

Birnbaum, F. (1935). The Individual Psychological Experimental School in Vienna. *International Journal of Individual Psychology, 1,* 118–124.

Birnbaum, F. (1961). Frankl's existential psychology from the viewpoint of Individual Psychology. *Journal of Individual Psychology, 17,* 162–166.

Boldt, R. (1994). Lifestyle types and therapeutic resistance: An Adlerian model for prediction and intervention of characterological resistance in therapy. Unpublished Psy.D. dissertation. Chicago: Adler School of Professional Psychology.

Bottome, P. (1939). *Alfred Adler: A biography.* New York: Putnam.

Brewer, D. H. (1976). The induction and alteration of state depression: A comparative study. Unpublished doctoral dissertation. University of Houston.

Brome, V. (1968). *Freud and his early circle.* New York: William Morrow.

Brown, C. (1965). *Manchild in the promised land.* New York: Signet Books.

Brown, J. F. (1976). Parallels between Adlerian psychology and the Afro-American value system. *Individual Psychologist, 13,* 29–33.

Bugental, J. F. T. (1963). Humanistic psychology: A new breakthrough. *American Psychologist, 18,* 563–567.

Clark, K. B. (1965). Problems of power and social change: Toward a relevant social psychology. *Journal of Social Issues, 21,* 4–20.

Clark, K. B. (1967a). *Dark ghetto.* New York: Harper Torchbooks.

Clark, K. B. (1967b). Implications of Adlerian theory for understanding of civil rights problems and action. *Journal of Individual Psychology, 23,* 181–190.

Colby, K. M. (1951). On the disagreement between Freud and Adler. *American Image, 8,* 229–238.

Corsini, R. J. (1953). The behind-the-back technique in group psychotherapy. *Group Psychotherapy, 6,* 102–109.

Corsini, R. J. (1977). Individual education. *Journal of Individual Psychology, 33,* 295–349.

Corsini, R. J. (1979). Individual education. In E. Ignas & R. J. Corsini (Eds.), *Alternative educational systems* (pp. 200–256). Itasca, IL: F E. Peacock.

Corsini, R. J., & Painter, G. (1975). *The practical parent.* New York: Harper & Row.

Crandall, J. E. (1981). *Theory and measurement of social interest.* New York: Columbia University Press.

Credner, L. (1930). Sicherungen. *Internationale Zeitschrzft für Individual-psychologie, 8,* 87–92. [Translated as Safeguards (1936). *International Journal of Individual Psychology, 2,* 95–102.]

Crookshank, F G. (1933). Individual Psychology and Nietzsche. *Individual Psychology Medical Pamphlets, 10,* 7–76.

Deutsch, D. (1967). Group therapy with married couples. *Individual Psychologist, 4,* 56–62.

Dinkmeyer, D. C., & Carlson, J. (1989). *Taking the time for love.* Englewood Cliffs, NJ: Prentice-Hall.

Dinkmeyer, D., & Dreikurs, R. (1963). *Encouraging children to learn: The encouragement process.* Englewood Cliffs, NJ: Prentice-Hall.

Dreikurs, R. (1944). The meaning of dreams. *Chicago Medical School Quarterly, 5*(3), 4–7.

Dreikurs, R. (1948). *The challenge of parenthood.* New York: Duell, Sloan & Pearch.

Dreikurs, R. (1949). The four goals of children's misbehavior. *Nervous Child, 6,* 3–11.

Dreikurs, R. (1950). Techniques and dynamics of multiple psychotherapy. *Psychiatric Quarterly, 24,* 788–799.

Dreikurs, R. (1951). The function of emotions. *Christian Register, 130*(3), 11–14, 24.

Dreikurs, R. (1957). Psychotherapy as correction of faulty social values. *Journal of Individual Psychology, 13,* 150–158.

Dreikurs, R. (1958). A reliable different diagnosis of psychological or somatic disturbances. *International Record of Medicine, 171,* 238–242.

Dreikurs, R. (1959). Early experiments with group psychotherapy. *American Journal of Psychotherapy, 13,* 882–891.

Dreikurs, R. (1961). The Adlerian approach to therapy. In Morris I. Stein (Ed.), *Contemporary psychotherapies* (pp. 80–94). Glencoe, IL: The Free Press.

Dreikurs, R. (1962). Can you be sure the disease is functional? *Consultant* (Smith, Kline & French Laboratories).

Dreikurs, R. (1963). Psychodynamic diagnosis in psychiatry. *American Journal of Psychiatry, 119,* 1045–1048.

Dreikurs, R. (1968). *Psychology in the classroom.* New York: Harper & Row.

Dreikurs, R. (1969). Social interest: The basis of normalcy. *The Counseling Psychologist, 1,* 45–48.

Dreikurs, R. (1971). *Social equality: The challenge of today.* Chicago: Henry Regnery.

Dreikurs, R. (1972). Technology of conflict resolution. *Journal of Individual Psychology, 28,* 203–206.

Dreikurs, R., Corsini, R. J., Lowe, R., & Sonstegard, M. (1959). *Adlerian family counseling.* Eugene, OR: University of Oregon Press.

Dreikurs, R., & Grey, L. (1968). *Logical consequences.* New York: Meredith.

Dreikurs, R., Grunwald, B., & Pepper, F. C. (1982). *Maintaining sanity in the classroom* (2nd ed.). New York: Harper & Row.

Dreikurs, R., & Mosak, H. H. (1966). The tasks of life. I. Adler's three tasks. *Individual Psychologist, 4,* 18–22.

Dreikurs, R., & Mosak, H. H. (1967). The tasks of life. II. The fourth life task. *Individual Psychologist, 4,* 51–55.

Dreikurs, R., Shulman, B. H., & Mosak, H. H. (1952a). Patient-therapist relationship in multiple psychotherapy. I. Its advantages to the therapist. *Psychiatric Quarterly, 26,* 219–227.

Dreikurs, R., Mosak, H. H., & Shulman, B. H. (1952b). Patient-therapist relationship in multiple psychotherapy. II. Its advantages for the patient. *Psychiatric Quarterly, 26,* 590–596.

Dreikurs, R., Shulman, B. H., & Mosak, H. H. (1982). *Multiple psychotherapy.* Chicago: Alfred Adler Institute.

Dreikurs, R., & Soltz, V. (1964). *Children: The challenge.* New York: Duell, Sloan & Pearce.

Dunlap, K. (1933). *Habits: Their making and unmaking.* New York: Liveright.

Edgar, T. (1975). Social interest—another view. *Individual Psychologist, 12,* 16–24.

Elam, H. (1969a). Cooperation between African and Afro-American, cultural highlights. *Journal of the National Medical Association, 61,* 30–35.

Elam, H. (1969b). Malignant cultural deprivation, its evolution. *Pediatrics, 44,* 319–326.

Ellenberger, H. F. (1970). *The discovery of the unconscious.* New York: Basic Books.

Ellis, A. (1957). Rational psychotherapy and Individual Psychology. *Journal of Individual Psychology, 13,* 38–44.

Ellis, A. (1963). Toward a more precise definition of "emotional" and "intellectual" insight. *Psychological Reports, 13*, 125–126.

Ellis, A. (1970). Humanism, values, rationality. *Journal of Individual Psychology, 26*, 37–38.

Ellis, A. (1971). Reason and emotion in the Individual Psychology of Adler. *Journal of Individual Psychology, 27*, 50–64.

Farau, A. (1953). The influence of Alfred Adler on current psychology. *American Journal of Individual Psychology, 10*, 59–76.

Farau, A. (1964). Individual psychology and existentialism. *Individual Psychologist, 2*, 1–8.

Federn, E. (1963). Was Adler a disciple of Freud? A Freudian view. *Journal of Individual Psychology, 19*, 80–81.

Fiedler, F. E. (1950). A comparison of therapeutic relationships in psychoanalytic, non-directive and Adlerian therapy. *Journal of Consulting Psychology, 14*, 436–445.

Forer, L. K. (1977). Bibliography of birth order literature of the 1970s. *Journal of Individual Psychology, 33*, 122–141.

Frank, L. K. (1939). Projective methods for the study of personality. *Journal of Personality, 8*, 389–413.

Frankl, V. E. (1963). *Man's search for meaning.* New York: Washington Square Press.

Frankl, V. E. (1970). Forerunner of existential psychiatry. *Journal of Individual Psychology, 26*, 38.

Fromm-Reichman, F. (1949). Notes on personal and professional requirements of a psychotherapist. *Psychiatry, 12*, 361–378.

Goldstein, K. (1939). *The organism.* New York: American Book Co.

Gottesfeld, H. (1966). Changes in feelings of powerlessness in a community action program. *Psychological Reports, 19*, 978.

Grunwald, B. (1954). The application of Adlerian principles in a classroom. *American Journal of Individual Psychology, 11*, 131–141.

Gushurst, R. S. (1971). The reliability and concurrent validity of an idiographic approach to the interpretation of early recollections. Unpublished doctoral dissertation. University of Chicago.

Heine, R. W. (1953). A comparison of patients' reports on psychotherapeutic experience with psychoanalytic, nondirective, and Adlerian therapists. *American Journal of Psychotherapy, 7*, 16–23.

Hemming, J. (1956). *Mankind against the killers.* London: Longmans, Green.

Hinrichsen, O. (1913). Unser Verstehen der seelischen Zusammenhänge in der Neurose and Freud's and Adler's Theorien. *Zentralblätter für Psychoanalyse, 3*, 369–393.

Horney, K. (1951). *Neurosis and human growth.* London: Routledge & Kegan Paul.

Jahn, E., & Adler, A. (1964). Religion and Individual Psychology. In H. L. Ansbacher & R. Ansbacher (Eds.), *Superiority and social interest.* Evanston, IL: Northwestern University Press. [Reprinted in *Individual Psychology*, 1987, *43*(4), 522–526.]

James, W. (1890). *Principles of psychology.* New York: Holt.

James, W. T. (1947). Karen Horney and Erich Fromm in relation to Alfred Adler. *Individual Psychology Bulletin, 6*, 105–116.

Kadis, A. L. (1956). Re-experiencing the family constellation in group psychotherapy. *American Journal of Individual Psychology, 12*, 63–68.

Kazan, S. (1978). Gemeinschaftsgefühl means caring. *Journal of Individual Psychology, 34*, 3–10.

Kramer, H. D. (1947). Preventive psychiatry. *Individual Psychology Bulletin, 7*, 12–18.

Krausz, E. O. (1935). The pessimistic attitude. *International Journal of Individual Psychology, 1*, 86–99.

Krausz, E. O. (1959). The commonest neurosis. In K. A. Adler & D. Deutsch (Eds.), *Essays in individual psychology* (pp. 108–118). New York: Grove Press.

La Porte, G. H. (1966). Social interest in action: A report on one attempt to implement Adler's concept. *Individual Psychologist, 4*, 22–26.

Lazarsfeld, S. (1952). Pitfalls in psychotherapy. *American Journal of Individual Psychology, 10*, 20–26.

Lazarsfeld, S. (1966). The courage for imperfection. *Journal of Individual Psychology, 22*, 163–165.

Lewin, K. (1935). *A dynamic theory of personality.* New York: McGraw-Hill.

Lombardi, D. M. (1969). The special language of the addict. *Pastoral Psychology, 20*, 51–52.

Low, A. A. (1952). *Mental health through will training.* Boston: Christopher.

Maslow, A. H. (1962). Was Adler a disciple of Freud? A note. *Journal of Individual Psychology, 18*, 125.

Maslow, A. H. (1970). Holistic emphasis. *Journal of Individual Psychology, 26*, 39.

May, R. (1970). Myth and guiding fiction. *Journal of Individual Psychology, 26*, 39.

McArthur, H. (1958). The necessity of choice. *Journal of Individual Psychology, 14*, 153–157.

Meerloo, J. A. M. (1970). Pervasiveness of terms and concepts. *Journal of Individual Psychology, 26*, 40.

Miley, C. H. (1969). Birth-order research, 1963–1967: Bibliography and index. *Journal of Individual Psychology, 25*, 64–70.

Mosak, H. H. (1954). The psychological attitude in rehabilitation. *American Archives of Rehabilitation Therapy, 2*, 9–10.

Mosak, H. H. (1958). Early recollections as a projective technique. *Journal of Projective Techniques, 22*, 302–311. [Also in G. Lindzey & C. S. Hall (Eds.). (1965). *Theories of personality: Primary sources and research.* New York: Wiley.]

Mosak, H. H. (1967). Subjective criteria of normality. *Psychotherapy, 4,* 159–161.

Mosak, H. H. (1968). The interrelatedness of the neuroses through central themes. *Journal of Individual Psychology, 24,* 67–70.

Mosak, H. H. (1971). Strategies for behavior change in schools: Consultation strategies. *Counseling Psychologist, 3,* 58–62.

Mosak, H. H. (1972). Life style assessment: A demonstration based on family constellation. *Journal of Individual Psychology, 28,* 232–247.

Mosak, H. H. (1985). Interrupting a depression: The pushbutton technique. *Individual Psychology, 41*(2), 210–214.

Mosak, H. H. (1987a). *Ha ha and aha: The role of humor in psychotherapy.* Muncie, IN: Accelerated Development.

Mosak, H. H. (1987b). Guilt, guilt feelings, regret and repentance. *Individual Psychology, 43*(3), 288–295.

Mosak, H. H. (1987c). Religious allusions in psychotherapy. *Individual Psychology, 43*(4), 496–501.

Mosak, H. H. (1991). "I don't have social interest": Social interest as construct. *Individual Psychology, 47,* 309–320.

Mosak, H. H., & Dreikurs, R. (1967). The life tasks. III. The fifth life task. *Individual Psychologist, 5,* 16–22.

Mosak, H. H., & Fletcher, S. J. (1973). Purposes of delusions and hallucinations. *Journal of Individual Psychology, 29,* 176–181.

Mosak, H. H., & Gushurst, R. S. (1971). What patients say and what they mean. *American Journal of Psychotherapy, 3,* 428–436.

Mosak, H. H., & Kopp, R. (1973). The early recollections of Adler, Freud, and Jung. *Journal of Individual Psychology, 29,* 157–166.

Mosak, H. H., & LaFevre, C. (1976). The resolution of "intrapersonal conflict." *Journal of Individual Psychology, 32,* 19–26.

Mosak, H. H., & Maniacci, M. P. (1998). *Tactics in counseling and psychotherapy.* Itasca, IL: F. E. Peacock.

Mosak, H. H., & Mosak, B. (1975a). *A bibliography for Adlerian psychology.* Washington, DC: Hemisphere.

Mosak, H. H., & Mosak, B. (1975b). Dreikurs' four goals: The clarification of some misconceptions. *Individual Psychologist, 12*(2), 14–16.

Mosak, H. H., & Schneider, S. (1977). Masculine protest, penis envy, women's liberation and sexual equality. *Journal of Individual Psychology, 33,* 193–201.

Mosak, H. H., & Shulman, B. H. (1963). *Individual psychotherapy: A syllabus.* Chicago: Alfred Adler Institute.

Mozdzierz, G. J., & Lottman, T. J. (1973). Games married couples play: Adlerian view. *Journal of Individual Psychology, 29,* 182–194.

Mullahy, P. (1955). *Oedipus: Myth and complex.* New York: Evergreen.

Murphy, G. (1947). *Personality: A biosocial approach to origins and structure.* New York: Harper.

Neuer, A. (1936). Courage and discouragement. *International Journal of Individual Psychology, 2,* 30–50.

Nikelly, A. G. (1971a). Basic processes in psychotherapy. In A. G. Nikelly (Ed.), *Techniques for behavior change* (pp. 27–32). Springfield, IL: Charles C. Thomas.

Nikelly, A. G. (1971b). Developing social feeling in psychotherapy. In A. G. Nikelly (Ed.), *Techniques for behavior change* (pp. 91–95). Springfield, IL: Charles C. Thomas.

Nikelly A. G. (1971c). The protesting student. In A. G. Nikelly (Ed.), *Techniques for behavior change* (pp. 159–164). Springfield, IL: Charles C. Thomas.

O'Reilly, C., Cizon, E., Flanagan, J., & Pflanczer, S. (1965). *Men in jail.* Chicago: Loyola University.

Painter, G., & Corsini, R. J. (1989). *Effective discipline in the home and the school.* Muncie, IN: Accelerated Development.

Pancner, K. R. (1978). The use of parables and fables in Adlerian psychotherapy. *Individual Psychologist, 15,* 19–29.

Papanek, E. (1971). Delinquency. In A. G. Nikelly (Ed.), *Techniques for behavior change* (pp. 177–183). Springfield, IL: Charles C. Thomas.

Papanek, H. (1954). Combined group and individual therapy in private practice. *American Journal of Psychotherapy, 8,* 679–686.

Papanek, H. (1956). Combined group and individual therapy in the light of Adlerian psychology. *International Journal of Group Psychotherapy, 6,* 135–146.

Papanek, H. (1959). Emotion and intellect in psychotherapy. *American Journal of Psychotherapy, 13,* 150–173.

Papanek, H., & Papanek, E. (1961). Individual Psychology today. *American Journal of Psychotherapy, 15,* 4–26.

Pelzman, O. (1952). Some problems in the use of psychotherapy. *Psychiatric Quarterly Supplement, 26,* 53–58.

Pew, M. L., & Pew, W. (1972). Adlerian marriage counseling. *Journal of Individual Psychology, 28,* 192–202.

Phillips, C. E., & Corsini, R. J. (1982). *Give in or give up.* Chicago: Nelson–Hall.

Rasey, M. I. (1956). Toward the end. In C. E. Moustakas (Ed.), *The self: Explorations in personal growth* (pp. 247–260). New York: Harper.

Reik, T. (1948). *Listening with the third ear.* New York: Farrar, Straus & Cudahy.

Rogers, C. R. (1951). *Client-centered therapy.* Boston: Houghton Mifflin.

Rosenthal, D., & Frank, J. D. (1956). Psychotherapy and the placebo effect. *Psychological Bulletin, 53,* 294–302.

Seidler, R. (1967). The individual psychologist looks at testing. *Individual Psychologist, 5,* 3–6.

Seidler, R., & Zilahi, L. (1949). The Vienna child guidance clinics. In A. Adler & Associates, *Guiding the child* (pp. 9–27). London: Allen & Unwin.

Shlien, J. M., Mosak, H. H., & Dreikurs, R. (1962). Effect of time limits: A comparison of two psychotherapies. *Journal of Counseling Psychology, 9,* 31–34.

Shoben, E. J., Jr. (1957). Toward a concept of normal personality. *American Psychologist, 12,* 183–189.

Shoobs, N. E. (1964). Role-playing in the individual psychotherapy interview. *Journal of Individual Psychology, 20,* 84–89.

Shulman, B. H. (1962). The meaning of people to the schizophrenic and the manic-depressive. *Journal of Individual Psychology, 18,* 151–156.

Shulman, B. H., & Klapman, H. (1968). Organ inferiority and psychiatric disorders in childhood. In E. Harms (Ed.), *Pathogenesis of nervous and mental diseases* (pp. 49–62). New York: Libra.

Shulman, B. H., & Mosak, H. H. (1977). Birth order and ordinal position. *Journal of Individual Psychology, 33,* 114–121.

Shulman, B. H., & Mosak, H. H. (1988). *Manual for lifestyle assessment.* Muncie, IN: Accelerated Development.

Sicher, L., & Mosak, H. H. (1967). Aggression as a secondary phenomenon. *Journal of Individual Psychology, 23,* 232–235.

Simpson, H. N. (1966). *Stoic apologetics.* Oak Park, IL: Author.

Smuts, J. C. (1961). *Holism and evolution.* New York: Viking Press.

Soltz, V. (1967). *Study group leader's manual.* Chicago: Alfred Adler Institute.

Spiel, O. (1962). *Discipline without punishment.* London: Faber & Faber.

Starr, A. (1977). *Psychodrama.* Chicago: Nelson-Hall.

Strupp, H. H. (1972). Freudian analysis today. *Psychology Today, 6,* 33–40.

Sullivan, H. S. (1954). *The psychiatric interview.* New York: Norton.

Sward, K. (1947). Review [Review of *Our inner conflicts*]. *Science,* December 1, 600–601.

Taylor, J. A. (1975). Early recollections as a projective technique: A review of some recent validation studies. *Journal of Individual Psychology, 31,* 213–218.

Toman, W. (1970). Never mind your horoscope, birth order rules all. *Psychology Today, 4,* 45–48, 68–69.

Vaihinger, H. (1965). *The philosophy of "as if."* London: Routledge & Kegan Paul.

Von Sassen, H. W. (1967). Adler's and Freud's concepts of man: A phenomenological comparison. *Journal of Individual Psychology, 23,* 3–10.

Watkins, C. E., Jr. (1982). A decade of research in support of Adlerian psychological theory. *Individual Psychology, 38*(1), 90–99.

Watkins, C. E., Jr. (1983). Some characteristics of research on Adlerian theory, 1970–1981. *Individual Psychology, 39*(1), 99–110.

Way, L. (1962). *Adler's place in psychology.* New York: Collier Books.

Wexberg, E. (1929). *Individual Psychology.* London: Allen & Unwin.

Wexberg, E. (1929/1970). *Individual psychological treatment.* Chicago: Alfred Adler Institute. (Originally published in 1929.)

White, R. W. (1957). Adler and the future of ego psychology. *Journal of Individual Psychology, 13,* 112–124.

Wittels, F. (1939). The neo-Adlerians. *American Journal of Sociology, 45,* 433–445.

Wolfe, W. B. (1932). *How to be happy though human.* London: Routledge & Kegan Paul.

Zborowski, R. (1997). The phenomenon of transference: An Adlerian perspective. Unpublished Psy.D. dissertation, Adler School of Professional Psychology.

Carl Jung, 1875–1961

© Bettmann /CORBIS

# 4 ANALYTICAL PSYCHOTHERAPY

*Claire Douglas*

## OVERVIEW

Analytical psychology, the psychodynamic system and personality theory created by Carl Gustav Jung, builds upon Freud's and Adler's perspectives, offering an expanded view of humanity's personal and collective realities. Analytical psychotherapy offers a map of the human psyche that encompasses conscious and unconscious elements, including both a transpersonal (archetypal) and personal layer in the unconscious. The goals of psychotherapy are reintegration, self-knowledge, and individuation, with a heartfelt awareness of the human condition, individual responsibility, and a connection to the transcendent replacing a wounded, one-sided, rationalistic, and limited sense of self. Therapy taps into the healing and self-regulating potential of the psyche by means of a profound encounter between the interacting personalities of patient and therapist.

### Basic Concepts

The cornerstone of Jung's psychological system is his concept of the psyche, the inner realm of personality that balances the outer reality of material objects. Jung defined *psyche* as a combination of spirit, soul, and idea; he viewed psychic reality as the sum of conscious and unconscious in processes. According to Jung, this inner world influences biochemical processes in the body, affects the instincts, and determines one's perception of outer reality. Jung proposed that physical matter can only be known through a person's psychic images of outside reality; thus, what people perceive is in large part determined by who they are.

The reality of the psyche was Jung's working hypothesis, confirmed through material he gathered from fantasy, myth, image, and the behavior of individual people. Jung mapped the psyche in terms of a whole made up of balancing and compensatory opposites. Key aspects of his map of the psyche are a personal and collective unconscious as well as a personal and collective consciousness.

Jung's description of the personal unconscious is similar to, but more extensive than, Freud's. In Jungian theory, an individual's personal unconscious contains not only material unacceptable to one's ego and superego and therefore repressed, but also material unimportant to the psyche, temporarily or permanently dropped from consciousness. It also contains undeveloped parts of one's personality not yet ready for or admitted to consciousness, as well as elements rising from the collective unconscious.

The *collective unconscious* is Jung's term for the vast, hidden psychic resource shared by all human beings. Jung discovered the collective unconscious through his patients' disclosures, his own self-analysis, and cross-cultural studies. He found the same basic motifs expressed in fantasies, dreams, symbols, or myths. Images that emerge out of the collective unconscious are shared by all people but modified by their personal experiences. Jung called these motifs archetypal images and depicted the collective unconscious as organized in underlying patterns.

An *archetype* is an organizing principle, a system of readiness, and a dynamic nucleus of energy. As an organizing principle, an archetype is analogous to the circuitry pattern in the brain that orders and structures reality; as a system of readiness, it parallels animals' instincts; as a dynamic nucleus of energy, it propels a person's actions and reactions in a patterned way. Jung believed that humans have an inherited predisposition to form their personalities and to view reality according to universal inner patterns.

Archetypes can be seen as pathways along whose course energy flows from the collective unconscious into consciousness and action. Jung wrote that there were as many archetypal images in the collective unconscious as there were typical situations in life, and that they have appeared in individual experience from time immemorial and will reappear in the future whenever analogous situations arise. Some archetypal patterns that became a major focus of Jung's work and a fertile source for popular psychology are the Heroic Quest; the Night Sea Journey; the Inner Child (often seen as the childlike part of one's own personality) and Divine Child; the Maiden, Mother, and Goddess; the Wise Old Man; and the Wild Man.

While the collective unconscious reveals itself to a person by means of such archetypal images, the personal unconscious makes itself known through *complexes.* Archetypal images flow from the collective unconscious into the personal unconscious by means of a *complex* (a sensitive, energy-filled cluster of emotions, such as an attitude toward one's father or anyone resembling him). Jung's idea of the complex came from his research on the Word Association Test. Jung would read a list of words aloud, asking subjects to respond with the first word that came to their minds; he then repeated the list, with the subjects attempting to recall their initial responses. Jung noticed pauses, failures to respond or remember, and bodily reactions, and he believed that such variations revealed sensitive, hidden areas. Jung named these reactions complexes—emotionally charged associations of ideas and feelings that act as magnets to draw a net of imagery, memories, and ideas into their orbit.

Jung believed the complex to be so important that when he broke from Freud and looked for a name for his form of psychoanalysis, his first choice was Complex Psychology. Though Freud and Adler adopted Jung's terminology of the complex, Jung's formulation was far richer than those of his colleagues. Jung believed that though a complex may have restricting, upsetting, or other disturbing consequences in some instances, it can also be positive, serving to bring matters of importance to consciousness. Complexes demand personal confrontation and response that can promote a person's development and growth. One can relate to a complex positively by meeting its demand, but this takes hard psychological work. Many people try to manage a complex by projecting its contents: A man with a negative mother complex, for instance, may see all women in an exaggeratedly negative light. (*Projection* means attributing to another person something that really belongs to one's own personality.) Another way a person may try to avoid a complex is by repression. Thus, a woman with a negative mother complex may cut herself off from all that she considers feminine so as not to resemble her mother in any way. Another woman with a mother complex might perceive herself as an all-good, "earth mother" type of woman. In more extreme cases, a complex may overpower an individual so that the person loses touch with reality, becoming psychotic; a psychotic woman who has a mother complex may believe she is Mother Nature and the mother of everything and everybody on earth.

Rather than seeing the unconscious as something needing to be cleaned out and made conscious, Jung felt that individuals grow toward wholeness when both conscious and unconscious parts of the mind work in harmony. Because of this natural movement toward balance and self-healing, Jung concluded that neurosis contained the seeds for its own cure and had the energy to bring about growth and healing. The Jungian analyst serves as a catalyst to promote balance, growth, and integration.

## Other Systems

Jung's theories have influenced contemporary religious, cultural, and sociological thought, as well as art, literature, and drama. Nevertheless, psychology in general, and modern psychotherapeutic systems in particular, frequently overlook or ignore Jung's influence. There are many reasons for this, including the difficulty of Jung's writing style and the bitter parochialism of some early psychoanalysts. The situation is compounded by the tendency of psychologists to believe what they have *heard* about Jung rather than reading what he wrote. Today's psychologists receive a rigorously scientific education that often leads them to fear "soft" science and to avoid a system that they have been told is mystical. In reality, the pragmatism of Jung's practical and inclusive approach to psychotherapy has contributed much to the general field of psychology. To ignore one of the three great early psychodynamic theoreticians of the twentieth century is to travel with an incomplete map of the human psyche.

Jung started to develop his own form of psychoanalysis and to treat patients before he met Freud. However, his debt to Freud is great. Perhaps most important to Jung was Freud's exploration of the unconscious through free association, his focus on the significance of dreams, and his stress on the role of early childhood experiences in the formation of personality (Ellenberger, 1981). Jung constructed a map of these areas that became broader and more inclusive than Freud's.

Jung focused on the complex as the royal road to the unconscious, while Freud emphasized the importance of dreams. Yet dreams play a more significant role in Jung's system than in Freud's, since Jung saw dreams as more meaningful than simple wish-fulfillments, requiring a more thorough and well-rounded technique of dream analysis. For Jung, Freud's Oedipus complex was only one of many possible complexes and not necessarily the most important one. Sexuality and aggression, rather than being the sole channels for the expression of libido, were only two of its many possible routes. Neurosis had many causes, including, but not limited to, sexual problems. Perhaps the most salient difference between Freud and Jung resulted from Jung's belief that the quest for meaning was as strong a need as the sex drive.

Jung believed that certain people would profit most from a Freudian analysis, others from an Adlerian analysis, and still others from a Jungian analysis. He viewed Adler's theory of dreams as similar to his own. Both theories held that dreams could reveal what an individual wanted not to recognize in himself or herself (what Jung called the *shadow* aspects of the personality). Both Jung and Adler believed that dreams reveal the underlying pattern of the way an individual relates to the world. Adler and Jung also stressed the importance of first memories, and of fulfilling life tasks and one's duties to society. Jung taught that unless these tasks were met, neurosis would result. They both met the individual patient on a more equal footing than Freud. Freud had his patients lie on a couch and free associate, but Jung and Adler sat face-to-face with their patients. Finally, both Adler and Jung believed that psychotherapy should look to the future as well as to the past. Jung's ideas of life goals and forward-looking (teleological) energy are similar to Adler's views.

Life-span psychologists owe much to Jung. Erik Erickson's life stages, as well as Lawrence Kohlberg's stages of moral development and Carol Gilligan's reevaluation and redefinition of Kohlberg's work to reflect women's development, all express Jung's ideas of individuation over the life span. Jung's theories inspired Henry A. Murray's Needs-Press Theory of Personology, and Jung's encouragement of fantasies inspired the Thematic Apperception Test (Christiana Morgan, its first author, and Murray were analyzed by Jung). Gestalt therapy can be seen as an extension of Jung's method of dream interpretation. Jungians such as E. C. Whitmont and Sylvia Perera (1992) use a combination of gestalt enactment and active imagination (a conscious exploration of one's fantasies) as core analytic tools. J. L. Moreno's psychodrama reflects Jung's encouragement of patients' enacting their dreams and fantasies; Moreno's ideas of role and of surplus reality mirror Jung's belief in a pluralistic psyche composed of many archetypal images and possible roles.

Harry Stack Sullivan's *good me* and *bad me* reflect Jung's concepts of positive and negative *shadow* (the rejected or unrecognized parts of one's personality). Alexander Lowen's bioenergetic theory follows Jung's theory of typology, and Jung's four functions of *thinking, feeling, sensation,* and *intuition* loosely parallel Lowen's hierarchy of personality functions. Holistic therapies of all varieties, from the Adlerian to the most modern, share with Jung the idea of a person made up of many parts in service to the whole, with the individual having a normal urge toward growth and healing. Self-actualizing theories, such as those derived from Abraham Maslow's work, stress the forward-looking and optimistic parts of Jung's psychology, while the person-centered psychology of Carl Rogers echoes Jung's human interest and personal devotion to his patients. Jung (1935a) insisted on the human quality in analysis, emphasizing the integrity of the patient who "inasmuch as he is an individual . . . can only become what he is and always was . . . the best thing the doctor can do is lay aside his whole apparatus of methods and theory" (p. 10) in order to be with the patient as a fellow human being.

Neo-Freudian ego psychology, such as Melanie Klein's and Erich Fromm's theories, shares so much with Jungian thought that they cross-fertilize each other and may produce a vigorous hybrid. Jungians have pointed out the similarity of their constructs to Jung's original formulations in realms such as the description of infancy and its tasks, the internalization of parts of others' personalities, projections, and the death instinct (e.g., Maduro & Wheelwright, 1977). Barbara Stephens (1999) sees the following Jungian themes fertilizing post-Freudian thought: the centrality of self and subjective experience; countertransference as helpful analytic data; the role of symbol and symbol formation; the importance of primitive (and infantile) affective states; and finally, Freudian feminists' focus on desire as a significant conduit of integration and healing.

Jung's emphasis on the value of being as well as doing, and his deep trust in religious or mystical feelings, are similar to many Asian psychotherapies. Jung's method for incubating fantasies in active imagination is a directed meditation. Jung lectured widely on

Asian systems of thought, comparing them to his own theories; perhaps his most cogent lecture was on yoga in relation to the analysis of one of his patients (Douglas, 1997c).

# HISTORY

## Precursors

Carl Gustav Jung (1875–1961), the eldest son of a clergyman, grew up in the German-speaking part of Switzerland during the final quarter of the nineteenth century. His mother came from a family of theologians; his father's father, a physician, had also been a renowned poet, philosopher, and classical scholar. Jung received a thorough education embedded not only in the Protestant theological tradition but also in classical Greek and Latin literature. He was influenced especially by the pre-Socratic philosopher Heraclitus, the mystic Jacob Boehme, by romantic philosophy and psychiatry, and by Asian philosophy. During an era that marked the rise of scientific positivism, Jung's teachers emphasized a rational, optimistic, and progressive view of human nature. Nevertheless, Jung was drawn instead to romanticism, which valued the irrational, the occult, the mysterious, and the unconscious. Romanticism had a more pessimistic view of human nature than positivism did. According to romantic philosophy, humans were divided and polarized; they yearned for a unity and wholeness that had been lost. This yearning manifested itself through the desire to plumb the depths of the natural world as well as the individual soul (Douglas, 1997a).

Romantic philosophy underlay nineteenth-century anthropology, linguistics, and archaeology, as well as research on sexuality and the inner worlds of the mentally ill—all topics that interested Jung. Romanticism also manifested itself in the exploration of parapsychological phenomena and the occult.

Tracing the specific sources of Jung's ideas would require many chapters. Perhaps the best brief coverage is by Henri Ellenberger (1981), who stresses Jung's debt to romantic philosophy and psychiatry. The theories of Goethe, Kant, Schiller, and Nietzsche were influential in forming Jung's style of thinking in terms of opposites.

Jung's fellow townsman, Johann Bachofen, was interested in the religious and philosophical importance of myths and the meaning of symbols. Nietzsche had borrowed Bachofen's concept of a Dionysian-Apollonian duality, which Jung, in turn, also adopted. (Dionysius stood for the sensual side of life, while Apollo represented the rational.) Nietzsche shared with Jung a sense of the tragic ambiguity of life and the presence of good and evil in every human interaction. Nietzsche's ideas about the origin of civilization, humanity's moral conscience, and the importance of dreams, together with his concern about evil, influenced Jung. Nietzsche's description of the Shadow, the Persona, the Superman, and the Wise Old Man were taken up by Jung as specific archetypal images.

Carl Gustav Carus and Arthur Schopenhauer also influenced Jung. Carus had written about the creative and healing functions of the unconscious 50 years before Freud or Jung. Carus outlined a tripartite model of the unconscious that prefigured Jung's concepts of the archetypal, collective, and personal unconscious. Schopenhauer possessed a view of life that attracted Jung. Both wrote about the irrational in human psychology, as well as the role played by human will, repression, and the power of the instincts. Schopenhauer and Nietzsche inspired Jung's theory of archetypes; also influential was Schopenhauer's emphasis on imagination, the role of the unconscious, the reality of evil, and the importance of dreams. Both Schopenhauer and Jung were interested in moral issues and in Eastern philosophy, and both shared a belief in the possibility of personal wholeness.

Ellenberger (1981) traces Jung's psychotherapeutic emphasis on transference and countertransference (*transference* refers to feelings the patient projects onto the analyst and *countertransference* to the ways in which the analyst is influenced by patients' projections) to a chain of thought that originated in the exorcism of devils, wound through Anton Mesmer's theory of animal magnetism, and lead to the early nineteenth-century use of hypnosis by Pierre Janet to cure mental illness. Janet also influenced Jung through his classifications of mental diseases and his interest in multiple personality and fixed ideas. For Janet, as for Jung, the dedication of the doctor and the personal harmony between doctor and patient were major elements in cures.

## Beginnings

Jung wrote, "Our way of looking at things is conditioned by what we are" (1929/1933/1960, p. 335). He believed all psychological theories were subjective, reflecting the personal history of their founders. Jung's parents had been raised in prosperous city families and were well educated; their discontent with their life in the poor rural parish of Kesswil, where Jung's father served as a country pastor, affected Jung's childhood. Jung described his youth as lonely. Until he went to high school, his companions were mostly uneducated farm children. His early experience with peasants brought out a practical and earthy side of Jung that balanced his tendency toward introspection (Jung, 1965).

Jung was close to his mother. He experienced her as having two sides. One side was intuitive, with an interest in parapsychology that he feared; the other side was warm and maternal, which comforted him. In his mind, Jung split her into a daytime/nighttime, good/bad person. Jung's later efforts to integrate these contrasting aspects of his mother found form in his emphasis on the importance of the Hero's quest to free himself from the Terrible Mother, as well as his depiction of powerful feminine archetypal images. Jung's unsatisfactory relationship with his father may have led to his later problems with men, especially male mentors and other authority figures.

Throughout his life, Jung was interested in and attracted to women. He married a woman with an earthy side similar to his mother's, but he remained captivated by intuitive women whom he described as his lost feminine half. In his autobiography, Jung remembered a nursemaid who took care of him when his mother was hospitalized for several months. This nurse became the prototype for a series of women who were to fascinate and inspire him. The parapsychological experiments of Jung's cousin, Helene Preiswerk, became the subject of his medical school dissertation. Her influence was seminal to the development of Jung's theories.

Much of Jung's reading during his university and medical school years concerned multiple personality, trance states, hysteria, and hypnosis. He brought this interest to his coursework and to his lectures to fellow students, as well as to his dissertation. His fascination with these subjects, and his reading of Richard von Krafft-Ebing's study of sexual psychopathology, propelled Jung into psychiatry (Jung, 1965). Soon after Jung finished his dissertation, he started work under Eugen Bleuler at the Burgholzli Psychiatric Hospital, then a famous center for research on mental illness. Jung lived at the Burgholzli Hospital from 1902 to 1909, and became intimately involved with the daily lives of mentally disturbed patients. Their inner worlds intrigued him, and his exploration of the symbolic universe of one of his schizophrenic patients, Babette, was a major source of Jung's study on schizophrenia, *The Psychology of Dementia Praecox* (1907/1961). At the Burgholzli, Jung developed and administered a number of psychological tests. His Word Association Test studies (1904–1907) gained him renown. These studies were the first demonstration of the reality of the unconscious. This work led Jung to begin a correspondence with Sigmund Freud.

Freud appreciated Jung's contributions to psychoanalytic theory and accepted Jung as his heir apparent. He appointed Jung president of the International Psychoanalytic Association and editor of the *Jahrbuch,* the first psychoanalytic journal. The two men traveled together to the United States in 1909 to lecture on their respective views of psychoanalysis at Clark University. Jung considered himself Freud's collaborator, not his disciple. Divergent perceptions, as well as their conflicting personalities, caused them to sever their alliance. Jung brought about his inevitable break with Freud through writing *The Psychology of the Unconscious* (1911, revised in 1956 as *Symbols of Transformation*). In this book, Jung set forth his own form of psychoanalysis, in which myth, cultural history, and personal psychology were interwoven; he also redefined *libido* more comprehensively than had Freud. During this period, Jung married and then left the Burgholzli for private practice. He began to train his followers in his own method and his wife, Emma Jung, became one of the first analytical psychotherapists.

After his break with Freud, Jung suffered a period of extreme introversion that Ellenberger (1981) called a creative illness. At this time, a third in the series of women who inspired him, his former patient and a future analyst, Toni Wolff, served as Jung's guide for his descent into the unconscious. Jung acknowledged his debt to her, as well as to the women who were the subjects of his first three books, and to his female patients when he wrote: "What this psychology owes to the direct influence of women . . . is a theme that would fill a large volume. I am speaking here not only of analytical psychology but of the beginnings of psychopathology in general" (Jung, 1927/1970, p. 124). He added that "I have had mainly women patients, who often entered into the work with extraordinary conscientiousness, understanding and intelligence. It was essentially because of them that I was able to strike out on new paths in therapy" (Jung, 1965, p. 145).

Jung's emergence from his period of creative introversion was signaled by the 1921 publication of his *Psychological Types.* Its inspiration came from Jung's reflection on the destructive antagonism among Freud, Adler, and himself. Jung made his private peace with them by creating a system of typology that allowed for and explained the different ways each experienced and reacted to the world.

## Current Status

Interest in Jungian psychology is growing as the incompleteness of positivistic science becomes more apparent and the world becomes increasingly complex. In spite of the dismissal of analytical psychology by some pragmatic psychologists, the fact that analytical psychology answers a strong need for many people can be seen in the growing number of Jungian professional training institutes and analysts. As of 2004, the International Association for Analytical Psychology had over 2,500 certified analyst members in 28 countries and 48 professional societies (17 in the United States). There are striving Jungian study groups and analytical psychology clubs in cities that have professional societies and in many places not large enough to have institutes, and there are increasing numbers of people who call themselves Jungian-oriented therapists but have not gone through an institute's rigorous training. Professional journals are associated with specific institutes; among the more important ones are the British *Journal of Analytical Psychology;* the *San Francisco Jung Institute Library Journal;* the Los Angeles Institute's *Psychological Perspectives;* the New York Institute's *Journal of Jungian Theory and Practice;* Chicago's series of *Chiron* monographs on clinical practice; and the post-Jungian journal of archetypal studies, *Spring.* Important non-English journals include the *Cahiers de Psychologie Jungienne* from Paris, the *Zeitschrift fur Analytische Psychologie* from Berlin, and Rome's *La Rivista di Psicologia Analitica.*

Training varies from institute to institute and country to country. Though Jung accepted lay analysts, the trend toward increasing professionalism grows. In the United States, institutes most often accept physicians, clinical psychologists, and social workers for training. Jung was the first psychoanalyst to insist that an analyst be personally analyzed. The cornerstone of Jungian training remains a thorough analysis over many years and often with two different analysts. Six or more years of case supervision comes next in importance. Coursework in the United States commonly takes four years and involves seminars that provide a thorough grounding in clinical theory and practice (from both a Jungian and neo-Freudian perspective), dream analysis, and archetypal psychology. Extensive personal reviews, oral and written examinations, and a clinical dissertation are generally required for professional certification as a Jungian analyst. The average length of training is from six to eight years.

There is an exciting ferment within Jungian studies at this time. Interest in child analysis, group work, body work, and art therapy is increasing, as is a concomitant interest in a hybrid of Jungian psychology and post-Freudian's object relations theory that focuses on the analysis of early childhood development and early childhood wounds (Stephens, 1999). *Object relations* is an unfortunate term for the way people relate to other people. This hybrid is becoming increasingly popular with a number of analysts in the United States. Others are revising or discarding the more time- or culture-bound aspects of Jung's theory. Two examples are a Jungian psychology of women that fits the reality of contemporary women and a reformulation of Jung's anima-animus concept. *Anima* is a feminine archetypal image most often represented through the feminine part of a man; *animus* is a masculine archetypal image most often represented through the masculine part of a woman. Jungians are currently reassessing what were once held to be traditionally "masculine" and "feminine" characteristics and are reappraising Jungian typological theory. There is also an extension of archetypal theory to images relevant to contemporary life, both in scholarly works and in popular works that reach a wide and receptive audience. There has been a gradual easing of the bad feelings and jealousy that divided the various schools of depth psychology since Freud, Adler, and Jung parted ways. Thus, for example, the National Accreditation Association for Psychoanalysis includes depth psychologists and institutes from many different, and formerly opposing, schools, while the British *Journal of Analytical Psychology* gives a yearly conference (last held in Prague) that is sponsored by the American Psychoanalytical Foundation and Jungian Institutes in Chicago and New York.

Multiculturalism can also be seen through the growing number of South American Institutes and Jungian societies, the small but growing number of Asian, African-American, Hispanic, gay, lesbian, and feminist analysts in the United States, and a newly active attention in training and in journals to multicultural, gender, and aging issues. Andrew Samuels, for example, in *Politics on the Couch* (2001) calls for psychotherapists to develop an active sense of sociocultural realities and social responsibility both in session with their clients and in the community at large.

Along with this important and growing emphasis, there is also a backlash among more conservative Jungians who argue that Jung's original words—even when considered socioculturally suspect by today's standards—should not be reinterpreted or "watered down" by contemporary standards or cross-fertilization, but accepted and taught as he first presented them. Some Jungian Institutes are experiencing a paradigm shift, accompanied by fruitful ferment and discussion (see Alschuler, 1997; Douglas, 1997c; and Withers, 2003, for discussion of these issues); other institutes (the LA Institute, for example) have split into two groups because of this issue.

# PERSONALITY

## Theory of Personality

Jung's theory of personality rests on the concept of a dynamic unity of all parts of a person. The psyche is made up of conscious and unconscious components with connections to the *collective unconscious* (underlying patterns of images, thoughts, behaviors, and experiences). According to Jungian theory, our conscious understanding of who we are comes from two sources: the first derives from encounters with social reality, such as the things people tell us about ourselves, the second from what we deduce from our observations of others. If others seem to agree with our self-assessment, we tend to think we are normal; if they disagree, we tend to see ourselves, or to be seen by others, as abnormal.

In addition, each individual has a personal unconscious. This is an area of personality that cannot be understood directly but can only be approached indirectly through dreams and through analysis. The personal unconscious is affected by what Jung called the collective unconscious, an inherited human factor that expresses itself in the personal unconscious by means of archetypal images and complexes.

So, in effect, there are two aspects to the human psyche: One is an accessible side referred to as consciousness, comprising one's senses, intellect, emotions, and desires, and the other is an inaccessible side—the personal unconscious, containing elements of personal experience we have forgotten or denied, as well as elements of the collective unconscious that can be discerned through archetypal images and complexes.

Jung defined the Self as archetypal energy that orders and integrates the personality, an encompassing wholeness out of which personality evolves. The Self is the goal of personal development. The infant starts in a state of initial wholeness, as a unitary Self that soon fragments into subsystems. Through this fragmentation, mind and consciousness develop; over the course of a lifetime, the healthy personality then reintegrates at a higher level of development.

The most important fragment of the Self, the ego, first appears as the young child gains some sense of identity as an independent being. The ego in early life is like an island of consciousness set in an ocean of personal and unconscious material. The island grows in size and definition as it gathers and digests the deposits from the sea around it. This ego becomes the "I"—an entity comprising everything a person believes himself or herself to be, including thoughts, feelings, wants, and bodily sensations. The ego, as the center of consciousness, mediates between the unconscious realm and the outer world. Part of human psychological development consists of creating a strong and resilient ego that can filter stimuli from each of these domains without identifying with or being overcome by either side.

The *personal shadow* balances the ego in the personal unconscious. The shadow contains everything that could or should be part of the ego but that the ego denies or refuses to develop. The personal shadow can contain both positive and negative aspects. Shadow elements often appear in dreams in attacking or frightening forms of the same gender as the dreamer; they also erupt into consciousness through projection onto hated or envied individuals or groups. The personal shadow tends to be the vehicle through which archetypal images of evil emerge out of the collective unconscious, as when, for instance, a mob gets carried away in mindless acts of violence. Confronting shadow material, making it and one's response to it conscious, can reclaim important parts of the personality to consciousness; these are essential tasks for the mature personality.

Jung believed in the reality of evil and viewed it as an increasing problem in the world. Jung felt that humans could confront evil by becoming conscious of it and aware of archetypal, inherited images of absolute evil. He thought that responsibly facing human evil meant becoming conscious of what is in one's own shadow, confronting archetypal images of evil instead of being overwhelmed by them, and taking personal responsibility for one's own evil propensities and actions rather than projecting shadow material and complexes onto others.

The *persona* is the public "face" of an individual in society. Jung named the persona for the Greek theatrical mask that hid the actor's face and indicated the part he chose to play. The persona shields the ego and reveals appropriate aspects of it, smoothing the individual's interactions with society. The development of an adequate persona allows for the privacy of thoughts, feelings, ideas, and perceptions, as well as for modulation in the way they are revealed. Just as people can identify with their egos, they can identify with their persona, believing they really *are* the role they have chosen to play.

Jung believed that the task of the first part of life was strengthening the ego, taking one's place in the world in relationships with others, and fulfilling one's duty to society. The task of the second half of life was to reclaim undeveloped parts of oneself, fulfilling these aspects of personality more completely. He called this process *individuation* and felt this life task drew many of his older patients into analysis. By individuation, Jung did not mean perfection; the idea refers to completion and wholeness, including acceptance of the more negative parts of one's personality and adoption of an ethical, though individual, response to them. Fordham (1996) and many other contemporary Jungians believe that individuation does not have to wait until middle age. Jung's emphasis on individuation as the task of the second half of life further differentiated his personality theory from Freud's because it allowed for growth and transformation throughout the life cycle. The mid-life crisis, looked at in this way, becomes a challenging opportunity for further development.

Part of the process of individuation concerns not only assimilation of personal shadow material but also awareness and integration of the contrasexual elements in the psyche—what Jung called the *anima* (an archetypal image of the feminine) and *animus* (an archetypal image of the masculine), which serve as bridges to the unconscious. The form and character of the archetypal images of anima and animus are highly individual, based on a person's experience of the opposite sex, cultural assumptions, and the archetype of the feminine or masculine. Since so much about gender and gender roles is in flux today, current images no longer match those of Jung's time and are changing as culture and experience change (Douglas, 1997c). Contemporary reevaluation of this concept holds much promise for a reappraisal of homosexuality as a natural occurrence.

Typology is one of the most important and best known contributions Jung made to personality theory. In *Psychological Types* (1921/1971), Jung describes varying ways individuals habitually respond to the world. Two basic responses are *introversion* and *extraversion*. Jung saw introversion as natural and basic. Energy for the introvert flows predominantly inward, with reality being the introvert's reaction to an event, object, or person. Introverts need solitude to develop and maintain their rich inner worlds; they value friendship, having few but deep relationships with others. The extravert's reality, on the other hand, consists of objective facts or incidents. The extravert connects with reality mainly through external objects. While the introvert adapts outer reality to inner psychology, the extravert adapts himself or herself to the environment and to people. Extraverts usually communicate well, make friends easily, and have a great deal of libido for interactions with other people. Jung described nations as well as people as being either predominantly introverted or extraverted. For instance, he saw Switzerland as basically introverted and the United States not only as being primarily extraverted but also as tending to look on introversion as unhealthy.

In his theory of typology, Jung went on to differentiate personality into functional types, based on people's tendency to perceive reality primarily through one of four mental functions: *thinking, feeling, sensation,* and *intuition.* Each of these four functions can be experienced in an extraverted or an introverted way. According to Jung:

> For complete orientation all four functions should contribute equally: thinking should facilitate cognition and judgment, feeling should tell us how and to what extent a thing is important or unimportant for us, sensation should convey concrete reality to us through seeing, hearing, tasting, sensing, etc., and intuition should enable us to divine the hidden possibilities in the background, since these too belong to the complete picture of a given situation. (1921/1971, p. 518)

According to Jung, a thinker finds rules, assigns names, makes classifications, and develops theories; a feeling person puts a value on reality, often by liking or disliking something; a sensing type uses the five senses to grasp inner or outer reality; and an intuitive person has hunches that seem to penetrate into past and future reality, as well as an ability to pick up accurate information from the unconscious of another person.

Most people seem to be born with one of these four primary functions dominant. The dominant function is used more and is developed more fully than the others. Often a secondary function will develop as the person matures, while a third, but weaker function—such as feeling for the thinker, or sensation for the intuitive person—remains shadowy and undeveloped. Jung stressed the importance of the least developed function. Largely unconscious, it is often seen first in shadow and animus/anima subpersonalities. This undeveloped function causes trouble when it breaks into consciousness, but it can also bring creativity and freshness, appearing when the mature personality feels lifeless and spent.

People tend to develop one primary attitude and function and then rely on these, sometimes inappropriately. For instance, a predominantly thinking type tends always to consider the facts of the case when it may be better simply to understand that something is right or wrong, good or bad, worthy of acceptance or rejection.

Everyone has access to all four functions as well as to introversion and extraversion. Part of personality development, according to Jungians, consists of first refining one's predominant type and then cultivating one's less-evolved functions. In life-span development, the secondary function matures after the first and is followed by the third; the blooming of the least-developed function comes last and can be a source of great creativity in the latter part of life. It is important to stress that typological theory is a blueprint or map far dearer than the terrain of the personality itself, which is full of individual differences.

## Variety of Concepts

### Opposites

Jung (1976) wrote, "Opposites are the ineradicable and indispensable preconditions for all psychic life" (p. 169). In line with the dualistic theories of his day, Jung saw the world in terms of paired opposites such as good and evil, light and dark, positive and negative. He designed his personality theory with *consciousness* opposing the *unconscious, masculine* opposing *feminine, good aspects* of an archetypal image opposing the *bad* (e.g., the *Nourishing* opposing the *Devouring* Mother), *ego* opposing *shadow,* and so on. These opposites engage in active struggle; personality development takes place through the tension this conflict produces in the psyche. For instance, a woman's conscious sexuality may war with her animus figure, who may appear in her dreams as a negative and judgmental male cleric. Caught in the conflict, she may go from one pole to the other and may develop neurotic symptoms from the split. Through bringing the fight between her eroticism and her spirituality into awareness, attentively following it, and allowing both sides their voice in fantasies and therapy, the woman may increase her consciousness and thus integrate the opposing sides of her sexuality and her religious feelings at a higher level of awareness.

### Enantiodromia

This word refers to Heraclitus's law that everything sooner or later turns into its opposite. To illustrate enantiodromia, Jung liked to tell the story of the man who laughed on the way up a precipitous mountain path and cried on the easy way down. While climbing, he anticipated the effortless descent, but while ambling down, he remembered the difficult ascent he had made. Jung believed enantiodromia governed the cycles of human history as well as personal development. He thought that one could escape such cycles only through consciousness. Jung's belief in Heraclitus's law underlies his theory of compensation.

## Compensation

Jung not only divided the world into paired opposites but formed a theory built on the idea that just as the opposites lay in dynamic balance, so everything in the personality balanced or supplemented its opposite in a self-regulatory way. Jung referred to this tendency as compensation. Thus, the personal unconscious balances an individual's consciousness, giving rise in dreams, fantasies, or somatic symptoms to its opposite; the more rigidly one holds the conscious position, the more strongly will its opposite appear in images or symbols and break through into consciousness. Thus, someone who consciously identifies with a harshly judgmental spirituality may have a prostitute figure active in his or her unconscious who, if further repressed, may induce a scandalous alliance in the outer world.

## The Transcendent Function

Jung called reconciling symbols, or images that form bridges between opposites, compensatory or transcendent functions. These symbols synthesize two opposing attitudes or conditions in the psyche by means of third forces different from both but uniting the two. Jung used the word *transcendent* because the image or symbol went beyond, as well as mediated between, the two opposites, allowing a new attitude or relationship between them. Bringing the opposites of one's conscious ego and the personal unconscious together generates a conflict in the personality that is highly charged and full of energy. The specific image that appears at the height of a seemingly unsolvable conflict between two opposites seems both unexpected and inevitable, holding an energy-filled charge capable of uniting and reconciling the opposing sides. The woman whose animus male cleric warred with her womanly sexuality had a fantasy in which she was crowned with grape leaves and led a snake to the foot of an altar; the snake slithered up the cross and wrapped itself about it (Douglas, 1997c). The crown of grape leaves was an emblem of sensuality, while the snake on the cross (connected with feminine energy in many myths, the most familiar being Eve and the Garden of Eden) reconciled the woman's opposing sides in a surprising new form of union.

## Mandala

Jung defined the mandala as a symbol of wholeness and of the center of the personality. The word *mandala* comes from the Sanskrit word for a geometric figure in which a circle and square lie within each other, and each is further subdivided. The mandala usually had religious significance. A mandala often appears in dreams, both as a symbol of wholeness and as a compensatory image during times of stress. An example of a mandala is shown on the next page (Figure 4.1).

## Preoedipal Development

In contrast to Freud's stress on the oedipal phase of personality development, Jung focused on *preoedipal experience*. He was one of the first psychoanalysts to stress the importance of early mother-child interactions. The initial relationship between mother and child affects personality development at its most basic and profound level. Jung paid far more attention to this stage and its problems than to the father-son complications of the

FIGURE 4.1   **Mandala**

Oedipus complex. He placed the archetypal image of the Good Mother and Bad Mother at the center of an infant's experience.

## Development of Consciousness

Jungian theory holds that the infant follows the pattern of the development of consciousness in general, first experiencing total merger with the mother in a state of primordial fusion, then partially splitting off from her through perceiving her as sometimes all good and sometimes all bad. The child follows humanity's general historical development, emerging into self-awareness in a patriarchal stage where the father and male values are paramount. This stage affects girls as well as boys and is considered a stumbling block to women's development. When the ego is firmly in place, however, a person can integrate the mother world and father world, uniting both energies to become a more complete personality (Jung, 1934a/1970; Whitmont, 1997).

## Psychopathology

Psychopathology derives in large part from problems and conflicts that arise in early mother-child relationships but is made worse by other stresses. The psyche directs attention to such disharmony and calls out for a response. Since the psyche is a self-regulating system, pathological symptoms derive from the frustrated urge toward wholeness and often contain within themselves the clue to their own healing. Thus, for instance, extreme switches between love and hate for the same person typify an individual with borderline personality disorder calling attention to faulty infantile development.

## Defense Mechanisms

Defense mechanisms are seen as attempts of the psyche to survive the onslaught of complexes. They can represent normal as well as destructive modes of protection. Jung felt that any rigidly held defense caused an imbalance and would become increasingly pathological if its calls for attention were ignored. *Regression,* for example, is a defense that becomes pathological only when a person remains stuck in it. Jung felt that regression was often a natural and necessary period of consolidation and regeneration that could herald an individual's subsequent personal growth.

# PSYCHOTHERAPY

## Theory of Psychotherapy

To Sigmund Freud's predominantly analytic, reductive system, Carl Jung added a synthesis that included the psyche's purposiveness. According to Jung, the personality not only has the capacity to heal itself but also becomes enlarged through experience. Jung (1934b/1966) built his system of psychotherapy on four tenets: (1) the psyche is a self-regulating system, (2) the unconscious has a creative and compensatory component, (3) the doctor-patient relationship plays a major role in facilitating self-awareness and healing, and (4) personality growth takes place at many stages over the life span.

Jung found that neurosis tends to appear when a person slights or shrinks back from some important worldly or developmental task. A neurosis is a symptom of disturbance in the personality's equilibrium; thus, the whole personality has to be considered, not only the symptom of distress. Rather than concentrating on isolated symptoms, the psychotherapist looks for an underlying complex. The symptom and the complex are important clues that both hide and reveal "the patient's secret, the rock against which he is shattered" (Jung, 1965, p. 117). Jung stated that when therapists discover their patients' secrets, they have the key to treatment.

Overt symptoms, dreams, and fantasies can reveal to the analyst a complex hidden from the patient's consciousness. Analytical psychotherapists deal with secrets, complexes, and neuroses by tracking their roots to past events and traumas, by seeing how they manifest themselves in the relationship between doctor and patient, and by recognizing the archetypal patterns that emerge into consciousness through the action of complexes.

Analytical psychotherapy also deals with "the mental and moral conflicts of normal people" (Jung, 1948/1980, p. 606). Jung differentiated normal from pathological conflicts according to the degree of consciousness a person has of the conflict and the amount of power exerted by the underlying complex. The level of dissociation between conscious and unconscious content reflects the intensity of the disturbance and the amount of pathology. Jung lectured frequently on his psychotherapeutic theory; yet he also declared that the practice of psychotherapy "does not involve intellectual factors only, but also feeling values and above all the important question of human relationship" (Jung, 1948/1980, p. 609). The dialogue and partnership between patient and analyst probably play the most essential roles in therapy. Jung himself was a notably effective therapist who followed the tenets of his theory, adapting it to the needs of each of his cases. This interaction between theory and the personal equation gives creative energy to analytical psychology as a whole and particularly to its practice of psychotherapy.

Analytical psychotherapy is, in essence, a dialogue between two people undertaken to facilitate growth, healing, and a new synthesis of the patient's personality at a higher level of functioning. By means of the analytic relationship, one works through personal problems and gains greater understanding of one's inner and outer worlds. Because of the importance of this relationship, the therapist's character, training, development, and individuation are crucial to the healing process. Jung insisted not only on the training analysis of the analyst but also on constant self-examination by the analyst. Next, and equal in importance, he valued the therapist's respect for patients, care for their values, and "supreme tact and . . . artistic sensitiveness" toward psychic material (Jung, 1934b/1966,

p. 169). Jung wrote of the therapist's need to consider the patient from many angles, including a sociocultural one: "Psychic modes of behavior are, indeed, of an eminently historical nature. The psychotherapist has to acquaint himself not only with the personal biography of his patient, but also with the mental and spiritual assumptions prevalent in his milieu, both present and past, where traditional and cultural influences play a part and often a decisive one" (Jung, 1957, pp. vii–viii).

Through his emphasis on the mutual influence of the two people in therapy, Jung was one of the first psychoanalysts to focus on both transference and countertransference phenomena. Rather than viewing therapy as something done by one person to another, Jung acknowledged that the therapist needs to be affected before transformation can occur in the patient. Jung emphasized the influence of the patient's unconscious on the analyst as well as the need for the analyst to be open to this power. The therapist's own analysis and continued self-examination are essential if the therapist is going to maintain a beneficial role.

The psychotherapeutic process can (and often should) stop when specific goals are reached or specific problems are overcome. Nevertheless, analytical psychotherapy in its most complete form has the goal of self-actualization—helping patients discover and live up to their full potential. Thus, Jungian psychotherapy goes beyond the resolution of complexes, the strengthening of the conscious mind, and ego development, to include a larger comprehension of the psyche. Through this process, patients achieve greater personal self-knowledge and the capacity for improved relationships with themselves, with others, and with the world at large.

Michael Fordham (1996) and his followers have enriched Jung's basic theory of psychotherapy by carefully observing young children's behavior and by analyzing children and childhood, focusing on the primary infantile wounds behind complexes. A growing number of Jungians stress the analysis of early childhood experiences, including the analysis of fantasy material. They also stress the value of verbal interpretation and explanations of present behavior. This approach has resulted in a synthesis of Jungian psychotherapy with neo-Freudian psychoanalysis.

Another major movement in Jungian psychotherapy questions the value of verbal interpretation as the primary mode of analysis. Instead, the patient's affect, feelings, and body awareness are emphasized, and therapists are more likely to use the traditionally feminine realm of subjective and shared experience (Wyman-McGinty, 1999). Wilmer (1994) finds emotion to be the core subject matter in a therapeutic setting where patient and therapist meet as equals. Sullivan (1989), Siegelman (1990), Beebe (1992), and Chodorow (1995) focus on the importance of subjective feelings. They emphasize the analyst's empathy, free-floating or hovering attention, and shared metaphoric images. They also provide a theoretical base for what has been a neglected but important aspect of analytical psychotherapy.

John Beebe stresses "active passivity," in which the analyst opens himself or herself to the wide range of stimuli emitted by the patient. Beebe points out that infringements of a person's privacy inevitably occur in psychotherapy, since its subject matter concerns sensitive secrets about which one is often ashamed. These secrets, when sensitively examined, may lead to the recall and healing of early infringements of bodily or psychological space. Because of sensitive subject matter, therapists need to adhere to an ethical code that honors and respects the integrity of their patients' boundaries. Beebe suggests that ethical principles in psychotherapy derive from the necessity of protecting patients' self-esteem while also protecting the integrity of the therapeutic setting and the beliefs that are essential for progress in analytical psychotherapy.

These views remain faithful to Jung's ideas of the primacy of patients and also preserve Jung's belief that the principle aim of psychotherapy is ultimately neither curing nor alleviating patients' unhappiness but increasing patients' self-respect and self-knowledge.

A sense of peace and a greater capacity for both suffering and joy can accompany this ex-panded sense of self, and patients are more likely to take personal responsibility for their behavior.

## Process of Psychotherapy

Psychotherapy takes place among fallible equals; however, Andrew Samuels's (1985) term *asymmetrical mutuality* may be preferred to *equals* insofar as it acknowledges the differing roles and responsibilities of patients and analysts. Jung (1933/1966) delin-eated four stages in the process of psychotherapy: *confession, elucidation, education,* and *transformation.*

### Confession

The first stage, confession, is a cathartic recounting of personal history. During this stage, the patient shares conscious and unconscious secrets with the therapist, who serves as a nonjudgmental, empathic listener. Jung found that confession brought the basic material of psychotherapy to the surface. Confession makes people feel less like outcasts, restor-ing them to their place in the human community. The analyst facilitates this process through an accepting attitude that drains the poison of guilt at the same time that it re-leases emotions long held hostage. The process of confession does, however, tend to bind the patient to the therapist through transference.

### Elucidation

During elucidation, the therapist draws attention to the transference relationship as well as to dreams and fantasies in order to connect the transference to its infantile origins. The goal of this stage is insight on both affective and intellectual levels. Jung describes the suc-cessful outcome of this procedure as leading to a person's "normal adaptation and for-bearance with his own shortcomings: these will be his guiding moral principles, together with freedom from sentimentality and illusion" (Jung, 1933/1966, p. 65).

### Education

The third stage, education, moves the patient into the realm of the individual as an adapted social being. Confession and elucidation primarily involve exploring the per-sonal unconscious, while education is concerned with persona and ego tasks. At this stage the therapist encourages the patient to develop an active and health-promoting role in everyday life. Insight, previously mostly intellectual, is now translated into responsible action.

### Transformation

Many people stop therapy at the completion of the first three stages, but Jung noted that some clients seemed impelled to go further, especially people in the second half of life. The transference does not go away for these patients, even though its infantile origins have been thoroughly explored. These people feel a desire for greater knowledge and in-sight leading them toward the final stage—*transformation.* Jung described this as a pe-riod of self-actualization; the person in this stage values unconscious as well as conscious experience. The archetypal image of the Self appears in the transference as well as in dream and fantasy; this archetypal image of wholeness inspires the patient to become a uniquely individual self, encompassing all that he or she can be, yet without losing a sense of responsible integrity.

In this most Jungian of stages, the transference-countertransference becomes even more profound, and what happens to the patient "must now happen to the doctor, so that his personality shall not react unfavorably on the patient. The doctor can no longer evade his own difficulty by treating the difficulties of others" (Jung, 1933/1966, p. 74). The analyst often has to face a challenge in his or her own life before something changes in the patient. Jung gave an example when he was becoming quite famous and was treating a woman patient who worshipped him. Nothing changed until he realized that he had become too removed from his patients and was starting to feel superior to this one especially; he then dreamed he was kneeling before her as if she were a female divinity. With this, he was brought back to reality, and the analysis started to progress again.

Jung spent the latter part of his career explaining this stage through a series of analogies to alchemy. He found that the symbols and processes of medieval alchemy were comparable to those of the psychotherapeutic process in that alchemists most often worked in pairs and left records showing that they were examining their own psyches while trying to transform some base material, through a series of stages, into gold. Jung's inclusion of self-realization as part of the process broadened the scope of psychology immeasurably, bringing analytical psychotherapy into the area of human potential, consciousness study, and field theory.

Jung became increasingly interested in the transformative stage and gathered much of the material in his case studies from it. He found the transference and dream symbols went from the personal to the archetypal during this stage. Jung illustrated the process with the case study of a patient who projected a personal father image onto Jung in the first three stages of her therapy. When she got to the transformative stage, however, her dreams of him as her good father changed. Now she dreamed of a giant father figure towering over a field of ripe wheat; as she nestled in the palm of this giant's hand, he rocked her in rhythm with the blowing wind. Jung interpreted this as an archetypal image of the Great Father in the form of a vegetation god and declared that it, along with the ripeness of the wheat, signaled that the patient was entering the final stage of analysis (Jung, 1935b/1966).

Jung noted that each stage of the analytical process seems to be accompanied by a sense of finality, as if it were a goal in itself. Though each can be a temporary goal or the endpoint of a partial analysis, all four belong in a complete analysis. The stages overlap and can be concurrent, with no stage excluding the others because neither their order nor duration is fixed.

## Mechanisms of Psychotherapy

### The Analysis of the Transference

Jungian psychotherapists agree with all practitioners of depth psychology that transference plays a crucial role throughout therapy; however, the idea takes on a different resonance and complexity in Jungian theory. In his Tavistock Lectures (Jung, 1935c/1980), Jung described four stages of analysis of the transference itself. In the first stage, transference projections onto the therapist mirror the personal history of the patient. Patients, in working through each of their earlier relationships, relate to the analyst as if he or she were the problematic person. This is an invaluable aid to therapy, as it brings the past into the consulting room. The three goals at this stage are to have one's patients realize that the projections belong to themselves and not to others, withdraw the projections from the analyst, and integrate them as conscious parts of the patient's own personalities. Jung, writing about this first stage, said "to establish a really mature attitude, [the patient] has to see the *subjective value* of all these images which seem to create trouble for him. He has to assimilate them into his own psychology; he has to find out in what way they are part of himself" (Jung, 1933/1966, p. 160).

Jung expanded the scope of transference by considering its sociocultural and archetypal components. These impersonal aspects also get projected onto the therapist. During the second stage of the analysis of the transference, patients learn to discriminate between the personal and the impersonal contents they project onto the therapist; they determine what belongs to their own psyches and what belongs to the collective realms of culture and archetype. The impersonal cannot be assimilated, but the act of projecting it can be stopped. In the case of the woman who dreamed of the Giant Vegetation God, Jung helped her see that this image was a transpersonal one reflecting a need for her personal connection to her image. When she had seen the difference between what belonged to her, to Jung, and to the impersonal archetypal image of the Great Father, she could establish a more healing relationship with the image's power.

In the third stage of analyzing the transference, the personal reality of the analyst becomes differentiated from the image assigned the healer by the patient. At this stage, the patient can begin to relate to the therapist as a normal human being, and the personality of the therapist plays a pivotal role. In the final stage, as the transference is resolved and greater self-knowledge and self-realization take place, a truer evaluation of the therapist emerges, along with a more straightforward and empathic connection between patient and therapist.

## Active Imagination

To help his patients get in touch with unconscious material, Jung taught a form of meditative imagery based on his own self-analysis. This came to be known as active imagination. The process calls for clearing the mind and concentrating intensely, so that inner images can be activated. The patient watches these, always returning his or her mind to them until movement is observed, upon which the patient enters into the scene, becoming part of the picture or action. Patients are instructed to pay relaxed meditative attention to what is going on. After the images stop, patients are to write, draw, paint, or even dance the story (Cwik, 1995; Douglas, 1997c; Rosen, 2002). The starting point for the exercise of active imagination can be a mood, a complex, an obsessive thought or feeling, or an image from a dream (Chodorow, 1997). Active imagination allows unconscious images to reveal themselves with little conscious intervention, yet it is more focused than dreams because of the presence of a witnessing consciousness. Therapists today emphasize that a patient must have a strong ego if unconscious images are to be dealt with in this way. Until then, the personal daily reality of the patient is the main focus of therapy; archetypal images or fantasies, if they appear, need to be grounded in a more objective, down-to-earth, and personal way than through active imagination.

## Dream Analysis

Not all people remember their dreams, nor do all people who enter Jungian therapy discuss their dreams. The perspective offered by a dream does, however, often compensate for one-sidedness of the waking ego. Dreams, according to Jung, don't necessarily conceal, as in the traditional Freudian view, nor do they always denote unfulfilled wishes, nor can they be interpreted according to a standard symbology. They are accurate renderings of something to which one may need to pay attention and take as seriously as a conscious event. Dreams may represent wishes and fears; they often express impulses the dreamer either represses or finds impossible to voice; they can also point to solutions to both exterior and interior problems. They are of great value in exposing a patient's hidden inner life, and through their evolving symbolic imagery, they reveal changes occurring in the patient's psyche. For example, at the start of therapy, a woman may dream of hostile men breaking into her house. As she deals with past traumas and begins to explore and integrate her own masculine energy, these malevolent male figures slowly change. In the latter part of a long dream series, the figures often turn into friends, helpers, and guides. Their positive and helpful behavior markedly contrasts with their earlier threatening demeanor. By watching the archetypal images of the unconscious through dreams, the personality is able to regulate itself.

An analytical psychotherapist looks for the role a dream may play in relation to the patient's conscious attitude. The therapist often explores the dream first on the objective level, considering in what ways it accurately portrays an actual person or situation. A dream is then probed for what it reveals about the patient's own behavior and character (Bosnak & Levertov, 1998). Jung gave the example of a young man who dreamed of a headstrong father smashing a car. Jung first investigated the objective reality but found little that resonated with his patient. On the subjective level, however, the dream compensated for the boy's tendency to overidealize his father and any other man in a position of authority as well as to ignore the heedless part of himself (Jung, 1934c/1966). In treating this patient, a Jungian therapist would ascertain if something akin to the image might be shadowing the therapy; for instance, if either the therapist or the patient were recklessly endangering the analysis by their attitudes or actions. In dream analysis, the unconscious and the dream are relied on far more than the therapist's interpretation. Jung believed that if the interpretation was not accurate, another dream would inevitably correct the faulty understanding.

## Types of Dreams

The initial dream, recurrent dreams, dreams containing shadow material, and dreams about the therapist or therapy are especially useful to the therapist. The initial dream at or near the start of therapy may indicate the path that a particular therapy may take and the type of transference that may occur. For instance, a short and unsuccessful therapy was predicted by an initial dream in which a female patient dreamed her therapist neither looked at nor listened to her but admired a beautiful jade figurine instead. The patient switched to a different analyst and then dreamed she was a baby lion being roughly groomed by the mother lion. This initial dream boded well for the course of the new therapy. Though the patient experienced some pain from what she felt was the therapist's fierce mothering, over the course of the therapy the patient regained a connection to her instinctual nature and discovered her own feminine power.

Recurrent dreams, especially those from early childhood, suggest problematic complexes and/or a repressed traumatic event. In trauma, the dream remains a photographic replay. Over the course of the therapy the dreams change from flashback accuracy to less realistic and more neutral imagery and finally include scenarios in which the patient exerts some control (Wilmer, 1986). Dreams that contain rage, violence, or immoral conduct provide a clearer illustration of the patient's shadow than the therapist's own observations (Kalsched, 1996). This is because the material comes from the patient, with the unconscious part of the personality commenting on another part. Dreams about the therapist, the setting, or the therapy itself bring to light transference feelings of which the patient is either unaware or fearful. They provide symbols and language for both the patient and the analyst.

Dreams can block therapy as well as advance it. This happens when patients bring in a flood of dream material and use it to fill up the therapy hour; when they prefer to remain in their dream worlds rather than confront life; or when they distance themselves from the dream by refusing to engage their emotions or feelings (Bosnak and Levertov, 1998; Whitmont & Perera, 1992). The therapist can observe this behavior for a while and then, at an appropriate moment, bring the situation to the patient's attention and explore the reasons for these defensive maneuvers.

# APPLICATIONS

## Problems

There is wide latitude in the type of patients Jungians see and the form of therapy they employ. Jungian therapists treat people of all ages and cultures, at all levels of functioning. Analytical therapy is suitable for people facing the common problems of life and accompanying symptoms of stress, anxiety, depression, and low self-esteem. It is also useful in dealing with people who have severe personality disorders or psychoses. The problems an analytical psychotherapist chooses to treat are dependent on that analyst's personality, ability, and training. Specific types of therapists seem to attract specific patients, yet each patient creates a different situation. The therapist's technique must be flexible enough to adapt to the particular patient and situation, and firm enough that the therapist works within his or her limits of expertise.

Some of the most interesting applications of analytical psychotherapy involve people with severe personality disorders; hospital and follow-up care of psychotics; and treatment of post-traumatic stress, disturbed children, the aging, the sick, and those gravely ill, dying, or preparing for death. Some Jungian therapists specialize in short-term psychodynamic psychotherapy, treating substance abusers, battered women, or the sexually abused. Some analysts integrate feminism with Jungian theory, often attracting patients who are reevaluating traditional gender roles or who are dealing with sexual trauma. Innovative work is also being done with people who have creative, religious, relationship, or sexual problems.

People who have undergone other depth analyses are increasingly undergoing a Jungian analysis because they feel their earlier analysis did not touch a dimension of their psyche. So, too, some Jungians, especially those who were more archetypally analyzed, seek some type of other therapy to fill gaps in their own self-knowledge.

Patients who adapt well to talking cures are those who have an ability for introspection and are able to regress and yet maintain a working alliance with the therapist. Analytical psychotherapists working with people who have less intact egos, such as borderline personalities, adapt their technique to focus on supportive ego building. Other patients may need to remain in any one of the first three stages of therapy—confession, elucidation, and education—so that they can learn to live more easily in the human community, have better relationships with others, and establish and maintain themselves through meaningful work.

Analytical psychotherapy is singularly beneficial for those people undergoing a midlife crisis and concerned with the problems of the second half of life. Dieckmann (1991) mentions three types of people who are drawn toward the process of individuation at midlife: those who find deep meaning within themselves and want to further explore their inner worlds; those who realize they have failed to reach the goals of their youth, or who find these goals are insufficient or no longer compelling; and finally, those who have reached their goals and are confronting problems that accompanied worldly success. Because the scope of Jung's theory is so wide and concerns final causes as well as the status quo, many who look for more profound meaning in their lives and who are concerned with people's impact on each other and on the world's survival are also drawn to analytical psychotherapy.

## Evaluation

### Evaluation of the Therapist

A Jungian analyst undergoes a rigorous training program during which he or she is evaluated in classes, in case seminars, in individual supervision, and through appearances before various committees that closely monitor the quality of candidates' patient care as well as their self-knowledge. A combination of clinical and theoretical exams and a written case study and/or thesis round out training based on the depth of the candidate's own analysis. Participation in peer supervision, in monthly meetings of individual analytic societies, regional yearly meetings, and international meetings is combined with reading or writing articles in various Jungian clinical journals. Each society of Jungian analysts has education and ethics committees that monitor and review the quality of care therapists deliver.

## Evaluation of Therapy

The most convincing and conclusive studies evaluating particular forms of psychodynamic psychotherapy conclude that therapy is more beneficial than no therapy, but that the type of therapy is less important than the quality of the person who delivers it and the match, and/or empathic bond, between patient and therapist. Thus, followers of a specific modality can make only modest claims for their theory's value, even though therapists' and patients' belief in that theory enhances positive outcomes.

The evaluation of the success of analytical psychotherapy comes from clinical observation, mainly through single case studies. In them as well as in patients' reports, the patient's quality of life usually improves slowly over the course of the therapy. Dreams can be evaluated by the evolution of the type of images and by changes in their affective content over the course of the analysis. For example, nightmares usually cease, and their terrifying images or threatening figures slowly change into more benign or friendly ones. A specific dream may indicate that the time for the termination of therapy has arrived; this could be as graphic as a dream in which the patient bids good-bye to the therapist before a positive move or journey, or as subtle as one in which the patient not only acquires a piece of beautiful fabric she once dreamed her therapist owned but is now weaving her own material as well.

Subjectively, the improving patient reports symptom relief, looks more alive, has more energy, and often can release and experience blocked or untapped channels of creativity. Relationships with other people improve markedly. The process of growth becomes independent of the therapist when patients start to do their own work between sessions, master new and enriching habits of introspection and self-examination, pay attention to their dreams and fantasies, and deal with themselves and others with integrity. An analytical psychotherapist would agree with Freud that learning to love and to work is the key to measuring the outcome of a successful analysis. Jungians would also want to see their patients develop a more complete knowledge of, a relationship with, and responsibility for all aspects of their psyche. This development often leads patients to grapple with philosophical and religious questions about the meaning of existence, including their personal responsibility to the world in which they find themselves and which they will pass on to others.

## Evaluation of Theory

Both qualitative and quantitative studies have examined Jung's theory of typology. These types, or personality dimensions, consist of the two basic attitudes of introversion and extraversion and the four functions of thinking, feeling, intuition, and sensation. We all have these qualities to different degrees, but we often prefer one mode over the others. The *Myers-Briggs* and the *Grey-Wheelwright* typology tests ascertain a person's predominant attitude and function as well as the relative amounts of each attitude and function in an individual's personality (Quenk, 1994). Both tests are questionnaires that follow Jung's original formulations, determining a person's predominance of introversion and extraversion as well as his or her relative preference for the thinking, feeling, sensing, and intuitive modes of experiencing reality. The tests give a more rounded view of character than does simply looking at a single function or attitude. The Myers-Briggs adds questions to determine whether one perceives things first (as Jung wrote of sensates and intuitives) or judges them first (as both feelers and thinkers do). It yields 16 different personality types. Many analysts find these typology tests especially beneficial when working with couples. By indicating differences in the way people of differing types tend to interpret their environment, they provide an objective explanation for many problems in communication.

Jung used statistics in his Word Association Tests to display evidence of his theory of complexes. Some analysts make use of these association tests to uncover material in patients who have difficulties in self-exploration. Projective tests such as the Rorschach test and the Thematic Apperception Test (TAT), which are based on Jung's theories of complex and projection, are also used. Contemporary studies of the validity of projective tests have been less persuasive, but the tests themselves still prove clinically useful. *The Journal of Analytical Psychology* has a research section as well as a directory of research in analytical psychology and sponsors a yearly conference.

## Treatment

Jung was open to a wide variety of modalities, settings, and styles in his treatment of patients. Today, analytical psychotherapy most often takes place at a regular time and place, for a set fee. The encounter is often face to face, with therapist and patient both seated, though many analysts use a couch from time to time or as a matter of course.

Jungian analysts also work with body movement, dramatization, art, sand trays, or an eclectic mixture of these methods. Just as the primary mode of therapy varies among analysts, so too does the timing. Most often sessions in the United States are for 50 minutes once or twice per week, though three times is not uncommon. The timing varies and often includes more frequent and shorter visits for hospitalized clients, disturbed children, and the ill or severely impaired.

The impact of managed care on the modality and length of treatment has led to some experimentation with brief therapy. It has also resulted in many more analysts practicing entirely outside the managed care system. The effect of these changes on the types of patient seen has yet to be studied.

### Group Therapy

Often as an adjunct to and amplification of individual therapy, individuals will meet in groups of approximately 6 to 10 people. Members are usually patients of the analyst who runs the group, although some analysts will accept referrals. The meetings customarily take place once a week and run for about 90 minutes. The group is usually carefully selected to create a balance of gender, typology, age, and type of problem. Some therapists run single-issue or single-gender groups, though an eclectic mixture of patients is more usual. Undergoing group therapy is often suggested or required of an analyst in training. Patients need adequate ego strength because the situation is apt to be confrontive as well as supportive. Group therapy has been found to be particularly suitable for introverts drawn to Jungian psychotherapy. It is also recommended for patients who tend to intellectualize or aestheticize their analysis or otherwise defend themselves from their feelings and for those who have been unable to translate what they have learned in private therapy into real life.

Group work focuses on therapeutic issues through discussions, dream analysis, active imagination, psychodrama, gestalt, and bioenergetic modalities. The group is most effective, however, when complexes become active and particular issues come to life through the various clashes, alliances, and confrontations between and among members of the group. Participating in group therapy allows individuals to experience themselves interacting with others, experiencing their shared humanity as they reality test, reveal themselves, and give clarifying feedback. Within the group, patients must agree to confidentiality. Whether patients socialize between meetings is up to the group and the particular therapist.

During the course of the meetings, the individual tends to project his or her own shadow (that part of the personality people cannot acknowledge in themselves) onto the group, while the group inevitably picks up on parts of the personality that the individual conceals. Resistances are often more visible in a group than in private therapy and can be dealt with more easily. The group reconstellates the family, so issues of family dynamics arise, including a re-creation of sibling rivalries or problems of an individual's position within the family. Each member of the group, therefore, is able to work on family issues in a way not possible in individual therapy. Transference issues with the analyst can be transferred to the group and worked on in this arena as well. An analyst's shadow can also be seen more clearly in the group. Patients who have felt the analyst to be too powerful in individual therapy may be able to express feelings toward the therapist in group work. Patients who have gone through group therapy remark on the difficulty of the process as well as on the depth of feeling engendered through the group's acceptance of their most vulnerable or wounded sides. They report a greater feeling of resiliency, more ease in social settings, and more acceptance of themselves after group work.

## Family and Marital Therapy

Jungian analysts often use or refer their patients to some mode of analytical family therapy. Analysts will see the couple or family sometimes as a unit and sometimes separately or will do conjoint family work. The use of Jungian terminology, especially the concepts of typology, *anima* and *animus, shadow,* and *projection,* forms a language through which the family or couple can discern and reflect on their own dynamics.

Therapists often administer a typology test to the couple or family members. Through its interpretations, family members realize that one source of their differences may be a typology problem. Dissimilarities can be accepted and worked with more easily when interpreted as a typological clash, while knowledge of each family member's various mixture of attitude and function types—introversion and extraversion, thinking, feeling, sensation, and intuition—can lead to improved family communication. Individual family members often have different typological ways of perceiving reality, and people often choose partners with a typology opposite to their own.

Analysts working with families and couples emphasize family dynamics caused by members' shadow and animus/anima projections onto other family members. Fights arise when a family member projects these, believing the other person is behaving in ways that really belong to the accuser's own shadow or anima/animus. Thus, a predominantly thinking-type man might fall prey to inferior feelings and fight his wife through moodiness while accusing her of his own sulkiness, and she, if she is predominantly a feeling type, might defend herself with theoretical arguments and blame her husband for her own judgmental stance. An argument of this sort is doomed to failure. Scapegoating of a specific individual frequently takes place when the scapegoated person is typologically different from the rest of the family or when the scapegoated person reminds a spouse or parent of a disliked parent or sibling.

## Body/Movement Therapy

Jung encouraged patients to engage in active imagination through body movement or dance. Jung found that by using his own body to mirror the gestures of his psychotic and withdrawn patients at the Burgholzli, he could better understand feelings they were trying to communicate. He found that the body stores, holds, experiences, and communicates psychological and emotional experience as much as, if not more than, words. Joan Chodorow (1995) has described movement as a type of active imagination that, in therapy, accompanies and is followed by discussion. She found that the transference as well as trauma, early or crisis experiences, grief, dreams, fantasies, feelings, and moods can be embodied and expressed in movement. As the patient moves, the therapist observes or serves as a mirror moving along with the patient.

## Art Therapy

Jung often suggested that a patient draw or paint an image from a dream or from active imagination. During his own self-analysis, Jung painted his dream and fantasy images; he perceived therapeutic value in doing this, in playing with stones like a child, and later, in sculpting in stone and carving at his retreat in Bollingen. Jung encouraged his patients to do the same in their own analysis through painting, sculpting, and other form-giving methods that provided a feeling and image through which the contents of the unconscious could find expression. He felt this was especially valuable for people who were out of touch with their feelings or who tried to deal with their experience solely through logic.

Analytical psychotherapy encourages art in therapy as a conscious way to express elements of the unconscious. Art therapy is especially useful in working through and integrating traumatic material when isolated images and feeling states tend to explode into consciousness. The expression of these images or feeling states through art releases their archetypal power and domesticates them in a way that gives the survivor a sense of control. Art therapy is useful, as well, in overcoming mental blocks or side-stepping an overly one-sided consciousness. The point of the therapy is not to produce a finished or aesthetically pleasing object but to allow an active dialogue with the unconscious.

## Sand Tray Therapy

This method was inspired by Jung's construction of stone "villages" during his self-analysis and then further developed by Dora Kalff, who combined Jung's ideas with Margaret Lowenfeld's World Technique. In Kalff's adaptation, a rectangular box measuring approximately $30 \times 20 \times 3$ inches is filled with sand and becomes a miniature world that a child or adult can shape and form, meanwhile arranging any of the hundreds of figurines the analyst provides. In therapy, the sand tray becomes a world through which complexes, pain, trauma, moods, emotions, and feelings are given expression. Use of the sand tray, like other forms of active imagination, provides a bridge to the unconscious; during the process the child or adult can also recover undeveloped elements of his or her character. Sand-play studies document the efficacy of the procedure (Bradway & McCoard, 1997). Over the course of therapy, the trays show a progressive change from a primitive and disorganized state, through images representative of vegetation, animals, the shadow and the human, toward more order, peacefulness, and integration. Symbols appearing toward the end of therapy often have a mandala form and tend to evoke a holy feeling. Sand-tray therapy with children is useful as a structured and healing form of free play that promotes the child's ego development and unblocks hidden feelings; in adults, it returns the patient to a world of childhood play where lost parts of the personality can again come alive and contribute to self-healing.

## Child Analysis

Children pick up and reflect what is going on in their surroundings. This happens to such a degree that Jung once analyzed a parent through the dreams and nightmares of his son. Training in child analysis is required at a growing number of Jungian Institutes and is based on core work by the Jungian analysts Frances Wickes, Erich Neumann, Dora Kalff, and Edith Sullwold. Treatment is based on the theory that children have within themselves what they need for a natural process of growth and self-healing to occur. The process works by providing a safe environment in which the therapist serves as witness, participant, and ally, who not only treats the child but intervenes appropriately so that the child's family and life situation can be improved. During therapy, the child slowly learns to integrate and humanize potentially overwhelming archetypal images. While children's therapy is similar to adults' analytical psychotherapy, it uses a wide variety of tactile and nonverbal modalities. A child finds expression for dreams, fantasies, and fears through sand-tray therapy, arts and crafts, clay modeling, musical instruments, and body movement as well as through stories and myths. The therapist provides boundaries and a safe space so that the child can work out problems, strengthen ego and resilience, and become more self-accepting, independent, and better functioning.

## Post-Traumatic Stress

In 1934, in a letter to a Dr. Birnie, Jung wrote of the profound biological (as well as psychological) changes that can follow the experience of an overwhelming trauma. He went on to write about repetitive dreams and the way the unconscious keeps bringing the trauma up as if to search for its healing through repetition. Modern research on post-traumatic stress disorder (PTSD) supports Jung's observations and documents similar physical and psychological changes in survivors of wars, abuse, torture, and other overwhelming situations. Werner Engel (1986) has described his work with Nazi concentration camp survivors and their long-lasting feelings of guilt. He states that the power of Jungian psychotherapy lies in the curative value of patient and therapist listening together to a patient's horrors, combined with a belief in self-healing and the application of archetypal theory.

Henry Wilmer (1986) studied 103 patients suffering from PTSD subsequent to their Vietnam service, focusing on their repetitive nightmares. He felt such photographic repetition must have a psychological and/or biological purpose. He shared the pain of one PTSD patient as expressed through his dreams and experience. Accompanying the patient in a receptive, noninterpretive way, Wilmer watched as the patient's nightmares finally began to change. The patient started to wake up, not caught in the frozen repetition of a flashback, but in tears. Healing took place when the patient mourned what had happened, found meaning in his experience, and finally saw his role in the dream shift into one in which he could actively change the outcome.

Donald Kalsched (1996) found that severe trauma during childhood can produce an internalization of the traumatizer that remains active in the now-adult psyche. He observes that the patients' self-attacking internal figures initially serve to defend the psyche but gradually change over the course of therapy until these isolating defenses are no longer needed.

## The Treatment of Psychosis

Jung as a psychiatrist treated a full range of severe mental problems. He discerned a pattern and internal logic in the psychotic utterances and fantasies of patients he treated and concluded that the personality of the patient in a psychosis is dominated by a complex split from reality and/or is overwhelmed by (and identifies with) archetypal images that belong to the collective unconscious. Jung believed that the psychotic's upheaval led to distinct psychosomatic changes as well as chemical changes in the brain. He also speculated that some bodily toxin could produce the psychosis. Today, analytical treatment of psychosis includes listening for the meaning or metaphor behind the symptom so that psychotics' mental worlds and imagery can be used in their healing. Group work, a safe living environment, and art therapy are valuable adjuncts to psychotherapy, as is medication. All help build an environment in which patients can emerge from their chaotic and mythic worlds and prepare for a more regular life. A minority of analytical therapists believe that medication blunts the regression of a psychotic person and prevents the individual from working through the psychosis. Some therapists have run types of home-based therapy, where patients and therapists interact in a homelike setting throughout the day. They report the successful treatment of a schizophrenic episode without the use of drugs and with no relapse; however, no long-range study of this form of therapy has been done.

## CASE EXAMPLE

Rochelle, a divorced white woman in her mid-30s, taught at a community college. Her self-consciousness and anxiety brought her into analysis, as did the nightmares that had plagued her since childhood. She was drawn to Jungian psychotherapy because of a life-long interest in dreams and a love of myths and fairy tales. She had been in therapy before; it had started off well but ended in disappointment, and she wondered if working with a female analyst this time would make a difference.

During the initial stages of therapy, Rochelle settled into twice-weekly sessions. The following facts emerged during the first months of treatment, often in association with dream material. She remembered little about her childhood except having had an active fantasy and dream life and having been happiest alone, outdoors, or daydreaming. Her family life had been chaotic. For several years while she was in grade school, partly because of her father's illness, Rochelle was sent by her mother to live with a series of relatives. Later she was dispatched to a girls' boarding school, where she did well. She was a good student who was active in student government. Rochelle had earned her own living since she was 18, putting herself through college with a scholarship and a series of part-time jobs.

She reported being close to neither parent but having more negative feelings toward her mother, blaming her for neglect. Rochelle had a form of negative mother complex expressed in her determination to do everything opposite from the way her mother did things. Rochelle kept clear of her mother psychically through the development of her thinking function, especially in academic work, in which she excelled. She typified Jung's further description of this type of unmothered daughter as being awkward, lacking body awareness, and suffering from a variety of uterine problems; in Rochelle's case, a hysterectomy had been suggested.

Though Rochelle most often appeared to be dryly rationalistic, there was also a charged emotional component in her personality that revealed itself in the outbursts of tears that accompanied early therapy sessions. Her therapist gave Rochelle typology tests. Rochelle was found to be markedly introverted, with thinking as her primary function followed by intuition; sensation and feeling were conspicuously low. Rochelle gained comfort from reading about these types and learning that she behaved fairly typically for a person with an undeveloped and primitive feeling function.

In the initial stages of therapy, Rochelle exhibited a strong idealizing transference and worked hard during the hour, though it felt to her therapist as if she were encased in ice. (The therapist was primarily an introverted sensation type and so tended to experience things first as inner images or sensations rather than as ideas or emotions.) However, Rochelle took great pleasure in having someone listen to the story of her life and take her dreams seriously. Her therapist kept interpretations to a minimum and directed attention as much as possible to Rochelle's daily life. Rochelle could not accept anything that seemed like criticism from her analyst, but flourished under the analyst's empathic reflection of Rochelle's feelings; gradually she started to look more relaxed and attractive as she felt herself valued and nurtured.

Rochelle had one or two women friends but had trouble relating to men. She tended to fall in love rapidly, idealize the man and often negate her own interests to meet his and to help him with his career. Overidealization and a romantic belief in living happily ever after, however, soon turned into hypercriticism and rejection, withdrawal, and flight. Some of these dynamics in her personal life started to appear in the consulting room. Though compliance and admiration marked Rochelle's conscious relationship to her therapist, she seemed to be always on guard. The therapist's countertransference was a strong bodily feeling of distance, at times as if her patient were miles away across the room or vanishing. There was something almost desperate behind the exaggeratedly "Jungian" quality and quantity of the material Rochelle brought to her therapy hour. It was as if Rochelle was trying very hard to produce what she thought her therapist would want, without noticing her therapist's efforts to focus on Rochelle's anxiety symptoms and her outer life. The therapist used the dream material sparingly, primarily as a doorway into the reality of Rochelle's experience. Rochelle concealed from herself her contempt for her analyst's continued emphasis on the here and now and her focus on Rochelle's physical and psychological condition. When this was brought to Rochelle's attention, she responded with a fierce burst of anger that brought the pain of her negative mother complex to the surface. There ensued a number of months of transference in which Rochelle attacked the analyst as the negative mother while the analyst subjectively felt the misery Rochelle had experienced under her mother's care.

Despite the negative transference, however, Rochelle kept turning up for sessions. In response to the therapist's support of Rochelle's sensation function and her need for autonomy, she sought out a second opinion concerning her hysterectomy and found that it was not indicated. Rochelle also started to pay attention to her body. About nine months after her decision not to undergo the operation, she enrolled in a dance class upon learning from an acquaintance that her analyst liked to dance.

The analyst did not interpret her behavior but held it in the back of her mind. She continued to pay a hovering, almost free-floating attention to Rochelle's behavior and words as well as to the images and sensations they brought up in her own mind. She noticed that the feeling quality in the room was growing warmer but still contained chilling voids that seemed to parallel Rochelle's own recollection of her past. The therapist felt a sense of foreboding building up with each visit as if Rochelle was accompanied by some chaotic and unspecific feeling of violence.

Rochelle attended a weekend dance/movement seminar at the local Jungian Institute; at the following session, as she started to describe a nightmare, her nose started to bleed. A look of horror came over Rochelle's face as she experienced the first of a series of flashbacks accompanied by recurrent nightmares. They concerned the sexual attacks she had endured as a child after she had been sent to live with a relative who was an elder in their church. He had coerced her into secrecy under the threat of God's wrath, and he had explained the blood on the child's bedclothes to the housekeeper as the result of a nosebleed.

Initially in therapy, Rochelle had professed herself untouched by this molestation, but now its full emotional impact flooded her. The slow recall of discrete images and memories marked a critical point in therapy. Rochelle fell into a depression and entered a needy and fearful regression during which her sessions were increased to four times a week. At this time, Rochelle made considerable use of the clay, art materials, and sand tray that her analyst kept in her office. Most of the emotional history of her trauma came first through her hands, and only later could it be put into words. It took many more months before the splits in Rochelle's feeling recall were slowly filled in and the story of her early life emerged in a linear way. Rochelle now looked to her therapist as a positive mother figure and felt entirely safe only in the therapy room and its boundaries, though she lashed out at her therapist for causing her to feel the reality of her memories and for taking away the lovely dreams into which she had escaped.

In her regression, Rochelle found weekends and holidays intolerable but got through them by borrowing a small figure from the sand tray. Her analyst felt great tenderness for her patient as she witnessed Rochelle's experience and shared her pain. She allied herself with her patient's efforts to recall secrets that had long been repressed. She let them unfold in their own order and time, without questioning or probing. Sometimes the therapist felt drained by the quantity of pain that was now flooding the room, and struggled with herself to neither block it nor silence Rochelle. For both analyst and patient, these were difficult times in the analysis, as both allowed the surfacing of the agony that Rochelle had not been able to permit herself to feel before. The therapist found herself increasingly inclined to comfort Rochelle and found herself tempted to break her own boundary rules by extending the hour or letting Rochelle stay on for a cup of tea. She considered how much of her feelings were countertransference and how much something she needed to process further in herself. The analyst knew how crucial it was for her to symbolically hold the transference in this charged arena and not act it out; she also knew that part of the force field generated by Rochelle's initial trauma came from the dangerous pull toward repetition that Rochelle and many trauma survivors experience. In order to check that she completely understood her own countertransference issues, the analyst went into supervision with a senior analyst. Through weeks of self-confrontive work, the analyst gained a deeper understanding of the powerfully destructive pull to reenactment that makes trauma survivors all too often fall victim to reinjury. Both Rochelle and her therapist succeeded in maintaining their boundaries without cutting off the current between them. [See Rutter (1997), Kalsched (1996), and Douglas (1997b) for a further discussion of this important subject from a Jungian standpoint.]

Shortly after her therapist had completed her own self-examination, Rochelle emerged from her depression and started intensive work on the transference on a different level. This was accompanied by Rochelle's reading about goddesses and images of powerful female archetypes. At this point, work on the archetypal image of incest started to accompany the personal work. Rochelle came into the session one day with an Irish myth she said both terrified and fascinated her. For a time, its analogies with her own trauma became the focus of much of Rochelle's interest, as she and the therapist began to use the myth as a common metaphor. This caused renewed work on Rochelle's childhood abuse at a deeper but also more universal level.

The myth was about a girl named Saeve, whose relative, a Druid named Dark, pursued her. Unable to escape his advances, she turned herself into a deer and vanished into the woods. Three years later a hero, Fionn, found her and led her to his castle, where she turned back into a beautiful young woman. They lived completely enraptured with each other until Fionn had to leave for battle. Soon after Fionn's departure, Saeve thought she saw him returning; she raced out of the castle to meet him but realized too late that it was the Druid disguised as Fionn. He tapped her with his hazel rod and turned her back into a deer, and they vanished.

Rochelle used this fairy tale to picture her own neurotic patterns of behavior. Through the story, she could start to view them objectively, without shame. The myth gave form and an image to the damage she had experienced from too potent and too early experience of an invasive other. Rochelle gained a feeling for her own horrors through her feelings for Saeve; she also began to understand her defense of splitting off from reality (becoming a deer) when scared and vanishing into daydreams. The story also helped

Rochelle comprehend why she seemed incapable of maintaining a relationship, turning every lover from a Fionn into a Druid. Eventually she even recognized that she had internalized the church elder into an inner negative animus who kept judgmentally assaulting her.

As Rochelle's therapy progressed, she stopped turning against the childlike parts of herself that needed to idealize someone as all-good, and she started to forgive herself for what had happened to her. She also started to understand the protective value of splitting off from an intolerable reality and assuming a deer-like disguise. As she did this, that particular defense started to drop away. Rochelle also grew to understand her desire for a savior: What she had experienced was so vile (the touch of the Druid) that what she longed for became impossibly pure (Fionn). She also better understood her self-consciousness and fear of people as well as her feelings of loneliness; she felt she had lived much of her life alone as a deer in the woods hiding in disguise, flight, and illusion instead of being able to maintain relationships.

Her therapist's accompanying Rochelle on this voyage of discovery allowed her the time to look at the world by means of the separation and division of opposites: the blackest of villains versus the noblest of heroes. Rochelle realized that she was repeatedly searching for Fionn, the hero, protector, and savior, whom she inevitably scanned for the slightest defect, and, just as inevitably, looked upon him, when he showed a failing or two, as an all-evil Druid. She then escaped in deer disguise and in a split-off little-girl vulnerability, yet behind her meltingly doe-like softness lay a self-destructive, self-hating, abusive, rapist animus tearing at her sad child's soul. On the other side, her inner hero tended to become icily rational or heady; he drove Rochelle into unmercifully heroic activity and disdained the dark, sensual, unmaidenly feminine inside her. The Druid animus brutalized her inner child-maiden and the deer, while the virtuous animus punished her for the very brutalization she experienced.

At this point Rochelle became kinder to herself. She stopped ricocheting from one opposite to the other and stopped mistaking the dark for the light or turning someone she had thought good into bad as soon as he made a mistake. Her impaired relations with others started to heal as she allowed her therapist to be neither all-light nor all-dark but intermingled. Through confronting and fighting with her analyst, Rochelle started to regain some of her own darkly potent female energy. Now she also started to be able to claim her own needs in a relationship rather than disguise herself as an all-giving woman.

Assimilation of her shadow, not identification with it, grounded Rochelle. Her nightmares lessened in intensity after a watchful and self-contained black cat, whom Rochelle associated with her therapist, started to appear in her dreams sitting on a round rug and silently witnessing the dream's turmoil. Rochelle felt that the female cat figure symbolized something old and complex, as if it held attributes of both a Wise Woman and a Terrible Mother in its centered witnessing. From this center and with the continued empathic witnessing support of her therapist, Rochelle's inner and outer lives gradually changed as she mulled over her life history and her powerfully archetypal myth and dream material. It was not enough for her to experience something of this intensity in the consulting room; she needed to see what the images meant in her own life. As Rochelle slowly reclaimed and integrated the cat as well as the animus figures and finally the good-enough mother analyst in herself, the black cat figure in her dreams assumed a human form. Rochelle decided to leave an analysis that had taken three and a half years; there followed a newly creative turn in her work, and she also risked loving a quiet and fallible man. Over the next few years, Rochelle returned to her therapy for brief periods in times of crisis or as her complexes reappeared, but she generally could rely on her inner therapist for recentering herself.

# SUMMARY

Jung pioneered an approach to the psyche that attracts a growing number of people through its breadth of vision and its deep respect for the individual. Rather than pathologizing, Jung looked for the meaning behind symptoms, believing that symptoms held the key to their own cure. Jung discovered methods and techniques for tapping into the self-healing potential in human beings and taught a process that engages therapist and patient alike in a profound and growth-promoting experience. Jung's purpose was to assist psychological development and healing by involving all aspects of the personality.

Analytical personality theory provides a map of the psyche that values the unconscious as much as consciousness, seeing each as complementing the other. In the personal realm, the personal conscious (the ego or I) and persona (the social mask) are matched with the personal unconscious. The personal unconscious contains things repressed, forgotten, or at the verge of consciousness as well as the personal shadow (what the ego does not accept in itself), and the animus and anima (ego-alien contrasexual elements). The impersonal or collective unconscious can never be known, but can be pictured as a vast deposit that flows into the personal unconscious and consciousness by means of archetypal images: propensities, motifs, and forms common to all humanity. The interface between the collective and personal unconscious may represent the most archaic and least mapped layer of the psyche.

Complexes grow in this interface. Complexes are energy-filled constellations of psychic elements that have an archetypal core and erupt into consciousness, often in an autonomous way. They are both personal and impersonal. The personal unconscious is created by the individual and ultimately is his or her personal responsibility. Since the collective unconscious is innate and impersonal, it would be an error for the individual to claim its powers or in any way identify with its contents. The unconscious itself is completely neutral and only becomes dangerous to the degree that the ego has a wrong relationship to it or represses it. The impersonal realm is home also to the collective consciousness, the giant matrix of the outer world in which an individual lives his or her life.

The archetype of the Self encompasses the personal unconscious and conscious and a bit of the other realms as they impinge on or seep into the personal. A newborn infant is immersed in the self; it soon splits (or deintegrates) into fragments of ego, consciousness, and unconscious. The task of psychotherapy is to consolidate the ego and let the psyche heal and responsibly enlarge itself so that all the parts of the self can develop, reintegrate, and maintain a more balanced and less egocentric relationship with each other. In analytical psychotherapy it is not enough to understand these concepts and their activity; they must be felt experientially by the individual in relation to the past and as they come into play in the therapy room through transference and countertransference. The new understanding then needs to be lived so that the individual can participate in life with integrity. To this end, experiential methods of analytical psychotherapy are especially valuable, as is the therapist's inclusion of the feminine dimension of receptive empathy, groundedness, nurturing, and ability to hold the personality as it develops. This generative approach allows growth and healing to take place alongside what can be gained from insight and interpretation.

Analytical psychotherapy stresses the patient-therapist encounter as one that involves empathy, trust, openness, and risk. Through the interaction of the two personalities and the quality of this relationship, the self-regulating and healing potential of the personality can come into play, repairing old wounds while allowing the individual to grow in self-knowledge. This is why analytical psychotherapy stresses the quality, training, analysis, and continuing self-analysis of therapists.

Depth psychotherapy, as it is understood today, is less than a century old. Jung often wrote of psychology being in its infancy, and he believed no one map of its realm could be complete. Depth-oriented psychotherapeutic systems of all types contain more similarities than differences. The systems reflect the language and style of their creator and attract those of like mind. It is as if the founders of the varied schools have each drawn slightly different maps of the same terrain—the human psyche. Though the particular style of these maps varies, those that are still useful have more and more in common as original rivalries are forgotten and each is freer to borrow what it needs from the others. At the same time, a specifically Jungian map may be best for one person, while someone else may need an Adlerian, a Rogerian, a neo-Freudian, or some other map.

Jungian psychology is especially inclusive, as its four stages of therapy cover essential elements of the others' theories while adding a particular emphasis on wholeness, completion, and individuation. Analytical psychotherapy allows room for the depths of the collective unconscious and the width of humanity's collective history, art, and culture while grounding itself solidly in the particular individual at a particular time and moment. It is a rich and diverse system that rests on a theory whose practice undergoes constant transformation as the experience and needs of the individual and society both change.

# ANNOTATED BIBLIOGRAPHY

## Primary Sources

Jung, C. G. (1954–1991). *The collected works of C. G. Jung.* (22 Volumes). Princeton, NJ: Princeton University Press.
See especially the following:

Jung, C. G. (1957). *The practice of psychotherapy. Collected works,* Vol. 16.
This collection of Jung's essays and lectures includes both basic and in-depth discussions of Jung's methods and techniques of psychotherapy. Part One concerns general problems in psychotherapy and clearly differentiates Jung's theory and practice from those of Freud and Adler. Part Two examines specific topics such as abreaction, Jungian dream analysis, and transference. Most of the book is highly suitable for general study; however, the article on the transference is steeped in Jung's alchemical studies and is somewhat arcane.

Jung, C. G. (1935/1956). *Two essays on analytical psychology. Collected works,* Vol. 17.
A clear, succinct portrayal of the basic concepts of analytical psychology, this book also gives a good account of the early history of depth psychology. Part One sets out Jung's ideas on the psychology of the unconscious, clearly differentiating the personal from the impersonal unconscious. Part Two deals with the ego and its relationship to the personal and collective unconscious and to the task of integration and individuation.

## Secondary Sources

Kalsched, D. (1998). Archetypal affect, anxiety and defense in patients who have suffered early trauma. In A. Casement (Ed.), *Post-Jungians today: Key papers in contemporary analytical psychology* (pp. 83–102). NY: Routledge.
Kalsched discusses the ways in which the psyche internalizes trauma and demonstrates the self's role in defending the psyche. He describes the way a self-care system often keeps the trauma victim at the mercy of sadistic, self-attacking internal figures and dreams. Kalsched considers dreams and dream images about these terrifying "dark forces" as well as a dream that demonstrated a core positive side to a patient's psyche and an opening toward healing. After a historical overview of depth psychologists' work on primitive anxiety and defense, he ends with a discussion of the transformation possible in therapy.

Mathers, D. (2001). *An introduction to meaning and purpose in analytical psychology.* Philadelphia: Taylor and Francis.
In a wide-ranging discussion of the importance of social purpose and personal meaning in psychotherapy, this book includes many helpful clinical examples. Mathers's work is grounded in analytical psychology which he presents as a practical and useful set of tools to help the client and promote individuation. He integrates into his analytical therapy insights from cognitive psychology, linguistics, systems theory, developmental theory, ecology politics, and religion that unite the search for individual meaning with social purpose.

Rosen, D. (2002). *Transforming depression: Healing the soul through creativity.* York Beach, ME: Nicholas-Hays.

A practical book on treating depression and suicide that offers a creative way for therapists to help their clients away from self-destruction and hopelessness and toward a more meaningful life. The book is a good overview of crisis points and suicidality as well as of current diagnosis and treatment from biological, sociological, psychological, and spiritual perspectives. Core sections of the book present and teach Jungian active imagination as a strongly effective therapeutic approach and clinical tool. Rosen finds it especially powerful in getting to the depths beneath depression's hopelessness and replacing this with a renewal of hope and meaning. Part Three of the book is particularly useful to the clinician as it follows in detail the treatment of four patients, and shows Rosen's theory put to practice.

Samuels, A. (2001). *Politics on the couch: Citizenship and the internal life.* New York: Kamac Books.

An activist book by a Jungian analyst and political consultant. Samuels' overarching theme is a vision of change and transformation rooted in psychotherapy and working from the ground up. He finds the roots of social change come from personal therapeutic work and an understanding of where personal gender, sexual, and "internal family" stereotypes may need transforming. His discussion of the "good enough" father and political leader (of whatever sex) contains an interesting analysis of the way a therapeutic term can become alive in a larger context. The "good enough" leader [and therapist] steers a middle course that avoids idealization and dependence and leads to personal responsibility. In the same way Jungian-based psychotherapy can help bring about a transformation that avoids both inflation and despair. Samuels advocates a pluralism that attempts to resolve differences by inclusion rather than exclusion, so that unity and diversity can be in balance. He discusses this from an individual therapeutic perspective as well as from a more global one.

Sedgwick, D. (2001). *Introduction to Jungian psychotherapy: The therapeutic relationship.* Philadelphia: Taylor and Francis.

This is a detailed account of analytical psychotherapy that focuses on the unique relationship between patient and therapist. Sedgwick's well-argued thesis is that this relationship constitutes the main healing factor in psychotherapy. He demonstrates this belief using both traditional Jungian theory and such post-Freudians as Bion, Klein, Kohut, and Winnicott. A clear, concise, and grounded basic teaching text on clinical issues, it is especially thorough on transference and countertransference in therapy and ways to set up and maintain the practical components of a good therapeutic relationship. Clinical examples are particularly well chosen.

Sullivan, B. S. (1989). *Psychotherapy grounded in the feminine principle.* Wilmette, IL: Chiron.

This pioneering book synthesizes all aspects of analytical theory while demonstrating the key role that a nurturing, receptive, accommodating stance plays in the therapeutic relationship. Sullivan examines the bias against these more feminine modes in both theory and process; she not only argues for the integration of the feminine dimension, but also sees it as a particularly healing aspect of therapy.

Withers, R. (2003). *Controversies in analytical psychology.* New York: Brunner-Routledge.

Eleven mostly clinical differences of approach in current analytical practice are discussed by 24 Jungian analysts or psychotherapists. The book is aimed at those who welcome diversity and an open acceptance of the variety of styles and influences on current analytical psychotherapy. Some of the issues debated are the prospects for a Jung/Klein synthesis; the status of developmental theory; working with the transference; the role of interpretation; frequency of sessions and keeping the analytic frame; integrating the body/mind split; and political, religious, and gender issues, as well as a rare discussion of the heterosexual framing of most theory and how this might affect homosexual analysts and patients.

Young-Eisendrath, P., and Dawson, T. (Eds.). (1997). *The Cambridge companion to Jung.* Cambridge, UK, and New York: Cambridge University Press.

A critical introduction to Jung's theory and work and their importance to current psychotherapy. The book is divided into three parts. Part One contains four chapters on Jung's ideas and their context. Part Two covers Jungian psychology in practice, with chapters on archetypal, developmental, and classical approaches to psychotherapy and a case study discussed from these three vantage points. Part Three focuses on analytical psychology in contemporary society, literature, gender studies, politics, and religion. each with an emphasis on a different style of Jungian therapy.

# CASE READINGS

Abramovich, H. (2002). Temenos regained: Reflections on the absence of the analyst. *Journal of Analytical Psychology, 47*(4), 583–598.

Two cases are used to illustrate boundary and containment issues. The first and lengthier discussion is of a woman who needed to preserve the analytic container while her therapist was away for several months. The case is explored in much detail, and a novel and healing way to provide a holding space is found. Abramovich's discussion of maternal reverie and maternal holding in therapy is of key interest. In the second case, the patient has a chance extra-analytical encounter with his therapist, who exits quickly. The patient perceives Abramovich's sacrifice of his self-interest as an effort to preserve the patient's space; he contrasts it with the way someone in his household took advantage of him over many years. For the first time, the patient could experience a safe place both within and outside of the therapy.

Beebe, J., McNeely, D., and Gordon, G. (1997). The case of Joan: Classical archetypal, and developmental approaches. In Young-Eisendrath and Dawson (Eds.), *Cambridge companion to Jung* (pp. 185–219). Cambridge, UK: Cambridge University Press.

Three analysts focus on the study of a 40-year-old woman suffering from an eating disorder, each with an emphasis on a different style of Jungian therapy.

Hinton, L. (2001). Dreams and the horizon of the unknown. *Journal of Jungian Theory and Practice, Spring, 3,* 25–38.

Hinton describes the gradual and difficult work of the first 16 months of therapy with a critical, depressed, and emotionally rigid 36-year-old man who was the only child of emotionally absent parents, the man's growing sense of pain, and his apperception of "a large black hole" inside him. A series of dreams, well discussed with the patient and in this paper, broke through the aloofness and lifted the depression. This came about by the force of the primitive imagery in the dreams and the therapist's ability to contain their anxiety, fear, anger, and terror. The transference provided a space where the patient felt that healing and transformation was possible.

Jung, C. G. (1968). An analysis of a patient's dream. *Analytical psychology: Its theory and practice.* New York: Pantheon.

This analysis of a patient's dream is taken from one of Jung's speeches. It demonstrates the ways in which dreams can be used to support clinical inferences.

Kalsched, D. (1996). The inner world of trauma in a diabolical form, and further clinical illustrations of the self-care system. In *The inner world of trauma: Archetypal defenses of the personal spirit,* Chapters One and Two (pp. 11–67). London and New York: Routledge.

Important case reading on trauma and post-traumatic stress, the two chapters comprise a series of nine cases, discussed and interpreted, in which early childhood trauma has produced similar defenses, repetition compulsions, and self-care systems that further isolate and attack each of the patients. Healing is shown as occurring in a similar manner across all cases.

Sullivan, B. S. (1989). Christina. In *Psychotherapy grounded in the feminine principle* (pp. 164–172). Wilmette, IL: Chiron. [Reprinted in D. Wedding & R. J. Corsini (Eds.). (2005). *Case studies in psychotherapy.* Belmont, CA: Wadsworth.]

This case deals with the therapy of a woman plagued with guilt over her decision to leave her husband and children to pursue her own psychological growth. The case is especially useful in highlighting issues of transference and countertransference.

# REFERENCES

Adams, M. V. (1996). *The multicultural imagination.* New York: Routledge.

Alschuler, L. R. (1997). Jung and politics. In P. Young-Eisendrath and T. Dawson (Eds.), *The Cambridge companion to Jung* (pp. 281–295). Cambridge, UK: Cambridge University Press.

Beebe, J. (1992). *Integrity in depth.* College Station, TX: Texas A & M Press.

Bosnak, R., & Levertov, D. (1998). *A little course in dreams.* New York: Shambhala Press.

Bradway, K., & McCoard, B. (1997). *Sandplay—Silent workshop of the psyche.* New York: Routledge.

Chodorow, J. (1995). Dance/movement and body experience in analysis. In Murray Stein (Ed.), *Jungian analysis* (pp. 391–404). La Salle, IL: Open Court.

Chodorow, J. (Ed.) (1997). *Jung on active imagination.* Princeton: Princeton University Press.

Cwik, A. J. (1995). Active imagination: Synthesis in analysis. In M. Stein (Ed.), *Jungian analysis* (pp. 137–169). LaSalle, IL: Open Court.

Dieckmann, H. (1991). *Methods in analytical psychology.* Wilmette, IL: Chiron.

Douglas, C. (1997a). The historical context of analytical psychology. In P. Young-Eisendrath and T. Dawson (Eds.), *The Cambridge companion to Jung* (pp. 17–36). Cambridge, UK: Cambridge University Press.

Douglas, C. (1997b). After such violence: A reconceptualization of Jung's incest theory. In Mattoon, M. A. (Ed.), *Zurich 95: Open questions in analytical psychology.* Einsiedeln, Switzerland: Daimon Verlag.

Douglas, C. (1997c). Introduction. In C. G. Jung, *The visions seminar* (pp. ix–xxxiii). Princeton: Princeton University Press.

Ellenberger, H. (1981). *The discovery of the unconscious.* New York: Basic Books.

Engel, W. H. (1986). Postscript. *Quadrant, 19*(1), 62.

Fordham, M. (1996). *Analyst-patient interaction: Collected papers on technique.* New York: Routledge.

Jung, C. G. (1904–1907/1973). Studies in word association. In *Experimental researches. Collected works,* Vol. 2 (pp. 3–482). Princeton: Princeton University Press.

Jung, C. G. (1907/1960). Psychology of dementia praecox. In *The psychogenesis of mental disease. Collected works,* Vol. 3 (pp. 1–151). Princeton: Princeton University Press.

Jung, C. G. (1911/1956). *The psychology of the unconscious.* Revised as *Symbols of transformation. Collected works,* Vol. 5. Princeton: Princeton University Press.

Jung, C. G. (1921/1971). *Psychological types. Collected works,* Vol. 6. Princeton: Princeton University Press.

Jung, C. G. (1927/1970). Woman in Europe. In *Civilization in transition. Collected works,* Vol. 10 (pp. 113–133). Princeton: Princeton University Press.

Jung, C. G. (1929/1933/1961). Freud and Jung: Contrasts. In *Freud and psychoanalysis. Collected works,* Vol. 4 (pp. 333–340). Princeton: Princeton University Press.

Jung, C. G. (1933/1966). Problems of modern psychotherapy. In *The practice of psychotherapy. Collected works,* Vol. 16. (pp. 53–75). Princeton: Princeton University Press.

Jung, C. G. (1934a/1970). *The development of personality. Collected works,* Vol. 17. Princeton: Princeton University Press.

Jung, C. G. (1934b/1966). The state of psychotherapy today. In *The practice of psychotherapy. Collected works,* Vol. 16 (pp. 157–173). Princeton: Princeton University Press.

Jung, C. G. (1934c/1966). The practical use of dream analysis. In *The practice of psychotherapy. Collected works,* Vol. 16 (pp. 139–161). Princeton: Princeton University Press.

Jung, C. G. (1935a/1966). Principles of practical psychotherapy. In *The practice of psychotherapy. Collected works,* Vol. 16 (pp. 3–20). Princeton: Princeton University Press.

Jung, C. G. (1935b/1966). The relations between the ego and the unconscious. In *Two essays on analytical psychology. Collected works,* Vol. 7 (pp. 132–134). Princeton: Princeton University Press.

Jung, C. G. (1935c/1980). The Tavistock lectures. In *Symbolic life: Miscellaneous writings. Collected works,* Vol. 18 (pp. 1–182). Princeton: Princeton University Press.

Jung, C. G. (1948/1980). Techniques of attitude change conducive to world peace. In *The symbolic life. Collected works,* Vol. 18 (pp. 606–613). Princeton: Princeton University Press.

Jung, C. G. (1957). *The practice of psychotherapy. Collected works,* Vol. 16. Princeton: Princeton University Press.

Jung, C. G. (1965). *Memories, dreams, reflections.* New York: Vintage.

Jung, C. G. (1976). *Mysterium Coniunctionis. Collected works,* Vol. 14. Princeton: Princeton University Press.

Kalsched, D. (1996). *The inner world of trauma: Archetypal defenses of the personal spirit.* New York: Routledge.

Maduro, R., & Wheelwright, J. B. (1977). Analytical psychology. In R. Corsini (Ed.), *Current personality theories* (pp. 83–124). Itasca, IL: F. E. Peacock.

Quenk, N. L. (1994). *Beside ourselves.* Palo Alto: CPP Books.

Rosen, D. (2002). *Transforming depression: Healing the soul through creativity.* York Beach, ME: Nicholas-Hays.

Rutter, P. (1997). *Sex in the forbidden zone: When men in power—therapists, doctors, clergy, teachers, and others—betray women's trust.* New York: Ballantine Books.

Samuels, A. (1985). Can the post-Jungians survive? *Psychological Perspectives, 31,* 55–59.

Samuels, A. (2001). *Politics on the couch: Citizenship and the internal life.* New York: Kamac Books.

Siegelman, E. Y. (1990). *Metaphor and meaning in psychotherapy.* New York: Guilford Press.

Stephens, B. D. (1999). The return of the prodigal: The emergence of Jungian themes in post-Freudian thought. *Journal of Analytical Psychology, 44*(2), 197–220.

Sullivan, B. S. (1989). *Psychotherapy grounded in the feminine principle.* Wilmette, IL: Chiron.

Whitmont, E. C. (1997). *Return of the goddess.* New York: Continuum.

Whitmont, E. C., & Perera, S. (1992). *Dreams, a portal to the source.* New York: Routledge.

Wilmer, H. A. (1986). The healing nightmare: A study of the war dreams of Vietnam combat veterans. *Quadrant, 19*(1), 47–61.

Wilmer, H. A. (1994). *Understandable Jung: The personal side of Jungian Psychology.* LaSalle, IL: Chiron.

Withers, R. (2003). *Controversies in analytical psychology.* New York: Brunner-Routledge.

Wyman-McGinty, W. (1999). The body in analysis. *Journal of Analytical Psychology, 43*(2), 239–260.

Carl R. Rogers, 1902–1987

© Bettmann /CORBIS

# 5 PERSON-CENTERED THERAPY

*Nathaniel J. Raskin and Carl R. Rogers*

## OVERVIEW

*Person-centered therapy* is based upon a phenomenological view of human life and helping relationships. Its essentials were formulated by psychologist Carl R. Rogers in 1940. A clearly stated theory, accompanied by the introduction of verbatim transcriptions of psychotherapy, stimulated a vast amount of research on a revolutionary hypothesis: that a self-directed growth process would follow the provision and reception of a particular kind of relationship characterized by genuineness, nonjudgmental caring, and empathy. This hypothesis has been tested over decades in situations involving teachers and students, administrators and staff, and facilitators and participants in cross-cultural groups, as well as psychotherapists and clients.

### Basic Concepts

Perhaps the most fundamental and pervasive concept in client-centered therapy is trust. The foundation of Rogers's approach is an *actualizing tendency* present in every living organism—in human beings, this tendency is most clearly reflected in movement toward the realization of an individual's full potential. Rogers (1980) described this actualizing force as part of a *formative tendency,* observable in the movement toward greater order, complexity, and interrelatedness that can be observed in stars, crystals, and microorganisms, as well as in human beings. Trust in the client's innate capacity for growth and development finds expression in the client-centered therapist's attitude of respect for the unique experience of every individual client and the client-centered therapist's intention to responsively follow the client's lead and to do nothing that might disempower the self-directing client. This valuing of the client's inalienable right to self-determination permeates the person-centered approach to therapy and has been described as "the nondirective attitude" (Raskin, 1947, 1948; Rogers, 1951).

On a practical level, the person-centered approach is built on trust that individuals and groups can set their own goals and monitor their progress toward these goals. This has special meaning in relation to children, students, and workers, who are often viewed as requiring detailed and constant guidance and supervision. In the context of psychotherapy, a client-centered approach assumes that clients can be trusted to select their own therapists, to choose the frequency and length of their therapy, to talk or to be silent, to decide what needs to be explored, to achieve their own insights, and to be the architects of their own lives. Groups are believed to be capable of developing the processes that are right for them, and of resolving conflicts within the group.

One particular person-centered application of trust involves the therapist or facilitator. In the early days of the movement, the focus was entirely on the client. The therapist provided continuous and consistent empathy for the client's perceptions, meanings, and feelings. With experience came growing recognition that it was important for the therapist to be appreciated as a person in the relationship and to be regarded with trust, as is the client.

Eugene Streich formulated one of the earliest statements of this trust:

> When the therapist's capacity for awareness is thus functioning freely and fully without limitations imposed by theoretical formulations of his role, we find that we have, not an individual who may do harm, not a person who must follow certain procedures, but a person able to achieve, through the remarkable integrative capacity of his central nervous system, a balanced, therapeutic, self-growing, other-growth facilitating behavior as a result of all these elements of awareness. To put it another way, when the therapist is less than fully himself—when he denies to awareness various aspects of his experience—then indeed we have all too often to be concerned about his effectiveness, as our failure cases would testify. But when he is most fully himself, when he is his most complete organism, when awareness of experience is most fully operating, then he is to be trusted, then his behavior is constructive. (1951, pp. 8–9)

Congruence

Over time there has been a growing recognition of the role of the relationship between therapist and client as a major component of constructive therapeutic change. The client-centered therapist's intention to provide the core therapeutic attitudes of *congruence, unconditional positive regard,* and *empathy* is infused with the nondirective attitude; in practice, all of these attitudes meld into the therapist's way of being in relationship with the client.

Congruence, unconditional positive regard, and empathy are the core concepts of person-centered therapy. While distinguishable, these three concepts are intimately related (Rogers, 1957). Congruence refers to the correspondence between the thoughts and the behavior of the therapist; thus, genuineness describes this characteristic. The therapist does not put up a professional front or personal facade.

The therapist also possesses unconditional positive regard for the client. This means the therapist accepts the client's moment-to-moment thoughts, feelings, wishes, intentions, and descriptions of him- or herself and others as unique, human, and appropriate to the present experience (i.e., the relationship with the therapist). The client may be reserved or talkative, address any issue of choice, and come to whatever insights and resolutions are personally meaningful. The therapist's regard for the client will not be affected by these particular choices, characteristics, or outcomes.

The therapist expresses this quality of genuine regard through empathy. Being empathic reflects an attitude of profound interest in the client's world of meanings and feelings. The therapist receives these communications and conveys appreciation and understanding. The notion that this involves nothing more than a repetition of the client's last words is erroneous. Instead, an interaction occurs in which one person is a warm, sensitive, respectful companion in the typically difficult exploration of another's emotional world. The therapist's manner of responding should be individual, natural, and unaffected. When empathy is at its best, the two individuals are participating in a process comparable to that of a couple dancing, with the client leading and the therapist following. This dance can take many forms. But always the counselor, as much as possible, assumes the client's internal frame of reference, perceiving the world and the client the way the client does and communicating this empathic understanding with the implicit attitude, "Did I understand you correctly?" (Raskin, 2001)

Basic concepts on the client side of the process include *self-concept, locus-of-evaluation,* and *experiencing.* In focusing on what is important to the person seeking help, client-centered therapists soon discovered that the person's perceptions and feelings about self were of central concern (Raimy, 1948).

A major component of self-concept is self-regard. Clients typically lacked self-esteem. Some of the earliest psychotherapy research projects showed that when clients were rated as successful in therapy, their attitudes toward self became significantly more positive (Sheerer, 1949).

Successful clients were also found to progress along a related dimension, *locus-of-evaluation.* At the same time that they gained self-esteem, they tended to shift the basis for their standards and values from other people to themselves. People commonly began therapy overly concerned with what others thought of them—their locus-of-evaluation was external. With success in therapy, their attitudes toward others, as toward themselves, became more positive, and they were less dependent on others for their values and standards (Raskin, 1952).

A third central concept in person-centered therapy is *experiencing,* a dimension along which successful clients improved (Rogers, Gendlin, Kiesler, & Truax, 1967), shifting from a rigid mode of experiencing self and world to an attitude of openness and flexibility.

The three therapist qualities and the three client constructs described in this section have been carefully defined, measured, and studied in scores of research projects relating therapist practice to the outcome of psychotherapy. There is considerable evidence that when clients receive congruence, unconditional positive regard, and empathy, their self-concepts become more positive and realistic, they become more self-expressive and self-directed, they become more open and free in their experiencing, their behavior is rated as more mature, and they deal better with stress (Rogers, 1986a).

## Other Systems

Person-centered therapy evolved predominantly out of Rogers's own experience. There are both important differences and conceptual similarities between the person-centered approach and other personality theories.

*Self-actualization,* a concept central to person-centered theory, was advanced most forcefully by Kurt Goldstein. His holistic theory of personality emphasizes that individuals must be understood as totalities and that they strive to actualize themselves (Goldstein, 1934/1959). Goldstein's work and ideas preceded those of Abraham Maslow, a founder of humanistic psychology, who was opposed to the Freudian and behavioral interpretations of human nature.

Heinz Ansbacher, a leading proponent of Adlerian theory, joined Maslow (1968) and Floyd Matson (1969) in recognizing a host of theories and therapists "united by six basic premises of humanistic psychology":

1. People's creative power is a crucial force, in addition to heredity and environment.
2. An anthropomorphic model of humankind is superior to a mechanomorphic model.
3. Purpose, rather than cause, is the decisive dynamic.
4. The holistic approach is more adequate than an elementaristic one.
5. It is necessary to take humans' subjectivity, their opinions and viewpoints, and their conscious and unconscious fully into account.
6. Psychotherapy is essentially based on a good human relationship (Ansbacher, 1977, p. 51).

Among those subscribing to such beliefs were Alfred Adler, William Stern, Gordon Allport, the gestalt psychologists (Max Wertheimer, Wolfgang Kohler, and Kurt Koffka), the neo-Freudians (Franz Alexander, Erich Fromm, Karen Horney, and Harry Stack Sullivan), post-Freudians (such as Judd Marmor and Thomas Szasz), phenomenological and existential psychologists (such as Rollo May), the cognitive theorist George A. Kelly, and of course, Carl Rogers (Ansbacher, 1977).

While some fundamental person-centered concepts and values are consonant with the proponents of other systems, Rogers and Sanford (1985) have listed a number of distinctive characteristics of client-centered therapy:

1. The hypothesis that certain attitudes in therapists constitute the necessary and sufficient conditions of therapeutic effectiveness
2. The concept of therapists being immediately present and accessible to clients, relying on moment-to-moment experiencing in each relationship
3. The intensive and continuing focus on the phenomenological world of the client (hence the term "client-centered")
4. A developing theory that the therapeutic process is marked by a change in the client's manner and immediacy of experiencing, with increasing ability to live more fully in the moment
5. A concern with the process of personality change, rather than with the structure of personality
6. Emphasis on the need for continuing research to learn more about psychotherapy
7. The hypothesis that the same principles of psychotherapy apply to all persons, whether they are categorized as psychotic, neurotic, or normal
8. A view of psychotherapy as one specialized example of all constructive interpersonal relationships
9. A determination to build all theoretical formulations out of the soil of experience, rather than twisting experience to fit a preformed theory
10. A concern with the philosophical issues that derive from the practice of psychotherapy

Meador and Rogers (1984) distinguished person-centered therapy from psychoanalysis and from behavior modification in these terms:

In psychoanalysis the analyst aims to interpret connections between the past and the present for the patient. In person-centered therapy, the therapist facilitates the client's discoveries of the meanings of his or her own current inner experiencing. The psychoanalyst takes the role of a teacher in interpreting insights to the patient and encouraging the development of a transference relationship, a relationship based on the neurosis of the patient. The person-centered therapist presents him- or herself as honestly and transparently as possible and attempts to establish a relationship in which he or she is authentically caring and listening.

In person-centered therapy, transference relationships may begin, but they do not become full-blown. Rogers has postulated that transference relationships develop in an evaluative atmosphere in which the client feels the therapist knows more about the client than the client knows about him- or herself, and therefore the client becomes dependent. Person-centered therapists tend to avoid evaluation. They do not interpret for clients, do not question in a probing manner, and do not reassure or criticize clients. Person-centered therapists have not found the transference relationship, central to psychoanalysis, a necessary part of a client's growth or change.

In behavior therapy, *behavior change* comes about through external control of associations to stimuli and the consequences of various responses. In practice, if not in theory, behavior therapy *does* pay attention to the therapy relationship; however, its major emphasis is on specific changes in specific behaviors. In contrast, person-centered therapists believe behavior change evolves from within the individual. Behavior therapy's goal is symptom removal. It is not particularly concerned with the relationship of inner experiencing to the symptom under consideration, or with the relationship between the therapist and the client, or with the climate of their relationship. It seeks to eliminate the symptom as efficiently as possible using the principles of learning theory. Obviously, this point of view is quite contrary to person-centered therapy, which maintains that fully functioning people rely on inner experiencing to direct their behavior. (p. 146)

Raskin (1974), in a comparison of Rogers's practice with those of leaders of five other orientations, found that client-centered therapy was distinctive in providing empathy and unconditional positive regard. Psychoanalytically oriented and eclectic psychotherapists agreed with client-centered theory on the desirability of empathy, warmth, and unconditional positive regard, but examples of rational-emotive, psychoanalytically oriented, and Jungian interviews were ranked low on these qualities.

This study provided a direct comparison of audiotaped samples of therapy done by Rogers and by Albert Ellis, the founder of rational emotive behavior therapy (REBT). Among 12 therapist variables rated by 83 therapist-judges, the only one on which Rogers and Ellis were alike was Self-Confident. The therapy sample by Rogers received high ratings on the following dimensions: Empathy, Unconditional Positive Regard, Congruence, and Ability to Inspire Confidence. The interview by Ellis was rated high on the Cognitive and Therapist-Directed dimensions. Rogers was rated low on Therapist-Directed, while Ellis received a low rating on Unconditional Positive Regard.

This research lends support to the following differences between person-centered therapy and rational emotive therapy.

1. Unlike REBT, the person-centered approach greatly values the therapeutic relationship.

2. Rational-emotive therapists provide much direction, while the person-centered approach encourages the client to determine direction.

3. Rational-emotive therapists work hard to point out deficiencies in their clients' thought processes; person-centered therapists accept and respect their clients' ways of thinking and perceiving.

4. Person-centered therapy characteristically leads to actions chosen by the client; rational-emotive methods include "homework" assignments by the therapist.

5. The person-centered therapist will relate to the client on a feeling level and in a respectful and accepting way; the rational-emotive therapist will be inclined to interrupt this affective process to point out the irrational harm that the client may be doing to self and interpersonal relationships.

While Rogers and Ellis have very different philosophies and methods of trying to help people, they share some very important beliefs and values:

1. A great optimism that people can change, even when they are deeply disturbed
2. A perception that individuals are often unnecessarily self-critical, and that negative self-attitudes can become positive
3. A willingness to put forth great effort to try to help people, both through individual therapy and through professional therapy and nontechnical writing
4. A willingness to demonstrate their methods publicly
5. A respect for science and research.

Similar differences and commonalities will be found when Rogers is compared to other cognitive therapists, such as Aaron Beck.

# HISTORY

## Precursors

One of the most powerful influences on Carl Rogers was learning that traditional child-guidance methods in which he had been trained did not work very well. At Columbia University's Teachers College he had been taught testing, measurement, diagnostic interviewing, and interpretive treatment. This was followed by an internship at the psycho-analytically oriented Institute for Child Guidance, where he learned to take exhaustive case histories and do projective personality testing. It is important to note that Rogers originally went to a Rochester child-guidance agency believing in this diagnostic, prescriptive, professionally impersonal approach, and it was only after actual experience that he concluded that it was not effective. As an alternative, he tried listening and following the client's lead rather than assuming the role of the expert. This worked better, and he discovered some theoretical and applied support for this alternative approach in the work of Otto Rank and his followers at the University of Pennsylvania School of Social Work and the Philadelphia Child Guidance Clinic. One particularly important event was a three-day seminar in Rochester with Rank (Rogers & Haigh, 1983). Another was his association with a Rankian-trained social worker, Elizabeth Davis, from whom "I first got the notion of responding almost entirely to the feelings being expressed. What later came to be called the reflection of feeling sprang from my contact with her" (Rogers & Haigh, 1983, p. 7).

Rogers's methodology and, later, his theory grew out of the soil of his own experience. At the same time, a number of links to Otto Rank are apparent in Rogers's early work.

The following elements of Rankian theory bore a close relationship to principles of nondirective therapy:

1. The individual seeking help is not simply a battleground of impersonal forces such as id and superego, but has personal creative powers.
2. The aim of therapy is acceptance by the individual of self as unique and self-reliant.
3. In order to achieve this goal, the client rather than the therapist must become the central figure in the therapeutic process.

4. The therapist can be neither an instrument of love, which would make the patient more dependent, nor an instrument of education, which attempts to alter the individual.

5. The goals of therapy are achieved by the patient not through an explanation of the past, which the client would resist if interpreted, and which, even if accepted, would lessen responsibility for present adjustment, but rather through experiencing the present in the therapeutic situation (Raskin, 1948, pp. 95–96).

Rank explicitly, eloquently, and repeatedly rejected therapy by technique and interpretation, stating:

> Every single case, yes every individual hour of the same case, is different, because it is derived momentarily from the play of forces given in the situation and immediately applied. My technique consists essentially in having no technique, but in utilizing as much as possible experience and understanding that are constantly converted into skill but never crystallized into technical rules which would be applicable ideologically. There is a technique only in an ideological therapy where technique is identical with theory and the chief task of the analyst is interpretation (ideological), not the bringing to pass and granting of experience. (1945, p. 105)

Rank is obscure about his actual practice of psychotherapy, particularly the amount and nature of his activity during the treatment hour. Unsystematic references in *Will Therapy, Truth and Reality* (1945) reveal that, despite his criticism of educational and interpretive techniques and his expressed value of the patient being his or her own therapist, he assumed a position of undisputed power in the relationship.

## Beginnings

Carl Ransom Rogers was born in Oak Park, Illinois, on January 8, 1902. Rogers's parents believed in hard work, responsibility, and religious fundamentalism and frowned on activities such as drinking, dancing, and card playing. The family was characterized by closeness and devotion but did not openly display affection. While in high school, Carl worked on the family farm, and he became interested in experimentation and the scientific aspect of agriculture. He entered the University of Wisconsin, following his parents and older siblings, as an agriculture major. Rogers also carried on his family's religious tradition. He was active in the campus YMCA and was chosen to be 1 of 10 American youth delegates to the World Student Christian Federation's Conference in Peking, China, in 1922. At that time he switched his major from agriculture to history, which he thought would better prepare him for a career as a minister. After graduating from Wisconsin in 1924 and marrying Helen Elliott, a childhood friend, he entered the Union Theological Seminary. Two years later, and in part as a result of taking several psychology courses, Rogers moved "across Broadway" to Teachers College, Columbia University, where he was exposed to what he later described as "a contradictory mixture of Freudian, scientific, and progressive education thinking" (Rogers & Sanford, 1985, p. 1374).

After Teachers College, Rogers worked for 12 years at a child-guidance center in Rochester, New York, where he soon became an administrator as well as a practicing psychologist. He began writing articles and became active at a national level. His book *The Clinical Treatment of the Problem Child* was published in 1939, and he was offered a professorship in psychology at Ohio State University. Once at Ohio State, Rogers began to teach newer ways of helping problem children and their parents.

In 1940, Rogers was teaching an enlightened distillation of child-guidance practices described in *The Clinical Treatment of the Problem Child*. From his point of view, this approach represented a consensual direction in which the field was moving and was evolutionary rather than revolutionary. The clinical process began with an assessment, including testing of children and interviewing of parents, and the results of assessment provided the basis for a treatment plan. In treatment, nondirective principles were followed.

Rogers's views became more radical. His presentation at the University of Minnesota on December 11, 1940, entitled "Some Newer Concepts in Psychotherapy," is the single event most often identified with the birth of client-centered therapy.

Rogers decided to expand this talk into a book titled *Counseling and Psychotherapy* (1942). The book, which included an electronically recorded eight-interview case, described the generalized process in which a client begins with a conflict situation and a predominance of negative attitudes and moves toward insight, independence, and positive attitudes. Rogers hypothesized that the counselor promoted such a process by avoiding advice and interpretation and by consistently recognizing and accepting the client's feelings. Research corroborating this new approach to counseling and psychotherapy was offered, including the first (Porter, 1943) of what soon became a series of pioneering doctoral dissertations on the process and outcomes of psychotherapy. In a very short time, an entirely new approach to psychotherapy was born, as was the field of psychotherapy research. This approach and its accompanying research led to the eventual acceptance of psychotherapy as a primary professional function of clinical psychologists.

After serving as Director of Counseling Services for the United Service Organizations during World War II, Rogers was appointed professor of psychology at the University of Chicago and became head of the university's counseling center. The 12 years during which Rogers remained at Chicago were a period of tremendous growth in client-centered theory, philosophy, practice, research, applications, and implications. In 1957, Rogers published a classic "necessary and sufficient conditions" paper in which congruence and unconditional positive regard were added to empathy as three essential therapist-offered conditions of therapeutic personality change. This was followed by a comprehensive and rigorous theory of therapy, personality, and interpersonal relationships (Rogers, 1959b). Rogers's philosophy of the "exquisitely rational" nature of the behavior and growth of human beings was further articulated and related to the thinking of Søren Kierkegaard, Abraham Maslow, and others. The practice of client-centered therapy deepened and broadened. The therapist was also more fully appreciated as a person in the therapeutic relationship. Psychotherapy research, which had begun so auspiciously at Ohio State, continued with investigations by Godfrey T. Barrett-Lennard (1962), John Butler and Gerard Haigh (1954), Desmond Cartwright (1957), Eugene Gendlin (1961), Nathaniel Raskin (1952), Julius Seeman (1959), John Shlien (1964), and Stanley Standal (1954), among others.

At Ohio State, there was a sense that client-centered principles had implications beyond the counseling office. At Chicago, this was made most explicit by the empowerment of students and the counseling center staff. About half of Rogers's *Client-Centered Therapy* (1951) was devoted to applications of client-centered therapy, with additional chapters on play therapy, group therapy, and leadership and administration.

In 1957, Rogers accepted a professorship in psychology and psychiatry at the University of Wisconsin. With the collaboration of associates and graduate students, a massive research project was mounted, based on the hypothesis that hospitalized schizophrenics would respond to a client-centered approach (Rogers et al., 1967). Two relatively clear conclusions emerged from a complex maze of results: (1) the most successful patients were those who had experienced the highest degree of accurate empathy, and (2) it was the client's, rather than the therapist's, judgment of the therapy relationship that correlated more highly with success or failure.

## Current Status

Rogers left the University of Wisconsin and full-time academia and began living in La Jolla, California, in 1964. He was a resident fellow for four years at the Western Behavioral Sciences Institute and then, starting in 1968, at the Center for Studies of the Person. In more than two decades in California, Rogers wrote books on a person-centered approach to teaching and educational administration, on encounter groups, on marriage and other forms of partnership, and on the "quiet revolution" that he believed would emerge with a new type of "self-empowered person." Rogers believed this revolution had the potential to change "the very nature of psychotherapy, marriage, education, administration, and politics" (Rogers, 1977). These books were based on observations and interpretations of hundreds of individual and group experiences.

A special interest of Rogers and his associates was the application of a person-centered approach to international conflict resolution. This resulted in trips to South Africa, Eastern Europe, and the Soviet Union, as well as in meetings with Irish Catholics and Protestants and with representatives of nations involved in Central American conflicts (Rogers & Ryback, 1984). In addition to Rogers's books, a number of valuable films and videotapes have provided data for research on the basic person-centered hypothesis that individuals and groups who have experienced empathy, congruence, and unconditional positive regard will go through a constructive process of self-directed change.

Since 1982, there have been biennial international forums on the Person-Centered Approach, meeting in Mexico, England, the United States, Brazil, the Netherlands, Greece, and South Africa. Alternating with these meetings have been international conferences on Client-Centered and Experiential Psychotherapy in Belgium, Scotland, Austria, and Portugal. There is now a World Association for Person-Centered and Experiential Psychotherapy and Counseling, which has been meeting every three years. However, some "purists" believe that there is a directive aspect to experiential therapy and object to client-centered or person-centered therapy, which they consider nondirective, being merged with it.

In September 1986, several months before his death, Rogers attended a meeting of the Association for the Development of the Person-Centered Approach held at International House on the campus of the University of Chicago. At this meeting, which was to be the last Carl Rogers attended, the idea for a workshop on the person-centered approach was developed. The workshop, organized by Professor Jerold Bozarth of the University of Georgia and several graduate students, began a week after Carl Rogers's death on February 4, 1987. It was held in Warm Springs, Georgia, February 11–15, 1987, at the Rehabilitation Institute, where Franklin Roosevelt was treated after being struck by polio. Forty participants, including Barbara Brodley, Chuck Devonshire, Nat Raskin, David Spahn, and Fred Zimring, came from Georgia, Florida, Illinois, Kansas, and Nevada. The group expressed its appreciation to Jerold Bozarth for allowing it to find its own direction and develop its own process. Workshops have been held annually at Warm Springs since 1987, and this nondirective climate has been maintained over the years.

The *Person-Centered Review,* "an international journal of research, theory, and application," was initiated by David Cain in 1986. The journal has an editorial board made up of scholars and practitioners from around the world. In 1992, the *Review* was succeeded by *The Person-Centered Journal,* coedited by Jerold Bozarth and Fred Zimring. Zimring and Raskin (1992), in a volume on the history of psychotherapy during the first hundred years of the American Psychological Association, wrote:

> The *Review* has published articles about many aspects of client-centered therapy. In addition, *Client-Centered and Experiential Psychotherapy in the Nineties* (Lietaer, Rombauts, & Van Balen, 1990) contains many papers about . . . the use of the ap-

proach with various populations . . . children and child therapy . . . family and couples therapy . . . disturbed clients . . . and clients who are working with fears of death and dying.

Raskin (1996) formulated significant steps in the evolution of the movement from individual therapy in 1940 to the concept of community in the 1990s.

# PERSONALITY

## Theory of Personality

Rogers moved from a disinterest in psychological theory to the development of a rigorous 19-proposition "theory of therapy, personality, and interpersonal relationships" (Rogers, 1959b). On one level, this signified a change in Rogers's respect for theory. On another, this comprehensive formulation can be understood as a logical evolution. His belief in the importance of the child's conscious attitudes toward self and self-ideal was central to the test of personality adjustment he devised for children (Rogers, 1931). The portrayal of the client's growing through a process of reduced defensiveness and of self-directed expansion of self-awareness was described in a paper on the processes of therapy (Rogers, 1940). Rogers wrote here of a gradual recognition and admission of a real self with its childish, aggressive, and ambivalent aspects as well as more mature components. As data on personality changes in psychotherapy started to accumulate rapidly, with the objective analyses of verbatim interviews, Rogers found support for his belief that the facts are always friendly, despite some results at variance with his hypotheses.

As outgoing president of the American Psychological Association, Rogers summed up this perspective:

> Client-centered therapy has led us to try to adopt the client's perceptual field as the basis for genuine understanding. In trying to enter this internal world of perception . . . we find ourselves in a new vantage point for understanding personality dynamics. . . . We find that behavior seems to be better understood as a reaction to this reality-as-perceived. We discover that the way in which the person sees himself, and the perceptions he dares not take as belonging to himself, seem to have an important relationship to the inner peace which constitutes adjustment. We discover . . . a capacity for the restructuring and reorganization of self, and consequently the reorganization of behavior, which has profound social implications. We see these observations, and the theoretical formulations which they inspire, as a fruitful new approach for study and research in various fields of psychology. (1947, p. 368)

Rogers expanded his observations into a theory of personality and behavior that he described in *Client-Centered Therapy* (1951). This theory is based on 19 basic propositions:

1.  Every individual exists in a continually changing world of experience of which he or she is the center.
2.  The organism reacts to the field as it is experienced and perceived. This perceptual field is, for the individual, "reality."
3.  The organism reacts as an organized whole to this phenomenal field.
4.  The organism has one basic tendency and striving—to actualize, maintain, and enhance the experiencing organism.
5.  Behavior is basically the goal-directed attempt of the organism to satisfy its needs as experienced, in the field as perceived.

*consummatory*

6. Emotion accompanies and in general facilitates such goal-directed behavior, the kind of emotion being related to the seeking versus the consummatory aspects of the behavior, and the intensity of the emotion being related to the perceived significance of the behavior for the maintenance and enhancement of the organism.

7. The best vantage point for understanding behavior is from the internal frame of reference of the individual.

8. A portion of the total perceptual field gradually becomes differentiated as the self.

9. As a result of interaction with the environment, and particularly as a result of evaluational interaction with others, the structure of self is formed—an organized, fluid, but consistent conceptual pattern of perceptions of characteristics and relationships of the "I" or the "me," together with values attached to these concepts.

10. The values attached to experiences, and the values which are a part of the self-structure, in some instances are values experienced directly by the organism, and in some instances are values introjected or taken over from others, but perceived in distorted fashion, as if they had been experienced directly.

11. As experiences occur in the life of the individual, they are either (a) symbolized, perceived, and organized into some relationship to the self, (b) ignored because there is no perceived relationship to the self-structure, or (c) denied symbolization or given a distorted symbolization because the experience is inconsistent with the structure of the self.

12. Most of the ways of behaving which are adopted by the organism are those which are consistent with the concept of self.

13. Behavior may, in some instances, be brought about by organic experiences and needs which have not been symbolized. Such behavior may be inconsistent with the structure of the self, but in such instances the behavior is not "owned" by the individual.

14. Psychological maladjustment exists when the organism denies to awareness significant sensory and visceral experiences, which consequently are not symbolized and organized into the gestalt of the self-structure. When this situation exists, there is a basis for potential psychological tension.

15. Psychological adjustment exists when the concept of the self is such that all the sensory and visceral experiences of the organism are, or may be, assimilated on a symbolic level into a consistent relationship with the concept of self.

16. Any experience which is inconsistent with the organization or structure of self may be perceived as a threat, and the more of these perceptions there are, the more rigidly the self-structure is organized to maintain itself.

17. Under certain conditions, involving primarily complete absence of any threat to the self-structure, experiences which are inconsistent with it may be perceived and examined, and the structure of self revised to assimilate and include such experiences.

18. When the individual perceives and accepts into one consistent and integrated system all his sensory and visceral experiences, then he is necessarily more understanding of others and is more accepting of others as separate individuals.

19. As the individual perceives and accepts into his self-structure more of his organic experiences, he finds that he is replacing his present value system—based so largely upon introjections which have been distortedly symbolized—with a continuing organismic valuing process. (pp. 481–533)

Rogers comments that:

This theory is basically phenomenological in character, and relies heavily upon the concept of the self as an explanatory construct. It pictures the end-point of personality development as being a basic congruence between the phenomenal field of experience and the conceptual structure of the self—a situation which, if achieved, would represent freedom from internal strain and anxiety, and freedom from potential strain; which would represent the maximum in realistically oriented adaptation; which would mean the establishment of an individualized value system having considerable identity with the value system of any other equally well-adjusted member of the human race. (1951, p. 532)

Further investigations of these propositions were conducted at the University of Chicago Counseling Center in the early 1950s in carefully designed and controlled studies. Stephenson's (1953) Q-sort technique was used to measure changes in self-concept and self-ideal during and following therapy and in a no-therapy control period. Many results confirmed Rogers's hypotheses, e.g., a significant increase in congruence between self and ideal occurred during therapy, and changes in the perceived self were toward better psychological adjustment (Rogers & Dymond, 1954).

Rogers's personality theory has been described as growth-oriented rather than developmental. While this is accurate, it does not acknowledge Rogers's sensitivity to the attitudes with which children are confronted, beginning in infancy:

> While I have been fascinated by the horizontal spread of the person-centered approach into so many areas of our life, others have been more interested in the vertical direction and are discovering the profound value of treating the infant, during the whole birth process, as a person who should be understood, whose communications should be treated with respect, who should be dealt with empathically. This is the new and stimulating contribution of Frederick Leboyer, a French obstetrician who . . . has assisted in the delivery of at least a thousand infants in what can only be called a person-centered way. (Rogers, 1977, p. 31)

Rogers goes on to describe the infant's extreme sensitivity to light and sound, the rawness of the skin, the fragility of the head, the struggle to breathe, etc., and the specific ways in which Leboyer has taught parents and professionals to provide a beginning life experience that is caring, loving, and respectful.

This sensitivity to children was further expressed in Rogers's explanation of his fourth proposition (*The organism has one basic tendency and striving—to actualize, maintain, and enhance the experiencing organism*):

> The whole process (of self-enhancement and growth) may be symbolized and illustrated by the child's learning to walk. The first steps involve struggle, and usually pain. Often it is true that the immediate reward involved in taking a few steps is in no way commensurate with the pain of falls and bumps. The child may, because of the pain, revert to crawling for a time. Yet the forward direction of growth is more powerful than the satisfactions of remaining infantile. Children will actualize themselves, in spite of the painful experiences of so doing. In the same way, they will become independent, responsible, self-governing, and socialized, in spite of the pain which is often involved in these steps. Even where they do not, because of a variety of circumstances, exhibit the growth, the tendency is still present. Given the opportunity for clear-cut choice between forward-moving and regressive behavior, the tendency will operate. (Rogers, 1951, pp. 490–491)

One of Rogers's hypotheses about personality (Proposition 8) was that a part of the developing infant's private world becomes recognized as "me," "I," or "myself." Rogers described infants, in the course of interacting with the environment, as building up concepts about themselves, about the environment, and about themselves in relation to the environment.

Rogers's next suppositions are crucial to his theory of how development may proceed either soundly or in the direction of maladjustment. He assumes that very young infants are involved in "direct organismic valuing," with very little or no uncertainty. They have experiences such as "I am cold, and I don't like it," or "I like being cuddled," which may occur even though they lack descriptive words or symbols for these examples. The principle in this natural process is that the infant positively values those experiences that are perceived as self-enhancing and places a negative value on those that threaten or do not maintain or enhance the self.

This situation changes once children begin to be evaluated by others (Holdstock & Rogers, 1983). The love they are given and the symbolization of themselves as lovable children become dependent on behavior. To hit or to hate a baby sibling may result in the child's being told that he or she is bad and unlovable. The child, to preserve a positive self-concept, may distort experience.

> It is in this way . . . that parental attitudes are not only introjected, but . . . are experienced . . . in distorted fashion, *as if* based on the evidence of one's own sensory and visceral equipment. Thus, through distorted symbolization, expression of anger comes to be "experienced" as bad, even though the more accurate symbolization would be that the expression of anger is often experienced as satisfying or enhancing. . . . The "self" which is formed on this basis of distorting the sensory and visceral evidence to fit the already present structure acquires an organization and integration which the individual endeavors to preserve. (Rogers, 1951, pp. 500–501)

This type of interaction may sow the seeds of confusion about self, self-doubt, and disapproval of self, as well as reliance upon the evaluation of others. Rogers indicated that these consequences may be avoided if the parent can accept the child's negative feelings and the child as a whole while refusing to permit certain behaviors such as hitting the baby.

## Variety of Concepts

Various terms and concepts appear in the presentation of Rogers's theory of personality and behavior that often have a unique and distinctive meaning in this orientation.

### Experience

Experience refers to the private world of the individual. At any moment, some of this is conscious; for example, we feel the pressure of the pen against our fingers as we write. Some of it may be difficult to bring into awareness, such as the idea, "I am an aggressive person." While people's actual awareness of their total experiential field may be limited, each individual is the only one who can know it completely.

### Reality

For psychological purposes, reality is basically the private world of individual perceptions, though for social purposes reality consists of those perceptions that have a high degree of communality among various individuals. Two people will agree on the reality that a particular person is a politician. One sees her as a good woman who wants to help people and, based on this reality, votes for her. The other person's reality is that the politician appropriates money to win favor, and therefore this person votes against her. In therapy, changes in feelings and perceptions will result in changes in reality.

## The Organism Reacts as an Organized Whole

A person may be hungry, but because of a report to complete, will skip lunch. In psychotherapy, clients often become more clear about what is more important to them, resulting in behavioral changes directed toward the clarified goals. A politician may choose not to run for office because he decides that his family life is more important.

## The Organism's Actualizing Tendency

This is a central tenet in the writings of Kurt Goldstein, Hobart Mowrer, Harry Stack Sullivan, Karen Horney, and Andras Angyal, to name just a few. The child's painful struggle to learn to walk is an example. It is Rogers's belief and the belief of most other personality theorists that, given a free choice and in the absence of external force, individuals prefer to be healthy rather than sick, to be independent rather than dependent, and in general to further the optimal development of the total organism.

## The Internal Frame of Reference

This is the perceptual field of the individual. It is the way the world appears and the meanings attached to experience and feelings. From the person-centered point of view, this internal frame of reference provides the fullest understanding of why people behave as they do. It is to be distinguished from external judgments of behavior, attitudes, and personality.

## The Self, Concept of Self, and Self-Structure

"These terms refer to the organized, consistent, conceptual gestalt composed of perceptions of the characteristics of the 'I' or 'me' and the perceptions of the relationships of the 'I' or 'me' to others and to various aspects of life, together with the values attached to these perceptions. It is a gestalt available to awareness although not necessarily in awareness. It is a fluid and changing process, but at any given moment it . . . is at least partially definable in operational terms" (Meador & Rogers, 1984, p. 158).

## Symbolization

This is the process by which the individual becomes aware or conscious of an experience. There is a tendency to deny symbolization to experiences at variance with the concept of self—e.g., people who think of themselves as truthful will tend to resist the symbolization of an act of lying. Ambiguous experiences tend to be symbolized in ways that are consistent with self-concept. A speaker lacking in self-confidence may symbolize a silent audience as unimpressed; one who is confident may symbolize such a group as attentive and interested.

## Psychological Adjustment or Maladjustment

This refers to the consistency, or lack of consistency, between an individual's sensory and visceral experiences and the concept of self. A self-concept that includes elements of weakness and imperfection facilitates the symbolization of failure experiences. The need to deny or distort such experiences does not exist and therefore fosters a condition of psychological adjustment.

## Organismic Valuing Process

This is an ongoing process in which individuals freely rely on the evidence of their own senses for making value judgments. This is in distinction to a fixed system of introjected values characterized by "oughts" and "shoulds" and by what is supposed to be right or wrong. The organismic valuing process is consistent with the person-centered hypothesis of confidence in the individual and, even though established by each individual, makes for a highly responsible socialized system of values and behavior. The responsibility derives from people making choices on the basis of their direct, organic processing of situations, in contrast to acting out of fear of what others may think of them or what others have taught them is the way to think and act.

## The Fully Functioning Person

Rogers defined those who rely on organismic valuing processes as fully functioning people, able to experience all of their feelings, afraid of none of them, allowing awareness to flow freely in and through their experiences. Seeman (1984) has been involved in a long-term research program to clarify and describe the qualities of such optimally functioning individuals. These empirical studies highlight the possession of a positive self-concept, greater physiological responsiveness, and an efficient use of the environment.

# PSYCHOTHERAPY

## Theory of Psychotherapy

The basic theory of person-centered therapy is that if the therapist is successful in conveying genuineness, unconditional positive regard, and empathy, then the client will respond with constructive changes in personality organization. Research has demonstrated that these qualities can be made real in a relationship and can be conveyed and appreciated in a short time. Changes in self-acceptance, immediacy of experiencing, directness of relating, and movement toward an internal locus-of-evaluation may occur in short-term intensive workshops or even in single interviews.

After a four-day workshop of psychologists, educators, and other professionals conducted by Rogers and R. C. Sanford in Moscow, participants reported their reactions. The following is a typical response:

> This is just two days after the experience and I am still a participant. I am a psychologist, not a psychotherapist. I have known Rogers's theory but this was a process in which we were personally involved. I didn't realize how it applied. I want to give several impressions. First was the effectiveness of this approach. It was a kind of process in which we all learned. Second, this process was moving, without a motor. Nobody had to lead it or guide it. It was a self-evolving process. It was like the Chekhov story where they were expectantly awaiting the piano player and the piano started playing itself. Third, I was impressed by the manner of Carl and Ruth [Sanford]. At first I felt they were passive. Then I realized it was the silence of understanding. Fourth, I want to mention the penetration of this process into my inner world. At first I was an observer, but then the approach disappeared altogether. I was not simply surrounded by this process, I was absorbed into it! It was a revelation to me. We started moving. I wasn't simply seeing people I had known for years, but their feelings. My fifth realization was my inability to control the flow of feelings, the flow of the process. My feelings tried to put on the clothes of my words. Sometimes people ex-

ploded; some even cried. It was a reconstruction of the system of perception. Finally, I want to remark on the high skill of Carl and Ruth, of their silences, their voices, their glances. It was always some response and they were responded to. It was a great phenomenon, a great experience. (Rogers, 1987, pp. 298–299)

This kind of experience speaks against the perception of the person-centered approach as safe, harmless, innocuous, and superficial. It is intended to be safe, but clearly it can also be powerful.

## Empathy

Empathy, in person-centered therapy, is an active, immediate, continuous process. Rogers quotes from a 1947 unpublished paper by Raskin on the "The Nondirective Attitude":

> "At this level, counselor participation becomes an active experiencing with the client of the feelings to which he gives expression, the counselor makes a maximum effort to get under the skin of the person with whom he is communicating, he tries to get within and to live the attitudes expressed instead of observing them, to catch every nuance of their changing nature; in a word, to absorb himself completely in the attitudes of the other. And in struggling to do this, there is simply no room for any other type of counselor activity or attitude; if he is attempting to live the attitudes of the other, he cannot be diagnosing them, he cannot be thinking of making the process go faster. Because he is another, and not the client, the understanding is not spontaneous but must be acquired, and this through the most intense, continuous and active attention to the feelings of the other, to the exclusion of any other type of attention." (Rogers, 1951)

The accuracy of the therapist's empathic understanding has often been emphasized, but more important is the therapist's interest in appreciating the world of the client and offering such understanding with the willingness to be corrected. This creates a process in which the therapist gets closer and closer to the client's meanings and feelings, developing an ever-deepening relationship based on respect for and understanding of the other person.

Person-centered therapists vary in their views of the empathic understanding process. Some aim to convey an understanding of just what the client wishes to communicate. For Rogers, it felt right not only to clarify meanings of which the client was aware, but also those just below the level of awareness. Rogers was especially passionate about empathy's not being exemplified by a technique such as "reflection of feeling," but by the therapist's sensitive immersion in the client's world of experience. Brodley (1993) has documented the high proportion of "empathic understanding responses" in Rogers's therapy transcripts.

## Unconditional Positive Regard

Other terms for this condition are *warmth, acceptance, nonpossessive caring,* and *prizing.*

> When the therapist is experiencing a positive, nonjudgmental, acceptant attitude toward whatever the client *is* at that moment, therapeutic movement or change is more likely. It involves the therapist's willingness for the client to *be* whatever immediate feeling is going on—confusion, resentment, fear, anger, courage, love, or pride. . . . When the therapist prizes the client in a total rather than a conditional way, forward movement is likely. (Rogers, 1986a, p. 198)

## Congruence

Rogers regarded congruence as:

> the most basic of the attitudinal conditions that foster therapeutic growth. . . . [It] does not mean that the therapist burdens the client with all of his or her problems or feelings. It does not mean that the therapist blurts out impulsively any attitudes that come to mind. It does mean, however, that the therapist does not deny to himself or herself the feelings being experienced and that the therapist is willing to express and to be open about any persistent feelings that exist in the relationship. It means avoiding the temptation to hide behind a mask of professionalism. (Rogers & Sanford, 1985, p. 1379)

Correspondingly, an effective way of dealing with the common occurrence of therapist fatigue is to express it. This strengthens the relationship because the therapist is not trying to cover up a real feeling. It may also reduce or eliminate the fatigue and restore the therapist to a fully attending and empathic state.

## Implied Therapeutic Conditions

There are three other conditions in addition to the "therapist-offered" conditions of empathy, congruence, and unconditional positive regard (Rogers, 1957):

1. The client and therapist must be in psychological contact.
2. The client must be experiencing some anxiety, vulnerability, or incongruence.
3. The client must receive or experience the conditions offered by the therapist.

Rogers described the first two as preconditions for therapy. The third, the reception by the client of the conditions offered by the therapist, sometimes overlooked, is essential. Research relating therapeutic outcome to empathy, congruence, and unconditional positive regard based on external judgments of these variables is moderately supportive of the person-centered hypothesis. If the ratings are done by clients themselves, the relationship to outcome is much stronger. Orlinsky and Howard (1978) reviewed 15 studies relating client perception of empathy to outcome and found that 12 supported the critical importance of perceived empathy.

## Process of Psychotherapy

The practice of person-centered therapy dramatizes its differences from most other orientations. Therapy begins immediately, with the therapist trying to understand the client's world in whatever way the client wishes to share it. The first interview is not used to take a history, to arrive at a diagnosis, to determine if the client is treatable, or to establish the length of treatment.

The therapist immediately shows respect for clients, allowing them to proceed in whatever way is comfortable for them. She or he listens without prejudice and without a private agenda. The therapist is open to either positive or negative feelings, speech or silence. The first hour may be the first of hundreds or it may be the only one; this is for the client to determine. If the client has questions, the therapist tries to recognize and to respond to whatever feelings are implicit in the questions. "How am I going to get out of this mess?" may be the expression of the feeling, "my situation seems hopeless." The therapist will convey recognition and acceptance of this attitude. If this question is actually a plea for suggestions, the therapist may reply that she or he does not have the answers, but hopes to help the client find the ones that are right for him or her. There is a willingness to stay with the client in moments of confusion and despair. There is an assumption that reassurance and easy answers are not helpful and show a lack of respect for the client. Some person-centered therapists consider replying directly to client questions a more respectful manner of responding (Brodley, 1999).

The therapist looks to the client for decisions about the timing and frequency of therapy. The therapist must respect her or his own availability, but is guided as much as possible by scheduling that feels right to the client. Person-centered therapists commonly share with their clients the responsibility for fee setting and manner of payment. In a money-oriented society, this is an opportune area for showing respect for the client.

Regard is also demonstrated through discussion of options such as group therapy and family therapy, in contrast to therapists of other orientations who "put" the client in a group or make therapy conditional on involvement of the whole family. This is not to be interpreted as meaning that the client is allowed to dictate the circumstances of therapy, but to make clear that the client is a vital partner in determining these conditions. On many issues, the client is regarded as the expert.

## An Interview Illustrating the Process of Therapy

It has always been characteristic of the person-centered approach to illustrate its principles with verbatim accounts. This has the advantage of depicting the interaction between therapist and client more exactly and gives readers the opportunity to agree or to differ with the interpretation of the data.

The following is a demonstration interview carried out by Carl Rogers with a client whose code name is "Jill." Because of space limitations, the middle third of the interview has been omitted. Asterisks indicate words that could not be made out in the transcription (T = Therapist; C = Client).

T-1:  OK, I think I'm ready. And you . . . ready?

C-1:  Yes.

T-2:  I don't know what you might want to talk about, but I'm very ready to hear. We have half an hour, and I hope that in that half an hour we can get to know each other as deeply as possible, but we don't need to strive for anything. I guess that's my feeling. Do you want to tell me whatever is on your mind?

C-2:  I'm having a lot of problems dealing with my daughter. She's 20 years old; she's in college; I'm having a lot of trouble letting her go. . . . And I have a lot of guilt feelings about her; I have a real need to hang on to her.

T-3:  A need to hang on so you can kind of make up for the things you feel guilty about—is that part of it?

C-3:  There's a lot of that. . . . Also, she's been a real friend to me, and filled my life . . . And it's very hard***a lot of empty places now that she's not with me.

T-4:  The old vacuum, sort of, when she's not there.

C-4:  Yes. Yes. I also would like to be the kind of mother that could be strong and say, you know, "Go and have a good life," and this is really hard for me to do that.

T-5:  It's very hard to give up something that's been so precious in your life, but also something that I guess has caused you pain when you mentioned guilt.

C-5:  Yeah, and I'm aware that I have some anger toward her that I don't always get what I want. I have needs that are not met. And, uh, I don't feel I have a right to those needs. You know . . . She's a daughter; she's not my mother—though sometimes I feel as if I'd like her to mother me . . . It's very difficult for me to ask for that and have a right to it.

T-6:  So it may be unreasonable, but still, when she doesn't meet your needs, it makes you mad.

C-6:  Yeah, I get very angry, very angry with her.

[PAUSE]

T-7:  You're also feeling a little tension at this point, I guess.

C-7:  Yeah. Yeah. A lot of conflict . . .

T-8:  Umm-hmm . . .

C-8:  A lot of pain.

T-9:  A lot of pain. Can you say anything more what that's about?

C-9:  [Sigh.] I reach out for her, and she moves away from me. And she steps back and pulls back . . . And then I feel like a really bad person. Like some kind of monster, that she doesn't want me to touch her and hold her like I did when she was a little girl . . .

T-10:  It sounds like a very double feeling there. Part of it is, "Damn it, I want you close." The other part of it is, "Oh my God, what a monster I am to not let you go."

C-10:  Umm-hmm. Yeah. I should be stronger. I should be a grown woman and allow this to happen.

T-11:  But instead, sometimes you feel like her daughter.

C-11:  Umm-hmm. Yeah. Sometimes when I cuddle her, I feel I'm being cuddled.

T-12:  Umm-hmm.

[PAUSE]

But you place a lot of expectations on yourself: "I should be different."

C-12:  Yeah. I should be more mature. I should have my needs met so that I don't have to get anything from her.

T-13:  You should find other ways and other sources to meet your needs, but somehow that doesn't seem to be happening?

C-13:  Well, I feel I get a lot of my needs met, but the need from her is very strong—it's the need from a woman really, I think . . . It doesn't quite make up the needs I get from men****** . . .

T-14:  There are some things that you just want from her.

C-14:  Umm-hmm. Yeah. Just from her. [Sigh.]

T-15:  When she pulls back, that's a very painful experience.

C-15:  Yeah, that really hurts. That really hurts. [Big sigh.]

[PAUSE]

T-16:  It looks like you're feeling some of that hurt right now.

C-16:  Yeah, I can really feel her stepping back.

T-17:  Umm-hmm. Umm-hmm.

[PAUSE]

T-18:  Pulling away from you.

C-17:  Yeah . . . Going away.

T-19:  ***you feel her sort of slipping away, and you . . . and it hurts . . . and—

C-18:  Yeah. I'm just sort of sitting here alone. I guess like, you know, I can feel her gone and I'm just left here.

T-20:  Umm-hmm. You're experiencing it right now: that she's leaving and here you are all alone.

C-19:  Yeah. Yeah. Yeah. I feel really lonely. [Cries.]

T-21:  Umm-hmm. Umm-hmm. If I understand right, not lonely in every respect, but lonely for her.

T-22:  I'm not a good therapist—I forgot a box of Kleenex, but . . . I think I've got . . . [Laughs.]

C-20:  Thank you. [Laughs.] I feel like I could cry a million tears about that. [Laughs.]

T-23:  Umm-hmm. It feels as if the tears could just flow and flow on that score.

C-21:  Yeah. Never stop.

T-24:  That just to have her leave, have her pull away is just more than you can take.

C-22:  Yeah. Yeah. It's really hard to go on without her. [Cries.]

T-25:  It sounds as though that is almost the center of your life.

C-23:  It's very close to that, you know. My husband, my children, my home . . . My work is important too, but there's something about the heart that's connected to her. [Sigh.]

T-26:  And there's a real ache in your heart with her leaving.

C-24:  Yeah. Yeah. [Cries.]

[PAUSE]

C-25:  Oh . . . I just don't want her to go.

T-27:  I want to keep her as my daughter, as my little girl, as the one I can cuddle . . .

C-26:  Yeah, yeah. The one I can cuddle. She likes to cuddle too.

T-28:  Umm-hmm. Umm-hmm.

C-27:  [Cries.] And you know, I'm also scared for her. I'm scared for her out in the world. I'm scared for her to have to go through all the things that I did and how painful that is. I'd like to save her from that.

T-29:  You'd like to protect her from that life out there and all the pain that you went through . . .

C-28:  Yeah, yeah. And all the new stuff that all the young people are going through . . . It's very hard. She's struggling.

T-30:  It's a hard world . . .

C-29:  Yeah, very hard . . .

T-31:  And you'd like to cushion it for her . . .

C-30:  Yeah, make it perfect . . .

[Middle third of interview omitted]

T-73:  Does that mean that you feel no one cares, no one accepts?

C-73:  No. I feel like now that there are people who do, who care and accept and hear and value me. But there's that little—

T-74:  So that the person who can't care and accept and value you is you.

C-74:  Umm-hmm. Yeah. It's mostly me.

T-75:  The person who sees those things as unforgivable is you.

C-75:  Yeah. Yeah. Nobody else is that hard on me.

T-76:  Umm-hmm. Nobody could be that cruel to you, or make such awful judgment.

C-76:  [Sigh.]

T-77:  Or hate you so.

C-77:  Or hate me so. Yeah.

T-78:  Sounds like you're the judge, the jury, and the executioner.

C-78:  Yeah, my own worst enemy.

T-79:  You pass a pretty tough sentence on yourself.

C-79:  Yeah. Yeah, I do. Not a very good friend to me.

T-80:  No.

C-80:  ***—

T-81:  You're not a very good friend to yourself. Umm-hmm.

C-81:  Umm-hmm.

T-82:  And you wouldn't think of doing to a friend what you do to yourself.

C-82:  That's right. I would feel terrible if I treated anyone the way I treat me.

T-83:  Umm-hmm. Umm-hmm. Umm-hmm.

[PAUSE]

T-84:  Because to you, your self is just unlovable.

C-84:  Well, there's a part of me that's lovable . . .

T-85:  OK. OK.

C-85:  Yeah.

T-86:  OK. So in some respects you do love yourself.

C-86:   Yeah. I love and appreciate the little child part of me—

T-87:   Umm-hmm—

C-87:   That's really struggled and come through—

T-88:   Umm-hmm—

C-88:   And survived—

T-89:   Umm-hmm—

C-89:   An awful lot.

T-90:   Umm-hmm. That's a damned nice little girl.

C-90:   Yeah. She's really special—

T-91:   Umm-hmm.

C-91:   She's like my daughter.

T-92:   Uh-huh.

C-92:   [Sigh.]

T-93:   And she's a daughter you can hold on to.

C-93:   Yeah. Yeah. I can still cuddle her. And tell her she's beautiful. And love her.

T-94:   And she's a survivor, and she's strong, and she's been through a lot, but she's OK.

C-94:   Yeah. Yeah, she is. She's real special.

[PAUSE]

T-95:   It must be nice to have such a special person in your life.

C-95:   Yeah. It is. That is nice. Yeah. She's very nice.

T-96:   Can she care for the other parts of you?

C-96:   She's starting to***—

T-97:   She's starting to.

C-97:   Yeah.

T-98:   Umm-hmm.

C-98:   Just beginning.

T-99:   Umm-hmm. She's not as hard on you as the adult you.

C-99:   No. That's right.

T-100: Umm-hmm.

C-100: She's much more understanding.

T-101: Umm-hmm.

C-101: And compassionate.

T-102: Umm-hmm.

C-102: [Sigh.]

[PAUSE]

T-103: Sounds like she loves you.

C-103: Yeah. She gives me all that unconditional love that I didn't feel like I got.

T-104: Umm-hmm. Umm-hmm. Umm-hmm. And she loves all of you.

C-104: Yeah. Yeah. She loves all of me.

T-105: To her, none of it is unforgivable.

C-105: No. It's all OK.

T-106: All OK.

C-106: Yeah. [Sigh.]

[PAUSE]

T-107: I like her.

C-107: I like her too. [Sigh.] She's going to save me.

T-108: Hmm?

C-108: She's going to save me.

T-109: She's going to save you.

C-109: [Laughs.] From hurting myself anymore.

T-110: Umm-hmm . . . She may really be able to keep you from being so hard on your-
        self. Really save you.

C-110: Yeah. I think she will; I think she will; I just have to give her a little help too.

T-111: Umm-hmm. Umm-hmm.

C-111: Like we'll work together . . . ***save me.

T-112: She's a good companion to have, isn't she?

C-112: Yeah, she is. [Sigh.] It's good to have a friend.

T-113: Yeah. Umm-hmm. To have that kind of a friend inside really touches you.

C-113: Yeah. It really does. It'll never go away.

T-114: Umm-hmm.

C-114: It'll always be there for me.

T-115: Umm-hmm. She's not going to pull away and—

C-115: Go out into the world and do her thing. Laughs.***gonna stay home with Mama.

T-116: Umm-hmm. Umm-hmm. And be a mother to Mama too, huh?

C-116: Yeah. Yeah.

[PAUSE]

[Sigh.]

T-117: What's that smile?

C-117: It's your eyes are twinkling. [Both laugh.]

T-118: Yours twinkle too.

[Laugh.]

[Sigh.]

Tape Over.[1]

## Commentary

The interview illustrates, in concrete form, many principles of the process of person-centered therapy:

In T-2, Rogers makes it clear that he is leaving it up to the client to talk about what she wishes. He indicates that this can be a deep exchange but that it does not have to be.

T-1 and T-2 signify that Rogers is ready to enter immediately into a person-to-person exchange in which he will be "very ready to hear" whatever the client chooses to bring up.

After this, his responses are consistent attempts to understand the client and to communicate, or check out, his understanding of her feelings. They show that he is open to whatever kinds of feelings the client verbalizes. In T-6, he recognizes a negative feeling, anger; in T-10, he responds to a mixture of feelings; in T-23, he accepts her feeling that her tears are endless; in T-85 and T-86 and many succeeding responses, he conveys his recognition of positive self-attitudes.

The therapist's last two statements (T-117 and T-118) reveal a mutuality in the relationship implicit throughout the interview but often not obvious on the printed page.

The client's tears and frequent expressions of self-depreciation could provide a stimulus for reassurance. However, Rogers consistently does not do this; he is a reliable, understanding partner who stays with the client as she lives with her various negative feelings and accompanies her as she finds the strength to rise above them.

## Mechanisms of Psychotherapy

The interview just quoted reveals many examples of the way in which change and growth are fostered in the person-centered approach. Rogers's straightforward statements in opening the interview (T-1 and T-2) allow the client to begin with a statement of the problem of concern to her and to initiate dialogue at a level comfortable for her.

---

[1] From a previously unpublished article by Carl Rogers given to me for this chapter. N. J. R.

Just as he does not reassure, Rogers does not ask questions. In response to C-2, he does not ask the myriad questions that could construct a logical background and case history for dealing with the presenting problem. Rogers does not see himself as responsible for arriving at a solution to the problem as presented, or determining whether *this* is the problem that will be focused on in therapy, or changing the client's attitudes. The therapist sees the client as having these responsibilities and respects her capacity to fulfill them.

In this excerpt from a person-centered interview are numerous examples of the client's expanding her view of the problem after the therapist recognized her stated percept, accepted it unconditionally, and communicated his understanding to her:

1. Rogers's recognition of the client's stated need to hang on to her daughter (T-3) is followed by the client's recognition that her daughter has been "a real friend to me" (C-3).

2. The therapist's appreciation of the difficulty the client has in letting go of her daughter (T-5) is followed by the revelation of anger felt toward her daughter because "I don't always get what I want" (C-5). The therapist's acceptance of the anger as stated (T-6) helps the client to bring out the extent of the emotion (C-6).

3. The therapist's continued recognition of the client's feelings (T-7 and T-8) helps her to express and share the extreme pain she feels (C-8).

Another result worth noting is the experiencing of emotion in the moment, as distinguished from the recounting of the emotion. This comes out in the exchange (T-15, C-15) and continues into the tears that begin in C-19.

In the final third of the interview, we see another result of the therapist's empathic way of being with the client. She has now shifted from her daughter to herself as the agent of bad self-treatment: "That's right. I would feel terrible if I treated anyone the way I treat me" (C-82).

The mechanism of therapist acceptance leading to change of self-attitude is shown operating powerfully in T-84, C-84: "Because to you, your self is just unlovable." "Well, there's a part of me that's lovable . . ." The client goes on to define that part as "the little child part of me" (C-86) and "She's really special" (C-90), relates that part of herself to her daughter (C-91), and sees that she herself can provide all the caring feelings she has been seeking unsuccessfully from her daughter (C-93). The remainder of the interview clarifies a reciprocal relationship in which she sees that a part of herself that she prizes and loves is also a part she can depend on as a permanent source of support.

The interview exemplifies empathy backed by genuineness and unconditional positive regard. It helps the client to (1) examine her problems in a way that shifts responsibility from others to herself, (2) experience emotions in the immediacy of the therapy encounter, (3) accept aspects of self formerly denied to awareness, and (4) raise her general level of self-regard.

Therapeutic change involves both cognitive and affective elements. The integration of intellect and feelings is occurring in the therapist and in his relationship with the client. He is grasping her perceptions of her external and internal worlds, doing so with warmth and genuine caring. The client is also looking at some of the most troubling aspects of her life, changing the way she looks at others and self, and experiencing anger, pain, loneliness, tearfulness, nurturance, disgust, tenderness, and compassion. The resolution that she introduces toward the end of the interview (C-114), "It'll always be there for me" [the part of herself that will never let her down], may be seen as the therapeutic blending of conation, cognition, and affect.

## An Early Formulation

In a paper given at the first meeting of the American Academy of Psychotherapists in 1956, Rogers (1959a) presented "a client-centered view" of "the essence of psychotherapy." He conceptualized a "molecule" of personality change, hypothesizing "therapy is made up of a series of such molecules, sometimes strung rather closely together, sometimes occurring at long intervals, always with periods of preparatory experiences in between" (p. 52). Rogers attributed four qualities to such a "moment of movement":

> (1) It is something which occurs in this existential moment. It is not a *thinking* about something, it is an *experience* of something at this instant, in the relationship. (2) It is an experiencing which is without barriers, or inhibitions, or holding back. She is consciously *feeling* as sorry for herself as she *is* sorry for herself. (3) This is . . . an experience which has been repeated many times in her past, but which has never been completely experienced. In the past she has felt it at some physiological level, but has "covered it up." This is the first time that it has been experienced completely. (4) This experience has the quality of being acceptable. It is . . . not "I feel sorry for myself, and that is reprehensible." It is instead an experience of "My feeling is one of sorrow for myself, and this is an acceptable part of me." (pp. 52–53)

This mechanism of psychotherapy described by Rogers in 1956 closely matches the experience of the client just discussed: She has a full, emotional experience of a part of herself, a lovable child, of which she has been aware but also covered up; she now experiences that part of herself, and accepts the child completely as part of a newly integrated self. Her laughter and twinkling eyes express the great emotional gratification that accompanies this reorganization.

# APPLICATIONS

## Problems

Person-centered therapists offer the same basic conditions to all prospective clients. These conditions do not include psychological tests, history taking, or other assessment procedures leading to diagnoses and treatment plans. Diagnostic labels take away from the person of the client; assuming a professional posture takes away from the person of the therapist. The therapist's task is uncluttered by the need to be an expert. Rogers expressed with passion and eloquence his belief in the strength of clients and his view of the facilitative role of the therapist:

> We have come to recognize that if we can provide understanding of the way the client seems to himself at this moment, he can do the rest. The therapist must lay aside his preoccupation with diagnosis and his diagnostic shrewdness, must discard his tendency to make professional evaluations, must cease his endeavors to formulate an accurate prognosis, must give up the temptation to subtly guide the individual, and must concentrate on one purpose only: that of providing deep understanding and acceptance of the attitudes consciously held at this moment by the client as he explores step-by-step into the dangerous areas which he has been denying to consciousness. (1946, p. 420)

A consequence of this position is that the person-centered approach has been used with individuals diagnosed by others as psychotic or retarded, as well as with people simply seeking a personal growth experience.

"James" was one of the patients in the Wisconsin study (Rogers et al., 1967). In the course of a detailed description of two interviews with this patient, a "moment of change" is described in which the patient's hard shell is broken by this perception of the therapist's warmth and caring, and he pours out his hurt and sorrow in anguished sobs. This followed an intense effort by Rogers, in two interviews a week for the better part of a year, to reach this 28-year-old man, whose sessions were filled with prolonged silences. Rogers stated, "We were relating as two . . . genuine persons. In the moments of real encounter the differences in education, in status, in degree of psychological disturbance, had no importance—we were two persons in a relationship" (Rogers et al., 1967, p. 411). Eight years later, this patient telephoned Rogers and reported continued success on his job and general stability in his living situation, and he expressed appreciation for the therapeutic relationship with Rogers (Meador & Rogers, 1984).

This clinical vignette emphasizes the person-centered rather than problem-centered nature of this approach. All people have feelings, like to be understood, and have issues of self-concept maintenance and enhancement. The person-centered approach respects the various ways people use to deal with these issues. In this regard, it may work particularly well with people who are "different."

This nonconcern with a person's "category" can be seen in person-centered cross-cultural and international conflict resolution. Empathy is provided in equal measure for Catholics and Protestants in Northern Ireland (Rogers & Ryback, 1984) and for oppressed blacks and troubled whites in South Africa (Rogers, 1986b). Conflict resolution is fostered when the facilitator appreciates the attitudes and feelings of opposing parties, and then the stereotyping of one side by the other is broken down by the protagonists' achievement of empathy.

## Evaluation

The heart of evaluation in person-centered therapy is the evaluative process in the client. The client evaluates whether therapy is useful and the specific ways in which he or she can use it. The client decides what to bring up, how much to explore any particular issue, the level of emotional intensity, and so on. The natural extension of this client-centered responsibility is that the client decides when it is time to terminate therapy.

Because the theory of personality development in person-centered therapy is based on how clients experience change, there is a smooth transition from clients' descriptions of change and those of therapists or external judges. Victor Raimy's (1948) pioneering dissertation on self-concept at Ohio State University was based on self-references in counseling interviews and on simple quantitative analysis of changes in self-approval in 14 complete series of counseling interviews. He defined a *self-reference* as "a group of words spoken by the client which directly or indirectly described him as he appears in his own eyes." Self-ratings of this type were used extensively in the "parallel studies" project analyzing the first 10 completely recorded cases at the University of Chicago Counseling Center (Rogers et al., 1949). Rogers described his experience involving clients' perceptions of the importance of self:

> In my early days as a therapist, I tended to scorn any thinking about the self . . . [it] seemed so ephemeral. . . . Another problem was that it had very different meanings for different people.
>
> But my clients kept pushing me toward its consideration. It cropped up so frequently in therapeutic interviews. "I can't be my real self;" "I think that underneath I have a solid self, if I could get to it;" "I don't understand my self;" "With my mother, I never show my true self;" "I'm always afraid that if I uncover the real me, I'll find there is nothing there." Clearly, it was important to find a way of defining, of thinking about, the self. But how? (1986c, p. 1)

Rogers eventually found an answer in William Stephenson's Q-sort technique. It was possible to study "the self as perceived by the individual," with items such as "I am assertive," "I feel inadequate," or "I am a responsible person." One hundred such items were sorted by the client into nine piles in a continuum from "most like me" to "least like me." This method allowed for quantified descriptions of self-concept and correlations between perceived self before and after therapy, between perceived self and ideal self, and so on.

After the formulation of "the necessary and sufficient conditions of constructive personality change" (Rogers, 1957), considerable research was generated on the measurement of empathy, congruence, and unconditional positive regard and their effects on the outcome of psychotherapy. In the early 1970s, the relationship of outcome to the provision of person-centered conditions was generally regarded as impressive (Bergin & Garfield, 1971). By the late 1970s, some psychotherapy researchers concluded that the "potency and generalizability" of the earlier evidence were "not as great as once thought" (Mitchell, Bozarth, & Krauft, 1977). More recently, Patterson (1984), Raskin (1985), and Stubbs and Bozarth (1994) have challenged the basis for questioning the strength of the original conclusions.

Through all of these assessments, a consistent finding has been that when the measurement of the therapist-offered conditions is based on client perception rather than external judgment, the relationship to outcome is stronger. Most of this research has utilized the Relationship Inventory (Barrett-Lennard, 1986).

Jerold Bozarth (1998) has summarized research on psychotherapy outcome and the person-centered approach. He states that the following conclusions have emerged from a number of reviews of outcome studies as well as his own three-decades-long inquiry into effective psychotherapy:

1. Effective psychotherapy is primarily predicated upon (a) the relationship between the therapist and the client and (b) the inner and external resources of the client.

2. The type of therapy and technique is largely irrelevant in terms of successful outcome.

3. Training, credentials, and experience of therapists are irrelevant to successful therapy.

4. Clients who receive psychotherapy improve more than clients who do not receive psychotherapy.

5. There is little evidence to support the position that there are specific treatments for particular disabilities.

6. The most consistent of the relationship variables related to effectiveness are the conditions of empathy, genuineness, and unconditional positive regard.

## Treatment

The process of the person-centered approach has been described particularly in the context of individual psychotherapy with adults, its original arena. The broadening of the "client-centered" designation to "person-centered" stemmed from the generalizability of client-centered principles to other areas of human relations.

### Play Therapy

Rogers deeply admired Jessie Taft's play therapy with children at the Philadelphia Child Guidance Clinic and was specifically impressed by her ability to accept the negative feelings verbalized or acted out by the child, which led to positive attitudes in the child.

One of Rogers's graduate student associates, Virginia Axline, formulated play therapy as a comprehensive system of treatment for children. Axline shared Rogers's deep conviction about self-direction and self-actualization and, in addition, was passionate in her interest in helping fearful, inhibited, sometimes abused children to develop the courage to express long-buried emotions and to experience the exhilaration of being themselves. She used play when children could not overcome the obstacles to self-realization by words alone.

Axline made major contributions to research on play therapy, group therapy with children, schoolroom applications, and parent-teacher as well as teacher-administrator relationships. She also demonstrated the value of play therapy for poor readers, for clarifying the diagnosis of mental retardation in children, and for dealing with race conflicts in young children (Axline, 1947; Rogers, 1951).

Ellinwood and Raskin (1993) offer a comprehensive chapter on client-centered play therapy that starts with the principles formulated by Axline and shows how they have evolved into practice with parents and children in the 1990s. Empathy with children and adults, respect for their capacity for self-directed change, and the congruence of the therapist are emphasized and illustrated.

## Client-Centered Group Process

Beginning as a one-to-one method of counseling in the 1940s, client-centered principles were being employed in group therapy, classroom teaching, workshops, organizational development, and concepts of leadership less than 10 years later. Teaching, intensive groups, and peace and conflict resolution exemplify the spread of the principles that originated in counseling and psychotherapy.

## Classroom Teaching

In Columbus, while Rogers was beginning to espouse the nondirective approach, he accepted the role of the expert who structured classes and graded students. At Chicago, he began to practice a new philosophy, which he later articulated in *Freedom to Learn:*

> I ceased to be a teacher. It wasn't easy. It happened rather gradually, but as I began to trust students, I found they did incredible things in their communication with each other, in their learning of content material in the course, in blossoming out as growing human beings. Most of all they gave me courage to be myself more freely, and this led to profound interaction. They told me their feelings, they raised questions I had never thought about. I began to sparkle with emerging ideas that were new and exciting to me, but also, I found, to them. I believe I passed some sort of crucial divide when I was able to begin a course with a statement something like this: "This course has the title 'Personality Theory' (or whatever). But what we do with this course is up to us. We can build it around the goals we want to achieve, within that very general area. We can conduct it the way we want to. We can decide mutually how we wish to handle these bugaboos of exams and grades. I have many resources on tap, and I can help you find others. I believe I am one of the resources, and I am available to you to the extent that you wish. But this is our class. So what do we want to make of it?" This kind of statement said in effect, "We are *free* to learn what we wish, *as* we wish." It made the whole climate of the classroom completely different. Though at the time I had never thought of phrasing it this way, I changed at that point from being *a teacher* and *evaluator,* to being *a facilitator of learning*—a very different occupation. (1983, p. 26)

The change was not easy for Rogers. Nor was it easy for students who were used to being led and experienced the self-evaluation method of grading as strange and unwelcome.

## The Intensive Group

The early 1960s witnessed another important development, the intensive group. Rogers's move to California in 1964 spurred his interest in intensive groups, and, in 1970, he published a 15-step formulation of the development of the basic encounter group.

Rogers visualized the core of the process, the "basic encounter," as occurring when an individual in the group responds with undivided empathy to another in the group who is sharing and also not holding back.

Rogers conceptualized the leader or facilitator's role in the group as exemplifying the same basic qualities as the individual therapist; in addition, he thought it important to accept and respect the group as a whole, as well as the individual members. An outstanding example of the basic encounter group can be seen in the film *Journey into Self,* which shows very clearly the genuineness, spontaneity, caring, and empathic behavior of co-facilitators Rogers and Richard Farson (McGaw, Farson, & Rogers, 1968).

## Peace and Conflict Resolution

Searching for peaceful ways to resolve conflict between larger groups became the cutting edge of the person-centered movement in the 1980s. The scope of the person-centered movement's interest in this arena extends all the way to conflicts between nations. In some instances opposing groups have met in an intensive format with person-centered leadership. This has occurred with parties from Northern Ireland, South Africa, and Central America. A meeting in Austria on the "Central American Challenge" included a significant number of diplomats and other government officials (Rogers, 1986d). A major goal accomplished at this meeting was to provide a model for person-centered experiences for diplomats in the hope that they would be strengthened in future international meetings by an increased capacity to be empathic. Rogers (1987) and his associates also conducted workshops on the person-centered approach in Eastern Europe and the Soviet Union.

Rogers offered a person-centered interpretation of the Camp David Accords and a proposal for avoiding nuclear disaster (Rogers & Ryback, 1984). One notion is central to all these attempts at peaceful conflict resolution: When a group in conflict can receive and operate under conditions of empathy, genuineness, and caring, negative stereotypes of the opposition weaken and are replaced by personal, human feelings of relatedness (Raskin & Zucconi, 1984).

## CASE EXAMPLE [2]

### Introduction

In 1964 Carl Rogers was filmed in a half-hour interview with a female client for a film series, *Three Approaches to Psychotherapy* (Rogers, 1965). That interview contains many of the elements of person-centered therapy discussed in this chapter and is a typical example of the person-centered way of working.

---

[2] This example is borrowed from Meador & Rogers, 1984, pp. 187–192.

Rogers had never seen the woman before the interview and knew his contact with her would be limited to a half-hour. In his introduction to the interview, he describes the way he hopes to be with her. He says he will, if he is fortunate, first of all, be real, try to be aware of his own inner feelings and to express them in ways that will not impose these feelings on her. Second, he hopes he will be caring of her, prizing her as an individual and accepting her. Third, he will try to understand her inner world from the inside; he will try to understand not just the surface meanings, but also the meanings just below the surface. Rogers says if he is successful in holding these three attitudes, he expects certain things to happen to the client. He expects she will move from a remoteness from her inner experiencing to a more immediate awareness and expression of it; from disapproving of parts of her self to greater self-acceptance; from a fear of relating to relating to him more directly; from holding rigid, black-and-white constructs of reality to holding more tentative constructs; and from seeing the locus-of-evaluation outside herself to finding the locus-of-evaluation in her own inner experiencing.

The fact that the interview lasted for only half an hour and the client was seen by the therapist only one time emphasizes that the person-centered approach depends on the here-and-now attitudes of the therapist, attitudes as valid and constant in a brief interaction as over a long period.

## The Interview

The interview is with a young woman, Gloria, a 30-year-old divorcée. The first portion of the interview concerns the problem Gloria presents initially, that she has not been honest with her nine-year-old daughter Pammy about the fact that she has had sexual relationships with men since her divorce. Gloria has always been honest with her children and is feeling great conflict over having lied to Pammy. She wants to know whether telling Pammy the truth about her sexual relationships would affect Pammy adversely.

At the very beginning Gloria tells Rogers, "I almost want an answer from you. I want you to tell me if it would affect her wrong if I told her the truth, or what." Later, on two occasions, she asks again for a direct answer to her question. Clearly, she wants an "authority" to tell her what to do. Rogers's responses assure her that he understands her dilemma and guide her to her own resources for answering. After each time that she asks the question and hears the response, Gloria explores her own feelings a little more deeply.

To her first request, Rogers replies, "And it's this concern about her (Pammy) and the fact that you really aren't—that this open relationship that has existed between you, now you feel it's kind of vanished?" After Gloria's reply, he says, "I sure wish I could give you the answer as to what you should tell her." "I was afraid you were going to say that," she says. Rogers replies, "Because what you really want is an answer."

Gloria begins to explore her relationship with Pammy and concludes that she feels real uncertainty about whether or not Pammy would accept her "devilish" or "shady" side. Gloria finds she is not certain she accepts that part of herself. Again she asks Rogers for an answer: "You're just going to sit there and let me stew in it and I want more." Rogers replies, "No, I don't want to let you just stew in your feelings, but on the other hand, I also feel this is the kind of very private thing that I couldn't possibly answer for you. But I sure as anything will try to help you work toward your own answer. I don't know whether that makes any sense to you, but I mean it." Gloria says she can tell he really does mean it and again begins to explore her feelings, this time focusing more on the conflict she herself feels between her actions and her inner standards. Shortly, she again says, "I want you very much to give me a direct answer."

Rogers replies:

I guess, I am sure this will sound evasive to you, but it seems to me that perhaps the person you are not being fully honest with is you, because I was very much struck by the fact that you were saying, 'If I feel all right about what I have done, whether it's going to bed with a man or what, if I really feel all right about it, then I do not have any concern about what I would tell Pam or my relationship with her.'

To this Gloria answers:

Right. All right. Now I hear what you are saying. Then all right, then I want to work on accepting *me* then. I want to work on feeling all right about it. That makes sense. Then that will come natural and then I won't have to worry about Pammy . . .

This statement indicates that Gloria has assimilated a real insight, an understanding that the solution to her problem is in herself rather than in an authoritative opinion on how knowledge of her sex life will affect Pammy.

From this point in the interview she focuses on her inner conflict. She tells Rogers what she "wishes he would tell her" and then says she can't quite take the risk of being the way she wants to be with her children "unless an authority tells me that." Rogers says with obvious feeling, "I guess one thing that I feel very keenly is that it's an awfully risky thing to live. You'd be taking a chance on your relationship with her and taking a chance on letting her know who you are, really." Gloria says she wishes very strongly that she could take more risks, that she could act on her own feelings of rightness without always needing encouragement from others. Again she says what she'd like to do in the situation with Pammy, and then adds, "Now I feel like 'Now that's solved'—and, I didn't even solve a thing; but I feel relieved."

> *Gloria:* I do feel like you have been saying to me—you are not giving me advice, but I do feel like you are saying, "You know what pattern you want to follow, Gloria, and go ahead and follow it." I sort of feel a backing up from you.
> *Rogers:* I guess the way I sense it, you've been telling me that you know what you want to do, and yes, I do believe in backing up people in what they want to do. It's a little different slant than the way it seems to you.

Gloria's expressing the feeling, "Now that's solved—and I didn't even solve a thing; but I feel relieved," exemplifies an awareness of inner experiencing, a felt meaning she has not yet put into words. She "feels relieved," as though her problem is solved. Therapeutic movement has occurred in her inner self before she understands its explicit meaning. It is interesting that she says in the same speech, "I feel a backing up from you." She *feels* the support of Rogers's empathic understanding and acceptance of her. From the person-centered point of view there is a relationship between her feeling understood and valued and her movement from seeking the locus-of-evaluation outside herself to depending on her own inner feeling of "rightness" for a solution to her problem.

The next portion of the interview involves Gloria's experience of her own inner valuing processes and the conflicts she sometimes feels. She explains her use of the word *utopia,* which refers to times she is able to follow her inner feelings: "When I do follow a feeling and I feel this good feeling inside of me, that's sort of utopia. That's what I mean. That's the way I like to feel whether it's a bad thing or a good thing. But I feel right about me." Rogers's response that in those moments she must feel "all in one piece" brings tears to Gloria's eyes, for those moments are all too few. In the midst of her weeping, she continues speaking.

> *Gloria:* You know what else I was just thinking? I . . . a dumb thing . . . that all of a sudden while I was talking to you, I thought, "Gee, how nice I can talk to you and

I want you to approve of me and I respect you, but I miss that my father couldn't talk to me like you are." I mean, I'd like to say, "Gee, I'd like you for my father." I don't even know why that came to me.

*Rogers:* You look to me like a pretty nice daughter. But you really do miss that fact that you couldn't be open with your own Dad.

Gloria is now quite close to her inner experiencing, allowing her tears to flow as she thinks of her rare moments of "utopia" and then expressing a feeling that comes into awareness of positive affection for Rogers. She then explores her relationship with her father, as she says, "You know, when I talk about it, it feels more flip. If I just sit still a minute, it feels like a great big hurt down there."

Gloria looks at and feels her deep inner hurt over her relationship to her father. She has moved significantly from seeking a solution outside herself to a problem with her children to looking inward at a painful hurt. She says she tries to soothe the hurt through relationships with fatherly men, pretending they are her father, as she is doing with Rogers.

*Rogers:* I don't feel that's pretending.
*Gloria:* Well, you're not really my father.
*Rogers:* No. I meant about the real close business.
*Gloria:* Well, see, I sort of feel that's pretending too, because I can't expect you to feel very close to me. You don't know me that well.
*Rogers:* All I can know is what I am feeling, and that is I feel close to you in this moment.

Here Rogers presents himself as he really is, offering Gloria the experience of genuine caring, an experience she missed in her relationship with her father. Shortly after this exchange, the interview ends.

## Evaluation

It is clear that the therapist's empathy, genuineness, and caring come through and are received by the client throughout the course of the interview. His acceptance helps her make important progress. For instance, she begins the interview looking for an authority to tell her what to do, and by its end has much greater faith in her own ability to make decisions. She moves from trying to keep some distance from her emotions to letting them be expressed without inhibition, going so far as to focus directly on the great hurt she feels about her relationship with her father. She also starts off not accepting part of herself, and then sees greater self-acceptance as an important task for future work. Her self-concept becomes more complete, her experiencing becomes less rigid, her locus-of-evaluation moves from external to more internal, and her self-regard increases. All the important qualities of the therapist and client are revealed in this brief interview.

The intensity of Rogers's genuineness and presence in the relationship is readily apparent from watching the film. The strength of his feelings comes through when he says, "It's an awfully risky thing to live," and when he clearly expresses his inner self: "All I can know is what I am feeling, and that is I feel close to you in this moment."

The therapeutic movement the client makes follows the direction and manner that Rogers initially predicted. First, he predicted she would move from a remoteness from her feelings to an immediate awareness and expression of them. She does in fact begin the interview wanting an answer to a troubling question and does move to a point toward the end where her feelings are flowing into awareness and she is expressing them as they occur. At one point she says, concerning her wanting a father like Rogers, "I don't even know why that came to me." She is allowing her feelings to come into expression without censoring, questioning, or even knowing where they are coming from.

Rogers also predicted that Gloria would move from disapproving of herself toward self-acceptance. In the beginning, Gloria says she is not sure she accepts her "shady" or "devilish" side. Later, she very explicitly asks to work on accepting herself and spends much of the remaining time exploring the nuances of her self-acceptance.

Initially, Gloria believes there is a true answer that will solve her problem. She construes reality in this black-and-white fashion. Later, she tentatively considers relying on her own inner experiencing for solutions as she says, "I wish I could take more risks." Finally, she describes the utopian experience of feeling so sure of herself that whatever she does comes out of her inner experience and feels "right." This same example demonstrates the therapeutic process of moving from finding the locus-of-evaluation outside oneself to finding it in one's inner self.

The quality of this interview is like a piece of music that begins on a thin persistent note and gradually adds dimension and levels until the whole orchestra is playing. The intuitive interaction and response of the therapist are not unlike the interplay in a creative improvisation. Whatever wisdom science can bring to how the instruments are made and which combinations make for harmony and growth will greatly enrich the players, but we must never lose sight of the primacy of the creative human beings making the music.

As a result of countless inquiries about Gloria from people who had viewed his interview with her, Rogers (1984) published a historical note in which he stated that for about 10 years after the interview, Gloria wrote to him approximately once or twice a year. Her last letter was written "shortly before her untimely death" 15 years following the interview. He also described her reactions at a weekend conference led by him a year or more after the interview, during which her interviews with Rogers and with Fritz Perls and Albert Ellis were shown. She expressed much anger about the fact that she had done all the things Perls had asked her to do and that she had given over her power to him. Having seen the interview at this point, she did not like it, which contrasted with her positive reaction soon after the interview.

Rogers also described Gloria's request, at the end of a luncheon with him and his wife, Helen, during the same weekend, that they allow her to think of them as "parents in spirit," parents she would have liked to have had. "We each replied that we would be pleased and honored to have that status in her life. Her warm feelings for us were reciprocated. . . . In the ensuing years she wrote me about many things in her life. . . . There were very good times, and there were tragic times . . . and she showed sensitivity, wisdom, and courage in meeting the different aspects of her experience." Rogers concludes, "I am awed by the fact that this 15-year association grew out of the quality of the relationship we formed in one 30-minute period in which we truly met as persons. It is good to know that even one half-hour can make a difference in a life" (pp. 423–425).

## SUMMARY

The central hypothesis of the person-centered approach is that individuals have within themselves vast resources for self-understanding and for altering their self-concepts, behavior, and attitudes toward others. These resources will become operative in a definable, facilitative, psychological climate. Such a climate is created by a psychotherapist who is empathic, caring, and genuine.

*Empathy,* as practiced in the person-centered approach, refers to a consistent, unflagging appreciation of the experience of the client. It involves a continuous process of checking with the client to see if understanding is complete and accurate. It is carried out in a manner that is personal, natural, and free-flowing; it is not a mechanical kind of reflection or mirroring. *Caring* is characterized by a profound respect for the individuality of the client and by unconditional, nonpossessive regard. *Genuineness* is marked by congruence between what the therapist feels and says, and by the therapist's willingness to relate on a person-to-person basis rather than through a professionally distant role.

The impetus given to psychotherapy research by the person-centered approach has resulted in substantial evidence demonstrating that changes in personality and behavior occur when a therapeutic climate is provided. Two frequent results of successful person-centered therapy are increased self-esteem and greater openness to experience.

Trust in the perceptions and the self-directive capacities of clients expanded client-centered therapy into a person-centered approach to education, group process, organizational development, and conflict resolution.

When Carl Rogers began his journey in 1940, psychotherapy was a field dominated by individuals who practiced in a manner that encouraged a view of themselves as experts. Rogers created a way of helping in which the therapist was a facilitator of a process that was directed by the client. More than half a century later, the person-centered approach remains unique in the magnitude of its trust of the client.

# ANNOTATED BIBLIOGRAPHY

Barrett-Lennard, G. T. (1998). *Carl Rogers's helping system: Journey and substance.* London: Sage Publications.
A comprehensive and scholarly presentation of the person-centered approach to psychotherapy and human relations. It starts with the beginnings of client-centered therapy and the social-political-economic milieu of the 1920s and 1930s and continues with a description of early practice and theory, detailed examinations of the helping interview and the course of therapy, applications to work with children and families, to groups, education, conflict resolution and the building of community, research and training; it concludes with a retrospective and prospective look at this system of helping.

Bozarth, J. (1998). *Person-centered therapy: A revolutionary paradigm.* Ross-on-Wye, UK: PCCS Books.
A collection of 20 revised and new papers by one of the movement's outstanding teachers and theoreticians. It is divided into sections: Theory and Philosophy, The Basics of Practice, Applications of Practice, Research, and Implications. The book reflects upon Carl Rogers's theoretical foundations, emphasizes the revolutionary nature of these foundations, and offers extended frames for understanding this radical approach to therapy.

Rogers, C. R. (1951). *Client-centered therapy.* Boston: Houghton Mifflin.
This book describes the orientation of the therapist, the therapeutic relationship as experienced by the client, and the process of therapy. It expands and de-velops the ideas expressed in the earlier book *Counseling and Psychotherapy* (1942).

Rogers, C. R. (1961). *On becoming a person.* Boston: Houghton Mifflin.
Perhaps Rogers's best-known work, this book helped to make his personal style and positive philosophy known globally. The book includes an autobiographical chapter and sections on the helping relationship; the ways in which people grow in therapy; the fully functioning person; the place of research; the implications of client-centered principles for education, family life, communication, and creativity; and the impact on the individual of the growing power of the behavioral sciences.

Rogers, C. R. (1980). *A way of being.* Boston: Houghton Mifflin.
As the book jacket states, this volume "encompasses the changes that have occurred in Dr. Rogers's life and thought during the decade of the seventies in much the same way *On Becoming a Person* covered an earlier period of his life. The style is direct, personal, clear—the style that attracted so many readers to the earlier book." There is a large personal section, including chapters on what it means to Rogers to listen and to be heard and one on his experience of growing as he becomes older (he was 78 when the book was published), as well as important theoretical chapters. An appendix contains a chronological bibliography of Rogers's publications from 1930 to 1980.

# CASE READINGS

Ellis, J., & Zimring, F. (1994). Two therapists and a client. *Person-Centered Journal, 1*(2), 77–92.
This article contains the transcripts of short interviews by two therapists with the same client. Because eight years intervened between the interviews, these type-scripts permit a glimpse of the changes in the client over the period, as well as allowing for the comparison of the style and effect of two client-centered therapists.

Raskin, N. J. (1996). The case of Loretta: A psychiatric in-patient. In B. A. Farber, D. C. Brink, & P. M. Raskin, *The psychotherapy of Carl Rogers: Cases and commentary* (pp. 33–56). New York: Guilford.
This is one of the few verbatim recordings of a therapy interview with a psychotic patient, and it provides a concrete example of the application of client-centered therapy to a psychiatric inpatient diagnosed as para-

noid schizophrenic. The interview shows a deeply disturbed individual responding positively to the therapist-offered conditions of empathy, congruence, and unconditional positive regard. It is especially dramatic because another patient can be heard screaming in the background while the interview is taking place.

Rogers, C. R. (1942). The case of Herbert Bryan. In C. R. Rogers, *Counseling and psychotherapy* (pp. 261–437). Boston: Houghton Mifflin.

This may be the first publication of a completely recorded and transcribed case of individual psychotherapy that illustrates the new nondirective approach. Rogers provides a summary of the client's feelings after each interview and additional commentary.

Rogers, C. R. (1967). A silent young man. In C. R. Rogers, G. T. Gendlin, D. V. Kiesler, & C. Truax (Eds.), *The therapeutic relationship and its impact: A study of psychotherapy with schizophrenics* (pp. 401–406). Madison: University of Wisconsin Press.

This case consists of two transcribed interviews that were conducted by Rogers as part of a year-long treatment of a very withdrawn hospitalized schizophrenic patient who was part of a client-centered research project on client-centered therapy with a schizophrenic population.

# REFERENCES

Ansbacher, H. L. (1977). Individual psychology. In R. J. Corsini (Ed.), *Current psychotherapies.* Itasca, IL: F. E. Peacock.

Axline, V. M. (1947). *Play therapy.* Boston: Houghton Mifflin.

Barrett-Lennard, G. T. (1962). Dimensions of therapist response as causal factors in therapeutic change. *Psychological Monographs, 76,* 1–33.

Barrett-Lennard, G. T. (1986). The relationship inventory now: Issues and advances in theory, method, and use. In L. S. Greenberg & W. M. Pinsof (Eds.), *The psychotherapeutic process: A research handbook* (pp. 439–476). New York: Guilford.

Bergin, A. E., & Garfield, S. L. (Eds.). (1971). *Handbook of psychotherapy and behavior change: An empirical analysis.* New York: Wiley.

Bozarth, J. D. (1998). *Person-centered therapy: A revolutionary paradigm.* Ross-on-Wye, UK: PCCS Books.

Brodley, B. T. (1993). Some observations of Carl Rogers's behavior in therapy interviews. *Person-Centered Journal, 1*(1), 37–47.

Brodley, B. T. (1999). Reasons for responses expressing the therapist's frame of reference in client-centered therapy. *Person-Centered Journal, 6*(1), 4–27.

Butler, J. M., & Haigh, G. V. (1954). Changes in the relation between self-concepts and ideal concepts consequent upon client-centered counseling. In C. R. Rogers & R. F. Dymond (Eds.), *Psychotherapy and personality change* (pp. 55–75). Chicago: University of Chicago Press.

Cartwright, D. S. (1957). Annotated bibliography of research and theory construction in client-centered therapy. *Journal of Counseling Psychology, 4,* 82–100.

Ellinwood, C. G., & Raskin, N. J. (1993). Client-centered/humanistic psychotherapy. In T. R. Kratochwill & R. J. Morris (Eds.), *Handbook of psychotherapy with children and adolescents* (pp. 258–287). Boston: Allyn & Bacon.

Gendlin, E. T. (1961). Experiencing: A variable in the process of therapeutic change. *American Journal of Psychotherapy, 15,* 233–245.

Goldstein, K. (1934/1959). *The organism: A holistic approach to biology derived from psychological data in man.* New York: American Book. (Originally published in 1934.)

Holdstock, T. L., & Rogers, C. R. (1983). Person-centered theory. In R. J. Corsini & A. J. Marsella (Eds.), *Personality theories, research and assessment.* Itasca, IL: F. E. Peacock.

Lietaer, G., Rombauts, J., & Van Balen, R. (1990). *Client-centered and experiential psychotherapy in the nineties.* Leuven, Belgium: Leuven University Press.

Maslow, A. H. (1968). *Toward a psychology of being* (2nd ed.). Princeton, NJ: Van Nostrand.

Matson, F. W. (1969). Whatever became of the Third Force? *American Association of Humanistic Psychology Newsletter, 6*(1), 1, 14–15.

McGaw, W. H., Farson, R. E., & Rogers, C. R. (Producers). (1968). *Journey into self* [Film]. Berkeley: University of California Extension Media Center.

Meador, B. D., & Rogers, C. R. (1984). Person-centered therapy. In R. J. Corsini (Ed.), *Current psychotherapies* (3rd ed.) (pp. 142–195). Itasca, IL: F E. Peacock.

Mitchell, K. M., Bozarth, J. D., & Krauft, C. C. (1977). A reappraisal of the therapeutic effectiveness of accurate empathy, non-possessive warmth, and genuineness. In A. S. Gurman & A. M. Razin (Eds.), *Effective psychotherapy: A handbook of research* (pp. 482–502). New York: Pergamon Press.

Orlinsky, D. E. & Howard, K. L. (1978). The relation of process to outcome in psychotherapy. In S. L. Garfield & A. E. Bergin (Eds.), *Handbook of psychotherapy and behavior change: An empirical analysis* (2nd ed.) (pp. 283–329). New York: Wiley.

Patterson, C. H. (1984). Empathy, warmth, and genuineness in psychotherapy: A review of reviews. *Psychotherapy, 21,* 431–438.

Porter, E. H., Jr. (1943). The development and evaluation of a measure of counseling interview procedures. *Educational and Psychological Measurement, 3,* 105–126, 215–238.

Raimy, V. C. (1948). Self-reference in counseling interviews. *Journal of Consulting Psychology, 12,* 153–163.

Rank, O. (1945). *Will therapy, truth and reality.* New York: Knopf.

Raskin, N. J. (1947). *The nondirective attitude.* Unpublished paper.

Raskin, N. J. (1948). The development of nondirective therapy. *Journal of Consulting Psychology, 12,* 92–110.

Raskin, N. J. (1952). An objective study of the locus-of-evaluation factor in psychotherapy. In W. Wolfe & J. A. Precker (Eds.), *Success in psychotherapy* (pp. 143–162). New York: Grune & Stratton.

Raskin, N. J. (1974). *Studies of psychotherapeutic orientation: Ideology and practice.* Research Monograph No. 1. Orlando, FL: American Academy of Psychotherapists.

Raskin, N. J. (1985). Client-centered therapy. In S. J. Lynn and J. P. Garske (Eds.), *Contemporary psychotherapies: Models and methods* (pp. 155–190). Columbus, OH: Charles F. Merrill.

Raskin, N. J. (1996). Person-centered psychotherapy: Twenty historical steps. In W. Dryden (Ed.), *Developments in psychotherapy: Historical perspectives.* London: Sage Publications.

Raskin, N. J. (2001). The history of empathy in the client-centered movement. In S. Haugh & T. Merry (Eds.), *Rogers' therapeutic condition,* Vol. 2: Empathy (pp. 1–15). Ross-on-Wye, UK: PCCS Books.

Raskin, N. J., & Zucconi, A. (1984). *Peace, conflict resolution, and the person-centered approach.* Program presented at the annual convention of the American Psychological Association, Toronto.

Rogers, C. R. (1931). *Measuring personality adjustment in children nine to thirteen.* New York: Teachers College, Columbia University, Bureau of Publications.

Rogers, C. R. (1939). *The clinical treatment of the problem child.* Boston: Houghton Mifflin.

Rogers, C. R. (1940). The process of therapy. *Journal of Consulting Psychology, 4,* 161–164.

Rogers, C. R. (1942). *Counseling and psychotherapy.* Boston: Houghton Mifflin.

Rogers, C. R. (1946). Significant aspects of client-centered therapy. *American Psychologist, 1,* 415–422.

Rogers, C. R. (1947). Some observations on the organization of personality. *American Psychologist, 2,* 358–368.

Rogers, C. R. (1951). *Client-centered therapy.* Boston: Houghton Mifflin.

Rogers, C. R. (1957). The necessary and sufficient conditions of therapeutic personality change. *Journal of Consulting Psychology, 21,* 95–103.

Rogers, C. R. (1959a). The essence of psychotherapy: A client-centered view. *Annals of Psychotherapy, 1,* 51–57.

Rogers, C. R. (1959b). A theory of therapy, personality and interpersonal relationships as developed in the client-centered framework. In S. Koch (Ed.), *Psychology: A study of science: Formulations of the person and the social context* (pp. 184–256). New York: McGraw-Hill.

Rogers, C. R. (1965). Client-centered therapy. Part I. In E. Shostrom (Ed.), *Three approaches to psychotherapy.* Santa Ana, CA: Psychological Films.

Rogers, C. R. (1977). *Carl Rogers on personal power.* New York: Delacorte Press.

Rogers, C. R. (1980). *A way of being.* Boston: Houghton Mifflin.

Rogers, C. R. (1983). *Freedom to learn for the 80s.* Columbus, OH: Charles E. Merrill.

Rogers, C. R. (1984). A historical note—Gloria. In R. F. Levant & J. M. Shlien (Eds.), *Client-centered therapy and the person-centered approach* (pp. 423–425). New York: Praeger.

Rogers, C. R. (1986a). Client-centered therapy. In I. L. Kutash & A. Wolf (Eds.), *Psychotherapist's casebook: Therapy and technique in practice* (pp. 197–208). San Francisco: Jossey-Bass.

Rogers, C. R. (1986b). The dilemmas of a South African white. *Person-Centered Review, 1,* 15–35.

Rogers, C. R. (1986c). Measuring the self and its changes: A forward step in research. *Archives of Humanistic Psychology, 26,* 1–13.

Rogers, C. R. (1986d). The Rust workshop: A personal overview. *Journal of Humanistic Psychology, 26,* 23–45.

Rogers, C. R. (1987). Inside the world of the Soviet professional. *Journal of Humanistic Psychology, 27,* 277–304.

Rogers, C. R., & Dymond, R. F. (Eds.). (1954). *Psychotherapy and personality change.* Chicago: University of Chicago Press.

Rogers, C. R., Gendlin, G. T., Kiesler, D. V., & Truax, C. (Eds.). (1967). *The therapeutic relationship and its impact: A study of psychotherapy with schizophrenics.* Madison: University of Wisconsin Press.

Rogers, C. R., & Haigh, G. (1983). I walk softly through life. *Voices: The Art and Science of Psychotherapy, 18,* 6–14.

Rogers, C. R., Raskin, N. J., Seeman, J., Sheerer, E. T., Stock, D., Haigh, G., Hoffman, A. E., & Carr, A. C. (1949). A coordinated research in psychotherapy. [Special Issue]. *Journal of Consulting Psychology, 13*(3), 149–153.

Rogers, C. R., & Ryback, D. (1984). One alternative to nuclear planetary suicide. In R. F. Levant & J. M. Shlien (Eds.), *Client-centered therapy and the person-centered approach: New directions in theory, research, and practice* (pp. 400–422). New York: Praeger.

Rogers, C. R., & Sanford, R. C. (1985). Client-centered psychotherapy. In H. I. Kaplan, B. J. Sadock, & A. M. Friedman (Eds.), *Comprehensive textbook of psychiatry* (4th ed.) (pp. 1374–1388). Baltimore: William & Wilkins,

Seeman, J. (1959). Toward a concept of personality integration. *American Psychologist, 14,* 794–797.

Seeman, J. (1984). The fully functioning person: Theory and research. In R. R. Levant & J. M. Shlien (Eds.), *Client-centered therapy and the person-centered approach: New directions in theory, research, and practice* (pp. 131–152). New York: Praeger.

Sheerer, E. T. (1949). An analysis of the relationship between acceptance of and respect for others in ten counseling cases. *Journal of Consulting Psychology, 13,* 169–175.

Shlien, J. M. (1964). Comparison of results with different forms of psychotherapy. *American Journal of Psychotherapy, 28,* 15–22.

Standal, S. (1954). The need for positive regard: A contribution to client-centered theory. Unpublished Ph.D. dissertation, University of Chicago.

Stephenson, W. V. (1953). *The study of behavior.* Chicago: University of Chicago Press.

Streich, E. R. (1951). The self-experience of the client-centered therapist. Unpublished paper, The University of Chicago Counseling Center.

Stubbs, J. P., & Bozarth, J. D. (1994). The dodo bird revisited: A qualitative study of psychotherapy efficacy research. *Journal of Applied and Preventive Psychology, 3,* 109–120.

Zimring, F. M., & Raskin, N. J. (1992). Carl Rogers and client/person-centered therapy. In D. K. Freedheim (Ed.), *History of psychotherapy: A century of change* (pp. 629–656). Washington, DC: American Psychological Association.

Courtesy of Dr. Albert Ellis, Albert Ellis Institute

Albert Ellis

# 6    RATIONAL EMOTIVE BEHAVIOR THERAPY

*Albert Ellis*

## OVERVIEW

*Rational emotive behavior therapy (REBT),* a theory of personality and a method of psychotherapy developed in the 1950s by Albert Ellis, a clinical psychologist, holds that when a highly charged emotional consequence (C) follows a significant activating event (A), event A may seem to, but actually does not, cause C. Instead, emotional consequences are largely created by B—the individual's *belief system.* When an undesirable emotional consequence occurs, such as severe anxiety, this usually involves the person's irrational beliefs, and when these beliefs are effectively disputed (at point D), by challenging them rationally and behaviorally, the disturbed consequences are reduced. From its inception, REBT has viewed cognition and emotion integratively, with thought, feeling, desires, and action interacting with each other. It is therefore a comprehensive cognitive-affective-behavioral theory and practice of psychotherapy (Ellis, 1962, 1994; Ellis & Dryden, 1997; Ellis & MacLaren, 1998).

Formerly known as rational emotive therapy (RET), this approach is more accurately referred to as rational emotive behavior therapy (REBT). From the beginning, REBT considered the importance of both mind and body, or of thinking/feeling/wanting (contents of the mind according to psychology) and of behavior (the operations of the body). It has stressed that personality change can occur in both directions: therapists can talk with people and attempt to change their minds so that they will behave differently, or they can help clients to change their behaviors and thus modify their thinking. As stated in several early writings on REBT that are reprinted in *The Albert Ellis Reader* (Ellis & Blau, 1998), REBT theory states that humans rarely change a profound self-defeating belief unless they *act* against it. Thus, it is most accurately called rational emotive behavior therapy.

## Basic Concepts

The main propositions of REBT can be described as follows:

1.  People are born with a potential to be rational (self-constructive) as well as irrational (self-defeating). They have predispositions to be self-preserving, to think about their thinking, to be creative, to be sensuous, to be interested in other people, to learn by mistakes, and to actualize their potentials for life and growth. They also tend to be self-destructive, to be short-range hedonists, to avoid thinking things through, to procrastinate, to repeat the same mistakes, to be superstitious, to be intolerant, to be perfectionistic and grandiose, and to avoid actualizing their potential for growth.

2.  People's tendency to irrational thinking, self-damaging habituations, wishful thinking, and intolerance is frequently exacerbated by their culture and their family group. Their suggestibility (or conditionability) is greatest during their early years, because they are dependent upon and are highly influenced by family and social pressures.

3.  Humans perceive, think, emote, and behave simultaneously. They are, therefore, at one and the same time cognitive, conative, and motoric. They rarely act without implicit thinking. Their sensations and actions are viewed in a framework of prior experiences, memories, and conclusions. People seldom emote without thinking, because their feelings include, and are usually triggered by, an appraisal of a given situation and its importance. People rarely act without perceiving, thinking, and emoting, because these processes provide reasons for acting. Just as "normal" human behavior is a function of malfunctioning, it is usually desirable to use a variety of perceptual-cognitive, emotive-evocative, and behavioralistic-reeducative methods (Bernard & Wolfe, 1993; Ellis, 1962, 1994, 2001a, 2001b, 2002, 2003a; Walen, DiGiuseppe, & Dryden, 1992).

4.  Although all the major psychotherapies employ a variety of cognitive, emotive, and behavioral techniques, and although all (including unscientific methods such as witch doctoring) may help individuals who have faith in them, they are probably not equally effective or efficient. Highly cognitive, active-directive, homework-assigning, and discipline-oriented therapies such as REBT are likely to be more effective, usually in briefer periods, and with fewer sessions.

5.  Rational emotive behavior therapists do not believe a warm relationship between client and counselor is a necessary or a sufficient condition for effective personality change, though it is quite desirable. They stress unconditional acceptance of and close collaboration with clients but also actively encourage them to unconditionally accept themselves with their inevitable fallibility. In addition, therapists may use a variety of practical methods, including didactic discussion, behavior modification, bibliotherapy, audiovisual aids, and activity-oriented homework assignments. To discourage clients from becoming unduly dependent, therapists often use hardheaded methods of convincing them that they had better resort to self-discipline and self-direction.

6.  Rational emotive behavior therapy uses role-playing, assertion training, desensitization, humor, operant conditioning, suggestion, support, and a whole bag of other "tricks." As Arnold Lazarus points out in his "multimodal" therapy, such wide-ranging

methods are effective in helping clients achieve deep-seated cognitive change. REBT is not just oriented toward symptom removal, except when it seems that this is the only kind of change likely to be accomplished. It is designed to help people examine and change some of their basic values—particularly those that keep them disturbed. If clients seriously fear failing on the job, REBT does not merely help them to give up this particular symptom, but also tries to show them how to minimize their basic "awfulizing" tendencies. The usual goal of REBT is to help people reduce their underlying symptom-creating propensities. There are two basic forms of rational emotive behavior therapy: (a) general REBT, which is almost synonymous with cognitive-behavior therapy; and (b) preferential REBT, which includes general REBT but which also emphasizes a profound philosophic change. General REBT tends to teach clients rational or healthy behaviors. Preferential REBT teaches them how to dispute irrational ideas and unhealthy behaviors and to become more creative, scientific, and skeptical thinkers.

7.    REBT holds that most neurotic problems involve unrealistic, illogical, self-defeating thinking and that if disturbance-creating ideas are vigorously disputed by logico-empirical and pragmatic thinking, they can be minimized. No matter how defective people's heredity may be, and no matter what trauma they may have experienced, the *main* reason they usually now overreact or underreact to adversities (at point A) is that they *now* have some dogmatic, irrational, unexamined beliefs (at point B). Because these beliefs are unrealistic, they will not withstand rational scrutiny. They are often deifications and devilifications of themselves and others and tend to wane when empirically checked, logically disputed, and shown to be impractical. Thus, a woman with severe emotional difficulties does not merely believe it is undesirable if her lover rejects her. She tends to believe, also, that (a) it is awful; (b) she cannot stand it; (c) she should not, must not be rejected; (d) she will never be accepted by a desirable partner; (e) she is a worthless person because one lover has rejected her; and (f) she deserves to be rejected for being so worthless. Such common covert hypotheses are illogical, unrealistic, and destructive. They can be revealed and disputed by a rational emotive behavior therapist who shows clients how to think more flexibly and scientifically, and the rational-emotive therapist is partly that: an exposing and skeptical scientist.

8.    REBT shows how activating events or adversities (A) in people's lives contribute to but do not directly "cause" emotional consequences (C); these consequences stem from people's interpretations of these events—their unrealistic and overgeneralized beliefs (B) about them. The "real" cause of upsets, therefore, mainly lies in people and not in what happens to them (even though gruesome experiences obviously have considerable influence over what people think and feel).

REBT provides clients with several powerful insights. Insight number 1 is that a person's self-defeating behavior usually follows from the interaction of A (adversity) and B (belief about A). Disturbed consequences (C) therefore usually follow the formula $A \times B = C$.

Insight number 2 is the understanding that although people have become emotionally disturbed (or have *made* themselves disturbed) in the past, they are *now* upset because they keep indoctrinating themselves with similar constructed beliefs. These beliefs do not continue because people were once "conditioned" and so now hold them "automatically." No! People still, here and now, actively reinforce them, and their present active self-propagandizations and constructions keep them alive. Unless they fully admit and face their own responsibilities for the continuation of their dysfunctional beliefs, it is unlikely they will uproot them.

Insight number 3 acknowledges that *only hard work and practice* will correct irrational beliefs—and keep them corrected. Insights 1 and 2 are not enough! Commitment to repeated rethinking of irrational beliefs and repeated actions designed to undo them will likely extinguish or minimize them.

9.    Historically, psychology was considered an S-R science, with the S meaning stimulus and the R meaning response. Later, it became evident that similar stimuli produced different responses in different people. This meant that there presumably was something between the S and the R that was responsible for variations.

An analogy may be helpful. If you hit the same billiard ball from the same spot with exactly the same force and let it bounce off the side of the billiard table, that ball will always come back to exactly the same spot. Otherwise, no one would play billiards. Therefore, hitting the billiard ball is the S (stimulus), and the movement of the ball is the R (response). However, let us suppose that inside a billiard ball was a little person who could control to some degree the direction and force of the ball after it was hit. Then it could move in different directions because the ball could be directed to different locations.

Exactly this concept came into scrutiny in psychology in the late 1800s because of the conceptualization of James McKeen Cattell, an American psychologist studying with Wilhelm Wundt in Leipzig, Germany. In so doing, he started an entirely different kind of psychology known as *idiographic psychology,* whereas the prior psychology that Wundt and his students were working on is known as *nomothetic psychology.*

Wundt and his followers were looking for average behavior, or S-R behavior, and were discounting individual variations. The truth was, according to them, the average. Cattell disagreed, and he started a new kind of psychology known as *individual differences.* As a result, the S-R concept changed to S-O-R. The O stood for organism, but what it really meant was that the ball (or the person) had a mind of its own, and it did not go precisely where a ball that had no mind of its own would go, because O had some degree of independence.

REBT has precisely the same concept. RE represents the contents of the mind: Rationality and Emotions; and it is these that REBT therapists attempt to reach, to change people's thinking and feelings (let us call the combination the *philosophy* of a person), with the goal of permitting them to change their behavior through having a new understanding and a new set of feelings about self and others. By showing their clients how to combine thinking and feeling, REBT therapists have given the little man in the billiard ball the ability to change directions. So when the ball is hit again (an event that previously would have generated a particular reaction), the ball no longer goes where it used to go.

In REBT, we want to empower individuals, by changing their thinking and feelings, to act differently—in a manner desired by the clients, by the therapist, and by society. At the same time, REBT encourages people to act differently—this is where the B (for behavior) comes in—and thereby to think and feel differently. The interaction goes both ways! Thinking, feeling, and behaving seem to be separate human processes, but as Ellis said in his first paper on REBT in 1956, they actually go together holistically and inevitably influence each other. When you think, you feel and act; when you feel, you think and act; and when you act, you think and feel. That is why REBT uses many cognitive, emotive, and behavioral methods to help clients change their disturbances.

## Other Systems

REBT differs from psychoanalytic schools of psychotherapy by eschewing free association, compulsive gathering of material about the client's history, and most dream analysis. It is not concerned with the presumed sexual origins of disturbance or with the Oedipus complex. When transference does occur in therapy, the rational therapist is likely to attack it, showing clients that transference phenomena tend to arise from the irrational belief that they must be loved by the therapist (and others). Although REBT practitioners are much closer to modern neoanalytic schools, such as those of Karen Horney, Erich Fromm, Harry Stack Sullivan, and Franz Alexander, than to the Freudian school, they employ considerably more persuasion, philosophical analysis, homework activity assignments, and other directive techniques than practitioners of these schools.

REBT overlaps significantly with Adlerian theory, but departs from the Adlerian practices of stressing early childhood memories and insisting that social interest is the heart of therapeutic effectiveness. REBT is more specific than Adler's Individual Psychology in disclosing, analyzing, and disputing clients' concrete internalized beliefs and is closer in this respect to general semantic theory and philosophical analysis than to Individual Psychology. It is also much more behavioral than Adlerian therapy.

Adler (1931, 1964) contended that people have basic fictional premises and goals and that they generally proceed quite logically on the basis of these false hypotheses. REBT, on the other hand, holds that people, when disturbed, may have both irrational premises and illogical deductions from these premises. Thus, in Individual Psychology, a male who has the unrealistic premise that he *should* be the king of the universe, but actually has only mediocre abilities, is shown that he is "logically" concluding that he is an utterly inferior person. But in REBT this same individual, with the same irrational premise, is shown that in addition to his "logical" deduction he may also be making several other illogical conclusions, for example, (1) he should be king of the universe because he was once king of his own family; (2) his parents will be impressed by him only if he is outstandingly achieving and *therefore* he must achieve outstandingly; (3) if he cannot be the king of the universe, he might as well do nothing and get nowhere in life; and (4) he deserves to suffer for not being the noble king that he should be.

REBT has much in common with parts of the Jungian therapeutic outlook, especially in that it views clients holistically, holds that the goals of therapy include growth and achievement of potential as well as relief of disturbed symptoms, and emphasizes enlightened individuality. However, REBT deviates radically from Jungian treatment because Jungians are preoccupied with dreams, fantasies, symbol productions, and the mythological or archetypal contents of their clients' thinking—most of which the REBT practitioner deems a waste of time.

REBT is in close agreement with person-centered or relationship therapy in some ways: they both emphasize what Carl Rogers (1961) calls *unconditional positive regard* and what in rational-emotive psychology is called *full acceptance* or *tolerance.* Rational therapists differ from Rogerian therapists in that they actively *teach* (1) that blaming is the core of much emotional disturbance; (2) that it leads to dreadful results; (3) that it is possible, although difficult, for humans to learn to avoid rating themselves even while continuing to rate their performances; and (4) that they can give up self-rating by challenging their grandiose (*must*urbatory), self-evaluating assumptions and by deliberately risking (through homework activity assignments) possible failures and rejections. The REBT practitioner is more active-directive and more emotive-evocative than the person-centered practitioner (Ellis, 1962, 2001a, 2001b; Hauck, 1992).

REBT is in many respects an existential, phenomenologically oriented therapy because its goals overlap with the usual existentialist goals of helping clients to define their own freedom, cultivate individuality, live in dialogue with others, accept their experiencing as highly important, be fully present in the immediacy of the moment, and learn to accept limits in life (Ellis, 2001b, 2002). Many who call themselves existential therapists, however, are rather anti-intellectual, prejudiced against the technology of therapy, and confusingly nondirective, while REBT makes much use of incisive logical analysis, clearcut techniques (including behavior modification procedures), and directiveness and teaching by the therapist.

REBT has much in common with behavior modification. Many behavior therapists, however, are mainly concerned with symptom removal and ignore the cognitive aspects of conditioning and deconditioning. REBT is therefore closer to cognitive and multimodal modifiers such as Aaron Beck, Arnold Lazarus, and Donald Meichenbaum.

# HISTORY

## Precursors

The philosophical origins of rational emotive behavior therapy go back to some of the Asian philosophers, such as Confucius, Lao-Tsu, and Buddha, and especially to Epicurus and the Stoic philosophers Epictetus and Marcus Aurelius. Although most early Stoic writings have been lost, their gist has come down to us through Epictetus, who in the first century AD wrote in *The Enchiridion,* "People are disturbed not by things, but by the view which they take of them."

The modern psychotherapist who was the main precursor of REBT was Alfred Adler. "I am convinced," he stated, "that *a person's behavior springs from his ideas*" (1964, italics in original). According to Adler (1964):

> The individual . . . does not relate himself to the outside world in a predetermined manner, as is often assumed. He relates himself always according to his own interpretation of himself and of his present problem. . . . It is his attitude toward life which determines his relationship to the outside world.

Adler (1931) put the A-B-C or S-O-R (Stimulus-Organism-Response) theory of human disturbance neatly: No experience is a cause of success or failure. We do not suffer from the shock of our experiences—the so-called *trauma*—but we make out of them just what suits our purposes. We are self-determined by the meaning we give to our experiences, and it is almost a mistake to view particular experiences as the basis of our future life. Meanings are not determined by situations, but we determine ourselves by the meanings we give to situations. In his first book on Individual Psychology, Adler's motto was *Omnia ex opinione suspense sunt* (Everything depends on opinion).

Another important precursor of REBT was Paul DuBois, who used persuasive forms of psychotherapy. Alexander Herzberg was one of the inventors of homework assignments. Hippolyte Bernheim, Andrew Salter, and a host of other therapists have employed hypnosis and suggestion in a highly active-directive manner. Frederick Thorne created what he called directive therapy. Franz Alexander, Thomas French, John Dollard, Neal Miller, Wilhelm Stekel, and Lewis Wolberg all practiced forms of psychoanalytic psychotherapy that diverged so far from the Freudian therapy that they more properly can be classified in the active-directive therapy column and are in many ways precursors of REBT.

In addition, a large number of individuals during the 1950s, when REBT was first being formulated, independently began to arrive at some theories and methodologies that significantly overlap with the methods outlined by Ellis (1962). These include Eric Berne, Jerome Frank, George Kelly, Abraham Low, E. Lakin Phillips, Julian Rotter, and Joseph Wolpe.

## Beginnings

After practicing psychoanalysis for several years during the late 1940s and early 1950s, Ellis discovered that no matter how much insight his clients gained or how well they seemed to understand events from their early childhood, they rarely lost their symptoms and still retained tendencies to create new ones. He realized that this was because they were not merely indoctrinated with irrational, mistaken ideas of their own worthlessness when they were young, but that they also *constructed* dysfunctional demands on themselves and others and kept *reindoctrinating* themselves with these commands (Ellis, 1962, 2001b, 2002, 2003a, 2004; Ellis & MacLaren, 1998).

Ellis also discovered that as he pressed his clients to surrender their basic irrational premises, they often tended to resist giving up these ideas. This was not, as the Freudians hypothesized, because they hated the therapist, or wanted to destroy themselves, or were still resisting parent images, but because they *naturally,* one might say *normally,* tended to *must*urbate. They insisted (a) that they *must* do well and win others' approval, (b) that other people *must* act considerately and fairly, and (c) that environmental conditions *must* be unfrustrating and gratifying. Ellis concluded that humans are *self-talking, self-evaluating,* and *self-construing.* They frequently take strong preferences, such as desires for love, approval, success, and pleasure, and misleadingly *define* them as needs. They thereby create many of their "emotional" difficulties.

People are not exclusively the products of social learning. Their so-called pathological symptoms are the result of *bio*social processes. *Because they are human,* they tend to have strong, irrational, empirically misleading ideas; and as long as they hold on to these ideas they tend to be what is commonly called "neurotic." These irrational ideologies are not infinitely varied or hard to discover. They can be listed under a few major headings and, once understood, quickly uncovered by REBT analysis.

Ellis also discovered that people's irrational assumptions were so biosocially deep-rooted that weak methods were unlikely to budge them. Passive, nondirective methodologies (such as reflection of feeling and free association) rarely changed them. Warmth and support often helped clients live more "happily" with unrealistic notions. Suggestion or "positive thinking" sometimes enabled them to cover up and live more "successfully" with underlying negative self-evaluations. Abreaction and catharsis frequently helped them to feel better but tended to reinforce rather than eliminate their demands. Classic desensitizing sometimes relieved clients of anxieties and phobias but did not undermine their anxiety-arousing, phobia-creating fundamental meanings and philosophies.

What *did* work effectively, Ellis found, was an active-directive, cognitive-emotive-behavioral attack on major self-defeating "musts" and commands. The essence of effective psychotherapy according to REBT is full tolerance of oneself and of others as *persons,* combined with a campaign against one's self-defeating *ideas, traits,* and *performances.*

As Ellis abandoned his previous psychoanalytic approaches, he obtained better results (Ellis, 1962). Other therapists who began to employ REBT also found that when they switched to its procedures, more progress was made in a few weeks than had been made in months or years of prior treatment (Ellis, 2002; Lyons & Woods, 1991; Walen et al., 1992).

## Current Status

The Albert Ellis Institute, a nonprofit scientific and educational organization, was founded in 1959 to teach the principles of healthy living. With headquarters in New York City and affiliates in several cities in the United States and other countries, it disseminates the rational emotive behavioral approach through (1) adult education courses and workshops in the principles of rational living, (2) postgraduate training programs, (3) moderately priced clinics for individual and group therapy, (4) special books, monographs, pamphlets, audiovisual materials, and the *Journal of Rational-Emotive and Cognitive-Behavior Therapy,* in which the latest developments of REBT are published.

The Institute has a register of hundreds of psychotherapists who have received training in REBT. In addition, thousands of other therapists primarily follow REBT principles, and a still greater number use some major aspects of REBT in their work. Cognitive restructuring, employed by almost all cognitive-behavior therapists today, stems mainly from REBT. But REBT also includes many other emotive and behavioral methods.

## Research Studies

Many researchers have tested the main hypotheses of REBT, and the majority of their findings support central REBT contentions (Hajzler & Bernard, 1991; Lyons & Woods, 1991; McGovern & Silverman, 1984; Silverman, McCarthy, & McGovern, 1992). These research studies show that (1) clients tend to receive more effective help from a highly active-directive approach than from a more passive one; (2) efficient therapy includes activity-oriented homework assignments; (3) people largely choose to disturb themselves and can choose to surrender these disturbances; (4) helping clients modify their beliefs helps them to make significant behavioral changes; and (5) many effective methods of cognitive therapy exist, including modeling, role-playing, skill training, and problem solving.

In addition, hundreds of clinical and research papers present empirical evidence supporting REBT's main theories of personality. Many of these studies are reviewed in Ellis and Whiteley (1979). These studies tend to substantiate the following hypotheses:

1. Human thinking and emotion do not constitute two disparate or different processes, but significantly overlap.

2. Although activating events or adversities (A) significantly contribute to emotional and behavioral consequences (C), people's beliefs (B) about A more importantly and more directly "cause" C.

3. The kinds of things people say to themselves, as well as the form in which they say these things, affect their emotions and behavior and often disturb them.

4. Humans not only think, and think about their thinking, but also think about thinking about their thinking. Whenever they have disturbances at C (consequence) after something unfortunate has happened in their lives at A (adversity), they tend to make C into a new A—to perceive and think about their emotional disturbances and thereby often create new ones.

5. People not only think about what happens to them in words, phrases, and sentences but also by images, fantasies, and dreams. Nonverbal cognitions contribute to their emotions and behaviors and can be used to change such behaviors.

6. Just as cognitions contribute to emotions and actions, emotions also contribute to or "cause" cognitions and actions, and actions contribute to or "cause" cognitions and emotions. When people change one of these three modalities of behaving, they concomitantly tend to change the other two (Ellis, 1994, 1998; Ellis & Dryden, 1997; Ellis & MacLaren, 1998).

# PERSONALITY

## Theories of Personality

### Physiological Basis of Personality

REBT emphasizes the biological aspects of human personality. Obliquely, some other systems do this, too, saying something like this: "Humans are easily influenced by their parents during early childhood and thereafter remain similarly influenced for the rest of their lives, unless some intervention, such as years of psychotherapy, occurs to enable them to give up this early suggestibility and to start thinking much more independently." These psychotherapeutic systems implicitly posit an "environmentalist's" position, which is actually physiologically and genetically based, because only a *special, innately predisposed* kind of person would be so prone to be "environmentally determined."

Although REBT holds that people are born constructivists and have considerable resources for human growth, and that they are in many important ways able to change their social and personal destinies, it also holds that they have powerful innate tendencies to think irrationally and to defeat themselves (Ellis, 1976, 2001b, 2003a, 2004).

Most such human tendencies may be summarized by stating that humans are born with a tendency to want, to "need," and to condemn (1) themselves, (2) others, and (3) the world when they do not immediately get what they supposedly "need." They consequently tend to think "childishly" (or "humanly") all their lives and are able only with real effort to achieve and maintain "mature" or realistic behavior. This is not to deny, as Abraham Maslow and Carl Rogers have pointed out, that humans have impressive self-actualizing capacities. They do, and these are strong inborn propensities, too. But, alas, people frequently defeat themselves by their inborn and acquired self-sabotaging ways.

There is a great deal of evidence that people's basic personality or temperament has strong biological, as well as environmental, influences. People are born, as well as reared, with greater or lesser degrees of demandingness, and therefore they can change from demanding to *desiring* only with great difficulty. If their demandingness is largely acquired rather than innate, they still seem to have difficulty in ameliorating this tendency toward disturbance. REBT emphasizes that people nonetheless have the *choice* of changing their dysfunctional behaviors and specifically shows them many ways of doing so. It particularly stresses flexible thinking and behaving that helps them remove the rigidities to which they often easily fall victim.

## Social Aspects of Personality

Humans are reared in social groups and spend much of their lives trying to impress, live up to the expectations of, and outdo the performances of other people. On the surface, they are "ego-oriented," "identity-seeking," or "self-centered." Even more importantly, however, they usually define their "selves" as "good" or "worthwhile" when they believe that others accept and approve of them. It is realistic and sensible for people to find or fulfill "themselves" in their interpersonal relations and to have a good amount of what Adler calls "social interest." For, as John Donne beautifully expressed it, no one is an island unto himself or herself. The healthy individual finds it enjoyable to love and be loved by significant others and to relate to almost everyone he or she encounters. In fact, the better one's interpersonal relations are, the happier one is likely to be.

However, what is called *emotional disturbance* is frequently associated with caring *too much* about what others think. This stems from people's belief that they can accept themselves *only* if others think well of them. When disturbed, they escalate their desire for others' approval, and the practical advantages that normally go with such approval, into an absolutistic *dire need* to be liked, and in so doing they become anxious and prone to depression. Given that we have our being-in-the-world, as the existentialists point out, it is quite *important* that others to some degree value us. But it is our tendency to exaggerate the importance of others' acceptance that often leads to self-denigration (Ellis, 1962, 2001a, 2002; Ellis & Harper, 1997; Hauck, 1992).

## Psychological Aspects of Personality

How, specifically, do people become psychologically disordered? According to REBT, they usually needlessly upset themselves as follows:

When individuals feel upset at point C, after experiencing an obnoxious adversity at point A, they almost always convince themselves of irrational beliefs (B), such as: "I *can't* stand adversity! It is *awful* that it exists! It *shouldn't exist!* I am a *worthless person* for not being able to get rid of it!" This set of beliefs is irrational because:

1.    People *can* stand obnoxious adversities, even though they may never like them.

2.    Adversities are hardly *awful,* because *awful* is an essentially indefinable term, with surplus meaning and little empirical referent. By calling the noxious events *awful,* the disturbed individual means they are (a) highly inconvenient, and (b) totally inconvenient, disadvantageous, and unbeneficial. But what noxious stimuli can be, in point of fact, totally inconvenient, disadvantageous, and unbeneficial? Or as bad as it could be?

3.    By holding that the unfortunate happenings in their lives *absolutely should not* exist, people really imply that they have godly power and that whatever they *want* not to exist, *must* not. This hypothesis is, to say the least, highly dubious!

4.    By contending that they are *worthless persons* because they have not been able to ward off unfortunate events, people hold that they should be able to control the universe and that because they are not succeeding in doing what they cannot do, they are obviously worthless. (What drivel!)

The basic tenet of REBT is that emotional *upsets,* as distinguished from feelings of sorrow, regret, annoyance, and frustration, largely stem from irrational beliefs. These beliefs are irrational because they magically insist that something in the universe *should, ought,* or *must* be different from the way it is. Although these irrational beliefs are ostensibly connected with reality (the adversity at point A), they are dogmatic ideas beyond the realm of empiricism. They generally take the form of the statement, "Because I *want* something, it is not only desirable and preferable that it exist, but it *absolutely should,* and it is awful when it doesn't!" No such proposition, obviously, can be substantiated. Yet, such propositions are devoutly held, every day, by literally billions of humans. That is how incredibly disturbance-prone most people are!

Once people become emotionally upset—or, rather, upset themselves!—a peculiar thing frequently occurs. Most of the time, they know they feel anxious, depressed, or otherwise agitated, and also know their symptoms are undesirable and (in our culture) socially disapproved. For who approves or respects highly agitated or "crazy" people? They therefore make their emotional consequence (C) or symptom into another activating event or adversity (A) and create a secondary symptom ($C_2$) about this new A!

Thus, if you originally start with something like (A): "I did poorly on my job today" and (B): "Isn't that horrible!", you may wind up with (C): feelings of anxiety, worthlessness, and depression. You may now start all over with ($A_2$): "I feel anxious and depressed, and worthless!" Then you proceed to ($B_2$): "Isn't *that* horrible!" Now you end up with ($C_2$): even greater feelings of anxiety, worthlessness, and depression. In other words, once you become anxious, you frequently make yourself anxious about *being* anxious; once you become depressed, you make yourself depressed about *being* depressed; and so on. You now have two consequences or symptoms for the price of one, and you often go around and around, in a vicious cycle of (1) condemning yourself for doing poorly at some task, (2) feeling guilty or depressed because of this self-condemnation, (3) condemning yourself for your feelings of guilt and depression, (4) condemning yourself for condemning yourself, (5) condemning yourself for seeing your disturbances and still not eliminating them, (6) condemning yourself for going for psychotherapeutic help and still not getting better, (7) condemning yourself for being more disturbed than other individuals, (8) concluding that you are indubitably hopelessly disturbed and that nothing can be done about it; and so on, in an endless spiral.

No matter what your original self-condemnation is about—and it hardly matters what it was, because your adversity (A) is often not that important—you eventually tend to end up with a chain of disturbed reactions only obliquely related to the original "traumatic events" of your life. That is why dramatic psychotherapies are often misleading—they overemphasize "traumatic events" rather than self-condemnatory attitudes *about* these events—and that is why these therapies fail to help with any secondary disturbance, such as being anxious about being anxious. Most major psychotherapies also concentrate either on A, the adversities, or on C, the emotional consequences, and rarely consider B, the belief system, which is a vital factor in creating self-disturbance.

Even assuming, moreover, that adversities and emotional consequences are important, as in post-traumatic stress disorder (PTSD), there is not too much we can do by concentrating our therapeutic attention on them. The adversities belong to the past. There is nothing that anyone can do to *change* the past.

As for clients' present feelings, the more we focus on them, the worse they are likely to feel. If we keep talking about their anxiety, and getting clients to reexperience this feeling, they can become still more anxious. The best point to interrupt their disturbed process is usually to help them to focus on their anxiety-creating belief system—point B—because that is the main (though not the only) cause of their disturbance.

If, for example, a male client feels anxious during a therapy session and the therapist reassures him that there is nothing for him to be anxious about, he may achieve a palliative "solution" to his problem by thinking, "I am afraid that I will act foolishly right here and now, and wouldn't that be awful! No, it really wouldn't be awful, because *this* therapist will accept me, anyway." He may thereby temporarily decrease his anxiety.

Or the therapist can concentrate on the past adversities in the client's life that are presumably making him anxious—by, for instance, showing him that his mother used to point out his deficiencies, that he was always afraid of speaking to authority figures who might disapprove of him, and that, *therefore,* because of all his prior and present fears, in situations $A_1, A_2, A_3 \ldots A_{11}$, he is *now* anxious with the therapist. Whereupon the client might convince himself, "Ah! Now I see that I am generally anxious when I am faced with authority figures. No wonder I am anxious even with my own therapist!" In which case, he might feel better and temporarily lose his anxiety.

It would be better for the therapist to show this client that he was anxious as a child and is still anxious with authority figures because he has always believed, and still believes, that he *must* be approved, that it is *awful* when an authority figure disapproves of him.

Whereupon the anxious client would tend to become diverted from concentrating on A (criticism by an authority figure) and from C (his feelings of anxiety) to a consideration of B (his irrational belief system). This diversion would help him become immediately nonanxious—for when he is focusing on "what am I telling myself (at B) to *make myself* anxious" he cannot focus upon the self-defeating, useless thought, "Wouldn't it be terrible if I said something stupid to my therapist and if even he disapproved of me!" He would begin actively to dispute (at point D) his irrational beliefs, and not only could he then temporarily change them (by convincing himself, "It would be *unfortunate* if I said something stupid to my therapist and he disapproved of me, but it would hardly be *terrible* or *catastrophic!*"), but he would also tend to have a much weaker allegiance to these self-defeating beliefs the next time. So he would obtain, by the therapist's helping him to focus primarily on B rather than on A and C, curative and preventive, rather than palliative, results in connection with his anxiety.

This is the basic personality theory of REBT: Humans largely create their own emotional consequences. They appear to be born with a distinct proneness to do so, and they learn, through social conditioning, to exaggerate (rather than to minimize) that proneness. They nonetheless have considerable ability to understand what they foolishly believe to cause their distress (because they have a unique talent for thinking about their thinking) and to train themselves to change their self-sabotaging beliefs (because they also have a unique capacity for self-discipline or self-reconditioning). If they *think* and *work* hard at understanding and contradicting their *must*urbatory belief systems, they can make amazing curative and preventative changes. And if they are helped to zero in on their crooked thinking and unhealthy emoting and behaving by a highly active-directive homework-assigning therapist, they are more likely to change their beliefs than if they only work with a dynamically oriented, client-centered, conventional existential, or classical behavior-modification-centered therapist.

Although REBT is mainly a theory of personality change, it is also a personality theory in its own right (Ellis, 1994, 2001b, 2002).

## Variety of Concepts

Ellis largely agrees with Sigmund Freud that the pleasure principle (or short-range hedonism) tends to run most people's lives; with Karen Horney and Erich Fromm that cultural influences as well as early family influences tend to play a significant part in bolstering people's irrational thinking; with Alfred Adler that fictitious goals tend to order and run human lives; with Gordon Allport that when individuals begin to think and act in a certain manner, they find it very difficult to think or act differently, even when they want very much to do so; with Ivan Pavlov that humans' large cerebral cortices provide them with a secondary signaling system through which they often become cognitively conditioned; with Jerome Frank that people are exceptionally prone to the influence of suggestion; with Jean Piaget that active learning is much more effective than passive learning; with Anna Freud that people frequently refuse to acknowledge their mistakes and resort to defenses and rationalizations to cover up underlying feelings of shame and self-deprecation; and with Abraham Maslow and Carl Rogers that humans, however disturbed they may be, have great untapped growth forces.

On the other hand, REBT has serious differences with certain aspects of many popular personality theories.

1.   It opposes the Freudian concept that people have clear-cut libidinous instincts, which if thwarted must lead to emotional disturbances. It also objects to the view of William Glasser and many other therapists that all humans *need* to be approved and to succeed—and that if these needs are blocked, they cannot possibly accept themselves or be happy. REBT, instead, posits strong human *desires,* which only become *needs* or *necessities* when people foolishly *define* them as such.

2.   REBT places the Oedipus complex as a relatively minor subheading under people's major irrational belief that they absolutely have to receive the approval of their parents (and others), that they *must not* fail (at lusting or almost anything else), and that when they are disapproved of and when they fail they are worthless. Many so-called sexual problems—such as sexual inadequacy, severe inhibition, and obsessive-compulsive behavior—partly result from people's irrational beliefs that they *need* approval, success, and immediate gratification.

3.   REBT holds that people's environment, particularly childhood parental environment, *reaffirms* but does not always *create* strong tendencies to think irrationally and to be disturbed. Parents and culture teach children standards and values, but they do not always teach them *musts* about these values. People *naturally* and *easily* add rigid commands to socially inhibited standards.

4.   REBT looks skeptically at anything mystical, devout, transpersonal, or magical, when these terms are used in the strict sense. It believes that reason itself is limited, ungodlike, and absolute (Ellis, 1962, 1994). It holds that humans may in some ways transcend themselves or experience altered states of consciousness—for example, hypnosis—that may enhance their ability to know themselves and the world and to solve some of their problems; but it does not believe that people can transcend their humanness and become su-

perhuman. They can become more adept and competent, but they still remain *fallible* and in no way godly! REBT holds that minimal disturbance goes with people's surrendering all pretensions to superhumanness and *accepting* while still *disliking* their own and the world's limitations.

5.    REBT believes that no part of a human is to be reified into an entity called the unconscious, although it holds that people have many thoughts, feelings, and even acts of which they are unaware. These "unconscious" or tacit thoughts and feelings are, for the most part, slightly below the level of consciousness, not often deeply repressed, and can usually be brought to consciousness by brief, incisive probing. Thus, suppose a wife is angrier with her husband than she is aware of, and that her anger is motivated by the unconscious grandiose thought, "After all I've done for him he *absolutely should* be having sex with me more frequently!" A rational emotive behavior therapist (who suspects that she has these unconscious feelings and thoughts) can usually induce her to (a) *hypothesize* that she is angry with her husband and look for some evidence with which to test that hypothesis and (b) *check* herself for grandiose thinking whenever she feels angry. In the majority of instances, without resorting to free association, dream analysis, analyzing the transference relationship, hypnosis, or other presumably "depth-centered" techniques for revealing unconscious thoughts and feelings, REBT practitioners can reveal these in short order—sometimes in a matter of minutes. They show the client her unconsciously held attitudes, beliefs, and values and, in addition, teach the client how to bring her self-defeating, hidden ideas to consciousness and to actively dispute them.

People often see how REBT differs significantly from psychoanalysis, Rogerianism, gestalt therapy, and orthodox behavior therapy but have difficulty seeing how it differs from more closely related schools, such as Adler's Individual Psychology. REBT agrees with almost all of Adlerian theory but has a more hardheaded and behavior-oriented practice (Ellis, 1994; Ellis & Dryden, 1997; Ellis & MacLaren, 1998). It also ignores most of the Adlerian emphasis on early childhood memories and the importance of birth order. But the *basic mistakes* that Adlerians emphasize are similar to the irrational beliefs of REBT.

REBT overlaps with Beck's cognitive therapy (CT) in several ways, but it also differs in significant ways: (1) It usually disputes clients' irrational beliefs more actively, directly, quickly, and forcefully than does CT. (2) It emphasizes absolutist *musts* more than CT and holds that most major irrationalities implicitly stem from dogmatic *shoulds* and *musts.* (3) It uses psychoeducational approaches—such as books, pamphlets, audiovisual cassettes, talks, and workshops—as intrinsic elements and stresses their use more than does CT. (4) It clearly distinguishes between healthy negative feelings (e.g., sadness and frustration) and unhealthy negative feelings (e.g., depression and hostility). (5) REBT emphasizes several emotive-evocative methods—such as shame-attacking exercises, rational emotive imagery, and *strong* self-statements and self-dialogues—that CT often neglects. (6) REBT favors in vivo desensitization, preferably done implosively, more than CT does. (7) REBT often uses penalties as well as reinforcements to help people do their homework (Ellis, 2001b, 2002, 2003a). (8) It emphasizes profound philosophic acceptance of oneself, other people, and the world more than does CT.

REBT is humanistic and to some degree existentialist. It first tries to help people minimize their emotional and behavioral disturbances, but it also encourages them to make themselves happier than they normally are and to strive for more self-actualization and human growth (Ellis, 1994). It is closer in some respects to Rogers's (1961) person-centered approach than to other therapies in that it mainly emphasizes unconditional self-acceptance (USA) as well as unconditional other-acceptance (UOA) no matter how well or badly people may perform (Ellis, 2001a, 2002, 2003a; Ellis & Blau, 1998; Ellis & Harper, 1997; Hauck, 1992).

# PSYCHOTHERAPY

## Theory of Psychotherapy

According to the theory of REBT, neurotic disturbance occurs when individuals *demand* that their wishes be satisfied, that they succeed and be approved, that others treat them fairly, and that the universe be more pleasant. When people's demandingness (and not their desirousness) gets them into emotional trouble, they tend to alleviate their pain in both inelegant and elegant ways.

### Distraction

Just as a whining child can be temporarily diverted by receiving a piece of candy, so can adult demanders be transitorily sidetracked by distraction. Thus, a therapist who sees someone who is afraid of being rejected (that is, one who *demands* that significant others accept him) can try to divert him into activities such as sports, aesthetic creation, a political cause, yoga exercises, meditation, or preoccupation with the events of his childhood. While the individual is so diverted, he will not be as inclined to demand acceptance by others and to make himself anxious. Distraction techniques are mainly palliative, given that distracted people are still demanders and as soon as they are not diverted, they will probably return to their destructive commanding.

### Satisfying Demands

If a client's insistences are always catered to, she or he will tend to feel better (but not necessarily get better). To arrange this kind of "solution," a therapist can give her or his love and approval, provide pleasurable sensations (for example, put the client in an encounter group to be hugged or massaged), teach methods of having demands met, or give reassurance that the client eventually will be gratified. Many clients will feel immensely better when given this kind of treatment, but may well have their demandingness reinforced rather than minimized.

### Magic and Mysticism

A boy who demands may be assuaged by magic; for example, by his parents saying that a fairy godmother will soon satisfy his demands. Similarly, adolescent and adult demanders can be led to believe (by a therapist or someone else) that their therapist is a kind of magician who will take away their troubles merely by listening to what bothers them. These magical solutions sometimes work beautifully by getting true believers to feel better and to give up disturbed symptoms, but they rarely work for any length of time and frequently lead to eventual disillusionment.

### Giving Up Demandingness

The most elegant solution to the problems resulting from irrational demandingness is to help individuals to become less demanding. As children mature, they normally become less childish and less insistent that they must have their desires immediately gratified. REBT encourages clients to achieve minimal demandingness and maximum tolerance. REBT practitioners may, at times, use temporary "solutions," such as distraction, satisfying the client's "needs," and even (on rare occasions) "magic." But they realize that these are low-level, inelegant, palliative solutions, mainly to be used with clients who refuse to accept a more elegant and permanent resolution. The therapist prefers to strive for the highest-order solution: minimization of *must*urbation, perfectionism, grandiosity, and low frustration tolerance.

In REBT, therapists help clients to minimize their absolutistic core philosophies by using cognitive, emotive, and behavioristic procedures.

1.    REBT cognitively attempts to show clients that giving up perfectionism can help them lead happier, less anxiety-ridden lives. It teaches them how to recognize their *shoulds, oughts,* and *musts;* how to separate rational (preferential) from irrational (absolutistic) beliefs; how to be logical and pragmatic about their own problems; and how to accept reality, even when it is pretty grim. REBT is oriented toward helping disturbed people philosophize more effectively and thereby uncreate the needless problems they have constructed. It not only employs a one-to-one Socratic-type dialogue between the client and the therapist, but it also, in group therapy, encourages other members of the group to discuss, explain, and reason with other ineffectually thinking clients. It teaches logical and semantic precision—that a man's being rejected does not mean that he will *always* be rejected and that a woman's failure does not mean she *cannot* succeed. It helps clients to keep asking themselves whether the worst things that could happen would really be as bad as they melodramatically fantasize they would be.

2.    REBT emotively employs various means of dramatizing preferences and *musts* so clients can clearly distinguish between the two. Thus, the therapist may employ *roleplaying* to show clients how to adopt different ideas; *humor* to reduce disturbance-creating ideas to absurdity; *unconditional acceptance* to demonstrate that clients are acceptable, even with their unfortunate traits; and *strong disputing* to persuade people to give up some of their crazy thinking and replace it with more efficient notions. The therapist may also encourage clients, either in individual or group counseling, to take risks (for example, telling another group member what they really think of him or her) that will prove to be not that risky; to reveal themselves (for example, by sharing the details of their sexual problems); to convince themselves that others can accept them with their failings; and to get in touch with their "shameful" feelings (such as hostility) so they can zero in on the exact things they are telling themselves to create these feelings. Experiential exercises are used to help clients overcome denial of their feelings and then work at REBT's ABCDs (the D refers to disputation) to change their self-defeating emotions. The therapist may also use pleasure-giving techniques, not merely to satisfy clients' unreasonable demands for immediate gratification, but to show them they are capable of doing many pleasant acts that they think, wrongly, they *cannot* do, and that they can seek pleasure for its own sake, even though others may frown upon them for doing so.

3.    *Behavior therapy* is employed in REBT not only to help clients to become habituated to more effective ways of performing, but also to help change their *cognitions.* Thus, their demandingness that they perform beautifully may be whittled away by their agreeing to do risk-taking assignments, such as asking a desired person for a date, deliberately failing at some task (for example, making a real attempt to speak badly in public), imagining themselves in failing situations, and throwing themselves into unusual activities that they consider especially dangerous. Clients' demandingness that others treat them fairly and that the world be kind may be challenged by the therapist's encouraging them to stay in poor circumstances and teach themselves, at least temporarily, to accept them; to take on hard tasks (such as enrolling in college); to imagine themselves having a rough time at something and making themselves not feel terribly upset or having to "cop out" of it; to allow themselves to do a pleasant thing, such as go to a movie or see their friends, only after they have done unpleasant but desirable tasks, such as studying French or finishing a report for their boss; and so on.

REBT often employs operant conditioning to reinforce people's efforts to change unde-sirable behavior (e.g., smoking or overeating) or to change irrational thinking (e.g., con-demning themselves when they smoke or overeat).

REBT accepts that there are many kinds of psychological treatment and that most of them work to some degree. An elegant system of therapy includes (a) economy of time and effort, (b) rapid symptom reduction, (c) effectiveness with a large percentage of dif-ferent kinds of clients, (d) depth of solution of the presenting problems, and (e) lasting-ness of the therapeutic results. Philosophically, REBT combats absoluteness and ruth-lessly persists at undermining childish demandingness—the main element of much neurotic disturbance (Ellis, 1962, 1994, 2002). It theorizes that if people learn to only strongly prefer, instead of grandiosely insisting, that their desires be fulfilled, they can make themselves remarkably less disturbed and less disturb*able* (Ellis, 1999, 2001a, 2001b, 2002).

## Process of Psychotherapy

REBT helps clients acquire a more realistic, tolerant philosophy of life. Because some of its methods are similar to methods used by other therapists, they are not detailed in this section. Most of the space here is devoted to the cognitive-persuasive aspects of REBT, one of its most distinguishing characteristics.

REBT practitioners generally do not spend a great deal of time listening to the client's history, encouraging long tales of woe, sympathetically getting in tune with emo-tionalizing, or carefully and incisively reflecting feelings. They may use all these methods, but they usually keep them short because they consider most long-winded dialogues a form of indulgence therapy, in which the client may be helped to *feel* better but rarely to *get* better. Even when these methods work, they are often highly inefficient and side-tracking (Ellis, 2001a).

Similarly, the rational emotive behavior therapist makes little use of free association, dream analysis, interpretations of the transference relationship, explanations of the cli-ent's present symptoms in terms of past experiences, disclosure, analysis of the so-called Oedipus complex, and other "dynamically" directed interpretations or explanations. When they are employed at all, they are used to help clients see some of their basic irra-tional ideas.

Thus, if a male therapist notes that a female client rebels against him just as she pre-viously rebelled against her father during childhood, he will not interpret the present re-belliousness as stemming from the prior pattern, but will instead probably say something like this:

> It looks like you frequently hated your father because he kept forcing you to follow certain rules you considered arbitrary and because you kept convincing yourself: "My father isn't being considerate of me and he *ought* to be! I'll get even with him!" I think you are now telling yourself approximately the same thing about me. But your angry rebelliousness against your father was senseless because (a) he was not a *total bastard* for perpetrating a bastardly act; (b) there was no reason why he *ought* to have been considerate of you (although there were several reasons why it *would have been preferable* if he had been); and (c) your getting angry at him and trying to "get even with him" would not, probably, encourage him to act more kindly, but actually to be more cruel.
>
> You consequently confused—as most children will—being displeased with your father's behavior with being "righteously" angry at him, and you needlessly made yourself upset about his real or imagined unfair treatment of you. In my case, too,

you may be doing much the same thing. You may be taking the risks that I encourage you to take and insisting that they are too onerous (when in fact, they are only onerous), and after assuming that I am wrong in suggesting them (which I indeed may be), you are condemning me for my supposedly wrong deeds. Moreover, you are quite possibly assuming that I am "wrong" and a "louse" for being wrong because I resemble, in some ways, your "wrong" and "lousy" father.

But this is another illogical conclusion (that I resemble him in all ways) and an irrational premise (that I, like your father, am a *bad person* if I do a wrong act). So you are not only *inventing* a false connection between me and your father, but you are creating today, as you have done for many years now, a renewed *demand* that the world be an easy place for you and that everyone *ought* to treat you fairly. Now, how can you challenge these irrational premises and illogical deductions?

REBT practitioners often employ a rapid-fire active-directive-persuasive-philosophic methodology. In most instances, they quickly pin clients down to a few basic dysfunctional beliefs. They challenge them to try to defend these ideas; show that they contain illogical premises that cannot be substantiated logically; analyze these ideas and actively dispute them; vigorously show why they cannot work and why they will almost inevitably lead to more disturbance; reduce these ideas to absurdity, sometimes in a humorous manner; explain how they can be replaced with more rational philosophies; and teach clients how to think scientifically, so they can observe, logically parse, and minimize any subsequent irrational ideas and illogical deductions that lead to self-defeating feelings and behaviors.

When working with certain clients who have suffered from extreme traumas, however, such as incest, rape, child abuse, or other violent situations, REBT practitioners may well be quite empathic and go more slowly before doing any vigorous disputing of clients' dysfunctional beliefs about these traumatic events or about anything else in their lives.

To show how REBT is sometimes, but hardly always, actively-directively done, here is a verbatim transcript of a session with a 25-year-old single woman, Sara, who worked as the head of a computer programming section of a firm and who, without any traumatic or violent history, was very insecure and self-denigrating.

T-1:    What would you want to start on first?
C-1:    I don't know. I'm petrified at the moment!
T-2:    You're petrified—of what?
C-2:    Of you!
T-3:    No, surely not of me—perhaps of yourself!
C-3:    [Laughs nervously.]
T-4:    Because of what I am going to do to you?
C-4:    Right! You are threatening me, I guess.
T-5:    But how? What am I doing? Obviously, I'm not going to take a knife and stab you. Now, in what way am I threatening you?
C-5:    I guess I'm afraid, perhaps, of what I'm going to find out—about me.
T-6:    Well, so let's suppose you find out something dreadful about you—that you're thinking foolishly or something. Now why would that be awful?
C-6:    Because I, I guess I'm the most important thing to me at the moment.
T-7:    No, I don't think that's the answer. It's, I believe, the opposite! You're really the least important thing to you. You are prepared to beat yourself over the head if I tell you that you're acting foolishly. If you were not a self-blamer, then you wouldn't care what I said. It would be important to you—but you'd just go around correcting it. But if I tell you something really negative about you, you're going to beat yourself mercilessly. Aren't you?
C-7:    Yes, I generally do.

T-8:    All right. So perhaps that's what you're really afraid of. You're not afraid of me. You're afraid of your own self-criticism.

C-8:    [Sighs.] All right.

T-9:    So why do you have to criticize yourself? Suppose I find you're the worst person I ever met? Let's just suppose that. All right, now *why* would you have to criticize yourself?

C-9:    [Pause.] I'd have to. I don't know any other behavior pattern, I guess, in this point of time. I always do. I guess I think I'm just a shit.

T-10:   Yeah. But that, that isn't so. If you don't know how to ski or swim, you could learn. You can also learn not to condemn yourself, no matter what you do.

C-10:   I don't know.

T-11:   Well, the answer is: You don't know how.

C-11:   Perhaps.

T-12:   I get the impression you're *saying,* "I *have* to berate myself if I do something wrong." Because isn't that where your depression comes from?

C-12:   Yes, I guess so. [Silence.]

T-13:   Now, what are you *mainly* putting yourself down for right now?

C-13:   I don't seem quite able, in this point of time, to break it down very neatly. The form [that our clinic gets clients to fill out before their sessions] gave me a great deal of trouble. Because my tendency is to say *everything,* I want to change everything; I'm depressed about everything, etc.

T-14:   Give me a couple of things, for example.

C-14:   What I'm depressed about? I, uh, don't know that I have any purpose in life. I don't know what I—what I am. And I don't know in what direction I'm going.

T-15:   Yeah, but that's—so you're saying, "I'm ignorant!" [Client nods.] Well, what's so awful about being ignorant? It's too bad you're ignorant. It would be nicer if you weren't—if you *had* a purpose and *knew* where you were going. But just let's suppose the worst: for the rest of your life you didn't have a purpose and you stayed this way. Let's suppose that. Now, why would *you* be so bad?

C-15:   Because everyone *should* have a purpose!

T-16:   Where did you get the *should?*

C-16:   'Cause it's what I believe in. [Silence.]

T-17:   I know. But think about it for a minute. You're obviously a bright woman. Now, where did that *should* come from?

C-17:   I, I don't know! I'm not thinking clearly at the moment. I'm too nervous! I'm sorry.

T-18:   Well, but you *can* think clearly. Are you now saying, "Oh, it's hopeless! I can't think clearly. What a shit I am for not thinking clearly!" You see: you're blaming yourself for *that.*

        [From C-18 to C-26 the client upsets herself about not reacting well to the session, but the therapist shows her this is not overly important and calms her down.]

C-27:   I can't imagine existing, uh, or that there would be any reason for existing without a purpose!

T-28:   No, but the vast majority of human beings don't have much purpose.

C-28:   [Angrily.] All right, then, I should not feel bad about it.

T-29:   No, no, no! Wait a minute, now. You just *jumped.* [Laughs.] You jumped from one extreme to another! You see, you said a sane sentence and an *insane* sentence. Now, if we could get you to separate the two—which you're perfectly able to do—you would solve the problem. What you really mean is "It *would be better* if I had a purpose. Because I'd be happier." Right?

C-29:   Yes.

T-30:   But then you magically jump to "Therefore I *should!*" Now do you see the difference between "It *would be better* if I had a purpose" and "I *should, I must, I've got to*"?

C-30:   Yes, I do.

T-31:   Well, what's the difference?

C-31:   [Laughs.] I just said that to agree with you!

T-32:   Yes! See, that won't be any good. We could go on that way forever, and you'll agree with me, and I'll say, "Oh, what a great woman! She agrees with me." And then you'll go out of here as nutty as you were before!

C-32:   [Laughs, this time with genuine appreciation and good humor.]

T-33:   You're perfectly able, as I said, to think—to stop giving up. That's what you've done most of your life. That's why you're disturbed. Because you refuse to think. And let's go over it again: "It would be better if I had a purpose in life; if I weren't depressed, etc., etc. If I had a good, nice, enjoyable purpose." We could give reasons why it would be better. "It's fairly obvious why it would be better!" Now, why is that a magical statement, that "I *should* do what would be better"?

C-33:   You mean, why do I feel that way?

T-34:   No, no. It's a belief. You feel that way because you believe that way.

C-34:   Yes.

T-35:   If you believed you were a kangaroo, you'd be hopping around and you'd *feel* like a kangaroo. Whatever you *believe* you feel. Feelings largely come from your beliefs. Now, I'm temporarily forgetting about your feelings, because we really can't change feelings without changing beliefs. So I'm showing you; you have two beliefs—or two feelings, if you want to call them that. One, "It would be better if I had a purpose in life." Do you agree? [Client nods.] Now that's perfectly reasonable. That's quite true. We could prove it. Two, "Therefore I *should* do what would be better." Now those are two different statements. They may seem the same, but they're vastly different. Now, the first one, as I said, is sane. Because we could prove it. It's related to reality. We can list the advantages of having a purpose—for almost anybody, not just for you.

C-35:   [Calm now, and listening intently to T's explanation.] Uh-huh.

T-36:   But the second one, "Therefore I *should* do what would be better," is crazy. Now, why is it crazy?

C-36:   I can't accept it as a crazy statement.

T-37:   Because who said you *should?*

C-37:   I don't know where it all began! Somebody said it.

T-38:   I know, but I say whoever said it was screwy!

C-38:   [Laughs.] All right.

T-39:   How could the world possibly have a *should?*

C-39:   Well, it does.

T-40:   But it *doesn't!* You see, that's what emotional disturbance is: believing in *shoulds, oughts,* and *musts* instead of *it would be betters.* That's exactly what makes people neurotic! Suppose you said to yourself, "I wish I had a dollar in my pocket right now," and you had only ninety cents. How would you feel?

C-40:   Not particularly upset.

T-41:   Yes, you'd be a little disappointed. *It would be better* to have a dollar. But now suppose you said, "I *should,* I *must* have a dollar in my pocket at all times," and you found you had only ninety cents. Now, how would you feel?

C-41:   Then I would be terribly upset, following your line of reasoning.

T-42:   But not because you had only ninety cents.

C-42:   Because I thought I *should* have a dollar.

T-43:   THAT'S RIGHT! The *should.* And what's more, let's just go one step further. Suppose you said, "I must have a dollar in my pocket at all times." And you found you had a dollar and ten cents. Now how would you feel?

C-43:  Superb, I guess!

T-44:  No—anxious!

C-44:  [Laughs.] You mean I'd be guilty: "What was I doing with the extra money?"

T-45:  No.

C-45:  I'm sorry, I'm not following you. I—

T-46:  Because you're not *thinking.* Think for a minute. Why, if you said, "I *must* have a dollar, I *should* have a dollar," and you had a dollar and ten cents, would you still be anxious? *Anybody* would be. Now why would anybody be anxious if they were saying, "I've got to have a dollar!" and they found they had a dollar and ten cents?

C-46:  Because it violated their *should.* It violated their rule of what they thought was right, I guess.

T-47:  Well, not at the moment. But they could easily lose twenty cents.

C-47:  Oh! Well.

T-48:  Yeah! They'd still be anxious. You see, because *must* means, "At *all* times I must—"

C-48:  Oh, I see what you mean! All right. I see what you mean. They could easily lose some of the money and would therefore feel insecure.

T-49:  Yeah. Most anxiety comes from *musts.*

C-49:  [Long silence.] Why do you create such an anxiety-ridden situation initially for someone?

T-50:  I don't think I do. I see hundreds of people and you're one of the few who *makes* this so anxiety provoking for yourself. The others may do it mildly, but you're making it very anxiety provoking. Which just shows that you may carry *must* into *everything,* including this situation. Most people come in here very relieved. They finally get to talk to somebody who knows how to help them, and they're very happy that I stop the horseshit, and stop asking about their childhood, and don't talk about the weather, etc. And I get *right away* to what bothers them. I tell them in five minutes. I've just explained to you the secret of most emotional disturbance. If you really followed what I said, and used it, you'd never be disturbed about practically anything for the rest of your life!

C-50:  Uh-huh.

T-51:  Because practically every time you're disturbed, you're changing *it would be better* to a *must!* That's all neurosis is! Very, very simple. Now, why should I waste your time and not explain this—and talk about irrelevant things?

C-51:  Because perhaps I would have followed your explanation a little better if I hadn't been so threatened initially.

T-52:  But then, if I pat you on the head and hold back, etc., then you'll think for the rest of your life you have to be patted on the head! You're a bright woman!

C-52:  All right—

T-53:  That's another *should.* "He *should* pat me on the head and take it slowly—*then* a shit like me can understand! But if he goes *fast* and makes me *think,* oh my God I'll make an error—and that is awful!" More horseshit! You don't have to believe that horseshit! You're perfectly able to follow what I say—if you stop worrying, "I *should* do perfectly well!" For that's what you're basically thinking, sitting there. Well, why *should* you do perfectly well? Suppose we had to go over it 20 times before you got it?

C-53:  I don't *like* to appear stupid!

T-54:  No. See. Now you're lying to yourself! Because again you said a sane thing—and then you added an insane thing. The sane thing was, "I don't like to appear stupid, because it's *better* to appear bright." But then you immediately jumped over to the insane thing: "And it's *awful* if I appear stupid—"

C-54:  [Laughs appreciatively, almost joyously.]

T-55:   "—I *should* appear bright!" You see?

C-55:   [With conviction.] Yes.

T-56:   The same crap! It's always the same crap. Now if you would look at the crap—instead of "Oh, how stupid I am! He hates me! I think I'll kill myself!"—then you'd be on the road to getting better fairly quickly.

C-56:   You've been listening! [Laughs.]

T-57:   Listening to what?

C-57:   [Laughs.] Those wild statements in my mind, like that, that I make.

T-58:   That's right! Because I know that you have to make those statements—because I have a good *theory*. And according to my theory, people wouldn't usually get upset *unless* they made those nutty statements to themselves.

C-58:   I haven't the faintest idea why I've been so upset—

T-59:   But you *do* have the faintest idea. I just told you.

C-59:   All right, I know!

T-60:   Why are you upset? Report it to me.

C-60:   I'm upset because I know, I—the role that I envisioned myself being in when I walked in here and what I [Laughs, almost joyously] and what I would do and should do—

T-61:   Yeah?

C-61:   And therefore you forced me to violate that. And I don't like it.

T-62:   "And isn't it *awful* that I didn't come out greatly! If I had violated that needed role *beautifully,* and I gave him the *right* answers immediately, and he beamed, and said, 'Boy, what a bright woman, this!' then it would have been all right."

C-62:   [Laughing good-humoredly.] Certainly!

T-63:   Horseshit! You would have been exactly as disturbed as you are now! It wouldn't have helped you a bit! In fact, you would have gotten nuttier! Because then you would have gone out of here with the same philosophy you came in here with: "That when I act well and people pat me on the head and say, 'What a great woman I am!' then everything is rosy!" It's a nutty philosophy! Because even if I loved you madly, the next person you talk to is likely to hate you. So I like brown eyes and he likes blue eyes or something else. So you're then dead! Because you really think: "I've got to be *accepted!* I've got to act intelligently!" Well, why?

C-63:   [Very soberly and reflectively.] True.

T-64:   You see?

C-64:   Yes.

T-65:   Now, if you will learn that lesson, then you've had a very valuable session. Because you *don't* have to upset yourself. As I said before, if I thought you were the worst shit who ever existed, well, that's my *opinion.* And I'm entitled to it. But does it make you a turd?

C-65:   [Reflective silence.]

T-66:   *Does* it?

C-66:   No.

T-67:   *What* makes you a turd?

C-67:   *Thinking* that you are.

T-68:   That's right! Your *belief* that you are. That's the only thing that could ever do it. And you never have to believe that. See? You control your thinking. I control *my* thinking—*my* belief about you. But you don't have to be affected by that. You *always* control what you think. And you believe you don't. So let's get back to that depression. The depression, as I said before, stems from self-castigation. That's where it comes from. Now what are you castigating yourself for?

C-68:   Because I can't live up to it—there's a basic conflict in what people appear to think I am and what I think I am.

T-69:   Right.

C-69:   And perhaps it's not fair to blame other people. Perhaps I thrust myself into a leader's role. But, anyway, my feeling right now is that all my life I've been forced to be something that I'm not, and the older I get the more difficult this *façade*, huh, this *appearance*, uh—that the veneer is becoming thinner and thinner and thinner, until I just can't do it anymore.

T-70:   Well, but really, yeah, I'm afraid you're a little wrong. Because oddly enough, almost the opposite is happening. You are thrust into this role. That's right: the role of something of a leader. Is that correct?

C-70:   Yes.

T-71:   And *they* think you're filling it.

C-71:   Everyone usually does.

T-72:   And it just so happens they're *right.*

C-72:   But it's taking more and more out of me.

T-73:   Because you're not doing something else. You see, you are fulfilling *their* expectations of you. Because, obviously, they wouldn't think you are a leader, they'd think you were nothing if you *were* acting like a nonleader. So you are filling their expectations. But you're not fulfilling your own idealistic and impractical expectations of leadership.

C-73:   [Verging on tears.] No, I guess I'm not.

T-74:   You see, that's the issue. So therefore you *are* doing O.K. by them—by your job. But you're not being an angel, you're not being *perfect!* And you *should* be, to be a real *leader.* And therefore you're a *sham!* You see? Now, if you give up those nutty expectations of yourself and go back to their expectations, you're in no trouble at all. Because obviously you're doing all right by them and *their* expectations.

C-74:   Well, I haven't been. I had to, to give up one very successful situation. And, uh, when I left, they thought it was still successful. But I just couldn't go on—

T-75:   "Because I must, I must *really* be a leader in *my* eyes, be pretty *perfect.*" You see, "If I satisfy the world, but I know I did badly, or less than I *should,* then I'm a slob! And they haven't found me out, so that makes me a *double* slob. Because I'm pretending to them to be a nonslob when I really am one!"

C-75:   [Laughs in agreement, then grows sober.] True.

T-76:   But it's all your silly *expectations.* It's not *them.* And oddly enough, you are—even with your *handicap,* which is depression, self-deprecation, etc.—you're doing remarkably well. Imagine what you might do *without* this nutty handicap! You see, you're satisfying them while you're spending most of your time and energy flagellating yourself. Imagine what you might do *without* the self-flagellation! Can you see that?

C-76:   [Stopped in her self-blaming tracks, at least temporarily convinced, speaks very meaningfully.] Yes.

## Mechanisms of Psychotherapy

From the foregoing partial protocol (which consumed about 15 minutes of the first session with the client), it can be seen that the therapist tries to do several things:

1.   No matter what *feelings* the client brings out, the therapist tries to get back to her main irrational *ideas* that most probably lie behind these feelings—especially her ideas that it would be *awful* if someone, including him, disliked her.

2.   The therapist does not hesitate to contradict the client, using evidence from the client's own life and from his knowledge of people in general.

3.   He usually is one step *ahead* of her—tells her, for example, that she is a self-blamer before she has said that she is. Knowing, on the basis of REBT theory, that she has *shoulds, oughts,* and *musts* in her thinking if she becomes anxious, depressed, and guilty, he helps her to admit these *shoulds* and then dispute them (T-16, T-17).

4.   He uses the strongest philosophic approach he can think of: "Suppose," he keeps saying to her, "the *worst* thing happened and you really did do badly and others hated you, would you *still* be so bad?" (T-15). He assumes if he can convince her that *none* of her behavior, no matter how execrable, denigrates *her,* he has helped her to make a *deep* attitudinal change.

5.   He is not thrown by her distress (C-17), is not too sympathetic about these feelings, but *uses* them to try to prove to her that, right now, she still believes in foolish ideas and thereby upsets herself. He does not dwell on her "transference" feelings. He interprets the *ideas* behind these feelings, shows her why they are self-defeating, and indicates why his acting sympathetically would probably reinforce instead of help change her demanding philosophy.

6.   He is fairly stern with her but also shows full acceptance and demonstrates confidence in her abilities, especially her constructive ability to change herself.

7.   Instead of merely *telling* her that her ideas are irrational, he keeps trying to get her to see this for *herself* (T-36). He doesn't merely want her to accept or parrot *his* rational philosophies but to think them through. He does, however, explain some relevant psychological processes, such as the client's *feelings* largely come from her *thinking* (T-35, T-68).

8.   He deliberately, on several occasions, uses strong language (T-18, T-50). This is done (a) to help loosen up the client, (b) to show that he, the therapist, is a down-to-earth human being, and (c) to give her an emotive jolt or shock, so his words may take a more dramatic effect. Note that in this case the client first calls herself a "shit" (C-9).

9.   Although hardly sympathetic to her ideas, he is really quite empathic. Rational emotive behavior therapists are usually attuned to the client's unexpressed thoughts (her negative ideas about herself and the world) rather than to her superficial feelings (her perceptions that she is doing poorly or that others are abusing her). They empathize with the client's *feelings* and with the *beliefs* that underlie these feelings. This is a double-headed form of empathy that many therapies miss out on.

10. The therapist keeps checking the client's ostensible understanding of what he is teaching her (T-65, T-66, T-67).

11. The therapist—as is common in early sessions of REBT—does most of the talking and explaining. He gives the client plenty of opportunity to express herself, but uses her responses as take-off points for further teaching. He tries to make each "lecture" brief and trenchant and to relate it specifically to her problems and feelings. Also, at times he stops to let ideas sink in.

As can be seen from the first part of this initial REBT session, the client does not receive feelings of love and warmth from the therapist. Transference and countertransference spontaneously occur, but they are quickly analyzed, the philosophies behind them are revealed, and they tend to evaporate in the process. The client's deep feelings (shame, self-pity, weeping, anger) clearly exist, but the client is not given too much chance to revel in these feelings or to abreact strongly about them. As the therapist points out and attacks the ideologies that underlie these feelings, they swiftly change and are sometimes almost miraculously transformed into other, contradictory feelings (such as humor, joy, and reflective contemplation). The therapist's "coolness," philosophizing, and encouraging insistence that the client can feel something besides anxiety and depression tends to help change her destructiveness into constructive feelings. That is why REBT is a constructivist rather than a purely rationalist kind of therapy (Ellis, 1994, 1999, 2001a, 2001b, 2002).

What the client does seem to experience, as the session proceeds, are (1) full acceptance of herself, in spite of her poor behavior; (2) renewed confidence that she can do certain things—e.g., think for herself; (3) the belief that it is her own perfectionistic *shoulds* that are upsetting her and not the attitudes of others (including the therapist); (4) reality testing, in her starting to see that even though she performs inefficiently (with the therapist and with some of the people she works with), she can still recover, try again, and probably do better in the future; and (5) reduction of some of her defenses in that she can stop blaming others (such as her therapist) for her anxiety and can start to admit that she is doing something herself to cause it.

In these 15 minutes the client is getting only *glimmerings* of these constructive thoughts and feelings. The REBT intent, however, is that she will *keep* getting insights—that is, *philosophic* rather than merely *psychodynamic* insights—into the self-causation of her disturbed symptoms; that she will use these insights to change some of her most enduring and deep-seated ways of thinking about herself, about others, and about the world; and that she will thereby eventually become ideationally, emotionally, and behaviorally less self-defeating. Unless she finally makes an *attitudinal* (as well as symptom-reducing) change, although helped to some degree, she will still be far from the ideal REBT goal of making a basic and lasting personality change.

## APPLICATIONS

### Problems

It is easier to state what kinds of problems are *not* handled than the kind that *are* handled in REBT. Individuals who are out of contact with reality, in a highly manic state, seriously autistic or brain injured, and in the lower ranges of mental deficiency are not normally treated by REBT (or most other practitioners). They are referred for medical treatment, for custodial or institutional care, or for behavior therapy along operant conditioning lines.

Most other individuals with difficulties are treated with REBT. These include (1) clients with maladjustment, moderate anxiety, or marital problems; (2) those with sexual difficulties; (3) run-of-the-mill "neurotics"; (4) individuals with character disorders; (5) truants, juvenile delinquents, and adult criminals; (6) borderline personalities and others with personality disorders; (7) overt psychotics, including those with delusions and hallucinations, when they are under medication and somewhat in contact with reality; (8) individuals with higher-grade mental deficiency; and (9) clients with psychosomatic problems.

Although varying types of problems are treated with REBT, no claim is made that they are treated with equal effectiveness. As is the case with virtually all psychotherapies, the REBT approach is more effective with clients who have a single major symptom (such as sexual inadequacy) than with seriously disordered clients (Ellis, 2001b, 2002). This conforms to the hypotheses of REBT theory that the tendency toward emotional distress is partly inborn and not merely acquired, that individuals with serious aberrations are more innately predisposed to have rigid and crooked thinking than are those with lesser aberrations, and that consequently they are less likely to make major advances. Moreover, REBT emphasizes commitment to changing one's thinking and to doing homework activity assignments, and it is clinically observable that many of the most dramatically symptom-ridden individuals (such as those who are severely depressed) tend to do considerably less work and more shirking (including shirking at therapy) than those with milder symptoms. Nevertheless, seasoned REBT practitioners claim they get better results with a wide variety of clients than do therapists from other schools of psychological thought (Ellis, 1994; Lyons & Woods, 1991; McGovern & Silverman, 1984; Silverman et al., 1992).

REBT is applicable for preventative purposes. Rational-emotive procedures are closely connected to the field of education and have enormous implications for emotional prophylaxis (Ellis 2003b). A number of clinicians have shown how they can help prevent normal children from eventually becoming seriously disturbed. Evidence shows that when nondisturbed grade school pupils are given, along with regular elements of an academic education, a steady process of REBT education, they can learn to understand themselves and others and to live more rationally and happily in this difficult world (Hajzler & Bernard, 1991; Vernon, 2001).

## Evaluation

REBT has directly or indirectly inspired scores of experiments to test its theories, and there are now hundreds of research studies that tend to validate its major theoretical hypotheses (Ellis & Whiteley, 1979). More than 200 outcome studies have been published showing that REBT is effective in changing the thoughts, feelings, and behaviors of groups of individuals with various kinds of disturbances (DiGiuseppe, Terjesen, Rose, Doyle, & Vadalakis, 1998). These studies tend to show that REBT disputing and other methods usually work better than no therapy and are often more effective than other methods of psychotherapy (DiGiuseppe, Miller, & Trexler, 1979; Engels, Garnefski, & Diekstra, 1993; Haaga & Davison, 1993; Hajzler & Bernard, 1991; Jorn, 1989; Lyons & Woods, 1991; McGovern & Silverman, 1984; Silverman et al., 1992).

Applications of REBT to special kinds of clients have also been shown to be effective. Thus, it has given particularly good results with individuals with anger disorders (Ellis, 2003a), with religious clients (Nielsen, Johnson, & Ellis, 2001), and with schoolchildren (Seligman, Revich, Jaycox, & Gillham, 1995).

In addition, hundreds of other outcome studies have been done by cognitive therapists—particularly by Aaron Beck (Alford & Beck, 1997) and his associates—that also support the clinical hypothesis of REBT. Finally, more than 1,000 other investigations have shown that the irrationality scales derived from Ellis's original list of irrational beliefs significantly correlate with the diagnostic disorders with which these scales have been tested (Hollon & Beck, 1994; Woods, 1992). Although much has yet to be learned about the effectiveness of REBT and other cognitive-behavior therapies, the research results that have been found so far are impressive.

### Individual Evaluations

REBT therapists may use various diagnostic instruments and psychological tests, and they especially employ tests of irrationality, such as the Jones Irrational Beliefs Test, the Beck Depression Inventory, and the Dysfunctional Attitude Scale. Many of these tests have been shown to have considerable reliability and validity in controlled experiments.

## Treatment

REBT employs virtually all forms of individual and group psychotherapy. Some of the main methods are described in this section.

### Individual Therapy

Most clients with whom REBT is practiced are seen for individual sessions, usually on a weekly basis, for from 5 to 50 sessions. They generally begin their sessions by telling their most upsetting feelings or consequences (C) during the week. REBT therapists then discover what adversities (A) occurred before clients felt so badly and help them to see what rational beliefs and what irrational beliefs (B) they hold in connection with these adversities. They teach clients to dispute (D) their irrational beliefs and often agree upon concrete homework activity assignments to help with this disputing. They then check up in the following session, sometimes with the help of an REBT Self-Help Report Form, to see how the clients have tried to use the REBT approach during the week. If clients work at REBT, they arrive at an effective new philosophy (E)—which they reach through *Effort* and *Exercise.*

In particular, REBT therapists try to show clients how to (1) minimize anxiety, guilt, and depression by unconditionally accepting themselves, (2) alleviate their anger, hostility, and violence by unconditionally accepting other people, and (3) reduce their low frustration tolerance and inertia by learning to unconditionally accept life even when it is grim (Ellis, 2001a; Ellis & Blau, 1998; Ellis & Dryden, 1997; Ellis & MacLaren, 1998).

## Group Therapy

REBT is particularly applicable to group therapy. Because group members are taught to apply REBT procedures to one another, they can help others learn the procedures and get practice (under the direct supervision of the group leader) in applying them. In group work, moreover, there is usually more opportunity for the members to agree upon homework assignments (some of which are to be carried out in the group itself), to get assertiveness training, to engage in role playing, to interact with other people, to take verbal and nonverbal risks, to learn by the experiences of others, to interact therapeutically and socially with each other in after-group sessions, and to have their behavior directly observed by the therapist and other group members (Ellis, 2001b; Ellis & Dryden, 1997).

## Rational Encounter Marathons and Intensives

REBT has successfully used marathon encounter groups and large-scale one-day intensive workshops that include many verbal and nonverbal exercises, dramatic risk-taking procedures, evocative lectures, personal encounters, homework agreements, and other emotive and behavioral methods. Research studies have shown that these marathons and intensive workshops have beneficial, immediate, and lasting effects (Ellis & Dryden, 1997; Ellis & Joffe, 2002).

## Brief Therapy

REBT is naturally designed for brief therapy. It is preferable that individuals with severe disturbances come to individual and/or group sessions for at least six months. But for individuals who are going to stay in therapy for only a short while, REBT can teach them, in 1 to 10 sessions, the A-B-C method of understanding emotional problems, seeing their main philosophic source, and beginning to change fundamental disturbance-creating attitudes (Ellis, 2001b).

This is particularly true for the person who has a specific problem—such as hostility toward a boss or sexual inadequacy—and who is not too *generally* disturbed. Such an individual can, with the help of REBT, be almost completely "cured" in a few sessions. But even clients with longstanding difficulties may be significantly helped as a result of brief therapy.

Two special devices often employed in REBT can help speed the therapeutic process. The first is to tape the entire session. These recordings are then listened to, usually several times, by the clients in their own home, car, or office so they can more incisively see their problems and the rational emotive behavioral way of handling them. Many clients who have difficulty in hearing what goes on during the face-to-face sessions

## <u>REBT Self-Help Form</u>

### A (ACTIVATING EVENTS OR ADVERSITIES)

- Briefly summarize the situation you are disturbed about (what would a camera see?)
- An *A* can be *internal* or *external, real* or *imagined.*
- An *A* can be an event in the *past, present,* or *future.*

### IBs (IRRATIONAL BELIEFS)

### D (DISPUTING IBs)

**To identify IBs, look for**

- Dogmatic Demands
  (musts, absolutes, shoulds)

- Awfulizing
  (It's awful, terrible, horrible)

- Low Frustration Tolerance
  (I can't stand it)

- Self/Other Rating
  (I'm/he/she is bad, worthless)

**To dispute, ask yourself:**

- Where is holding this belief getting me? Is it *helpful* or *self-defeating?*

- Where is the evidence to support the existence of my irrational belief? Is it *consistent with social reality?*

- Is my belief *logical?* Does it follow from my preferences?

- Is it really *awful* (as bad as it could be)?

- Can I really not *stand* it?

© Windy Dryden & Jane Walker 1992. Revised by Albert Ellis, 1996.

**REBT Self-Help Form** (*continued*)

## C (CONSEQUENCES)

Major unhealthy negative **emotions:**

Major self-defeating **behaviors:**

Unhealthy negative emotions include

- Anxiety
- Depression
- Rage
- Low Frustration Tolerance
- Shame/Embarrassment
- Hurt
- Jealousy
- Guilt

## E (EFFECTIVE NEW PHILOSOPHIES)

## E (EFFECTIVE EMOTIONS & BEHAVIORS)

New healthy
**negative emotions:**

New constructive
**behaviors:**

**To think more rationally, strive for:**

- Non-Dogmatic Preferences
  (wishes, wants, desires)
- Evaluating Badness
  (it's bad, unfortunate)
- High Frustration Tolerance
  (I don't like it, but I can stand it)
- Not Globally Rating Self or Others
  (I—and others—are fallible human
  beings)

**Healthy negative emotions include:**

- Disappointment
- Concern
- Annoyance
- Sadness
- Regret
- Frustration

(because they are too intent on talking themselves, are easily distractible, or are too anxious) are able to get more from listening to a recording of these sessions than from the original encounter.

Second, an REBT Self-Help Form is frequently used with clients to help teach them how to use the method when they encounter emotional problems between therapy sessions or after therapy has ended. This form is reproduced on the previous two pages.

## Marriage and Family Therapy

From its beginning, REBT has been used extensively in marriage and family counseling (Ellis, 1962, 2001b; Ellis & Dryden, 1997; Ellis & Harper, 1997, 2003). Usually marital or love partners are seen together. REBT therapists listen to their complaints about each other, then try to show that even if the complaints are justified, making themselves unduly upset is not. Work is done with either or both participants to minimize anxiety, depression, guilt, and (especially) hostility. As they begin to learn and apply the REBT principles, they usually become much less disturbed, often within a few sessions, and then are much better able to minimize their incompatibilities and maximize their compatibilities. Sometimes, of course, they decide that they would be better off separated or divorced, but usually they decide to work at their problems to achieve a happier marital arrangement. They are frequently taught contracting, compromising, communication, and other relating skills. The therapist is concerned with each of them as individuals who can be helped emotionally, whether or not they decide to stay together. But the more they work at helping themselves, the better their relationship tends to become (Ellis, 2001b; Ellis & Crawford, 2000; Ellis & Harper, 2003).

In family therapy, REBT practitioners sometimes see all members of the same family together, see the children in one session and the parents in another, or see them all individually. Several joint sessions are usually held to observe the interactions among family members. Whether together or separately, parents are frequently shown how to accept their children and to stop condemning them, and children are similarly shown that they can accept their parents and their siblings. The general REBT principles of unconditionally accepting oneself and others are repeatedly taught. As is common with other REBT procedures, bibliotherapy supplements counseling with REBT materials such as *A Guide to Rational Living* (Ellis & Harper, 1997), *A Rational Counseling Primer* (Young, 1974), *How to Make Yourself Happy and Remarkably Less Disturbable* (Ellis, 1999), and *Feeling Better, Getting Better, Staying Better* (Ellis, 2001a).

The *setting* of REBT sessions is much like that for other types of therapy. Most individual sessions take place in an office, but there may well be no desk between the therapist and the client, and REBT therapists tend to be informally dressed and to use simple language. Because they have relatively secure professional identities, they tend to be more open, authentic, and less "professional" than the average therapist. The main special equipment used is a cassette tape recorder. The client is likely to be encouraged to make a recording of the session to take home for replaying.

REBT therapists are highly active, give their own views without hesitation, usually answer direct questions about their personal lives, are quite energetic and often directive in group therapy, and do a good deal of speaking, particularly during early sessions. At the same time, they unconditionally accept clients. They may engage in considerable explaining, interpreting, and "lecturing" and may easily work with clients they personally do not like. Because they tend to have complete tolerance for all individuals, REBT therapists are often seen as warm and caring by their clients.

Resistance is usually handled by showing clients that they resist changing because they would like to find a magical, easy solution rather than work at changing themselves. Resistance is not usually interpreted as their particular feelings about the therapist. If a client tries to seduce a therapist, this is not usually explained in terms of "transference" but in terms of (1) the client's need for love, (2) normal attraction to a helpful person, and (3) the natural sex urges of two people who have intimate mental-emotional contact. If the therapist is attracted to the client, he or she usually admits the attraction, but explains why it is unethical to have sexual or personal relations with a client (Ellis, 2002).

## Multicultural Aspects of REBT

It is important for all therapists to appreciate the multicultural aspects of psychotherapy, since this is a vital issue (Sue & Sue, 2003). REBT has always taken a multicultural position, and aids flexibility and open-mindedness, so that practitioners who use it can deal with clients who follow different family, religious, and cultural customs. This is because it practically never gets people to dispute or fight against their cultural goals, values, and ideals but only their grandiose insistences that these goals *absolutely must* be achieved.

Suppose a client lives in an American city that has largely middle-class white Protestant citizens, and she is a relatively poor, dark-skinned, Pakistani-born Muslim. She will naturally have some real differences with her neighbors and coworkers and may upset herself about these differences. Her REBT therapist would give her unconditional acceptance, even though the therapist was a member of the majority group in the client's region and viewed some of her views and leanings as "peculiar." Her cultural and religious values would be respected as being legitimate and good for her, in spite of her differences with her community's values.

This client would be supported in following her goals and purposes—as long as she was willing to accept the consequences of displeasing some of the townspeople by sticking to them. She could be shown, with REBT, how to refuse to put herself down if she suffered from community criticism, and her "peculiar" cultural and religious ways would only be questioned if they were so rigidly held that they interfered with her basic aims. Thus, if she flouted the social-sexual mores of her own religion and culture, and concluded that she was worthless for not following them perfectly, she would be shown that it was her rigid demand that she *absolutely must* inflexibly adhere to them that was leading to her feelings of worthlessness and depression. If she changed her *must* to a *preference,* she could choose to follow or not follow these cultural rules and not feel worthless and depressed.

REBT, then, has three main principles relevant to cross-cultural psychotherapy: (1) Clients can unconditionally accept themselves and other individuals and can achieve high frustration tolerance when faced with life adversities; (2) if the therapist follows these rules and encourages her or his clients to follow them and to lead a flexible life, multicultural problems may sometimes seriously exist but can be resolved with minimum intercultural and intracultural prejudice; and (3) most multicultural issues involve bias and intolerance—which REBT particularly works against.

## Client Problems

No matter what the presenting problem may be, REBT therapists first help clients to express their disturbed emotional and behavioral reactions to their practical difficulties, and to see and tackle the basic ideas or philosophies that underlie these reactions. This is notably shown in the course of workshops for executives. In these workshops, the executives constantly bring up business, management, organizational, personal, and other problems. But they are shown that these practical problems often are tied to their self-defeating belief systems and it is *this* problem that REBT mainly helps them resolve (Ellis, Gordon, Neenan, & Palmer, 1998).

Some individuals, however, may be so inhibited or defensive that they do not permit themselves to feel and therefore may not even be aware of some of their underlying emotional problems. Thus, the successful executive who comes for psychological help only because his wife insists they have a poor relationship, and who claims that nothing really bothers him other than his wife's complaints, may have to be jolted out of his complacency by direct confrontation. REBT group therapy may be particularly helpful for such an individual, so that he finally expresses underlying anxieties and resentments and begins to acknowledge he has emotional problems.

Extreme emotionalism in the course of REBT sessions—such as crying, psychotic behavior, and violent expressions of suicidal or homicidal intent—are naturally difficult to handle. But therapists handle these problems by their own presumably rational philosophy of life and therapy, which includes these ideas: (1) Client outbursts make things difficult, but they are hardly *awful, terrible,* or *catastrophic.* (2) Behind each outburst is some irrational idea. Now, what is this idea? How can it be brought to the client's attention and what can be done to help change it? And (3) No therapist can possibly help every client all the time. If this particular client cannot be helped and has to be referred elsewhere or lost to therapy, this is unfortunate. But it does not mean that the therapist is a failure.

REBT therapists usually handle clients' profound depressions by showing them, as quickly, directly, and vigorously as possible, that they are probably creating or exacerbating their depression by (1) blaming themselves for what they have done or not done, (2) castigating themselves for being depressed and inert, and (3) bemoaning their fate because of the hassles and harshness of environmental conditions. Their self-condemnation is not only revealed but firmly disputed and, in the meantime, the therapist may give clients reassurance and support, may refer them for supplementary medication, may speak to their relatives or friends to enlist their aid, and may recommend temporary withdrawal from some activities. Through an immediate and direct disputing of clients' extreme self-deprecation and self-pity, the therapist often helps deeply depressed and suicidal people in a short period.

The most difficult clients are usually the chronic avoiders or shirkers who keep looking for magical solutions. These individuals are shown that no such magic exists; that if they do not want to work hard to get better, it is their privilege to keep suffering; and that they are not *terrible persons* for goofing off, but that they could live much more enjoyably if they worked at helping themselves. To help them get going, a form of people-involved therapy, such as group therapy, is frequently a method of choice. Results with unresponsive clients are still relatively poor in REBT (and virtually all other therapies), but persistence and vigor on the part of the therapist often eventually overcomes this kind of resistance (Ellis, 1994, 2002; Ellis & Tafrate, 1998).

## CASE EXAMPLE

This section is relatively brief because it concerns the 25-year-old computer programmer whose initial session was presented in this chapter (pp. 182–187). Other case material on this client follows.

### Background

Sara came from an Orthodox Jewish family. Her mother died in childbirth when Sara was two years of age, so Sara was raised by a loving but strict and somewhat remote father and a dominating paternal grandmother. She did well in school but had few friends up to and through college. Although fairly attractive, she was always ashamed of her body, did little dating, and occupied herself mainly with her work. At the age of 25, she was head of a section in a data processing firm. She was highly sexed and masturbated several times a week, but she had had intercourse with a man only once, when she was too drunk to know what she was doing. She had been overeating and overdrinking steadily since her college days. She had had three years of classical psychoanalysis. She thought her analyst was "a very kind and helpful man" but she had not really been helped by the process. She was quite disillusioned about therapy as a result of this experience and returned to it only because the president of her company, who liked her a great deal, told her that he would no longer put up with her constant drinking and insisted that she come to see the author of this chapter.

## Treatment

Treatment continued for six sessions along the same lines indicated in the transcript included previously in this chapter. This was followed by 24 weeks of REBT group therapy and a weekend-long rational encounter marathon.

*Cognitively,* the client was shown repeatedly that her central problem was that she devoutly believed she *had* to be almost perfect and that she *must not* be criticized in any major way by significant others. She was persistently shown, instead, how to refrain from rating her *self* but only to measure her *performances;* to see that she could never be, except by arbitrary definition, a "worm" even if she never succeeded in overcoming her overeating, compulsive drinking, and foolish symptoms; to see that it was highly desirable but not necessary that she relate intimately to a man and win the approval of her peers and her bosses at work; and first to accept herself *with* her hostility and then to give up her childish *demands* on others that led her to be so hostile to them. Although she devoutly believed in the "fact" that she and others *should* be extremely efficient and follow strict disciplinary rules, and although time and again she resisted the therapist's and the group members' assaults against her moralistic *shoulds,* she was finally induced to replace them, in her vocabulary as well as in her internalized beliefs, with *it would be betters.* She claimed to have completely overthrown her original religious orthodoxy, but she was shown that she had merely replaced it with an inordinate demand for certainty in her personal life and in world affairs, and she was finally induced to give this up, too (Ellis, 2003b).

*Emotively,* Sara was fully accepted by the therapist *as a person,* even though he strongly assailed many of her *ideas* and sometimes humorously reduced them to absurdity. She was assertively confronted by some of the group members, who helped her see how she was angrily condemning other group members for their stupidities and their shirking, and she was encouraged to accept these "bad" group members (as well as people outside the group) in spite of their inadequacies. The therapist and some of the others in her group and in the marathon weekend of rational encounter in which she participated used vigorous, down-to-earth language with her. This initially horrified Sara, but she later began to loosen up and to use similar language. When she went on a drinking bout for a few weeks and felt utterly depressed and hopeless, two group members brought out their own previous difficulties with alcohol and drugs and showed how they had managed to get through that almost impossible period in their lives. Another member gave her steady support through many phone calls and visits. At times when she clammed up and sulked, the therapist and other group members pushed her to open up and voice her real feelings. Then they went after her defenses, revealed her foolish ideas (especially the idea that she had to be terribly hurt if others rejected her), and showed how these could be uprooted. During the marathon, she was able, for the first time in her life, to let herself be really touched emotionally by a man who, up to that time, was a perfect stranger to her, and this showed her that she could afford to let down her long-held barriers to intimacy and allow herself to love.

*Behaviorally,* Sara was given homework assignments that included talking to attractive men in public places and thereby overcoming her fears of being rejected. She was shown how to stay on a long-term diet (which she had never done before) by only allowing herself rewarding experiences (such as listening to classical music) when she had first maintained her diet for a certain number of hours. Using role-playing with the therapist and other group members, she was given training in being assertive with people at work and in her social life without being aggressive (Ellis, 2003a; Wolfe, 1992).

## Resolution

Sara progressed in several ways: (1) She stopped drinking completely, lost 25 pounds, and appeared to be maintaining both her sobriety and her weight loss. (2) She became considerably less condemnatory of both herself and others and began to make some close friends. (3) She had satisfactory sexual relations with three different men and began to steadily date one of them. (4) She only rarely made herself guilty or depressed, accepted herself with her failings, and began to focus much more on enjoying than on rating herself.

## Follow-up

Sara had REBT individual and group sessions for six months—and occasional follow-up sessions the next year. She married her steady boyfriend about a year after she had originally begun treatment, after having two premarital counseling sessions with him following their engagement. Two and a half years after the close of therapy, she and her husband reported that everything was going well in their marriage, at her job, and in their social life. Her husband seemed particularly appreciative of the use she was making of REBT principles and noted "she still works hard at what she learned with you and the group and, frankly, I think that she keeps improving, because of this work, all the time." She smilingly and enthusiastically agreed.

## SUMMARY

Rational emotive behavior therapy (REBT) is a comprehensive system of personality change that incorporates cognitive, emotive, and behavior therapy methods. It is based on a clear-cut theory of emotional health and disturbance, and the many techniques it employs are usually related to that theory. Its major hypotheses also apply to child-rearing, education, social and political affairs, the extension of people's intellectual-emotional frontiers, and support of their unique potential for growth. REBT psychology is hardheaded, empirically oriented, rational, and nonmagical. It fosters the use of reason, science, and technology. It is humanistic, existentialist, and hedonistic. It aims for reduced emotional disturbance as well as increased growth and self-actualization in people's intrapersonal and interpersonal lives.

REBT theory holds that people are biologically and culturally predisposed to choose, create, and enjoy, but that they are also strongly predisposed to overconform, be suggestible, hate, and foolishly block their enjoying. Although they have remarkable capacities to observe, reason, imaginatively enhance their experiencing, and transcend some of their own essential limitations, they also have strong tendencies to ignore social reality, misuse reason, and invent absolutist musts that frequently sabotage their health and happiness. Because of their refusals to accept social reality, their continual *must*urbation, and their absorption in deifying and devil-ifying themselves and others, people frequently wind up with emotional disturbances.

More specifically, when noxious stimuli occur in people's lives at point A (their adversities), they usually observe these events objectively and conclude, at point rB (their rational belief), that this event is unfortunate, inconvenient, and disadvantageous and that they wish it would change. Then they healthily feel, at point C (the consequence), sad, regretful, frustrated, or annoyed. These healthy negative feelings usually help them to try to do something about their adversities to improve or change them. Their inborn and acquired hedonism and constructivism encourage them to have, in regard to adversities, rational thoughts ("I don't like this; let's see what I can do to change it") and healthy negative feelings (sorrow and annoyance) that enable them to reorder their environment and to live more enjoyably.

Very often, however, when similar adversities occur in people's lives, they observe these events intolerantly and grandiosely and conclude, at point iB (their irrational beliefs), that these events are awful, horrible, and catastrophic; that they *must* not exist; and that they absolutely cannot stand them. They then self-defeatingly feel the consequence, at point C, of worthlessness, guilt, anxiety, depression, rage, and inertia. Their disturbed feelings usually interfere with their doing something constructive about the adversities, and they tend to condemn themselves for their unconstructiveness and to experience more feelings of shame, inferiority, and hopelessness. Their inborn and acquired person-downing, antihumanistic, and deifying and devil-ifying philosophies encourage them to have, in regard to unfortunate activating events, foolish thoughts ("How awful this is and I am! There's nothing I can do about it!") and dysfunctional feelings (hatred of themselves, of others, and of the world) that encourage them to whine and rant and live less enjoyably.

REBT is a cognitive-emotive-behavioristic method of psychotherapy uniquely designed to enable people to observe, understand, and persistently dispute their irrational, grandiose, perfectionistic *shoulds, oughts,* and *musts* and their *awfulizing.* It employs the logico-empirical method of science to encourage people to surrender magic, absolutes, and damnation; to acknowledge that nothing is sacred or all-important (although many things are exceptionally unpleasant and inconvenient); and to gradually teach themselves and to practice the philosophy of desiring rather than demanding and of working at changing what they can change and gracefully accepting what they cannot change about themselves, about others, and about the world (Ellis, 1994, 2002; Ellis & Blau, 1998; Ellis & Dryden, 1997; Ellis & MacLaren, 1998).

In conclusion, rational emotive behavior therapy is a method of personality change that quickly and efficiently helps people resist their tendencies to be too conforming, suggestible, and anhedonic. It actively and didactically, as well as emotively and behaviorally, shows people how to abet and enhance one side of their humanness while simultaneously changing and living more happily with (and not repressing or squelching) another side. It is thus realistic and practical as well as idealistic and future-oriented. It helps individuals to more fully actualize, experience, and enjoy the here and now, but it also espouses long-range hedonism, which includes planning for their own (and others') future. It is what its name implies: rational *and* emotive *and* behavioral, realistic *and* visionary, empirical *and* humanistic. As, in all their complexity, are humans.

## ANNOTATED BIBLIOGRAPHY

Ellis, A., & Dryden, W. (1997). *The practice of rational-emotive behavior therapy.* New York: Springer.
This book presents the general theory and basic practice of rational emotive behavior therapy (REBT), with special chapters on how it is used in individual, couples, family, group, and sex therapy. It brings the original seminal book on REBT, *Reason and Emotion*

*in Psychotherapy* (Ellis, 1962) up to date and gives many details about REBT therapy procedures.

Ellis, A., & Harper, R. A. (1997). *A guide to rational living.* North Hollywood, CA: Wilshire Books.
This completely revised and rewritten version of the REBT self-help classic is one of the most widely read

self-help books ever published, and it is often recommended by cognitive-behavior therapists to their clients. It is a succinct, straightforward approach to

REBT based on self-questioning and homework and shows how readers can help themselves with various emotional problems.

## CASE READINGS

Ellis, A. (1971). A twenty-three-year-old woman, guilty about not following her parents' rules. In A. Ellis, *Growth through reason: Verbatim cases in rational-emotive therapy* (pp. 223–286). Hollywood: Wilshire Books. [Reprinted in D. Wedding & R. J. Corsini (Eds.). (2005). *Case studies in psychotherapy.* Belmont, CA: Wadsworth.]

Ellis presents a verbatim protocol of the first, second, and fourth sessions with a woman who comes for help because she is self-punishing, impulsive and compulsive, afraid of males, has no goals in life, and is guilty about her relations with her parents. The therapist quickly zeroes in on her main problems and shows her that she need not feel guilty about doing what she wants to do in life, even if her parents keep upsetting themselves about her beliefs and actions.

Ellis, A. (1977). Verbatim psychotherapy session with a procrastinator. In A. Ellis & W. J. Knaus, *Overcoming procrastination* (pp. 152–167). New York: New American Library.

Ellis presents a single verbatim session with a procrastinator who was failing to finish her doctoral thesis in sociology. He deals with her problems in a direct, no-nonsense manner typical of rational emotive behavior therapy, and as a result of a single session, she later reports she finished her thesis, although she had previously been procrastinating on it for a number of years.

Ellis, A., & Dryden, W. (1996). Transcript of a demonstration session, with comments on the session by Windy Dryden and Albert Ellis. In W. Dryden, *Practical skills in rational emotive behavior therapy* (pp. 91–117). London: Whurr.

Ellis presents a verbatim protocol with a therapist who volunteers to bring up problems of feeling inadequate as a therapist and as a person. Albert Ellis shows her some core beliefs leading to her self-downing and how to actively dispute and surrender these beliefs. Ellis and Windy Dryden then review the protocol to analyze its REBT aspects.

## REFERENCES

Adler, A. (1931). *What life should mean to you.* New York: Blue Ribbon Books.

Adler, A. (1964). *Social interest: A challenge to mankind.* New York: Capricorn.

Alford, B. A., & Beck, A. T. (1997). *The integrative power of cognitive therapy.* New York: Guilford Press.

Barlow, D. H., Esler, J. L., & Vitali, A. E. (1998). Psychosocial treatment for panic disorders, phobias, and general anxiety disorder. In P. E. Nathan & J. M. Gorman (Eds.), *A guide to treatments that work* (pp. 228–318). New York: Oxford University Press.

Bernard, M. E., & Wolfe, J. W. (Eds.). (1993). *The RET resource book for practitioners.* New York: Institute for Rational-Emotive Therapy.

DiGiuseppe, R. A., Miller, N. K., & Trexler, L. D. (1979). A review of rational-emotive psychotherapy outcome studies. In A. Ellis & J. M. Whiteley (Eds.), *Theoretical and empirical foundations of rational-emotive therapy* (pp. 218–235). Monterey, CA: Brooks/Cole.

DiGiuseppe, R. A., Terjesen, M., Rose, R., Doyle, K., & Vadalakis, N. (1998, August). *Selective abstractions errors in reviewing REBT outcome studies: A review of reviews.* Poster presented at the 106th Annual Convention of the American Psychological Association, San Francisco, CA.

Ellis, A. (1962). *Reason and emotion in psychotherapy.* Secaucus, NJ: Citadel.

Ellis, A. (1976). The biological basis of human irrationality. *Journal of Individual Psychology, 32,* 145–168.

Ellis, A. (1994). *Reason and emotion in psychotherapy* (rev. ed.). New York: Citadel.

Ellis, A. (1998). *How to control your anxiety before it controls you.* New York: Citadel.

Ellis, A. (1999). *How to make yourself happy and remarkably less disturbable.* San Luis Obispo, CA: Impact Publishers.

Ellis, A. (2001a). *Feeling better, getting better, staying better.* Atascadero, CA: Impact Publishers.

Ellis, A. (2001b). *Overcoming destructive beliefs, feelings, and behaviors.* Amherst, NY: Prometheus Books.

Ellis, A. (2002). *Overcoming resistance: A rational emotive behavior therapy integrative approach.* New York: Springer.

Ellis, A. (2003a). *Anger: How to live with it and without it* (rev. ed.). New York: Citadel Press.

Ellis, A, (2003b). *Sex without guilt in the twenty-first century.* Teaneck, NJ: Battleside Books.

Ellis, A. (2004). *Rational emotive behavior therapy: It works for me, it can work for you.* Amherst, NY: Prometheus Books.

Ellis, A., & Blau, S. (1998). (Eds.). *The Albert Ellis reader.* Secaucus, NJ: Carol Publishing Group.

Ellis, A., & Crawford, T. (2000). *Making intimate connections.* Atascadero, CA: Impact Publishers.

Ellis, A., & Dryden, W. (1996). Transcript of demonstration session. Commentary on Albert Ellis' demonstration session by Windy Dryden and Albert Ellis. In W. Dryden, *Practical skills in rational emotive behavior therapy* (pp. 91–117). London: Whurr.

Ellis, A., & Dryden, W. (1997). *The practice of rational emotive behavior therapy.* New York: Springer.

Ellis, A., Gordon, J., Neenan, M., & Palmer, S. (1998). *Stress counseling.* New York: Springer.

Ellis, A., & Harper, R. A. (1997). *A guide to rational living.* North Hollywood, CA: Melvin Powers.

Ellis, A., & Harper, R. A. (2003). *Dating, mating, and relating.* New York: Citadel.

Ellis, A., & Joffe, D. (2002). A study of volunteer clients who experience live sessions of rational emotive behavior therapy in front of a public audience. *Journal of Rational-Emotive and Cognitive-Behavior Therapy, 20,* 151–158.

Ellis, A., & MacLaren, C. (1998). *Rational emotive behavior therapy: A therapist's guide.* Atascadero, CA: Impact Publishers.

Ellis, A., & Tafrate, R. C. (1998). *How to control your anger before it controls you.* Secaucus, NJ: Birch Lane Press.

Ellis, A., & Whiteley, J. (1979). *Theoretical and empirical foundations of rational-emotive therapy.* Pacific Grove, CA: Brooks/Cole.

Engels, G. I., Garnefski, N., & Diekstra, R. F. W. (1993). Efficacy of rational-emotive therapy: A quantitative analysis. *Journal of Consulting & Clinical Psychology, 61,* 1083–1090.

Haaga, D. A. F., & Davison, G. C. (1993). An appraisal of rational-emotive therapy. *Journal of Consulting & Clinical Psychology, 61,* 215–220.

Hajzler, D., & Bernard, M. E. (1991). A review of rational-emotive outcome studies. *School Psychology Studies, 6*(1), 27–49.

Hauck, P. A. (1992). *Overcoming the rating game: Beyond self-love—Beyond self-esteem.* Louisville, KY: Westminster/John Knox.

Hollon, S. D., & Beck, A. T. (1999). Cognitive and cognitive-behavioral therapies. In A. E. Bergin & S. L. Garfield (Eds.), *Handbook of psychotherapy and behavior change* (4th ed., pp. 428–466). New York: Wiley.

Jorn, A. F. (1989). Modifiability and neuroticism: A meta-analysis of the literature. *Australian and New Zealand Journal of Psychiatry, 23,* 21–29.

Lyons, L. C., & Woods, P. J. (1991). The efficacy of rational-emotive therapy: A quantitative review of the outcome research. *Clinical Psychology Review, 11,* 357–369.

McGovern, T. E., & Silverman, M. S. (1984). A review of outcome studies of rational-emotive therapy from 1977 to 1982. *Journal of Rational-Emotive Therapy, 2*(1), 7–18.

Nielsen, S., Johnson, W. B., & Ellis, A. (2001). *Counseling and psychotherapy with religious persons.* Mahwah, NJ: Erlbaum.

Rogers, C. R. (1961). *On becoming a person.* Boston: Houghton Mifflin.

Seligman, M. E. P., Revich, K., Jaycox, L., & Gillham, J. (1995). *The optimistic child.* Boston: Houghton Mifflin.

Silverman, M. S., McCarthy, M., & McGovern, T. (1992). A review of outcome studies of rational-emotive therapy from 1982–1989. *Journal of Rational-Emotive and Cognitive-Behavior Therapy, 10*(3), 111–186.

Smith, M., & Glass, G. (1977). Meta-analysis of psychotherapy outcome studies. *American Psychologist, 32,* 752–760.

Sue, D. W., & Sue, D. (2003). *Counseling with the culturally diverse.* New York: Wiley.

Vernon, A. (2001). *The passport program.* 3 vols. Champaign, IL: Research Press.

Walen, S. R., Digiuseppe, R., & Dryden, W. (1997). *A practitioner's guide to rational-emotive therapy* (2nd ed.). New York: Oxford.

Wolfe, J. L. (1992). *What to do when he has a headache.* New York: Hyperion.

Woods, P. J. (1992). A study of belief and non-belief items from the Jones irrational beliefs test with implications for the theory of RET. *Journal of Rational-Emotive and Cognitive-Behavior Therapy, 10,* 41–52.

Young, H. S. (1974). *A rational counseling primer.* New York: Albert Ellis Institute.

Ivan Pavlov
(1849–1936)
© Bettmann /CORBIS

B. F. Skinner
(1904–1990)
© Bettmann /CORBIS

Joseph Wolpe
(1915–1997)
Courtesy of Professor Joseph Wolpe

Albert Bandura
University of Akron,
Psychology Archives

# 7    BEHAVIOR THERAPY

*G. Terence Wilson*

## OVERVIEW

Behavior therapy is a relative newcomer on the psychotherapy scene. Not until the late 1950s did it emerge as a systematic approach to the assessment and treatment of psychological disorders. In its early stages, behavior therapy was defined as the application of modern learning theory to the treatment of clinical problems. The phrase *modern learning theory* referred to the principles and procedures of classical and operant conditioning. Behavior therapy was seen as the logical extension of behaviorism to complex forms of human activities.

Behavior therapy has undergone significant changes in both nature and scope, and it has been responsive to advances in experimental psychology and innovations in clinical practice. It has grown more complex and sophisticated. Behavior therapy can no longer be defined simply as the clinical application of classical and operant conditioning theory.

Behavior therapy today is marked by a diversity of views. It now comprises a broad range of heterogeneous procedures with different theoretical rationales and open debate about conceptual bases, methodological requirements, and evidence of efficacy. As behavior therapy expands, it increasingly overlaps with other psychotherapeutic approaches. Nevertheless, the basic concepts characteristic of the behavioral approach are clear and its commonalities with and differences from nonbehavioral therapeutic systems can be readily identified.

## Basic Concepts

Three main approaches in contemporary behavior therapy include (1) *applied behavior analysis,* (2) a *neobehavioristic mediational stimulus-response model,* and (3) *social-cognitive theory.* These three approaches differ in the extent to which they use cognitive concepts and procedures. At one end of this continuum is *applied behavior analysis,* which focuses exclusively on observable behavior and rejects all cognitive mediating processes. At the other end is *social-cognitive theory,* which relies heavily on cognitive theories.

### Applied Behavior Analysis

This approach is a direct extension of Skinner's (1953) radical behaviorism. It relies on operant conditioning, the fundamental assumption being that behavior is a function of its consequences. Accordingly, treatment procedures are based on altering relationships between overt behaviors and their consequences. Applied behavior analysis makes use of reinforcement, punishment, extinction, stimulus control, and other procedures derived from laboratory research. Cognitive processes are considered private events and are not regarded as proper subjects of scientific analysis.

### The Neobehavioristic Mediational Stimulus-Response (S-R) Model

This approach features the application of the principles of classical conditioning, and it derives from the learning theories of Ivan Pavlov, E. R. Guthrie, Clark Hull, O. H. Mowrer, and N. E. Miller. Unlike the operant approach, the S-R model is mediational, with intervening variables and hypothetical constructs prominently featured. S-R theorists have been particularly interested in the study of anxiety; the techniques of systematic desensitization and flooding, both closely associated with this model, are directed toward the extinction of the underlying anxiety assumed to maintain phobic disorders. Private events, especially imagery, have been an integral part of this approach, including systematic desensitization. The rationale is that covert processes follow the laws of learning that govern overt behaviors.

### Social-Cognitive Theory

The social-cognitive approach depends on the theory that behavior is based on three separate but interacting regulatory systems (Bandura, 1986). They are (1) external stimulus events, (2) external reinforcement, and (3) cognitive mediational processes.

In the social-cognitive approach, the influence of environmental events on behavior is largely determined by cognitive processes governing how environmental influences are perceived and how the individual interprets them. Psychological functioning, according to this view, involves a reciprocal interaction among three interlocking sets of influences: behavior, cognitive processes, and environmental factors. Bandura put it as follows:

> Personal and environmental factors do not function as independent determinants; rather, they determine each other. Nor can "persons" be considered causes independent of their behavior. It is largely through their actions that people produce the environmental conditions that affect their behavior in a reciprocal fashion. The experiences generated by behavior also partly determine what individuals think, expect, and can do, which in turn affect their subsequent behavior. (1977, p. 345)

In social-cognitive theory, the person is the agent of change. The theory emphasizes the human capacity for self-directed behavior change. Strongly influenced by the social-cognitive model, the clinical practice of behavior therapy has increasingly included cognitive methods, especially those described by Aaron Beck (see Chapter 8). A primary focus of both cognitive and behavioral techniques is to change the cognitive processes viewed as essential to therapeutic success. The basic assumption is that it is not so much experience itself, but rather the person's interpretation of that experience, that produces psychological disturbance. This position is also reflected in the work of Albert Ellis (see Chapter 6). Both cognitive and behavioral methods are used to modify faulty perceptions and interpretations of important life events. For these reasons it is now common to refer to "cognitive behavior therapy" (CBT) instead of "behavior therapy." As Jacobson (1987) has pointed out, "incorporation of cognitive theory and therapy into behavior therapy has been so total that it is difficult to find pure behavior therapists working with outpatients" (pp. 4–5). The term "behavior therapy" is used throughout this chapter, although it could just as easily be replaced with "CBT." Behavior therapy, in a broad sense, refers to practice based primarily on social-cognitive theory and encompassing a range of cognitive principles and procedures.

## Common Characteristics

Although the three preceding behavior therapy approaches involve conceptual differences, behavior therapists subscribe to a common core of basic concepts. The two foundations of behavior therapy are (1) a psychological model of human behavior that differs fundamentally from the traditional psychodynamic model, and (2) a commitment to the scientific method.

The emphasis on a psychological model of abnormal behavior and the commitment to a scientific approach have the following consequences:

1. Many types of abnormal behavior formerly regarded as illnesses or as signs and symptoms of illness are better construed as nonpathological "problems of living" (key examples include anxiety reactions, as well as sexual and conduct disorders). This position is similar to that of Alfred Adler.

2. Most abnormal behavior is assumed to be acquired and maintained in the same manner as normal behavior. It can be treated through the application of behavioral procedures.

3. Behavioral assessment focuses on the current determinants of behavior rather than on the analysis of possible historical antecedents. Specificity is the hallmark of behavioral assessment and treatment, and it is assumed that the person is best understood and described by what the person does in a particular situation.

4. Treatment requires a prior analysis of the problem into components or subparts. Procedures are then systematically targeted at specific components.

5. Treatment strategies are individually tailored to different problems in different individuals.

6. Understanding the origins of a psychological problem is not essential for producing behavior change. Conversely, success in changing a problem behavior does not imply knowledge about its etiology.

7. Behavior therapy involves a commitment to the scientific approach. This includes an explicit, testable conceptual framework; treatment derived from or at least consistent with the content and method of experimental-clinical psychology; therapeutic techniques that have measurable outcomes and can be replicated; the experimental evaluation of treatment methods and concepts; and the emphasis on innovative research strategies that

allow rigorous evaluation of specific methods applied to particular problems instead of global assessment of ill-defined procedures applied to heterogeneous problems.

## Other Systems

Behavior therapy has much in common with other psychological therapies, particularly those that tend to be brief and directive. In some cases, behavior therapy has "borrowed" concepts and methods from other systems. For example, behavioral marital therapy places great emphasis on communication skills (Jacobson & Margolin, 1979), an approach that was derived from the clinical tradition of client-centered therapy (Knudson, Gurman, & Kniskern, 1979).

Cognitive-behavioral treatment strategies have incorporated some of the concepts of Albert Ellis's rational emotive behavior therapy and especially Beck's cognitive therapy (Hawton, Salkovskis, Kirk, & Clark, 1989; O'Leary & Wilson, 1987). CBT is closer to Beck's cognitive therapy than Ellis's approach because Beck emphasizes the importance of behavioral procedures in correcting the dysfunctional beliefs assumed to cause emotional distress. Ellis's REBT, despite the later inclusion of *behavior* in the name, is mainly a semantic treatment in which the goal is to alter the person's basic philosophy of life through reason and logic. The overlap between BT and Beck's cognitive therapy is more extensive, especially in the treatment of unipolar depression and some anxiety disorders. Both systems include cognitive and behavioral components but may differ in how these components are combined and especially in their theories about mechanisms of therapeutic change (Hawton et al., 1989; Hollon & Beck, 1994).

In terms of clinical practice, behavior therapy and multimodal therapy are similar. The majority of the techniques that Arnold Lazarus (1981) lists as the most frequently used in multimodal therapy (see Chapter 11) are standard behavior therapy strategies. This is not surprising, given that Lazarus (1971) was one of the pioneers of clinical behavior therapy.

Therapists are guided in their formulations and treatment of different problems either by clearly stated principles or by their personal experience and intuition. Behavior therapy represents an attempt to move beyond idiosyncratic practices and to base clinical practice on secure scientific foundations. This does not mean that clinical practice by behavior therapists is always based on solid empirical evidence. Behavior therapists, not unlike therapists from other approaches, have developed their own clinical lore, much of which is not based on experimental research. Lacking sufficient information and guidelines from research, behavior therapists often adopt a trial-and-error approach. Nonetheless, behavior therapy is clearly linked to a specifiable and testable conceptual framework.

Behavior therapy differs fundamentally from psychodynamic approaches to treatment. Based on a learning or educational model of human development, it rejects the psychoanalytic model, in which abnormal behavior is viewed as a symptom of underlying unconscious conflicts. Psychoanalytic therapy has difficulty explaining successes of behavior therapy that contradict basic concepts that psychoanalysts claim are crucial for therapeutic change. Some psychodynamic therapists state that behavioral treatments result in symptom substitution because behavioral treatment allegedly overlooks the "real" cause of the problem. Yet the evidence is clear that symptom substitution does not occur in successful behavior therapy (e.g., Sloane, Staples, Cristol, Yorkston, & Whipple, 1975).

Family and systems therapists assert that individuals can best be understood and treated by changing the interpersonal system within a family. Behavior therapy has increasingly emphasized the importance of including family members in treatment. However, behavior therapists reject the assumption that every problem requires a broad-scale intervention in the family system. The findings of outcome studies show that this is not always necessary (Mathews, Gelder, & Johnston, 1981). For example, not only does individual behavior therapy for agoraphobics produce long-term improvement in phobic avoidance, it often also results in increases in marital satisfaction and improvements in other aspects of interpersonal functioning (Marks, 1981). Data such as these discredit the claims of some family systems theorists.

Most forms of psychotherapy are limited to specific populations. Traditional psychoanalytic therapy, for instance, has focused predominantly on white, well-educated, socially and economically advantaged clients. Behavior therapy is more broadly applicable to the full range of psychological disorders than is traditional psychotherapy (Kazdin & Wilson, 1978). In the Sloane et al. (1975) study, for example, behavior therapy appeared to be more effective than traditional psychotherapy, particularly with the complex problems of severely disturbed patients. Areas of successful application of behavior therapy procedures are found in education, rehabilitation, and medicine (Franks, Wilson, Kendall, & Brownell, 1982; Kazdin, 1978b). Finally, behavior therapy is the preferred treatment for certain problems, such as phobic and obsessive-compulsive disorders, sexual dysfunction, and a number of childhood disorders.

Overall evaluation of the comparative efficacy of behavior therapy versus other psychotherapies is uncertain. Nevertheless, in no comparative outcome study to date has behavior therapy been shown to be less effective than any alternative form of psychotherapy (Kazdin & Wilson, 1978). The evidence, unsatisfactory as it is, indicates that behavior therapy is more effective than psychoanalytic and other verbal psychotherapies (see Hollon & Beck, 1994; O'Leary & Wilson, 1987).

# HISTORY

## Precursors

Two historical events stand out as foundations for behavior therapy. The first was the rise of behaviorism in the early 1900s. The key figure in the United States was J. B. Watson, who criticized the subjectivity and mentalism of the psychology of the time and advocated behaviorism as the basis for the objective study of behavior. Watson's emphasis on the importance of environmental events, his rejection of covert aspects of the individual, and his claim that all behavior could be understood as a result of learning became the formal bases of behaviorism.

Watson's position has been widely rejected by behavior therapists, and more refined versions of behaviorism have been developed by theorists such as B. F. Skinner, whose radical behaviorism has had a significant impact not only on behavior therapy but also on psychology in general. Like Watson, Skinner insisted that overt behavior is the only acceptable subject of scientific investigation.

The second event was experimental research on the psychology of learning. In Russia, around the turn of the twentieth century, Ivan Pavlov, a Nobel laureate in physiology, established the foundations of classical conditioning. About the same time in the United States, pioneering research on animal learning by E. L. Thorndike showed the influence of consequences (rewarding and punishing events) on behavior.

Research on conditioning and learning principles, conducted largely in the animal laboratory, became a dominant part of experimental psychology in the United States following World War II. Workers in this area, in the traditions of Pavlov and Skinner, were committed to the scientific analysis of behavior using the laboratory rat and pigeon as their prototypic subjects. Among the early applications of conditioning principles to the treatment of clinical problems were two particularly notable studies. In 1924, Mary Cover Jones described different behavioral procedures for overcoming children's fears.

In 1938, O. Hobart Mowrer and E. Mowrer extended conditioning principles to the treatment of enuresis. The treatment they developed is now an effective and widely used approach (Ross, 1981). These isolated and sporadic efforts had scant impact on psychotherapy at the time partly because conditioning principles, demonstrated with animals, were rejected as too simplistic for treating complex human problems. Conditioning treatments were rejected as superficial, mechanistic, and naive. In addition, a schism existed between academic-experimental and clinical psychologists. The former were trained in scientific methods, with an emphasis on controlled experimentation and quantitative measurement. The latter concerned themselves with the "soft" side of psychology, including uncontrolled case studies, speculative hypotheses, and psychodynamic hypotheses. Some efforts were made to integrate conditioning principles with psychodynamic theories of abnormal behavior, but these formulations only obscured crucial differences between behavioral and psychodynamic approaches.

The advent of behavior therapy was marked by its challenge of the status quo through the presentation of a systematic and explicitly formulated clinical alternative that attempted to bridge the gap between the laboratory and the clinic.

## Beginnings

The formal beginnings of behavior therapy can be traced to separate but related developments in the 1950s in three countries.

Joseph Wolpe (1958), in South Africa, presented procedural details and results of his application of learning principles to adult neurotic disorders in his book *Psychotherapy by Reciprocal Inhibition*. Wolpe introduced several therapeutic techniques based on Pavlov's conditioning principles, Hull's S-R learning theory, and his own experimental research on fear reduction in laboratory animals. Anxiety was regarded as the causal agent in all neurotic reactions. It was defined as a persistent response of the autonomic nervous system acquired through classical conditioning. Wolpe developed specific techniques designed to extinguish these conditioned autonomic reactions, including systematic desensitization, one of the most widely used methods of behavior therapy. Wolpe made the controversial claim that 90 percent of his patients were either "cured" or "markedly improved." Moreover, this unprecedented success rate was apparently accomplished within a few months, or even weeks. Wolpe influenced Arnold Lazarus and Stanley Rachman, both of whom became leading figures in the development of behavior therapy. Wolpe's conditioning techniques in therapy were consistent with similar proposals that had been put forward by Andrew Salter (1949) in New York.

Another landmark in the development of behavior therapy was the research and writings of Hans J. Eysenck and his students at the Institute of Psychiatry of London University. In a seminal paper published in 1959, Eysenck defined behavior therapy as the application of modern learning theory to the treatment of behavioral and emotional disorders. Eysenck emphasized the principles and procedures of Pavlov and Hull, as well as learning theorists such as Mowrer (1947) and Miller (1948). In Eysenck's formulation, behavior therapy was an applied science, the defining feature of which was that it was testable and falsifiable. In 1963 Eysenck and Rachman established the first journal devoted exclusively to behavior therapy —*Behaviour Research and Therapy.*

A third force in the emergence of behavior therapy was the publication in 1953 of Skinner's book *Science and Human Behavior,* in which he criticized psychodynamic concepts and reformulated psychotherapy in behavioral terms. The most important initial clinical application of operant conditioning was with children, work carried out under the direction of Sidney Bijou at the University of Washington. The broad application of operant conditioning to the whole range of psychiatric disorders reached full expression in the 1965 publication of Leonard Ullmann and Leonard Krasner's *Case Studies in Be-*

*havior Modification*. In 1968, the first issue of the *Journal of Applied Behavior Analysis* was published. This journal provided the premier outlet for research on the modification of socially significant problems through the use of operant conditioning.

Toward the end of the 1960s, the theoretical and research bases of behavior therapy began to expand. Increasingly, behavior therapists turned to social, personality, and developmental psychology as sources of innovative therapeutic strategies. Particularly noteworthy in this regard was Bandura's (1969) social learning theory, with its emphases on vicarious learning (modeling), symbolic processes, and self-regulatory mechanisms. The 1970s witnessed an increased emphasis on cognitive processes and procedures in behavior therapy.

The 1980s and 1990s have been marked by an even broader focus on developments in other areas of psychology. Particular attention has been paid to the role of affect in therapeutic change. The experimental analysis of the complex interactions among cognition, affect, and behavior is one of the more important areas of theory and research in contemporary behavior therapy. There is also increasing recognition of the importance of biological factors in many of the disorders commonly treated with behavioral methods (e.g., anxiety disorders and obesity). The study of biobehavioral interactions is an increasingly significant part of behavior therapy (O'Leary & Wilson, 1987). (See Kazdin [1978b] for details of the early history of behavior therapy.)

## Current Status

Behavior therapy has had a profound impact on the field of psychotherapy. An important measure of the influence of behavior therapy is the degree to which psychotherapists use cognitive-behavioral principles and procedures in their clinical practice. Based on his survey of the theoretical orientations of clinical psychologists in the United States, Darrell Smith (1982) concluded that "No single theme dominates the present development of professional psychotherapy. Our findings suggest, however, that cognitive-behavioral options represent one of the strongest, if not the strongest, theoretical emphases today" (p. 310). Nine years ago, a committee of the American Psychological Association constructed a list of psychological treatments that had been shown to be effective in controlled empirical research (Task Force on Promotion and Dissemination of Psychological Procedures, 1995). Behavior therapy methods dominated this list of empirically supported treatments.

It seems likely that behavior therapy techniques will be increasingly used to treat a broad range of psychological problems. In the early 1990s, a panel of 75 expert psychotherapists comprising representatives of a wide range of different theoretical orientations in the United States was asked to predict what would happen to the practice of psychotherapy in the future (regardless of their personal preferences) (Norcross, Alford, & DeMichele, 1992). The panel largely agreed in ranking CBT techniques as those most likely to be used in the future. The reason? As health care policy in the U.S. is changing to contain costs and provide coverage to more people, the emphasis is switching to problem-focused, time-limited psychological treatment. Moreover, future third-party reimbursement for mental health services will not only emphasize cost containment, but also demand that treatments be demonstrably effective in producing specified goals. Behavior therapy will be an important part of those interventions.

In its formative years in the 1950s and 1960s, behavior therapy was a radical minority movement that challenged the then-dominant psychoanalytic establishment. Today behavior therapy is part of the psychotherapeutic establishment. Beginning in the 1960s in the United States, several graduate clinical programs in some of the country's most distinguished universities placed primary emphasis on a behavioral orientation in their training of predoctoral students. Many others began to include behavior therapy as part of an eclectic approach to clinical training. In their analysis of the orientations of faculty in doctoral programs accredited by the American Psychological Association, Sayette and Mayne (1990) found that 14 percent could be described as having an applied behavioral or radical behavioral approach, while an additional 42 percent emphasized cognitive-behavioral or social learning approaches.

In contrast to the impact on the training and practice of clinical psychologists, behavior therapy has had little influence on that of other mental health professionals in the United States (Glass & Arnkoff, 1992). The minimal impact on psychiatry is ironic, given the seminal contributions of some psychiatrists to the development of cognitive-behavioral therapy (e.g., Joseph Wolpe and Aaron Beck). This is probably due to the total dominance of psychoanalysis in American psychiatry for more than 40 years. More recently, biological psychiatry has often supplanted the psychoanalytic model in training programs. As a result, psychological treatment has been deemphasized in the training of psychiatrists.

The first behavior therapy journal, *Behaviour Research and Therapy,* was published in 1963 in part because the psychodynamically inclined editors of existing clinical journals were unreceptive to behavior therapy. Today there are numerous journals devoted to behavior therapy in different countries. Moreover, behavior therapists have been editors and editorial board members of major all-purpose clinical psychology journals, such as the *Journal of Clinical and Consulting Psychology* in the United States.

# PERSONALITY

## Theory of Personality

There are specific theoretical differences within the broad framework of contemporary behavior therapy. These differences are most noticeable in the personality theories on which the respective approaches are based. For example, Eysenck (1967) has developed an elaborate trait theory of personality. Briefly, Eysenck classifies people on two major personality dimensions. The first, *introversion-extraversion,* refers to characteristics usually associated with the words *introverted* and *extraverted.* The second dimension is *neuroticism–emotional stability,* ranging from moody and touchy at one extreme to stable and even-tempered at the other. Eysenck believes these personality dimensions are genetically determined and that introverts are more responsive to conditioning procedures than extraverts. In general, however, personality theory appears to have had little impact on clinical behavior therapy, and most behavior therapists have rejected trait theories of personality.

Applied behavior analysis, derived directly from Skinner's radical behaviorism, restricts itself to the study of overt behavior and environmental conditions that presumably regulate behavior. Covert, unobservable elements, such as needs, drives, motives, traits, and conflicts, are disregarded. Skinner's analyses of behavior, for example, are couched in terms of conditioning processes, such as reinforcement, discrimination, and generalization.

Radical behaviorism has been criticized for losing sight of the importance of the person and for lacking a theory of personality. Humanistic psychologists believe applied behavior analysts treat people as though they were controlled only by external, situational forces. A solution to this clash between two extreme viewpoints is to recognize that the characteristics of the environment *interact* with the nature of the people in it. Both commonsense and experimental findings demonstrate the folly of ignoring either side of this crucial interaction. A social learning framework of personality development and change provides a detailed and sophisticated analysis of this interaction between person and situation (Bandura, 1969; Mischel, 1968, 1981).

Many people have debated whether the person or the situation is more important in predicting behavior. However, this question is unanswerable. The relative importance of individual differences and situations will depend on the situation selected, the type of behavior assessed, the particular individual differences sampled, and the purpose of the assessment (Mischel, 1973).

Evidence clearly shows that an individual's behavioral patterns are generally stable and consistent over time. However, the specificity of behavior in different situations poses a problem for trait theories of personality. The central assumption of such theories is that stable and generalized personality traits determine behavioral consistency in a wide variety of different situations. Yet, as Mischel (1968) has pointed out, the correlations between different measures of the same trait are usually very low, and there is little consistency in behavior patterns across different situations.

Psychodynamic conceptualizations of personality assume that the underlying personality structure is stable across situations. Overt behavior is of interest to psychodynamic theorists only to the extent that the behavior provides signs of deep-seated personality traits. Psychodynamic theorists believe that behavior cannot be taken at face value but must be interpreted symbolically because the personality's defense mechanisms disguise and distort the "real" motivations being expressed. However, "the accumulated findings give little support for the utility of clinical judgments. . . . Clinicians guided by concepts about underlying genotypic dispositions have not been able to predict behavior better than have the person's own direct self-report, simple indices of directly relevant past behavior, or demographic variables" (Mischel, 1973, p. 254).

Social-cognitive theory readily accounts for the discriminatory nature of human behavior. A person would be predicted to act consistently in different situations only to the extent that similar behavior leads, or is expected to lead, to similar consequences. An illustration from Mischel will help clarify this key concept:

> Consider a woman who seems hostile and fiercely independent some of the time but passive, dependent, and feminine on other occasions. What is she really like? Which one of these two patterns reflects the woman that she really is? Is one pattern in the service of the other, or might both be in the service of a third motive? Must she be a really aggressive person with a facade of passivity—or is she a warm, passive-dependent woman with a surface defense of aggressiveness? Social learning theory suggests that it is possible for her to be all of these—a hostile, fiercely independent, passive, dependent, feminine, aggressive, warm person all in one. Of course, which of these she is at any particular moment would not be random and capricious; it would depend on discriminative stimuli—who she is with, when, how, and much, much more. But each of these aspects of herself may be a quite genuine and real aspect of her total being. (1976, p. 86)

The difference between the behavioral and psychodynamic approaches in explaining the development of abnormal behavior can be illustrated by Freud's case of Little Hans. This child developed a phobia for horses, which Freud attributed to castration anxiety and oedipal conflict. In their reinterpretation of this case, Wolpe and Rachman (1960) point out that Little Hans had recently experienced four incidents in which horses were associated with frightening events that could have created a classically conditioned phobic reaction. For example, Hans was terrified when he saw a horse that was pulling a loaded cart knocked down and apparently killed. From a psychodynamic viewpoint, the external stimuli (what Little Hans saw) had little effect on the phobia; the fear of horses per se was less significant than the underlying conflict. As Freud put it, "the anxiety originally had no reference to horses but was transposed onto them secondarily." This interpretation does not account for the discriminative pattern of the boy's reactions. For example, he was fearful of a single horse pulling a loaded cart (viewed by Freud as a symbol of pregnancy) but not of two horses, of large horses but not small ones, and of rapidly moving horse-drawn carts but not slowly moving ones. How is this pattern predicted by a global, internal construct such as an oedipal conflict? In the accident that the boy witnessed, a single, large horse, moving rapidly, was believed to have been killed. A conditioning explanation emphasizes that specific stimulus elements elicit particular responses and therefore accounts plausibly for the discriminative fear responses of Little Hans.

Trait theories emphasize differences among people on dimensions selected by the clinician. For some purposes, such as gross screening (e.g., administering the Minnesota Multiphasic Personality Inventory [MMPI] to a client) or group comparisons, a trait approach is useful. But it does not aid the therapist in making treatment decisions about a particular individual. For example, consider the trait of introversion-extraversion. According to Eysenck's theory, particular treatments will have different effects on clients who vary along these dimensions. In a well-controlled study, Paul (1966) correlated performance on paper-and-pencil personality tests measuring extraversion, emotionality, and anxiety, among other traits, with the therapeutic success obtained by treating public speaking anxiety with systematic desensitization. His results revealed no relationship whatsoever between global personality measures and therapeutic outcome. This result is typical of other outcome studies.

## Variety of Concepts

### Learning Principles

The case of Little Hans illustrates the role of classical conditioning. When a previously neutral stimulus is paired with a frightening event (the unconditioned stimulus, or US), it can become a *conditioned stimulus* (CS) that elicits a *conditioned response* (CR) such as anxiety. Current analyses of classical conditioning have moved away from the once-popular notion that what was learned consisted of simple S-R bonds. Rather, people learn that there are correlational or contingent relationships between the CS and US. This learning defines the conditioning process. Classical conditioning is no longer seen as the simple pairing of a single CS with a single US. Instead, correlations between entire classes of stimulus events can be learned. People may be exposed to traumatic events (contiguity) but not develop phobic reactions unless a correlational or contingent relationship is formed between the situation and the traumatic event.

*Operant conditioning* emphasizes that behavior is a function of its environmental consequences. Behavior is strengthened by positive and negative reinforcement; it is weakened by punishment. *Positive reinforcement* refers to an increase in the frequency of a response followed by a favorable event. An example would be a teacher or parent praising a child for obtaining a good report card. *Negative reinforcement* refers to an increase in behavior as a result of avoiding or escaping from an aversive event that one would have expected to occur. For example, an agoraphobic, fearing loss of control and panic in a crowded shopping mall, will escape this aversive prospect by staying at home. This individual then experiences relief from anxiety by having avoided this panic and finds it increasingly difficult to leave the house.

In *punishment,* an aversive event is contingent on a response; the result is a decrease in the frequency of that response. If a child is criticized or punished by his parents for speaking up, he is likely to become an inhibited and unassertive adult.

*Extinction* refers to the cessation or removal of a response. For example, the family of an obsessive-compulsive client might be instructed to ignore requests for reassurance from the client that he has not done something wrong. The reinforcer that is no longer presented is inappropriate attention.

*Discrimination learning* occurs when a response is rewarded (or punished) in one situation but not in another. Behavior is then under specific *stimulus control.* This process is particularly important in explaining the flexibility of human behavior. For example, an obese client who goes on eating binges may show good food self-control under some circumstances but lose control in predictable situations (e.g., when alone and feeling frustrated or depressed). *Generalization* refers to the occurrence of behavior in situations other than that in which it was acquired. A therapist might help a client to become more assertive and expressive during treatment sessions. But the ultimate goal of therapy is to have the client act more assertively in real-life situations.

Social-cognitive theory recognizes both the importance of awareness in learning and the person's active cognitive appraisal of environmental events. Learning is facilitated when people are aware of the rules and contingencies governing the consequences of their actions. Reinforcement does not involve an automatic strengthening of behavior. Learning is a consequence of the informative and incentive functions of rewards. By observing the consequences of behavior, a person learns what action is appropriate in what situation. By symbolic representation of anticipated future outcomes of behavior, one generates the motivation to initiate and sustain current actions (Bandura, 1977). Often, people's expectations and hypotheses about what is happening to them may affect their behavior more than the objective reality.

The importance social-cognitive theory attaches to *vicarious learning (modeling)* is consistent with its emphasis on cognitive processes. In this form of learning, people acquire new knowledge and behavior by observing other people and events, without engaging in the behavior and without any direct consequences to themselves. Vicarious learning may occur when people watch what others do. The influence of vicarious learning on human behavior is pervasive, and this concept greatly expands the power of social-cognitive theory.

## Person Variables

People do not passively interact with situations with empty heads or an absence of feelings. Rather, they actively attend to environmental stimuli, interpret them, encode them, and selectively remember them. Mischel (1973) has spelled out a series of *person variables* that explain the interchange between person and situation. These person variables are the products of each person's social experience and cognitive development that, in turn, determine how future experiences influence him or her. Briefly, they include the individual's *competencies* to construct diverse behaviors under appropriate conditions. In addition, there is the person's *categorization* of events and people, including the self. To understand how a person will perform in particular situations also requires attention to his or her *expectancies,* the *subjective values* of any expected outcomes, and the individual's *self-regulatory systems and plans.*

A full discussion of these person variables is beyond the scope of the present chapter, but some illustrative examples may be given. For example, consider the role of *personal constructs.* It is common in clinical practice to find clients who constantly "put themselves down," even though it is clear to the objective onlooker that they are competent and that they are distorting reality. In cases like these, behavior is mainly under the control of internal stimuli rather than environmental events. Different people might respond differently to the same objective stimulus situation, depending on how they interpret what is happening to them. Therapy concentrates on correcting such faulty cognitive perceptions. But the behavior therapist must also assess a client's cognitive and behavioral *competencies* to ascertain whether he or she really can respond in a particular way. A client may be depressed not because he misperceives the situation but because he actually lacks the appropriate skills to secure rewards. A case in point would be a shy, underassertive college freshman who is motivated to date but who realizes he does not have the social skills needed to establish relationships with women. Therapy would be geared to overcoming his behavioral deficit, helping the student acquire the requisite interpersonal skills.

*Self-efficacy* refers to one's belief about being able to perform certain tasks or achieve certain goals (Bandura, 1998). Self-efficacy is assessed simply by asking a person to indicate the degree of confidence that he or she can do a particular task.

Such person variables differ from traits in that they do not assume broad cross-situational consistency but depend on specific contexts. Constructs such as generalized expectancies have not proved fruitful in predicting behavior. However, specific evaluations of individuals' efficacy expectations with respect to particular tasks are useful.

Applied behavior analysts reject cognitive mediating processes and have little use for person variables. They agree that the environment interacts with the person but contend that the role of the person is best explained in terms of *past history of reinforcement.* To illustrate the differences between the social-cognitive approach and the radical behaviorist position, imagine a client who is phobic about flying. This client typically becomes highly anxious when he hears the plane's landing gear retracting. A therapist with a social-cognitive view might attribute this anxiety reaction to the client's perception that something is wrong. The radical behaviorist would suggest that the client is reacting, not only to the present environment (the sudden noise), but also to stories he has heard in the past about engines falling off and planes crashing. This example makes it clear that radical behaviorism is not free from inferential reasoning. The question is not whether inferences will be made in trying to account for human behavior, but what sort of inference is the most useful. There is now evidence to demonstrate that taking person variables into account improves prediction about behavior and enhances therapeutic efficacy (O'Leary & Wilson, 1987).

## PSYCHOTHERAPY

### Theory of Psychotherapy

#### Learning

Behavior therapy emphasizes corrective learning experiences in which clients acquire new coping skills, improve communication, or learn to break maladaptive habits and overcome self-defeating emotional conflicts. These corrective learning experiences involve broad changes in cognitive, affective, and behavioral functioning: They are not limited to modifications of narrow response patterns in overt behavior.

The learning that characterizes behavior therapy is carefully structured. Perhaps more than any other form of treatment, behavior therapy involves asking a patient to do something such as practice relaxation training, self-monitor daily caloric intake, engage in assertive acts, confront anxiety-eliciting situations, and refrain from carrying out compulsive rituals. The high degree to which behavior therapists emphasize the client's activities in the real world between therapy sessions is one of the distinctive features of the behavioral approach. However, behavior therapy is not a one-sided influence process by the therapist to effect changes in a client's beliefs and behavior. It involves both dynamic interaction between therapist and client and directed work on the part of the client. A crucial factor in all forms of therapy is the client's motivation, the willingness to cooperate in the arduous and challenging task of making significant changes in real-life behavior. Resistance to change and lack of motivation are common reasons for treatment failures in behavior therapy. Much of the art in therapy involves coping with these issues (Lazarus & Fay, 1982).

## The Therapeutic Relationship

Behavior therapy demands skill, sensitivity, and clinical acumen. Brady et al. underscore the importance of the therapeutic relationship as follows:

> There is no question that qualitative aspects of the therapist-patient relationship can greatly influence the course of therapy for good or bad. In general, if the patient's relationship to the therapist is characterized by belief in the therapist's competence (knowledge, sophistication, and training) and if the patient regards the therapist as an honest, trustworthy, and decent human being with good social and ethical values (in his own scheme of things), the patient is more apt to invest himself in the therapy. Equally important is the quality and tone of the relationship he has with the therapist. That is, if he feels trusting and warm toward the therapist, this generally will facilitate following the treatment regimen, will be associated with higher expectations of improvement, and other generally favorable factors. The feelings of the therapist toward the patient are also important. If the therapist feels that his patient is not a desirable person or a decent human being or simply does not like the patient for whatever reasons, he may not succeed in concealing these attitudes toward the patient, and in general they will have a deleterious effect. (1980, pp. 285–286)

A survey of behavior practitioners indicated that treatment frequently aims at improving the therapeutic relationship (Swan & MacDonald, 1978). O'Leary, Turkewitz, and Tafel (1973) found that virtually all parents whose children were treated at a child-guidance clinic rated their behavior therapists as understanding, warm, sincere, and interested. Similarly, in a study of marital therapy by Turkewitz and O'Leary (1981), clients' ratings of their behavior therapists were positive.

As opposed to the neutral and detached role that the psychoanalytically oriented therapist is taught to assume, the behavior therapist is directive and concerned—a problem solver and a coping model. In their comparative study of behavior therapy and psychoanalytically oriented psychotherapy, Staples, Sloane, Whipple, Cristol, and Yorkston concluded:

> Differences between behavior therapy and analytically-oriented psychotherapy . . . involved the basic patterns of interactions between patient and therapist and the type of relationship formed. Behavior therapy is not psychotherapy with special "scientific techniques" superimposed on the traditional therapeutic paradigm; rather, the two appear to represent quite different styles of treatment although they share common elements. (1975, p. 1521)

The behavior therapists in this study were rated as more directive, more open, more genuine, and more disclosing than their psychoanalytically oriented counterparts.

Both behavioral and psychodynamic treatments attempt to modify underlying causes of behavior. The difference is what proponents of each approach regard as causes. Behavior analysts look for current variables and conditions that control behavior. Some psychodynamic approaches (e.g., psychoanalysis) ask, "How did the client become this kind of person?" Others (e.g., Adlerian psychotherapy) ask, "What is this person trying to achieve?" Behavioral approaches ask, "What is causing this person to behave in this way right now, and what can we do right now to change that behavior?"

## Ethical Issues

In behavior therapy the client is encouraged to participate actively. Consider, for example, the important issue of who determines the goals of therapy. Because it is fundamental to behavior therapy that the client should have the major say in setting treatment goals, it is important that the client is fully informed and consents to and participates in setting goals. A distinction is drawn between how behavior is to be changed—in which the therapist is presumably expert—and the objectives of therapy. The latter must ultimately be determined by the client. The client controls what; the therapist controls how. The major contribution of the therapist is to assist clients by helping them to generate alternative courses of action and to analyze the consequences of pursuing various goals. Because this process involves an expression of the therapist's own values, the therapist should identify them and explain how they might affect his or her analysis of therapeutic goals.

Selecting goals is far more complicated in the case of disturbed clients (such as institutionalized patients who are struggling with psychosis) who are unable to participate meaningfully in deciding treatment objectives. To ensure that treatment is in the client's best interests, it is important to monitor program goals and procedures through conferences with other professionals (Risley & Sheldon-Wildgen, 1982).

All forms of therapy involve social influence. The critical ethical question is whether therapists are aware of this influence. Behavior therapy entails an explicit recognition of the influence process and emphasizes specific, client-oriented behavioral objectives. Behavior therapists have formulated procedures to guarantee the protection of human rights and personal dignity of all clients (Stolz, 1978; Wilson & O'Leary, 1980).

## Process of Psychotherapy

### Problem Identification and Assessment

The initial task of a behavior therapist is to identify and understand the client's presenting problem(s). The therapist seeks detailed information about the specific dimensions of problems, such as initial occurrence, severity, and frequency. What has the client done to cope with the problems? What does the client think about his or her problem and any previous therapeutic contacts? Obtaining answers to such searching questions is facilitated by a relationship of trust and mutual understanding. To achieve this, the therapist is attentive, trying to be objective and empathic. The therapist then proceeds to make a functional analysis of the client's problem, attempting to identify specific environmental and person variables that are thought to be maintaining maladaptive thoughts, feelings, or behavior. The emphasis on variables currently maintaining the problem does not mean that the client's past history is ignored. However, past experiences are important only to the degree that they directly contribute to the client's present distress.

### Assessment Methods

In the behaviorally oriented interview the therapist seldom asks the client *why* questions, e.g., "Why do you become anxious in crowded places?" Questions starting with *how, when, where,* and *what* are more useful. The therapist does not necessarily take everything the client says at face value and is constantly looking for inconsistencies, evasiveness, or apparent distortions. Nevertheless, the therapist relies heavily on clients' self-reports, particularly in assessing thoughts, fantasies, and feelings. Self-report has often proved to be a superior predictor of behavior as compared to clinicians' judgments or scores on personality tests (Mischel, 1981). Of course, therapists must ask the right questions if they are to get meaningful answers. Given the tendency of most people to describe themselves with broad personality labels, therapists may have to help clients to identify specific behavioral referents for global subjective impressions.

## Guided Imagery

A useful method for assessing clients' reactions to particular situations is to have them symbolically recreate a problematic life situation. Instead of asking clients simply to talk about an event, the therapist has them imagine the event actually happening to them. When clients have conjured up an image of a situation, they are then asked to verbalize any thoughts that come to mind, an especially useful way of uncovering the specific thoughts associated with particular events.

## Role-Playing

Another option is to ask clients to role-play a situation. This method lends itself to the assessment of interpersonal problems, with the therapist adopting the role of the person with whom the client reports problems. Role-playing provides the therapist with a sample of the problem behavior, albeit under somewhat artificial circumstances. If the therapist is assessing a client couple, the two partners are asked to discuss chosen issues that enable the therapist to observe first-hand the extent of their interpersonal skills and their ability to resolve conflict.

## Physiological Recording

Technological progress in monitoring different psychophysiological reactions has made it possible to objectively measure a number of problems. Monitoring a client's sexual arousal in response to specific stimuli that cause changes in penile or vaginal blood flow (Rosen & Keefe, 1978) is an example of the use of physiological recording instruments in behavioral assessment and treatment strategies.

## Self-Monitoring

Clients are typically instructed to keep detailed, daily records of particular events or psychological reactions. Obese clients, for example, are asked to self-monitor daily caloric intake, the degree to which they engage in planned physical activities, the conditions under which they eat, and so on. In this way it is possible to detect behavioral patterns in clients' lives functionally related to their problems.

## Behavioral Observation

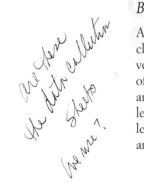

Assessment of overt problem behavior, ideally, is based on actual observation of the client's behavior in the natural environment. Accordingly, behavior therapists have developed sophisticated behavioral observation rating procedures. These procedures most often have been used with children and hospitalized patients. Parents, teachers, nurses, and hospital aides have been trained as behavioral observers. Once these individuals have learned to observe behavior, they can be taught to make a behavioral analysis of a problem and then instructed to alter their own behavior to influence the problem behavior of another person.

## Psychological Tests and Questionnaires

In general, behavior therapists do not use standardized psychodiagnostic tests. Tests such as the MMPI may be useful for providing an overall picture of the client's personality profile, but they do not yield the kind of information necessary for a functional analysis or for the development of therapeutic interventions. Projective tests are widely rejected because of a lack of acceptable evidence for their validity or utility (Mischel, 1968). Behavior therapists do use checklists and questionnaires, such as the Marks and Mathews Fear Questionnaire (1979), self-report scales of depression like the Beck Depression Inventory (Beck, Rush, Shaw, & Emery, 1979), assertion inventories like the Rathus (1973) questionnaire, and paper-and-pencil measures of marital satisfaction such as the Locke and Wallace inventory of marital adjustment (1959). These assessment devices are not sufficient for carrying out a functional analysis of the determinants of a problem, but are useful in establishing the initial severity of the problem and charting therapeutic efficacy over the course of treatment.

## Treatment Techniques

Behavior therapy offers a wide range of different treatment methods and attempts to tailor the principles of social-cognitive theory to each individual's unique problem. In selecting treatment techniques, the behavior therapist relies heavily on empirical evidence about the efficacy of that technique applied to the particular problem. In many cases the empirical evidence is unclear or largely nonexistent. Here the therapist is influenced by accepted clinical practice and the basic logic and philosophy of a social-cognitive approach to human behavior and its modification. In the process, the therapist must often use intuitive skill and clinical judgment to select appropriate treatment methods and determine the best time to implement specific techniques. Both science and art influence clinical practice, and the most effective therapists are aware of the advantages and limitations of each.

The following are some selective illustrations of the varied methods the typical behavior therapist is likely to employ in clinical practice.

*Imagery–Based Techniques*   In systematic desensitization, after isolating specific events that trigger unrealistic anxiety, the therapist constructs a stimulus hierarchy in which different situations that the client fears are ordered along a continuum from mildly stressful to very threatening. The client is instructed to imagine each event while he or she is deeply relaxed. Wolpe (1958) adapted Jacobson's (1938) method of progressive relaxation training as a means of producing a response incompatible with anxiety. Briefly, this consists of training clients to concentrate on systematically relaxing different muscle groups. When any item produces excessive anxiety, the client is instructed to cease visualizing the particular item and to restore feelings of relaxation. The item is then repeated, or the hierarchy adjusted, until the client can visualize the scene without experiencing anxiety. Only then does the therapist present the next item of the hierarchy. Real-life exposure, where possible, is even more powerful than using imagination and is the technique of choice for treating anxiety disorders. An example of exposure treatment for an agoraphobic client is described in the "Applications" section.

Symbolically generated aversive reactions are used to treat diverse problems such as alcoholism and sexual disorders (e.g., exhibitionism). In this procedure the client is asked to imagine aversive consequences associated with the problem behavior. An alcoholic might be asked to imagine experiencing nausea at the thought of a drink. As illustrated in the "Case Example," an exhibitionist might be asked to imagine being apprehended by the police. This method is often referred to as covert sensitization (Cautela, 1967). A hierarchy of scenes that reliably elicit the problem urge or behavior is developed, and each scene is systematically presented until the client gains control over the problem.

*Cognitive Restructuring*    The treatment techniques in this category are based on the assumption that emotional disorders result, at least in part, from dysfunctional thinking. The task of therapy is to alter this maladaptive thinking. Although there is some overlap with Ellis's REBT, the cognitive restructuring method most commonly used by behavior therapists is derived from Beck's cognitive therapy. An example of this method is illustrated in the following excerpt from a therapy session. Notice how the therapist prompts the patient to examine his dysfunctional assumptions and how behavioral tasks are used to help the patient to alter his assumption (P = Patient; T = Therapist):

P:  In the middle of a panic attack, I usually think I am going to faint or collapse . . .
T:  Have you ever fainted in an attack?
P:  No.
T:  What is it then that makes you think you might faint?
P:  I feel faint, and the feeling can be very strong.
T:  So, to summarize, your evidence that you are going to faint is the fact that you feel faint?
P:  Yes.
T:  How can you then account for the fact that you have felt faint many hundreds of times and have not yet fainted?
P:  So far, the attacks have always stopped just in time or I have managed to hold onto something to stop myself from collapsing.
T:  Right. So one explanation of the fact that you have frequently felt faint, had the thought that you would faint, but have not actually fainted, is that you have always done something to save yourself just in time. However, an alternative explanation is that the feeling of faintness that you get in a panic attack will never lead to you collapsing, even if you don't control it.
P:  Yes, I suppose.
T:  In order to decide which of these two possibilities is correct, we need to know what has to happen to your body for you to actually faint. Do you know?
P:  No.
T:  Your blood pressure needs to drop. Do you know what happens to your blood pressure during a panic attack?
P:  Well, my pulse is racing. I guess my blood pressure must be up.
T:  That's right. In anxiety, heart rate and blood pressure tend to go together. So, you are actually less likely to faint when you are anxious than when you are not.
P:  That's very interesting and helpful to know. However, if it's true, why do I feel so faint?
T:  Your feeling of faintness is a sign that your body is reacting in a normal way to the perception of danger. Most of the bodily reactions you are experiencing when anxious were probably designed to deal with the threats experienced by primitive people, such as being approached by a hungry tiger. What would be the best thing to do in that situation?
P:  Run away as fast as you can.
T:  That's right. And in order to help you run, you need the maximum amount of energy in your muscles. This is achieved by sending more of your blood to your muscles and relatively less to the brain. This means that there is a small drop in oxygen to the brain and that is why you feel faint. However, this feeling is misleading because your overall blood pressure is up, not down.

P:   That's very clear. So next time I feel faint, I can check out whether I am going to faint by taking my pulse. If it is normal, or quicker than normal, I know I won't faint. (Clark, 1989, pp. 76–77)

*Assertiveness and Social Skills Training*    Unassertive clients often fail to express their emotions or to stand up for their rights. They are often exploited by others, feel anxious in social situations, and lack self-esteem. In behavior rehearsal the therapist may model the appropriate assertive behavior and may ask the client to engage repeatedly in a graduated sequence of similar actions. Initially, the therapist focuses on expressive behavior (e.g., body posture, voice training, and eye contact). The therapist then encourages the client to carry out assertive actions in the real world to ensure generalization. Behavior therapy is frequently conducted in a group as well as on an individual basis (Upper & Ross, 1981). Behavior rehearsal for assertiveness training is well suited to group therapy, because group members can provide more varied sources of educational feedback and can also offer a diversified range of modeling influences.

The instructional, modeling, and feedback components of behavior rehearsal facilitate a broad range of communication competencies, including active listening, giving personal feedback, and building trust through self-disclosure. These communication principles, drawn from nonbehavioral approaches to counseling but integrated within a behavioral framework, are an important ingredient of behavioral marital therapy (Jacobson & Margolin, 1979).

*Self–Control Procedures*    Behavior therapists use a number of self-control procedures (Bandura, 1977; Kanfer, 1977). Fundamental to successful self-regulation of behavior is self-monitoring, which requires helping the client set goals or standards that guide behavior. In the treatment of obesity, for example, daily caloric goals are mutually selected. Behavioral research has identified certain properties of goals that increase the probability of successful self-control. For example, one should set highly specific, unambiguous, and short-term goals, such as consumption of no more than 1,200 calories each day. Compare this to the goal of "cutting back" on eating for the "next week." Failure to achieve such vague goals elicits negative self-evaluative reactions by clients, whereas successful accomplishment of goals produces self-reinforcement that increases the likelihood of maintaining the new behavior.

Self-instructional training, described above, is often used as a self-control method for coping with impulsivity, stress, excessive anger, and pain. Similarly, progressive relaxation training is widely applied as a self-control method for reducing different forms of stress, including insomnia, tension headaches, and hypertension (O'Leary & Wilson, 1987). Biofeedback methods used to treat a variety of psychophysiological disorders also fall under the category of self-control procedures (Yates, 1980).

*Real–Life Performance–Based Techniques*    The foregoing techniques are applied during treatment sessions, and most are routinely coupled with instructions to clients to complete homework assignments in their natural environment.

The diversity of behavioral treatment methods is seen in the application of operant conditioning principles in settings ranging from classrooms to institutions for the retarded and the mentally ill. An excellent illustration is the use of a *token economy*. The main elements of a token reinforcement program can be summarized as follows: (a) carefully specified and operationally defined target behaviors, (b) backup reinforcers, (c) tokens that represent the backup reinforcers, and (d) rules of exchange that specify the number of tokens required to obtain backup reinforcers.

A token economy in a classroom might consist of the teacher, at regular intervals, making ratings indicating how well a student had behaved, both academically and so-

cially. At the end of the day, good ratings could be exchanged for various small prizes. These procedures reduce disruptive social behavior in the classroom and can improve academic performance (O'Leary & O'Leary, 1977). In the case of psychiatric inpatients the staff might make tokens contingent upon improvements in self-care activities, reductions in belligerent acts, and cooperative problem-solving behavior (Kazdin, 1977). The behavior therapist designs the token economy and monitors its implementation and efficacy. The procedures themselves are implemented in real-life settings by teachers, parents, nurses, and psychiatric aides—whoever has most direct contact with the patient. Ensuring that these psychological assistants are well trained and supervised is the responsibility of the behavior therapist.

*Length of Treatment*    Much of behavior therapy is short-term treatment, but therapy lasting from 25 to 50 sessions is commonplace, and still longer treatment is not unusual. Therapy in excess of 100 sessions is relatively rare. There are no established guidelines for deciding on the length of therapy. The usual approach in clinical practice is to carry out a detailed behavioral assessment of a client's problem(s) and to embark upon interventions as rapidly as possible. Assessment is an ongoing process, as the consequences of initial treatment interventions are evaluated against therapeutic goals. Unless treatment time is explicitly limited from the start, the length of therapy and the scheduling of the treatment sessions are contingent upon the patient's progress.

Typically, a behavior therapist might contract with a patient to pursue a treatment plan for two to three months (approximately 8 to 12 sessions) and reevaluate progress at the end of this period. The relative absence of any discernible improvement is cause for the therapist to reevaluate whether he or she conceptualized the problem accurately, whether he or she is using the appropriate techniques or needs to switch tactics, whether there is some personal problem with him or her as the therapist, or whether a referral to another therapist or another form of treatment might be necessary.

In terminating a successful case, the behavior therapist usually avoids abruptness. A typical procedure is to lengthen gradually the time between successive therapy sessions, from weekly to fortnightly to monthly and so on. These concluding sessions may be shorter than earlier ones, with occasional telephone contact.

*Manual–Based Treatments*    The use of standardized, manual-based treatments in clinical practice represents a new and controversial development with far-reaching implications for clinical practice. Cognitive behavioral therapists have been at the forefront of this development (Wilson, 1998). For example, there are now evidence-based CBT treatment manuals for a variety of clinical disorders, including different anxiety disorders, depressions, and eating disorders.

A treatment manual describes a limited and set number of techniques for treating a specific clinical disorder. Moreover, these techniques are implemented in the same sequence over a more or less fixed number of treatment sessions, and all patients diagnosed with the disorder in question are treated with the same manual-based approach. For example, all patients with the eating disorder of bulimia nervosa would be treated in essentially the same fashion using the cognitive behavior therapy manual developed specifically for this disorder by Fairburn and his colleagues (Fairburn, Marcus, & Wilson, 1993).

A particular strength of these manuals is that they describe treatment programs that have been evaluated in controlled clinical trials. Treatment manuals make psychological therapy, whatever its particular form, more consistent and more widely available. They make it easier for therapists to learn specific treatment strategies and to acquire skill in using them. They not only facilitate the training of therapists but make it easier for supervisors to monitor their trainees' expertise. The structured and time-limited nature of treatment manuals results in more highly focused treatment than might otherwise be the case.

Nonetheless, manual-based treatments have been criticized by practitioners, including some behavior therapists, because the standardized approach limits the role of the therapist's clinical judgment in tailoring specific interventions to the individual patient's needs (Davison & Lazarus, 1995). In response, proponents of manual-based treatments argue that therapists' clinical judgments are often highly subjective, relying more on intuition than empirical evidence. The limitations of clinical judgment have been well documented. Clinical judgment as a form of human inference is no better, and is worse in some situations, than actuarial prediction in which patients' behavior is predicted by viewing them as members of an aggregate (e.g., a diagnostic category) and by determining what variables generally predict for that aggregate or diagnostic category (Dawes, 1994). Empirically supported, manual-based treatments are consistent with the actuarial approach. The relative effectiveness of manual-based behavior therapy versus reliance on the therapist's clinical judgment is the subject of ongoing clinical investigation.

## Mechanisms of Psychotherapy

Research on behavior therapy has demonstrated that particular treatment methods are effective and has identified what components of multifaceted treatment methods and programs are responsible for therapeutic success. For example, empirical evidence has established that the changes produced by token reinforcement programs are due to the learning principles of operant conditioning on which they are based (Kazdin, 1977).

### Learning Processes

Ayllon and Azrin (1965) described a pioneering token reinforcement program with predominantly schizophrenic patients on a psychiatric hospital ward. The target behaviors in this investigation were self-care and improved capacity for productive work. Rewards were made contingent on improvement in these two areas. Following a period during which the job assignments of all 44 patients on the entire ward were rewarded contingently (phase A), tokens were administered on a noncontingent basis (phase B). In phase B, patients were given tokens each day regardless of their performance, which broke the contingency between reinforcer and response. This ensured that the amount of social interaction between the attendants and ward staff who administered the tokens and the patients remained unchanged. Any deterioration in performance was then directly attributable to the precise functional relationship between behavior and reinforcement.

Phase C marked a return to contingent reinforcement as in phase A. The results showed that "free" reinforcement (phase B) was totally ineffective. Similarly, the complete withdrawal of all tokens resulted in performance decreasing to less than one-fourth the rate at which it had previously been maintained by contingently rewarding the patients with tokens.

No single, monolithic theory encompasses the diverse methods and applications of the different behavior therapies. Although operant conditioning principles explain the efficacy of a broad range of behavioral procedures, they do not account for the success of a number of other methods. Classical conditioning and different cognitive processes all play a part in determining the effects of the various cognitive behavioral treatment methods described in this chapter. In many cases, the mechanisms responsible for the therapeutic success of a method remain unclear. Consider exposure treatment for phobic and obsessive-compulsive disorders. The effectiveness of this method has been well established, but its explanation is still a matter of some controversy. Originally, the explanation was based on Mowrer's (1947) two-factor theory of learning, according to which repeated exposure to anxiety-eliciting situations, as in systematic desensitization, resulted in the extinction of the classically conditioned anxiety that mediates phobic avoidance behavior. However, other research (Bandura, 1986) casts doubt on the validity of this explanation.

## Cognitive Mechanisms

In terms of social-cognitive theory, exposure leads not to the extinction of any underlying anxiety drive state, but rather to modification of the client's expectations of self-efficacy (Bandura, 1982). Self-efficacy refers to clients' beliefs that they can cope with formerly feared situations. For efficacy expectations to change, the client must make a self-attribution of behavioral change. For example, it is not uncommon for an agoraphobic client to approach situations she has avoided without increases in self-efficacy or reductions in fear. The explanation seems to be that some clients do not credit themselves for the behavioral change. The agoraphobic might say that she was "lucky" that she did not have a panic attack or that she just happened to have one of those rare "good days." The therapist must be prepared to help the client use cognitive methods to attribute changes to herself so that her sense of personal efficacy increases.

Initial studies with phobic subjects have generally provided empirical support for self-efficacy theory, although the findings are mixed. Experiments by Bandura and his associates have shown that efficacy expectations accurately predicted reductions in phobic avoidance regardless of whether they were created by real-life exposure or symbolic modeling, covert modeling, or systematic desensitization. Moreover, measures of personal efficacy predicted differences in coping behavior by different individuals receiving the same treatment and even specific performance by subjects in different tasks. Consistent with the theory, participant modeling, a performance-based treatment, produced greater increases in level and strength of efficacy expectations and in related behavior change (Bandura, 1986).

# APPLICATIONS

## Problems

Behavior therapy can be used to treat a full range of psychological disorders in different populations (Kazdin & Wilson, 1978). It also has broad applicability to problems in education, medicine, and community living. The following are selected examples of problems for which behavior therapy is an effective treatment.

## Anxiety Disorders

Several well-controlled studies have established that behavior therapy is an effective form of treatment for anxiety disorders. Simple phobias are successfully eliminated within a short number of sessions by using guided exposure treatment in which patients are helped to gradually approach and confront the objects or situations they fear and avoid. Even more importantly, behavior therapy is the treatment of choice for more complex and debilitating disorders such as panic disorder and obsessive-compulsive disorder.

*Panic Disorder*   Panic disorder is defined by a discrete period of intense fear that develops suddenly and involves physiological symptoms such as a pounding heart, shortness of breath, sweating, dizziness, and fear of going crazy. Effective treatment typically combines both behavioral and cognitive components. Studies by David Barlow and his colleagues have evaluated the effects of a panic control treatment (PCT) that includes both behavioral and cognitive components. PCT was more effective than a wait list control condition (in which patients were assessed but their treatment delayed) or relaxation training alone. A two-year follow-up showed that 81 percent of patients treated with PCT were panic-free (Craske, Brown, & Barlow, 1991). At Oxford University in England, David Clark and his colleagues tested the effects of a treatment that focused mainly on changing panic patients' catastrophic interpretation of bodily sensations. This cognitive-behavioral treatment proved to be superior to pharmacological therapy with imipramine, an antidepressant often assumed to be the therapy of choice for panic disorder. At the end of treatment, 90 percent of patients treated with cognitive-behavior therapy were panic-free, compared with only 55 percent of patients treated with imipramine. Patients treated with cognitive-behavioral therapy maintained their improvement over a one-year follow-up period, whereas patients treated with imipramine tended to relapse when the drug was discontinued (Clark, Salkovskis, Hackmann, Middleton, & Gelder, 1994). A recent controlled study, the largest ever conducted on panic disorder, showed that both CBT and imipramine were effective treatments in the short-term. Again, the therapeutic effects of CBT were maintained over follow-up, whereas patients withdrawn from their medication tended to relapse (Barlow, Gorman, Shear, & Woods, 2000).

*Obsessive-Compulsive Disorders*   Traditional psychotherapy is ineffective in treating obsessive-compulsive disorder (OCD). A significant advance was made in the 1970s with the development of specific behavioral methods. The most effective treatment is exposure and response prevention, which can be illustrated with compulsive hand washers. The different objects or activities leading the patient to wash his or her hands are first identified through behavioral assessment. Then, following a thorough explanation of the technique and its rationale, and with the patient's fully informed consent, touching objects that trigger hand washing is systematically encouraged. This is the exposure part of treatment. Once the patient has touched what is unrealistically viewed as contaminated, he or she refrains from washing. This is the response prevention part of treatment. The patient's anxiety typically rises after initially touching the object and then decreases over the course of the session. Focusing the patient's attention on fear of contamination assists the treatment. The goal of treatment is to break the negative reinforcing value of the compulsion, extinguish the anxiety elicited by the contaminated object, and enhance the patient's self-efficacy in coping with this kind of situation. Imaginal exposure is used in cases when in vivo exposure is impractical or impossible. Patients are instructed to conjure up detailed imagery of compulsive activities and stay with these images until their anxiety decreases.

Research has shown that roughly 65 to 75 percent of patients with OCD show marked improvement following behavioral treatment (Barlow, 1988). This therapeutic success is maintained during follow-ups as long as two years after treatment. Of particular interest is the finding that exposure treatment influences the biological basis of OCD. Successfully treated patients show significant changes in glucose metabolism in a specific region of the brain that is known to be connected with anxiety, the caudate nucleus. These changes are identical to those produced by successful pharmacological treatment (Baxter et al., 1992).

## Sexual Disorders

Behavior therapy is an effective and widely used treatment for male and female sexual problems, such as erectile disorder, premature ejaculation, orgasmic dysfunction, and vaginismus. Perhaps the best-known form of behavioral treatment for sexual dysfunction in both heterosexual and homosexual men and women is Masters and Johnson's (1970, 1979) two-week rapid therapy program. These pioneers of research on sexuality and its disorders reported a treatment success rate of roughly 80 percent. Subsequent sex therapists have made more modest claims.

Simple sexual problems, uncomplicated by other personal or interpersonal difficulties, are relatively easy to treat. Women can become orgasmic and males overcome premature ejaculation using self-help manuals with minimal instruction from a therapist. Clinical experience, nevertheless, shows that relationship problems tend to complicate sex therapy and hinder its success. This is additionally significant if, as sex therapists widely believe, the population seeking sex therapy today is more likely to have fundamental relationship problems than the patients treated in the early 1970s. Successful therapy for these more complex cases may take months or even years.

A variety of other sexual disorders, such as exhibitionism, transvestism, and sadomasochism, are commonly treated with cognitive-behavioral methods.

## Depression

Beck's cognitive therapy (CT) for depression is described in Chapter 8. CT is a mix of cognitive and behavioral strategies. Accordingly, in a major treatment outcome study, Jacobson and his colleagues conducted a component analysis of CT (1996). They compared the full CT treatment package, which by definition focused on modifying dysfunctional cognitions, to the behavioral component that they labeled behavioral activation (BA). The focus in BA is helping patients to become more active. They learn to self-monitor their daily activities, assess pleasure from engaging in different activities, complete increasingly difficult tasks designed to promote a sense of mastery, and overcome deficits in social skills. This behavioral component is especially prominent during the early stages of therapy, during which most of the improvement produced by CT takes place (Ilardi & Craighead, 1994).

The results showed that BA was as effective as the full CT package in decreasing depression both at the end of therapy and at six-month and two-year follow-ups (Gortner, Gollan, Dobson, & Jacobson, 1998). Furthermore, BA was equally effective in altering negative thinking in these depressed patients. Jacobson et al. (1996) concluded that CT is no more effective than the behavioral component of the full treatment package.

Two additional forms of behavior therapy have been used successfully to treat depression. One, developed by Peter Lewinsohn, combines many of the cognitive strategies of Beck's approach with a more traditional behavioral emphasis on increasing the range of patients' positive reinforcers. It has been shown to be effective in overcoming depression in adolescents (Lewinsohn, Clarke, Hops, & Andrews, 1990). The other is a form of behavioral marital therapy. The goal in this treatment is to modify the interpersonal influences on unipolar depression by reducing marital conflict and facilitating increased feelings of closeness and open sharing of thoughts and feelings (O'Leary & Beach, 1990). This treatment seems especially effective with depressed women who also have marital problems.

## Interpersonal and Marital Problems

Social skills training and assertiveness training are used to treat a broad range of interpersonal problems, from limited social-behavioral repertoires to social anxiety. Behavioral marital therapy is a relatively recent development, the central focus of which is helping partners to learn more positive and productive means of achieving desired behavioral changes in one another (Jacobson & Margolin, 1979). As in the case of anxiety and sexual disorders, specialized behavior marital therapy clinics are now in operation. Behavior therapy has shown clear promise as an effective and efficient treatment for marital problems, but comprehensive investigations of severely distressed couples, with longer follow-ups, are necessary before definitive conclusions can be reached.

## Chronic Mental Patients

Behavior therapy is not useful in treating acute psychotic reactions, and most behavior therapists favor pharmacotherapy as the treatment of choice for schizophrenic disorders. Yet behavioral programs are clearly indicated for treating the chronically mentally ill. Paul and Lentz (1977) studied chronic mental patients, all of whom were diagnosed as process schizophrenic and were of low socioeconomic status. These patients had been confined to a mental hospital for an average of 17 years, and had been treated previously with drugs and other methods without success. Approximately 90 percent were taking medication at the onset of the study. Their level of self-care was too low and the severity of their bizarre behavior too great to permit community placement. According to Paul and Lentz, these subjects were "the most severely debilitated chronically institutionalized adults ever subjected to systematic study" (p. v). In the most detailed, comprehensive, and well-controlled evaluation of the treatment of chronic mental hospital patients ever conducted, Paul and Lentz produced a wealth of objective data, including evidence of cost-effectiveness, showing that behavioral procedures (predominantly a sophisticated token reinforcement program) are the treatment of choice.

## Childhood Disorders

Children have been treated from the earliest days of behavior therapy. Treatment programs have addressed problems ranging from circumscribed habit disorders in children to multiple responses of children who suffer all-encompassing excesses, deficits, or bizarre behavior patterns. These problems include conduct disorders, aggression, and delinquency. Hyperactivity is widely treated by behavioral methods, such as token reinforcement programs. The documented success of the behavioral approach, particularly in improving the academic performance of these children, suggests that it can sometimes be used as an alternative to drug treatment (O'Leary, 1980).

Autism is a particularly severe early childhood disorder with a very poor prognosis. Traditional psychological and medical treatments have proved ineffective. Behavioral methods, however, have achieved notable success. Lovaas (1987) has recently reported that intensive, long-term behavioral treatment of autistic children resulted in 47 percent achieving normal intellectual and educational functioning. Another 40 percent were mildly retarded and assigned to special classes for the language delayed. Of a control group of autistic children, only 2 percent achieved normal functioning. These findings are the most positive ever obtained with autistic children and illustrate the efficacy of behavioral methods with serious childhood disorders.

Childhood psychoses have also been treated with behavioral techniques. Self-stimulatory and self-destructive behavior such as biting and head banging have been eliminated with aversive procedures. Positive behaviors have been developed to improve language and speech, play, social interaction and responsiveness, and basic academic skills (O'Leary & Carr, 1982).

One of the most effectively treated childhood problems has been enuresis. The bell-and-pad method has produced improvement rates greater than 80 percent in many reports. Toileting accidents have been effectively altered with other behavioral procedures (Ross, 1981).

## Eating and Weight Disorders

*Binge Eating and Bulimia Nervosa*    *Bulimia nervosa* (BN) is an eating disorder that occurs mainly in adolescent and young adult women. It is characterized by a severe disturbance of eating in which determined attempts to restrict food intake are punctuated by binge eating, namely, episodes of uncontrolled consumption of very large amounts of food. Binges are commonly followed by purging (self-induced vomiting or the misuse of laxatives). BN patients have dysfunctional concerns about body shape and weight, judging their self-worth in terms of shape and weight. Other psychiatric disorders, such as depression, substance abuse, and personality disorders, are commonly associated with BN. Binge eating disorder (BED) is diagnosed if patients show recurrent binge eating in the absence of extreme attempts at weight control such as purging. Whereas BN patients are typically of normal weight, BED patients are usually overweight or obese.

Manual-based CBT for BN (Fairburn et al., 1993) is designed to eliminate binge eating and purging, replace rigid dieting with more normal and flexible eating patterns, and modify dysfunctional thoughts and feelings about the personal significance of body weight and shape. Patients are helped to achieve enhanced self-acceptance instead of struggling to conform to unrealistic societal ideals of feminine beauty. In addition, cognitive and behavioral strategies are used to help patients cope more adaptively with stressful events instead of resorting to binge eating.

Numerous controlled studies in the United States and Europe have demonstrated the effectiveness of CBT in treating BN (Wilson & Fairburn, 2002). CBT has proved to be more effective than several other psychological treatments, including supportive-psychotherapy, supportive-expressive psychotherapy, stress management therapy, and a form of behavior therapy that did not address cognitive features of bulimia nervosa. The exception is interpersonal psychotherapy (IPT). A major comparative outcome study found that at the end of treatment IPT was less effective than CBT, but during a one-year follow-up the difference between the two treatments disappeared due to continuing improvement among the patients who received IPT (Fairburn et al., 1995).

Antidepressant medication has also been shown to be an effective treatment for BN. Research studies evaluating the relative and combined effectiveness of CBT and antidepressant drug treatment have, as a whole, shown that CBT is superior to medication alone. Combining CBT with medication is significantly more effective than medication alone. Combining the two has produced few benefits over CBT alone on the reduction of the core features of bulimia nervosa. In contrast to the data on CBT, there is virtually no evidence of the long-term effect of pharmacological treatment on BN (Wilson, 1997).

CBT is also effective in treating binge eating and associated psychopathology in BED patients, but does not produce significant weight loss (Wilson & Fairburn, 2002).

*Obesity*    A comprehensive behavioral weight control program, comprising components of improved eating habits, lifestyle change, sound nutrition, and increased exercise, is widely viewed as the treatment of choice for mild to moderate cases of obesity. Short-term results are good. Following five months of treatment, behavioral treatment combined with moderate dietary restriction (1,200 calories of self-selected foods daily) results in a mean weight loss of roughly 20 pounds, together with significant decreases in depression and body image dissatisfaction. The problem is that these treatment effects are not maintained over time.

The pattern of weight loss and regain in behavioral treatment is consistent. The rate of initial weight loss is rapid but then slowly declines. The low point is reached after approximately six months. Weight regain then begins and continues gradually until weight stabilizes near baseline levels. Obesity is a chronic condition that may require treatment of indefinite duration. Continuing therapist contact appears to be a key element in successful maintenance programs (Perri, 1998).

## Behavioral Medicine

Behavioral medicine has been defined as the "interdisciplinary field concerned with the development and integration of behavioral and biomedical science knowledge and techniques relevant to health and illness and application of this knowledge and these techniques to prevention, diagnosis, treatment and rehabilitation" (Schwartz & Weiss, 1978, p. 250). Behavior therapy has helped to catalyze the rapid growth of this field.

## Prevention and Treatment of Cardiovascular Disease

Specific behavior patterns appear to increase the risk of needless or premature cardiovascular disease. Modification of these behavior patterns is likely to produce significant reductions in cardiovascular disease. Among the risk factors that have been the target of behavioral treatment programs are cigarette smoking, obesity, lack of exercise, stress, hypertension, and excessive alcohol consumption. Substance abuse is typically treated with a combination of the self-control procedures. Stress and hypertension have been successfully treated using methods such as relaxation training. Behavior intervention methods have been applied not only to identified clients in both individual and group therapy sessions, but also to essentially healthy individuals in the workplace and the community in programs designed to prevent cardiovascular disease.

## Other Applications

Behavioral techniques have been successfully applied to such diverse health-related problems as tension headaches, different forms of pain, anorexia nervosa, asthma, epilepsy, sleep disorders, nausea reactions in cancer patients (resulting from radiation therapy), and children's fears about being hospitalized and undergoing surgery (Melamed & Siegel, 1980). Finally, cognitive-behavioral principles show promise in increasing compliance with medical treatments.

# Evaluation

Evaluation of therapy outcome must be guided by the question "*What* treatment, by *whom,* is most effective for *this* individual with *that* specific problem and under *which* set of circumstances?" (Paul, 1967, p. 111). "On what measures" and "at what cost" round off this appeal to specificity of therapy outcome evaluation.

## What Treatment Methods?

Behavior therapy consists of a broad range of different techniques, some of which are differentially effective for different problems. Hence, it is difficult to evaluate some global entity called "behavior therapy." Instead, evaluation must be directed at specific methods applied to particular problems.

## What Measures Should Be Used to Evaluate Therapy Outcome?

A major contribution of behavior therapy to the evaluation of therapy outcome has been the development of a wide range of measurement strategies for the assessment and modification of various disorders. Examples include behavioral measures of phobic avoidance and compulsive rituals, coding systems for direct behavioral observation of diverse behaviors across different situations, and psychophysiological systems for anxiety and sexual disorders. Adequate assessment of treatment outcome will necessarily require multiple objective and subjective measures. In the treatment of anxiety-related disorders, for example, it is now clear that measures of three response systems—avoidance behavior, physiological arousal, and self-report—are necessary. The correlations among these systems are often low; thus, by simply measuring one dimension, one might miss important changes in the other two. Moreover, there is evidence that these response systems may change at different speeds and be differentially reactive to different treatment methods.

## Treatment at What Cost?

Behavior therapy is cost-effective. Paul and Lentz (1977) found that their behavioral treatment program was less expensive than either of the two alternative approaches with which it was compared: milieu therapy and traditional psychiatric care typical of state hospitals in the United States. This benefit, added to the significantly greater efficacy of the behavioral program, makes it the cost-effective choice. In England, Marks (1981) and his colleagues improved on the cost-effectiveness of the behavioral treatment of agoraphobics and obsessive-compulsives by using nurses as therapists instead of more highly trained clinical psychologists and psychiatrists. No decrement in efficacy was observed.

## Evaluating Therapy Outcomes

Behavior therapists have developed various research strategies for evaluating therapy outcome. Single-case experimental designs are particularly important because they enable cause-effect relationships to be drawn between treatments and outcome in the individual case. The ABA, or reversal, design was illustrated in the Ayllon and Azrin study previously described (1965). In the multiple-baseline design, different responses are continuously measured. Treatment is then applied successively to each response. If the desired behavior changes maximally only when treated, then a cause-effect relationship can be inferred. Single-case experimental designs can be used to study individual clinical problems that are unsuitable for group designs. Limitations of single-subject methodology include the inability to examine the interaction of subject variables with specific treatment effects and difficulty in generalizing findings to other cases. Laboratory-based studies permit the evaluation of specific techniques applied to particular problems under tightly controlled conditions; for example, evaluating fear reduction methods with snake-phobic subjects (Bandura, 1986). The advantages of this methodology include the use of multiple objective measures of outcome, the selection of homogeneous subject samples and therapists, and the freedom to assign subjects to experimental and control groups. Limitations include the possibility that findings with only mildly disturbed subjects might not be generalizable to more severely disturbed clients.

The treatment package strategy evaluates the effect of a multifaceted treatment program. If the package proves to be successful, its effective components are analyzed in subsequent research. One way of doing this is to use the dismantling strategy, in which components of the treatment package are systematically eliminated and the associated decrement in treatment outcome is measured.

The comparative research strategy is directed toward determining whether some therapeutic techniques are superior to others. Comparative studies are appropriate after specific techniques have been shown to be effective in single-subject or laboratory-based research and the parameters that maximize their efficacy are known. Different group designs require different control groups, depending on the research question addressed. The no-treatment control group controls for the possible therapeutic effects of assessment of outcome, maturation, and other changes in clients' behavior that occur independently of formal treatment. Attention-placebo control groups are used to parcel out the contribution to treatment effects of factors that are common to all forms of therapy. These factors include the relationship between therapist and client, expectations of therapeutic progress, and suggestion.

## Treatment

Some clinical details of a cognitive-behavioral approach to therapy may be illustrated by the treatment of agoraphobia, a complex anxiety disorder. Initially, the therapist carries out a careful assessment of the nature of the problem and the variables that seem to be maintaining it. Subsequent treatment may vary, but it is probable that some form of real-life exposure will be a central part of therapy. Together, therapist and client work out a hierarchy of increasingly fear-eliciting situations that the client has been avoiding. Repeated and systematic exposure to these situations occurs until avoidance is eliminated and fear is decreased.

The therapist is careful to distinguish systematic exposure from the unsystematic and ill-considered attempts clients have typically made to enter feared situations too quickly. Preparation for each exposure experience involves anticipating the inevitable fearful reactions and teaching clients appropriate coping skills. This includes recognizing and accepting feelings of fear, identifying cognitive distortions that elicit or exacerbate fear, and counteracting cognitive distortions.

The therapist might accompany the client during real-life exposure sessions, providing encouragement, support, and social reinforcement. Although empathic, the therapist remains firm about the necessity for systematic exposure. Once the client enters the feared situation it is important for the client not to leave until his or her anxiety has decreased.

Following exposure, therapist and client analyze what happened. This provides the therapist an opportunity to see how the client interprets his or her experience and to uncover any faulty cognitive processing. For example, agoraphobics tend to discount positive accomplishments, do not always attribute success experiences to their own coping ability, and therefore do not develop greater self-efficacy.

Clients are given specific instructions about exposure homework assignments between therapy sessions and are asked to keep detailed daily records of what they attempted, how they felt, and what problems they encountered. These self-recordings are reviewed by the therapist at the beginning of each session. In addition to providing the therapist with information on clients' progress (or lack of progress), these daily records facilitate the process of changing clients' cognitive sets about their problems. By directing their attention to the records of their own experience, the therapist helps clients to gain a more objective and balanced view of their problems and progress.

Homework assignments typically require the active cooperation of the client's spouse (or some other family member). The therapist invites the spouse to one or more therapy sessions to assess his or her willingness and ability to provide the necessary support and to explain what is required. Mathews et al. (1981) have developed treatment manuals for both the client and the spouse in which they detail each step of real-life exposure treatment and describe mutual responsibilities. In many cases, these manuals can greatly reduce the number of sessions the couple spends with the therapist.

It is common for clients to fail to complete homework assignments. There are several possible reasons for lack of compliance, ranging from poorly chosen homework assignments to resistance to change. Another possibility is that the spouse is uncooperative or tries to sabotage therapy. One of the advantages of including the spouse in treatment is that this resistance to progress is rapidly uncovered and can be addressed directly in the therapy sessions.

To supplement real-life exposure, some clients need assertiveness training, whereas others need to acquire ways of coping with suppressed anger. Before terminating successful treatment, the therapist works on relapse prevention training with clients. Briefly, clients are told that it is possible that they might experience an unexpected return of some fear at unpredictable points in the future. Using imagery to project ahead to such a recurrence of fear, clients learn to cope with their feelings by reinstituting previously successful coping responses. They are reassured that these feelings are quite normal and time-limited and do not necessarily signal a relapse. Clients learn that it is primarily the way they interpret these feelings that determines whether or not they experience a relapse. Specifically, the therapist tries to inoculate them against such anxiety-inducing cognitive errors as catastrophizing or selective focus on an isolated anxiety symptom.

## CASE EXAMPLE[1]

Mr. B was a 35-year-old man, married, with two sons aged eight and five, from a successful, middle-class family. He was a persistent exhibitionist whose pattern over the past 20 years had been to expose his genitals to unsuspecting adult women as often as five or six times a week. Fifteen years of intermittent psychoanalytic treatment, several hospitalizations at psychiatric institutions in the United States, and a six-year prison sentence for his deviant sexual behavior had failed to help Mr. B change his apparently uncontrollable behavior. He was currently under grand jury indictment for exposing himself to an adult woman in the presence of a group of young children. There was every prospect that he would receive a life sentence in view of his repeated offenses and numerous failures to show improvement. At least one psychiatrist had diagnosed him as untreatable and had advocated lifelong incarceration. Shortly before Mr. B came to trial, his psychoanalyst referred him to a behavior therapist as a last resort.

Mr. B was hospitalized and treated on a daily basis for six weeks, receiving a total of about 50 hours of therapy. After spending some time to develop a trusting personal relationship so that Mr. B would feel comfortable in disclosing intimate details about his problems, the therapist conducted a series of intensive interviews to ferret out the specific environmental circumstances and psychological factors that were maintaining Mr. B's deviant behavior. With Mr. B's permission, his parents and wife were also interviewed to obtain more information and to corroborate aspects of his own description of the development and present status of the problem. To obtain a sample of his actual exhibitionist behavior, a situation was arranged in a hospital office that closely resembled the conditions under which Mr. B would normally expose himself in real life. Two attractive female professional colleagues of the therapist were seated in a simulated doctor's waiting room, reading magazines, and the patient was instructed to enter, sit across from them, and expose himself. Despite the artificial setting, he proceeded to expose himself, became highly aroused, and nearly masturbated to orgasm. This entire sequence was videotaped, and objective measures of his response to this scene as well as to various other adult sexual stimuli were obtained by recording the degree of penile erection he showed while observing the videotape and selected other erotic films.

[1] This case example, with minor modifications, is taken from G. T. Wilson and K. D. O'Leary, *Principles of Behavior Therapy* (Englewood Cliffs, NJ: Prentice-Hall, 1980). Reprinted with permission.

A detailed picture was developed of the sequence of internal and external stimuli and responses that preceded his acts of exposure. For example, a woman standing alone at a bus stop as he drove past in his car often triggered a pattern of thoughts and images that caused him to circle the block and eventually expose himself. Alternatively, the anger he experienced after a heated argument with his father would also elicit the urge to expose himself. The more Mr. B thought about exposing himself, the more obsessed he became with a particular woman and her anticipated reactions. Because he tuned out everything except his immediate feelings and intentions, he became oblivious to the consequences of his actions. His behavior was out of control. Mr. B hoped that his victim would express some form of approval, either by smiling or making some sexual comment. Although this did happen occasionally, most women ignored him, and some called the police.

Mr. B believed he would be passively "conditioned" through therapy so that his problem would disappear. The therapist systematically disabused him of this notion by explaining that success could be achieved only with his active cooperation in all phases of the treatment program. He was told that there was no automatic "cure" for his problem, but that he could learn new behavioral self-control strategies, which, if practiced conscientiously and applied at the right time, would enable him to avoid further deviant behavior.

As in most complex clinical cases, treatment was multifaceted. Mr. B's own belief about his problem was that he was suddenly seized by a desire, which he could not consciously control, and that his subsequent actions were "involuntary." Analysis of the sequence of events that always preceded exposure altered Mr. B's expectation that he was unable to control his behavior. He was shown how he himself was instrumental in transforming a relatively weak initial urge into an overpowering compulsion to expose because he attended to inappropriate thoughts and feelings and engaged in behaviors that increased, rather than decreased, the temptation. It was explained that the time to break this behavioral chain and to implement the self-control strategies was at the beginning, when the urge was weakest. In order to do this, he would have to learn to be aware of his thoughts, feelings, and behavior and to recognize the early danger signals.

Specific tension states had often precipitated exposure. Accordingly, Mr. B was trained to reduce this tension with progressive relaxation. Instead of exposing himself, he learned to relax, an activity incompatible with exposure behavior. Assertion training was used to help Mr. B cope constructively with feelings of anger and to express them appropriately. Using role-playing, the therapist modeled an appropriate reaction and then provided Mr. B with reinforcing feedback as he rehearsed more effective ways of responding to anger-inducing events. In covert modeling, Mr. B was taught to imagine himself in a range of situations that customarily resulted in exposure and to see himself engaging in alternative responses to exposure; for example, relaxing away tension, expressing anger appropriately, reminding himself of the consequences of being caught, or simply walking away from a tempting situation.

Aversion conditioning was used to decrease the positive appeal of exposure. During repeated presentations of the videotape of his exposure scene, on an unpredictable schedule, a loud, subjectively aversive police siren was blared over earphones. Whereas Mr. B initially found watching the videotape pleasurable and sexually arousing, he progressively lost all sexual interest in it. He reported that he experienced marked difficulty in concentrating on the scene because he began to anticipate the disruptive—and given his personal social learning history, understandably frightening—police siren in connection with thoughts of exposure. The siren was also paired systematically with a range of fantasies of different situations in which he would expose himself. In addition to the siren, Mr. B learned how to associate self-administered aversive cognitive events with deviant thoughts or images. For example, imagery of an aversive event, such as being apprehended by the police, was coupled with thoughts of exposure. Periodically, Mr. B's sexual arousal to the videotape was assessed directly by measuring penile erection to provide an evaluation of his progress.

Following every session with the therapist, Mr. B was given specific homework assignments. These included monitoring and recording any urges to expose himself in order to ensure awareness about any signs of reverting back to old habits. Other assignments involved (1) practicing relaxation exercises and recording the degree to which the relaxation was associated with reduced tension; (2) rehearsing the association of aversive imagery with fantasies of exposure and recording the intensity of the aversive imagery and the clarity of the exposure fantasies on 10-point rating scales; and (3) engaging in assertive behavior, where appropriate, during interactions with other patients and staff on his assigned ward. Direct observation of his interpersonal behavior on the hospital ward provided an index of his utilization of assertive behavior.

Finally, after speaking with the therapist about cooperation and apparent progress in the treatment program, Mr. B's wife agreed to several joint therapy sessions that used behavioral methods for improving marital communication and interaction. Although the behavioral assessment had indicated that Mr. B's exhibitionist behavior was not directly caused by an unhappy marriage or lack of sexual satisfaction from his wife, the therapist believed improvement in these spheres of functioning would help consolidate and support Mr. B's self-control.

On leaving the hospital at the end of treatment, Mr. B continued to self-monitor thoughts or feelings about exposing himself, relax systematically, assert himself, and rehearse the pairing of aversive imagery with thoughts of exposure. Every week he mailed these records to the therapist, a procedure designed to generalize treatment-produced improvement to the real world and to maintain self-control over time. Another facet of this maintenance strategy was a series of booster sessions scheduled approximately four months after therapy in which he returned to the hospital for a week of intensive treatment along the same lines as described above.

In large part owing to the therapist's strong recommendation, the court gave Mr. B a suspended sentence. A five-year follow-up showed that Mr. B had refrained from any exhibitionism, had experienced very few such desires, and felt confident in his newly found ability to control his behavior.

## SUMMARY

Behavior therapy helped to change the face of psychotherapy in the latter half of the twentieth century by generating innovative treatment strategies and influencing how we conduct research on psychological treatment. In turn, behavior therapy itself has changed and continues to evolve. Its theoretical foundations have broadened and its treatment techniques have become more diverse. In the process, its overlaps with other systems of psychotherapy have become more apparent. Nonetheless, it remains a distinctive approach to assessment and treatment. Methodological rigor and innovation have been major contributions of behavior therapy to the field of psychotherapy. Behavioral treatments have been subjected to more rigorous evaluation than any other psychological therapy.

Behavior therapy faces two immediate challenges in the twenty-first century. One is the need to improve the dissemination and adoption of demonstrably effective behavioral treatments for a number of common disorders. Although behavior therapy has become an accepted part of the psychotherapeutic establishment, its methods are not being used as widely as the evidence would warrant (Persons, 1997). As noted earlier in this chapter, the growing demand for accountability in health care will provide an impetus for more widespread application of behavioral methods.

The evidence supporting behavior therapy comes mainly from well-controlled research studies conducted at universities where therapists are carefully selected and highly trained and patients are recruited specifically for the treatment studies. However, many practitioners question the relevance of this type of research to actual clinical practice in which they are confronted with a diverse mix of patients and varying clinical problems. In the future we can anticipate an increased emphasis on clinical research focused on evaluating the generalizability of the findings from tightly controlled, university-based research to different service settings such as mental health clinics and independent practice.

Another likely trend will be the use of a stepped-care approach to treatment services. In a stepped-care framework, which is widely used in medicine, treatments are provided sequentially according to need. Initially all patients receive the lowest step—the simplest, least intrusive, and most cost-effective treatment. More complex or intensive interventions are administered to patients who do not respond to these initial efforts. To date, most behavior therapy treatments have been designed for use within specialist settings and require professional training. Relatively few therapists are sufficiently well-trained in these specialized, manual-based treatments (Wilson, 1998). Moreover, there are unlikely ever to be sufficient specialist treatment resources for all patients. Briefer and simpler methods that can be used by a wide range of different mental health professionals are needed. It will be challenging but critical to identify reliable predictors of patients for whom these cost-effective methods are appropriate.

The second major challenge confronting behavior therapy is the need to develop more effective treatments for a broader range of problems. At present, even the most effective treatments are often not good enough. Clinical researchers and practitioners need to cooperate in devising innovative and improved methods for treating patients who do not respond to the best available treatments.

Whereas considerable progress has been made in developing effective treatments, the field has lagged behind in understanding how these treatments achieve their therapeutic effects. We need to learn more about the mechanisms of therapeutic change. Understanding the mechanisms through which behavior therapy methods operate is vital to the development of innovative, more potent interventions. With respect to current manual-based treatments, active therapeutic procedures could be enhanced and inactive elements discarded. Theory-driven, experimental analysis of therapy outcome and its mechanisms of action is a priority for future research.

Finally, to fulfill its original promise of linking clinical practice to advances in scientific research, behavior therapy must be responsive to developments both in experimental psychology and in biology. Dramatic breakthroughs in genetics and neuroscience have already revolutionized the biological sciences. Progress will continue in unlocking the secrets of the brain. A better understanding of the role of brain mechanisms in the development and maintenance of clinical disorders will lead to better theories and therapies for behavior change.

## ANNOTATED BIBLIOGRAPHY

Barlow, D. H. (Ed.). (2001). *Clinical handbook of psychological disorders* (3rd ed.). New York: Guilford Press.
This edited volume provides detailed clinical descriptions of the behavioral treatment of several adult clinical disorders. A particularly informative feature is the extensive use of transcripts from actual therapy sessions with individual patients.

Clark, D. M., & Fairburn, C. G. (Eds.). (1997). *Science and practice of cognitive behaviour therapy.* New York: Oxford University Press.
This text presents a comprehensive analysis of the most recent theoretical and practical developments in the theory and practice of CBT for major adult clinical problems. It illustrates how CBT is based on

specific conceptual models of the psychological and biological factors responsible for the maintenance of each disorder and provides state-of-the-art evaluations of treatment outcome.

Hawton, K., Salkovskis, P., Kirk, J., & Clark, D. M. (Eds.). (1989). *Cognitive behaviour therapy for psychiatric disorders.* New York: Oxford University Press.

This edited volume details how CBT is applied in actual practice. Written for therapists, it provides specific guidance on how to assess and treat different clinical disorders. The volume is invaluable for training graduate students in clinical psychology.

# CASE READINGS

Barlow, D. (1993). Covert sensitization for paraphilia. In J. R. Cautela, A. J. Kearney, L. Ascher, A. Kearney, & M. Kleinman (Eds.), *Covert conditioning casebook* (pp. 188–197). Pacific Grove, CA: Thomson Learning. [Reprinted in D. Wedding & R. J. Corsini (Eds.). (2005). *Case studies in psychotherapy.* Belmont, CA: Wadsworth.]

This is a detailed case that demonstrates the use of covert sensitization in the treatment of a deeply troubled minister.

Barlow, D. H., & Cerny, J. A. (1988). *Psychological treatment of panic.* New York: Guilford Press.

Chapter 8 of this treatment manual provides a detailed description of the cognitive-behavioral treatment of a patient with panic disorder.

Melamed, B., & Siegel, L. (1975). Self-directed in vivo treatment of an obsessive-compulsive checking ritual. *Journal of Behavior Therapy and Experimental Psychiatry, 6,* 31–35.

This case illustrates the application of exposure and response prevention, among other techniques, in the treatment of compulsions. The case also describes the detailed, ongoing assessment of treatment progress characteristic of behavior therapy.

Novaco, R. (1977). Stress inoculation: A cognitive therapy for anger and its application to a case of depression. *Journal of Consulting and Clinical Psychology, 45,* 600–608.

This case illustrates the use of cognitive techniques within behavior therapy. It also shows how cognitive-behavioral methods are used to treat problems of anger, which, together with anxiety and depression, are the most common emotions encountered by clinicians.

Wilson, G. T., & Pike, K. (1993). Eating disorders. In D. H. Barlow (Ed.), *Clinical handbook of psychological disorders* (2nd ed.). New York: Guilford Press.

This chapter provides an in-depth illustration of the treatment of a female patient with bulimia nervosa, an eating disorder that is common among college-aged and young adult women.

Wolf, M. M., Risley, T., & Mees, H. (1965). Application of operant conditioning procedures to the behavior problems of an autistic child. In L. P. Ullmann & L. Krasner (Eds.), *Case studies in behavior modification* (pp. 138–145). New York: Holt, Rinehart and Winston.

This classic case study illustrates the application of operant principles and procedures to the treatment of an autistic child. The assessment and treatment approach described here provide a model for the use of behavioral methods with a wide range of problems among the developmentally disabled.

Wolpe, J. (1991). A complex case. *The practice of behavior therapy* (4th ed.). New York: Pergamon. [Reprinted in D. Wedding & R. J. Corsini (Eds.). (1995). *Case studies in psychotherapy.* Itasca, IL: F. E. Peacock.]

This case study describes the way one of the founders of behavior therapy treated a 31-year-old man who presented with symptoms of anxiety and an obsession about his wife's premarital loss of virginity.

# REFERENCES

Ayllon, T., & Azrin, N. H. (1965). The measurement and reinforcement of behavior of psychotics. *Journal of the Experimental Analysis of Behavior, 8,* 357–383.

Bandura, A. (1969). *Principles of behavior modification.* New York: Holt, Rinehart and Winston.

Bandura, A. (1977). *Social learning theory.* Englewood Cliffs, NJ: Prentice-Hall.

Bandura, A. (1982). Self-efficacy mechanism in human agency. *American Psychologist, 37,* 122–147.

Bandura, A. (1986). *Social foundations of thought and action: A social cognitive theory.* Englewood Cliffs, NJ: Prentice-Hall.

Bandura, A. (1998). Personal and collective efficacy in human adaptation and change. In J. G. Adair, D. Belanger, & K. L. Dion (Eds.), *Advances in psychological science* (pp. 51–72). East Sussex, UK: Psychology Press.

Barlow, D. H. (1988). *Anxiety and its disorders.* New York: Guilford Press.

Barlow, D. H., Gorman, J. M., Shear, M. K., & Woods, S. W. (2000). Cognitive behavioral therapy, imipramine, or their combination for panic disorder. *Journal of the American Medical Association, 283,* 2529–2536.

Baxter, L. R., Schwartz, J. M., Bergman, K. S., Szuba, M. P., Guze, B. H., Mazziotata, J. C., et al. (1992).

Caudate glucose metabolic rate changes with both drug and behavior therapy for obsessive-compulsive disorder. *Archives of General Psychiatry, 49,* 681–689.

Beck, A. T., Rush, A. J., Shaw, B. E., & Emery, G. (1979). *Cognitive therapy of depression.* New York: Guilford Press.

Brady, J., Davison, G., Dewald, P., Egan, G., Fadiman, J., Frank, J., et al. (1980). Some views on effective principles of psychotherapy, cognitive therapy and research. *Cognitive Therapy and Research, 4,* 269–306.

Cautela, J. (1967). Covert sensitization. *Psychological Reports, 20,* 459–468.

Clark, D. M. (1989). Anxiety states. In K. Hawton, P. M. Salkovskis, J. Kirk, & D. M. Clark (Eds.), *Cognitive behaviour therapy for psychiatric problems* (pp. 52–96). New York: Oxford Medical Publications.

Clark, D. M., Salkovskis, P. M., Hackmann, A., Middleton, H., & Gelder, M. (1994). A comparison of cognitive therapy, applied relaxation and imipramine in the treatment of panic disorder. *British Journal of Psychiatry, 164,* 759–769.

Craske, M. G., Brown, T. A., & Barlow, D. H. (1991). Behavioral treatment of panic disorder: A two-year follow-up. *Behavior Therapy, 22,* 289–304.

Davison, G. C., & Lazarus, A. A. (1995). The dialectics of science and practice. In S. C. Hayes, V. M. Follette, R. M. Dawes, & K. E. Grady (Eds.), *Scientific standards of psychological practice: Issues and recommendations* (pp. 95–120). Reno, NV: Context Press.

Dawes, R. M. (1994). *House of cards.* New York: Free Press.

Eysenck, H. J. (1959). Learning theory and behavior therapy. *British Journal of Medical Science, 105,* 61–75.

Eysenck, H. J. (1967). *The biological basis of personality.* Springfield, IL: Charles C. Thomas.

Fairburn, C. G., Marcus, M. D., & Wilson, G. T. (1993). Cognitive behaviour therapy for binge eating and bulimia nervosa: A comprehensive treatment manual. In C. G. Fairburn & G. T. Wilson (Eds.), *Binge eating: Nature, assessment and treatment* (pp. 361–404). New York: Guilford Press.

Fairburn, C. G., Norman, P. A., Welch, S. L., O'Connor, M. E., Doll, H. A., & Peveler, R. C. (1995). A prospective study of outcome in bulimia nervosa and the long-term effects of three psychological treatments. *Archives of General Psychiatry, 52,* 304–312.

Franks, C. M., Wilson, G. T., Kendall, P., & Brownell, K. (1982). *Annual review of behavior therapy: Theory and practice* (Vol. 8). New York: Guilford Press.

Glass, C. R., & Arnkoff, D. B. (1992). Behavior therapy. In D. K. Freedheim, H. J. Freudenberger, J. W. Kessler, S. B. Messer, D. R. Peterson, H. H. Strupp, et al. (Eds.), *History of psychotherapy: A century of change* (pp. 587–628). Washington, DC: American Psychological Association.

Gortner, E. T., Gollan, J. K., Dobson, K. S., & Jacobson, N. S. (1998). Cognitive-behavioral treatment for depression: Relapse prevention. *Journal of Consulting and Clinical Psychology, 66,* 377–384.

Hawton, K., Salkovskis, P. M., Kirk, J., & Clark, D. M. (Eds.). (1989). *Cognitive behaviour therapy for psychiatric problems.* Oxford University Press.

Hollon, S. D., & Beck, A. (1994). Cognitive and cognitive-behavioral therapies. In S. L. Garfield & A. E. Bergin (Eds.), *Handbook of psychotherapy and behavior change: An empirical analysis* (4th ed.). New York: Wiley.

Ilardi, S. S., & Craighead, W. E. (1994). The role of nonspecific factors in cognitive-behavior therapy for depression. *Clinical Psychology, 1,* 138–156.

Jacobson, E. (1938). *Progressive relaxation.* Chicago: University of Chicago Press.

Jacobson, N. S. (Ed.). (1987). *Psychotherapists in clinical practice: Cognitive and behavioral perspectives.* New York: Guilford Press.

Jacobson, N. S., Dobson, K. S., Truax, P. A., Addis, M. E., Koerner, K., Gollan, J. K., et al. (1996). A component analysis of cognitive-behavioral treatment for depression. *Journal of Consulting and Clinical Psychology, 64,* 295–304.

Jacobson, N., & Margolin, G. (1979). *Marital therapy.* New York: Brunner/Mazel.

Jones, M. C. (1924). The elimination of children's fears. *Journal of Experimental Psychology, 7,* 382–390.

Kanfer, F. H. (1977). The many faces of self-control, or behavior modification changes its focus. In R. B. Stuart (Ed.), *Behavioral self-management.* New York: Brunner/Mazel.

Kazdin, A. E. (1977). *The token economy.* New York: Plenum.

Kazdin, A. E. (1978a). The application of operant techniques in treatment, rehabilitation, and education. In S. L. Garfield & A. E. Bergin (Eds.), *Handbook of psychotherapy and behavior change* (2nd ed.; pp. 549–590). New York: Wiley.

Kazdin, A. E. (1978b). *History of behavior modification.* Baltimore, MD: University Park Press.

Kazdin, A. E., & Wilson, G. T. (1978). *Evaluation of behavior therapy: Issues, evidence and research strategies.* Cambridge, MA: Ballinger.

Knudson, R. M., Gurman, A. S., & Kniskern, D. P. (1979). Behavioral marriage therapy: A treatment in transition. In C. M. Franks & G. T. Wilson (Eds.), *Annual review of behavior therapy: Theory and practice* (Vol. 7; pp. 543–574). New York: Brunner/Mazel.

Lazarus, A. A. (1971). *Behavior therapy and beyond.* New York: McGraw-Hill.

Lazarus, A. A. (1981). *The practice of multimodal therapy.* New York: McGraw-Hill.

Lazarus, A. A., & Fay, A. (1982). Resistance or rationalization? A cognitive-behavioral perspective. In P. L. Wachtel (Ed.), *Resistance: Psychodynamic and behavioral approaches* (pp. 94–107). New York: Plenum.

Lewinsohn, P. M., Clarke, G. N., Hops, H., & Andrews, J. (1990). Cognitive-behavioral treatment for depressed adolescents. *Behavior Therapy, 21,* 385–401.

Locke, H. J., & Wallace, K. M. (1959). Short marital adjustment and prediction tests: Their reliability and validity. *Marriage and Family Living, 21,* 251–255.

Lovaas, O. I. (1987). Behavioral treatment and normal educational and intellectual functioning in young autistic children. *Journal of Consulting and Clinical Psychology, 55,* 3–9.

Marks, I. M. (1981). *Cure and care of the neuroses.* New York: Wiley.

Marks, I., & Mathews, A. (1979). Brief standard self-rating for phobic patients. *Behaviour Research and Therapy, 17,* 263–267.

Masters, W., & Johnson, V. (1970). *Human sexual inadequacy.* Boston: Little, Brown.

Masters, W., & Johnson, V. (1979). *Homosexuality in perspective.* Boston: Little, Brown.

Mathews, A. M., Gelder, M. G., & Johnston, D. W. (1981). *Agoraphobia: Nature and treatment.* New York: Guilford Press.

Melamed, B., & Siegel, L. (1980). *Behavioral medicine.* New York: Springer.

Miller, N. E. (1948). Studies of fear as an acquirable drive. I. Fear as motivation and fear reduction as reinforcement in the learning of new responses. *Journal of Experimental Psychology, 38,* 89–101.

Mischel, W. (1968). *Personality and assessment.* New York: Wiley.

Mischel, W. (1973). Toward a cognitive social learning reconceptualization of personality. *Psychological Review, 80,* 252–283.

Mischel, W. (1976). *Introduction to personality.* New York: Holt, Rinehart and Winston.

Mischel, W. (1981). A cognitive social learning approach to assessment. In T. V. Merluzzi, C. R. Glass, & M. Genest (Eds.), *Cognitive assessment* (pp. 479–500). New York: Guilford Press.

Mowrer, O. H. (1947). On the dual nature of learning—A reinterpretation of "conditioning" and "problem solving." *Harvard Educational Review, 17,* 102–148.

Mowrer, O. H., & Mowrer, E. (1938). Enuresis: A method for its study and treatment. *American Journal of Orthopsychiatry, 4,* 436–459.

Norcross, J. C., Alford, B. A., & DeMichele, J. T. (1992). The future of psychotherapy: Delphi data and concluding observations. *Psychotherapy, 29,* 150–158.

O'Leary, K. D. (1980). Pills or skills for hyperactive children. *Journal of Applied Behavior Analysis, 13,* 191–204.

O'Leary, K. D., & Beach, S. R. H. (1990). Marital therapy: A viable treatment for depression. *American Journal of Psychiatry, 147,* 183–186.

O'Leary, K. D., & Carr, E. G. (1982). Childhood disorders. In G. T. Wilson & C. M. Franks (Eds.), *Contemporary behavior therapy: Conceptual and empirical foundations* (pp. 495–496). New York: Guilford.

O'Leary, K. D., & O'Leary, S. G. (1977). *Classroom management.* New York: Pergamon Press.

O'Leary, K. D., Turkewitz, H., & Tafel, S. (1973). Parent and therapist evaluation of behavior therapy in a child psychological clinic. *Journal of Consulting and Clinical Psychology, 41,* 289–293.

O'Leary, K. D., & Wilson, G. T. (1987). *Behavior therapy: Application and outcome* (2nd ed.). Englewood Cliffs, NJ: Prentice-Hall.

Paul, G. L. (1966). *Insight versus desensitization in psychotherapy.* Stanford: Stanford University Press.

Paul, G. L. (1967). Outcome research in psychotherapy. *Journal of Consulting Psychology, 31,* 109–188.

Paul, G. L., & Lentz, R. J. (1977). *Psychological treatment of chronic mental patients.* Cambridge, MA: Harvard University Press.

Perri, M. G. (1998). The maintenance of treatment effects in the long-term management of obesity. *Clinical Psychology: Theory and Practice, 5,* 526–543.

Persons, J. B. (1997). Dissemination of effective methods: Behavior therapy's next challenge. *Behavior Therapy, 28,* 465–471.

Rathus, S. A. (1973). A 30-item schedule for assessing assertive behavior. *Behavior Therapy, 4,* 398–406.

Risley, T., & Sheldon-Wildgen, J. (1982). Invited peer review: The AABT experience. *Professional Psychology, 13,* 125–131.

Rosen, R. C., & Keefe, F. J. (1978). The measurement of human penile tumescence. *Psychophysiology, 15,* 366–376.

Ross, A. (1981). *Child behavior therapy.* New York: Wiley.

Salter, A. (1949). *Conditioned reflex therapy.* New York: Farrar, Straus.

Sayette, M., & Mayne, T. (1990). Survey of current clinical and research trends in clinical psychology. *American Psychologist, 45,* 1263–1266.

Schwartz, G. E., & Weiss, S. M. (1978). Behavioral medicine revisited: An amended definition. *Journal of Behavioral Medicine, 1,* 249–252.

Skinner, B. E. (1953). *Science and human behavior.* New York: Macmillan.

Sloane, R. B., Staples, F. R., Cristol, A. H., Yorkston, J. J., & Whipple, K. (1975). *Psychotherapy versus behavior therapy.* Cambridge, MA: Harvard University Press.

Smith, D. (1982). Trends in counseling and psychotherapy. *American Psychologist, 37,* 802–809.

Staples, F. R., Sloane, R. B., Whipple, K., Cristol, A. H., & Yorkston, N. (1975). Differences between behavior therapists and psychotherapists. *Archives of General Psychiatry, 32,* 1517–1522.

Stolz, S. G. (1978). *Ethical issues in behavior modification.* San Francisco: Jossey-Bass.

Swan, G. E., & MacDonald, M. D. (1978). Behavior therapy in practice: A national survey of behavior therapists. *Behavior Therapy, 9,* 799–807.

Task Force on Promotion and Dissemination of Psychological Procedures. (1995). Training in and dissemination of empirically validated psychological treatments:

Report and recommendations. *The Clinical Psychologist, 48,* 3–24.

Turkewitz, H., & O'Leary, K. D. (1981). A comparative outcome study of behavioral marital and communication therapy. *Journal of Marital and Family Therapy, 7,* 159–169.

Ullmann, L. P., & Krasner, L. (1965). *Case studies in behavior modification.* New York: Holt, Rinehart and Winston.

Upper, D., & Ross, S. M. (Eds.). (1981). *Behavioral group therapy.* Champaign, IL: Research Press.

Wilson, G. T. (1997). Cognitive behavioral treatment of bulimia nervosa. *The Clinical Psychologist, 50*(2), 10–12.

Wilson, G. T. (1998). Manual-based treatment and clinical practice. *Clinical Psychology: Science and Practice, 5,* 363–375.

Wilson, G. T., & Fairburn, C. G. (2002). Eating disorders. In P. E. Nathan & J. M. Gorman (Eds.), *A guide to treatments that work* (2nd ed.; pp. 559–592). New York: Oxford University Press.

Wilson, G. T., & O'Leary, K. D. (1980). *Principles of behavior therapy.* Englewood Cliffs, NJ: Prentice-Hall.

Wolpe, J. (1958). *Psychotherapy by reciprocal inhibition.* Stanford: Stanford University Press.

Wolpe, J., & Rachman, S. (1960). Psychoanalytic evidence: A critique based on Freud's case of Little Hans. *Journal of Nervous and Mental Disorders, 131,* 135–145.

Yates, A. J. (1980). *Biofeedback and the modification of behavior.* New York: Plenum.

Aaron T. Beck

 *Collective consciousness*

# 8   COGNITIVE THERAPY

*Aaron T. Beck and Marjorie E. Weishaar*

## OVERVIEW

Cognitive therapy is based on a theory of personality which maintains that people respond to life events through a combination of cognitive, affective, motivational, and behavioral responses. These responses are based in human evolution and individual learning history. The cognitive system deals with the way that individuals perceive, interpret, and assign meanings to events. It interacts with the other affective, motivational, and physiological systems to process information from the physical and social environments, and to respond accordingly. Sometimes responses are maladaptive because of misperceptions, misinterpretations, or dysfunctional, idiosyncratic interpretations of situations.

Cognitive therapy aims to adjust information-processing and initiate positive change in all systems by acting through the cognitive system. In a collaborative process, the therapist and patient examine the patient's beliefs about himself, other people, and the world. The patient's maladaptive conclusions are treated as testable hypotheses. Behavioral experiments and verbal procedures are used to examine alternative interpretations and to generate contradictory evidence that supports more adaptive beliefs and leads to therapeutic change.

## Basic Concepts

Cognitive therapy can be thought of as a theory, a system of strategies, and a series of techniques. The theory is based on the idea that the processing of information is crucial for the survival of any organism. If we did not have a functional apparatus for taking in relevant information from the environment, synthesizing it, and formulating a plan of action on the basis of this synthesis, we would soon die or be killed.

Each system involved in survival—cognitive, behavioral, affective, and motivational—is comprised of structures known as *schemas.* Cognitive schemas contain people's perceptions of themselves and others, their goals and expectations, memories, fantasies, and previous learning. These greatly influence, if not control, the processing of information.

In various psychopathological conditions such as anxiety disorders, depressive disorders, mania, paranoid states, obsessive-compulsive neuroses, and others, a specific bias affects how the person incorporates new information. Thus, a depressed person has a negative bias, including a negative view of self, world, and future. In anxiety, there is a systematic bias or *cognitive shift* toward selectively interpreting themes of danger. In paranoid conditions, the dominant shift is toward indiscriminate attributions of abuse or interference, and in mania the shift is toward exaggerated interpretations of personal gain.

Contributing to these shifts are certain specific attitudes that predispose people under the influence of certain life situations to interpret their experiences in a biased way. These are known as *cognitive vulnerabilities.* For example, a person who has the belief that any minor loss represents a major deprivation may react catastrophically to even the smallest loss. A person who feels vulnerable to sudden death may overinterpret normal body sensations as signs of impending death and have a panic attack.

Previously, cognitive theory emphasized a linear relationship between the activation of cognitive schemas and changes in the other systems; that is, cognitions (beliefs and assumptions) triggered affect, motivation, and behavior. Current cognitive theory, benefiting from recent developments in clinical, evolutionary, and cognitive psychology, views all systems acting together as a *mode.* Modes are networks of cognitive, affective, motivational, and behavioral schemas that compose personality and interpret ongoing situations. Some modes, like the anxiety mode, are *primal,* meaning they are universal and tied to survival. Other modes, like conversing or studying, are minor and under conscious control. Although primal modes are thought to have been adaptive in an evolutionary sense, individuals may find them maladaptive in everyday life when they are triggered by misperceptions or overreactions. Even personality disorders may be viewed as exaggerated versions of formerly adaptive strategies. In personality disorders, primal modes are operational almost continuously.

Primal modes include primal thinking, which is rigid, absolute, automatic, and biased. Nevertheless, conscious intentions can override primal thinking and make it more flexible. Automatic and reflexive responses can be replaced by deliberate thinking, conscious goals, problem solving, and long-term planning. In cognitive therapy, a thorough understanding of the mode and all its integral systems is part of the case conceptualization. This approach to therapy teaches patients to use conscious control to recognize and override maladaptive responses.

*this is opposed to existentialist beliefs about death?*

### *Strategies*

The overall strategies of cognitive therapy involve primarily a collaborative enterprise between the patient and the therapist to explore dysfunctional interpretations and try to modify them. This *collaborative empiricism* views the patient as a practical scientist who lives by interpreting stimuli but who has been temporarily thwarted by his or her own in-formation-gathering and integrating apparatus (cf. Kelly, 1955).

The second strategy, *guided discovery,* is directed toward discovering what threads run through the patient's present misperceptions and beliefs and linking them to analo-gous experiences in the past. Thus, the therapist and patient collaboratively weave a tap-estry that tells the story of the development of the patient's disorder.

The therapy attempts to improve reality testing through continuous evaluation of personal conclusions. The immediate goal is to shift the information-processing appara-tus to a more "neutral" condition so that events will be evaluated in a more balanced way.

There are three major approaches to treating dysfunctional modes: (1) deactivating them, (2) modifying their content and structure, and (3) constructing more adaptive modes to neutralize them. In therapy, the first and third approaches are often accom-plished simultaneously, for the particular belief may be demonstrated to be dysfunctional and a new belief to be more accurate or adaptive. The deactivation of a dysfunctional mode can occur through distraction or reassurance, but lasting change is unlikely unless a person's underlying, core beliefs are modified.

## Techniques

Techniques used in cognitive therapy are directed primarily at correcting errors and bi-ases in information processing and modifying the core beliefs that promote faulty con-clusions. The purely cognitive techniques focus on identifying and testing the patient's beliefs, exploring their origins and basis, correcting them if they fail an empirical or log-ical test, or problem solving. For example, some beliefs are tied to one's culture, gender role, religion, or socioeconomic status. Therapy may be directed toward problem solving with an understanding of how these beliefs influence the patient.

Core beliefs are explored in a similar manner and are tested for their accuracy and adaptiveness. The patient who discovers that these beliefs are not accurate is encouraged to try out a different set of beliefs to determine if the new beliefs are more accurate and functional.

Cognitive therapy also uses behavioral techniques such as skills training (e.g., relax-ation, assertiveness training, social skills training), role-playing, behavioral rehearsal, and exposure therapy.

## Other Systems

Procedures used in cognitive therapy, such as identifying common themes in a patient's emotional reactions, narratives, and imagery, are similar to the *psychoanalytic method.* However, in cognitive therapy the common thread is a meaning readily accessible to conscious interpretation, whereas in psychoanalysis the meaning is unconscious (or re-pressed) and must be inferred.

Both psychodynamic psychotherapy and cognitive therapy assume that behavior can be influenced by beliefs of which one is not immediately aware. However, cognitive ther-apy maintains that the thoughts contributing to a patient's distress are not deeply buried in the unconscious. Moreover, the cognitive therapist does not regard the patient's self-report as a screen for more deeply concealed ideas. Cognitive therapy focuses on the linkages among symptoms, conscious beliefs, and current experiences. Psychoanalytic approaches are oriented toward repressed childhood memories and motivational con-structs, such as libidinal needs and infantile sexuality.

Cognitive therapy is highly structured and short-term, lasting from 12 to 16 weeks. The therapist is actively engaged in collaboration with the patient. Psychoanalytic ther-apy is long-term and relatively unstructured. The analyst is largely passive. Cognitive therapy attempts to shift biased information processing through the application of logic to dysfunctional ideas and the use of behavioral experiments to test dysfunctional beliefs. Psychoanalysts rely on free association and depth interpretations to penetrate the encapsulated unconscious residue of unresolved childhood conflicts.

Cognitive therapy and Rational Emotive Behavior Therapy (REBT) share emphases on the primary importance of cognition in psychological dysfunction, seeing the task of therapy as changing maladaptive assumptions and the stance of the therapist as active and directive. There are some differences, nevertheless, between these two approaches.

Cognitive therapy, using an information-processing model, is directed toward modifying the "cognitive shift" by addressing biased selection of information and distorted interpretations. The shift to normal cognitive processing is accomplished by testing the erroneous inferences that result from biased processing. Continual disconfirmation of cognitive errors, working as a feedback system, gradually restores more adaptive functioning. However, the dysfunctional beliefs that contributed to the unbalanced cognitive processing in the first place also require further testing and invalidation.

REBT theory states that a distressed individual has irrational beliefs that contribute to irrational thoughts and that by modifying these through confrontation, they will disappear and the disorder will clear up. The cognitive therapist, operating from an inductive model, helps the patient translate interpretations and beliefs into hypotheses, which are then subjected to empirical testing. An REBT therapist is more inclined to use a deductive model to point out irrational beliefs. The cognitive therapist eschews the word "irrational" in favor of "dysfunctional" because problematic beliefs are nonadaptive rather than irrational. They contribute to psychological disorders because they interfere with normal cognitive processing, not because they are irrational.

A profound difference between these two approaches is that cognitive therapy maintains that each disorder has its own typical cognitive content or *cognitive specificity*. The *cognitive profiles* of depression, anxiety, and panic disorder are significantly different and require substantially different techniques. REBT, on the other hand, does not conceptualize disorders as having cognitive themes, but rather focuses on the "musts," "shoulds," and other imperatives presumed to underlie all disorders.

The cognitive therapy model emphasizes the impact of cognitive deficits in psychopathology. Some clients experience problems because their cognitive deficits do not let them foresee delayed or long-range negative consequences. Others have trouble with concentration, directed thinking, or recall. These difficulties occur in severe anxiety, depression, and panic attacks. Cognitive deficits produce perceptual errors as well as faulty interpretations. Further, inadequate cognitive processing may interfere with use of coping abilities or techniques and with interpersonal problem solving, as occurs in suicidal people.

Finally, REBT views patients' beliefs as philosophically incongruent with reality. Meichenbaum (1977) criticizes this perspective, stating that nonpatients have irrational beliefs as well but are able to cope with them. Cognitive therapy teaches patients to *self-correct* faulty cognitive processing and to bolster assumptions that allow them to cope. Thus, REBT views the problem as philosophical; cognitive therapy views it as functional.

Cognitive therapy shares many similarities with some forms of *behavior therapy* but is quite different from others. Within behavior therapy are numerous approaches that vary in their emphasis on cognitive processes. At one end of the behavioral spectrum is applied behavioral analysis, an approach that ignores "internal events," such as interpretations and inferences, as much as possible. As one moves in the other direction, cognitive mediating processes are given increasing attention until one arrives at a variety of cognitive-behavioral approaches. At this point, the distinction between the purely cognitive and the distinctly behavioral becomes unclear.

Cognitive therapy and behavior therapy share some features: They are empirical, present-centered, problem-oriented, and require explicit identification of problems and the situations in which they occur as well as the consequences resulting from them. In contrast to radical behaviorism, cognitive therapy applies the same kind of functional analysis to internal experiences—to thoughts, attitudes, and images. Cognitions, like behaviors, can be modified by active collaboration through behavioral experiments that foster new learning. Also, in contrast to behavioral approaches based on simple conditioning paradigms, cognitive therapy sees individuals as active participants in their environments, judging and evaluating stimuli, interpreting events and sensations, and judging their own responses.

Studies of some behavioral techniques, such as exposure methods for the treatment of phobias, demonstrate that cognitive and behavioral changes work together. For example, in agoraphobia, cognitive improvement has been concomitant with behavioral improvement (Williams & Rappoport, 1983). Simple exposure to agoraphobic situations while verbalizing negative automatic thoughts may lead to improvement on cognitive measures (Gournay, 1986). Bandura (1977) has demonstrated that one of the most effective ways to change cognitions is to change performance. In real-life exposure, patients confront not only the threatening situations, but also their personal expectations of danger and their assumed inability to cope with their reactions. Because the experience itself is processed cognitively, exposure can be considered a cognitive procedure.

Cognitive therapy maintains that a comprehensive approach to the treatment of anxiety and other disorders includes targeting anxiety-provoking thoughts and images. Work with depressed patients (Beck, Rush, Shaw, & Emery, 1979) demonstrates that desired cognitive changes do not necessarily follow from changes in behavior. For this reason, it is vital to know the patient's expectations, interpretations, and reactions to events. Cognitive change must be demonstrated, not assumed.

# HISTORY

## Precursors

Cognitive therapy's theoretical underpinnings are derived from three main sources: (1) the phenomenological approach to psychology, (2) structural theory and depth psychology, and (3) cognitive psychology. The phenomenological approach posits that the individual's view of self and the personal world are central to behavior. This concept was originally founded in Greek Stoic philosophy and can be seen in Immanuel Kant's (1798) emphasis on conscious subjective experience. This approach is also evident in the writings of Adler (1936), Alexander (1950), Horney (1950), and Sullivan (1953).

The second major influence was the structural theory and depth psychology of Kant and Freud, particularly Freud's concept of the hierarchical structuring of cognition into primary and secondary processes.

More recent developments in cognitive psychology also have had an impact. George Kelly (1955) is credited with being the first among contemporaries to describe the cognitive model through his use of "personal constructs" and his emphasis on the role of beliefs in behavior change. Cognitive theories of emotion, such as those of Magda Arnold (1960) and Richard Lazarus (1984), which give primacy to cognition in emotional and behavioral change, have also contributed to cognitive therapy.

## Beginnings

Cognitive therapy began in the early 1960s as the result of Aaron Beck's research on depression (Beck, 1963, 1964, 1967). Trained in psychoanalysis, Beck attempted to validate Freud's theory of depression as having at its core "anger turned on the self." To substantiate this formulation, Beck made clinical observations of depressed patients and investigated their treatment under traditional psychoanalysis. Rather than finding retroflected anger in their thoughts and dreams, Beck observed a negative bias in their cognitive processing. With continued clinical observations and experimental testing, Beck developed his theory of emotional disorders and a cognitive model of depression.

The work of Albert Ellis (1962) gave major impetus to the development of cognitive-behavior therapies. Both Ellis and Beck believed that people can consciously adopt reason, and both viewed the patient's underlying assumptions as targets of intervention. Similarly, they both rejected their analytic training and replaced passive listening with active, direct dialogues with patients. While Ellis confronted patients and persuaded them that the philosophies they lived by were unrealistic, Beck "turned the client into a colleague who researches verifiable reality" (Wessler, 1986, p. 5).

The work of a number of contemporary behaviorists influenced the development of cognitive therapy. Bandura's (1977) concepts of expectancy of reinforcement, self and outcome efficacies, the interaction between person and environment, modeling, and vicarious learning catalyzed a shift in behavior therapy toward the cognitive domain. Mahoney's (1974) early work on the cognitive control of behavior and his continuing theoretical contributions also influenced cognitive therapy. Along with cognitive therapy and rational emotive behavior therapy, Meichenbaum's (1977) cognitive-behavior modification is recognized as one of the three major self-control therapies (Mahoney & Arnkoff, 1978). Meichenbaum's combination of cognitive modification and skills training in a coping skills paradigm is particularly useful in treating anxiety, anger, and stress. The Constructivist movement in psychology and the modern movement for psychotherapy integration have been recent influences shaping contemporary cognitive therapy.

## Current Status

### Research: Cognitive Model and Outcome Studies

Controlled studies have demonstrated the efficacy of cognitive therapy in the treatment of panic disorder (Clark, 1996; Clark, Salkovskis, Hackmann, Middleton, & Gelder, 1992), social phobia (Clark, 1997; Eng, Roth, & Heimberg, 2001), generalized anxiety disorder (Butler, Fennell, Robson, & Gelder, 1991), substance abuse (Woody et al., 1983), eating disorders (Bowers, 2001; Fairburn, Jones, Peveler, Hope, Carr, Solomon, et al., 1991; Garner et al., 1993; Vitousek, 1996), marital problems (Baucom, Sayers, & Sher, 1990), obsessive-compulsive disorder (Freeston et al., 1997), post-traumatic stress disorder (Ehlers and Clark, 2000; Gillespie, Duffy, Hackmann, & Clark, 2002; Resick, 2001), and schizophrenia (Rector & Beck, 2001).

In addition, cognitive therapy appears to lead to lower rates of relapse than other treatments for anxiety and depression (Clark, 1996; Eng, Roth, & Heimberg, 2001; Hollon, DeRubeis, & Evans, 1996; Strunk & DeRubeis, 2001).

### Suicide Research

Beck has developed key theoretical concepts regarding suicide and its prevention. Chief among his findings about suicide risk is the notion of *hopelessness*. Longitudinal studies of both inpatients and outpatients who had suicidal ideation have found that a cut-off score of nine or more on the Beck Hopelessness Scale is predictive of eventual suicide (Beck, Brown, Berchick, Stewart, & Steer, 1990; Beck, Steer, Kovacs, & Garrison, 1985). Hopelessness as a predictor of eventual suicide has been confirmed in subsequent studies.

Current research is investigating the efficacy of a brief cognitive therapy treatment for those at high risk of attempting suicide who have significant psychopathology and substance abuse problems. Preliminary results indicate that cognitive therapy reduces the frequency of subsequent suicide attempts and prolongs the time period before an individual makes another suicide attempt (Beck, 2002).

## Assessment Scales

Beck's work has generated a number of assessment scales, most notably the Beck Depression Inventory (BDI) (Beck, Steer, & Brown, 1996; Beck, Ward, Mendelson, Mock, & Erbaugh, 1961), the Scale for Suicide Ideation (SSI) (Beck, Kovacs, & Weissman, 1979), the Suicide Intent Scale (Beck, Schuyler, & Herman, 1974), the Beck Hopelessness Scale (Beck, Weissman, Lester, & Trexler, 1974), Beck Anxiety Inventory (Beck & Steer, 1990), Beck Self-concept Test (Beck, Steer, Brown, & Epstein, 1990), Dysfunctional Attitude Scale (Weissman & Beck, 1978), Sociotropy-Autonomy Scale (Beck, Epstein, & Harrison, 1983), Beck Youth Inventories (Beck & Beck, 2002), and Clark-Beck Obsessive-Compulsive Inventory (Clark & Beck, 2002). The Beck Depression Inventory is the best known of these. It has been used in hundreds of outcome studies and is routinely employed by psychologists, physicians, and social workers to monitor depression in their patients and clients.

## Training

The Center for Cognitive Therapy, affiliated with the University of Pennsylvania Medical School, provides outpatient services and is a research institute that integrates clinical observations with empirical findings to develop theory. The Beck Institute in Bala Cynwyd, Pennsylvania, provides both outpatient services and training opportunities. In addition, there are 10 other training centers for cognitive therapy in the United States. Research and treatment efforts in cognitive therapy are being conducted in a number of universities and hospitals in the United States and Europe. The *International Cognitive Therapy Newsletter* began in 1985 for the exchange of information among cognitive therapists. Therapists from five continents participate in the newsletter network. In 2003, the XXXIII Annual Congress of the European Association of Behavior and Cognitive Therapy was held in Prague.

The Academy of Cognitive Therapy, a nonprofit organization, was founded in 1999 by a group of leading clinicians, educators, and researchers in the field of cognitive therapy. The academy administers an objective evaluation to identify and certify clinicians skilled in cognitive therapy. In 1999 the Accreditation Council of Graduate Medical Education mandated that psychiatry residency training programs train residents to be competent in the practice of cognitive behavior therapy.

Cognitive therapists routinely contribute to psychology, psychiatry, and behavior therapy journals. The primary journals devoted to research in cognitive therapy are *Cognitive Therapy and Research,* the *Journal of Cognitive Psychotherapy: An International Quarterly,* and *Cognitive and Behavioral Practice.*

Cognitive therapy is represented at the annual meetings of the American Psychological Association, the American Psychiatric Association, the American Orthopsychiatric Association, the Phobia Society of America, and others. It is a major force in the Association for the Advancement of Behavior Therapy. As of 2000, there had been five world congresses of the International Association of Cognitive Therapy, in the United States, Sweden, England, and Canada. The next conference of the International Association of Cognitive Therapy will be held in 2005.

Because of its efficacy as a short-term form of psychotherapy, cognitive therapy is achieving wider use in settings that must demonstrate cost-effectiveness or that require short-term contact with patients. It has applications in both inpatient and outpatient settings.

Many talented researchers and innovative therapists have contributed to the development of cognitive therapy. Controlled outcome studies comparing cognitive therapy with other forms of treatment are conducted with anxiety disorders, panic, drug abuse, anorexia and bulimia, geriatric depression, acute depression, and dysphoric disorder. Beck's students and associates do research on the nature and treatment of depression, anxiety, loneliness, marital conflict, eating disorders, agoraphobia, pain, personality disorders, substance abuse, bipolar disorder, and schizophrenia.

# PERSONALITY

## Theory of Personality

Cognitive therapy emphasizes the role of information processing in human responses and adaptation. When an individual perceives that the situation requires a response, a whole set of cognitive, emotional, motivational, and behavioral schemas gets mobilized. Previously, cognitive therapy viewed cognition as largely determining emotions and behaviors. Current thinking views all aspects of human functioning acting simultaneously as a mode.

Cognitive therapy views personality as shaped by the interaction between innate disposition and environment (Beck, Freeman, & Davis, 2003). Personality attributes are seen as reflecting basic schemas or interpersonal "strategies" developed in response to the environment.

Cognitive therapy sees psychological distress as being "caused" by a number of factors. While people may have biochemical predispositions to illness, they respond to specific stressors because of their learning history. The phenomena of psychopathology (but not necessarily the cause) are on the same continuum as normal emotional reactions, but they are manifested in exaggerated and persistent ways. In depression, for example, sadness and loss of interest are intensified and prolonged, in mania there is heightened investment in self-aggrandizement, and in anxiety there is an extreme sense of vulnerability and danger.

Individuals experience psychological distress when they perceive a situation as threatening their vital interests. At such times, their perceptions and interpretations of events are highly selective, egocentric, and rigid. This results in a functional impairment of normal cognitive activity. There is a decreased ability to turn off idiosyncratic thinking, to concentrate, recall, or reason. Corrective functions, which allow reality testing and refinement of global conceptualizations, are attenuated.

### Cognitive Vulnerability

Each individual has a set of idiosyncratic vulnerabilities and sensitivities that predispose him or her to psychological distress. These vulnerabilities appear to be related to personality structure. Personality is shaped by temperament and cognitive schemas. Cognitive schemas are structures that contain the individual's fundamental beliefs and assumptions. Schemas develop early in life from personal experience and identification with significant others. These concepts are reinforced by further learning experiences and, in turn, influence the formation of beliefs, values, and attitudes.

Cognitive schemas may be adaptive or dysfunctional. They may be general or specific in nature. A person may have competing schemas. Cognitive schemas are generally latent but become active when stimulated by specific stressors, circumstances, or stimuli. In personality disorders, they are triggered very easily and often, so that the person over-responds to a wide range of situations in a stereotyped manner.

### Dimensions of Personality

The idea that certain clusters of personality attributes or cognitive structures are related to certain types of emotional response has been studied by Beck, Epstein, and Harrison (1983), who found two major personality dimensions relevant to depression and possibly other disorders: social dependence (sociotropy) and autonomy. Beck's research revealed that dependent individuals became depressed following disruption of relationships. Autonomous people became depressed after defeat or failure to attain a desired goal. The sociotropic dimension is organized around closeness, nurturance, and dependency; the autonomous dimension around independence, goal setting, self-determination, and self-imposed obligations.

Research has also established that while "pure" cases of sociotropy and autonomy do exist, most people display features of each, depending on the situation. Thus, sociotropy and autonomy are styles of behavior, not fixed personality structures. This position stands in marked contrast with psychodynamic theories of personality, which postulate fixed personality dimensions.

Thus, cognitive therapy views personality as reflecting the individual's cognitive organization and structure, which are both biologically and socially influenced. Within the constraints of one's neuroanatomy and biochemistry, personal learning experiences help determine how one develops and responds.

## Variety of Concepts

Cognitive therapy emphasizes the individual's learning history, including the influence of significant life events, in the development of psychological disturbance. It is not a reductionistic model but recognizes that psychological distress is usually the result of many interacting factors.

Cognitive therapy's emphasis on the individual's learning history endorses social learning theory and the importance of reinforcement. The social learning perspective requires a thorough examination of the individual's developmental history and his or her own idiosyncratic meanings and interpretations of events. Cognitive therapy emphasizes the idiographic nature of cognition, for the same event may have very different meanings for two individuals.

The conceptualization of personality as reflective of schemas and underlying assumptions also relates to social learning theory. The way a person structures experience is based on consequences of past behavior, vicarious learning from significant others, and expectations about the future.

### Theory of Causality

Psychological distress is ultimately caused by many innate, biological, developmental, and environmental factors interacting with one another, and so there is no single "cause" of psychopathology. Depression, for instance, is characterized by predisposing factors such as hereditary susceptibility, diseases that cause persistent neurochemical abnormalities, developmental traumas leading to specific cognitive vulnerabilities, inadequate personal experiences that fail to provide appropriate coping skills, and counterproductive cognitive patterns, such as unrealistic goals, assumptions, or imperatives. Physical disease, severe and acute stress, and chronic stress are also precipitating factors.

## Cognitive Distortions

Systematic errors in reasoning called *cognitive distortions* are evident during psychological distress (Beck, 1967). These include:

*Arbitrary inference:* Drawing a specific conclusion without supporting evidence or even in the face of contradictory evidence. An example of this is the working mother who concludes after a particularly busy day, "I'm a terrible mother."

*Selective abstraction:* Conceptualizing a situation on the basis of a detail taken out of context, ignoring other information. An example is a man who becomes jealous upon seeing his girlfriend tilt her head toward another man to hear him better at a noisy party.

*Overgeneralization:* Abstracting a general rule from one or a few isolated incidents and applying it too broadly and to unrelated situations. After a discouraging date, a woman concluded, "All men are alike. I'll always be rejected."

*Magnification and minimization:* Seeing something as far more significant or less significant than it actually is. A student catastrophized, "If I appear the least bit nervous in class it will mean disaster." Another person, rather than facing the fact that his mother is terminally ill, decides that she will soon recover from her "cold."

*Personalization:* Attributing external events to oneself without evidence supporting a causal connection. A man waved to an acquaintance across a busy street. After not getting a greeting in return, he concluded, "I must have done something to offend him."

*Dichotomous thinking:* Categorizing experiences in one of two extremes; for example, as complete success or total failure. A doctoral candidate stated, "Unless I write the best exam they've ever seen, I'm a failure as a student."

## Systematic Bias in Psychological Disorders

A bias in information processing characterizes most psychological disorders (see Table 8.1). This bias is generally applied to "external" information, such as communications or threats, and may start operating at early stages of information processing. A person's orienting schema identifies a situation as posing a danger or loss, for instance, and signals the appropriate mode to respond.

**TABLE 8.1    The Cognitive Profile of Psychological Disorders**

| Disorder | Systematic Bias in Processing Information |
| --- | --- |
| Depression | Negative view of self, experience, and future |
| Hypomania | Inflated view of self and future |
| Anxiety disorder | Sense of physical or psychological danger |
| Panic disorder | Catastrophic interpretation of bodily/mental experiences |
| Phobia | Sense of danger in specific, avoidable situations |
| Paranoid state | Attribution of bias to others |
| Hysteria | Concept of motor or sensory abnormality |
| Obsession | Repeated warning or doubts about safety |
| Compulsion | Rituals to ward off perceived threat |
| Suicidal behavior | Hopelessness and deficiencies in problem solving |
| Anorexia nervosa | Fear of being fat |
| Hypochondriasis | Attribution of serious medical disorder |

## Cognitive Model of Depression

A *cognitive triad* characterizes depression (Beck, 1967). The depressed individual has a negative view of the self, the world, and the future, and perceives the self as inadequate, deserted, and worthless. A negative view is apparent in beliefs that enormous demands exist and that immense barriers block access to goals. The world seems devoid of pleasure or gratification. The depressed person's view of the future is pessimistic, reflecting the belief that current troubles will not improve. This hopelessness may lead to suicidal ideation.

Motivational, behavioral, emotional, and physical symptoms of depression are also activated in the depressed mode. These symptoms influence a person's beliefs and assumptions, and vice versa. For example, motivational symptoms of paralysis of will are related to the belief that one lacks the ability to cope or to control an event's outcome. Consequently, there is a reluctance to commit oneself to a goal. Suicidal wishes often reflect a desire to escape from unbearable problems.

The increased dependency often observed in depressed patients reflects the view of self as incompetent, an overestimation of the difficulty of normal life tasks, the expectation of failure, and the desire for someone more capable to take over. Indecisiveness similarly reflects the belief that one is incapable of making correct decisions. The physical symptoms of depression—low energy, fatigue, and inertia—are also related to negative expectations. Work with depressed patients indicates that initiating activity actually reduces inertia and fatigue. Moreover, refuting negative expectations and demonstrating motor ability play important roles in recovery.

## Cognitive Model of Anxiety Disorders

Anxiety disorders are conceptualized as excessive functioning or malfunctioning of normal survival mechanisms. Thus, the basic mechanisms for coping with threat are the same for both normal and anxious people: physiological responses prepare the body for escape or self-defense. The same physiological responses occur in the face of psychosocial threats as in the case of physical dangers. The anxious person's perception of danger is either based on false assumptions or exaggerated, while the normal response is based on a more accurate assessment of risk and the magnitude of danger. In addition, normal individuals can correct their misperceptions using logic and evidence. Anxious individuals have difficulty recognizing cues of safety and other evidence that would reduce the threat of danger. Thus, in cases of anxiety, cognitive content revolves around themes of danger, and the individual tends to maximize the likelihood of harm and minimize his or her ability to cope.

## Mania

The manic patient's biased thinking is the reverse of the depressive's. Such individuals selectively perceive significant gains in each life experience, blocking out negative experiences or reinterpreting them as positive, and unrealistically expecting favorable results from various enterprises. Exaggerated concepts of abilities, worth, and accomplishments lead to feelings of euphoria. The continued stimulation from inflated self-evaluations and overly optimistic expectations provide vast sources of energy and drive the manic individual into continuous goal-directed activity.

## Panic Disorder

Patients with panic disorder are prone to regard any unexplained symptom or sensation as a sign of some impending catastrophe. Their cognitive processing system focuses their attention on bodily or psychological experiences and shapes these sources of internal information into a belief in impending disaster. Each patient has a specific "equation." For one, distress in the chest or stomach equals heart attack; for another, shortness of breath means the cessation of all breathing; and for another, lightheadedness is a sign of imminent unconsciousness.

Some patients regard a sudden surge of anger as a sign that they will lose control and injure somebody. Others interpret a mental lapse, momentary confusion, or mild disorientation as a sign they are losing their mind. A crucial characteristic of people having panic attacks is the conclusion that vital systems (cardiovascular, respiratory, or central nervous system) will collapse. Because of their fear, they tend to be overly vigilant toward internal sensations and thus detect and magnify sensations that pass unnoticed in other people.

Patients with panic disorder show a specific cognitive deficit—an inability to view their symptoms and catastrophic interpretations realistically.

## Agoraphobia

Patients who have had one or more panic attacks in a particular situation tend to avoid that situation. For example, people who have had panic attacks in supermarkets will avoid going there. If they push themselves to go, they become increasingly vigilant toward their sensations and begin to anticipate having another panic attack.

The anticipation of such an attack triggers a variety of autonomic symptoms that are then misinterpreted as signs of an impending disaster (e.g., heart attack, loss of consciousness, suffocation), which can lead to a full-blown panic attack. Patients with a panic disorder that goes untreated frequently develop agoraphobia. They may eventually become housebound or so restricted in their activities that they cannot travel far from home and require a companion to venture any distance.

## Phobia

In phobias, there is anticipation of physical or psychological harm in specific situations. As long as patients can avoid these situations, they do not feel threatened and may be relatively comfortable. When they enter into these situations, they experience the typical subjective and physiological symptoms of severe anxiety. As a result of this unpleasant reaction, their tendency to avoid the situation in the future is reinforced.

In *evaluation phobias,* there is fear of disparagement or failure in social situations, examinations, and public speaking. The behavioral and physiological reactions to the potential "danger" (rejection, devaluation, failure) may interfere with the patient's functioning to the degree that these responses can produce just what the patient fears will happen.

## Paranoid States

The paranoid individual is biased toward attributing prejudice to others. The paranoid persists in assuming that other people are deliberately abusive, interfering, or critical. In contrast to depressed patients, who believe that supposed insults or rejections are justified, paranoid patients persevere in thinking others treat them unjustly.

Unlike depressed patients, paranoid patients do not experience low self-esteem. They are more concerned with the *injustice* of the presumed attacks, thwarting, or intrusions than with the actual loss, and they rail against the presumed prejudice and malicious intent of others.

## Obsessions and Compulsions

Patients with obsessions introduce uncertainty into the appraisal of situations that most people would consider safe. The uncertainty is generally attached to circumstances that are potentially unsafe and is manifested by continual doubts—even though there is no evidence of danger.

Obsessives continually doubt whether they have performed an act necessary for safety (for example, turning off a gas oven or locking the door at night). They may fear contamination by germs, and no amount of reassurance can alleviate the fear. A key characteristic of obsessives is this *sense of responsibility* and the belief that they are accountable for having taken an action—or having failed to take an action—that could harm them or others. Cognitive therapy views such intrusive thoughts as universal. It is the meaning assigned to the intrusive thought—that the patient has done something immoral or dangerous—that causes distress.

Compulsions are attempts to reduce excessive doubts by performing rituals designed to neutralize the anticipated disaster. A hand-washing compulsion, for instance, is based on the patients' belief that they have not removed all the dirt or contaminants from parts of their body. Some patients regard dirt as a source of danger, either as a cause of physical disease or as a source of offensive, unpleasant odors, and they are compelled to remove this source of physical or social danger.

## Suicidal Behavior

The cognitive processing in suicidal individuals has two features. First, there is a high degree of hopelessness. The greater the hopelessness, the more the likelihood of suicide increases (Beck & Emery, 1985). A second feature is a cognitive deficit—a difficulty in solving problems. Although the hopelessness accentuates poor problem solving and vice versa, the difficulties in coping with life situations can, by themselves, contribute to the suicidal potential.

## Anorexia Nervosa

Anorexia nervosa and bulimia represent a constellation of maladaptive beliefs that revolve around one central assumption: "My body weight and shape determine my worth and/or my social acceptability." Centered around this assumption are such beliefs as "I will look ugly if I gain much more weight," "The only thing in my life that I can control is my weight," and "If I don't starve myself, I will let go completely and become enormous."

Anorexics show typical distortions in information processing. They misinterpret symptoms of fullness after meals as signs they are getting fat. And they misperceive their image in a mirror or photograph as being much fatter than it actually is.

# PSYCHOTHERAPY

## Theory of Psychotherapy

The goals of cognitive therapy are to correct faulty information processing and to help patients modify assumptions that maintain maladaptive behaviors and emotions. Cognitive and behavioral methods are used to challenge dysfunctional beliefs and to promote more realistic adaptive thinking. Cognitive therapy initially addresses symptom relief, but its ultimate goals are to remove systematic biases in thinking and modify the core beliefs that predispose the person to future distress.

Cognitive therapy fosters change in patients' beliefs by treating beliefs as testable hypotheses to be examined through behavioral experiments jointly agreed upon by patient and therapist. The cognitive therapist does not tell the client that the beliefs are irrational or wrong or that the beliefs of the therapist should be adopted. Instead, the therapist asks questions to elicit the meaning, function, usefulness, and consequences of the patient's beliefs. The patient ultimately decides whether to reject, modify, or maintain all personal beliefs, being well aware of their emotional and behavioral consequences.

Cognitive therapy is not the substitution of positive beliefs for negative ones. It is based in reality, not in wishful thinking. Similarly, cognitive therapy does not maintain that people's problems are imaginary. Patients may have serious social, financial, or health problems as well as functional deficits. In addition to real problems, however, they have biased views of themselves, their situations, and their resources that limit their range of responses and prevent them from generating solutions.

Cognitive change can promote behavioral change by allowing the patient to take risks. In turn, experience in applying new behaviors can validate the new perspective. Emotions can be moderated by enlarging perspectives to include alternative interpretations of events. Emotions play a role in cognitive change, for learning is enhanced when emotions are triggered. Thus, the cognitive, behavioral, and emotional channels interact in therapeutic change, but cognitive therapy emphasizes the primacy of cognition in promoting and maintaining therapeutic change.

Cognitive change occurs at several levels: voluntary thoughts, continuous or automatic thoughts, and assumptions. According to the cognitive model, cognitions are organized in a hierarchy, with each level differing from the next in its accessibility and stability. The most accessible and least stable cognitions are voluntary thoughts. At the next level are automatic thoughts, which come to mind spontaneously when triggered by circumstances. They are the thoughts that intercede between an event or stimulus and the individual's emotional and behavioral reactions.

An example of an automatic thought is "Everyone will see I'm nervous," experienced by a socially anxious person before going to a party. Automatic thoughts are accompanied by emotions and at the time they are experienced seem plausible, are highly salient, and are internally consistent with individual logic. They are given credibility without ever being challenged. Though automatic thoughts are more stable and less accessible than voluntary thoughts, patients can be taught to recognize and monitor them. Cognitive distortions are evident in automatic thoughts.

Automatic thoughts are generated from underlying assumptions. For example, the belief "I am responsible for other people's happiness" produces numerous negative automatic thoughts in people who perceive themselves as causing distress to others. Assumptions shape perceptions into cognitions, determine goals, and provide interpretations and meanings to events. They may be quite stable and outside the patient's awareness.

Core beliefs are contained in cognitive schemas. Therapy aims at identifying these assumptions and counteracting their effects. If the assumptions themselves can be changed, the patient is less vulnerable to future distress.

## The Therapeutic Relationship

The therapeutic relationship is collaborative. The therapist assesses sources of distress and dysfunction and helps the patient clarify goals. In cases of severe depression or anxiety, patients may need the therapist to take a directive role. In other instances, patients may take the lead in determining goals for therapy. As part of the collaboration, the patient provides the thoughts, images, and beliefs that occur in various situations as well as the emotions and behaviors that accompany the thoughts. The patient also shares re-

sponsibility by helping to set the agenda for each session and by doing homework between sessions. Homework helps therapy to proceed more quickly and gives the patient an opportunity to practice newly learned skills and perspectives.

The therapist functions as a guide who helps the patient understand how beliefs and attitudes interact with affect and behavior. The therapist is also a catalyst who promotes corrective experiences that lead to cognitive change and skills acquisition. Thus, cognitive therapy employs a learning model of psychotherapy. The therapist has expertise in examining and modifying beliefs and behavior but does not adopt the role of a passive expert.

Cognitive therapists actively pursue the patient's point of view. By using warmth, accurate empathy, and genuineness (see Rogers, 1951), the cognitive therapist appreciates the patient's personal world view. However, these qualities alone are not sufficient for therapeutic change. The cognitive therapist specifies problems, focuses on important areas, and teaches specific cognitive and behavioral techniques.

Along with having good interpersonal skills, cognitive therapists are flexible. They are sensitive to the patient's level of comfort and use self-disclosure judiciously. They provide supportive contact, when necessary, and operate within the goals and agenda of the cognitive approach. Flexibility in the use of therapeutic techniques depends on the targeted symptoms. For example, the inertia of depression responds best to behavioral interventions, while the suicidal ideation and pessimism of depression respond best to cognitive techniques. A good cognitive therapist does not use techniques arbitrarily or mechanically, but with sound rationale and skill, and with an understanding of each individual's needs.

To maintain collaboration, the therapist elicits feedback from the patient, usually at the end of each session. Feedback focuses on what the patient found helpful or not helpful, whether the patient has concerns about the therapist, and whether the patient has questions. The therapist may summarize the session or ask the patient to do so. Another way the therapist encourages collaboration is by providing the patient with a rationale for each procedure used. This demystifies the therapy process, increases patients' participation, and reinforces a learning paradigm in which patients gradually assume more responsibility for therapeutic change.

## Definitions

Three fundamental concepts in cognitive therapy are *collaborative empiricism, Socratic dialogue,* and *guided discovery.*

*Collaborative Empiricism*    The therapeutic relationship is collaborative and requires jointly determining the goals for treatment, eliciting and providing feedback, thereby demystifying how therapeutic change occurs. The therapist and patient become co-investigators, examining the evidence to support or reject the patient's cognitions. As in scientific inquiry, interpretations or assumptions are treated as testable hypotheses.

Empirical evidence is used to determine whether particular cognitions serve any useful purpose. Prior conclusions are subjected to logical analysis. Biased thinking is exposed as the patient becomes aware of alternative sources of information. This process is conducted as a partnership between patient and therapist, with either taking a more active role as needed.

*Socratic Dialogue*    Questioning is a major therapeutic device in cognitive therapy (Beck & Young, 1985), and Socratic dialogue is the preferred method. The therapist carefully designs a series of questions to promote new learning. The purposes of the therapist's questions are generally to (1) clarify or define problems, (2) assist in the identification of thoughts, images, and assumptions, (3) examine the meanings of events for the patient, and (4) assess the consequences of maintaining maladaptive thoughts and behaviors.

Socratic dialogue implies that the patient arrives at logical conclusions based on the questions posed by the therapist. Questions are not used to "trap" patients, lead them to inevitable conclusions, or attack them. Questions enable the therapist to understand the patient's point of view and are posed with sensitivity so that patients may look at their assumptions objectively and nondefensively.

Beck and Young describe how questions change throughout the course of therapy:

> In the beginning of therapy, questions are employed to obtain a full and detailed picture of the patient's particular difficulties. They are used to obtain background and diagnostic data; to evaluate the patient's stress tolerance, capacity for introspection, coping methods and so on; to obtain information about the patient's external situation and interpersonal context; and to modify vague complaints by working with the patient to arrive at specific target problems to work on.
>
> As therapy progresses, the therapist uses questioning to explore approaches to problems, to help the patient weigh advantages and disadvantages of possible solutions, to examine the consequences of staying with particular maladaptive behaviors, to elicit automatic thoughts, and to demonstrate maladaptive assumptions and their consequences. In short, the therapist uses questioning in most cognitive therapeutic techniques. (1985, p. 223)

*Guided Discovery*   Through guided discovery the patient modifies maladaptive beliefs and assumptions. The therapist serves as a "guide" who elucidates problem behaviors and errors in logic by designing new experiences (*behavioral experiments*) that lead to the acquisition of new skills and perspectives. Guided discovery implies that the therapist does not exhort or cajole the patient to adopt a new set of beliefs. Rather, the therapist encourages the patient's use of information, facts, and probabilities to obtain a realistic perspective.

## Process of Psychotherapy

### Initial Sessions

The goals of the first interview are to initiate a relationship with the patient, to elicit essential information, and to produce symptom relief. Building a relationship with the patient may begin with questions about feelings and thoughts about beginning therapy. Discussing the patient's expectations helps put the patient at ease, provides information to the therapist regarding the patient's expectations, and presents an opportunity to demonstrate the relationship between cognition and affect (Beck, Rush, et al., 1979). The therapist also uses the initial sessions to socialize the patient to cognitive therapy, establish a collaborative framework, and deal with any misconceptions about therapy. The types of information the therapist seeks in the initial session regard diagnosis, past history, present life situation, psychological problems, attitudes about treatment, and motivation for treatment.

Problem definition and symptom relief begin in the first session. Although problem definition and background may take several sessions, it is often critical to focus on a very specific problem and provide rapid relief in the first session. For example, a suicidal patient needs direct intervention to undermine hopelessness immediately. Symptom relief can come from several sources: specific problem solving, clarifying vague or general complaints into workable goals, or gaining objectivity about a disorder (e.g., that a patient's symptoms represent anxiety, and nothing worse, or that difficulty concentrating is a symptom of depression and not a sign of brain disease).

Problem definition entails both functional and cognitive analyses of the problem. A functional analysis identifies elements of the problem: how it is manifested; situations in which it occurs; its frequency, intensity, and duration; and its consequences. A cognitive analysis of the problem identifies the thoughts and images a person has when emotion is triggered. It also includes investigation of the extent to which the person feels in control of thoughts and images, what the person imagines will happen in a distressing situation, and the probability of such an outcome actually occurring.

In the early sessions, the cognitive therapist plays a more active role than does the patient. The therapist gathers information, conceptualizes the patient's problems, socializes the patient to cognitive therapy, and actively intervenes to provide symptom relief. The patient is assigned homework beginning at the first session.

Homework, at this early stage, is usually directed at recognizing the connections among thoughts, feelings, and behavior. Some patients might be asked to record their automatic thoughts when distressed. Others might practice recognizing thoughts by counting them, as they occur, on a wrist counter. Thus, the patient is trained from the outset to self-monitor thoughts and behaviors. In later sessions, the patient plays an increasingly active role in determining homework, and assignments focus on testing very specific assumptions.

During the initial sessions, a problem list is generated. A problem list may include specific symptoms, behaviors, or pervasive problems. These problems are assigned priorities as targets for intervention. Priorities are based on the relative magnitude of distress, the likelihood of making progress, the severity of symptoms, and the pervasiveness of a particular theme or topic.

If the therapist can help the patient solve a problem early in treatment, this success can motivate the patient to make further changes. As each problem is approached, the therapist chooses the appropriate cognitive or behavioral technique to apply and provides the patient with a rationale for the technique. Throughout therapy, the therapist elicits the patient's reactions to various techniques to ascertain whether they are being applied correctly, whether they are successful, and how they can be incorporated into homework or practical experience outside the session.

## Middle and Later Sessions

As cognitive therapy proceeds, the emphasis shifts from the patient's symptoms to the patient's patterns of thinking. The connections among thoughts, emotions, and behavior are chiefly demonstrated through the examination of automatic thoughts. Once the patient can challenge thoughts that interfere with functioning, he or she can consider the underlying assumptions that generate such thoughts.

There is usually a greater emphasis on cognitive rather than behavioral techniques in later sessions, which focus on complex problems that involve several dysfunctional thoughts. Often these thoughts are more amenable to logical analysis than to behavioral experimentation. For example, the prophecy "I'll never get what I want in life" is not easily tested. However, one can question the logic of this generalization and look at the advantages and disadvantages of maintaining it as a belief.

Often such assumptions outside the patient's awareness are discovered as themes of automatic thoughts. By observing automatic thoughts over time and across situations, assumptions appear or can be inferred. Once these assumptions and their power have been recognized, therapy aims at modifying them by examining their validity, adaptiveness, and utility for the patient.

In later sessions, the patient assumes more responsibility for identifying problems and solutions and for creating homework assignments. The therapist takes on the role of advisor rather than teacher as the patient becomes more able to use cognitive techniques to solve problems. The frequency of sessions decreases as the patient becomes more self-sufficient. Therapy is terminated when goals have been reached and the patient feels able to practice his or her new skills and perspectives.

## Ending Treatment

Length of treatment depends primarily on the severity of the client's problems. The usual length for unipolar depression is 15 to 25 sessions at weekly intervals (Beck, Rush, et al., 1979). Moderately to severely depressed patients usually require sessions twice a week for 4 to 5 weeks and then require weekly sessions for 10 to 15 weeks. Most cases of anxiety are treated within a comparable period of time.

Some patients find it extremely difficult to tolerate the anxiety involved in giving up old ways of thinking. For them, therapy may last for several months. Still others experience early symptom relief and leave therapy early. In these cases, little structural change has occurred and problems are likely to recur.

From the outset, the therapist and patient share the expectation that therapy is time-limited. Because cognitive therapy is present-centered and time-limited, there tend to be fewer problems with termination than in longer forms of therapy. As the patient develops self-reliance, therapy sessions become less frequent.

Termination is planned for, even in the first session as the rationale for cognitive therapy is presented. Patients are told that a goal of the therapy is for them to learn to be their own therapists. The problem list makes explicit what is to be accomplished in treatment. Behavioral observation, self-monitoring, self-report, and sometimes questionnaires (e.g., the Beck Depression Inventory) measure progress toward the goals on the problem list. Feedback from the patient aids the therapist in designing experiences to foster cognitive change.

Some patients have concerns about relapse or about functioning autonomously. Some of these concerns include cognitive distortions, such as dichotomous thinking ("I'm either sick or 100 percent cured") or negative prediction ("I'll get depressed again and won't be able to help myself"). It may be necessary to review the goal of therapy: to teach the patient ways to handle problems more effectively, not to produce a "cure" or restructure core personality (Beck, Rush, et al., 1979). Education about psychological disorders, such as the possibility of recurrent depression, is done throughout treatment so that the patient has a realistic perspective on prognosis.

During the usual course of therapy, the patient experiences both successes and setbacks. Such problems give the patient the opportunity to practice new skills. As termination approaches, the patient can be reminded that setbacks are normal and have been handled before. The therapist might ask the patient to describe how prior specific problems were handled during treatment. Therapists can also use cognitive rehearsal prior to termination by having patients imagine future difficulties and report how they would deal with them.

Termination is usually followed by one to two booster sessions, usually one and two months after termination. Such sessions consolidate gains and assist the patient in employing new skills.

## Mechanisms of Psychotherapy

Several common denominators cut across effective treatments. Three mechanisms of change common to all successful forms of psychotherapy are (1) a comprehensible framework, (2) the patient's emotional engagement in the problem situation, and (3) reality testing in that situation.

Cognitive therapy maintains that the modification of dysfunctional assumptions leads to effective cognitive, emotional, and behavioral change. Patients change by recognizing automatic thoughts, questioning the evidence used to support them, and modify-

ing cognitions. Next, the patient behaves in ways congruent with new, more adaptive ways of thinking.

Change can occur only if the patient experiences a problematic situation as a real threat. According to cognitive therapy, core beliefs are linked to emotions, and with affective arousal, those beliefs become accessible and modifiable. One mechanism of change, then, centers on making accessible those cognitive constellations that produced the maladaptive behavior or symptomatology. This mechanism is analogous to what psychoanalysts call "making the unconscious conscious."

Simply arousing emotions and the accompanying cognitions is not sufficient to cause lasting change. People express emotion, sometimes explosively, throughout their lives without benefit. However, the therapeutic milieu allows the patient to simultaneously experience emotional arousal and reality testing. For a variety of psychotherapies, what is therapeutic is the patient's ability to be engaged in a problem situation and yet respond to it adaptively. In terms of cognitive therapy, this means to experience the cognitions and to test them within the therapeutic framework.

## APPLICATIONS

### Problems

Cognitive therapy is a present-centered, structured, active, cognitive, problem-oriented approach best suited for cases in which problems can be delineated and cognitive distortions are apparent. It was originally developed for the treatment of Axis I disorders but has been elaborated to treat Axis II disorders as well. It has wide-ranging applications to a variety of clinical and nonclinical problems. While originally used in individual psychotherapy, it is now used with couples, families, and groups. It can be applied alone or in combination with pharmacotherapy in inpatient and outpatient settings.

Cognitive therapy is widely recognized as an effective treatment for unipolar depression. Beck, Rush, et al. (1979, p. 27) list criteria for using cognitive therapy alone or in combination with medication. It is the treatment of choice in cases in which the patient refuses medication, prefers a psychological treatment, has unacceptable side effects to antidepressant medication, has a medical condition that precludes the use of antidepressants, or has proven to be refractory to adequate trials of antidepressants.

Cognitive therapy is not recommended as the exclusive treatment in cases of bipolar affective disorder or psychotic depression. It is also not used alone for the treatment of other psychoses, such as schizophrenia. While some patients with anxiety may begin treatment on medication, cognitive therapy teaches them to function without relying on medication.

Cognitive therapy produces the best results with patients who have adequate reality testing (i.e., no hallucinations or delusions), good concentration, and sufficient memory functions. It is ideally suited to patients who can focus on their automatic thoughts, accept the therapist-patient roles, are willing to tolerate anxiety in order to do experiments, can alter assumptions permanently, will take responsibility for their problems, and are willing to postpone gratification in order to complete therapy. Although these ideals are not always met, this therapy can proceed with some adjustment of outcome expectations and flexibility of structure. For example, therapy may not permanently alter schemas but may improve the patient's daily functioning.

Cognitive therapy is effective for patients with different levels of income, education, and background (Persons, Burns, & Perloff, 1988). As long as the patient can recognize the relationships among thoughts, feelings, and behaviors and takes some responsibility for self-help, cognitive therapy can be beneficial.

# Evaluation

## Therapists

Therapists who are beginning training at the Center for Cognitive Therapy are evaluated prior to training through live observation and videotaped role-playing. A confederate plays the role of the patient, and raters, using the Competency Checklist for Cognitive Therapists (Young & Beck, 1980), observe the role-play through a one-way mirror as the session is videotaped. At the end of a year's training, another role-play interview is done and the therapist's progress is assessed. The Competency Checklist for Cognitive Therapists is divided into three parts. Part One, General Interview Procedures, assesses collaboration and mutual understanding. Part Two evaluates the use of specific cognitive and behavioral techniques. Part Three assesses the personal and professional characteristics of the therapist.

Therapists in training are supervised by experienced therapists. Supervision consists of weekly meetings during which trainees and supervisors review videotapes, audiotapes, or notes of cases in progress.

## Patients

Patients' presenting problems are evaluated by clinical interviews and psychological tests. The intake interview at the Center for Cognitive Therapy is part of a three-hour protocol during which patients also complete psychological tests and questionnaires. The clinical interview contributes to a diagnosis and provides a thorough description of the background factors contributing to the patient's distress. Current level of functioning, prominent symptoms, and expectations for therapy are also explored.

The psychological tests most frequently used are the BDI, the SSI, the Beck Anxiety Inventory, and the Dysfunctional Attitudes Scale. These self-report inventories increase the efficiency of therapy by quickly providing the therapist with information that would otherwise have to be elicited in interview. Questionnaires like the BDI and the SSI may also alert a therapist to suicide risk. These questionnaires are not projective tests, and their purposes are obvious to the patient. Cognitive therapists do not generally use standard personality tests but may use the Sociotropy-Autonomy Scale (Beck, Epstein, & Harrison, 1983) to determine how best to work with the patient's style of interaction.

## Progress in Therapy

Progress evaluation depends on the goals of therapy. In general, relief from symptoms is indicated by changes in scores on standardized inventories such as the BDI, changes in behavior as indicated through self-monitoring and observation by others, and changes in thinking as evident in such measures as the Daily Record of Dysfunctional Thoughts (Beck, Kovacs, & Weissman, 1979). Because patients have weekly homework designed for their particular goals, progress can be assessed by the outcome of the homework assignments. Progress in therapy is apparent in the relative ease with which a patient challenges automatic thoughts, the decrease in frequency of maladaptive cognitions and behaviors, the increase in ability to generate solutions to problems, and improved mood.

If there are problems in the progress of therapy, several factors must be considered: The patient may have dysfunctional beliefs about therapy or the therapist; the therapist may lack rapport or may have failed to provide a rationale for a procedure; an assignment may be too difficult for the patient or the patient may have higher-order anxieties; or there may be a lack of consensus on the aims and goals of therapy (see Beck, Rush, et al., 1979, and Golden, 1983). Feedback during each session is designed to clarify misunderstandings and increase collaboration, thereby reducing the likelihood of problems in the progress of therapy.

## Treatment

Cognitive therapy consists of highly specific learning experiences designed to teach patients (1) to monitor their negative, automatic thoughts (cognitions), (2) to recognize the connections among cognition, affect, and behavior, (3) to examine the evidence for and against distorted automatic thoughts, (4) to substitute more reality-oriented interpretations for these biased cognitions, and (5) to learn to identify and alter the beliefs that predispose them to distort their experiences (Beck, Rush, et al., 1979).

Both cognitive and behavioral techniques are used in cognitive therapy to reach these goals. The technique used at any given time depends on the patient's level of functioning and the particular symptoms and problems presented.

### Cognitive Techniques

Verbal techniques are used to elicit the patient's automatic thoughts, analyze the logic behind the thoughts, identify maladaptive assumptions, and examine the validity of those assumptions. Automatic thoughts are elicited by questioning the patient about those thoughts that occur during upsetting situations. If the patient has difficulty recalling thoughts, imagery or role-playing can be used. Automatic thoughts are most accurately reported when they occur in real-life situations. Such "hot" cognitions are accessible, powerful, and habitual. The patient is taught to recognize and identify thoughts and to record them when upset.

Cognitive therapists do not interpret patients' automatic thoughts, but explore their meanings, particularly when a patient reports fairly neutral thoughts yet displays strong emotions. In such cases, the therapist asks what those thoughts mean to the patient. For example, after an initial visit, an anxious patient called his therapist in great distress. He had just read an article about drug treatments for anxiety. His automatic thought was, "Drug therapy is helpful for anxiety." The meaning he ascribed to this was, "Cognitive therapy can't possibly help me. I am doomed to failure again."

*Automatic thoughts* are tested by direct evidence or by logical analysis. Evidence can be derived from past and present circumstances, but true to scientific inquiry, it must be as close to the facts as possible. Data can also be gathered in behavioral experiments. For example, if a man believes he cannot conduct a conversation, he might try to initiate brief exchanges with three people. The empirical nature of behavioral experiments allows patients to think in a more objective way.

Examination of the patient's thoughts can also lead to cognitive change. Questioning may uncover logical inconsistencies, contradictions, and other errors in thinking. Identifying and labeling cognitive distortions is in itself helpful, for patients then have specific errors to correct.

*Maladaptive assumptions* are usually much less accessible to patients than are automatic thoughts. While some patients are able to articulate their assumptions, most find it difficult. Assumptions appear as themes in automatic thoughts. The therapist may ask the patient to abstract rules underlying specific thoughts. The therapist might also make assumptions from these data and present these assumptions to the patient for verification. A patient who had trouble identifying her assumptions broke into tears upon reading an assumption inferred by her therapist, an indication of the salience of that assumption. Patients always have the right to disagree with the therapist and find more accurate statements of their beliefs.

Once an assumption has been identified, it is open to modification. This can occur in several ways: by asking the patient if the assumption seems reasonable, by having the patient generate reasons for and against maintaining the assumption, and by presenting evidence contrary to the assumption. While a particular assumption may seem reasonable in a specific situation, it may appear dysfunctional when universally applied. For example, being highly productive at work is generally reasonable. To be highly productive during recreational time may be unreasonable. A physician who believed he should work to his top capacity throughout his career may not have considered the prospect of early burnout. Thus, what may have made him successful in the short run could lead to problems in the long run. Specific cognitive techniques include decatastrophizing, reattribution, redefining, and decentering.

*Decatastrophizing,* also known as the "what if" technique (Beck & Emery, 1979), helps patients prepare for feared consequences. This is helpful in decreasing avoidance, particularly when combined with coping plans (Beck & Emery, 1985). If anticipated consequences are likely to happen, these techniques help to identify problem-solving strategies. Decatastrophizing is often used with a time-projection technique to widen the range of information and broaden the patient's time perspective.

*Reattribution* techniques test automatic thoughts and assumptions by considering alternative causes of events. This is especially helpful when patients personalize or perceive themselves as the cause of events. It is unreasonable to conclude, in the absence of evidence, that another person or single factor is the sole cause of an event. Reattribution techniques encourage reality testing and appropriate assignment of responsibility by requiring examination of all the factors that impinge on a situation.

*Redefining* is a way to mobilize a patient who believes a problem to be beyond personal control. Burns (1985) recommends that lonely people who think, "Nobody pays any attention to me," redefine the problem as, "I need to reach out to other people and be caring." Redefining a problem may include making it more concrete and specific and stating it in terms of the patient's own behavior.

*Decentering* is used primarily in treating anxious patients who wrongly believe they are the focus of everyone's attention. After examining the logic behind why others would stare at them and be able to read their minds, behavioral experiments are designed to test these particular beliefs. For example, one student who was reluctant to speak in class believed his classmates watched him constantly and noticed his anxiety. By observing them instead of focusing on his own discomfort, he saw some students taking notes, some looking at the professor, and some daydreaming. He concluded his classmates had other concerns.

The cognitive domain comprises thoughts and images. For some patients, pictorial images are more accessible and easier to report than thoughts. This is often the case with anxious patients. Ninety percent of anxious patients in one study reported visual images before and during episodes of anxiety (Beck, Laude, & Bohnert, 1974). Gathering information about imagery, then, is another way to understand conceptual systems. Spontaneous images provide data on the patient's perceptions and interpretations of events. Other specific imagery procedures used to modify distorted cognitions are discussed by Beck and Emery (1979, 1985).

In some cases, imagery is modified for its own sake. Intrusive imagery, such as imagery related to trauma, can be directly modified to reduce its impact. Patients can change aspects of an image by "rewriting the script" of what happened, making an attacker shrink in size to the point of powerlessness, or empowering themselves in the image. The point of restructuring such images is not to deny what actually happened, but to reduce the ability of the image to disrupt daily functioning.

Imagery is also used in role-plays because of its ability to access emotions. Experiential techniques, such as dialogues between one's healthy self and one's negative thoughts, are used to mobilize affect and help patients both believe and feel they have the right to be free of harmful and self-defeating patterns.

## Behavioral Techniques

Cognitive therapy uses behavioral techniques to modify automatic thoughts and assumptions. It employs behavioral experiments designed to challenge specific maladaptive beliefs and promote new learning. In a behavioral experiment, for example, a patient may

predict an outcome based on personal automatic thoughts, carry out the agreed-upon behavior, and then evaluate the evidence in light of the new experience.

Behavioral techniques are also used to expand patients' response repertoires (skills training), to relax them (progressive relaxation) or make them active (activity scheduling), to prepare them for avoided situations (behavioral rehearsal), or to expose them to feared stimuli (exposure therapy). Because behavioral techniques are used to foster cognitive change, it is crucial to know the patient's perceptions, thoughts, and conclusions after each behavioral experiment.

*Homework* gives patients the opportunity to apply cognitive principles between sessions. Typical homework assignments focus on self-observation and self-monitoring, structuring time effectively, and implementing procedures for dealing with concrete situations. Self-monitoring is applied to the patient's automatic thoughts and reactions in various situations. New skills, such as challenging automatic thoughts, are also practiced as homework.

*Hypothesis testing* has both cognitive and behavioral components. In framing a "hypothesis" it is necessary to make it specific and concrete. A resident who insisted, "I am not a good doctor," was asked to list what was needed to arrive at that conclusion. The therapist contributed other criteria as well, for the physician had overlooked such factors as rapport with patients and the ability to make decisions under pressure. The resident then monitored his behavior and sought feedback from colleagues and supervisors to test his hypothesis, coming to the conclusion, "I am a good doctor after all."

*Exposure therapy* serves to provide data on the thoughts, images, physiological symptoms, and self-reported level of tension experienced by the anxious patient. Specific thoughts and images can be examined for distortions, and specific coping skills can be taught. By dealing directly with a patient's idiosyncratic thoughts, cognitive therapy is able to focus on that patient's particular needs. Patients learn that their predictions are not always accurate and they then have data to challenge anxious thoughts in the future.

*Behavioral rehearsal* and *role-playing* are used to practice skills or techniques that are later applied in real life. Modeling is also used in skills training. Often role-playing is videotaped so that an objective source of information is available with which to evaluate performance.

*Diversion techniques,* which are used to reduce strong emotions and to decrease negative thinking, include physical activity, social contact, work, play, and visual imagery.

*Activity scheduling* provides structure and encourages involvement. By rating the degree of mastery and pleasure (using a scale of 0 to 10) experienced during each activity of the day, several goals are accomplished: Patients who believe their depression is at a constant level see mood fluctuations; those who believe they cannot accomplish or enjoy anything are contradicted by the evidence; and those who believe they are inactive because of an inherent defect are shown that activity involves some planning and is reinforcing in itself.

*Graded task assignment* calls for the patient to initiate an activity at a nonthreatening level while the therapist gradually increases the difficulty of assigned tasks. For example, someone who has difficulty socializing might begin interacting with one other person or a small group of acquaintances, or might socialize with people for just a brief period of time. Step by step, the patient comes to increase the time spent with others.

Cognitive therapists work in a variety of settings. Patients are referred by physicians, schools and universities, and other therapists who believe that cognitive therapy would be especially helpful to a patient. Many patients are self-referred. The Center for Cognitive Therapy maintains an international referral list of therapists.

Cognitive therapists generally adhere to 45-minute sessions. Because of the structure of cognitive therapy, much can be accomplished in this time. Patients are frequently asked to complete questionnaires, such as the BDI, prior to the start of each session. Most sessions take place in the therapist's office. However, real-life work with anxious patients occurs outside the therapist's office. A therapist might travel on public transportation with an agoraphobic, go to a pet store with a rodent phobic, or fly in an airplane with someone afraid of flying.

Confidentiality is always maintained, and the therapist obtains informed consent for audiotaping and videotaping. Such recording is used in skills training or as a way to present evidence contradicting the patient's assumptions. For example, a patient who believes she looks nervous whenever she converses might be videotaped in conversation to test her assumption. Her appearance on camera may convince her that her assumption was in error or help her to identify specific behaviors to improve. Occasionally, patients take home audiotaped sessions to review content material between sessions.

Sessions are usually conducted on a weekly basis, with severely disturbed patients seen more frequently in the initial sessions. Cognitive therapists give their patients their home phone numbers in case of emergency.

Whenever possible, and with the patient's permission, significant others, such as friends and family members, are included in a therapy session to review the treatment goals and to explore ways in which the significant others might be helpful. This is especially important when family members misunderstand the nature of the illness, are overly solicitous, or are behaving in counterproductive ways. Significant others can be of great assistance in therapy, helping to sustain behavioral improvements by encouraging homework and assisting the patient with reality testing.

Problems may arise in the practice of cognitive therapy. For example, patients may misunderstand what the therapist says, resulting in anger, dissatisfaction, or hopelessness. When the therapist perceives such a reaction, he or she elicits the patient's thoughts, as with any other automatic thoughts. Together the therapist and client look for alternative interpretations. The therapist who has made an error accepts responsibility and corrects the mistake.

Problems sometimes result from unrealistic expectations about how quickly behaviors should change, from the incorrect or inflexible application of a technique, or from lack of attention to central issues. Problems in therapy require that the therapist attend to his or her own automatic thoughts and look for distortions in logic that create strong affect or prevent adequate problem solving.

Beck, Rush, et al. (1979) provide guidelines for working with difficult patients and those who have histories of unsuccessful therapy: (1) avoid stereotyping the patient as *being* the problem rather than *having* the problem; (2) remain optimistic; (3) identify and deal with your own dysfunctional cognitions; (4) remain focused on the task instead of blaming the patient; and (5) maintain a problem-solving attitude. By following these guidelines, the therapist is able to be more resourceful with difficult patients. The therapist also can serve as a model for the patient, demonstrating that frustration does not automatically lead to anger and despair.

## CASE EXAMPLE

This case example of the course of treatment for an anxious patient illustrates the use of both behavioral and cognitive techniques.

### Presenting Problem

The patient was a 21-year-old male college student who complained of sleep onset insomnia and frequent awakenings, halting speech and stuttering, shakiness, feelings of nervousness, dizziness, and worrying. His sleep difficulties were particularly acute prior to exams or athletic competitions. He attributed his speech problems to his search for the "perfect word."

The patient was raised in a family that valued competition. As the eldest child, he was expected to win all the contests. His parents were determined that their children should surpass them in achievements and successes. They so strongly identified with the patient's achievements that he believed, "My success is their success."

The patient was taught to compete with other children outside the family as well. His father reminded him, "Never let anyone get the best of you." As a consequence of viewing others as adversaries, he developed few friends. Feeling lonely, he tried desperately to attract friends by becoming a prankster and by telling lies to enhance his image and make his family appear more attractive. Although he had acquaintances in college, he had few friends, for he was unable to self-disclose, fearing that others would discover he was not all that he would like to be.

## Early Sessions

After gathering initial data regarding diagnosis, context, and history, the therapist attempted to define how the patient's cognitions contributed to his distress (T = Therapist; P = Patient).

T: What types of situations are most upsetting to you?
P: When I do poorly in sports, particularly swimming. I'm on the swim team. Also, if I make a mistake, even when I play cards with my roommates. I feel really upset if I get rejected by a girl.
T: What thoughts go through your mind, let's say, when you don't do so well at swimming?
P: I think people think much less of me if I'm not on top, a winner.
T: And how about if you make a mistake playing cards?
P: I doubt my own intelligence.
T: And if a girl rejects you?
P: It means I'm not special. I lose value as a person.
T: Do you see any connections here, among these thoughts?
P: Well, I guess my mood depends on what other people think of me. But that's important. I don't want to be lonely.
T: What would that mean to you, to be lonely?
P: It would mean there's something wrong with me, that I'm a loser.

At this point, the therapist began to hypothesize about the patient's organizing beliefs: that his worth is determined by others, that he is unattractive because there is something inherently wrong with him, that he is a loser. The therapist looked for evidence to support the centrality of these beliefs and remained open to other possibilities.

The therapist assisted the patient in generating a list of goals to work on in therapy that included (1) decreasing perfectionism, (2) decreasing anxiety symptoms, (3) decreasing sleep difficulties, (4) increasing closeness in friendships, and (5) developing his own values apart from those of his parents. The first problem addressed was anxiety. An upcoming exam was chosen as a target situation. This student typically studied far beyond what was necessary, went to bed worried, finally fell asleep, woke during the night thinking about details or possible consequences of his performance, and went to exams exhausted. To reduce ruminations about his performance, the therapist asked him to name the advantages of dwelling on thoughts of the exam.

P: Well, if I don't think about the exam all the time I might forget something. If I think about the exam constantly, I think I'll do better. I'll be more prepared.

T: Have you ever gone into a situation less "prepared"?

P: Not an exam, but once I was in a big swim meet and the night before I went out with friends and didn't think about it. I came home, went to sleep, got up, and swam.

T: And how did it work out?

P: Fine. I felt great and swam pretty well.

T: Based on that experience, do you think there's any reason to try to worry less about your performance?

P: I guess so. It didn't hurt me not to worry. Actually, worrying can be pretty distracting. I end up focusing more on how I'm doing than what I'm doing.

The patient came up with his own rationale for decreasing his ruminations. He was then ready to consider giving up his maladaptive behavior and risk trying something new. The therapist taught the patient progressive relaxation and the patient began to use physical exercise as a way to relieve anxiety.

The patient was also instructed in how cognitions affect behavior and mood. Picking up on the patient's statement that worries can be distracting, the therapist proceeded.

T: You mentioned that when you worry about your exams you feel anxious. What I'd like you to do now is imagine lying in your bed the night before an exam.

P: Okay, I can picture it.

T: Imagine that you are thinking about the exam and you decide that you haven't done enough to prepare.

P: Yeah, OK.

T: How are you feeling?

P: I'm feeling nervous. My heart is beginning to race. I think I need to get up and study some more.

T: Good. When you think you're not prepared, you get anxious and want to get up out of bed. Now, I want you to imagine that you are in bed the night before the exam. You have prepared in your usual way and are ready. You remind yourself of what you have done. You think that you are prepared and know the material.

P: OK. Now I feel confident.

T: Can you see how your thoughts affect your feelings of anxiety?

The patient was instructed to record automatic thoughts, recognize cognitive distortions, and respond to them. For homework, he was asked to record his automatic thoughts if he had trouble falling asleep before an exam. One automatic thought he had while lying in bed was, "I should be thinking about the exam." His response was, "Thinking about the exam is not going to make a difference at this point. I did study." Another thought was, "I must go to sleep now! I must get eight hours of sleep!" His response was, "I have left leeway, so I have time. Sleep is not so crucial that I have to worry about it." He was able to shift his thinking to a positive image of himself floating in clear blue water.

By observing his automatic thoughts across a variety of situations—academic, athletic, and social—the patient identified dichotomous thinking (e.g., "I'm either a winner or a loser") as a frequent cognitive distortion. Perceiving the consequences of his behavior as either totally good or completely bad resulted in major shifts in mood. Two techniques that helped with his dichotomous thinking were reframing the problem and building a continuum between his dichotomous categories.

Here the problem is reframed:

T: Can you think of reasons for someone not to respond to you other than because you're a loser?

P:  No. Unless I really convince them I'm great, they won't be attracted.

T:  How would you convince them of that?

P:  To tell you the truth, I'd exaggerate what I've done. I'd lie about my grade point average or tell someone I placed first in a race.

T:  How does that work out?

P:  Actually, not too well. I get uncomfortable and they get confused by my stories. Sometimes they don't seem to care. Other times they walk away after I've been talking a lot about myself.

T:  So in some cases, they don't respond to you when you focus the conversation on yourself.

P:  Right.

T:  Does this have anything to do with whether you're a winner or a loser?

P:  No, they don't even know who I am deep down. They're just turned off because I talk too much.

T:  Right. It sounds like they're responding to your conversational style.

The therapist reframed the problem from a situation in which something was inherently wrong with the patient to one characterized by a problem of social skills. Moreover, the theme "I am a loser" appeared so powerful to the patient that he labeled it as his "main belief." This assumption was traced historically to the constant criticism from his parents for mistakes and perceived shortcomings. By reviewing his history, he was able to see that his lies prevented people from getting closer, reinforcing his belief that they didn't want to be close. In addition, he believed that his parents made him whatever success he was and that no achievement was his alone. This had made him angry and lacking in self-confidence.

## Later Sessions

As therapy progressed, the patient's homework increasingly focused on social interaction. He practiced initiating conversations and asking questions in order to learn more about other people. He also practiced "biting his tongue" instead of telling small lies about himself. He monitored people's reactions to him and saw that they were varied, but generally positive. By listening to others, he found that he admired people who could openly admit shortcomings and joke about their mistakes. This experience helped him understand that it was useless to categorize people, including himself, as winners and losers.

In later sessions, the patient described his belief that his behavior reflected on his parents and vice versa. He said, "If they look good, it says something about me and if I look good, they get the credit." One assignment required him to list the ways in which he was different from his parents. He remarked, "Realizing that my parents and I are separate made me realize I could stop telling lies." Recognizing how he was different from his parents freed him from their absolute standards and allowed him to be less self-conscious when interacting with others.

Subsequently, the patient was able to pursue interests and hobbies that had nothing to do with achievement. He was able to set moderate and realistic goals for schoolwork, and he began to date.

## SUMMARY

Cognitive therapy has grown quickly because of its empirical basis and demonstrated efficacy. Borrowing some of its concepts from cognitive theorists and a number of techniques from behavior therapy and client-oriented psychotherapy, cognitive therapy consists of a broad theoretical structure of personality and psychopathology, a set of well-defined therapeutic strategies, and a wide variety of therapeutic techniques. Similar in many ways to rational emotive behavior therapy, which preceded but developed parallel to cognitive therapy, this new system of psychotherapy has acquired strong empirical support for its theoretical foundations. A number of outcome studies have demonstrated its efficacy, especially in the treatment of depression. The related theoretical formulations of depression have been supported by more than 100 empirical studies. Other concepts, such as the cognitive triad in depression, the concept of specific cognitive profiles for specific disorders, cognitive processing, and the relationship of hopelessness to suicide, have also received strong support.

Outcome studies have investigated cognitive therapy with major depressive disorders, generalized anxiety disorder, dysthymic disorder, drug abuse, alcoholism, panic disorder, anorexia, and bulimia. In addition, cognitive therapy has been applied successfully to the treatment of obsessive-compulsive disorder, hypochondriasis, and various personality disorders. In conjunction with psychotropic medication, it has been used for the treatment of delusional disorders and manic-depressive disorder.

Much of the popularity of cognitive therapy is attributable to strong empirical support for its theoretical framework and the large number of outcome studies with clinical populations. In addition, there is no doubt that the zeitgeist represented by the "cognitive revolution" has made the field of psychotherapy more receptive to this new therapy. A further attractive feature of cognitive therapy is the fact that it is not only testable but is readily teachable. The various therapeutic strategies and techniques have been described and defined in such a way that one year's training is usually sufficient for a psychotherapist to attain a reasonable level of competence as a cognitive therapist.

Although cognitive therapy focuses on understanding the patient's problems and applying appropriate techniques, it also attends to the nonspecific therapeutic characteristics of the therapist. Consequently, the basic qualities of empathy, acceptance, and personal regard are highly valued.

Because therapy is not conducted in a vacuum, cognitive therapists pay close attention to patients' interpersonal relations and confront patients continuously with problems they may be avoiding. Further, therapeutic change can take place only when patients are emotionally engaged with their problems. Therefore, the experience of emotion during therapy is a crucial feature. The patient's reactions to the therapist, and vice versa, are also important. Excessive and distorted responses to the therapist are elicited and evaluated just like any other type of ideational material. In the presence of the therapist, patients learn to correct their misconceptions, which were often derived from early experiences.

Cognitive therapy may offer an opportunity for a rapprochement between psychodynamic therapy and behavior therapy. In many ways it provides a common ground for these two disciplines. At the present time, the number of cognitive therapists within the behavior therapy movement is growing. In fact, many behavior therapists view themselves as cognitive-behavior therapists.

Looking to the future, it is anticipated that there will be a gradual expansion of the boundaries of the theoretical background of cognitive therapy that will encompass or penetrate the fields of cognitive psychology and social psychology. There is already an enormous amount of interest in social psychology, which provides the theoretical background of cognitive therapy.

In an era of cost containment, this short-term approach will prove to be increasingly attractive to third-party payers as well as to patients. Future empirical studies of its processes and effectiveness will undoubtedly be conducted to determine whether cognitive therapy can fulfill its promise.

# ANNOTATED BIBLIOGRAPHY

Beck, A. T., Rush, A. J., Shaw, B. F., & Emery, G. (1979). *Cognitive therapy of depression.* New York: Guilford Press.

Perhaps Beck's most influential book, this work presents the cognitive model of depression and treatment interventions. This book served to codify what actually happens in cognitive therapy and thus set a standard for other psychotherapies to follow.

Beck, J. S. (1995). *Cognitive therapy: Basics and beyond.* New York: Guilford Press.

Dr. Judith Beck presents an updated manual for cognitive therapy. She begins with how to develop a cognitive case conceptualization and instructs the reader on how to identify deeper-level cognitions, prepare for termination, and anticipate problems.

Greenberger, D., & Padesky, C. A. (1995). *Mind over mood: A cognitive therapy treatment manual for clients.* New York: Guilford Press.

Padesky, C. A., & Greenberger, D. (1995). *Clinician's guide to mind over mood.* New York: Guilford Press. These companion volumes are designed as step-by-step guides to the techniques and strategies of cognitive therapy. The manual is designed as a self-help workbook, and the clinician's guide provides therapists with instructions on how to incorporate the workbook into individual and group psychotherapy.

Salkovskis, P. M. (Ed.). (1996). *Frontiers of cognitive therapy.* New York: Guilford Press.

This edited volume presents contemporary developments in cognitive theory and current applications of cognitive therapy by leading experts. Topics include the empirical status of the model of anxiety and depression, treatment of depression, personality disorders, substance abuse, and eating disorders.

Weishaar, M. E. (1993). *Aaron T. Beck.* London: Sage Publications.

This book is a biography of Aaron Beck and includes chapters on the theoretical and practical contributions of cognitive therapy to psychotherapy, as well as criticisms of cognitive therapy, rebuttals to the criticisms, and a review of the overall contributions of Beck's cognitive therapy to psychotherapy and counseling.

# CASE READINGS

Beck, A. T., Rush, J., Shaw, B., & Emery, G. (1979). Interview with a depressed and suicidal patient. In *Cognitive therapy of depression* (pp. 225–243). New York: Guilford Press. [Reprinted in D. Wedding & R. J. Corsini (Eds.) (2005). *Case studies in psychotherapy.* Belmont, CA: Wadsworth.]

This interview with a suicidal patient features an outline of the types of assessments and interventions made by cognitive therapists in an initial session. Substantial change occurs in one session, as demonstrated in the verbatim transcript of the interview.

Beck, A. T., & Young, J. E. (1985). Cognitive therapy of depression. In D. Barlow (Ed.), *Clinical handbook of psychological disorders: A step-by-step treatment manual* (pp. 206–244). New York: Guilford Press.

This case of a depressed young woman demonstrates how a therapist elicits and challenges maladaptive thoughts and assumptions throughout the course of treatment.

Freeman, A., & Dattilio, E. M. (Eds.). (1992). *Comprehensive casebook of cognitive therapy.* New York: Plenum Press.

This edited volume contains a variety of cases using cognitive therapy.

Greenberger, D., & Padesky, C. A. (1995). *Mind over mood: A cognitive therapy treatment manual for clients.* New York: Guilford Press.

This treatment manual describes how to apply various cognitive therapy strategies, using cases throughout the book.

# REFERENCES

Adler, A. (1936). The neurotic's picture of the world. *International Journal of Individual Psychology, 2,* 3–10.

Alexander, E. (1950). *Psychosomatic medicine: Its principles and applications.* New York: Norton.

Arnold, M. (1960). *Emotion and personality* (vol. 1). New York: Columbia University Press.

Bandura, A. (1977). *Social learning theory.* Englewood Cliffs, NJ: Prentice Hall.

Baucom, D., Sayers, S., & Sher, T. (1990). Supplementary behavioral marital therapy with cognitive restructuring and emotional expressiveness training: An outcome investigation. *Journal of Consulting & Clinical Psychology, 58,* 636–645.

Beck, A. T. (1963). Thinking and depression. 1. Idiosyncratic content and cognitive distortions. *Archives of General Psychiatry, 9,* 324–333.

Beck, A. T. (1964). Thinking and depression. 2. Theory and therapy. *Archives of General Psychiatry, 10,* 561–571.

Beck, A. T. (1967). *Depression: Clinical, experimental, and theoretical aspects.* New York: Hoeber. (Republished as *Depression: Causes and treatment.* Philadelphia: University of Pennsylvania Press, 1972.)

Beck, A. T. (1978). *Anxiety checklist.* Philadelphia: Center for Cognitive Therapy.

Beck, A. T. (2002). *Cognitive therapy of borderline personality disorder and attempted suicide.* Paper presented at the conference of the Treatment and Research Advancements Association for Personality Disorders, Bethesda, MD.

Beck, J. S., & Beck, A. T. (2002). *Beck Youth Inventories of Emotional and Social Impairment.* San Antonio, TX: The Psychological Corporation.

Beck, A. T., Brown, G., Berchick, R. J., Stewart, B. L., & Steer, R. A. (1990). Relationship between hopelessness and ultimate suicide: A replication with psychiatric outpatients. *American Journal of Psychiatry, 147*(2), 190–195.

Beck, A. T., & Emery, G. (1979). *Cognitive therapy of anxiety and phobic disorders.* Philadelphia: Center for Cognitive Therapy.

Beck, A. T., & Emery, G. (1985). *Anxiety disorders and phobias: A cognitive perspective.* New York: Basic Books.

Beck, A. T., Epstein, N., & Harrison, R. (1983). Cognitions, attitudes and personality dimensions in depression. *British Journal of Cognitive Psychotherapy, 1*(1), 1–16.

Beck, A. T., Freeman, A., & Davis, D. D. (2003). *Cognitive therapy of personality disorders.* New York: Plenum.

Beck, A. T., Kovacs, M., & Weissman, A. (1979). Assessment of suicidal intention: The scale for suicidal ideation. *Journal of Consulting and Clinical Psychology, 47,* 343–352.

Beck, A. T., Laude, R., & Bohnert, M. (1974). Ideational components of anxiety neurosis. *Archives of General Psychiatry, 31,* 319–325.

Beck, A. T., Rush, A. J., Shaw, B. F., & Emery, G. (1979). *Cognitive therapy of depression.* New York: Guilford Press.

Beck, A. T., Schuyler, D., & Herman, I. (1974). Development of the suicidal intent scales. In A. T. Beck, H. L. P. Resnik, & D. J. Lettieri (Eds.), *The prediction of suicide* (pp. 45–56). Bowie, MD: Charles Press.

Beck, A. T., Sokol, L., Clark, D. A., Berchick, R. J., & Wright, F. D. (1992). A crossover study of focused cognitive therapy for panic disorder. *American Journal of Psychiatry, 149,* 778–783.

Beck, A. T., & Steer, R. A. (1990). *Beck anxiety inventory manual.* San Antonio, TX: The Psychological Corporation.

Beck, A. T., Steer, R. A., & Brown, G. K. (1996). *The Beck depression inventory manual* (2nd ed.). San Antonio, TX: The Psychological Corporation.

Beck, A. T., Steer, R. A., Brown, G., & Epstein, N. (1990). The Beck Self-concept Test. *Psychological Assessment: A Journal of Consulting and Clinical Psychology, 2,* 191–197.

Beck, A. T., Steer, R. A., Kovacs, M., & Garrison, B. (1985). Hopelessness and eventual suicide: A 10-year study of patients hospitalized with suicidal ideation. *American Journal of Psychiatry, 412,* 559–563.

Beck, A. T., Ward, C. H., Mendelson, M., Mock, J. E., & Erbaugh, J. K. (1961). An inventory for measuring depression. *Archives of General Psychiatry, 4,* 561–571.

Beck, A. T., Weissman, A., Lester, D., & Trexler, L. (1974). The measurement of pessimism: The hopelessness scale. *Journal of Consulting and Clinical Psychology, 42,* 861–865.

Beck, A. T., & Young, J. E. (1985). Cognitive therapy of depression. In D. Barlow (Ed.), *Clinical handbook of psychological disorders: A step-by-step treatment manual* (pp. 206–244). New York: Guilford Press.

Bowers, W. A. (2001). Cognitive model of eating disorders. *Journal of Cognitive Psychotherapy: An International Quarterly, 15,* 331–340.

Burns, D. D. (1985). *Intimate connections.* New York: Morrow.

Butler, G., Fennell, M., Robson, D., & Gelder, M. (1991). Comparison of behavior therapy and cognitive-behavior therapy in the treatment of generalized anxiety disorder. *Journal of Consulting & Clinical Psychology, 59,* 167–175.

Clark, D. A., & Beck, A. T. (2002). *Clark-Beck Obsessive-Compulsive Inventory.* San Antonio, TX: The Psychological Corporation.

Clark, D. A., Beck, A. T., & Alford, B. A. (1999). *Scientific foundations of cognitive theory and therapy of depression.* New York: John Wiley & Sons, Inc.

Clark, D. M. (1996). Panic disorder: From theory to therapy. In P. Salkovskis (Ed.), *Frontiers of cognitive therapy* (pp. 318–344). New York: Guilford.

Clark, D. M. (1997). Panic disorder and social phobia. In D. M. Clark & C. G. Fairburn (Eds.), *Science and practice of cognitive behavior therapy* (pp. 122–153). New York: Oxford University Press.

Clark, D. M., Salkovskis, P. M., Hackmann, A., Middleton, H., & Gelder, M. (1992). A comparison of cognitive therapy, applied relaxation, and imipramine in the treatment of panic disorder. *British Journal of Psychiatry, 164,* 759–769.

Dobson, K. S. (1989). A meta-analysis of the efficacy of cognitive therapy for depression. *Journal of Consulting and Clinical Psychology, 57*(3), 414–419.

Ehlers, A., & Clark, D. M. (2000). A cognitive model of posttraumatic stress disorder. *Behaviour Research and Therapy, 38,* 319–345.

Ellis, A. (1962). *Reason and emotion in psychotherapy.* New York: Lyle Stuart.

Eng, W., Roth, D. A., & Heimberg, R. G. (2001). Cognitive behavioral therapy for social anxiety. *Journal of Cognitive Psychotherapy: An International Quarterly, 15,* 311–319.

Fairburn, C. C., Jones, R., Peveler, R. C., Hope, R. A., Carr, S. J., Solomon, R. A., et al. (1991). Three psychological treatments for bulimia nervosa: A comparative trial. *Archives of General Psychiatry, 48,* 463–469.

Freeston, M. H., Ladoucer, R., Gagnon, F., Thibodeau, N., Rheaume, J., Letarte, H., et al. (1997). Cognitive-behavioral treatment of obsessive thoughts: A controlled study. *Journal of Consulting and Clinical Psychology, 65,* 405–413.

Garner, D. M., Rockert, W., Davis, R., Garner, M. V., Olmsted, M. P., & Eagle, M. (1993). Comparison of cognitive-behavioral and supportive-expressive therapy for bulimia nervosa. *American Journal of Psychiatry, 150,* 37–46.

Gillespie, K., Duffy, M., Hackmann, A., & Clark, D. M. (2002). Community-based cognitive therapy in the treatment of posttraumatic stress disorder following the Omagh bomb. *Behaviour Research and Therapy, 40,* 345–357.

Golden, W. L. (1983). Resistance in cognitive-behavior therapy. *British Journal of Cognitive Psychotherapy, 1*(2), 33–42.

Gournay, K. (1986). Cognitive change during the behavioral treatment of agoraphobia. Paper presented at Congress of European Association for Behavior Therapy, Lucerne, Switzerland.

Haaga, D. A. E., Dyck, M. J., & Ernst, D. (1991). Empirical status of cognitive theory of depression. *Psychological Bulletin, 110*(2), 215–236.

Hollon, S. D., DeRubeis, R. J., & Evans, M. D. (1996). Cognitive therapy in the treatment and prevention of depression. In P. Salkovskis (Ed.), *Frontiers of cognitive therapy* (pp. 293–317). New York: Guilford.

Horney, K. (1950). *Neurosis and human growth: The struggle toward self-realization.* New York: Norton.

Kant, I. (1798). *The classification of mental disorders.* Konigsberg, Germany: Nicolovius.

Kelly, G. (1955). *The psychology of personal constructs.* New York: Norton.

Lazarus, R. (1984). On the primacy of cognition. *American Psychologist, 39,* 124–129.

Mahoney, M. J. (1974). *Cognition and behavior modification.* Cambridge, MA: Ballinger.

Mahoney, M. J., & Arnkoff, D. (1978). Cognitive and self-control therapies. In S. L. Garfield & A. E. Bergin (Eds.), *Handbook of psychotherapy and behavior change: An empirical analysis* (pp. 689–722). New York: Wiley.

Meichenbaum, D. (1977). *Cognitive-behavior modification: An integrative approach.* New York: Plenum.

Persons, J. B., Burns, D. D., & Perloff, J. M. (1988). Predictors of dropout and outcome in cognitive therapy for depression in a private practice setting. *Cognitive Therapy and Research, 12,* 557–575.

Rector, N. A., & Beck, A. T. (2001). Cognitive behavioral therapy for schizophrenia: An empirical review. *Journal of Nervous and Mental Disease, 189,* 278–287.

Resick, P. A. (2001). Cognitive therapy for posttraumatic stress disorder. *Journal of Cognitive Psychotherapy: An International Quarterly, 15,* 321–329.

Rogers, C. (1951). *Client-centered therapy.* Boston: Houghton Mifflin.

Strunk, D. R., & DeRubeis, R. J. (2001). Cognitive therapy for depression: A review of its efficacy, *Journal of Cognitive Psychotherapy: An International Quarterly, 15,* 289–297.

Sullivan, H. S. (1953). *The interpersonal theory of psychiatry.* New York: Norton.

Vitousek, K. M. (1996). The current status of cognitive-behavioral models of anorexia nervosa and bulimia nervosa. In P. Salkovskis (Ed.), *Frontiers of cognitive therapy* (pp. 383–418). New York: Guilford.

Weissman, A., & Beck, A. T. (1978). Development and validation of the Dysfunctional Attitude Scale. Paper presented at the 12th annual meeting of the Association for Advancement of Behavior Therapy, Chicago.

Wessler, R. L. (1986). Conceptualizing cognitions in the cognitive-behavioral therapies. In W. Dryden & W. Golden (Eds.), *Cognitive-behavioural approaches to psychotherapy* (pp. 1–30). London: Harper & Row.

Williams, S. L., & Rappoport, A. (1983). Cognitive treatment in the natural environment for agoraphobics. *Behavior Therapy, 14,* 299–313.

Woody, G. E., Luborsky, L., McClellan, A. T., O'Brien, C. P., Beck, A. T., Blaine, J., et al. (1983). Psychotherapy for opiate addicts: Does it help? *Archives of General Psychiatry, 40,* 639–645.

Young, J. E., & Beck, A. T. (1980). *Development of an instrument for rating cognitive therapy: The Cognitive Therapy Rating Scale.* Philadelphia: University of Pennsylvania.

Rollo May (1909–1994)
Courtesy of Professor Rollo May

Irvin Yalom
Courtesy of Professor Irvin Yalom

# 9   EXISTENTIAL PSYCHOTHERAPY

*Rollo May and Irvin Yalom*

## OVERVIEW

Existential psychotherapy arose spontaneously in the minds and works of a number of psychologists and psychiatrists in Europe in the 1940s and 1950s who were concerned with finding a way of understanding human beings that was more reliable and more basic than the then-current psychotherapies. The "existential orientation in psychiatry," wrote Ludwig Binswanger, "arose from dissatisfaction with the prevailing efforts to gain scientific understanding in psychiatry" (1956, p. 144). These existential therapists believed drives in Freudian psychology, conditioning in behaviorism, and archetypes in Jungianism all had their own significance. But where was the actual, *immediate person* to whom these things were happening? Are we seeing patients as they really are, or are we simply seeing a projection of our theories *about* them?

These therapists were keenly aware that we are living in an age of transition, when almost every human being feels alienated from fellow humans, threatened by nuclear war and economic upsets, perplexed by the radical changes in marriage and almost all other mores in our culture—in short, almost everyone is beset by anxiety.

Existential psychotherapy is not a specific technical approach that presents a new set of rules for therapy. It asks deep questions about the nature

269

*anomie*

of the human being and the nature of anxiety, despair, grief, loneliness, isolation, and anomie. It also deals centrally with the questions of creativity and love. Out of the understanding of the meaning of these human experiences, existential psychotherapists have devised methods of therapy that do not fall into the common error of distorting human beings in the very effort of trying to help them.

## Basic Concepts

### The "I-Am" Experience

The realization of one's being—"I am now living and I could take my life"—can have a salutary effect on a patient. "The idea of suicide has saved many lives," said Nietzsche. The human being will be victimized by circumstances and other people until he or she is able to realize, "I am the one living, experiencing. I choose my own being."

It is not easy to define *being* because in our society we often subordinate the sense of being to our economic status or the external type of life that we lead. A person is known (and knows self) not as a being or a self, but as a ticket seller in the subway, a grocer, a professor, a vice president of AT&T, or as whatever his or her economic function may be. This loss of the sense of being is related to mass collectivist trends and widespread conformist tendencies in our culture. The French existentialist Gabriel Marcel (May, Angel, & Ellenberger, 1958, p. 40), makes this trenchant challenge: "Indeed I wonder if a psychoanalytic method, deeper and more discerning than any that has been evolved until now, would not reveal the morbid effects of the repression of this sense [of being] and of the ignoring of this need."

Existential therapy endeavors to be this "deeper and more discerning" type of therapy. A patient, the daughter of a prostitute, had been an illegitimate child and had been brought up by relatives. She said:

> I remember walking that day under the elevated tracks in a slum area, feeling the thought, *I am an illegitimate child.* I recall the sweat pouring forth in my anguish in trying to accept that fact. Then I understood what it must feel like to accept "I am a Negro in the midst of privileged whites," or "I am blind in the midst of people who see." Later on that night I woke up and it came to me this way, "I accept the fact that I am an illegitimate child." But "I am not a child anymore." So it is "I am illegitimate." That is not so either. "I was born illegitimate." Then what is left? What is left is this, "I Am." This act of contact and acceptance with "I am," once gotten hold of, gave me the experience "Since I Am, I have the right to be." (May et al., 1958)

This "I-Am" experience is not in itself a solution to an individual's problems. It is, rather, the *precondition* for the solution. The patient in the preceding example spent some two years thereafter working through specific psychological problems, which she was able to do on the basis of her experience of being.

This experience of being points also to the experience of *not being,* or nothingness. Nonbeing is illustrated in the threat of death, or destructive hostility, severe incapacitating anxiety, or critical sickness. The threat of nonbeing is present in greater or lesser intensity at all times. When we cross the street while looking both ways to guard against being struck by an automobile, when someone makes a remark that disparages us, or when we go into an examination ill-prepared—all of these represent the threat of nonbeing.

The "I-Am" experience, or the experience of being, is known in existential therapy as an *ontological* experience. This word comes from two Greek words, *ontis* meaning "to be" and *logical* meaning "the science of." Thus it is the "science of being." The term *ontological* is valuable in existential psychotherapy.

*ontological*

## Normal and Neurotic Anxiety

Existential therapists define anxiety more broadly than other psychotherapeutic groups. *Anxiety arises from our personal need to survive, to preserve our being, and to assert our being.* Anxiety shows itself physically in faster beating of the heart, rising blood pressure, preparation of the skeletal muscles for fighting or fleeing, and a sense of apprehension. Rollo May defines anxiety as "the threat to our existence or to values we identify with our existence" (1977, p. 205).

Anxiety is more basic than fear. In psychotherapy, one of our aims is to help the patient confront anxiety as fully as possible, thus reducing anxiety to fears, which are then objective and can be dealt with. But the main therapeutic function is to help the patient confront the normal anxiety that is an unavoidable part of the human condition.

*Normal anxiety* has three characteristics. First, it is proportionate to the situation confronted. Second, normal anxiety does not require repression: We can come to terms with it, as we come to terms with the fact that we all face eventual death. Third, such anxiety can be used creatively, as a stimulus to help identify and confront the dilemma out of which the anxiety arose.

*Neurotic anxiety,* on the other hand, is not appropriate to the situation. For example, parents may be so anxious that their child will be hit by a car that they never let the child leave the house. Second, it is repressed, in the way most of us repress the fear of nuclear war. Third, neurotic anxiety is destructive, not constructive. Neurotic anxiety tends to paralyze the individual rather than stimulate creativity.

The function of therapy is *not* to do away with all anxiety. No person could survive completely without anxiety. Mental health is living as much as possible without *neurotic* anxiety, but *with* the ability to tolerate the unavoidable existential anxiety of living.

## Guilt and Guilt Feelings

The experience of guilt has special meaning for the existential therapist. Guilt can, like anxiety, take both normal and neurotic forms. Neurotic guilt feelings (generally called *guilt*) often arise out of fantasized transgressions. Other forms of guilt, which we call *normal guilt,* sensitize us to the ethical aspects of our behavior.

Still another form is guilt toward ourselves for failure to live up to our potentialities, for "forgetting being" as Medard Boss puts it. The attitude toward such guilt in existential therapy is well illustrated in a case Medard Boss (1957b) cites of a severe obsessive-compulsive whom he treated. This patient, a physician suffering from hand-washing compulsions, had gone through both Freudian and Jungian analyses. He had had for some time a recurrent dream involving church steeples, interpreted in the Freudian analysis in terms of phallic symbols and in the Jungian in terms of religious archetypal symbols. The patient could discuss these interpretations intelligently and at length, but his neurotic compulsive behavior, after temporary abeyance, continued, as crippling as ever. During the first months of his analysis with Boss, the patient reported a recurrent dream in which he would approach a lavatory door that would always be locked. Boss confined himself only to asking each time why the door needed to be locked. Finally the patient had a dream in which he opened the door and found himself inside a church. He was waist deep in feces and was tugged by a rope wrapped around his waist and leading up to the bell tower. The patient was suspended in such tension that he thought he would be pulled to pieces. He then went through a psychotic episode of four days, after which the analysis continued with an eventual successful outcome.

Boss (1957b) points out that the patient was guilty because he had locked up some essential potentialities in himself. *Therefore* he had guilt feelings. "If you lock up poten-

tialities, you are guilty . . . (or indebted to) . . . what is given you in your origin, in your 'core.' In this . . . condition of being indebted and being guilty are founded all guilt feelings." This patient had locked up both the bodily and the spiritual possibilities of his experience. The patient had previously accepted the libido and archetype explanations and knew them all too well; but that is a good way, says Boss, to escape the whole thing. Because the patient did not accept and take into his existence these two aspects, he was guilty, indebted to himself. This was the origin of his neurosis and psychosis.

## The Three Forms of World

Another basic concept in existential psychotherapy is called *being-in-the-world.* We must understand the phenomenological world in which the patient exists and participates.

A person's world cannot be comprehended by describing the environment, no matter how complex the description. The environment is only one mode of world. The biologist Jakob von Uexküll argues that one is justified in assuming as many environments as there are animals. "There is not one space and time only," he goes on to say, "but as many spaces and times as there are subjects" (von Uexküll, cited in May et al., 1958). How much more is it true that the human being also has his or her own world? This confronts us with no easy problem: for we cannot describe world in purely objective terms, nor is world to be limited to our subjective, imaginative participation in the structure around us.

*The human world is the structure of meaningful relationships in which a person exists and in the design of which he or she participates.* That is, the same past or present circumstances can mean very different things to different people. Thus, one's world includes the past events that condition one's existence and all the vast variety of deterministic influences that operate upon one. But it is these *as one relates to them,* as one is aware of them, molds, and constantly reforms them. For to be aware of one's world means at the same time to be designing it, *constituting* one's world.

From the point of view of existential psychotherapy, there are three modes of world. The first is *Umwelt,* meaning "world around," the biological world, the environment. The second is *Mitwelt,* literally the "with-world," the world of one's fellow human beings. The third is *Eigenwelt,* the "own-world," the relationship to one's self.

*Umwelt* is the world of objects about us, the natural world. All organisms have an *Umwelt.* For animals and human beings the Umwelt includes biological needs, drives, and instincts. It is the world of natural law and natural cycles, of sleep and awakeness, of being born and dying, of desire and relief, the world of finiteness and biological determinism to which each of us must in some way adjust. Existential analysts accept the reality of the natural world. "The natural law is as valid as ever," as Kierkegaard put it.

The *Eigenwelt,* or "own-world," has been least adequately dealt with or understood in modern psychology and depth-psychology. Own-world presupposes self-awareness and self-relatedness and is uniquely present in human beings. It is a grasping of what something in the world personally means to the individual observer. D. T. Suzuki has remarked that in Eastern languages, such as Japanese, adjectives always include the implication of "for-me-ness." That is to say, "This flower is beautiful" means "For me, this flower is beautiful."

One implication of this analysis of the modes of being-in-the-world is that it gives us a basis for understanding love. The human experience of love obviously cannot be adequately described within the confines of *Umwelt.* We can never accurately speak of human beings as "sexual objects," because once a person is a sexual object, we are not talking about a person anymore. The interpersonal schools of personality theory have dealt with love as an interpersonal relationship. Without an adequate concept of *Umwelt,* love becomes empty of vitality, and without *Eigenwelt,* it lacks power and the capacity to fructify itself. The importance of *Eigenwelt* was stressed by Friedrich Nietzsche and Søren Kierkegaard, who continually insisted that to love presupposes that one must already have become the "true individual," the "Solitary One," the one who "has comprehended the deep secret that also in loving another person one must be sufficient unto oneself."

## The Significance of Time

Existential psychotherapists are struck by the fact that the most profound human experiences, such an anxiety, depression, and joy, occur more in the dimension of time than in space.

Existential therapists agree with Henri Bergson that "time is the heart of existence" and that our error in the modern day has been to think of ourselves primarily in terms of space, as though we were objects that could be located like substances at this spot or that. By this distortion we lost our genuine existential relation with ourselves, and indeed also with other persons around us. As a consequence of this overemphasis on spatial thinking, says Bergson, "the moments when we grasp ourselves are rare, and consequently we are seldom free" (Bergson, cited in May et al., 1958, p. 56).

But in the with-world, the mode of personal relations and love, we can see particularly that quantitative time has much less to do with the significance of an occurrence. The nature or degree of one's love, for example, can never be measured by the number of years one has known the loved one. It is true, of course, that clock time has much to do with *Mitwelt*. We are referring rather to the inner meaning of the events. "No clock strikes for the happy one," says a German proverb. Indeed, the most significant events in a person's psychological existence are likely to be precisely the ones which are "immediate," breaking through the usual steady progression of time, like a sudden insight or a view of beauty that one sees in an instant, but which may remain in one's memory for days and months.

Finally, the *Eigenwelt,* the world of self-relatedness, self-awareness, and insight into the meaning of an event for one's self, has practically nothing whatever to do with clock time. The essence of self-awareness and insight is that they are there—instantaneous and immediate—and the moment of awareness has its significance for all time. One can see this easily by noting what happens in oneself at the instant of an insight. The instant occurs with suddenness; it is born whole, so to speak. One will discover that, though meditating on an insight for an hour or so may reveal many of its further implications, the insight is not dearer—and disconcertingly enough, often not as dear—at the end of the hour as it was at the beginning.

Whether or not a patient can even recall the significant events of the past depends upon his or her decision with regard to the future. Every therapist knows that patients may bring up past memories ad nauseam without any memory ever moving them, the whole recital being flat, inconsequential, and tedious. From an existential point of view, the problem is not that these patients endured impoverished pasts; it is rather that they cannot or do not commit themselves to the present and future. Their past does not become alive because nothing matters enough to them in the future. Some hope and commitment to work toward changing something in the immediate future, be it overcoming anxiety or other painful symptoms or integrating the self for further creativity, are necessary before a patient's uncovering of the past will have reality.

## Our Human Capacity to Transcend the Immediate Situation

If we are to understand a given person as existing, dynamic, at every moment becoming, we cannot avoid the dimension of transcendence. Existing involves a continual emerging, in the sense of emergent evolution, a transcending of one's past and present in order to reach the future. Thus *transcendere*—literally "to climb over and beyond"—describes what every human being is engaged in doing every moment when not seriously ill or temporarily blocked by despair or anxiety. One can, of course, see emergent evolution in all life processes. Nietzsche has his old Zarathustra proclaim, "And this secret spake Life herself to me. 'Behold' said she, 'I am that which must ever surpass itself'" (cited in May et al., 1958, p. 72).

The neurobiological base for this capacity is classically described by Kurt Goldstein (cited in May et al., 1958, p. 72). He found that brain-injured patients—chiefly soldiers with portions of the frontal cortex shot away—had specifically lost the ability to abstract, to think in terms of the possible. They were tied to any immediate concrete situation in which they happened to be. When their closets happened to be in disarray, they were thrown into profound anxiety and disordered behavior. They exhibited compulsive orderliness—which is a way of holding oneself at every moment rigidly to the concrete situation. When asked to write their names on a sheet of paper, they would typically write in the very corner, any venture out from the specific boundaries of the edges of the paper representing too great a threat. Goldstein held that the distinctive capacity of the normal human being is precisely this capacity to abstract, to use symbols, to orient oneself beyond the immediate limits of the given time and space, to think in terms of "the possible." The injured, or "ill," patients were characterized by loss of range of possibility. Their world space was shrunk, their time curtailed, and they suffered a consequent radical loss of freedom.

We human beings possess the ability to transcend time and space. We can transport ourselves back 2,000 years to ancient Greece and watch the drama of Oedipus being performed in ancient Athens. We can instantaneously transport ourselves to the future, conceiving what life will be like in, say, the year 2500. These forms of transcendence are part and parcel of human consciousness. This capacity is exemplified in the human being's unique capacity to think and talk in symbols. Thus, to make promises presupposes conscious self-relatedness and is a very different thing from simple conditioned social behavior, acting in terms of the requirements of the group or herd or hive. Jean-Paul Sartre writes that dishonesty is a uniquely human form of behavior. "The lie is a behavior of transcendence," because to lie we must at the same moment know we are departing from the truth (Sartre, 1956, p. 1203).

This capacity to transcend the immediate situation is not a "faculty." It is, rather, given in the ontological nature of being human. To abstract, to objectivate, are evidences of it, but as Martin Heidegger puts it, "transcendence does not consist of objectivation, but objectivation presupposes transcendence" (cited in May et al., 1958, p. 75). The fact that human beings can be self-related gives them the capacity to objectify their world, to think and talk in symbols. This is Kierkegaard's point when he reminds us that to understand the self we must see clearly that "imagination is not one faculty on a par with others, but, if one would so speak, it is the faculty for all faculties. What feeling, knowledge, or will a man has depends upon what imagination he has, that is to say, upon how these things are reflected. Imagination is the possibility of all reflection, and the intensity of this medium is the possibility of the intensity of the self" (Kierkegaard, 1954, p. 163).

## Other Systems

### Behaviorism

First we shall consider the differences between existential theory and the theory of *behaviorism*. This radical distinction can be seen when we note the chasm between abstract truth and existential reality.

Kenneth W. Spence (1956), a leader of one wing of behavior theory, wrote: "The question of whether any particular realm of behavior phenomena is more real or closer to real life and hence should be given priority in investigation does not, or at least should not, arise for the psychologist as scientist." That is to say, it does not primarily matter whether what is being studied is real or not.

What realms, then, should be selected for study? Spence gives priority to phenomena that lend themselves "to the degrees of control and analysis necessary for the formulation of abstract laws." Nowhere has this point been put more clearly than by Spence—what can be reduced to abstract laws is selected, and whether what is studied has *reality* or not is irrelevant to this goal. Many an impressive system in psychology has been erected, with abstraction piled high upon abstraction until an admirable and imposing structure is built. The only trouble is that the edifice has often been separated from reality in its very foundations.

Psychiatrists and psychologists in the existential psychotherapy movement insist that it is necessary and possible to have a science that studies human beings in their reality.

## Orthodox Freudianism

Ludwig Binswanger and some other existential therapists differed from Freud in several important respects, including rejection of the concept of the patient propelled by instincts and drives. As Sartre put it, Freudians have lost the human being *to whom* these things happen.

The existentialists also question the view of the unconscious as a reservoir of tendencies, desires, and drives from which the motivation for behavior arises. This "cellar" view of the unconscious leads patients in therapy to avoid responsibility for their actions by such phrases as, "My unconscious did it, not I." Existentialists always insist that the patient in therapy accept responsibility by asking such questions as, "Whose unconscious is it?"

The differences between existentialism and Freudianism are also seen in the modes of the world. The genius and the value of Freud's work lie in uncovering the mode of instincts, drives, contingency, and biological determinism. But traditional Freudianism has only a shadowy concept of the interrelation of persons as subjects.

## The Interpersonal School of Psychotherapy

A consideration of the three modes of world discloses the differences between existential therapy and the interpersonal school. Interpersonal schools do have a theoretical basis for dealing directly with *Mitwelt.* Though they should not be considered identical, *Mitwelt* and interpersonal theory have a great deal in common. The danger of this point, however, is that if *Eigenwelt,* one's own-world, is omitted, interpersonal relations tend to become hollow and sterile. H. S. Sullivan argued against the concept of individual personality and went to great efforts to define the self in terms of "reflected appraisal" and social categories—that is, the roles the person plays in the interpersonal world. Theoretically, this approach suffers from considerable logical inconsistency and indeed goes directly against other contributions of Sullivan. Practically, it tends to make the self a mirror of the group around one, to empty the self of vitality and originality, and to reduce the interpersonal world to mere "social relations." It opens the way to a tendency directly opposed to the goals of Sullivan and other interpersonal thinkers, namely, social conformity.

## Jungian Psychology

There are similarities between Jungian and existential therapy. But the main criticism existentialists make is that Jungians too quickly avoid the immediate existential crises of patients by leaping into theory. This is illustrated in Medard Boss's case related in the previous section titled "Guilt and Guilt Feelings." A patient who was afraid to go out of the house alone was analyzed by a Jungian therapist for six years, in the course of which the therapist interpreted several dreams as indicating that "God is speaking to you." The patient was flattered, but still couldn't go out of the house alone. She later was enabled to get over her crippling neurosis by an existential therapist who insisted that she could overcome her problem only if she actively *wanted* to, which was a way of insisting that she, not God, needed to take responsibility for her problem.

## Client–Centered Approach

The difference between existentialism and Rogerian therapy is seen in statements made by Rollo May when he was acting as a judge of client-centered therapy in the client-centered experiment at the University of Wisconsin. Twelve outside experts were sent tapes of the therapy to judge. Rollo May (1982), as one of the outside experts, reported that he often felt that there were not two distinct people in the room. When the therapist only reflects the patient's words, there transpires "only an amorphous kind of identity rather than two subjects interacting in *a world in which both participate, and in which love and hate, trust and doubt, conflicts and dependence, come out and can be understood and assimilated*" (p. 16). May was concerned that the therapist's overidentification with the patient could "take away the patient's opportunity to experience himself as a subject in his own right or to take a stand against the therapist, to experience being in an interpersonal world" (p. 16).

In spite of the fact that client-centered therapists, both individually and collectively, have advocated openness and freedom in the therapeutic relationship, the outside judges concluded that "the therapist's rigid and controlling nature closed him off to many of his own as well as to the patient's experiences" (p. 16).

One of the Rogerian therapists, after experience as an independent therapist, wrote this criticism:

> I used the early concept of the client-centered therapist to bolster the inhibition of my anger, my aggression, etc. I got some feedback at that time that it was difficult for people, because I was so nice, to tell me things that were not nice, and that it was hard for people to get angry at me. (Raskin, 1978, p. 367)

In other words, client-centered therapy is not fully existential in that it does not confront the patient directly and firmly.

# HISTORY

## Precursors

There are two streams in the history of human thought. One is of *essences,* seen most clearly in Plato's belief that there are perfect forms of everything and that things such as a specific chair are imperfect copies. These essences are clearest if we imagine mathematics: a perfect circle and a perfect square exist in heaven, of which our human circles and squares are imperfect copies. This requires an abstraction that leaves the *existence* of the individual thing out of the picture. A proposition can be true without being real. Perhaps just because this approach has worked in certain areas of science, we tend to forget that it omits *the living individual.*

But there is another stream of thought coming down through history: namely, *existence.* This viewpoint holds that truth depends upon the existing person, existing in a given situation (world) at that *time.* Hence the term *existential.* This is what Sartre meant in his famous statement, "Existence precedes essence." The human being's awareness (i.e., his or her existence) precedes everything he or she has to say about the surrounding world.

Down through history, the existential tradition is exemplified by many thinkers. These include Augustine, who held that "Truth dwells in the inner man"; Duns Scotus, who argued against Thomas Aquinas's rational essences and insisted that human *will* must be taken as basic to any statement; and Blaise Pascal, as in his famous statement, "The heart has its reasons which reason knows nothing of."

There remains in our day the chasm between truth and reality. And the crucial question that confronts us in psychology is precisely this chasm between what is abstractly true and what is existentially real for the given living person.

## Beginnings

Kierkegaard, Nietzsche, and those existentialists who followed them foresaw this growing split between truth and reality in Western culture, and they opposed the delusion that reality can be comprehended in an abstracted, detached way. Though they protested vehemently against arid intellectualism, they were by no means simple activists, nor were they antirational. Anti-intellectualism and other movements that make thinking subordinate to feeling must not be confused with existentialism. Either alternative—making a human being entirely subject or object—results in *losing the living, existing person.* Kierkegaard and the existential thinkers appealed to a reality underlying *both* subjectivity and objectivity. We must not only study a person's experience as such, they held, but even more, we must study the one who is doing the experiencing.

It is by no means accidental that the greatest existentialists in the nineteenth century, Kierkegaard and Nietzsche, happen also to be among the most remarkable psychologists of all time. A contemporary leader of existential philosophy, Karl Jaspers, originally a psychiatrist, wrote a notable text on psychopathology. When one reads Kierkegaard's profound analyses of anxiety and despair or Nietzsche's amazingly acute insights into the dynamics of resentment and the guilt and hostility that accompany repressed emotional powers, it is difficult to realize that one is reading works written more than 100 years ago and not a contemporary psychological analysis.

Existential therapists are centrally concerned with rediscovering the living person amid the dehumanization of modern culture, and in order to do this they engage in in-depth psychological analysis. Their concern is not with isolated psychological reactions in themselves but rather with the psychological being of the living person doing the experiencing. They use psychological terms with an ontological meaning.

Existential therapy sprang up spontaneously in different parts of Europe and among different schools and has a diverse body of researchers and creative thinkers. There were psychiatrists—Eugene Minkowski in Paris, Erwin Straus in Germany and then in America, V. E. von Gebsattel in Germany—who represent chiefly the first, phenomenological stage of this movement. Ludwig Binswanger, A. Storch, Medard Boss, G. Bally, Roland Kuhn in Switzerland and J. H. Van Den Berg and F. J. Buytendijk in Holland represented the second, or existential, stage.

## Current Status

Existential psychotherapy was introduced to the United States in 1958 with the publication of *Existence: A New Dimension in Psychiatry and Psychology,* edited by Rollo May, Ernest Angel, and Henri Ellenberger. The main presentation and summary of existential therapy was in the first two chapters, written by May: "The Origins of the Existential Movement in Psychology" and "Contributions of Existential Psychology." The remainder of the book is made up of essays and case studies by Henri Ellenberger, Eugene Minkowski, Erwin Straus, V E. von Gebsattel, Ludwig Binswanger, and Ronald Kuhn. The first comprehensive textbook in existential psychiatry was written by Irvin Yalom (1981) and entitled *Existential Psychotherapy.*

The spirit of existential psychotherapy has never supported the formation of specific institutes because it deals with the *presuppositions underlying therapy of any kind.* Its concern was with concepts about human beings and not with specific techniques. This leads to the dilemma that existential therapy has been quite influential, but there are very few adequate training courses in this kind of therapy simply because it is not a specific training in technique.

The founders of the existential movement always stated that specific training in techniques of therapy could be obtained at any number of schools of therapy, and that the student was responsible for molding his or her own presuppositions in existential form.

Rollo May, an existentialist before he knew the word, found that the existing person was the important consideration, and not a theory *about* this person. He had argued in his Ph.D. dissertation, published under the title *The Meaning of Anxiety* in 1950, for a concept of normal anxiety as the basis for a theory of human beings. He had already, before his training in the William Alanson White Institute, experienced the futility of going to analysis five times a week for two years. He was trained as a psychoanalyst in the William Alanson White Institute, the neo-Freudian institute in New York, and was already a practicing analyst when he read in the early 1950s about existential therapies in Europe. He felt these new concepts in existential psychology were the ones he needed but had never been able to formulate.

The founders of existential psychotherapy believe that its contributions will be absorbed into other schools. Fritz Perls, in the foreword of *Gestalt Therapy Verbatim* (1969), states quite accurately that gestalt therapy is a form of existential psychotherapy. Therapists trained in different schools can legitimately call themselves existential if their assumptions are similar to those described in this chapter. Irvin Yalom was trained in the neo-Freudian tradition. Even such an erstwhile behavior therapist as Arnold Lazarus uses some existential presuppositions in his multimodal psychotherapy. All of this is possible because existential psychotherapy is a way of conceiving the human being. It goes deeper than the other forms of psychotherapy to emphasize the assumptions underlying all systems of psychotherapy.

Major works include May's *The Meaning of Anxiety* (1977), *Man's Search for Himself* (1953), and *Existential Psychology* (1961). Others are James Bugental's *The Search for Existential Identity* (1976), Medard Boss's *The Analysis of Dreams* (1957a) and *Psychoanalysis and Daseinanalysis* (1982), and Viktor Frankl's *Man's Search for Meaning* (1963). Helmut Kaiser has written valuably on existential therapy in his *Effective Psychotherapy* (1965). Leslie Farber (1966, 1976), Avery Weisman (1965), and Lester Havens (1974) have also contributed significantly to the existential literature.

# PERSONALITY

## Theory of Personality

Existential psychotherapy is a form of *dynamic psychotherapy* that posits a dynamic model of personality structure. *Dynamic* is a commonly used term in psychology and psychotherapy. We often, for example, speak of the patient's "psychodynamics," or a "dynamic" approach to therapy. *Dynamic* has both lay and technical meanings, and it is necessary to be precise about its meaning in the context of personality theory. In its lay meaning *dynamic* has the connotation of vitality.

The technical meaning of *dynamic* relevant to personality theory refers to the concept of force. Its use in personality theory was first invoked by Freud, who viewed the personality as a system consisting of forces in conflict with one another. The result of this conflict is the constellation of emotions and behavior (both adaptive and pathological) that constitute personality. Furthermore (and this is an essential part of the definition), these forces in conflict *exist at different levels of awareness.* Indeed, some of the forces are entirely out of awareness and exist on an unconscious plane.

Thus, when we speak of the "psychodynamics" of an individual, we refer to that individual's conflicting conscious and unconscious forces, motives, and fears. "Dynamic psychotherapy" is psychotherapy based upon this dynamic model of personality structure.

There are many dynamic models of personality. To differentiate these various models and to define the existential model of personality structure, we must ask: What is the content of the internal, conscious, and unconscious struggle? Forces, motives, and fears conflict with one another within the personality. But which forces? Which motives? Which fears?

The existential view of the internal struggle can be made clearer by contrasting it with two other common dynamic views of personality: the Freudian model and the interpersonal (neo-Freudian) model.

## The Freudian Model of Psychodynamics

The Freudian model posits that the individual is governed by innate instinctual forces that inexorably unfurl throughout the psychosexual developmental cycle. Freud postulated conflicts on several fronts: dual instincts collide with one another (ego instincts versus libido instincts in Freud's first theory or, in the second theory, Eros versus Thanatos); the instincts also collide with the demands of the environment, and later the instincts collide with the superego (the internalized environment).

We can summarize the nature of the conflict in the Freudian dynamic model by stating that an instinctually driven being is at war with a world that prevents the satisfaction of these innate aggressive and sexual drives.

## The Interpersonal (Neo-Freudian) Model of Psychodynamics

In the interpersonal model of personality the individual is not instinct-guided and preprogrammed, but is instead almost entirely shaped by the cultural and interpersonal environment. The child desperately requires acceptance and approval by important survival figures. But the child also has an inner press toward growth, mastery, and autonomy, and these tendencies are not always compatible with the demands of significant adults in the child's life. If the child is unlucky enough to have parents who are too caught up in their own neurotic struggles to provide the child security *and* encourage the child's autonomous development, then a conflict develops between the child's need for security and natural growth inclinations. In such a struggle, growth is always compromised for the sake of security.

## Existential Psychodynamics

The existential model of personality rests on a different view of inner conflict. It postulates that the basic conflict is not with suppressed instinctual drives or with the significant adults in the individual's early life; instead the conflict is between the individual and the "givens" of existence.

What are these "givens"? The reflective individual can discover them without a great deal of effort. If we "bracket" the outside world, if we put aside the everyday concerns with which we ordinarily fill our lives and reflect deeply upon our situation in the world, then we must confront certain "ultimate concerns" that are an inescapable part of the human being's existence in the world.

Yalom (1981) identifies four ultimate concerns that have considerable relevance for psychotherapy: *death, freedom, isolation,* and *meaninglessness.* The individual's confrontation with each of these constitutes the content of the inner conflict from the existential frame of reference.

*Death*    Death is the most obvious ultimate concern. It is apparent to all that death will come and that there is no escape. It is a terrible truth, and at the deepest levels we respond to it with mortal terror. "Everything," as Spinoza states, "wishes to persist in its own being" (1954, p. 6). From the existential point of view a core inner conflict is between awareness of inevitable death and the simultaneous wish to continue to live.

Death plays a major role in one's internal experience. It haunts the individual as nothing else. It rumbles continuously under the membrane of life. The child at an early age is pervasively concerned with death, and one of the child's major developmental tasks is to deal with the terror of obliteration.

To cope with this terror, we erect defenses against death awareness. These defenses are denial-based; they shape character structure and, if maladaptive, result in clinical maladjustment. Psychopathology, to a very great extent, is the result of failed death transcendence; that is, symptoms and maladaptive character structure have their origin in the individual terror of death.

*Freedom*    Ordinarily we do not think of freedom as a source of anxiety. Quite the contrary, freedom is generally viewed as an unequivocally positive concept. The history of Western civilization is punctuated by a yearning and striving toward freedom. Yet freedom in the existential frame of reference has a technical meaning—one that is riveted to dread.

In the existential frame of reference, freedom means that, contrary to everyday experience, the human being does not enter and ultimately exit from a structured universe with a coherent, grand design. Freedom refers to the fact that the human being is responsible for and the author of his or her own world, own life design, and own choices and actions. The human being, as Sartre puts it, is "condemned to freedom" (1956, p. 631). Rollo May (1981) holds that freedom, in order to be authentic, requires the individual to confront the limits of his or her destiny.

The existential position that the human being constitutes a personal world has been germinating for a long time in philosophic thought. The heart of Kant's revolution in philosophy was his postulate that human consciousness, the nature of the human being's mental structures, provides the external form of reality. Kant stated that even space "is not something objective and real but something subjective and ideal; it is, as it were, a schema issuing by a constant law from the nature of the mind for the coordinating of all outer sensa [sense data]" (1954, p. 308).

This existential view of freedom has terrifying implications. If it is true that we create our own selves and our own world, then it also means that there is no ground beneath us: there is only an abyss, a void, nothingness.

An important internal dynamic conflict emanates from our confrontation with freedom: conflict issues from our awareness of freedom and groundlessness on the one hand and, on the other hand, our deep need and wish for ground and structure.

The concept of freedom encompasses many themes that have profound implications for psychotherapy. The most apparent is *responsibility.* Individuals differ enormously in the degree of responsibility they are willing to accept for their life situation and in their modes of denying responsibility. For example, some individuals displace responsibility for their situation onto other people, onto life circumstances, onto bosses and spouses, and, when they enter treatment, they transfer responsibility for their therapy to their psychotherapist. Other individuals deny responsibility by experiencing themselves as "innocent victims" who suffer from external events (and remain unaware that they themselves have set these events into motion). Still others shuck responsibility by temporarily being "out of their minds"—they enter a temporary irrational state in which they are not accountable even to themselves for their behavior.

Another aspect of freedom is *willing*. To be aware of responsibility for one's situation is to enter the vestibule of action or, in a therapy situation, of change. Willing represents the passage from responsibility to action. Willing, as May (1969) points out, consists first of wishing and then of deciding. Many individuals have enormous difficulties in experiencing or expressing a wish. Wishing is closely aligned to feeling, and affect-blocked individuals cannot act spontaneously because they cannot feel and thus cannot wish. *Impulsivity* avoids wishing by failing to discriminate among wishes. Instead, individuals act impulsively and promptly on all wishes. *Compulsivity,* another disorder of wishing, is characterized by individuals not pro-acting, but instead being driven by ego-alien inner demands that often run counter to their consciously held desires.

Once an individual fully experiences a wish, he or she is faced with *decision*. Many individuals can be extremely clear about what they wish but still not be able to decide or to choose. Often they experience a decisional panic; they may attempt to delegate the decision to someone else, or they act in such a way that the decision is made for them by circumstances that they, unconsciously, have brought to pass.

*Isolation*    A third ultimate concern is isolation. It is important to differentiate *existential isolation* from other types of isolation. *Interpersonal isolation* refers to the gulf that exists between oneself and other people—a gulf that results from deficient social skills and psychopathology in the sphere of intimacy. *Intrapersonal isolation,* a term first introduced by Freud, refers to the fact that we are isolated from parts of ourselves. Enclaves of self (of experience, affect, desire) are dissociated out of awareness, and the goal of psychotherapy is to help the individual reclaim these split-off parts of self.

Existential isolation cuts beneath other forms of isolation. No matter how closely we relate to another individual, there remains a final unbridgeable gap. Each of us enters existence alone and must depart from it alone. Each individual in the dawn of consciousness created a primary self (*transcendental ego*) by permitting consciousness to curl back upon itself and to differentiate a self from the remainder of the world. Only after that does the individual, now "self-conscious," begin to constitute other selves. Beneath this act, as Mijuskovic (1979) notes, there is a fundamental loneliness; the individual cannot escape the knowledge that (1) he or she constitutes others and (2) he or she can never fully share his consciousness with others.

There is no stronger reminder of existential isolation than a confrontation with death. The individual who faces death invariably becomes acutely aware of isolation.

The third dynamic conflict is between the awareness of our fundamental isolation and the wish to be protected, to merge and to be part of a larger whole.

Fear of existential isolation (and the defenses against it) underlies a great deal of interpersonal psychopathology. This dynamic offers a powerful, parsimonious explanatory system for understanding many miscarried interpersonal relationships in which one *uses* another for some function rather than *relates* to the other out of caring for that person's being.

Although no relationship can eliminate isolation, it can be shared with another in such a way that the pain of isolation is assuaged. If one acknowledges one's isolated situation in existence and confronts it with resoluteness, one will be able to turn lovingly toward others. If, on the other hand, one is overcome with dread in the face of isolation, one will not be able to turn toward others but instead will use others as a shield against isolation. In such instances relationships will be out-of-joint miscarriages and distortions of what might have been authentic relationships.

Some individuals (and this is particularly true of individuals with a borderline personality disturbance) experience panic when they are alone that emanates from a dissolution of ego boundaries. These individuals begin to doubt their own existence and believe that they exist only in the presence of another, that they exist only so long as they are responded to or are thought about by another individual.

Many attempt to deal with isolation through *fusion:* they soften their ego boundaries and become part of another individual. They avoid personal growth and the sense of isolation that accompanies growth. Fusion underlies the experience of being in love. The wonderful thing about romantic love is that the lonely "I" disappears into the "we." Others may fuse with a group, a cause, a country, a project. To be like everyone else— to conform in dress, speech, and customs, to have no thoughts or feelings that are different—saves one from the isolation of the lonely self.

Compulsive sexuality is also a common response to terrifying isolation. Promiscuous sexual coupling offers a powerful but temporary respite for the lonely individual. It is temporary because it is only a caricature of a relationship. The sexually compulsive individual does not relate to the whole being of the other but relates only to the part of that individual that meets his or her need. Sexually compulsive individuals do not know their partners; they show and see only those parts that facilitate seduction and the sexual act.

*Meaninglessness*     The fourth ultimate concern is meaninglessness. If each person must die, and if each person constitutes his or her own world, and if each is alone in an indifferent universe, then what possible meaning can life have? Why do we live? How shall we live? If there is no preordained design in life, then we must construct our own meaning in life. The fundamental question then becomes, "Is it possible that a self-created meaning is sturdy enough to bear one's life?"

The human being appears to require meaning. Our perceptual neuropsychological organization is such that we instantaneously pattern random stimuli. We organize them automatically into figure and ground. When confronted with a broken circle, we automatically perceive it as complete. When any situation or set of stimuli defies patterning, we experience dysphoria, which persists until we fit the situation into a recognizable pattern. In the same way individuals organize random stimuli, so too do they face existential situations: In an unpatterned world an individual is acutely unsettled and searches for a pattern, an explanation, a meaning of existence.

A sense of meaning of life is necessary for still another reason: From a meaning schema we generate a hierarchy of values. Values provide us with a blueprint for life conduct; values tell us not only *why* we live but *how* to live.

The fourth internal conflict stems from this dilemma: *How does a being who requires meaning find meaning in a universe that has no meaning?*

## Variety of Concepts

The content of the internal conflict from the existential frame of reference consists of ultimate concerns and the conscious and unconscious fears and motives spawned by them. The dynamic existential approach retains Freud's basic dynamic *structure* but has a radically different *content.* The old Freudian formula of:

$$\text{DRIVE} \rightarrow \text{ANXIETY} \rightarrow \text{DEFENSE MECHANISM}$$

is replaced in the existential system by:

## AWARENESS OF ULTIMATE CONCERN → ANXIETY → DEFENSE MECHANISM[1]

Both psychoanalysis and the existential system place anxiety at the center of the dynamic structure. Anxiety fuels psychopathology: Conscious and unconscious psychic operations (i.e., defense mechanisms) are generated to deal with anxiety. These psychic operations constitute psychopathology: They provide safety, but they also restrict growth.

An important difference is that Freud's sequence begins with drive, whereas an existential framework begins with awareness. The existential frame of reference views the individual primarily as fearful and suffering rather than as driven.

To an existential therapist, anxiety springs from confrontation with death, groundlessness (freedom), isolation, and meaninglessness. The individual uses two types of defense mechanisms to cope with anxiety. The first, the conventional mechanisms of defense, thoroughly described by Sigmund Freud, Anna Freud, and Harry Stack Sullivan, defend the individual against anxiety regardless of source. The second are specific defenses that serve to cope with specific primary existential fears.

For example, consider the individual's defense mechanism for dealing with the anxiety emerging from awareness of death. Yalom (1981, p. 115) describes two major, specific intrapsychic defenses: an irrational belief in personal "specialness" and an irrational belief in the existence of an "ultimate rescuer." These defenses resemble delusions in that they are fixed, false beliefs. However, they are not delusions in the clinical sense, but are universally held irrational beliefs.

### Specialness

Individuals have deep, powerful beliefs in personal inviolability, invulnerability, and immortality. Although, at a rational level, we recognize the foolishness of these beliefs, nonetheless, at a deeply unconscious level, we believe that the ordinary laws of biology do not apply to us.

If this defense is weak or absent, then the individual manifests one of a number of clinical syndromes: for example, the narcissistic character, the compulsive workaholic consumed by a search for glory, the self-aggrandizing, paranoid individual. The crisis in the lives of these individuals occurs when their belief system is shattered and a sense of unprotected ordinariness intrudes. They frequently seek therapy when the defense of specialness is no longer able to ward off anxiety—for example, at times of severe illness or at the interruption of what had always appeared to be an eternal, upward spiral.

### The Belief in the Existence of an Ultimate Rescuer

The other major mechanism of defense that serves to block death awareness is our belief in a personal omnipotent servant who eternally guards and protects our welfare, who may let us get to the edge of the abyss but who will always bring us back. A hypertrophy of this particular defense mechanism results in a character structure displaying passivity, dependency, and obsequiousness. Often such individuals dedicate their lives to locating and appeasing an ultimate rescuer. In Silvano Arieti's terms, they live for the "dominant other" (1977, p. 864)—a life ideology that precedes and prepares the ground for clinical depression. These individuals may adapt well to life while basking in the presence of the

*[handwritten margin note: obsequiousness]*

---

[1] To Freud, anxiety is a signal of danger (i.e., if instinctual drives are permitted expression, the organism becomes endangered; either the ego is overwhelmed or retaliation by the environment is inevitable). The defense mechanisms restrict direct expression of drives but provide indirect expression—that is, in displaced, sublimated, or symbolic form.

dominant other, but they decompensate and experience extraordinary distress at the loss of this dominant other.

Another major difference between the existential dynamic approach and other dynamic approaches lies in temporal orientation. The existential therapist works in the present tense. The individual is to be understood and helped to understand himself or herself from the perspective of a here-and-now *cross-section,* not from the perspective of a historical *longitudinal section.* Consider the use of the word *deep.* Freud defines *deep* as "early," and so the deepest conflict meant the earliest conflict in the individual's life. Freud's psychodynamics are developmentally based. *Fundamental* and *primary* are to be grasped chronologically: Each is synonymous with "first." Thus, the fundamental sources of anxiety, for example, are considered to be the earliest calamities: separation and castration.

From the existential perspective, deep means the most fundamental concerns facing the individual at that moment. The past (i.e., one's memory of the past) is important only insofar as it is part of one's current existence and has contributed to one's current mode of facing ultimate concerns. The immediate, currently existing ground beneath all other ground is important from the existential perspective. Thus, the existential conception of personality is in the awareness of the depths of one's immediate experiences. Existential therapy does not attempt to excavate and understand the past; instead it is directed toward the future's becoming the present and explores the past only as it throws light on the present. The therapist must continually keep in mind that we create our past and that our present mode of existence dictates what we choose to remember of the past.

## PSYCHOTHERAPY

### Theory of Psychotherapy

A substantial proportion of practicing psychotherapists consider themselves existentially (or "humanistically") oriented. Yet few, if any, have received any systematic training in existential therapy. One can be reasonably certain of this because there are few comprehensive training programs in existential therapy. Although many excellent books illuminate some aspect of the existential frame of reference (Becker, 1973; Bugental, 1956; Koestenbaum, 1978; May, 1953, 1977; May et al., 1958), Yalom's book (1981) is the first to present a systematic, comprehensive view of the existential therapeutic approach.

Existential therapy is *not* a comprehensive psychotherapeutic system; it is a frame of reference—a paradigm by which one views and understands a patient's suffering in a particular manner.

Existential therapists begin with presuppositions about the sources of a patient's anguish and view the patient in human rather than behavioral or mechanistic terms. They may employ any of a large variety of techniques used in other approaches insofar as they are consistent with basic existential presuppositions and a human, authentic therapist-patient encounter.

The vast majority of experienced therapists, regardless of adherence to some particular ideological school, employ many existential insights and approaches. All competent therapists realize, for example, that an apprehension of one's finiteness can often catalyze a major inner shift of perspective, that it is the relationship that heals, that patients are tormented by choice, that a therapist must catalyze a patient's "will" to act, and that the majority of patients are bedeviled by a lack of meaning in their lives.

It is also true that the therapist's belief system determines the type of clinical data that he or she encounters. Therapists subtly or unconsciously cue patients to provide them with certain material. Jungian patients have Jungian dreams. Freudian patients discover themes of castration, anxiety, and penis envy. The therapist's perceptual system is affected by her or his ideological system. Thus, the therapist "tunes in" to the material that she or he wishes to obtain. So too with the existential approach. If the therapists tune their mental apparatus to the right channel, it is astounding how frequently patients discuss concerns emanating from existential conflicts.

The basic approach in existential therapy is strategically similar to other dynamic therapies. The therapist assumes that the patient experiences anxiety which issues from some existential conflict that is at least partially unconscious. The patient handles anxiety by a number of ineffective, maladaptive defense mechanisms that may provide temporary respite from anxiety but ultimately so cripple the individual's ability to live fully and creatively that these defenses merely result in still further secondary anxiety. The therapist assists the patient to embark on a course of self-investigation in which the goals are to understand the unconscious conflict, to identify the maladaptive defense mechanisms, to discover their destructive influence, to diminish secondary anxiety by correcting these heretofore restrictive modes of dealing with self and others, and to develop other ways of coping with primary anxiety.

Although the basic strategy in existential therapy is similar to other dynamic therapies, the content is radically different. In many respects, the process differs as well; the existential therapist's different mode of understanding the patient's basic dilemma results in many differences in the strategy of psychotherapy. For example, because the existential view of personality structure emphasizes the depth of experience at any given moment, the existential therapist does not spend a great deal of time helping the patient to recover the past. The existential therapist strives for an understanding of the patient's *current* life situation and *current* enveloping unconscious fears. The existential therapist believes, as do other dynamic therapists, that the nature of the therapist-client relationship is fundamental in good psychotherapeutic work. However, the accent is not upon transference but instead upon the relationship as fundamentally important in itself.

## Process of Psychotherapy

Each of the ultimate human concerns (death, freedom, isolation, and meaninglessness) has implications for the process of therapy. Let us examine the practical, therapeutic implications of the ultimate concern of freedom. A major component of freedom is *responsibility*—a concept that deeply influences the existential therapist's therapeutic approach.

Sartre equates responsibility to authorship: To be responsible means to be the author of one's own life design. The existential therapist continually focuses upon each patient's responsibility for his or her own distress. Bad genes or bad luck do not cause a patient to be lonely or chronically abused or neglected by others. Until patients realize that they are responsible for their own conditions, there is little motivation to change.

The therapist must identify methods and instances of responsibility avoidance and then make these known to the patient. Therapists may use a wide variety of techniques to focus the patient's attention on responsibility. Many therapists interrupt the patient whenever they hear the patient avoiding responsibility. When patients say they "can't" do something, the therapist immediately comments, "You mean you 'won't' do it." As long as one believes in "can't," one remains unaware of one's active contribution to one's situation. Such therapists encourage patients to *own* their feelings, statements, and actions. If a patient comments that he or she did something "unconsciously," the therapist might inquire, "Whose unconscious is it?" The general principle is obvious: Whenever the patient laments about his or her life situation, the therapist inquires how the patient created that situation.

Often it is helpful to keep the patient's initial complaints in mind and then, at appropriate points in therapy, juxtapose these initial complaints with the patient's in-therapy behavior. For example, consider a patient who sought therapy because of feelings of isolation and loneliness. During the course of therapy the patient expressed at great length his sense of superiority and his scorn and disdain of others. These attitudes were rigidly maintained; the patient manifested great resistance to examining, much less changing, these opinions. The therapist helped this patient to understand his responsibility for his personal predicament by reminding the patient, whenever he discussed his scorn of others, "And you are lonely."

Responsibility is one component of freedom. Earlier we described another, *willing,* which may be further subdivided into *wishing* and *deciding.* Consider the role of *wishing.* How often does the therapist participate with a patient in some such sequence as this:

"What shall I do? What shall I do?"

"What is it that stops you from doing what you want to do?"

"But I don't *know* what I want to do! If I knew that, I wouldn't need to see you!"

These patients actually know what they should do, ought to do, or must do, but they do not experience what they *want* to do. Many therapists, in working with patients who have a profound incapacity to wish, have shared May's inclination to shout "Don't you ever *want* anything?" (1969, p. 165). These patients have enormous social difficulties because they have no opinions, no inclinations, and no desires of their own.

Often the inability to wish is imbedded in a more global disorder—the inability to feel. In many cases, the bulk of psychotherapy consists of helping patients to dissolve their affect blocks. This therapy is slow and grinding. Above all, the therapist must persevere and, time after time, must continue to press the patient with, "What do you feel?" "What do you want?" Repeatedly the therapist will need to explore the source and nature of the block and of the stifled feelings behind it.

The inability to feel and to wish is a pervasive characterological trait, and considerable time and therapeutic perseverance are required to effect enduring change.

There are other modes of avoiding wishing in addition to blocking of affect. Some individuals avoid wishing by not discriminating among wishes, by acting impulsively on all wishes. In such instances, the therapist must help the patient to make some internal discrimination among wishes and assign priorities to each. The patient must learn that two wishes which are mutually exclusive demand that one be relinquished. If, for example, a meaningful, loving relationship is a wish, then a host of conflicting interpersonal wishes—such as the wish for conquest or power or seduction or subjugation—must be denied.

*Decision* is the bridge between wishing and action. Some patients, even though they are able to wish, are still unable to act because they cannot *decide.* One of the more common reasons that deciding is difficult is that every yes involves a no. Renunciation invariably accompanies decision, and a decision requires a relinquishment of other options—often options that may never come again. There are other patients who cannot decide because a major decision makes them more aware of the degree to which they constitute their own lives. Thus, a major, irreversible decision is a boundary situation in the same way that awareness of death may be a boundary situation.

The therapist must help patients make choices. The therapist must help patients recognize that they themselves, not the therapist, must generate and choose among options. In helping patients to communicate effectively, therapists teach that one must *own* one's feelings. It is equally important that one owns one's decisions. Some patients are panicked by the various implications of each decision. The "what ifs" torment them. *What if I leave my job and can't find another? What if I leave my children alone and they get hurt?* It is often useful to ask the patient to consider the entire scenario of each "what if" in turn, to fantasize it happening with all the possible ramifications, and then to experience and analyze emerging feelings.

A general posture toward decision making is to assume that the therapist's task is not to *create* will but instead to *disencumber* it. The therapist cannot flick the decision switch or inspirit the patient with resoluteness. But the therapist can influence the factors that influence willing. After all, no one has a congenital inability to decide. Decision making is blocked by obstacles, and it is the therapist's task to help move obstacles. Once that is done, the individual will naturally move into a more autonomous position in just the way, as Karen Horney (1950) put it, an acorn develops into an oak tree.

The therapist must help patients understand that decisions are unavoidable. One makes decisions all the time and often conceals from oneself the fact that one is deciding. It is important to help patients understand the inevitability of decisions and to identify how they make decisions. Many patients decide *passively* by, for example, letting another person decide for them. They may terminate an unsatisfactory relationship by unconsciously acting in such a way that the partner makes the decision to leave. In such instances the final outcome is achieved, but the patient may be left with many negative repercussions. The patient's sense of powerlessness is merely reinforced and he or she continues to experience himself or herself as one to whom things happen rather than as the author of his or her own life situation. The *way* one makes a decision is often as important as the content of the decision. An active decision reinforces the individual's active acceptance of his or her own power and resources.

## Mechanisms of Psychotherapy

We can best understand the mechanisms of the existential approach by considering the therapeutic leverage inherent in some of the ultimate concerns.

### Death and Psychotherapy

There are two distinct ways in which the concept of death plays an important role in psychotherapy. First, an increased awareness of one's finiteness stemming from a personal confrontation with death may cause a radical shift in life perspective and lead to personal change. Second, the concept that death is a primary source of anxiety has many important implications for therapy.

*Death as a Boundary Situation*   A *boundary situation* is a type of urgent experience that propels the individual into a confrontation with an existential situation. The most powerful boundary situation is confrontation with one's personal death. Such a confrontation has the power to provide a massive shift in the way one lives in the world. Some patients report that they learn simply that "existence cannot be postponed." They no longer postpone living until some time in the future; they realize that one can really live only in the present. The neurotic individual rarely lives in the present but is either continuously obsessed with events from the past or fearful of anticipated events in the future.

A confrontation with a boundary situation persuades individuals to count their blessings, to become aware of their natural surroundings: the elemental facts of life, changing seasons, seeing, listening, touching, and loving. Ordinarily what we *can* experience is diminished by petty concerns, by thoughts of what we cannot do or what we lack, or by threats to our prestige.

Many terminally ill patients, when reporting personal growth emanating from their confrontation with death, have lamented, "What a tragedy that we had to wait till now, till our bodies were riddled with cancer, to learn these truths." This is an exceedingly important message for therapists. The therapist can obtain considerable leverage to help "everyday" patients (i.e., patients who are not physically ill) increase their awareness of

*Teaching children*

death earlier in their life cycle. With this aim in mind, some therapists have employed structured exercises to confront the individual with personal death. Some group leaders begin a brief group experience by asking members to write their own epitaph or obituary, or they provide guided fantasies in which group members imagine their own death and funeral.

Many existential therapists do not believe that artificially introduced death confrontations are necessary or advisable. Instead they attempt to help the patient recognize the signs of mortality that are part of the fabric of everyday life. If the therapist and the patient are "tuned-in," there is considerable evidence of death anxiety in every psychotherapy. Every patient suffers losses through death of parents, friends, and associates. Dreams are haunted with death anxiety. Every nightmare is a dream of raw death anxiety. Everywhere around us are reminders of aging: Our bones begin to creak, age spots appear on our skin, we go to reunions and note with dismay how everyone *else* has aged. Our children grow up. The cycle of life envelops us.

An important opportunity for confrontation with death arises when patients experience the death of someone close to them. The traditional literature on grief primarily focuses on two aspects of grief work: loss and the resolution of ambivalence that so strongly accentuates the dysphoria of grief. But a third dimension must be considered: The death of someone close to us confronts us with our own death.

Often grief has a very different tone, depending upon the individual's relationship with the person who has died. The loss of a parent confronts us with our vulnerability: If our parents could not save themselves, who will save us? When parents die, nothing remains between ourselves and the grave. At the moment of our parents' death, we ourselves constitute the barrier between our children and their death.

The death of a spouse often evokes the fear of existential isolation. The loss of the significant other increases our awareness that, try as hard as we can to go through the world two by two, there is nonetheless a basic aloneness we must bear. Yalom reports a patient's dream the night after learning that his wife had inoperable cancer.

> I was living in my old house in _____ [a house that had been in the family for three generations]. A Frankenstein monster was chasing me through the house. I was terrified. The house was deteriorating, decaying. The tiles were crumbling and the roof leaking. Water leaked all over my mother. [His mother had died six months earlier.] I fought with him. I had a choice of weapons. One had a curved blade with a handle, like a scythe. I slashed him and tossed him off the roof. He lay stretched out on the pavement below. But he got up and once again started chasing me through the house. (1981, p. 168)

The patient's first association to this dream was "I know I've got a hundred thousand miles on me." Obviously his wife's impending death reminded him that his life and his body (symbolized in the dream by the deteriorating house) were also finite. As a child this patient was often haunted by the monster who returned in this nightmare.

Children try many methods of dealing with death anxiety. One of the most common is the personification of death—imagining death as some finite creature: a monster, a sandman, a bogeyman, and so on. This is very frightening to children but nonetheless far less frightening than the truth—that they carry the spores of their own death within them. If death is "out there" in some physical form, then possibly it may be eluded, tricked, or pacified.

Milestones provide another opportunity for the therapist to focus the patient on existential facts of life. Even simple milestones, such as birthdays and anniversaries, are useful levers. These signs of passage are often capable of eliciting pain (consequently, we often deal with such milestones by reaction formation, in the form of a joyous celebration).

*Reaction formation*

Major life events, such as a threat to one's career, a severe illness, retirement, commitment to a relationship, and separation from a relationship, are important boundary situations and offer opportunities for an increased awareness of death anxiety. Often these experiences are painful, and therapists feel compelled to focus entirely on pain alleviation. In so doing, however, they miss rich opportunities for deep therapeutic work that reveal themselves at those moments.

*Death as a Primary Source of Anxiety*   The fear of death constitutes a primary fount of anxiety: It is present early in life, it is instrumental in shaping character structure, and it continues throughout life to generate anxiety that results in manifest distress and the erection of psychological defenses. However, it is important to keep in mind that death anxiety exists at the very deepest levels of being, is heavily repressed, and is rarely experienced in its full sense. Often death anxiety per se is not easily visible in the clinical picture. There are patients, however, who are suffused with overt death anxiety at the very onset of therapy. There are often life situations in which the patient has such a rush of death anxiety that the therapist cannot evade the issue. In long-term, intensive therapy, explicit death anxiety is always to be found and must be considered in the therapeutic work.

In the existential framework, anxiety is so riveted to existence that it has a different connotation from the way anxiety is regarded in other frames of reference. The existential therapist hopes to alleviate crippling levels of anxiety but not to eliminate it. Life cannot be lived (nor can death be faced) without anxiety. The therapist's task, as May reminds us (1977, p. 374), is to reduce anxiety to tolerable levels and then to use the anxiety constructively.

It is important to keep in mind that, even though death anxiety may not explicitly enter the therapeutic dialogue, a theory of anxiety based on death awareness may provide therapists with a frame of reference that greatly enhances their effectiveness. Therapists, as well as patients, seek to order events into some coherent sequence. Once that is done, the therapist begins to experience a sense of control and mastery that allows organization of clinical material. The therapist's self-confidence and sense of mastery will help patients develop trust and confidence in the therapy process.

The therapist's belief system provides a certain consistency. It permits the therapist to know what to explore so that the patient does not become confused.

The therapist may, with subtlety and good timing, make comments that at an unspoken level click with the patient's unconscious and allow the patient to feel understood.

## Existential Isolation and Psychotherapy

Patients discover in therapy that interpersonal relationships may temper isolation but cannot eliminate it. Patients who grow in psychotherapy learn not only the rewards of intimacy but also its limits: They learn what they *cannot* get from others. An important step in treatment consists of helping patients address existential isolation directly. Those who lack sufficient experiences of closeness and true relatedness in their lives are particularly incapable of tolerating isolation. Otto Will[2] made the point that adolescents from loving, supportive families are able to grow away from their families with relative ease and to tolerate the separation and loneliness of young adulthood. On the other hand, those who grow up in tormented, highly conflicted families find it extremely difficult to leave the family. The more disturbed the family, the harder it is for children to leave—they are ill equipped to separate and therefore cling to the family for shelter against isolation and anxiety.

[2] Oral communication. Child psychiatry grand rounds. Stanford University, Department of Psychiatry, 1978.

Many patients have enormous difficulty spending time alone. Consequently they construct their lives in such a way that they eliminate alone time. One of the major problems that ensues from this is the desperation with which they seek certain kinds of relationships and use others to avoid some of the pain accompanying isolation. The therapist must find a way to help the patient confront isolation in a dosage and with a support system suited to that patient. Some therapists, at an advanced stage of therapy, advise periods of self-enforced isolation during which the patient is asked to monitor and record thoughts and feelings.

## Meaninglessness and Psychotherapy

To deal effectively with meaninglessness, therapists must first increase their sensitivity to the topic, listen differently, and become aware of the importance of meaning in the lives of individuals. For some patients the issue of meaninglessness is profound and pervasive. Carl Jung once estimated that more than 30 percent of his patients sought therapy because of a sense of personal meaninglessness (1966, p. 83).

The therapist must be attuned to the overall focus and direction of the patient's life. Is the patient reaching beyond himself or herself? Or is he or she entirely immersed in the daily routine of staying alive? Yalom (1981) reported that his therapy was rarely successful unless he was able to help patients focus on something beyond these pursuits. Simply by increasing their sensitivity to these issues, the therapist can help them focus on values outside themselves. Therapists, for example, can begin to wonder about the patient's belief systems, inquire deeply into the loving of another, ask about long-range hopes and goals, and explore creative interests and pursuits.

Viktor Frankl, who placed great emphasis on the importance of meaninglessness in contemporary psychopathology, stated that "happiness cannot be pursued, it can only ensue" (1969, p. 165).

The more we deliberately search for self-satisfaction, the more it eludes us, whereas the more we fulfill some self-transcendent meaning, the more happiness will ensue.

Therapists must find a way to help self-centered patients develop curiosity and concern for others. The therapy group is especially well suited for this endeavor: The pattern in which self-absorbed, narcissistic patients take without giving often becomes highly evident in the therapy group. In such instances therapists may attempt to increase an individual's ability and inclination to empathize with others by requesting, periodically, that patients guess how others are feeling at various junctures of the group.

But the major solution to the problem of meaninglessness is engagement. Wholehearted engagement in any of the infinite array of life's activities enhances the possibility of one's patterning the events of one's life in some coherent fashion. To find a home, to care about other individuals and about ideas or projects, to search, to create, to build—all forms of engagement are twice rewarding: They are intrinsically enriching, and they alleviate the dysphoria that stems from being bombarded with the unassembled brute data of existence.

The therapist must approach engagement with the same attitudinal set used with wishing. The desire to engage life is always there with the patient, and therefore the therapist's activity should be directed toward the removal of obstacles in the patient's way. The therapist begins to explore what prevents the patient from loving another individual. Why is there so little satisfaction from his or her relationships with others? Why is there so little satisfaction from work? What blocks the patient from finding work commensurate with his or her talents and interests or finding some pleasurable aspects of current work? Why has the patient neglected creative or religious or self-transcendent strivings?

# APPLICATIONS

## Problems

The clinical setting often determines the applicability of the existential approach. In each course of therapy, the therapist must consider the goals appropriate to the clinical setting. To take one example, in an acute inpatient setting where the patient will be hospitalized for approximately one to two weeks, the goal of therapy is crisis intervention. The therapist hopes to alleviate symptoms and to restore the patient to a precrisis level of functioning. Deeper, more ambitious goals are unrealistic and inappropriate to that situation.

In situations where patients desire not only symptomatic relief but also hope to attain greater personal growth, the existential approach is generally useful. A thorough existential approach with ambitious goals is most appropriate in long-term therapy, but even in briefer approaches some aspect of the existential mode (e.g., an emphasis on responsibility, deciding, an authentic therapist-patient encounter, grief work, and so on) is often incorporated into the therapy.

An existential approach to therapy is appropriate with patients who confront some boundary situation—that is, a confrontation with death, the facing of some important irreversible decision, a sudden thrust into isolation, milestones that mark passages from one life era into another. But therapy need not be limited to these explicit existential crises. In every course of therapy, there is abundant evidence of patients' anguish stemming from existential conflicts. The availability of such data is entirely a function of the therapist's attitudinal set and perceptivity. The decision to work on these levels should be a joint patient-therapist decision.

## Evaluation

Psychotherapy evaluation is always a difficult task. The more focused and specific the approach and the goals, the easier it is to measure outcome. Symptomatic relief or behavioral change may be quantified with reasonable precision. But more ambitious therapies, which seek to affect deeper layers of the individual's mode of being in the world, defy quantification. These problems of evaluation are illustrated by the following vignettes reported by Yalom (1981, p. 336).

A 46-year-old mother accompanied the youngest of her four children to the airport, from which he departed for college. She had spent the last 26 years rearing her children and longing for this day. No more impositions, no more incessantly living for others, no more cooking dinners and picking up clothes. Finally she was free.

Yet as she said good-bye she unexpectedly began sobbing loudly, and on the way home from the airport a deep shudder passed through her body. "It is only natural," she thought. It was only the sadness of saying good-bye to someone she loved very much. But it was much more than that, and the shudder soon turned into raw anxiety. The therapist whom she consulted identified it as a common problem: the empty-nest syndrome. Of course she was anxious. How could it be otherwise? For years she had based her self-esteem on her performance as a mother and suddenly she found no way to validate herself. The whole routine and structure of her life had been altered. Gradually, with the help of Valium, supportive psychotherapy, an assertiveness training group, several adult education courses, a lover or two, and a part-time volunteer job, the shudder shrunk to a tremble and then vanished. She returned to her premorbid level of comfort and adaptation.

This patient happened to be part of a psychotherapy research project, and there were outcome measures of her psychotherapy. Her treatment results could be described as excellent on each of the measures used—symptom checklists, target problem evaluation, and self-esteem. Obviously she had made considerable improvement. Yet, despite this, it is entirely possible to consider this case as one of missed therapeutic opportunities.

Consider another patient in almost precisely the same life situation. In the treatment of this second patient the therapist, who was existentially oriented, attempted to nurse the shudder rather than to anesthetize it. This patient experienced what Kierkegaard called "creative anxiety." The therapist and the patient allowed the anxiety to lead them into important areas for investigation. True, the patient suffered from the empty-nest syndrome; she had problems of self-esteem; she loved her child but also envied him for the chances in life she had never had; and, of course, she felt guilty because of these "ignoble" sentiments.

The therapist did not simply allow her to find ways to help her fill her time but plunged into an exploration of the *meaning* of the fear of the empty nest. She had always desired freedom but now seemed terrified of it. Why?

A dream illuminated the meaning of the shudder. The dream consisted simply of herself holding in her hand a 35-mm photographic slide of her son juggling and tumbling. The slide was peculiar, however, in that it showed movement; she saw her son in a multitude of positions all at the same time. In the analysis of the dream her associations revolved around the theme of time. The slide captured and framed time and movement. It kept everything alive but made everything stand still. It froze life. "Time moves on," she said, "and there's no way I can stop it. I didn't want John to grow up . . . whether I like it or not time moves on. It moves on for John and it moves on for me as well."

This dream brought her own finiteness into clear focus and, rather than rush to fill time with various distractions, she learned to appreciate time in richer ways than previously. She moved into the realm that Heidegger described as authentic being: She wondered not so much at the *way* things are but *that* things are. Although one could argue that therapy helped the second patient more than the first, it would not be possible to demonstrate this conclusion on any standard outcome measures. In fact, the second patient probably continued to experience more anxiety than the first did; but anxiety is a part of existence and no individual who continues to grow and create will ever be free of it.

## Treatment

Existential therapy has its primary applications in an individual therapy setting. However, various existential themes and insights may be successfully applied in a variety of other settings including group therapy, family therapy, couples therapy, and so forth.

The concept of responsibility has particularly widespread applicability. It is a keystone of the group therapeutic process. Group therapy is primarily based on interpersonal therapy; the group therapeutic format is an ideal arena in which to examine and correct maladaptive interpersonal modes of behavior. However, the theme of responsibility underlies much interpersonal work. Consider, for example, the following sequence through which group therapists, explicitly or implicitly, attempt to guide their patients:

1. *Patients learn how their behavior is viewed by others.* (Through feedback from other group members, patients learn to see themselves through others' eyes.)

2. *Patients learn how their behavior makes others feel.* (Members share their personal affective responses to one another.)

3. *Patients learn how their behavior creates the opinions others have of them.* (By sharing here-and-now feelings, members learn that, as a result of their behavior, others develop certain opinions and views of them.)

4.  *Patients learn how their behavior influences their opinions of themselves.* (The information gathered in the first three steps leads to the patient formulating certain kinds of self-evaluations.)

Each of these four steps begins with the patients' own behavior, which underscores their role in shaping interpersonal relations. The end point of this sequence is that group members begin to understand that they are responsible for how others treat them and for the way in which they regard themselves.

This is one of the most fascinating aspects of group therapy: All members are "born" simultaneously. Each starts out on an equal footing. Each gradually scoops out and shapes a particular life space in the group. Thus, each person is responsible for the interpersonal position he or she scoops out for himself in the group (and in life). The therapeutic work in the group then not only allows individuals to change their way of relating to one another but also brings home to them in a powerful way the extent to which they have created their own life predicament—clearly an existential therapeutic mechanism.

Often the therapist uses his or her own feelings to identify the patient's contribution to his or her life predicament. For example, a depressed 48-year-old woman complained bitterly about the way her children treated her: They dismissed her opinions, were impatient with her, and, when some serious issue was at stake, addressed their comments to their father. When the therapist tuned in to his feelings about this patient, he became aware of a whining quality in her voice that tempted *him* not to take her seriously and to regard her somewhat as a child. He shared his feelings with the patient, and it proved enormously useful to her. She became aware of her childlike behavior in many areas and began to realize that her children treated her precisely as she "asked" to be treated.

Not infrequently, therapists must treat patients who are panicked by a decisional crisis. Yalom (1981) describes one therapeutic approach in such a situation. The therapist's basic strategy consisted of helping the patient uncover and appreciate the existential implications of the decision. The patient was a 66-year-old widow who sought therapy because of her anguish about a decision to sell a summer home. The house required constant attention to gardening, maintenance, and protection and seemed a considerable burden to a frail elderly woman in poor health. Finances affected the decision as well, and she asked many financial and realty consultants to assist her in making the decision.

The therapist and the patient explored many factors involved in the decision and then gradually began to explore more deeply. Soon a number of painful issues emerged. For example, her husband had died a year ago and she mourned him yet. The house was still rich with his presence, and drawers and closets brimmed with his personal effects. A decision to sell the house also required a decision to come to terms with the fact that her husband would never return. She considered her house as her "drawing card" and harbored serious doubts whether anyone would visit her without the enticement of her lovely estate. Thus, a decision to sell the house meant testing the loyalty of her friends and risking loneliness and isolation. Yet another reason centered on the great tragedy of her life—her childlessness. She had always envisioned the estate passing on to her children and to her children's children. The decision to sell the house thus was a decision to acknowledge the failure of her major symbolic immortality project. The therapist used the house-selling decision as a springboard to these deeper issues and eventually helped the patient mourn her husband, herself, and her unborn children.

Once the deeper meanings of a decision are worked through, the decision generally glides easily into place, and after approximately a dozen sessions the patient effortlessly made the decision to sell the house.

Existentially oriented therapists strive toward honest, mutually open relationships with their patients. The patient-therapist relationship helps the patient clarify other relationships. Patients almost invariably distort some aspect of their relationship to the therapist. The therapist, drawing from self-knowledge and experience of how others view him or her, is able to help the patient distinguish distortion from reality.

The experience of an intimate encounter with a therapist has implications that extend beyond relationships with other people. For one thing, the therapist is generally someone whom the patient particularly respects. But even more important, the therapist is someone, often the only one, who *really* knows the patient. To tell someone else all one's darkest secrets and still to be fully accepted by that person is enormously affirmative.

Existential thinkers such as Erich Fromm, Abraham Maslow, and Martin Buber all stress that true caring for another means to care about the other's growth and to want to bring something to life in the other. Buber uses the term *unfolding,* which he suggests should be the way of the educator and the therapist: One uncovers what was there all along. The term *unfolding* has rich connotations and stands in sharp contrast to the goals of other therapeutic systems. One helps the patient unfold by *meeting,* by existential communication. The therapist is, in Sequin's terms, a "possibilitator" (1965, p. 123).

Perhaps the most important concept of all in describing the patient-therapist relationship is what May et al. term *presence* (1958, p. 80). The therapist must be fully present, striving for an authentic encounter with the patient.

## CASE EXAMPLE

### A Simple Case of Divorce

A 50-year-old scientist, whom we will call David, had been married for 27 years and had recently decided to separate from his wife. He applied for therapy because of the degree of anxiety he was experiencing in anticipation of confronting his wife with his decision.

The situation was in many ways a typical midlife scenario. The patient had two children; the youngest had just graduated from college. In David's mind the children had always been the main element binding him and his wife together. Now that the children were self-supporting and fully adult, David felt there was no reasonable point in continuing the marriage. He reported that he had been dissatisfied with his marriage for many years and on three previous occasions had separated from his wife, but, after only a few days, had become anxious and returned, crestfallen, to his home. Bad as the marriage was, David concluded that it was less unsatisfactory than the loneliness of being single.

The reason for his dissatisfaction with his marriage was primarily boredom. He had met his wife when he was 17, a time when he had been extremely insecure, especially in his relationships with women. She was the first woman who had ever expressed interest in him. David (as well as his wife) came from a blue-collar family. He was exceptionally intellectually gifted and was the first member of his family to attend college. He won a scholarship to an Ivy League school, obtained two graduate degrees, and embarked upon an outstanding academic research career. His wife was not gifted intellectually, chose not to go to college, and during the early years of their marriage worked to support David in graduate school.

For most of their married life his wife immersed herself in the task of caring for the children while David ferociously pursued his professional career. He had always experienced his relationship to his wife as empty and had always felt bored with her company. In his view she had an extremely mediocre mind and was so restricted characterologically that he found it constraining to be alone with her and embarrassing to share her with friends. He experienced himself as continually changing and growing, whereas his wife, in his opinion, had become increasingly rigid and unreceptive to new ideas.

The prototypic scenario of the male in midlife crisis seeking a divorce was made complete by the presence of the "other woman"—an intelligent, vivacious, attractive woman 15 years younger than himself.

David's therapy was long and complex, and several existential themes emerged during the course of therapy.

Responsibility was an important issue in his decision to leave his wife. First, there is the moral sense of responsibility. After all, his wife gave birth to and raised his children and had supported him through graduate school. He and his wife were at an age where he was far more "marketable" than she; that is, he had significantly higher earning power and was biologically able to father children. What moral responsibility, then, did he have to his wife?

David had a high moral sense and would, for the rest of his life, torment himself with this question. It had to be explored in therapy, and, consequently, the therapist confronted him explicitly with the issue of moral responsibility during David's decision-making process. The most effective mode of dealing with this anticipatory dysphoria was to leave no stone unturned in his effort to improve and, thus, to save the marriage.

The therapist helped David examine the question of his responsibility for the failure of the marriage. To what degree was he responsible for his wife's mode of being with him? For example, the therapist noted that he himself felt somewhat intimidated by David's quick, facile mind: The therapist also was aware of a concern about being criticized or judged by David. How judgmental was David? Was it not possible that he squelched his wife, that he might have helped his wife to develop greater flexibility, spontaneity, and self-awareness?

The therapist also helped David explore another major issue. Was he displacing onto the marriage dissatisfaction that belonged elsewhere in his life? A dream pointed the way toward some important dynamics:

> I had a problem with liquefaction of earth near my pool. John [a friend who was dying from cancer] sinks into the ground. It was like quicksand. I used a giant power auger to drill down into the quicksand. I expect to find some kind of void under the ground but instead I found a concrete slab five to six feet down. On the slab I found a receipt of money someone had paid me for $501. I was very anxious in the dream about that receipt since it was greater than it should have been.

One of the major themes of this dream had to do with death and aging. First, there was the theme of his friend who had cancer. David attempted to find his friend by using a giant auger. In the dream, David experienced a great sense of mastery and power during the drilling. The symbol of the auger seemed clearly phallic and initiated a profitable exploration of sexuality—David had always been sexually driven, and the dream illuminated how he used sex (and especially sex with a young woman) as a mode of gaining mastery over aging and death. Finally, he is surprised to find a concrete slab (which elicited associations of morgues, tombs, and tombstones).

He was intrigued by the numerical figures in the dream (the slab was "five to six feet" down and the receipt was for precisely $501). In his associations David made the interesting observation that he was 50 years old and the night of the dream was his 51st birthday. Though he did not consciously dwell on his age, the dream made it clear that at an unconscious level he had considerable concern about being over 50. Along with the slab that was between five and six feet deep and the receipt that was just over $500, there was his considerable concern in the dream about the amount cited in the receipt being too great. On a conscious level he denied his aging.

If David's major distress stemmed from his growing awareness of his aging and diminishment, then a precipitous separation from his wife might have represented an attempt to solve the wrong problem. Consequently, the therapist helped David plunge into a thorough exploration of his feelings about his aging and his mortality. The therapist's view was that only by fully dealing with these issues would he be more able to ascertain the true extent of the marital difficulties. The therapist and David explored these issues over several months. He attempted to deal more honestly with his wife than before, and soon he and his wife made arrangements to see a marital therapist for several months.

After these steps were taken, David and his wife decided that there was nothing salvageable in the marriage and they separated. The months following his separation were exceedingly difficult. The therapist provided support during this time but did not try to help David eliminate his anxiety; instead, he attempted to help David use his anxiety in a constructive fashion. David's inclination was to rush into an immediate second marriage, whereas the therapist persistently urged him to look at the fear of isolation that on each previous separation had sent him back to his wife. It was important now to be certain that fear did not propel him into an immediate second marriage.

David found it difficult to heed this advice because he felt so much in love with the new woman in his life. The state of being "in love" is one of the great experiences in life. In therapy, however, being in love raises many problems; the pull of romantic love is so great that it engulfs even the most well-directed therapeutic endeavors. David found his new partner to be the ideal woman, no other woman existed for him, and he attempted to spend all his time with her. When with her he experienced a state of continual bliss: All aspects of the lonely "I" vanished, leaving only a very blissful state of "we-ness."

What finally made it possible for David to work in therapy was that his new friend became somewhat frightened by the power of his embrace. Only then was he willing to look at his extreme fear of being alone and his reflex desire to merge with a woman. Gradually he became desensitized to being alone. He observed his feelings, kept a journal of them, and worked hard on them in therapy. He noted, for example, that Sundays were the worst time. He had an extremely demanding professional schedule and had no difficulties during the week. Sundays were times of extreme anxiety. He became aware that part of that anxiety was that he had to take care of himself on Sunday. If he wanted to do something, he himself had to schedule the activity. He could no longer rely on that being done for him by his wife. He discovered that an important function of ritual in culture and the heavy scheduling in his own life was to conceal the void, the total lack of structure beneath him.

These observations led him, in therapy, to face his need to be cared for and shielded. The fears of isolation and freedom buffeted him for several months, but gradually he learned how to be alone in the world and what it meant to be responsible for his own being. In short, he learned how to be his own mother and father—always a major therapeutic objective of psychotherapy.

## SUMMARY

Existential psychotherapy perceives the patient as an existing, immediate person, not as a composite of drives, archetypes, or conditioning. Instinctual drives and history are obviously present, but they come into existential therapy only as parts of the living, struggling, feeling, thinking human being in unique conflicts and with hopes, fears, and relationships. Existential therapy emphasizes that normal anxiety and guilt are present in all of life and that only the neurotic forms of these need to be changed in therapy. The person can be freed from neurotic anxiety and guilt only as he or she recognizes normal anxiety and guilt at the same time.

The original criticism of existential therapy as "too philosophical" has lessened as people recognize that all effective psychotherapy has philosophical implications.

Existential therapy is concerned with the "I-Am" (being) experience, the culture (world) in which a patient lives, the significance of time, and the aspect of consciousness called transcendence.

Karl Jaspers put his finger on the harmfulness of a therapist's lack of presence and of its importance: "What we are missing! What opportunities of understanding we let pass

archetypes

by because at a single, decisive moment we were, with all our knowledge, lacking in the simple virtue of *a full human presence!*" It is this presence that existential therapy seeks to cultivate.

The central aim of the founders of existential psychotherapy was that its emphases would influence therapy of all schools. That this has been occurring is quite clear.

The depth of existential ideas is shown in what is called the existential neurosis. This refers to the condition of the person who feels life is meaningless.

Existential therapy always sees the patient in the center of his or her own culture. Most people's problems are now loneliness, isolation, and alienation.

Our present age is one of disintegration of cultural and historical mores, of love and marriage, the family, the inherited religions, and so forth. This disintegration is the reason psychotherapy of all sorts has burgeoned in the twentieth century; people cried for help for their multitudinous problems. Thus, the existential emphasis on different aspects of the world (environment, social world, and subjective world) will, in all likelihood, become increasingly important. It is predicted that the existential approach in therapy will then become more widely used.

## ANNOTATED BIBLIOGRAPHY

May, R. (1977). *The meaning of anxiety* (rev. ed.). New York: Norton. (First edition published in 1950.)
A discussion of the prevalence of anxiety in the twentieth century and its roots in philosophy, biology, psychology, and modern culture, this is the first book written in America on the central theme of anxiety and the third book in history on this topic. The others were written by Sigmund Freud and Søren Kierkegaard. *The Meaning of Anxiety* was the first firm presentation of anxiety as a normal as well as a neurotic condition, and it argues that normal anxiety has constructive uses in human survival and human creativity.

Yalom, I. D. (1980). *Existential psychotherapy*. New York: Basic Books.
This volume offers a comprehensive clinical overview of the field of existential psychotherapy. A major task of the book is to build a bridge between theory and clinical application. It posits that psychopathology issues from the individual's confrontation with the ultimate concerns of death, freedom, isolation, and meaninglessness and explores the implications of each ultimate concern for the practice of psychotherapy.

Yalom, I. D. (1989). *Love's executioner and other tales of psychotherapy*. New York: Basic Books.
This collection of stories is based on cases of existential therapy and gives an intimate view of the clinical application of existential therapeutic principles and techniques.

Yalom, I. D. (1991). *When Nietzsche wept*. New York: Basic Books.
This teaching novel examines a thought experiment: What might have happened if Nietzsche had turned his attention to the invention of a psychotherapy based on his own published philosophical insights?

Yalom, I. D. (2001). *The gift of therapy: An open letter to a new generation of therapists*. New York: Harper Collins.
This book encapsulates Irvin Yalom's thoughts on psychotherapy after a lifetime of practice.

## CASE READINGS

Binswanger, L. (1958). The case of Ellen West. In R. May, E. Angel, & H. Ellenberger (Eds.), *Existence: A new dimension in psychology and psychiatry* (pp. 237–364). New York: Basic Books.

This is a classic case of considerable historical importance. It should be read by all serious students of psychotherapy.

Holt, H. (1966). The case of Father M: A segment of an existential analysis. *Journal of Existentialism, 6,* 369–495. [Also in D. Wedding & R. J. Corsini (Eds.). (1979). *Great cases in psychotherapy.* Itasca, IL: F. E. Peacock.]

This is a well-written case study that offers insight into the manner in which an existential analysis might unfold.

May, R. (1973). Black and impotent: The life of Mercedes. In *Power and innocence* (pp. 81–97). New York: Norton. [Reprinted in D. Wedding & R. J. Corsini (Eds.). (1995). *Case studies in psychotherapy.* Itasca, IL: F. E. Peacock.]

This brief case history illustrates the existential treatment by Rollo May of a young black woman dealing with core issues of power and self-esteem.

Yalom, I. (1989). Fat lady. In *Love's executioner and other tales of psychotherapy* (pp. 87–117). New York: Basic Books. [Reprinted in D. Wedding & R. J. Corsini (Eds.). (2005). *Case studies in psychotherapy.* Belmont, CA: Wadsworth.]

This provocative case study illustrates the problem all therapists confront as they attempt to cope with countertransference. Yalom is quite open about his revulsion and antipathy for obese people, and this case helps students appreciate how even very experienced therapists continue to grow professionally and personally.

# REFERENCES

Arieti, S. (1977). Psychotherapy of severe depression. *American Journal of Psychiatry, 134,* 864–868.

Becker, E. (1973). *Denial of death.* New York: Free Press.

Binswanger, L. (1956). Existential analysis and psychotherapy. In E. Fromm-Reichmann & J. L. Moreno (Eds.), *Progress in psychotherapy* (pp. 144–168). New York: Grune & Stratton.

Boss, M. (1957a). *The analysis of dreams.* London: Rider & Co.

Boss, M. (1957b). *Psychoanalyse and daseinsanalytik.* Bern & Stuttgart: Verlag Hans Huber.

Boss, M. (1982). *Psychoanalysis and daseinanalysis.* New York: Simon & Schuster.

Bugental, J. (1956). *The search for authenticity.* New York: Holt, Rinehart and Winston.

Bugental, J. (1976). *The search for existential identity.* San Francisco: Jossey-Bass.

Farber, L. (1966). *The ways of the will: Essays toward a psychology and psychopathology of will.* New York: Basic Books.

Farber, L. (1976). *Lying, despair, jealousy, envy, sex, suicide, drugs, and the good life.* New York: Basic Books.

Frankl, V. (1963). *Man's search for meaning: An introduction to logotherapy.* New York: Pocket Books.

Frankl, V. (1969). *Will to meaning.* New York: World Publishing.

Havens, L. (1974). The existential use of the self. *American Journal of Psychiatry, 131.*

Horney, K. (1950). *Neurosis and human growth.* New York: Norton.

Jung, C. G. (1966). *Collected works: The practice of psychotherapy* (Vol. 16). New York: Pantheon, Bollingen Series.

Kaiser, H. (1965). *Effective psychotherapy.* New York: Free Press.

Kant, I. (1954). *The encyclopedia of philosophy* (Vol. 4). P. Edwards (Ed.). New York: Macmillan and Free Press.

Kierkegaard, S. (1954). *Fear and trembling and the sickness unto death.* Garden City, NY: Doubleday.

Koestenbaum, P. (1978). *The new image of man.* Westport, CT: Greenwood Press.

May, R. (1953). *Man's search for himself.* New York: Norton.

May, R. (1961). *Existential psychology.* New York: Random House.

May, R. (1969). *Love and will.* New York: Norton.

May, R. (1977). *The meaning of anxiety* (rev. ed.). New York: Norton.

May, R. (1981). *Freedom and destiny.* New York: Norton.

May, R. (1982). The problem of evil: An open letter to Carl Rogers. *Journal of Humanistic Psychology, 3,* 16.

May, R., Angel, E., & Ellenberger, H. (Eds.). (1958). *Existence: A new dimension in psychiatry and psychology.* New York: Basic Books.

Mijuskovic, B. (1979). *Loneliness in philosophy, psychology and literature.* Assen, Netherlands: Van Gorcum.

Perls, F. (1969). *Gestalt therapy verbatim.* Moab, UT: Real People Press.

Raskin, N. (1978). Becoming—A therapist, a person, a partner, and a parent. *Psychotherapy: Theory, Research and Practice, 4,* 15.

Sartre, J. P. (1956). *Being and nothingness.* New York: Philosophical Library.

Sequin, C. (1965). *Love and psychotherapy.* New York: Libra Publishers.

Spence, K. (1956). *Behavior therapy and conditioning.* New Haven, CT: Yale University.

Spinoza, B. (1954). Cited by M. De Unamuno in *The tragic sense of life* (E. Flitch, Trans). New York: Dover.

Weisman, A. (1965). *Existential core of psychoanalysis: Reality sense and responsibility.* Boston: Little, Brown.

Yalom, I. (1981). *Existential psychotherapy.* New York: Basic Books.

(1893–1970)

# 10

## OVERVIEW

Gestalt therapy was founded by Frederick "Fritz" Perls and collaborators Laura Perls and Paul Goodman. They synthesized various cultural and intellectual trends of the 1940s and 1950s into a new gestalt, one that provided a sophisticated clinical and theoretical alternative to the two other main theories of their day: behaviorism and classical psychoanalysis.

Gestalt therapy started as a revision of psychoanalysis (F. Perls, 1942/ 1992) and quickly developed as a wholly independent, integrated system (F. Perls, Hefferline, & Goodman, 1951/1994). While retaining the psychoanalytic view of therapy as a search for change through understanding, gestalt therapy changed the nature of understanding and the methodology for gaining understanding. For instance, since gestalt therapy is an experiential and humanistic approach, it works with patients' awareness and awareness skills rather than using the classic psychoanalytic reliance on the analyst's interpretation of the unconscious. Also, in gestalt therapy the therapist is actively and personally engaged with the patient, rather than fostering transference by remaining in the analytic role of neutrality. In gestalt therapy theory, a process-based postmodern field theory replaces the mechanistic, simplistic, Newtonian system of psychoanalysis.

The gestalt therapist is actively engaged with the patient, and frequently discloses his or her own experience, both experience of the moment in the therapy hour and life experience, in a relationship based on mutuality. The

299

gestalt therapist is not seen as someone who has a more objective view of reality than the patient, but rather someone who works cooperatively with the patient and the patient's sense of reality.

The gestalt therapist uses active methods that not only develop patients' awareness, but also develop patients' repertoires of awareness and behavioral tools. The active methods and active personal engagement of gestalt therapy are used to increase the awareness, freedom, and self-direction of the patient and are not used to direct patients toward preset goals as in behavior therapy and encounter groups.

The gestalt therapy system is truly holistic and includes utilization of affective, sensory, cognitive, interpersonal, and behavioral components. In gestalt therapy, therapists and patients are encouraged to be creative in doing the awareness work. There are no prescribed or proscribed techniques in gestalt therapy.

## Basic Concepts

### Holism and Field Theory

Most humanistic theories of personality are holistic. Holism asserts that humans are inherently self-regulating, that they are growth-oriented, and that persons and their symptoms cannot be understood apart from their environment. Holism and field theory are interrelated in gestalt theory.

Field theory is one way of understanding how one's context influences one's experiencing. Field theory, described elegantly by Einstein's theory of relativity, is a theory about the nature of reality and our relationship to reality. It represents one of the first attempts to articulate a contextualist view of reality (Philippson, 2001).

Fields have certain properties that lead to a specific contextual theory. As with all contextual theories, a field is understood to be comprised of mutually interdependent elements. But there are other properties as well. For one thing, variables that contribute to shaping a person's behavior and experience are said to be present in the current field, therefore people cannot be understood without understanding the field, or context, in which they live. A patient's life story cannot tell you what actually happened in his or her past, but it can tell you how the patient experiences his or her history in the here and now. That rendition of history is shaped to some degree by the current field conditions.

An event that happened three years ago is not a part of the current field; and therefore cannot affect one's experience. What *does* shape one's experience is how one holds a memory of the event, and also the fact that an event three years ago has altered how one may organize one's perception in the field. Another property of the field is that the organization of one's experience occurs in the here and now, and is ongoing and subject to change based on field conditions. Another property is that no one can transcend embeddedness in a field; therefore, all attributions about the nature of reality are *relative* to the subject's position in the field. Field theory renounces the belief that anyone, including a therapist, can have an objective perspective on reality.

Field theory, born in science, was an early contributor to the current postmodern sensibility that influences almost all psychological theories today. Schools of thought that emphasize dependence upon context build on the work of Einstein and other field theorists. The combination of field theory, holism, and gestalt psychology form the bedrock for the gestalt theory of personality.

The *Paradoxical Theory of Change* is the heart of the gestalt therapy philosophy (Beisser, 1970). The paradox is that the more one tries to become who one is not, the more one stays the same. Health is largely a matter of being whole, and healing occurs when one is made whole again. The more one tries to force oneself into a mold that does not fit, the more one is fragmented rather than whole.

*Organismic self-regulation* requires knowing and owning, i.e., identifying with what one senses, feels emotionally, observes, needs or wants, and believes. True growth starts with conscious awareness of what is occurring in one's current existence, including how one is affected and how one affects others. One moves toward wholeness by clearly identifying with ongoing experience, being in contact with what is actually happening, identifying and trusting what one genuinely feels and wants, and being honest with self and others about what one is actually able and willing to do—or not do.

When one knows, senses, and feels one's self here and now, including the possibilities for change, one can be fully present, accepting or changing what is not satisfying. Living in the past, worrying about the future, and/or clinging to illusions about what one should be or could have been, diminishes emotional and conscious awareness and the immediacy of experience that is the key to organismic living and growth.

Gestalt therapy aims for self-knowledge, acceptance, and growth by immersion in current existence, aligning contact, awareness, and experimentation with what is actually happening at the moment. It focuses on the here and now, and not what should be, could be, or was. From this present-centered focus, one can become clear about one's needs, wishes, goals, and values.

The concepts emphasized in gestalt therapy are contact, conscious awareness, and experimentation. Each concept is described below.

*Contact* refers to being in touch with what is emerging here and now, moment to moment. *Conscious awareness* is a focusing of attention on what one is in touch with in situations requiring such attention. Awareness, i.e., focused attention, is required in situations requiring higher contact ability, situations involving complexity or conflict, and situations in which habitual modes of thinking and acting are not working and in which one does not learn from experience. For example, in a situation that produces numbness, one can focus on the experience of numbness, and cognitive clarity can emerge.

*Experimentation* is the act of trying something new in order to increase understanding. The experiment may result in enhanced emotions or the realization of something that had been kept from awareness. Experimentation, trying something new, is an alternative to the purely verbal methods of psychoanalysis and the behavior control techniques of behavior therapy.

Trying something new, without commitment to either the status quo or the adoption of a new pattern, can facilitate organismic growth. For example, patients often repeat stories of unhappy events without any evidence of increased clarity or relief. In this situation, a gestalt therapist might suggest that the patient express affect directly to the person involved (either live or through role playing). This often results in the patient experiencing relief and the emergence of other feelings, e.g., sadness or appreciation.

Contact, awareness, and experimentation have technical meanings, but these terms are also used in a colloquial way. The gestalt therapist improves his or her practice by knowing the technical definitions. However, for the sake of this introductory chapter the authors will try to use the colloquial form of these terms. Gestalt therapy starts with the therapist making contact with the patient by getting in touch with what the patient is experiencing and doing. The therapist helps the patient focus on and clarify what he or she is in contact with and deepens the exploration by helping focus the patient's awareness.

## Awareness Process

Gestalt therapy focuses on the awareness process. The awareness process refers to the continuum of one's flow of awareness. People have patterned processes of awareness that become foci for the work of therapy. This focus enables the patient to become clear about what he or she thinks, feels, and decides in the current moment—and how he or she does it. This includes a focus on what does not come to awareness. Careful attention to the sequence of the patient's continuum of awareness and observation of nonverbal behavior can help a patient recognize interruptions of contact and become aware of what has been kept out of awareness. For example, whenever Jill starts to look sad she does not report feeling sad, but moves immediately into anger. The anger cannot end as long as it functions to block Jill's sadness and vulnerability. In this situation, Jill can not only gain awareness of her sadness but also gain in skill at self-monitoring by being made aware of her tendency to block her sadness. That second order of awareness (how she interrupts awareness of her sadness) is referred to as awareness of one's awareness process.

Awareness of awareness can empower by helping the patient gain greater access to him- or herself and clarify processes that had been confusing, improving the accuracy of perception and unblocking previously blocked emotional energy. Jill had felt stymied by her lover's defensive reaction to her anger. When she realized that she actually felt hurt and sad, and not just angry, she could express her vulnerability, hurt, and sadness. Her lover was much more receptive to this than he was to her anger. In further work Jill realized that blocking her sadness resulted from being shamed by her family when as a child she had expressed hurt feelings.

The gestalt therapist focuses on the patient's awareness and contact processes with respect, compassion, and commitment to the validity of the patient's subjective reality. The therapist models the process by disclosing his or her own awareness and experience. The therapist is present in as mutual a way as possible in the therapeutic relationship and takes responsibility for his or her own behavior and feelings. In this way the therapist can be active and make suggestions but also can fully accept the patient consistent with the paradoxical theory of change.

## Other Systems

In the decades up to and including the 1970s, it seemed simple to compare gestalt therapy with other systems. There were three major systems: classical Freudian psychoanalysis, behavior therapy, and the existential and humanistic therapies. In the 1960s gestalt therapy became the most visible of the humanistic existential therapies and a salient alternative to psychoanalysis and behavior modification. However, the theoretical boundaries supporting various schools of therapy have become less distinct over the ensuing decades.

### Classical Freudian Psychoanalysis and Gestalt Therapy

At the heart of Freudian psychoanalysis was a belief in the centrality of basic biological drives and the establishment of relatively permanent structures created by the inevitable conflict between these basic drives and social demands, both necessary demands and those stemming from parental and societal neurosis. All human development, behavior, thinking, and feeling were believed to be determined by these unconscious biological and social conflicts.

Patients' statements of their feelings, thoughts, beliefs, wishes, and so forth were not considered reliable since they merely disguised deeper motivations stemming from the unconscious. The unconscious was a structure to which the patient did not have direct access, at least before completing analysis. However, the unconscious manifested itself in the transference neurosis, and through the analyst's interpretation of the transference "truth" was discovered and understood.

Psychoanalysis, the only treatment psychoanalysts believed has any real effect, proceeded by a simple paradigm. Through free association, i.e., talking without censoring or focusing, the patient provided data for psychoanalytic treatment. These data were interpreted by the analyst according to the particular version of drive theory that he or she espoused.

The analyst provided no details about his or her own life or person. He or she was supposed to be completely objective, eschewing all emotional reactions. The analyst had two fundamental rules: The *rule of abstinence* (gratifying no patient wish) and the *rule of neutrality* (the analyst had no preferences in the patient's conflict). Any deviation by the analyst was considered to be countertransference. Any attempt by the patient to know something about the analyst was interpreted as resistance. Since the patient could not and should not know anything of the analyst as a person, any view of the analyst was a projection from the unconscious of the patient.

Of course, the analytic situation could not be as neutral as claimed. Patients are affected by the behavior of the analyst and the atmosphere in the analytic situation. The analytic situation makes it very difficult for the warmth and caring of the analyst to come through to the patient.

The interpretation of the transference helped bring the focus back to the here and now. Unfortunately, the potential of the here-and-now relationship is not realized in classical psychoanalysis because focus is drawn away from the actual contemporaneous relationship, and the patients' feelings are interpreted as the result of unconscious drives and unresolved conflicts. Discussion in psychoanalysis is usually focused on the past and not on what is actually happening between analyst and patient *in the moment.*

This simple summary of psychoanalysis is not completely accurate since Adler, Rank, Jung, Reich, Horney, Fromm, Sullivan, and other analysts deviated from core Freudian assumptions in many ways and provided the soil from which the gestalt therapy system arose. In these derivative systems, as in gestalt therapy, the pessimistic Freudian view of a patient driven by unconscious forces was replaced by a belief in the potential for human growth and appreciation for the power of relationships and conscious awareness. These approaches did not limit the data to free association; instead, they valued an explicitly compassionate attitude by the therapist and allowed a wider range of interventions. However, these approaches were still fettered by remaining in the psychoanalytic tradition. Gestalt therapy took a more radical position.

*Behavior modification* provided a simple alternative: Observe the behavior, disregard the subjective reports of the patient, and control problematic behavior by using either classical or operant conditioning to manipulate stimulus-response relationships. In the behavioral approaches the emphasis was on what could be measured, counted, and "scientifically" proven.

The behavioral approach was the inverse of the intrapsychic, strictly mental approach of Freudian psychoanalysis. Here-and-now behavior was observed and taken as important data in its own right, but the patient's subjective, conscious experience was not considered reliable data.

A third choice was provided by gestalt therapy. In gestalt therapy the patient's awareness is not assumed to be merely a cover for some other, deeper, motivation. Unlike psychoanalysis, gestalt therapy uses any and all available data. Like behavior modification, gestalt therapy carefully observes behavior, including observation of the body, and it focuses on the here and now and uses active methods. The patient's self-report is considered real data. Unlike both behavior modification and psychoanalysis, the therapist and the patient codirect the work of therapy.

## Person–Centered Therapy, Rational Emotive Behavior Therapy, and Gestalt Therapy

Gestalt therapy and person-centered therapy share common roots and philosophy. Both believe in the potential for human growth, and both believe that growth results from a relationship in which the therapist shows warmth and authenticity (congruence). Both person-centered and gestalt therapy are phenomenological therapies that work with the subjective awareness of the patient. However, gestalt therapy has a more active phenomenological approach. The gestalt therapy phenomenology is an experimental phenomenology. The patient's subjective experience is made clearer by using awareness experiments. These experiments are often similar to behavioral techniques, but they are designed to clarify the patient's awareness rather than control his or her behavior.

Another difference is that the gestalt therapist is more oriented to an encounter in which the subjectivity of both patient and therapist is valued. The gestalt therapist is much more likely than a person-centered therapist to tell the patient about his or her own feelings or experience.

Gestalt therapy provides an alternative to both the confrontive approach of REBT and the nondirective approach of Carl Rogers. A person-centered therapist completely trusts the patient's subjective report, whereas a practitioner of rational emotive behavior therapy (REBT) confronts the patient about his or her irrational or dysfunctional ways of thinking. Gestalt therapy uses focused awareness experiments and personal disclosure to help patients enlarge their awareness. During the 1960s and 1970s Fritz Perls popularized a very confrontive model for dealing with avoidance; this is only one model of gestalt therapy and is not representative of gestalt therapy as it is practiced today.

Gestalt therapy has become more like the person-centered approach in two important ways. First, gestalt therapists have become more supportive, compassionate, and kind. In addition, it has become clear that the therapist does not have an "objective" truth that is more accurate than the truth that the patient experiences.

## Newer Models of Psychoanalysis and Relational Gestalt Therapy

There have been parallel developments in gestalt therapy and psychoanalysis. Although the concept of the relationship in gestalt therapy was modeled on Martin Buber's I-Thou relationship, it was not well explicated until the late 1980s (Hycner, 1985; Jacobs, 1996; Yontef, 1993). In its emerging focus on the relationship, gestalt therapy has moved away from classical psychoanalysis and drive theory, away from confrontation as a desired therapeutic tool, and away from the belief that the therapist is healthy and the patient is sick.

Psychoanalysis has undergone a fundamental paradigm shift, as has gestalt therapy, and there has been a convergence between the two systems. This is in part possible because contemporary psychoanalytic theories (interpersonal, relational, and intersubjective analysis) have rejected the limitations of classical Freudian psychoanalysis. The new theories eschew reductionism and determinism, and reject the tendency to minimize the patients' own perspective. This movement brings psychoanalysis closer to the theory and practice of gestalt therapy. Gestalt therapy was formed in reaction to the same aspects of psychoanalysis that contemporary psychoanalysis is now rejecting.

Gestalt therapy has also changed and has moved in the same direction as contemporary psychoanalysis. In part this has been a parallel development, and in part gestalt therapy has been influenced by the changes that have occurred in psychoanalysis. These new tenets, new in psychoanalysis and newly elaborated in gestalt therapy, include the following: an emphasis on the whole person and sense of self rather than on static, mechanistic, structural concepts (e.g., id, ego, and superego); an emphasis on process thinking; an emphasis on subjectivity and affect; an appreciation of the impact of life events (e.g., childhood sexual abuse) on personality development; a belief that people are motivated toward growth and development rather than regression; a belief that infants are born with a basic motivation and capacity for personal interaction, attachment, and satisfaction; a belief that there is no "self" without an "other," and a belief that the structure and contents of the mind are shaped by interactions with others, rather than by instinctual urges. For the contemporary analyst, as for the gestalt therapist, it is meaningless to speak of a person in isolation from the relationships that shape and define his or her life.

## Cognitive Behavior Therapy, REBT, and Gestalt Therapy

The assumption that gestalt therapy does not work with patients' thinking processes is inaccurate. Gestalt therapy has always paid attention to what the patient is thinking. Gestalt therapists, like their cognitive therapy colleagues, stress the role of "futurizing" in creating anxiety and, like REBT therapists, discuss the creation of guilt by moralistic thinking and thoughts of unreasonable conditions of worth ("shoulds"). Many of the thoughts that would be labeled as irrational in REBT or cognitive behavior therapy have also traditionally been an important focus for gestalt therapy.

This emphasis on cognition has been more salient in gestalt therapy in the last decade or two. Clinical experience and the research literature have indicated the importance of cognition in creating, maintaining, and exacerbating psychopathology, and these findings have significantly influenced the practice of gestalt therapy.

There is one major difference between contemporary gestalt therapy and REBT or cognitive behavior therapy. In modern gestalt therapy the therapist does not pretend to know the truth about what is irrational. The gestalt therapist observes the process, directs the patient to observe his or her thoughts, and explores alternate ways of thinking in a manner that values and respects what the patient experiences and comes to believe.

# HISTORY

## Precursors

Gestalt therapy was less an originator of substantial original "discoveries" than a groundbreaking integrative system for understanding personality and therapy that developed out of a seedbed of rich and varied sources. Fritz and Laura Perls, and their later American collaborators (Isadore From, Paul Goodman, and others) with whom they wrote, taught, and practiced from the 1940s through the 1960s, swam in the turbulent and daring waters of the twentieth-century revolutions in science, philosophy, religion, psychology, art, literature, and politics. There was tremendous cross-fertilization between intellectuals in all disciplines during this period.

Frankfurt-am-Main of the 1920s, where Fritz Perls got his M.D. and Laura Perls got her D.Sc., was a center of intellectual ferment in psychology. They were directly or indirectly exposed to leading gestalt psychologists, existential and phenomenological philosophers, liberal theologians, and psychoanalytic thinkers.

Fritz Perls was intimately acquainted with psychoanalysis and in fact was a training analyst. However, Perls chafed under the dogmatism of classical psychoanalysis. For Perls the revolutionary basic idea that Freud brought to Western culture—the existence of motivations which lay outside of conscious awareness—had to be woven into other streams of thought, particularly holism, gestalt psychology, field theory, phenomenology, and existentialism.

These intellectual disciplines, each in its own way, were attempting to create a new vision of what it means to be human. Their vision came to be called a "humanistic" vision, and gestalt therapy introduced that vision to the world of psychotherapy. Freudian analysts asserted the essential truth that human life is biologically determined, conflicted, and in need of constraint; the existentialists asserted the primacy of existence over essence, the belief that people choose the direction of their life, and the argument that human life is not biologically determined. Within psychoanalysis, Perls was influenced by the more "renegade" analysts, especially Otto Rank and Wilhelm Reich. Both Rank and Reich emphasized conscious experience, the body as "carrier" of emotional wisdom and conflicts, and the active process of engagement between the therapist and the patient in the here and now. Reich introduced the important notion of "character armor," repetitive patterns of experience, behavior, and body posture that keep the individual in fixed, socially determined roles. Reich also thought that how a patient spoke or moved was more important than what the patient said.

Rank emphasized the creative powers and uniqueness of the individual and argued that the client was his or her own best therapist. Like Fritz Perls, Rank stressed the importance of the experience of the here-and-now therapeutic relationship.

Providing a major source of inspiration to Fritz and Laura Perls were European continental philosophers who were breaking away from Cartesian dualism, arguing that the split between subject and object, self and world, was an illusion. This included the existentialists, phenomenologists, and philosophers such as Ludwig Wittgenstein.

The new approach was influenced by field theory, the gestalt psychologists, the holism of Jan Smuts (Smuts 1926/1996), and Zen thought and practice. This thinking was blended by Fritz Perls with the gestalt psychology of figure/ground perception, and with the strongly gestalt-psychology-influenced work of psychologists Kurt Goldstein (1939/1963) and Kurt Lewin (1938).

In his first book, *Ego, Hunger and Aggression* (1942/1992), Perls described people as imbedded in a person-environment field; this field was developed by the emergence into consciousness of those needs that organized perception. Perls also wrote about a "creative indifference" that enables a person to differentiate according to what is really needed in a particular situation. With the differentiation emerges the experience of contrast and awareness of the polarities that shape our experience of ourselves as separate. Perls thought of this as a western equivalent to eastern Zen practice (Wulf, 1998).

Fritz and Laura left Germany during the Nazi era and later fled Nazi-occupied Holland. They went to South Africa, where they started a psychoanalytic training center. During this same period Jan Smuts, South African prime minister in the 1940s, coined the term "holism" and wrote about it. In time, Fritz and Laura Perls left South Africa because of the beginning of the apartheid policies that Jan Smuts helped to initiate.

The fundamental precept of *holism* is that the organism is a self-regulating entity. For Fritz Perls, gestalt psychology, organismic theory, field theory, and holism formed a happy union. Gestalt psychology provided Perls with the organizing principles for gestalt therapy and provided a cognitive scheme that would integrate the varied influences in his life.

The word *gestalt* has no literal English translation. It refers to a perceptual whole or configuration of experience. People do not perceive in bits and pieces, which are then added up to form an organized perception; instead, they perceive in patterned wholes. Patterns reflect an interrelationship among elements such that the whole cannot be gleaned by a study of component parts, but only by a study of the relationship of parts to each other and to the whole. The leading figures in the development of gestalt psychology were Max Wertheimer, Kurt Koffka, and Wolfgang Kohler.

Kurt Lewin extended this work by applying gestalt principles to areas other than simple perceptual psychology and by explicating the theoretical implications of gestalt psychology. He is especially known for his explication of the field theory philosophy of gestalt psychology, although this concept did not originate with him. Lewin (1938) discussed the principles by which field theory differed from Newtonian and positivistic thinking. In field theory, the world is studied as a systematic web of relationships, continuous in time, and not as discrete or dichotomous particles. In this view, everything is in the process of becoming, and nothing is static. Reality in this field view is configured by the relationship between the observer and the observed. "Reality," then is a function of perspective, not a true positivist fact. There may be multiple realities, of equal legitimacy. Such a viewpoint toward the nature of reality opens gestalt theory to a variety of formerly disenfranchised voices, such as those of women, gays, and non-Europeans.

Lewin carried on the work of the gestalt psychologists by hypothesizing and researching the idea that a gestalt is formed by the interaction between environmental possibilities and organismic needs. Needs organize perception and action. Perception is organized by the state of the person-in-relation and the environmental surround. A gestalt therapy theory of organismic functioning was drawn based on the gestalt psychology principles of perception and holism. The theory of organismic self-regulation became a cornerstone of the gestalt therapy theory of personality.

The philosophical tenets of phenomenology and existentialism were popular during the Perlses' years in Germany and in the United States. Gestalt therapy was influenced profoundly by the work of the dialogic existential thinkers, especially Martin Buber, with whom Laura Perls studied directly. Buber's belief in the inextricable existential fact that a self is always a self-with-other was a natural fit with gestalt thinking, and his theory of the I-Thou relation became, through the teachings of Laura Perls, the basis for the patient-therapist relationship in gestalt therapy.

## Beginnings

Although Fritz Perls's earliest publication was *Ego, Hunger, and Aggression* (1942/1992), the first comprehensive integration of gestalt therapy system is found in *Gestalt Therapy* (F. Perls et al., 1951/1994). This seminal publication represented the synthesis, integration, and new gestalt formed by the authors' exposure to the intellectual zeitgeist described above. A New York Institute of Gestalt Therapy was soon formed, and the early seminar participants became teachers who spread the word to other cities by running regular training workshops, especially in New York, Cleveland, Miami, and Los Angeles. Intensive study groups formed in each of these cities. Learning was supplemented by the regular workshops of the original study group members, and eventually each of these cities developed their own gestalt training institutes. The Gestalt Institute of Cleveland has made a special effort to bring in diverse trainees and to develop a highly diverse faculty.

Gestalt therapy pioneered many ideas that have influenced humanistic psychotherapy. For instance, gestalt therapy has a highly developed methodology for attending to experience phenomenologically, and for attending to how the therapist and patient experience each other in the therapeutic relationship. *Phenomenology* assumes the reality is formed in the relationship between the observed and the observer. In short, reality is interpreted.

The dialogic relationship in gestalt therapy derived three important principles from Martin Buber's thought. First, in a dialogic therapeutic relationship the therapist practices inclusion, which is similar to empathic engagement. In this the therapist puts him- or herself into the experience of the patient, imagines the existence of the other, feels it as if it were a sensation within his or her own body, and simultaneously maintains a sense of self. Inclusion is a developed form of contact rather than a merger with the experience of the patient. Through imagining the patient's experience in this way, the dialogic therapist confirms the existence and potential of the patient. Second, the therapist discloses him or herself as a person who is authentic and congruent and someone who is striving to be transparent and self-disclosing. Third, the therapist in a dialogic therapy is committed to the dialogue, surrenders to what happens between the participants, and thus does not control the outcome. In such a relationship, the therapist is changed as well as the patient.

Underlying most existential thought is the existential phenomenological method. Gestalt therapy's phenomenology is a blend of the existential phenomenology of Edmund Husserl and the phenomenology of gestalt psychology.

Phenomenological understanding is achieved by taking initial perceptions and separating what is actually experienced at the moment from what was expected or merely logically derived. The phenomenological method increases the clarity of awareness by descriptively studying the awareness process. In order to do this, phenomenologists put aside assumptions, especially assumptions about what constitutes valid data. All data are considered valid initially, although they are likely to be refined by continuing phenomenological exploration. This is quite consistent with the gestalt therapy view that the patient's awareness is valid and should be explored rather than explained away in terms of unconscious motivation.

While other theories have not fully incorporated the I-Thou relation, or systematic phenomenological focusing, they have been influenced by the excitement and vitality of direct contact between therapist and patient; the emphasis on direct experience; the use of experimentation; emphasis on the here and now, emotional process, and awareness; trust in organismic self-regulation; emphasis on choice; and attention to the patient's context as well as his or her "inner" world.

## Current Status

Gestalt Institutes, literature, and journals have proliferated worldwide in the past 40 years. There is at least one gestalt therapy training center in every major city in the United States, and multiple gestalt therapy training institutes in most countries of Europe, North and South America, and Australia. Gestalt therapists practice all over the world.

Various countries and regions have begun to form umbrella organizations that sponsor professional meetings, set standards, and support research and public education. In the United States, there is the Association for the Advancement of Gestalt Therapy, with both national and international membership. This organization is not limited to professionals. The association was formed with the intention of governing itself through adherence to gestalt therapy principles enacted at an organizational level. Regional conferences are also sponsored by a European gestalt therapy association, the European Association for Gestalt Therapy, and by a New Zealand and Australian association, GANZ. The International Gestalt Therapy Association is a new organization attempting to form a thoroughly international governance and meeting structure, something made more feasible by the Internet and the widespread use of e-mail.

Gestalt therapy is known for a rich oral tradition, and historically gestalt writings have not reflected the full depth of its theory and practice. Gestalt therapy has tended to attract therapists inclined to an experiential approach. The gestalt therapy approach is almost impossible to teach without a strong experiential component.

Since the publication of a seminal book by the Polsters (Polster & Polster, 1973), the gap between the oral and written traditions of gestalt therapy has closed. There is now an extensive gestalt therapy literature, and a growing number of books address various aspects of gestalt therapy theory and practice. For many years there was only one English-language journal devoted to gestalt therapy, *The Gestalt Journal.* There are now four English-language gestalt journals: The *International Gestalt Journal* (formerly *The Gestalt Journal*), the *British Gestalt Journal,* the *Gestalt Review,* and the *Australian Gestalt Journal.* The Gestalt Journal Press also lists a comprehensive bibliography of gestalt books, articles, videotapes, and audiotapes. The listing can be accessed through the Internet at www.gestalt.org. Gestalt therapy literature has also flourished around the world. There is at least one journal in most languages in Europe, North and South America, and Australia. In addition to the books written in English, translated, and widely read in other countries, there have been important original theoretical works published in French, German, Italian, Portuguese, Danish, and Spanish.

The past decade has witnessed a major shift in gestalt therapy's understanding of personality and therapy. There has been a growing, albeit sometimes controversial, change in understanding the relational conditions for growth both in general and especially in the therapeutic relationship. There is an increased appreciation for interdependence, a better understanding of the shaming effect of the cultural value placed on self-sufficiency, and greater realization of how shame is created in childhood and triggered in interpersonal relationships (Lee & Wheeler, 1996).

As gestalt therapists have come to understand shame more thoroughly, and how shame is triggered, they have become less confrontive and more accepting and supportive than in earlier years. There is more interest in and acceptance of patients' subjective experience. This issue continues to be a subject of controversy and debate.

# PERSONALITY

## Theory of Personality

Gestalt theory has a highly developed, somewhat complicated theory of personality. The notions of healthy functioning and neurotic functioning are actually quite simple and clear, but they are built upon a paradigm shift, not always easy to grasp, from linear cause-and-effect thinking to a process, field theory world view.

Gestalt therapy is a radical ecological theory that maintains there is no meaningful way to consider any living organism apart from interactions with its environment, i.e., apart from the organism-environment field of which it is a part (F. Perls et al., 1951/1994). Psychologically there is no meaningful way to consider a person apart from interpersonal relations, just as there is no meaningful way to perceive the environment except through someone's perspective. According to gestalt therapy field theory, it is impossible for perception to be totally "objective."

The "field" that human beings inhabit is replete with other human beings. In gestalt theory, there is no self separate from one's organism/environmental field; more specifically, self does not exist without other. Self implies self-in-relation. While contact is an integral aspect of all experience—in fact, experience does not exist without contact—it is the contact between humans that dominates the formation and functions of our personalities.

The field is differentiated by *boundaries*. The contact boundary has dual functions: It connects people with each other but it also maintains separation. Without emotional connecting with others, one starves; without emotional separation, one does not maintain a separate autonomous identity. Connecting meets biological, social, and psychological needs; separation creates and maintains autonomy and protects against harmful intrusion or overload.

Needs are met and people grow through contact with and withdrawal from others. By separating and connecting, a person establishes boundary and identity. Effective self-regulation includes contact in which one is aware of what is newly emerging that potentially may be either nourishing or harmful. One identifies with that which is nourishing and rejects that which is harmful. This kind of differentiated contact leads to growth (Polster & Polster, 1973). The crucial processes regulating this discrimination are awareness and contact.

The most important processes for psychological growth are interactions in which two persons each acknowledge the experience of the other, with awareness and respect for the needs, feelings, beliefs, and customs of the other. This form of dialogic contact is essential in therapy.

## Organismic Self-Regulation

Gestalt therapy theory holds that people are inherently self-regulating and motivated to solve their own problems. Needs and desires are organized hierarchically so that one's most urgent need takes precedence and claims one's attention until this need is met. When this need is met, the next need or interest becomes the center of one's attention.

## Gestalt (Figure/Ground) Formation

A corollary to the concept of organismic self-regulation is called gestalt formation. Gestalt psychology has taught us that we perceive in unified wholes, and also that we perceive through the phenomenon of contrast. A figure of interest forms in contrast to a relatively dull background. For instance, the words on this page are a visual figure to the reader, whereas other aspects of the room are visually less clear and vivid until this reference to them leads the reader to allow the words on the page to slip into the background, at which time the figure of a table, chair, book, or soda emerges. One can only perceive one clear figure at a time, although figures and grounds may shift very rapidly.

## Consciousness and Unconsciousness

A most important consequence of adapting gestalt psychology to a theory of personality functioning is that ideas about consciousness and unconsciousness are radically different than those of Freud. Freud believed the unconscious was filled with impersonal, biologically based urges that constantly pressed for release. Competent functioning depended on the successful use of repression and sublimation to keep the contents of the unconscious hidden; these urges could only be experienced in symbolic form.

Gestalt therapy's "unconscious" is quite different. In gestalt theory, the concepts of awareness and unawareness replace the unconscious. One is unaware when something vital, powerful, and relevant is not allowed to emerge into foreground. Gestalt therapists use the concepts of awareness/unawareness to reflect the belief in the fluidity between what is momentarily in awareness and what is momentarily outside of awareness. This is in keeping with the gestalt psychology understanding of perception, which is the formation of a figure against a background. What is background is, for the moment, outside of awareness, but it could instantly become the figure in awareness.

In neurotic patients, some aspect of the phenomenological field is purposely and regularly relegated to the background. This concept is roughly similar to the Freudian dynamic unconscious. However, gestalt therapists do not believe in a "primary process" unconscious that needs to be translated by the therapist before it can be comprehensible to the patient.

Gestalt therapists maintain that what is being relegated to a permanent background status reflects the patient's current conflicts as well as the patient's perspective of current field conditions. When a patient perceives the conditions of the therapy relationship to be safe enough, more and more aspects of previously sequestered subjective states can be brought into awareness through the therapeutic dialogue.

## Health

The gestalt therapy notion of health is actually quite simple. In healthy organismic self-regulation one is aware of shifting need states, i.e., what is of most importance becomes the figure of one's awareness. Being whole, then, is simply identifying with one's ongoing, moment-by-moment experiencing and allowing this identification to organize one's behavior.

Healthy organismic awareness includes awareness of the human and nonhuman environment and is not unreflective or inconsiderate of the needs of others. For example, compassion, love, and care for the environment are all part of organismic functioning.

Healthy functioning requires being in contact with what is actually occurring in the person-environment field. Contact is the quality of being in touch with one's experience in relation to the field. By being aware of and allowing action to be organized by what is emerging, people interact in the world and learn from the experience. By trying something new, one learns what works and does not work in various situations. When a figure is not allowed to emerge, when it is somehow interrupt or misdirected, there is a disturbance in awareness and contact.

## Tendency Toward Growth

Gestalt therapists believe that people are inclined toward growth and will develop as fully as conditions will allow. Gestalt therapy is holistic and asserts that people are inherently self-regulating and growth-oriented and that people and their behavior, including symptoms, cannot be understood apart from their environment.

Gestalt therapy is interested in the existential themes of existence—connection and separation, life and death, choice and responsibility, authenticity and freedom. Gestalt therapy's theory of awareness is a bedrock phenomenological orientation toward experience derived from an existential and humanistic ethos. Gestalt therapy attempts to understand human beings by the study of experience. Meaning is understood in terms of what is experienced and how it is experienced.

## Life Is Relational

Gestalt therapy regards awareness and human relations as inseparable. Awareness develops in early childhood through a matrix of relations that continues throughout life. Relationships are regulated by how people experience them. People define themselves by how they experience themselves in relation to others. This derives from how people are regarded by others and how they think and behave toward others. In gestalt therapy theory, derived from Martin Buber, there is no "I," no sense of self, other than self in relation to others. There is only the "I" of the "I-Thou" or the "I" of the "I-it." As Buber said, "All real living is meeting" (1923/1970, p. 11).

Living is a progression of needs, met and unmet. One achieves homeostatic balance and moves on to whatever need emerges next. In health, the boundary is permeable enough to allow exchange with that which promotes health (connecting) and firm enough to preserve autonomy and exclude that which is unhealthy (separation). This requires the identification of those needs that are most pressing at a particular time and in a particular environment.

## Variety of Concepts

### Disturbances at the Boundary

Under optimum conditions, there is ongoing movement between connecting and withdrawal. When the experience of coming together is blocked repetitively, one is left in a state of *isolation,* which is a boundary disturbance. It is a disturbance because it is fixed, does not respond to a whole range of needs, and fails to allow close contact to emerge. By the same token, if the need to withdraw is blocked, there is a corresponding boundary disturbance, *confluence.* Confluence is the loss of the experience of separate identity.

In optimum functioning, when something is taken in—whether it is an idea, food, or love—there is contact and awareness. The person makes discriminations about what to take in and what meaning to attach to that which is taken in. When things (ideas, identity, beliefs, etc.) are taken in without awareness, the boundary disturbance of *introjection* results. Introjects are not fully integrated into organismic functioning.

To integrate and be whole, what is taken in must be assimilated. *Assimilation* is the process of experiencing what is to be taken in, deconstructing it, keeping what is useful and discarding what is not. When listening to a lecture, the process of assimilation allows the listener to select and keep only what is useful.

When a phenomenon that occurs in one's self is falsely attributed to another person in an effort to avoid awareness of one's own experience, the boundary disturbance of *projection* occurs. When an impulse or desire is turned into a one-person event instead of a two-person event, e.g., stroking oneself when one wants another person to do the stroking, there is the boundary disturbance of *retroflection*. In each of these processes some part of the person is disowned, and not allowed to become figural or to organize and energize action.

## Creative Adjustment

When all the pieces are put together, people function according to an overarching principle called *creative adjustment*. "All contact is creative adjustment of the organism and the environment" (F. Perls et al., 1951/1994). All organisms live in an environment to which they must adjust. Nevertheless, people also need to shape the environment so that it conforms to human needs and values.

The concept of creative adjustment follows from the notion that people are growth-oriented and will try to solve their problems in living in the best way possible. This means solving the problem in a way that makes the most complete use of their own resources and those of the environment. Since awareness can only be concentrated on one figure at a time, those processes that are not the object of creative awareness operate in a habitual mode of adjustment until it is their turn to come into full awareness.

The term *creative adjustment* reflects a creative balance between changing the environment and adjusting to current conditions. Since people only live in relation, they must balance adjusting to the demands of the situation, e.g., societal demands and the needs of others, and creating something new according to their own, individual interests. This is a continual, mutual, reciprocal negotiation between one's self and one's environment (Spagnuolo-Lobb & Amendt-Lyon, 2003).

The process whereby a need becomes figural, is acted upon, then recedes as a new figure emerges is called a *gestalt formation cycle*. Every gestalt formation cycle requires creative adjustment. Both sides of the polarity are necessary for the resolution of a state of need. If one is hungry, one must eat new food taken from the environment. Food that has already been eaten will not resolve the problem. New actions must occur and the environment must be contacted and adapted to meet the individual's needs.

On the other hand, one cannot be so balanced on the side of creating new experience that one does not draw upon prior learning and experience, established wisdom, and societal mores. For example, one must use yesterday's learning to be able to recognize aspects of the environment that might be used as a source of food while at the same time being creative in experimenting with new food possibilities.

## Maturity

Good health has the characteristics of a good gestalt. The *good gestalt* describes a perceptual field organized with clarity and good form. A well-formed figure clearly stands out against a broader and less distinct background. The relation between that which stands out (figure) and the context (ground) is meaning. In a good gestalt, meaning is clear.

Health and maturity result from creative adjustment that occurs in a context of environmental possibility. It requires a person whose gestalt formation process is freely functioning and one whose contact and awareness processes are relatively free of excessive anxiety, inhibition, or habitual selective attention.

In health, the figure changes as needed; that is, it shifts to another focus when a need is met or superseded by a more urgent need. It does not change so rapidly as to prevent satisfaction (as in hysteria) or so slowly that new figures have no room to assume dominance (as in compulsivity). When the figure and ground polarity are dichotomized, one is left with a figure out of context or a context without focus (as in impulsivity) (F. Perls et al., 1951/1994).

The healthy person is in creative adjustment with the environment. The person adjusts to the needs of the environment and adjusts the environment to his or her own needs. Adjustment alone is conformity and breeds stagnation. On the other hand, unbridled creativity in the service of the isolated individual would result in pathological narcissism.

## Disrupted Personality Functioning

Mental illness is simply the inability to form clear figures of interest and identify with one's moment-by-moment experience and/or to respond to what one becomes aware of. People whose contact and awareness processes are disrupted often have been shaped by environments that were chronically impoverished. Impoverished environments diminish one's capacity for creative adjustment.

However, even neurotic self-regulation is considered to be a creative adjustment. Gestalt therapists assume neurotic regulation is the result of a creative adjustment that was made in a difficult situation in the past and then not readjusted as field conditions changed. For example, one patient's father died when she was eight years old. The patient was terribly bereft, frightened, and alone. Her grief-stricken mother, the only adult in her life, was unavailable to help her assimilate her painful and frightening reactions to her father's death. The patient escaped her unbearable situation by busying herself to the point of distraction. That was a creative adjustment to her needs in a field with limited resources. However, even as an adult she continues to use the same means of adjustment, even though the field conditions have changed. This patient's initial creative adjustment became hardened into a repetitive character pattern. This often happens because the original solution worked well enough in an emergency, and current experiences which mimic the original emergency trigger one's emergency adaptation.

Neurotic self-regulation tends to replace organismic self-regulation. Patients frequently cannot trust their own self-regulation, because repeated use of a solution from an earlier time erodes their ability to respond with awareness to the current self-in-field problem. Organismic self-regulation is replaced by "shoulds," that is, by attempts to control and manage one's experience rather than accepting one's experience. Part of the task of therapy is to create a new "emergency" in the therapy situation, but a "safe emergency," one wherein some of the elements reminiscent of the old situation may be present (such as rising emotional intensity), but one which also contains health-facilitating elements that can be utilized (for instance, the therapist's affirming and calming presence). The new situation, if safe enough, can promote a new, more flexible and responsive creative adjustment.

## Polarities

Experience forms as a gestalt, a figure against a ground. Figure and ground stand in a polar relation to each other. In healthy functioning, figures and grounds shift according to changing needs and field conditions. What was previously an aspect of the ground can emerge almost instantly as the next figure.

Life is dominated by polarities, e.g., life/death, strength/vulnerability, connection/separation. When one's creative adjustments are flowing and responsive to current field conditions, the interaction and continually recalibrating balance of these polarities make up the rich tapestry of existence.

In neurotic regulation, some aspects of one's ground must be kept out of awareness (for instance, the patient's unbearable loneliness), and polarities lose their fluidity and become hardened into dichotomies. In neurotic regulation, a patient may readily identify with his or her strength, but ignore or disavow the experience of vulnerability. Such selective awareness results in a life filled with insoluble conflicts, and plagued by crises or dulled by passivity.

## Resistance

The ideas of holism and organismic self-regulation have turned the theory of resistance on its head. Its original meaning in psychoanalysis referred to a reluctance to face a painful truth about one's self. However, the theory of self-regulation posits that all phenomena, even resistance, when taken in context, can be shown to serve an organismic purpose.

In gestalt theory, resistance is an awkward but crucially important expression of the organism's integrity. Resistance is the process of opposing the formation of a figure (a thought, feeling, impulse, or need) that threatens to emerge in a context that is judged to be dangerous. For instance, someone may choke back tears, believing that crying would expose them to ridicule, or someone who has been ridiculed in the past for showing any vulnerability may assume that the current environmental surround is harsh and unforgiving. The inhibited experience is resisted—usually without awareness. For example, a patient may have pushed all experience of vulnerability out of awareness; however, the experience of vulnerability still lives in the background, quietly shaping and shadowing the figure formation process. It cannot disappear, as it is but one side of a polarity that is part of life. Therefore, instead of a fluid polar relationship between those two attributes, the patient develops a hardened dichotomy between strength and vulnerability, and inevitably experiences anxiety whenever he or she feels vulnerable. The result may be a man who takes risks demonstrating great physical courage, but who is inexplicably frightened by the thought of committing himself to a woman he loves. As the conflict is explored in therapy, he becomes aware he is terribly frightened of his vulnerable feelings and resists allowing those feelings to be activated and noticed. The resistance protects him by ensuring his habitual mode of self-regulation remains intact. When the original creative adjustment occurred, the identification with his strength and the banishment of his vulnerability were adaptive. Gestalt theory posits that he has "forgotten" that he made such an adjustment and so remains unaware that he even has any vulnerability that might be impeding his ability to make decisions in support of his current figure of interest, the commitment.

Even when the patient becomes vaguely aware, he may not be sure that the current context is sufficiently different that he can dare to change his dichotomized adjustment. Repetitive experiments within the relative safety of the therapeutic relationship may enable him to contact his vulnerable side enough to re-enliven the polarity of strength/vulnerability such that he can resume a more moment-by-moment creative adjustment process.

*Emotions* are central to healthy functioning because they orient one to one's relationship to the current field, and they help establish the relative urgency of an emergent figure. Emotional process is integral to the gestalt formation process and functions as a "self-signal" in a healthy individual. For instance, when one suddenly experiences shame, the healthy person takes that as a sign that he or she should not persist in whatever he or she is doing. Unfortunately, the person whose self-regulation has been disrupted cannot experience shame as a signal, but instead tends to be overwhelmed by it.

## Contact and Support

"*Contact* is possible only to the extent that *support* for it is available. . . . *Support* is everything that facilitates the ongoing assimilation and integration of experience for a person, relationship or society." (L. Perls, 1992).

Adequate support is a function of the total field. It requires both self-support and environmental support. One must support oneself by breathing, but the environment must provide the air.

In health one is not out of touch with the present set of self and environmental needs, and does not live in the past (unfinished business) or future (catastrophizing). It is only in the present that individuals can support themselves and protect themselves.

## Anxiety

Gestalt therapy is concerned with the process of anxiety rather than the content of anxiety (i.e., what one is anxious about). Fritz Perls first defined anxiety as excitement minus support (F. Perls, 1942/1992; F. Perls et al., 1951/1994). Anxiety can be created cognitively or through unsupportive breathing habits.

The cognitive creation of anxiety results from "futurizing" and failing to remain centered in the present. Negative predictions, misinterpretations, and irrational beliefs can all trigger anxiety. When people "futurize" they focus their awareness on something that is not yet present. For example, someone about to give a speech may be preoccupied with the potentially negative reaction of the audience. Fears about future failure can have a very negative effect on current performance. Stage fright is a classic example in which physical arousal is mislabeled and misattribution triggers a panic attack.

Anxiety can also be created by unsupported breathing. With arousal there is an organismic need for oxygen. "A healthy, self-regulating individual will automatically breathe more deeply to meet the increased need for oxygen which accompanies mobilization and contact" (Clarkson & Mackewn, 1993, p. 81).

When people breathe fully, tolerate increased mobilization of energy, are present-centered and cognitively flexible, and put energy into action, they experience excitement rather than anxiety. Breath support requires full inhalation and exhalation, and breathing at a rate that is neither too fast nor too slow. When one breathes rapidly without sufficient exhaling, fresh, oxygenated blood cannot reach the alveoli because the old air with its load of carbon dioxide is not fully expelled. Then the person has the familiar sensations of anxiety, e.g., increased pulse rate, inability to get enough air, and hyperventilation (Acierno, Hersen, & Van Hasselt, 1993; Garssen, de Ruiter, & van Dyck, 1992; F. Perls, 1942/1992, 1973/1976; F. Perls et al., 1951/1994).

The gestalt therapy method, with its focus on both body orientation and characterological issues, is ideal for the treatment of anxiety. Patients learn to master anxiety cognitively and physically through cognitive and body-oriented awareness work (Yontef, 1993).

## Impasse

An impasse is experienced when a person's customary supports are not available and new supports have not yet been mobilized. The experience is existentially one of terror. The person cannot go back and does not know if he or she can survive going forward. People in the impasse are paralyzed, with forward and backward energy fighting each other. This experience is often expressed in metaphorical terms, e.g., void, hollow, blackness, going off a cliff, drowning, or being sucked into a whirlpool (F. Perls, 1969/1992, 1970).

The patient who stays with the experience of the impasse may experience authentic existence, i.e., existence with minimal illusion, good self-support, vitality, creativity, and good contact with the human and nonhuman environment. In this mode, gestalt formation is clear and lively, and a maximum effort is put into what is important. When support is not mobilized to work through the impasse, the person continues to repeat old and maladaptive behaviors.

## Development

Gestalt therapy does not have a well-developed theory of childhood development, but current psychoanalytic research and theory support a perspective that gestalt therapists have held for quite awhile. This theory maintains that infants are born with the capacity for self-regulation, that the development and refinement of self-regulatory skills are contingent on mutual regulation between caretaker and infant, that the contact between caretaker and infant must be attuned to the child's emotional states for self-regulation to develop best, and that children seek relatedness through emotionally attuned mutual regulation (Stern, 1985).

# PSYCHOTHERAPY

## Theory of Psychotherapy

People grow and change all through life. Gestalt therapists believe growth is inevitable as long as one is engaged in contact. Ordinarily, people develop increasing emotional, perceptual, cognitive, motoric, and organismic self-regulatory competence. Sometimes, however, the process of development becomes impaired or derailed. To the extent that people learn from mistakes and grow, psychotherapy is not necessary. Psychotherapy is indicated when people routinely fail to learn from experience. People need psychotherapy when their self-regulatory abilities do not lead them beyond the maladaptive repetitive patterns that were developed originally as creative adjustments in difficult circumstances, but which now make them or those around them unhappy. Psychotherapy is also indicated with patients who do not deal adequately with crises, or feel ill equipped to deal with others in their lives, or who need guidance for personal or spiritual growth.

Gestalt therapy concentrates on helping patients become aware of how they avoid learning from experience, how their self-regulatory processes may be closed-ended rather than open-ended, and how inhibitions in the area of contact limit access to the experience necessary to broaden awareness. Of course, awareness is developed through interactions with other people. From the earliest moment of a person's life, both functional and dysfunctional patterns emerge from a matrix of relationships.

Psychotherapy is primarily a relationship between a patient and a therapist, a relationship in which the patient has another chance to learn, to unlearn, and to learn how to keep learning. The patient and the therapist make explicit the patterns of thought and behavior that are manifest in the psychotherapy situation. Gestalt therapists hold that the patterns that emerge in therapy recapitulate the patterns that are manifest in the patient's life.

## Goal of Therapy

The only goal of gestalt therapy is awareness. This includes achieving greater awareness in particular areas and also improving the ability to bring automatic habits into awareness as needed. In the former sense awareness refers to content; in the latter sense it refers to process, specifically the kind of self-reflective awareness that is called "awareness of awareness." Awareness of awareness is the patient's ability to use his or her skills with awareness to rectify disturbances in his or her awareness process. Both awareness as content and awareness as process broaden and deepen as the therapy proceeds. Awareness requires self-knowledge, knowledge of the environment, responsibility for choices, self-acceptance, and the ability to contact.

Beginning patients are chiefly concerned with the solution of problems, often thinking that the therapist will "fix" them the way a physician cures a disease. However, gestalt therapy does not focus on curing disease, nor is it restricted to talking about problems. Gestalt therapy uses an active relationship and active methods to help patients gain the self-support necessary to solve problems. Gestalt therapists provide support through therapeutic relationship and show patients how they block their awareness and functioning. As therapy goes on, the patient and the therapist turn more attention to general personality issues. By the end of successful gestalt therapy the patient directs much of the work and is able to integrate problem solving, characterological themes, relationship issues with the therapist, and the regulation of his or her own awareness.

## How Is the Therapy Done?

Gestalt therapy is an exploration rather than a direct attempt to change one's behavior. The goal is growth and autonomy through an increase in consciousness. The method is one of direct engagement, whether that engagement is the meeting between the therapist and patient or engagement with problematic aspects of the patient's contacting and awareness process. The model of engagement comes directly from the gestalt concept of contact. Contact is the means whereby living and growth occur, so lived experience almost always takes precedence over explanation. Rather than maintaining an impersonal professional distance and making interpretations, the gestalt therapist relates to the patient with an alive, excited, warm, and direct presence.

In this open, engaged relationship, patients not only get honest feedback, but also in the authentic contact can see, hear, and be told how they are experienced by the therapist, learn how they affect the therapist, and, if interested, patients can learn something about the therapist. They have the healing experience of being listened to by someone who profoundly cares about their perspectives, feelings, and thoughts.

## What and How; Here and Now

In gestalt therapy there is a dual focus of a constant and careful emphasis on *what* the patient does and *how* it is done and also a similar focus on the interactions between therapist and patient. What does the patient do to support him- or herself in the therapy hour in relation to the therapist and in the rest of his or her life?

Direct experience is the primary tool of gestalt therapy, and the focus is always on the here and now. The present is a transition between past and future. Not being primarily present-centered reflects a time disturbance—but so does not being able to contact the relevant past or not planning for the future. Frequently patients lose their contact with the present and live in the past. In some cases, patients live in the present as if they had no past, with the unfortunate consequence that they cannot learn from the past. The most common time disturbance is living in anticipation of what could happen in the future as if the future were now.

*Now* starts with the present awareness of the patient. In a gestalt therapy session, what happens first is not childhood, but what is experienced *now.* Awareness takes place *now.* Prior events may be the object of present awareness, but the awareness process is *now.*

*Now* I can contact the world around me, or *now* I can contact memories or expectations. "Now" refers to *this moment.* When patients refer to their lives outside of the therapy hour, or even earlier in the hour, the content is not considered *now* while the action of speaking *is* now. In gestalt therapy we orient more to the now than in any other form of psychotherapy. This "what and how; here and now" method frequently is used to work on characterological and developmental themes. Exploration of past experience is anchored in the present, e.g., what in the present field triggers this old memory? Whenever possible, methods are used that bring the old experience directly into present experience rather than just recounting the past.

There is an emerging awareness in gestalt therapy that the best therapy requires a binocular viewpoint: Gestalt therapy requires technical work on the patient's awareness process, but at the same time it involves a personal relationship in which careful attention is paid to nuances of what is happening in the contact between therapist and patient.

## Awareness

One of the pillars of gestalt therapy is developing awareness of the awareness process. Does the awareness deepen and develop fully—or is it truncated? Is any particular figure of awareness allowed to recede from the mind to make room for other awarenesses—or does one figure repeatedly capture the mind and shut out the development of other awareness?

Ideally processes that need to be in awareness come into awareness when and as needed, in the ongoing flow of living. When transactions get complex, more conscious self-regulation is needed. If this develops and the person behaves mindfully, a person is likely to learn from experience.

The concept of awareness exists along a continuum. For example, gestalt therapy distinguishes merely *knowing* about something and *owning* what one is doing. Merely knowing about something marks the transition between something being totally out of awareness and it being in focal awareness. When people report being aware of something and yet claim they are totally helpless to make desired changes, they are usually referring to a situation in which they *know* about something but do not fully feel it, do not know the details of how it works, and do not genuinely *own* it.

Being fully aware means turning one's attention to the processes that are most important for the person and environment; this is a natural occurrence in healthy self-regulating. One must know what is going on and how it is happening. What am I needing and what am I doing? What is needed by others? Who is doing what? Who needs what? For full awareness, this more detailed descriptive awareness must be allowed to affect the patient—and he or she has to be able to own it and respond in a relevant way.

## Contact

Contact refers to the relationship between patient and therapist; it is another pillar of gestalt therapy. The relationship is contact over time. What happens in the relationship is crucial. This is more than what the therapist says to the patient, and it is more than the techniques that are used. Of most importance is the nonverbal subtext (posture, tone of voice, syntax, and interest level) that communicates tremendous amounts of information to the patient about how the therapist regards the patient, what is important, and how therapy works.

In a good therapy relationship the therapist pays close attention to what the patient is doing moment to moment and to what is happening between the therapist and patient. The therapist not only pays close attention to what the patient experiences, but deeply believes that the patient's subjective experience is as real and valid as the therapist's "reality."

The therapist is in a powerful position in relation to the patient. If the therapist regards the patient with honesty, affection, compassion, kindness, and respect, an atmosphere of safety can be created in which it is relatively safe for the patient to become more deeply aware of what has been kept from awareness. This allows the patient to express thoughts and emotions that the patient has habitually not felt safe to share.

The therapist is in a position to guide the awareness work by entering into the patient's experience as deeply and completely. Martin Buber refers to "inclusion" as feeling the experience of the other much as one would feel something within one's own body while simultaneously being aware of one's own self.

There is some tension between the humane urge of the therapist to relieve the patient's pain and the indispensable need of the patient for someone to willingly enter into and understand his or her subjective pain. The therapist's empathic experience of the patient's pain brings the patient into the realm of human contact. However, trying to get the patient to feel better is often experienced by a patient as evidence that the patient is only acceptable to the extent that he or she feels good. The therapist may not intend to convey this message, but this reaction is often triggered when the therapist does not abide by the paradoxical theory of change.

## Experiment

In person-centered therapy the phenomenological work by the therapist is limited to reflecting what the patient subjectively experiences. In modern psychoanalytic work, the therapist is limited to interpretations or reflections. These interventions are both in the gestalt therapy repertoire, but gestalt therapy has an additional experimental phenomenological method. Put simply, the patient and therapist can experiment with different ways of thought and action to achieve genuine understanding rather than mere changes in behavior. As in any research, the experiment is designed to get more data. In gestalt therapy, the data is the phenomenological experience of the patient.

The greatest risk with experiments is that vulnerable patients may believe that change has been mandated. This danger is magnified if a therapist's self-awareness becomes clouded or if he or she strays from a commitment to the paradoxical theory of change. It is vitally important in gestalt therapy that the therapist remain clear that the mode of change is the patient's knowledge and acceptance of self, knowing and supporting what emerges in contemporaneous experience. If the therapist is clear that the experiments are experiments in awareness and not criticism of what is observed, the risk of adding to the patient's self-rejection is minimized.

## Self-Disclosure

One powerful and different aspect of gestalt therapy is that therapists are both permitted and encouraged to disclose their personal experience, both in the moment and in their lives. Unlike classical psychoanalysis, in gestalt therapy data is provided by both the patient and the therapist, and both the patient and the therapist take part in directing therapy through a process of mutual phenomenological exploration.

This kind of therapeutic relationship requires that therapists be at peace with the differences between themselves and their patients. In addition, therapists most truly believe that the patient's sense of subjective reality is as valid as their own. With an appreciation of the relativity of one's subjectivity, it becomes possible for therapists to disclose their reactions to patients without *requiring* that patients change. These conversations, entered into with care and sensitivity, are generally quite interesting and evocative, and often enhance the patient's sense of efficacy and worthiness.

*Dialogue* is the basis of the gestalt therapy relationship. In dialogue, the therapist practices inclusion, empathic engagement, and personal presence, e.g., self-disclosure. In the process of doing this, the therapist confirms the existence and potential of the patient, the therapist imagines the reality of the patient's experience and in doing so confirms existence of the patient. However, this is not enough to make the interaction a real dialogue.

Real dialogue between the therapist and patient must also include the therapist surrendering to the interaction and to what emerges from that interaction. The therapist must be open to being changed by the interaction. This sometimes requires the therapist to acknowledge having been wrong, hurtful, arrogant, or mistaken. This kind of acknowledgment puts therapist and patient on a horizontal plane. This sort of open disclosure requires personal therapy for the therapist to reduce defensiveness and the need to pridefully maintain his or her personal self-image.

## Process of Psychotherapy

People form their sense of self and their style of awareness and behavior in childhood. These become habitual and often are not refined or revised by new experiences. As a person moves out of the family and into the world, new situations are encountered and the old ways of thinking, feeling, and acting are no longer needed or adaptive in new situations. But the old ways continue because they are not in awareness.

In gestalt therapy the patient encounters someone who takes his or her experience seriously, and through this different, respectful relationship, a new sense of self is formed. By combining the gestalt therapy relationship with phenomenological focusing techniques, the patient becomes aware of processes that previously could not be changed because they were out of awareness. Gestalt therapists believe the contact between therapist and patient sets the stage for the development of the capacity to be in contact with one's shifting figures of interest on a moment-by-moment basis.

Gestalt therapy probably has a greater range of styles and modalities than any other system. Therapy can be short term or long term. Specific modalities include individual, couple, family, group, and large systems. Styles vary in degree and type of structure; quantity and quality of techniques used; frequency of sessions; confrontation versus compassionate relating; focus on body, cognition, affect, or interpersonal contact; knowledge of and work with psychodynamic themes; the emphasis on dialogue and presence; use of techniques; and so forth.

All styles of gestalt therapy share a common emphasis on direct experience and experimenting, use of direct contact and personal presence, and a focus on the what and how; here and now. The therapy varies according to context and the personalities of both therapist and patient.

Gestalt therapy starts with the first contact between therapist and patient. The therapist inquires about the desires or needs of the patient and describes how he or she practices therapy. From the beginning the focus is on what is happening now and what is needed now. The therapist begins immediately to help clarify the patient's awareness of self and environment. In this case the potential relationship with the therapist is part of the environment.

The therapist and prospective gestalt therapy patient work together to become clear about what the patient needs and whether this particular therapist is suitable. If there seems to be a match between the two, then the therapy proceeds with getting acquainted. The patient and therapist begin to relate and understand each other, and the process of sharpening awareness begins. In the beginning it is often not clear whether the therapy will be short or long term or even if, on further examination, the match between patient and therapist will prove to be satisfactory.

Typically therapy will begin with attention to the immediate feelings of the patient, the current needs of the patient, and some sense of the patient's life circumstances and history. A long social history is rarely taken, although there is nothing in gestalt theory to prevent it. Usually history is gathered in the process of therapy as it is relevant to current therapy work and at a pace comfortable for the patient.

Some patients start with their life story, while others start with a contemporaneous focus. The therapist helps patients become aware of what is emerging and what they are feeling and needing as they tell their stories. This is done by reflective statements of the therapist's understanding of what the patient is saying and feeling, and by suggestions about how to focus awareness (or questions that accomplish that same goal).

For example, a patient might start telling a story of recent events but not say how he was affected by the events. The therapist might ask either what the patient felt when the reported event happened or what the patient is feeling in telling the story. The therapist also might go back over the story, focusing on recognizing and verbalizing the feelings associated with various stages in the story.

The therapist also makes an assessment of the strengths and weaknesses of patients, including personality style. The therapist looks for how, and in what specific ways, the patient's self-support is either precarious or robust.

There is considerable controversy in gestalt therapy over the use of formal diagnosis. Some gestalt therapists are allied with those humanists who think diagnosis impedes authentic relating. Others see assessment of personality, culture, situation, and pathology as an indispensable part of psychotherapy practice. Those who take this position believe accurate assessment and diagnosis can inform and shape how therapy is practiced (Yontef, 1993).

Gestalt therapy can be adapted and practiced with virtually any patient for whom psychotherapy is indicated. However, the practice must be adopted to the particular needs of each person. The competent gestalt therapist, as any other kind of therapist, must have the training and ability to make this discrimination. A good therapist knows the limits of his or her experience and training and practices within these limits.

Treatment usually starts with either individual or couples therapy—or both. Group therapy is sometimes added to the treatment plan, and the group may become the sole modality for treatment. Fritz Perls made claims that patients could be treated by gestalt group therapy alone. This was never accepted by most gestalt therapists, and this belief is thoroughly rejected today. Gestalt group therapy complements individual and couples work but does not replace it.

Gestalt therapists work with all ages, although specialized training is required for work with young children. Gestalt therapy with children is done individually, as part of Gestalt family therapy, and occasionally in groups (Lampert, 2003; Oaklander, 1969/1988).

## Mechanisms of Psychotherapy

All techniques in gestalt therapy are considered experiments, and patients are repeatedly told to "Try this and see what you experience." There are many "gestalt therapy techniques," but the techniques themselves are of little importance. Any technique consistent with gestalt therapy principles can and will be used. In fact, gestalt therapy explicitly encourages therapists to be creative in their interventions (Zinker, 1977).

### Focusing

The most common techniques are the simple interventions of focusing. Focusing runs the range from simple inclusion or empathy to exercises arising mostly from the therapist's experience while being with the patient. Everything in gestalt therapy is secondary to the actual and direct experience of the participants. The therapist helps clarify what is important by helping the patient focus his or her awareness.

The prototypical experiment is some form of the question, "What are you aware of, or experiencing, right here and now?" Awareness occurs continuously moment to moment, and the gestalt therapist pays particular attention to the *awareness continuum*. This important focus is on the flow or sequence of awareness from one moment to another.

The gestalt therapist also draws attention to key moments in therapy. Of course, this requires that the therapist have the sensitivity and experience to recognize these moments when they occur. Some patients feel abandoned if the therapist is quiet for long periods; others feel it is intrusive when the therapist is active. Therefore, the therapist must balance the possible disruption of the patient's awareness continuum if he or she offers guiding observation or suggestion against the facilitative benefit that can be derived from focusing. This is regulated by the ongoing communication between the therapist and patient and is not solely directed by the therapist.

One key moment occurs when a patient interrupts ongoing awareness before it is completed. The gestalt therapist recognizes signs of this interruption, including the nonverbal indications, by paying close attention to shifts in tension states, muscle tone, or excitement levels. The therapist's observation and interpretation of the moment is not presumed to be relevant or useful unless the patient can confirm or disconfirm it. One patient may tell a story about events with someone in his life, and at a key moment grit his teeth, hold his breath and not exhale. This may turn out to be an interruption of awareness or an expression of anger. Alternately, a therapist might notice that an angry look is beginning to change to a look of sadness—but a sadness that is not reported. The patient might change to another subject or begin to intellectualize. In this case the sadness may be interrupted either at the level of self-awareness or at the level of expression of the affect.

When the patient reports a feeling, another technique is to "stay with it." This encourages the patient to continue with the feeling being reported and builds the patient's capacity to deepen and work through a feeling. The following vignette illustrates this technique (P = Patient; T = Therapist).

P: [Looks sad.]
T: What are you aware of?
P: I'm sad.
T: Stay with it.
P: [Tears well up. The patient tightens up, looks away, and becomes thoughtful.]
T: I see you are tightening. What are you aware of?
P: I don't want to stay with the sadness.
T: Stay with the not wanting to. Put words to the not wanting to. [This intervention is likely to bring awareness of the patient's resistance to vulnerability. The patient might respond "I won't cry here—it doesn't feel safe," or "I am ashamed," or "I am angry and don't want to admit I'm sad."]

There is an emerging awareness in gestalt therapy that the moments in which patients change subjects often reflect something happening in the interaction between the therapist and patient. Something the therapist says or his or her nonverbal behavior may trigger insecurity or shame in the patient. Most often this is not in the patient's awareness until attention is focused on it by the therapist and explored by dialogue (Jacobs, 1996).

## Enactment

The patient is asked to experiment with putting feelings or thoughts into action. This technique might be as simple as encouraging the patient to "say it to the person" (if the person involved is present) or might be enacted using role playing, psychodrama, or gestalt therapy's well-known empty-chair technique.

Sometimes enactment is combined with the technique of asking the patient to exaggerate. This is not done to achieve catharsis, but is a form of experiment that sometimes results in increased awareness of the feeling.

*Creative expression* is another form of enactment. For some patients creative expression can help clarify feelings in a way that talking alone cannot. The techniques of expression include journal writing, poetry, art, and movement. Creative expression is especially important in work with children (Lederman, 1970; Oaklander, 1969/1988).

## Mental Experiments, Guided Fantasy, and Imagery

Sometimes visualizing an experience here and now increases awareness more effectively than enacting it, as is illustrated in the following brief vignette (P = Patient; T = Therapist).

P:  I was with my girlfriend last night. I don't know how it happened but I was impotent. [Patient gives more details and history.]

T:  Close your eyes. Imagine it is last night and you are with your girlfriend. Say out loud what you experience at each moment.

P:  I am sitting on the couch. My friend sits next to me and I get excited. Then I go soft.

T:  Let's go through that again in slow motion, and in more detail. Be sensitive to every thought or sense impression.

P:  I am sitting on the couch. She comes over and sits next to me. She touches my neck. It feels so warm and soft. I get excited—you know, hard. She strokes my arm and I love it. [Pause. Looks startled.] Then I thought, I had such a tense day, maybe I won't be able to get it up.

One can use imagery to explore and express an emotion that does not lend itself to simple linear verbalization. For example, a patient might imagine being alone on a desert, eaten alive by insects, being sucked in by a whirlpool, and so forth. There are infinite possible images that can be drawn from dreams, waking fantasy, and the creative use of fantasy. The gestalt therapist might suggest that the patient imagine the experience happening right now, rather than simply discussing it. "Imagine you are actually in that desert, right now. What do you experience?" This is often followed by some version of "stay with it."

An image may arise spontaneously in the patient's awareness as a here-and-now experience, or it might be consciously created by the patient and/or therapist. The patient might suddenly report, "Just now I feel cold, like I'm alone in outer space." This might indicate something about what is happening between the therapist and the patient at that moment, i.e., perhaps the patient is experiencing the therapist as not being emotionally present.

Imagery techniques can also be used to expand the patient's self-supportive techniques. For example, in working with patients who have strong shame issues, at times it is helpful for them to imagine a metaphorical Good Mother, one who is fully present and loving and accepts and loves the patient just as he or she is (Yontef, 1993).

Meditative techniques, many of which are borrowed from Asian psychotherapies, can also be very helpful experiments.

## Body Awareness

Awareness of body activity is an important aspect of gestalt therapy, and there is a specific gestalt therapy methodology for working with body awareness (Kepner, 1987). The gestalt therapist is especially interested in patterns of breathing. For example, when a person is breathing in a manner that does not support centering and feeling, he or she will often experience anxiety. Usually the breathing of the anxious patient involves rapid inhalation and a failure to fully exhale. One can work with experiments in breathing in the context of an ordinary therapy session. One can also practice a thoroughly body oriented gestalt therapy (Frank, 2001; Kepner, 1987).

### Loosening and Integrating Techniques

Some patients are so rigid in their thinking that they do not even consider alternative possibilities. This rigidity is sometimes the result of psychological factors, such as denial or repression, but it can also result from cultural factors. Loosening techniques such as fantasy, imagination, or mentally experimenting with the opposite of what is believed can help break down this rigidity so alternatives can at least be considered.

Integrating techniques bring together processes that the patient doesn't bring together or actively keeps apart (splitting). Asking the patient to join the positive and negative poles of a polarity can be very integrating, e.g., "I love him and I abhor his flippant attitude." Putting words to sensations, or finding the sensations that accompany words ("see if you can locate it in your body") are other important integrating techniques.

## APPLICATIONS

### Problems

During the 1960s gestalt therapy was known for its treatment of individuals who were primarily constricted, anxious and/or depressed, in conflict with themselves, and without serious pathology (Fagan & Shepherd, 1970). Although gestalt therapy was and is quite effective with this population, its effectiveness and safety is not limited to such individuals. In fact, gestalt therapy might well be the treatment of choice for some personality disorders, e.g., borderline personality disorder (Yontef, 1993).

Because gestalt therapy is a process theory, it can be used effectively with any patient population the therapist understands and feels comfortable with. If the therapist can relate to the patient and understands the basic principles of gestalt therapy and how to adjust these principles to fit the unique needs of each new patient, the gestalt therapy principles of *awareness* (direct experience), *contact* (relationship), and *experimenting* (phenomenological focusing and experimentation) can be applied. Gestalt therapy does not advocate a cookbook of prescribed techniques for specialized groups of individuals. Therapists who wish to work with patients who are culturally different from themselves find support by attending to the field conditions that influence their understanding of the patient's life and culture (for example, see Jacobs, 2000). The gestalt therapy attitude of dialogue and the phenomenological assumption of multiple valid realities support the therapist in working with a patient from another culture, enabling patient and therapist to mutually understand the difference in background, assumptions, and so forth.

Both gestalt therapy philosophy and methodology dictate that *general principles must always be adapted for each particular clinical situation.* The manner of relating and the choice and execution of techniques must be tailored to each new patient's needs. Therapy will be ineffective or harmful if the patient is made to conform to the system rather than having the system adjust to the patient.

It has long been accepted that gestalt therapy in the confrontive and theatrical style of a 1960s Fritz Perls workshop is much more limited in application than the gestalt therapy that is described in this chapter. The effectiveness of more confrontive styles of gestalt therapy has not been well established, and confrontation should always be used with caution (Dolliver, 1981; Dublin, 1976).

Common sense, professional background, flexibility, and creativity are especially important in diagnosis and treatment planning. Methods, emphases, precautions, limitations, commitments, and auxiliary support (such as medication, day treatment, and nutritional guidance) must be modified with different patients depending on their personality organization, e.g., the presence of psychosis, sociopathy, or a personality disorder.

*The competent practice of gestalt therapy requires a strong general clinical background and training in more than gestalt therapy.* In addition to training in the theory and practice of gestalt therapy, gestalt therapists need to have a firm grounding in personality theory, psychopathology and diagnosis, theories and applications of other systems of psychotherapy, knowledge of psychodynamics, comprehensive personal therapy, and advanced clinical training, supervision, and experience.

This background is especially important in gestalt therapy because therapists and patients are encouraged to be creative and to experiment with new behavior in and out of the session. The individual clinician has a great deal of discretion in gestalt therapy. Modifications are made by the individual therapist and patient according to therapeutic style, personality of therapist and patient, and diagnostic considerations. A good knowledge of research, other systems, and the principles of personality organization are needed to guide and limit the spontaneous creativity of the therapist. The gestalt therapist is expected to be creative, but he or she cannot abdicate responsibility for professional discrimination, judgment, and proper caution.

Gestalt therapy has been applied in almost every setting imaginable. Applications have varied from intensive individual therapy multiple times per week to crisis intervention. Gestalt therapists have also worked with organizations, schools (Brown, 1970, 1971/1990; Lederman, 1969, 1970; Maurer, 2002; Nevis, 1987; Nevis, Lancourt, & Vasallo, 1996), and groups; they have worked with patients with psychoses, patients suffering from psychosomatic disorders, and patients with post-traumatic stress disorders. Many of the details about how to modify gestalt techniques in order to work effectively with these populations have been disseminated in the oral tradition, e.g., through supervision, consultation, and training.

In applications in which intense and disorganizing affective experiences emerge from gestalt therapy, especially in work marked by expressive or confrontive techniques that break down defenses, it is necessary for the therapist or group leader to engage in a manner that establishes sufficient contact with and between participants to provide safety in and after the work. A commitment by the therapist to continuity of treatment is also required in these situations.

The gestalt therapy system includes means of reestablishing good orientation when the affective work becomes very intense. The patient may be encouraged to make visual, tactile, or other contact with the therapist or with one or more group members, and of course he or she will be encouraged to talk about the experience. Another safety technique is to suggest that the patient shuttle back and forth between making contact in the *now* with the therapist or group members and with the emotional material that is being uncovered.

## Evaluation

There is an anarchistic tradition within gestalt therapy that prefers to train patients to evaluate for themselves what works and does not work rather than trusting research results. This tradition maintains that changes on measurable and narrowly defined scales do not give patients the information needed for their personal evaluation.

Perls admitted he offered no quantified, statistical evidence that gestalt therapy works. He did say, "we present nothing that you cannot verify for yourself in terms of your own behavior" (F. Perls et al., 1951/1994, p. 255). The book *Gestalt Therapy* offers a series of experiments that one can use to test the validity of gestalt therapy.

The emphasis on phenomenological observation, focusing, and experimentation provides data for the patient and to the therapist. The patient is aided in using phenomenological focusing skills and dialogic contact to evaluate what is and is not working. In this sense gestalt therapy values dialogue and spontaneity more than a precise treatment regime with set procedures that are scientifically proven.

The primary sources of evaluative data for both therapist and patient are observations, bodily and affective feelings, and feedback from others. Successful gestalt therapy is expected to improve perception and receptivity to self and others. and advance and develop behaviors that are effective in the person's environment, i.e., adjusting to the environment, changing environments, and/or improving the environment.

Gestalt therapy is evaluated based on improvement in the clarity of the patient's perception of self and the rest of the world, self-acceptance, and creative adjustment. An important part of the evaluation of success is a relatively accurate and honest self-appraisal and the ability to acknowledge strengths and weaknesses while still liking and respecting one's self. In successful gestalt therapy, this clarity and cohesion of one's sense of self is maintained over time and across situations.

One sign of successful gestalt therapy is a change in awareness. Successful patients develop insight, i.e., they experience and express "aha!" reactions, realize how the parts and the whole fit together and change over time, and come to appreciate how the whole is configured and how parts fit into that whole. The successful former gestalt therapy patient has clearer boundaries; he or she is clear about connecting and separating and knows what is self and what is other.

With this increase in awareness comes the ability to take more responsibility for what is under one's control and not take responsibility for what is not under one's control. Awareness includes awareness of personal motivation; of the links between present thinking, feeling, and behavior and one's own past history; and of the ability to identify with ongoing, moment-by-moment experiencing.

Improved patients look and feel livelier, and they make better contact with other people and with the environment. These patients also experience an improved ability to state accurately what they want and deal with the needs of the environment. Successful gestalt therapy patients often look more graceful: They are literally and figuratively better grounded, and they are able to move with more fluidity. A particularly sensitive indication of therapeutic success is the quality of breathing (Kepner, 1987). The improved patient is less tense and inhales and exhales smoothly.

These changes are reported by the patient and are also observed during sessions by the therapist, the patient, and other patients in group therapy. There is an increase in social interactions, and the patient is more aware of differences between people.

## Research

There is increasing research support for gestalt therapy (reviewed in Yontef, 1995). Cain and Seeman (2001) review issues of validation of humanistic therapies, including gestalt therapy (Staemmler, 2003). They cite relevant research and describe the general results using Carl Rogers's words: "The facts are friendly" (Rogers, 1961/1995, p. 25).

The best research is the ongoing research program of Les Greenberg and associates (Greenberg, 1986, 1991; Greenberg & Paivio, 1997; Greenberg, Rice, & Elliott, 1993) in which process and outcome studies are brought together with attention to context. Many of their research reports relate specific interventions with three types of outcome (immediate, intermediate, and final) and three levels of process (speech act, episode, and relationship).

Greenberg continues to conduct research in what he calls process-directive experiential therapy. He considers this form of active experiential therapy a combination of a Rogerian client-centered relationship and gestalt therapy techniques. For purposes of research, we can consider modern, relational gestalt therapy equivalent to process-directive experiential therapy, with the exception that gestalt therapy practice uses a wider range of techniques than have so far been studied in Greenberg's program.

Greenberg, Elliott, and Lietaer (1994) reviewed 13 studies comparing experiential therapies with cognitive and behavioral treatments using meta-psychological statistics and found the cognitive and behavioral interventions were slightly more effective. However, when the seven studies compared directive experiential therapy with cognitive or behavioral treatment, there was a small, statistically significant difference in favor of the directive experiential. This indicates that the directive experiential approach was more effective than either a pure client-centered approach lacking active phenomenological experimentation or the cognitive and behavioral treatments.

The same group has conducted a number of experiments in which using the gestalt therapy two-chair technique resulted in a greater depth of experience than empathic reflection alone (Greenberg, 1982; Greenberg & Clarke, 1979; Greenberg & Dompierre, 1981; Greenberg & Higgins, 1980; Greenberg & Rice, 1981). Paivio and Greenberg (1992) demonstrated that the empty-chair dialogue was effective for resolving unfinished emotional issues with significant others. Pre- and post-testing showed that general distress was reduced, and there was a reduction in unfinished business. The two-chair technique has been shown to be effective in healing internal splits because of an increase in the depth of experiencing (Greenberg, 1979; Greenberg & Higgins, 1980).

An introjected harsh, critical, self-rejecting voice prevents healing and growth. Research shows that the two-chair technique is effective in softening the "harsh internal critic" (Greenberg, 1980). Greenberg also has demonstrated that conflict resolution using the two-chair dialogue occurs by deeper experiencing of previously rejected aspects of self. This is a confirmation of gestalt therapy's paradoxical theory of change.

Research that is relevant, realistic, and valid for gestalt therapy would account for the importance of the therapeutic relationship and also allow the full range of interventions that are integral to the gestalt therapy method. Limiting the therapist's interventions in order to achieve scientific precision would achieve uniformity for the research at the expense of misrepresenting the gestalt therapy methodology. It would also contradict the main tenets of humanistic psychology (Cain & Seeman, 2001; Staemmler, 2003).

Specific techniques like the empty-chair and two-chair technique can be conveniently studied. However, these tools are not representative of all patients or the range of techniques used in gestalt therapy. Some patients are too inhibited or cannot generate sufficient affect to use the empty chair effectively. A wide range of techniques can be used in clinical practice that accomplish the same function as the empty chair. One advantage of gestalt therapy is that the therapist has support for using a wide range of techniques within the context of a cohesive theoretical framework.

Gestalt therapists take nomothetic data seriously and will utilize information from such research. One example is the impact of cognitive-behavioral research on the treatment of depression by strengthening cognitive awareness. However, most gestalt therapists agree with Norcross and Rossi (1994) that "psychotherapy is more fruitfully conceived and researched as a human relationship than as a technical, manualized treatment. The outcomes of particular therapist-patient dyads are probably more illuminating than the group means" (p. 537).

## Treatment

Patients often present similar issues but need different treatment because of differences in their personality organization and what unfolds in the therapeutic relationship. In the following two examples, each of two patients was raised by emotionally abandoning parents.

Tom was a 45-year-old man proud of his intelligence, self-sufficiency, and independence. He was not aware that he had unmet dependency needs and resentment. This man's belief in his self-sufficiency and denial of dependency required respect and sensitivity by his therapist. The belief in self-sufficiency met a need, was in part constructive, and was the foundation for the patient's self-esteem. The therapist was able to respond to the patient's underlying need without threatening the patient's pride (P = Patient; T = Therapist).

P:   [With pride.] When I was a little kid my mom was so busy I just had to learn to rely on myself.
T:   I appreciate your strength, but when I think of you as such a self-reliant kid, I want to stroke you and give you some parenting.
P:   [Tearing a little.] No one ever did that for me.
T:   You seem sad.
P:   I'm remembering when I was a kid . . .

[Tom evoked a sympathetic response in the therapist that was expressed directly to the patient. His denial of needing anything from others was not directly challenged. Exploration led to awareness of a shame reaction to unavailable parents and a compensatory self-reliance.]

Bob was a 45-year-old man who felt shame and isolated himself in reaction to any interaction that was not totally positive. He was consistently reluctant to support himself, conforming to and relying totally on others. Previous empathic or sympathetic responses only served to reinforce the patient's belief in his own inadequacy.

P:   [Whiny voice.] I don't know what to do today.
T:   [Looks and does not talk. Previous interventions of providing more direction had resulted in the patient following any slight lead by the therapist into talk that was not felt by the patient.]
P:   I could talk about my week. [Looks questioningly at therapist.]
T:   I feel pulled on by you right now. I imagine you want me to direct you.
P:   Yes, what's wrong with that?
T:   Nothing. I prefer not to direct you right now.
P:   Why not?
T:   You can direct yourself. I believe you are directing us now away from your inner self. I don't want to cooperate with that. [Silence.]
P:   I feel lost.
T:   [Looks alert and available but does not talk.]
P:   You are not going to direct me, are you?
T:   No.
P:   Well, let's work on my believing I can't take care of myself. [The patient had real feelings about this issue, and initiated a fruitful piece of work that led to awareness of abandonment anxiety and feelings of shame in response to unavailable parents.]

## Groups

Group treatment is frequently part of an overall gestalt therapy treatment program. There are three general models for doing group gestalt therapy (Frew, 1988; Yontef, 1990). In the first model participants work one-on-one with the therapist while the other participants remain relatively quiet and work vicariously. The work is then followed by feedback and interaction with other participants with an emphasis on how people are affected by the work. In the second model participants talk with each other with emphasis on direct here-and-now communication between the group members. This model is similar to Yalom's model for existential group therapy. A third model mixes these two activities in the same group (Yontef, 1990). The group and therapist creatively regulate movement and balance between interaction and the one-on-one focus.

All the techniques discussed in this chapter can be used in groups. In addition there are possibilities for experimental focusing that are special to groups. Gestalt therapy groups usually start with some procedure for bringing participants into the here and now and contacting each other. This is often called "rounds" or "check in."

A simple and obvious example of gestalt group work occurs when the therapist has each group member look at the other members of the group and express what he or she is experiencing in the here and now. Some gestalt therapists also use structured experiments, such as experiments in which participants express a particular emotion, e.g., "I resent you for . . . ," "I appreciate you for. . . ." The style of other gestalt therapists is fluid and organized by what emerges in the group.

## Couples and Families

Couples and family work are similar to groups in that there is a combination of work with each person in the session and work with interaction per se. Gestalt therapists vary in their preferences in this balance. There is also variation in how structured the intervention style of the therapist is and how much the therapist follows, observes, and focuses the spontaneous functioning of the couple or family.

Partners often start couple therapy by complaining and blaming each other. The work at this point involves calling attention to this dynamic and to alternative modes of interaction. The gestalt therapist will also explore what is behind the blaming. Frequently one party experiences the other as shaming him or her and blames the other, without awareness of the defensive function of the blaming.

*Circular causality* is a frequent pattern in unhappy couples. In circular causality A causes B and B causes A. Regardless of how an interaction starts, A triggers a response in B to which A then reacts negatively, without being aware of his or her role in triggering the negative response. B likewise triggers a negative response by A without being aware of his or her role in triggering the negative response. Circular causality is illustrated in the following example.

A wife expresses frustration with her husband for coming home late from work every night and not being emotionally available when he comes home. The husband feels unappreciated, attacked, and at an unaware level also feels ashamed of being criticized. The husband responds with anger, blaming the wife for not being affectionate. The wife accuses the husband of being defensive, aggressive, insensitive, and emotionally unavailable. The husband responds in kind. Each response in this circle makes it worse. In the worst cases this circular causality can lead to total disruption in the relationship and may trigger drinking, violence, or sexual acting out.

Underneath the wife's frustration is the fact that she misses her husband, is lonely, worries about him working so hard, really wants to be with him, and assumes that he does not want to be home with her because she is no longer attractive. However, these fears are not expressed clearly. The husband might want to be home with his wife and resent having to work so hard but also feel a need to unwind from the stress of work before being emotionally available. The caring and interest of each spouse for the other often gets lost in the circular defensive/offensive battle.

Often blaming statements trigger shame and shame defense. In this kind of toxic atmosphere, no one listens. There is no true contact and no repair or healing. Expressing actual experience, rather than judgments, and allowing oneself to really hear the experience of the spouse are first steps toward healing. Of course, that requires that the partners each know or learn how to recognize their actual experience.

Sometimes structured experiments are helpful. In one experiment the couple is asked to face each other, pulling their chairs toward each other until they are close enough to touch knees, and then instructed to look at each other and express what they are aware of at each moment. Other experiments include completing sentences such as "I resent you for . . ." and "I appreciate you for. . . ." Or, "I spite you by . . ." or "I feel bad about myself when you. . . ."

It is critical in couples therapy for the therapist to model the style of listening he or she thinks will enhance each spouse's ability to verbalize his or her experience, and to encourage each partner to listen as well as to speak. The various experiments help to convey to patients that verbal statements are not something written in stone but are part of an ongoing dialogue. The restoration of dialogue is a sign that therapy is progressing.

As described in the earlier section on psychotherapy, patients may move into various treatment modalities throughout treatment. They may have individual therapy, group therapy, or couples therapy, and they may occasionally participate in workshops. It is not unusual for patients to make occasional use of adjunctive workshops while engaged in ongoing individual therapy.

Gestalt therapists tend to see patients on a weekly basis. As more attention comes to be focused on the therapist/patient relationship, patients are eager to come more often, so some gestalt therapists see people more often than once a week. Many gestalt therapists also run groups, and there are therapists who teach and conduct workshops for the general public. Others primarily teach and train therapists. The shape of one's practice is limited only by one's interests and by the exigencies of the work environment.

## CASE EXAMPLE

### Background

Miriam often spoke in a flat voice, seemingly disconnected from her feelings, or even any sense of the meaningfulness of her sentences. She had survived terrifying and degrading childhood abuse, and now, some 35 years after leaving home, she had the haunted, pinched look of someone who expected the abuse to begin again at any minute. She could not even say that she wanted therapy for herself, as she claimed not to want or need people in her life. She thought that being in therapy could help her to develop her skills as a consultant more fully. Miriam was quite wary of therapy, but she had attended a lecture given by the therapist, and had felt a slight glimmer of hope that this particular therapist might actually be able to understand her.

Miriam's experiential world was characterized by extreme isolation. She was ashamed of her isolation but it made her feel safe. When she moved about in the world of people she felt terrified, often enraged, and deeply ashamed. She was unrelentingly self-critical. She believed she was a toxic presence, unwillingly destructive of others. She was unable to acknowledge wants or needs of her own, for such an acknowledgment made her vulnerable, and (in her words) a "target" for humiliation and annihilation. Finally, she was plagued by a sense of unreality. She never knew if what she thought or perceived was "real" or imagined. She knew nothing of what she felt, believed that she had no feelings, and did not even know what a feeling was. At times these feelings were so strong she fantasized she was an alien.

Miriam's fundamental conflicts revolved around the polarity of isolation versus confluence. Although she was at most times too ashamed of her desires to even recognize them, when her wish to be connected to others became figural she was overcome with dread. She recognized that she wanted to just "melt" into the other person, and could not bear even a hint of distance, for the distance signaled rejection, which she believed would be unbearable to her. She was rigidly entrenched in her isolated world. A consequence of her rigidity was that she was unable to flow back and forth in a rhythm of contact and withdrawal. The only way she could regulate the states of tension and anxiety that emerged as she dared to move toward contact, with the therapist and others, was to suddenly shrink back in shame, retreat into isolation, or become dissociated, which happened quite often. Then she would feel stuck, too ashamed and defeated to dare to venture forward again. She was unable to balance and calibrate the experience of desiring contact while at the same time being afraid of contact.

The following sequence occurred about four years into therapy. She was much better at this point in being able to identify with and express feeling, but navigating a contact boundary with another person was still daunting. She had begun this session with a deep sense of pleasure because she finally felt a sense of continuity with the therapist, and reported that for the first time in her life she was also connected to some memories. The air of celebration gave way to desperation and panic later, as therapist and patient struggled together with her wishes and fears for a closer connection to the therapist.

In a conversation which had been repeated at various times, Miriam's desperation grew as she wanted the therapist to "just reach past" her fear, to touch the tiny, disheveled, and lonely "cave girl" who hid inside. Miriam felt abandoned by the therapist's "patience" (Miriam's word).

P:   You're so damn patient!
T:   . . . and this is a bad thing? . . . [Said tentatively.]
P:   Right now it is.
T:   Because you need . . .
P:   [Pause.] Something that indicates *something.* [Sounding frightened and exasperated, and confused.]
T:   What does my patience indicate to you right now?
P:   That I am just going to be left scrambling forever!
T:   It sounds like I am watching from too far away—rather than going through this with you—does that sound right?
P:   Sounds right . . .
T:   So you need something from me that indicates we will get through this together, that I won't just let you drown. [Said softly and seriously.]

[A few minutes later, the exploration of her need for contact and her fear has continued, with Miriam even admitting to a wish to be touched physically, which is a big admission for her to make. Once again Miriam is starting to panic. She is panicked with fear of what may happen now that she has exposed her wish to be touched. She fears the vulnerability of allowing the touch, and is also panicky about being rejected or cruelly abandoned. The therapist has been emphasizing that Miriam's wish for contact is but one side of the conflict, and that the other side, her fear, needs to be respected as well. The patient was experiencing the therapist's caution as an abandonment, whereas the therapist was concerned that "just reaching past" the patient's fear would reenact a boundary violation and would trigger greater dissociation.]

T:   . . . so, we need to honor *both* your fear and your wish. . . . [Miriam looks frightened, on the verge of dissociating.] . . . now you are moving into a panic—speak to me . . .
P:   [Agonized whisper.] It's too much.
T:   [Softly.] yeah, too much . . . what's that . . . "it's too much"?
P:   Somehow if you touch me I will disappear. And I don't want to—I want to—I want to use touch to *connect,* not to disappear!
T:   Right, OK, so the fear side of you is saying that the risk in touching is that you'll disappear.

Now we have to take that fear into account. And I have a suggestion—that I will move and we sit so that our fingertips can be just an inch or so from each other—and see how that feels to you. Do you want to try? [Therapist moves as patient nods assent. Miriam is still contorted with fear and desperation.] Okay, now, I am going to touch one of your fingers—keep breathing—how is that?

P:  [crying] How touch-phobic I am! I shift between "it feels nice" and "it feels horrid!"

T:  That is why we have to take this slowly. . . . Do you understand that . . . if we didn't take it slowly you would have to disappear—the horror would make you have to disappear [all spoken slowly and carefully and quietly] . . . do you understand that . . . so it's worth going slowly . . . your fingers feel to me . . . full of feeling?

P:  Yes . . . as if all my life is in my fingers . . . not disappeared here, warm . . .

The patient attended a weeklong workshop the next week, after which she reported, with a sense of awe, that she had stayed "in her body" for the whole week, even when being touched. Since this session this patient has reported that she feels a greater sense of continuity, and as we continue to build on it (even the notion of being able to "build" is new and exciting), she feels less brittle, more open, more "in touch."

As more time has passed, and we continue to work together several times per week, longstanding concerns about feeling "alien" and about being severely dissociated and fragmented have begun to be resolved. The patient feels increasingly "human," able to engage more freely in intimate participation with others.

## SUMMARY

Gestalt therapy is a system of psychotherapy that is philosophically and historically linked with gestalt psychology, field theory, existentialism, and phenomenology. Fritz Perls, his wife Laura Perls, and their collaborator, Paul Goodman, initially developed and described the basic principles of gestalt therapy.

Gestalt therapists focus on contact, conscious awareness, and experimentation. There is a consistent emphasis on the present moment and the validity and reality of the patient's phenomenological awareness. Most of the change that occurs in gestalt therapy results from an I-Thou dialogue between the therapist and patient, and gestalt therapists are encouraged to be self-disclosing and candid, both about their personal history and about their feelings in therapy.

The techniques of gestalt therapy include focusing exercises, enactment, creative expression, mental experiments, guided fantasy, imagery, and body awareness. However, these techniques themselves are relatively insignificant and are only the tools traditionally employed by gestalt therapists. Any mechanism consistent with the theory of gestalt therapy can and will be used in therapy.

Therapeutic practice is in turmoil, in a time when the limitations associated with managed care have encroached on clinical practice. At a time of humanistic growth in theorizing, clinical practice seems to be narrowing, with more focus on particular symptoms and an emphasis on people as products who can be fixed by following the instructions in a procedure manual.

The wonderful array of gestalt-originated techniques for which gestalt therapy is famous can be easily misused for just such a purpose. The authors caution the reader not to confuse the use of technique for symptom removal, however imaginative, with gestalt therapy. The fundamental precepts of gestalt therapy, including the paradoxical theory of change, are thoroughly geared toward the development of human freedom, not human conformity, and in that sense gestalt therapy rejects the view of persons implied in the managed care ethos. Gestalt practice, when true to its principles, is a protest against the reductionism of mere symptom removal and adjustment; it is a protest for a client's right to develop fully enough to be able to make conscious and informed choices that shape his or her life.

Since gestalt therapy is so flexible, creative, and direct, it is very adaptable to short-term as well as long-term therapy. The direct contact, focus, and experimentation can sometimes result in important insight. This adaptability is an asset in dealing with managed care and related issues of funding mental health treatment.

In the 1960s, Fritz Perls prophesied that gestalt therapy would come into its own during the decade ahead and become a significant force in psychotherapy during the 1970s. His prophesy has been more than fulfilled.

In 1952, there were perhaps a dozen people actively involved in the gestalt therapy movement. Today there are hundreds of training institutes here and abroad, and there are thousands of well-trained gestalt therapists practicing worldwide. Unfortunately, there are also large numbers of poorly trained therapists who call themselves gestalt therapists after attending a few workshops and/or without adequate academic preparation. It behooves students and patients who are interested in exposure to gestalt therapy to inquire in depth about the training and experience of anyone who claims to be a gestalt therapist.

Gestalt therapy has pioneered many useful and creative innovations in psychotherapy theory and practice that have been incorporated into the general psychotherapy field. Now gestalt therapy is moving to further elaborate and refine these innovations. Regardless of label, the principles of existential dialogue, the use of direct phenomenological experience for both patient and therapist, the trust of organismic self-regulation, the emphasis on experimentation and awareness, the paradoxical theory of change, and close attention to the contact between the therapist and the patient all form a model of good psychotherapy that will continue to be used by gestalt therapists and others.

# ANNOTATED BIBLIOGRAPHY

Hycner, R., & Jacobs, L. (1995). *The healing relationship in gestalt therapy: A dialogic, self psychology approach.* Highland, NY: The Gestalt Journal Press.
Hycner and Jacobs' book is the most complete description of the gestalt theory of the therapist-patient relationship in the literature. It articulates the attitude and praxis of an I-Thou orientation as it would be applied in gestalt therapy. There are extensive case examples presented by both authors. The book also reaches outside of gestalt theory for insights from contemporary psychoanalysis, so it has a more specific slant than the other books, and probably is best suited for the advanced reader. It would also be of interest to readers who wish to integrate psychoanalytic ideas with a humanistic clinical approach.

Kepner, J. (1993). *Body process: Working with the body in psychotherapy.* San Francisco: Jossey-Bass.
Kepner's book can be read by people who may have no particular interest in gestalt therapy but who want to work effectively with patients while attending to body process as well as verbal communication. It is a beautiful illustration of the holistic approach that gestalt therapy espouses. Kepner describes how to attend to body process, both observed and experienced, and how to weave work with bodily experience into ongoing psychotherapy. Readers will also get a hint as to how the therapist's creativity, coupled with the readiness of the patient, can yield fertile gestalt awareness experiments.

Korb, M., Gorrell, J., & Van De Reit, V. (1989). *Gestalt therapy: Practice and theory* (2nd ed.). New York: Pergamon Press.
This book is a lucid introduction to the theory and practice of gestalt therapy. Much of the language and many of the core concepts of gestalt therapy are unfamiliar to the general practitioner, and these writers render the unfamiliar terms and concepts understandable and useable. The authors review the theoretical foundations of gestalt therapy, and describe the process perspective of personality, health, and disease. They also describe some of the basics of the therapeutic process and offer a picture of the therapist's use of self as an essential contribution to the therapeutic dialogue. This book, coupled with the clinical flavor of the Polsters' book *Gestalt Therapy Integrated,* provides a well-rounded beginning for the interested clinician.

Polster, E., & Polster, M. (1973). *Gestalt therapy integrated.* New York: Vintage Books.
This is one of the most readable and enjoyable therapy books around. There are many illustrative vignettes for people who want to get a sense of the "feel" of gestalt therapy. The book is written at the level of clinical theory, and covers the basics of gestalt therapy:

process, here and now, contact, awareness, and experiments. The writing is so lively that the reader is bound to come away with a feel for the gestalt therapy experience as practiced by some of its finest senior practitioners.

Yontef, G. (1993). *Awareness, dialogue and process: Essays on gestalt therapy.* Highland, NY: The Gestalt Journal Press.

These essays are a compendium of articles written over a span of 25 years. Some of the articles are for those who are new to gestalt therapy, but most are for the advanced reader. The essays are sophisticated probes into some of the thornier theoretical and clinical problems that any theory must address. The book presents a comprehensive picture of the evolution of gestalt theory and practice and provides theoretical scaffolding for its future.

## CASE READINGS

Fagan, J. (1947). Three sessions with Iris. *The Counseling Psychologist, 4,* 42–59. [Also in C. Hatcher and P. Himelstein (Eds.). (1976). *The handbook of gestalt therapy* (pp. 673–721). New York: Jason Aronson.]

Dr. Fagan describes her work with Iris as "an example of good, hard, routine work with a resistant patient in individual therapy in a heavily gestalt style" (1976, p. 674). The patient was a volunteer for a doctoral dissertation. She agreed to be videotaped and had no previous experience with gestalt therapy.

Feder, B., & Ronall, R. (1997). *A living legacy of Fritz and Laura Perls: Contemporary case studies.* New York: Feder Publishing.

This edited collection provides a look at how different clinicians work from a gestalt perspective. The variety of styles encourages the reader to find his or her own.

Hycner, R., & Jacobs, L. (1995). Simone. *The healing relationship in gestalt therapy: A dialogic, self-psychology approach* (pp. 85–90). Highland, NY: The Gestalt Journal Press.

Hycner, R., & Jacobs, L. (1995). Transference meets dialogue. *The healing relationship in gestalt therapy: A dialogic, self-psychology approach* (pp. 171–195). Highland, NY: The Gestalt Journal Press.

The first case is an example from a workshop conducted in Israel; the second, an interesting case report by a psychoanalytically oriented gestalt therapist, including verbatim transcripts of three sessions. The second case is analyzed in a panel discussion by two gestalt therapists and two psychoanalysts in Alexander, Brickman, Jacobs, Trop, & Yontef (1992).

Lampert, R. (2003). *A child's eye view: Gestalt therapy with children, adolescents and their families.* Highland, NY: The Gestalt Journal Press.

Case material is provided throughout the book.

Perls, F. S. (1992). Jane's three dreams. In *Gestalt therapy verbatim* (pp.284–310). Highland, NY: The Gestalt Journal Press.

Three dreams are presented verbatim. The third dreamwork is a continuation of unfinished work from the second dream. Portions of this case are also found in D. Wedding and R. J. Corsini (Eds.). (2005). *Case studies in psychotherapy.* Belmont, CA: Wadsworth.

Perls, L. P. (1956). Two instances of gestalt therapy. In P. D. Purlsglove (Ed.). (1968). *Recognition in gestalt therapy* (pp. 42–68). New York: Funk and Wagnalls.

Laura Perls presents the case of Claudia, a 25-year-old woman of color who comes from a lower-middle-class West Indian background, and the case of Walter, a 47-year-old Central European Jewish refugee.

Simkin, J. S. (1967). *Individual gestalt therapy* [Film]. Orlando, FL: American Academy of Psychotherapists. 50 minutes.

In this tape of the eleventh hour of therapy with a 34-year-old actor, emphasis is on present, nonverbal communications leading to production of genetic material. The use of fantasy dialogue is also illustrated.

Simkin, J. S. (1972). The use of dreams in gestalt therapy. In C. J. Sager and H. S. Kaplan (Eds.), *Progress in group and family therapy* (pp. 95–104). New York: Brunner/Mazel.

In a verbatim transcript, a patient works on a dream about his youngest daughter.

## REFERENCES

Acierno, R., Hersen, M., & Van Hasselt, V. (1993). Interventions for panic disorder: A critical review of the literature. *Clinical Psychology Review, 13,* 561–578.

Alexander, R., Brickman, B., Jacobs, L., Trop, J., & Yontef, G. (1992). Transference meets dialogue. *The Gestalt Journal, 15,* 61–108.

Beisser, A. (1970). The paradoxical theory of change. In J. Fagan & I. Shepherd (Eds.). *Gestalt therapy now* (pp. 77–80). Palo Alto: Science & Behavior Books.

Brown, G. (1970). Teaching creativity to teachers and others. *Journal of Teacher Education, 21,* 210–216.

Brown, G. (1971/1990). *Human teaching for human learning: An introduction to confluent education.* New York: The Gestalt Journal Press.

Buber, M. (1923/1970). *I and thou* (W. Kaufmann, Trans.). New York: Scribner's.

Cain, D. J., & Seeman, J. (Eds.). (2001). *Handbook of research and practice.* Washington, DC: American Psychological Association Press.

Clarkson, P., & Mackewn, J. (1993). *Fritz Perls.* London: Sage.

Crocker, S. (1999). *A well-lived life: Essays in gestalt therapy.* Cambridge, MA: GIC Press.

Dolliver, R. (1981). Some limitations in Perls' gestalt therapy. *Psychotherapy, Research and Practice, 8,* 38–45.

Dublin, J. (1976). Gestalt therapy: Existential-Gestalt therapy and/versus "Perls-ism." In E. Smith (Ed.), *The growing edge of gestalt therapy* (pp. 124–150). New York: Brunner/Mazel.

Fagan, J., & Shepherd, I. (Eds.). (1970). *Gestalt therapy now* (pp. 77–80). Palo Alto, CA: Science & Behavior Books.

Frank, R. (2001). *Body of awareness: A somatic and developmental approach to psychotherapy.* Hillsdale, NJ: GIC/Analytic Press.

Frew, J. (1988). The practice of Gestalt therapy in groups. *The Gestalt Journal, 11,* 1, 77–96.

Garssen, B., de Ruiter, C., & van Dyck, R. (1992). Breathing retraining: A rational placebo? *Clinical Psychology Review, 12,* 141–153.

Golden, W., & Dryden, W. (1987). Cognitive-behavioural therapies: Commonalities, divergences and future developments. In W. Dryden & W. Golden (Eds.), *Cognitive behavioural approaches to psychotherapy* (pp. 356–378). New York: Harper and Row.

Goldstein, K. (1939/1963). *The organism.* Boston: Beacon.

Greenberg, L. (1979). Resolving splits: The two-chair technique. *Psychotherapy: Theory, Research and Practice, 16,* 310–318.

Greenberg, L. (1980). The intensive analysis of recurring events from the practice of Gestalt therapy. *Psychotherapy: Theory, Research and Practice, 17,* 143–152.

Greenberg, L. (1982). Toward a task analysis of conflict resolution in Gestalt therapy. *Psychotherapy: Theory, Research and Practice, 20,* 190–201.

Greenberg, L. (1986). Change process research. *Journal of Consulting and Clinical Psychology, 54,* 4–9.

Greenberg, L. (1991). Research in the process of change. *Psychotherapy Research, 1,* 14–24.

Greenberg, L., & Clarke, K. (1979). Differential effects of the two-chair experiment and empathic reflections at a conflict maker. *Journal of Counseling Psychology, 26,* 1–9.

Greenberg, L., & Dompierre, L. (1981). Specific effects of Gestalt two-chair dialogue on intrapsychic conflict in counseling. *Journal of Counseling Psychology, 28,* 288–295.

Greenberg, L., Elliott, R., & Lietaer, G. (1994). Research on experiential psychotherapies. In A. Bergin & S. Garfield (Eds.). *Handbook of psychotherapy and behavior change* (pp. 509–539). New York: Wiley.

Greenberg, L., & Higgins, H. (1980). The differential effects of two-chair dialogue and focusing on conflict resolution. *Journal of Counseling Psychology, 27,* 221–225.

Greenberg, L., & Paivio, S. C. (1997). *Working with emotions in psychotherapy.* New York: Guilford.

Greenberg, L., & Rice, L. (1981). The specific effects of Gestalt therapy intervention. *Psychotherapy: Theory, Research and Practice, 18,* 31–38.

Greenberg, L., Rice, L., & Elliott, R. (1993). *Facilitating emotional change: The moment-by-moment process.* New York: Guilford.

Hycner, R. (1985). Dialogical gestalt therapy: An initial proposal. *The Gestalt Journal, 8*(1), 23–49.

Hycner, R., & Jacobs, L. (1995). *The healing relationship in gestalt therapy: A dialogic, self psychology approach.* Highland, NY: The Gestalt Journal Press.

Jacobs, L. (1996). Shame in the therapeutic dialogue. In R. Lee and G. Wheeler (Eds.). *The voice of shame* (pp. 297–314). San Francisco: Jossey-Bass.

Jacobs, L. (2000). For whites only. *British Gestalt Journal, 9*(1), 3–14.

Kepner, J. (1987). *Body process: A gestalt approach to working with the body in psychotherapy.* New York: Gestalt Institute of Cleveland Press.

Lampert, R. (2003). *A child's eye view: Gestalt therapy with children, adolescents, and their families.* Highland, NY: The Gestalt Journal Press.

Lederman, J. (1969). *Anger and the rocking chair.* New York: McGraw-Hill.

Lederman, J. (1970). Anger and the rocking chair. In J. Fagan & I. Shepherd (Eds.), *Gestalt therapy now* (pp. 285–294). Palo Alto, CA: Science and Behavior Books.

Lee, R., & Wheeler, G. (Eds.). (1996). *The voice of shame: Silence and connection in psychotherapy.* San Francisco: Jossey-Bass.

Lewin, K. (1938). The conflict between Aristotelian and Galilean modes of thought in contemporary psychology. In K. Lewin, *A dynamic theory of personality* (pp. 1–42). London: Routledge & Kegan Paul.

Maurer, R. (2002). *Why don't you want what I want? How to win support for your ideas without hardsell, manipulation or power plays.* London: Bard Press.

Nevis, E. (1987). *Organizational consulting: A gestalt approach.* Hillsdale, NJ: GIC/Analytic Press.

Nevis, E., Lancourt, J., & Vasallo, H. G. (1996). *Intentional revolutions: A seven point strategy for transforming organizations.* San Francisco: Jossey-Bass.

Norcross, J., & Rossi, J. (1994). Looking weakly in all the wrong places? *Journal of Consulting and Clinical Psychology, 6*(3), 535–538.

Oaklander, V. (1969/1988). *Windows to our children: A gestalt therapy approach to children and adolescents.* New York: The Gestalt Journal Press.

Paivio, S., & Greenberg, L. (1992). Resolving unfinished business: A study of effects. Paper presented at the annual meeting of the Society for Psychotherapy Research, Berkeley, CA.

Perls, F. (1942/1992). *Ego, hunger and aggression.* New York: The Gestalt Journal Press.

Perls, F. (1969/1992). *Gestalt therapy verbatim.* Highland, NY: The Gestalt Journal Press.

Perls, F. (1970). Four lectures. In J. Fagan & I. Shepherd (Eds.), *Gestalt therapy now* (pp. 14–38). Palo Alto, CA: Science and Behavior Books.

Perls, F. (1973/1976). *The Gestalt approach and eyewitness to therapy.* New York: Bantam.

Perls, F., Hefferline, R., & Goodman, P. (1951/1994). *Gestalt therapy: Excitement & growth in the human personality.* New York: The Gestalt Journal Press.

Perls, L. (1992). *Living at the boundary.* New York: The Gestalt Therapy Press.

Philippson, P. (2001). *Self in relation.* New York: The Gestalt Journal Press.

Polster, E., & Polster, M. (1973). *Gestalt therapy integrated.* New York: Brunner/Mazel.

Rogers, C. (1961/1995). *On becoming a person.* New York: Houghton Mifflin.

Smuts, J. (1926/1996). *Holism & evolution.* Highland, New York: The Gestalt Journal Press.

Spagnuolo-Lobb, M., & Amendt-Lyon, N. (2003). *Creative license: The art of gestalt therapy.* New York: Springer Wein.

Staemmler, F.-M. (2003). The "friendly facts" of "normal science." [Book review of Cain & Seeman (2001)]. In *International Gestalt Journal, 26,* 131–134.

Stern, D. (1985). *The interpersonal world of the infant.* New York: Basic Books.

Wallen, R. (1957/1970). Gestalt psychology and gestalt therapy. Paper presented at Ohio Psychological Association Symposium. In J. Fagan & I. Shepherd (Eds.), *Gestalt therapy now* (pp. 8–13). Palo Alto: Science & Behavior Books.

Weishaar, M., & Beck, A. (1987). Cognitive therapy. In W. Dryden & W. Golden (Eds.), *Cognitive behavioural approaches to psychotherapy.* New York: Harper and Row.

Wheeler, G. (2000). *Beyond Individualism.* Hillsdale, NJ: GIC/Analytic Press.

Wulf, R. (1998). The historical roots of gestalt therapy. *The Gestalt Journal, 21, 1.*

Yontef, G. (1990). Gestalt therapy in groups. In I. Kutash & A. Wolf (Eds.), *Group psychotherapist's handbook.* New York: Columbia University Press.

Yontef, G. (1993). *Awareness, dialogue and process: Essays on gestalt therapy.* New York: The Gestalt Journal Press.

Yontef, G. (1995). Gestalt therapy. In A. Gurman & S. Messer (Eds.), *Essential psychotherapies* (pp. 261–303). New York: Guilford.

Yontef, G. (1996). Shame and guilt in Gestalt therapy theory and practice. In R. Lee & G. Wheeler (Eds.), *The voice of shame: Silence and connection in psychotherapy* (pp. 351–380). San Francisco: Jossey-Bass.

Yontef, G. (2002). The relational attitude in gestalt therapy theory and practice. *International Gestalt Journal, 25*(1), 15–36.

Zinker, J. (1977). *Creative process in Gestalt therapy.* New York: Brunner/Mazel.

Arnold A. Lazarus

# 11 MULTIMODAL THERAPY

*Arnold A. Lazarus*

## OVERVIEW

*Multimodal therapy* is a systematic and comprehensive psychotherapeutic approach developed by Arnold Lazarus, a clinical psychologist. While respecting the assumption that clinical practice should adhere firmly to the principles, procedures, and findings of psychology as an experimental science, the multimodal orientation transcends the behavioral tradition by adding unique assessment procedures and by dealing in great depth and detail with sensory, imagery, cognitive, and interpersonal factors and their interactive effects. A basic premise is that patients are usually troubled by a multitude of specific problems that should be dealt with by a broad range of specific methods. A multimodal assessment examines each area of a person's BASIC I.D.:

B = Behavior

A = Affect

S = Sensation

I = Imagery

C = Cognition

I = Interpersonal relationships

D = Drugs/Biology

It provides an operational way of answering the questions, What works? For whom? Under which conditions?

## Basic Concepts

Multimodal therapy is personalized and individualistic. Scrutiny for individual exceptions to general rules and principles characterizes the search for appropriate interventions for each person. Clinical effectiveness is predicated on the therapist's flexibility, versatility, and technical eclecticism. The technical eclectic uses procedures drawn from different sources without necessarily subscribing to the theories or disciplines that spawned them (Lazarus, 1992a). The upshot is a consistent, systematic, and testable set of beliefs and assumptions about human beings and their problems, and an armamentarium of effective therapeutic strategies for remedying their afflictions.

While remaining technically eclectic, multimodal therapy rests primarily on the theoretical base of *social learning theory* (Bandura, 1969, 1977, 1986; Rotter, 1954) while also drawing from *general system theory* (Bertalanffy, 1974; Buckley, 1967) and *group and communications theory* (Watzlawick, Weakland, & Fisch, 1974). These diverse theories blend harmoniously into a congruent framework. (See Lazarus, 1996.)

Most of our experiences comprise moving, feeling, sensing, imagining, thinking, and relating to one another. In the final analysis, we are biochemical-neurophysiological entities. Human life and conduct are products of ongoing *b*ehaviors, *a*ffective processes, *s*ensations, *i*mages, *c*ognitions, *i*nterpersonal relationships, and *b*iological functions. BASIC I.B. is derived from the first letters of each of these modalities, but by referring to the biological modality as "Drugs/Biology" (because one of the most common biological interventions is the use of psychotropic medication), we have the acronym BASIC I.D. It is crucial to remember that D stands not only for drugs, medication, or pharmacological intervention, but also includes nutrition, hygiene, exercise, and all basic physiological and pathological inputs. (See C. N. Lazarus, 1998.)

The BASIC I.D. is presumed to comprise human temperament and personality, and it is assumed that everything from anger, disappointment, disgust, greed, fear, grief, awe, contempt, and boredom to love, hope, faith, ecstasy, optimism, and joy can be explained by examining components and interactions within a person's BASIC I.D. It is also essential to recognize and include factors that fall outside the BASIC I.D., such as sociocultural, political, and other macroenvironmental events. While external realities are not part of temperament and personality, "psychopathology and society are inextricably bound together" (Nathan & Harris, 1980, p. xvii). There are obviously crucial differences in adaptive interpersonal styles between people raised and living in New York and New Guinea, but regardless of an individual's background, detailed descriptions of salient behaviors, affective responses, sensory reactions, images, cognitions, interpersonal dealings, and biological propensities will provide the principal ingredients of a person's psychological makeup. To appreciate further the interactions among the various modalities—for example, how certain behaviors influence and are influenced by affects, sensations, images, cognitions, and significant relationships—is to know a great deal about individuals and their social networks.

While multimodal theory (MMT) draws heavily from several systems (especially behavior therapy, rational emotive behavior therapy, and cognitive therapy), six distinctive features set MMT apart from all other approaches:

1. The specific and comprehensive attention given to the entire BASIC I.D.
2. The use of *second-order* BASIC I.D. assessments
3. The use of *modality profiles*
4. The use of *structural profiles*
5. Deliberate *bridging* procedures
6. *Tracking* the modality firing order

Each of these features will be discussed in this chapter.

The term *bespoke therapy,* which has been used to describe the multimodal orientation (see Zilbergeld, 1982), aptly conveys the custom-made, personalistic emphasis. The form, style, and cadence of therapy are fitted, whenever possible, to each client's perceived requirements. The basic question is, *Who or what is best for this particular individual?* Some clients respond best to therapists who are warm and empathic; others do better with more distant and formal relationships (Lazarus, 1993). Quiet, passive, reflective listeners are especially suited to some clients; others want therapists who are active, directive, and bluntly outspoken. The same client may respond favorably to various therapeutic styles at different times. How is the therapist to gauge whether pensive reflection is more likely to succeed than direct disputation? The answer can be found largely by noting the client's implicit and explicit expectations and by observing the impact of applying various tactics (cf., Howard, Nance, & Myers, 1987). Even effective therapists will make mistakes in gauging clients' expectations and in tactics applied, but capable therapists, on noticing these errors, will usually make adjustments to change the course of therapy. The choice of a particular therapeutic style and the selection of techniques are not capricious affairs. After drawing up a detailed modality profile (a chart depicting excesses and deficits across the client's BASIC I.D.), the multimodal therapist resorts to two main procedures—bridging and tracking.

## Bridging

*Bridging* refers to a procedure in which the therapist deliberately tunes into the client's preferred modality before branching off into other dimensions that seem likely to be more productive. For example, instead of challenging a client or even pointing out that he or she tends to eschew the expression of feelings by erecting intellectual barriers, we find it better first to enter into the client's domain and then gently lead him or her into other (potentially more meaningful) channels. Here is an example (C = Client; T = Therapist):

C: I think that Molly resorts to what I call a three-down maneuver when we disagree about virtually anything. In other words, I am not placed in a one-down position, but I am seen as the lowest man on the totem pole.

T: How does that make you feel?

C: I realize why she does it. It is exactly what her mother does to her father, and Molly is very much like her mother in many ways.

T: [Going along with client's cognitive leanings.] So Molly has imitated her mother and uses her tactics. What are some of the other things she does that remind you of her mother?

C: Well, there are a couple of things that come to mind immediately. First . . . [Client intellectualizes about the alleged similarities between Molly and her mother.]

T: [Bridging.] When you think about all these ties that Molly has to her mother and the way she puts you down, are you aware of any feelings or sensations in your body?

C: Right now I've got a knot in my stomach.

T: Can you concentrate fully on that stomach tension? Can you focus on that knot?

C: It feels like a vise is gripping it.

T: Do you feel tension anywhere else in your body?

C: My jaws feel tight.

T: Will you concentrate on the tension in your jaws and your stomach and tell me what feelings or mental pictures come to mind?

C: I feel sad. I think it gets down to the fact that I am afraid that my relationship with Molly will be a carbon copy of her parents' marriage.

T: Let's hear more about your fears and your feelings of sadness.

The therapist wanted to move into affective areas right from the start but instead went along with the client's apparent desire to dwell on cognitive components. Shortly thereafter, when the therapist again inquired about affective and sensory responses, the client was willing to reveal his sensations and then to verbalize his feelings. Failure to tune into the client's presenting modality often leads to feelings of alienation—the client feels misunderstood or may conclude that the therapist does not speak his or her language. Thus, multimodal therapists *start where the client is* and then bridge into more productive areas of discourse.

## Tracking

*Tracking* refers to a careful examination of the "firing order" of the different modalities. For example, some clients tend to generate negative emotions by dwelling first on sensations (S) (e.g., a slight dizziness accompanied by mild heart palpitations), to which they attach negative cognitions (C) (e.g., ideas of illness and death), immediately followed by aversive images (I) (e.g., pictures of hospitals and catastrophic disease), culminating in maladaptive behavior (B) (e.g., unnecessary avoidance or extreme withdrawal). Other people tend to experience a different firing order. Rather than a sensory-cognitive-imagery-behavioral sequence as just outlined, they may display a CISB pattern (cognitive-imagery-sensory-behavior), an I.BSCA order (interpersonal-behavior-sensory-cognitive-affective), or any other combination. An example of an I.BSCA firing order can be seen at a social gathering where a man insults one of his friends (I.) and walks out of the room (B). He starts feeling hot and shaky and develops a severe tension headache (S). He then regrets having acted aggressively and impulsively, but starts rationalizing his conduct (C). Nonetheless, he concludes that he is a stupid and unbalanced person. Soon he begins to feel depressed (A).

In studying panic disorders, Margraf, Ehlers, and Roth (1986) identified positive feedback loops in which unpleasant body sensations are followed by "catastrophizing cognitions," resulting in full-blown panic attacks. Clark (1986) also discusses trigger stimuli (excitement, anger), followed by bodily sensations (dizziness, breathlessness), followed by cognitive appraisals, culminating in a panic attack.

Firing orders are not fixed tendencies. A person may generate negative affect through a particular sequence on some occasions and follow a different pattern at other times. Different emotions may follow distinct firing orders. Thus, a client, when anxious, found that a CISB sequence was operative, but when depressed, an IBI.S order was established. Most people, however, report a reasonably stable proclivity toward a particular firing order much of the time. By tracking the precise sequence of events that results in the affective disturbance, the therapist enables the client to gain insight into the antecedent events and also enables him or her to intercede appropriately. The therapist may elect to track the I.BSCA order more closely. Thus, questions might be asked to determine what thoughts or feelings had led the client to insult his friend in the first place, thereby uncovering additional antecedent factors. Such precise information permits intervention at any of several entry points in the sequence.

Tracking also enables one to select the most appropriate intervention techniques. An agoraphobic woman complained of panic and anxiety. Medication helped to control her outbreaks of panic, but when she exposed herself to feared situations (such as shopping in a supermarket), she nevertheless experienced considerable anxiety. When asked to take particular note of how these anxious feelings arose, she observed a cognitive-imagery-sensory-affective sequence (CISA). First, she tended to *think* about the probability of becoming anxious, and this, in turn, led to other negative self-statements such as, "What if I pass out?" and "What if I start feeling weak and dizzy?" Soon, she formed mental images of these unpleasant events—in her mind's eye she would see herself hyperventilating and fainting. As these thoughts and images grew stronger, she would notice a *sensation* of lightheadedness, and her palms would sweat. She would immediately feel tense and anxious.

Following her firing order, she was first given *self-instructional training* (Meichenbaum, 1977) in which her irrational, self-defeating thoughts were replaced with self-statements that tend to mitigate anxiety. ("I will handle the situation." "I will remain in control." "I will stay cool, calm, and collected.") Next, she was taught *coping imagery* (Lazarus, 1978, 1982), which involves picturing oneself coping, vividly imagining oneself remaining calm and in control. In the sensory modality, she was taught slow abdominal breathing and differential muscle relaxation. While shopping in the supermarket, she was to follow a specified sequence—first to use positive self-instructions, then to add positive mental imagery, and then to employ breathing while deliberately relaxing those muscles she was not using at the time.

If the client had reported a different firing order, say sensory-imagery-cognitive-affect (SICA), she would have been advised to commence with slow abdominal breathing and differential relaxation and follow with coping images. The positive self-statements would have been her third line of defense. Our clinical observations suggest that when one selects techniques that follow the client's habitual sequence, the positive impact is greater than if one follows any other order. If a client who follows, say, a CSI sequence is treated first with sensory procedures, followed by imagery techniques, and then with cognitive methods (i.e., an SIC treatment order) the results are less impressive than outcomes that adhere to the client's firing order.

## Other Systems

All systems of psychotherapy, and most therapists, advocate a stance of respect and regard for clients or patients. Therapists generally serve as facilitators who provide direct or indirect guidance. It is widely agreed that it is often necessary to alter clients' self-perceptions as well as the ways in which they perceive the world. These and many other commonalities can be delineated, but upon close scrutiny, these similarities between systems are more specious than real.

For example, both multimodal therapy and psychoanalysis regard "conflict resolution" as necessary for successful treatment outcomes. Upon closer scrutiny, these phenotypical similarities reflect genotypical differences. The meaning of "conflict," its origins, functions, effects, and overall impact, as well as the best ways of dealing with or resolving conflicts, are all quite different according to psychoanalytic and multimodal tenets (Lazarus, 1989a). It is a serious error to emphasize insignificant similarities at the expense of significant differences.

There are hundreds of different schools of psychological thought and practice (Corsini, 2000; Herink, 1980; Karasu, 1986). When examining the claims and counterclaims of their proponents, one discerns a number of trends or clusters. Some advocate particular techniques or procedures and tout them as virtual panaceas. Thus, one finds relaxation pundits, meditation gurus, scream advocates, and promulgators of megavitamins, hypnosis, psychodrama, rebirthing, or other unimodal interventions. These one-track procedures are the antithesis of multimodal therapy, which views human disquietude as multilayered and multileveled and calls for the correction of deviant behaviors, unpleasant feelings, negative sensations, intrusive images, irrational beliefs, stressful relationships, and physiological difficulties. Yet multimodal therapy is equally opposed to those theoretical eclectics who endeavor to unite the morass of competing systems, models, vocabularies, and personal idiosyncrasies into a unified whole, thus ending up with an agglomerate of incompatible and contradictory notions (which might be called *multimuddle therapy*).

Each system can be evaluated on the extent to which it assesses and treats—or ignores—each modality of the BASIC I.D. For example, gestalt therapy tends to neglect the cognitive domain in favor of "gut reactions." Cognitive-behavior therapy does not delve thoroughly into sensory and imagery modalities, nor are behavior therapists sufficiently sensitive to interpersonal factors or unexpressed emotions. Beck's cognitive therapy places heavy emphasis on dysfunctional thoughts and on reparative behaviors but pays insufficient attention to specific sensory components, the rich array of imagery procedures, and the client's interpersonal networks. (See Zilbergeld & Lazarus, 1988, for a detailed account of the synergistic properties of mental imagery and muscular relaxation.) The polar opposite of the multimodal approach is the person-centered approach that offers the therapist's genuineness, empathy, and unpossessive caring to all clients and regards these conditions as necessary and sufficient for therapeutic growth and change. The multimodal position emphasizes that people have diverse needs and expectancies, come from different molds, and require a wide range of stylistic, tactical, and strategic maneuvers from the therapist. No amount of empathy, genuineness, or unpossessive caring is likely to fill the gaps left by impoverished learning histories (behavioral and attitudinal deficits). These require teaching, coaching, training, modeling, shaping, and directing.

When a multimodal therapist is consulted by a client who requires a genuine, empathic, unpossessive listener, nothing prevents the multimodalist from adopting a Rogerian stance. Multimodal therapists constantly ask, *"What works, for whom, and under which particular circumstances?"* Thus, they take care *not* to attempt to fit the client to a predetermined treatment. With most practitioners, the client seems to get only what the therapist practices—which may not necessarily be what is best for the client. In multimodal therapy, there is a deliberate attempt to determine precisely what type of relationship or what type of interactive posture each client will respond to. The multimodal orientation emphasizes therapeutic flexibility and versatility above all else. There is no unitary way to approach people's problems. To exude empathy and warmth to a client who prefers distant, formal, businesslike interactions is likely to impede treatment (Lazarus, 1993). In some cases, instead of attempting to match the client to the therapy and therapist, the multimodal therapist may prescribe *no therapy.* For example, I was consulted by a middle-aged woman who had been seeing therapists on and off for years. She complained of vague anxiety, depression, tension, and general dissatisfaction with her life. After conducting a BASIC I.D. assessment I gave the following advice: "Use the money that you would have spent on therapy to have someone clean your house, have your hair done, and take tennis lessons. You will still have some money left over to meet friends for coffee or a snack. Be sure to engage in these activities on four different days each week, and after doing this for two months, please call and let me know if you are enjoying life more, if you feel less tense, anxious, and depressed." This no-treatment prescription resulted in a distinct amelioration of her problems.

Many therapists express the need for flexibility. Thus, Haley (1976) stated, "A skillful therapist will approach each new person with the idea that a unique procedure might be necessary for this particular person and social situation" (p. 10). Nevertheless, he then goes on to say, "Today it is assumed that to begin therapy by interviewing one person is to begin with a handicap" (p. 10). Haley then stresses that "at every stage of the interview *all* family members should be involved in the action, and particularly during the greeting stage" (p. 15). We have seen clients at Multimodal Therapy Institutes who were upset by family therapists' insistence that significant others had to be present at initial meetings. After working with these individuals and gaining their trust and confidence, we were then able to get them to bring family members into the treatment (if and when indicated). The multimodal therapist will shift the focus of attention back and forth from the individual and his or her personal responses to the individual in his or her social settings.

Multimodal clinicians may draw on Haley's strategic therapy, Beck's cognitive therapy, Skinner's operant conditioning, or any other school without being locked into that system. Whereas Beck employs a Socratic method of asking questions, multimodal therapists are apt to employ a directive stance because it exemplifies the psychoeducational thrust of multimodal therapy. For detailed discussions of the differences between rational emotive behavior therapy and multimodal therapy, see Lazarus (1988) and a very thoughtful article by Kwee and Ellis (1997).

Were an observer to watch a multimodal therapist in action, he or she might observe the therapist behaving in a rather cold and austere manner with one client on a particular day, but in a warm and effusive mode with the same client at a different time. Yet another client might be exposed to a question-and-answer session. The next one might be treated in a directive, demanding manner, whereas a different client would receive a soft, warm, and accepting mode. Multimodal therapists constantly adjust to the client in terms of that mode of interaction most likely to achieve the desired aims of the therapy (Lazarus, 1993).

Zilbergeld summarized the multimodal position succinctly and accurately:

> The aim of MMT is to come up with the best methods for each client rather than force all clients to fit the same therapy. . . . Three depressed clients might be given very different treatments depending on their therapists' assessments and the methods they prefer. . . . The only goal is helping clients make desired changes as rapidly as possible. (1982, p. 85)

Given that the BASIC I.D. is presumed to represent the pillars of human temperament and personality, any system that glosses over any of these seven dimensions is bound to be incomplete. The reader should have no difficulty, when reading the other chapters in this book, in determining which systems deal *explicitly* with maladaptive behaviors + affective disorders + negative sensations + intrusive images + faulty cognitions + interpersonal difficulties + biological factors. It seems to us that most systems are based on unimodal, bimodal, or, at best, trimodal conceptions of human functioning—stressing affect, behavior, and cognition.

# HISTORY

## Precursors

Hippocrates (c. 400 B.C.) was aware that human personality is multilayered. He underscored the need for eliciting a complete life history of all patients and he recognized the importance of relationship factors in therapy. Galen in the second century and Swiss psychiatrist Paul Dubois in the nineteenth century foreshadowed many of the best tactics advocated by multimodal therapists. One may also note many similarities between present-day multimodal conceptions and more recent writings. Thus, in 1874, Franz Brentano's *Psychologie vom Empirischen Standpunkte* underscored the importance of acts (including ideation), together with feeling states and "sensory judgments." There is considerable overlap between multimodal eclecticism and the theory of functionalism put forth by William James (1890). W. H. Burnham's *The Normal Mind* (1924) was decidedly "multimodal" in its scope.

The direct precursors date back to the 1950s, when Lazarus was a student at the University of the Witwatersrand in Johannesburg, South Africa, where the psychotherapeutic climate was predominantly Freudian and Rogerian. There were some followers of Melanie Klein, Harry Stack Sullivan, and Carl Jung. Two behavioristic faculty members—C. A. L. Warffemius and Alma Hannon—underscored the internal inconsistencies in psychoanalytic theory and emphasized the untestable nature of most Freudian postulates. The contributions of James Taylor of the University of Cape Town and visiting lectures by Joseph Wolpe, a medical practitioner who was applying "conditioning methods" to his patients, led to the formation of a coterie of "neobehaviorists." The members of this group embraced animal analogues, extrapolated from infrahuman to human levels of functioning, and focused heavily on classical conditioning paradigms.

It became apparent to these individuals that performance-based methods were usually better than purely verbal and cognitive approaches at effecting change. Whereas the psychotherapeutic establishment viewed behavior as the outward manifestation of psychic processes, the neobehaviorists stressed that behavior per se is often clinically significant. It became clear that people could acquire insight or alter significant beliefs and still engage in self-destructive behavior. Yet, after behaving differently, it was evident that people were inclined to feel and think differently. (Unfortunately, most professionals still view overt behavior as the tip of the iceberg, as symptoms of underlying disease, or as symbols of unconscious complexes.)

To legitimize behavioral intervention as an essential part of effective clinical practice, Lazarus (1958) introduced the terms *behavior therapy* and *behavior therapist* into the scientific and professional literature. The observation and quantification of significant actions became established as a starting point for effective clinical interventions. Coupled with a search for relevant antecedents as well as maintaining variables, the focus on maladaptive behaviors and their remediation resulted in positive outcomes. But when follow-up studies revealed a disappointingly high relapse rate for people who were exposed to behavioral methods alone, it became necessary to employ techniques that were considered outside the boundaries of traditional behavior therapy (Lazarus, 1971, 1989a, 1997).

## Beginnings

In 1965 Lazarus wrote a paper on the need to treat alcoholism from a multidimensional perspective. The following components were involved:

1. Medical care to return the patient to physical well-being

2. Aversion therapy and anxiety-relief conditioning to mitigate the patient's uncontrolled drinking

3. A thorough assessment to identify "specific stimulus antecedents of anxiety" in the patient's environment

4. The use of additional techniques, including systematic desensitization, assertiveness training, behavior rehearsal, and hypnosis

5. The development of a cooperative relationship with the patient's spouse

This was foreshadowed by Lazarus's earlier (1956) statement that "the emphasis in psychological rehabilitation must be on a *synthesis* which would embrace a diverse range of effective therapeutic techniques, as well as innumerable adjunctive measures, to form part of a wide and all-embracing re-educative programme" (p. 710).

These earlier publications reveal a definite penchant for broad-based, or comprehensive, psychotherapeutic procedures. By 1966 Lazarus had become suspicious of what he subsequently termed *narrow-band behavior therapy* and published "Broad-Spectrum Behavior Therapy and the Treatment of Agoraphobia" (Lazarus, 1966). This article not only challenged narrow stimulus-response formulations, but also elaborated on the notion that dyadic transactions, or interpersonal systems, are an integral part of the genesis and maintenance of agoraphobia. The durability of narrow-band behavior therapy was seriously questioned, and in *Behavior Therapy and Beyond* (Lazarus, 1971), a "broad-spectrum" approach was advocated. The work of Salter (1949) and Ellis (1962) had an enduring impact on underscoring the crucial significance of emotional freedom and rational thinking as integral elements of the broad-spectrum therapy.

While Lazarus was gathering outcome and follow-up data, a number of questions arose repeatedly. When do behavior therapy techniques suffice? What sorts of people with what types of problems seem to require more than behavior therapy? When the clinician steps outside the bounds of behavior therapy, which effective nonbehavioral methods are best incorporated into what types of specific treatment programs for which particular problems, under what set of circumstances, and with which individuals (cf. Paul, 1967)? The careful scrutiny of case notes revealed that positive results were obtained by individuals with situational crises, circumscribed phobias, specific adjustment problems, transient or relatively mild sexual inadequacies, stress and tension-related difficulties, and some psychobiological disorders. Enduring benefits seemed to accrue to those who needed support over a trying period or reassurance about difficult life decisions and to those who lacked assertiveness and other social skills. Less impressive results were obtained with obsessive-compulsive individuals (despite the use of flooding and response prevention procedures), in cases with self-destructive tendencies, with addicts (whether addicted to drugs, food, or alcohol), and with highly anxious individuals who were prone to panic attacks.

The search for additional systematic interventions led to an awareness that cognitive restructuring often called for more than the correction of misconceptions or the straightforward alteration of negative self-talk. For example, when intrusive images conjure up a gloomy and troubled future, no amount of rational self-talk seems to alter the depressive affect—it is necessary to change the negative imagery itself. Thus, a wide range of specific imagery techniques was added to the clinical armamentarium—goal rehearsal, time projection, coping imagery, and many others (see Lazarus, 1978, 1982, 1997). Similarly, people with sensory complaints (e.g., tension headaches, muscle spasms, bruxism) required specific sensory techniques (e.g., deep muscle relaxation, biofeedback, muscle-toning exercises) in addition to behavioral change, cognitive shifts, affective expression, and attention to other aspects of functioning. It seemed important to separate affect from sensation as well as imagery from cognition. The importance of overt behavior was well documented in the writings and practices of behavior therapists, but they seemed to gloss over crucial interpersonal factors. A comprehensive appraisal of human interactions called for an examination of Behavior, Affect, Sensation, Imagery, Cognition, and Interpersonal relationships (the first letters of which form the acronym BASIC I.). To ignore the physical-medical aspects would obviously bypass the fundamental realities of the neurophysiological-biochemical elements that contribute to human personality and temperament. Hence the D. modality was added to the BASIC I. (It should be emphasized again that the D. stands for Drugs/Biology and represents far more than an awareness that some people require medication.)

While multimodal therapy is essentially behavioral, it has evolved into an approach that employs additional (extrabehavioral) assessment and treatment procedures and strategies. Kwee, in a critical review of multimodal therapy, concludes that "whether or not multimodal therapy can be classified as behavior therapy is less important than the method itself" (1981, p. 65).

## Current Status

Since the appearance of multimodal therapy as a distinctive orientation (Lazarus, 1973), a considerable number of clinicians have been using the BASIC I.D. framework. The first book on multimodal procedures had 11 contributors (Lazarus, 1976). One issue of the *Journal of Humanistic Education and Development* (1985, Volume 23) and two issues of *Elementary School Guidance and Counseling* (1978, Volume 13, and 1982, Volume 16) were devoted to multimodal approaches. Nieves (1978a) has provided a multimodal self-assessment procedure dealing with self-control systems for minority college students and (1978b) has described a multimodal self-help program for college achievement. Detailed accounts of multimodal assessment and therapy have been presented in several textbooks

(Anchor, 1991; Dryden, 1992; Dryden & Golden, 1986; Jacobson, 1987; Leiblum & Rosen, 1988; Norcross, 1986; Norcross & Goldfried, 1992). Numerous articles in professional journals have focused on the BASIC I.D. format. Books, articles, and chapters on multimodal therapy have been written or translated into several languages—German, Italian, Portuguese, Spanish, and Dutch. In Holland, Kwee (1978, 1979, 1981, 1984, 1990; Kwee & Roborgh, 1987; Kwee & Kwee-Taams, 1994) has been most prolific. There are, at present, nine books on multimodal therapy (Brunell & Young, 1982; Keat, 1979, 1990; Lazarus, 1976, 1981, 1985, 1989a, 1997; Palmer & Dryden, 1995). Multimodal therapy has been applied in such diverse environments as mental hospitals, residential facilities, day hospitals, and other complete care systems (e.g., Brunell & Young, 1982; O'Keefe & Castaldo, 1981b; Roberts, Jackson, & Phelps, 1980).

Training in multimodal therapy has been a formal aspect of the clinical doctoral program at Rutgers University since 1972, and a number of former Rutgers students teach multimodal therapy at various universities and centers throughout the United States. Several unpublished doctoral dissertations have focused on specific aspects of the approach (e.g., Aigen, 1980; Ferrise, 1978; Herman, 1992; Landes, 1988; Lawler, 1985; Mann, 1985; Olson, 1979; Rosenblad, 1985). Students here and abroad frequently write to inform me about studies they are conducting, and many Spanish-speaking centers are studying aspects of MMT, especially in South America and Costa Rica. There are several multimodal therapy institutes in the United States, and a multimodal therapy center opened about six years ago in London, England.

# PERSONALITY

## Theory of Personality

Traditionally, American psychologists have tended to be environmentalists, but as geneticists have shed more light on the impact of DNA on various behaviors, the crucial relevance of our genetic heritage has grudgingly been brought back into the picture. It seems foolhardy to deny the biological substrate or the physiological basis of temperament and personality.

At the physiological level, the concept of *thresholds* is most compelling. While psychological interventions can undoubtedly modify various thresholds, the genetic diathesis will usually prevail in the final analysis. Thus, a person with an extremely low pain-tolerance threshold may, through hypnosis and other psychological means, be brought to a level of withstanding pain at somewhat higher intensities, but a penchant for over-reacting to pain stimuli will nevertheless remain omnipresent. The person whose autonomic nervous system is *stable* will have a different "personality" from someone with *labile* autonomic reactions. The latter are anxiety-prone and are apt to become pathologically anxious under stressful conditions (Tyrer, 1982).

People tend to favor some BASIC I.D. modalities over others. Thus, we may speak of a "sensory reactor," an "imagery reactor," or a "cognitive reactor." This does not imply that a person will always favor or react in a given modality but that over time, a tendency to value certain response patterns can be noted. Thus, when a person's most highly valued representational system is visual, he or she is inclined to respond to the world and organize it in terms of mental images.

A person with a high frustration tolerance but a low pain tolerance, someone who is extremely active and whose mental imagery is penetratingly clear, is bound to have a very different "personality" from someone who succumbs easily to frustration, who is at best moderately active, deeply analytical (cognitive), and incapable of forming more than

FIGURE 11.1    **Rating Scales**

1. *Behavior:* How active are you? How much of a doer are you? Do you like to keep busy?

   Rating:  6 5 4 3 2 1 0

2. *Affect:* How emotional are you? How deeply do you feel things? Are you inclined to impassioned or soul-stirring inner reactions?

   Rating:  6 5 4 3 2 1 0

3. *Sensation:* How much do you focus on the pleasures and pains derived from your senses? How tuned in are you to your bodily sensations—to sex, food, music, art?

   Rating:  6 5 4 3 2 1 0

4. *Imagery:* Do you have a vivid imagination? Do you engage in fantasy and daydreaming? Do you think in pictures?

   Rating:  6 5 4 3 2 1 0

5. *Cognition:* How much of a thinker are you? Do you like to analyze things, make plans, reason things through?

   Rating:  6 5 4 3 2 1 0

6. *Interpersonal:* How much of a social being are you? How important are other people to you? Do you gravitate to people? Do you desire intimacy with others?

   Rating:  6 5 4 3 2 1 0

7. *Drugs/Biology:* Are you healthy and health conscious? Do you take good care of your body and physical health? Do you avoid overeating, ingestion of unnecessary drugs, excessive amounts of alcohol, and exposure to other substances that may be harmful?

   Rating:  6 5 4 3 2 1 0

fleeting visual images. *Structural profiles*[1] may readily be drawn up from the following instructions: "Here are seven rating scales that pertain to various tendencies that people have. Using a scale of 0 to 6 (6 is high—it characterizes you, or you rely on it greatly; 0 means that it does not describe you, or you rarely rely on it) please rate yourself in each of the seven areas." (See Figure 11.1.)

These subjective ratings are easily depicted on a graph. A 35-item Structured Profile Inventory (SPI) has been developed, factor-analyzed, and tested for validity and reliability (see Herman, 1993a, 1993b; Landes, 1991; Lazarus, 1989a). Herman (1998b) showed that the SPI predicted psychotherapy outcome. Therapists and clients who have similar SPI scores tend to find greater clinical improvements than those clients whose scores are dissimilar to those of their therapists.

In couples' therapy, it can prove illuminating for partners to compare their structural profiles and also to anticipate what ratings their mates will give them in each modality (see Lazarus, 1989a, 1997). Despite the arbitrary and subjective nature of these ratings, useful clinical information is often derived. When the therapist asks the client about the meaning and relevance of each rating, important insights are often gained. In addition, structural profiles may be obtained for specific areas of functioning. For example, in the realm of sexuality, the degree of activity, emotionality, sensuality, imagery, or fantasy may be rated on separate scales, together with questions about how highly valued sexual par-

[1] These differ from "modality profiles" that list problems and proposed treatments across the BASIC I.D.

ticipation is, its specific interpersonal importance, and the rater's overall biological adequacy. (See Herman, 1998a.)

How, when, where, and why are certain behaviors, outlooks, ideas, fantasies, and interpersonal patterns acquired?

Association plays a key role in all learning processes. Events that occur simultaneously or in close succession are more likely to be connected. Two stimuli that occur frequently in temporal proximity are likely to become associated. An association may be said to exist when responses evoked by one stimulus are similar to those provoked by another stimulus. Without becoming embroiled in the controversies and intricacies of learning theory or classical and operant conditioning, it is clear that a good deal of human thoughts, feelings, and behaviors are due to conditioning. Many aversions appear to result from classical conditioning. A client stated: "After undergoing surgery a few years ago, I experienced postoperative nausea for two days, during which time the man in the next bed kept playing a recording of Beethoven's Moonlight Sonata. Now every time I hear any part of that composition, I feel sick to my stomach!"

Operant conditioning is based on the observation that behavior is frequently a function of its consequences. Another client stated, "I now realize that my headaches were in large part due to the fact that the only time my husband showed me any real caring was when I was in pain."

In therapy, one endeavors to overcome classically conditioned problems by introducing new associations. Difficulties engendered by operant conditioning call for a reorganization of consequential behaviors.

How else do we acquire the habits that make up our personalities? If we had to rely solely on conditioning for all our responses, errors made during the acquisition phase of various skills would prove hazardous. It would probably prove fatal to rely on trial and error or successive approximation methods when learning to swim or to drive a car. In mastering these tasks and many complex occupational and social requirements, success often depends on imitation, observational learning, and identification (Bandura, 1969, 1977, 1986). Human personality (if not survival) is strongly determined by our ability to acquire new responses by watching someone else perform an activity and then doing it ourselves.

## To Reiterate

Our personalities stem from the interplay among our genetic endowment, our physical environment, and our social learning history. The basic social learning triad—classical (respondent) conditioning, operant (instrumental) conditioning, and modeling and vicarious processes—does not account for the fact that people are capable of overriding the best-laid plans of contiguity, reinforcements, and example by their idiosyncratic perceptions. People do not respond to their real environment but rather to their perceived environment. This includes the personalistic use of language, expectancies, selective attention, goals, and performance standards as well as the impact of numerous values, attitudes, and beliefs. As Bandura's (1986) principle of *reciprocal determinism* underscores, people do not react automatically to external stimuli. Their thoughts will determine which stimuli are noticed, how they are noticed, how much they are valued, and how long they are remembered.

This brief outline has not addressed the specific ways in which mental and emotional disorders arise. The main learning factors are our conditioned associations (respondent and operant responses) and the models with whom we identified and whom we imitated—deliberately or inadvertently. During the course of exposure to these inputs, we may have acquired conflicting information, faulty cognitions, and a variety of inhibitions and needless defenses.

Emotional problems and disorders also arise from inadequate or insufficient learning. Here the problems do not arise from conflicts, traumatic events, or false ideas. Rather, gaps in people's repertoires—they were never given necessary information and essential coping processes—make them ill-equipped to deal with societal demands.

The multimodal view emphasizes that most clients suffer from conflicts, the aftermaths of unfortunate experiences, and various deficits in their social and personal repertoires. Hence, unimodal remedies are bound to leave significant areas untouched.

## Variety of Concepts

What concepts are necessary for a full understanding of human personality? Can we do without instincts, racial unconscious, oedipal desires, archetypes, organ inferiority, psychic energy, the soul, and scores of other notions that are employed to account for the intricacies of human interaction? Psychotherapists could communicate their ideas with greater precision if they used everyday language instead of esoteric jargon. It could be argued that certain technical terms are useful for rapid and shorthand communication, but couldn't we keep these to the bare minimum? Moreover, if we heed *Occam's razor* (which holds that explanatory principles should not be needlessly multiplied), we can avoid much of the psychobabble that has risen in psychotherapy (Rosen, 1977).

In accounting for the structure and content of human personality, the previous section underscored the role of the biological substrate and the impact of learning (classical and operant conditioning, modeling, vicarious processes, and private events—thoughts, feelings, images, and sensations). Given that much of our learning is neither conscious nor deliberate (Shevrin & Dickman, 1980), is it not essential to include the unconscious in our compendium of basic concepts? Unfortunately, the unconscious has become a reified entity, and we prefer the term *nonconscious processes.* This merely acknowledges (1) that people have different degrees and levels of self-awareness, and (2) that despite a lack of awareness or conscious comprehension, unrecognized (subliminal) stimuli can nevertheless influence conscious thoughts, feelings, and behaviors. This completely bypasses the psychoanalytic notions of the unconscious, with its topographical boundaries, putative complexes, and intrapsychic functions, all tied into the intricate mosaic of elaborate inferences about state, stage, and trait theories of personality development.

Similarly, psychodynamic theory views the defense mechanisms as perceptual, attitudinal, or attentional shifts that aid the ego in neutralizing overbearing id impulses. In the multimodal orientation these convoluted theories are not necessary to account for the fact that people are capable of truncating their awareness, beguiling themselves, mislabeling their feelings, and losing touch with themselves (and others) in various ways. We are apt to defend against or avoid pain, discomfort, or negative emotions such as anxiety, depression, guilt, and shame. The term *defensive reactions* avoids the surplus meanings that psychodynamic theory attaches to the mechanisms of defense. Empirically, it is clear that one may overintellectualize and rationalize. While attempting to reduce dissonance, we may deny the obvious or falsely attribute our own feelings to others (projection). We can readily displace our aggressions onto other people, animals, or things.

The addition of *nonconscious processes* and *defensive reactions* to our assemblage of basic concepts should not be misconstrued as falling into the quagmire of Freudian constructs. But it is impossible to have a comprehensive understanding of human personality without admitting that people are capable of disowning, denying, and projecting numerous thoughts, feelings, wishes, and impulses. Furthermore, it has been demonstrated time and again that during altered states of consciousness one may have access to memories and skills not amenable to conscious recall. In acknowledging and accounting for these important reactions, it is not necessary to resort to psychoanalytic hypotheses.

Multimodal therapy is not a conglomeration of psychoanalysis, behavior therapy, and many other systems. While effective techniques may be drawn from many available sources, one need not subscribe to any of their underlying theories.

As we enter the interpersonal modality and examine various complex interactions, communication breaks down (literally and figuratively) unless we add another explanatory concept. People not only communicate, they also metacommunicate (i.e., communicate about their communications). Effective communication requires one to step back, as it were, and examine the content and process of patterns of communication in ongoing relationships.

# PSYCHOTHERAPY

## Theory of Psychotherapy

A fundamental premise of the multimodal approach is that clients are usually troubled by specific problems that should be dealt with through specific treatments. Multimodal therapy is different from systems that cluster presenting problems into ill-defined constructs and then employ one or two treatment procedures. The basic assumption of the multimodal approach is that durability of results is a function of the amount of effort expended by client and therapist across the seven dimensions of personality (BASIC I.D.). The more adaptive and coping responses clients learn in therapy, the less likely they are to relapse. Lasting change at the very least seems to depend upon combinations of techniques, strategies, and modalities. This outlook vitiates the search for a panacea—a single therapeutic modality.

Multimodal therapy overlaps cognitive behavior therapy and rational emotive behavior therapy in many important respects. They have several major points in common, including the following:

1. Most problems are presumed to arise from deficient or faulty social learning processes.

2. The therapist-client relationship is more that of a trainer and trainee than a doctor treating a sick patient.

3. Transfer of learning (generalization) from therapy to the client's everyday environment is not considered automatic but is deliberately fostered by means of homework assignments.

4. Labels such as diagnostic categories are operational definitions based on overt behavior.

There are important differences between MMT and other cognitive and behavioral orientations. MMT goes beyond the lip service often paid to tailoring treatment procedures to different problems in different people. The goodness of fit in terms of clients' expectancies, therapist-client compatibility, matching, and the selection of techniques is examined in great detail by multimodal therapists. Moreover, the scope of assessment and specific information obtained when examining sensory, imagery, cognitive, and interpersonal factors, and their interactive effects, goes beyond the confines of the usual stimulus and functional analyses conducted by some therapists.

Another assumption is that without new experiences there can be no change. In multimodal therapy clients are inspired and encouraged to do different things and to do things differently. Therapeutic change usually follows methods that are performance based. Purely cognitive or verbal methods are often less effective. Yet before certain clients can take effective action, they require help in eliminating barriers in their interpersonal domain, in their sensory reactions, mental images, and cognitive processing. Indeed, from the multimodal perspective, some of the most important insights are gained when clients develop an awareness and understanding of content areas and interactive relationships within their BASIC I.D. patterns. As one client put it:

> I never realized what an impact my mother and her older sister had on my life—how I let them shape my attitudes, how I treated my husband and children the way they treated my father, my uncle, my cousins, and me. Now I see that I even copied their aches and pains. . . . When I get a mental image I see their faces and hear their words. . . . Now I'm rewriting my BASIC I.D. the way I want to be. I'm tuning into my thoughts, my feelings, my images. . . . If I catch myself thinking the way they think, I crowd out their ideas with my ideas, and then I picture myself coping. I see myself succeeding. This has ended my tensions, my headaches, and all the neurotic cop-outs.

MMT disagrees with those who believe that as long as the client-therapist relationship is good, techniques are of little concern. Certainly, it is necessary for the therapist to be respected by clients and to be trusted enough for them to confide personal and emotionally significant material. Without the attainment of rapport, there will be little inclination for people to disclose distressing, embarrassing, and anxiety-provoking information. Woody stressed that an effective therapist "must be more than a 'nice guy' who can exude prescribed interpersonal conditions—he must have an armamentarium of scientifically derived skills and techniques to supplement his effective interpersonal relations" (1971, p. 8). In keeping with the pluralistic philosophy of the multimodal tradition, we see the client-therapist relationship on a continuum extending from a rather formal, businesslike investment at the one end to a close-knit, dependent bonding at the other (Lazarus, 1993). In multimodal therapy, the client-therapist relationship is examined or discussed only when there is reason to suspect that it is impeding therapeutic progress. When therapy is proceeding well, why waste time analyzing the interpersonal feelings between the client and therapist? (See Lazarus, 1981.)

Multimodal therapy is predicated on the assumption that the more disturbed the client is, the greater the specific excesses and deficits will be throughout the BASIC I.D. The model employed may be viewed as based on actualization and self-determination rather than on pathology. Everyone can benefit from a change in behavior that eliminates unwanted or surplus reactions while increasing the frequency, intensity, and duration of creative, fulfilling responses. Likewise, the control or elimination of unpleasant emotions and the augmentation of positive feelings are worthy goals.

In the sensory modality, it is eminently worthwhile to extinguish negative sensations and to derive more pleasure and meaning from each of our five basic senses (see Ackerman, 1995). Our mental imagery—those mental pictures that ultimately coalesce in a series of self-images—has a direct impact on the tone and cadence of our actions and feelings. Thus, we would do well to focus heavily on various coping images and try to keep them overridingly positive. Faulty assumptions, misconceptions, and irrational cognitions clearly undermine effective living. They are best replaced with as many reality-oriented, factual, and rational assumptions as can be mustered. Everyone would do well to cultivate the specific skills and prosocial interactions that produce good, close, and rewarding interpersonal relationships. The role that hypnosis plays in MMT has been explicated in a recent book (Lazarus, 1999).

## Process of Psychotherapy

Multimodal therapy places primary emphasis on the uniqueness of each person. Hence, there is no typical treatment format. When tuning into the expectancies and demand characteristics of one client, the therapist may adopt a passive-reflective stance. At other times, or with someone else, the same therapist may be extremely active, directive, and confrontative. Bearing in mind the fundamental question of who or what is best for this individual, the first issue is whether the therapist will work with the client or refer him or her to someone else. If clients display grossly bizarre or inappropriate behaviors, delusions, thought disorders, and other signs of "psychosis," nonmedical therapists refer them to a psychiatrist or a psychiatric facility. Similarly, evidence of strong homicidal or suicidal tendencies often requires medical and custodial intervention.

In general, the initial interview focuses on presenting complaints and their main precipitants. Antecedent events are carefully assessed, as are those factors that appear to be maintaining the client's maladaptive behaviors. One endeavors to ascertain what the client wishes to derive from therapy. It is also useful to elucidate the client's strengths and positive attributes. Overriding each of these specific details is the question of adequate client-therapist compatibility. The therapist also tries to determine whether there are any clear indications or contraindications for the adoption of particular therapeutic styles (e.g., directive or nondirective postures) (see Lazarus, 1993).

The initial meeting may be with an individual, a couple, or a family. To put the client(s) at ease, a therapist may begin the first session with small talk, noting formal details, such as name, address, phone numbers, marital status, and occupation. This gives the client an opportunity to adjust to the environment of the consulting room, to experience a verbal interchange, and to be primed for the detailed inquiry that soon follows. After taking down formal details, the therapist may simply say, "What seems to be troubling you?" As various complaints are mentioned, the therapist pays particular attention to which modality of the BASIC I.D. they apply to, and two additional interlocking factors are carefully noted: (1) What has led to the current situation? and (2) Who or what is maintaining it?

In multimodal therapy, it is not uncommon for specific interventions to be made during the initial interview. One does not wait until the full assessment procedures are completed before commencing to alleviate distress, to correct misconceptions, or to redefine the presenting complaint. Here is an example from the initial interview with a 38-year-old man (T = Therapist; C = Client):

T:  What seems to be troubling you?
C:  Well, according to my wife, I'm a premature ejaculator.
T:  Exactly what does that mean?
C:  I was married before for 10 years. I got married because she was pregnant, but we really never should have gotten together because we just were too different and never got along. I met my present wife about a year ago, and we've been married almost three months. She's a psychiatric social worker.
T:  Just how rapidly do you ejaculate? Do you last 2 seconds, 30 seconds, 60 seconds?
C:  Well, I can go for about um, 10 vigorous thrusts. If I go slower, I can last longer, I've tried adding numbers in my head, pinching my thigh, thinking of work, wearing two condoms . . .
T:  Do these things help?
C:  To some extent, but it sure takes most of the pleasure away.
T:  Have you ever ejaculated before entering your wife, or immediately after penetration?
C:  No. Like I said, if I do it vigorously, I come on the stroke of 10. [Laughs.]
T:  At which point you turn into a pumpkin.
C:  I become a jerk. My wife says I need help, so here I am!
T:  Is your pattern the same with other women? For example, were you the same with your first wife?
C:  Pretty much, but it never seemed to bother her or any of the others. If I wait 15 or 20 minutes and do it a second time, I can last almost indefinitely.
T:  Even with vigorous movements?

C: That's right. If I feel myself getting too excited, I just stop for a few moments and then I can keep going.

T: Well, from what you've told me, you are not a "premature ejaculator." You come fairly rapidly the first time, but after a rest pause you have excellent control. Do you usually want intercourse a second time, or after the first orgasm are you fully satisfied and maybe drop off to sleep?

C: Let's put it this way. If the woman remains interested, I'm always willing and ready to give it a second go round. But I'm really happy to hear you say that I'm not a sexual cripple.

T: Have you ever masturbated before having sex with your wife so that you will last longer right from the start of intercourse?

C: Yes, but my wife says I shouldn't have to resort to that.

T: If I may put it bluntly, I think your wife has several false ideas and you are a victim of her irrational shoulds.

C: Her what?

T: Shoulds. That you should do this and shouldn't do that. That this is a must. That everything is black or white.

C: That's her all right! You've hit the nail on the head.

T: I have the feeling that you take all this crap, that you allow yourself to be labeled, put down, and led by the nose. And my guess is that you endured a different type of abuse from your first wife until you reached a breaking point and got a divorce.

C: I've always put women on a pedestal.

T: What does that imply? That you treat woman as your superiors, that you look up to them, that you do not see men and women as equal but different?

C: [30-second silence.] I can't really say for sure. I know this sounds awfully Freudian, but my mother has always been sort of scary. [He appears to be deep in thought.]

T: Well, if I can sum up my impressions, it seems to me that your problem is not premature ejaculation but lack of assertiveness, plus some subtle attitudes and values that are tied into this whole perception. What do you think?

C: I think you're right. I know you're right. A long time ago one of my buddies—he's a psychologist with Bell Labs—said I seem to be attracted to castrating bitches. You seem to be saying the same thing.

T: Well, I wouldn't put it that way. Frankly, my guess is that you bring out the worst in women by the way you react to them. At any rate, I feel you and I have a few things to sort out, and maybe a bit later, you and your wife might meet with me so that we can perhaps establish better communication and upgrade your marriage.

[As the multimodal assessment continued, several additional inadequacies were brought to light that called for extensive attention to behavioral, cognitive, imagery, and interpersonal domains. The wife, a woman apparently riddled with many problems of her own, elected to see a female therapist and refused marital therapy. After about 15 months the couple met with the original therapist for an evaluation session, and both claimed that individually and maritally, things were decidedly better.]

At the end of the initial interview, the usual adult outpatient is given a *Multimodal Life History Inventory* (Lazarus & Lazarus, 1991), a 15-page printed booklet that asks crucial questions about antecedent events, ongoing problems, and maintaining factors (see Koocher, Norcross, & Hill, 1998). The answers are divided into BASIC I.D. categories.

The client is asked to bring the completed questionnaire to the second session. (Obviously, young children and many mental hospital patients are incapable of filling out questionnaires. Keat [1979, 1990] has addressed the multimodal treatment of children, and Brunell and Young [1982] have provided a multimodal handbook for mental hospitals.)

By the start of the third session, the therapist usually has gleaned sufficient information from the first two meetings and the life history inventory to construct a preliminary modality profile (i.e., a list of specific problems in each area of the client's BASIC I.D.). Typically, the client is invited to scrutinize the profile and to comment upon or modify specific items. Client and therapist then discuss strategies and techniques, and a general treatment plan is instituted.

A 33-year-old client with the presenting complaint of "depression" agreed that the following modality profile summed up her main problems:

| | |
|---|---|
| Behavior: | Withdrawal, avoidance, inactivity |
| Affect: | Depression, guilt, self-recrimination |
| Sensation: | Heavy, sluggish, enervated |
| Imagery: | Death images, visions of family rejection |
| Cognition: | Monologue about past failures, self-statements about personal worthlessness |
| Interpersonal: | Unassertive, passive |
| Drugs/Biology: | After having taken an antidepressant for three months, the client was given a new medication by her physician about four weeks ago. |

The interview with the client went as follows (T = Therapist; C = Client):

T:  Is there anything else we should add to the list?

C:  I don't know. The medicine helps me sleep better and I'm eating more, but I still don't feel any better.

T:  Well, three things stand out. First, regardless of how you feel, we've got to get you to do more things, to get out, to stop hiding from the world.

C:  [Shakes her head.]

T:  It's tough but necessary. The two other things are your negative images and all that nonsense you tell yourself about being utterly worthless. That needs to be changed.

C:  [On the verge of tears.] My brother was right. He said to me, "You're nothing!" God, how that hurt. I always heard that from my father. We girls were nothing. But I looked up to my brother, and coming from him . . . [Cries.]

T:  It seems that you desperately want approval from your father, your brother, perhaps all the men in the world before you will feel adequate. Can you close your eyes and picture saying to your father and to your brother, "I don't need your approval!"

C:  I wish I could say that and mean it.

T:  Shall we try some role-playing? I'll be your brother. "You're nothing! You are just a complete zero!" Now will you challenge that?
    [Role-playing, with considerable role reversal, in which the therapist modeled assertive answers, ensued for about 20 minutes.]

C:  I can say the right words, but the wrong feelings are still there.

T:  As long as you start with the right words and use them in the right places and to the relevant people, the feelings will soon start to change.

\* \* \* \* \*

C:  I just have these awful ideas about death. I dream about being at funerals, or getting lost in a cemetery . . . And my mind often goes back to my cousin's death, and how my brother cried for him, all these horrible thoughts.

T:  Let's deal with that, but first, I'd like to review the treatment plan. First, I want to be sure that you will increase your activity level, go out and do things. I want you to keep notes of the things you do, of the activities you wanted to avoid but did not avoid. Second, I want to be sure that you will express your feelings and not be passive, especially with your husband and your brother. No matter how miserable you feel, can you promise me that you will do these two things this week?

C: I'll try.

T: Promise me you'll do it.

C: [Cries.]

T: If I'm coming on too strong, tell me to back off.

C: I realize it's for my own good.

T: So can I count on you?

C: I'll do my best.

T: Good. Now let's delve into those death images. Why don't we start with your dream about being lost in the cemetery? Close your eyes. Settle back and relax. You're in your dream, lost in the cemetery. Tell me what happens.

C: [30-second pause] I feel awfully afraid. The ground is soggy as if it just rained. I see the tombstones but I can't make out the names. . . . There's someone else there. [Pause.] I'm frightened. [Pause.] I've seen him before, but his features are indistinct, he's too far from me to make out who it is.

T: You have binoculars or a zoom lens. Look through the eyepiece. Who is it?

C: It's . . . no it's not. It looked like my cousin for a moment. He went away.

T: Let's bring your cousin into the dream so that he can talk to you. Can you bring him into the picture?

C: [Pause.] Peculiar! He's dressed like a funeral director in a black suit.

[Over several sessions, guided imagery was used to conjure up encounters with several of her deceased relatives—her cousin, maternal grandmother, and several paternal aunts and uncles. A theme emerged. She had been close to all of her deceased relatives for the first 12 to 20 years of her life and had what gestalt therapists call *unfinished business* with each of them. Imaginary dialogues ensued with each one in turn. The therapist encouraged her to assume an assertive position throughout, which seemed to serve an important function. Problems in the other BASIC I.D. areas received equal attention. She was constantly encouraged to increase her activity level and to express her feelings, and her cognitive errors were corrected by emphasizing their irrational underpinnings.]

When treatment impasses arise, it is often helpful to introduce a second-order BASIC I.D. assessment. This consists of subjecting a problematic item on the initial modality profile to more detailed inquiry in terms of behavior, affect, sensation, imagery, cognition, interpersonal factors, and drugs or biological considerations. For example, the aforementioned woman remained extremely resistant to implementing assertive behaviors. While she acknowledged feeling less depressed and stated that her images and cognitions were more positive and rational, she remained interpersonally passive and unassertive. When asked for her BASIC I.D. associations to the concept of assertiveness, the following emerged:

| Behavior: | Attacking |
| Affect: | Angry |
| Sensation: | Tension |
| Imagery: | Bombs bursting |
| Cognition: | Get even |
| Interpersonal: | Hurting |
| Drugs/Biology: | High blood pressure |

She had been told, and paid lip service to understanding, the essential differences between assertion and aggression. Nevertheless, the second-order BASIC I.D. indicated that in her mind, an assertive response was tantamount to a vicious attack. This alerted the therapist to model, explain, rehearse, and define assertive behaviors in much greater detail.

With a different depressed individual, the treatment, while addressing all BASIC I.D. problem areas, might be quite dissimilar (Fay & Lazarus, 1981; Lazarus, 1992b).

## Mechanisms of Psychotherapy

Consonant with the pluralistic outlook of the multimodal tradition, different mechanisms are responsible for positive change in different people. Thus, for some, the mere non-judgmental acceptance of a highly respected outsider is sufficient to offset faulty attitudes and behaviors. For others, the main mechanism is largely didactic—they have learned, through discussions with the therapist, more effective ways of processing information, of responding to significant others, of coping with the exigencies of life.

Some of the main mechanisms and ingredients of psychotherapeutic change and the modalities to which they apply are described below.

### Behavior

*Extinction* (e.g., by applying methods such as massed practice, response prevention, and flooding). *Counterconditioning* (e.g., in using incompatible response techniques such as graded exposure and desensitization). *Positive reinforcement, negative reinforcement,* and *punishment* (e.g., when using operant procedures such as token economies, contingent praise, time-out, and aversion therapy).

### Affect

*Abreaction* (e.g., when reliving and recounting painful emotions, usually in the presence of a supportive, trusted ally). *Owning* and *accepting feelings* (e.g., when therapy permits the client to acknowledge affect-laden materials that were nonconscious).

### Sensation

*Tension release* (e.g., through biofeedback, relaxation, or physical exercise). *Sensory pleasuring* (e.g., the acquisition of positive tactile sensations during sexual retraining).

### Imagery

*Changes in self-image* (e.g., when success in any modality is sustained). *Coping images* (e.g., when able to picture self-control or self-achievement in situations where these images previously had been impossible to evoke).

### Cognition

*Cognitive restructuring* (e.g., changes in dichotomous reasoning, self-downing, overgeneralization, categorical imperatives, non sequiturs, and excessive desires for approval). *Awareness* (e.g., understanding antecedents and their relation to ongoing behaviors, appreciation of how specific firing orders culminate in various affective reactions).

### Interpersonal

*Modeling* (e.g., the therapist as role model or through selective self-disclosure and deliberate modeling as during role-reversal exercises). *Dispersing unhealthy collusions* (e.g., changing counterproductive alliances). *Paradoxical maneuvers* (e.g., when countering double-binding responses). *Nonjudgmental acceptance* (e.g., when clients realize that in therapy they are offered considerations not usually available in most social relationships).

## Drugs/Biology

In addition to medical examinations and interventions when warranted, the implementation of better exercise and nutrition, substance abuse cessation, or psychotropic medication is sometimes essential—particularly in the treatment of schizophrenia, affective disorders, and some anxiety states.

In the broadest terms, psychological problems may be due to *learning* and/or *lesions.* The latter falls into the D modality; learning is exemplified by the BASIC I. Full understanding of the exact mechanisms of change in any modality is yet to be achieved. Indeed, even in the D modality, while new knowledge about receptor sites, neurotransmitters, biological markers, and other biochemical parameters have emerged, much remains unknown. Perusal of the psychotropic drugs listed in the *Physician's Desk Reference* reveals that for most, the description under "Clinical Pharmacology" states that the mechanism of action is not definitely known. In the psychological sphere, the exact and precise "mechanisms of action" are even less well elucidated.

# APPLICATIONS

## Problems

The multimodal orientation has implications for both prevention and treatment. Its purview extends from individuals, couples, families, and groups to broader community and organizational settings. Thus, some multimodal therapists have special expertise in dealing with children (Keat, 1979, 1990) or applying these methods in classroom settings (Gerler, 1979), in a child care agency (O'Keefe & Castaldo, 1980), in parent training (Judah, 1978), in mental retardation (Pearl & Guarnaccia, 1976), in management (O'Keefe & Castaldo, 1981a), and in institutional settings (Roberts et al., 1980). Brunell and Young's (1982) *Multimodal Handbook for a Mental Hospital* shows the versatility of this framework in a variety of inpatient problem areas. The multimodal framework was even shown to have relevance when dealing with a community disaster (Sank, 1979) and when confronted by a nondisclosing black client (Ridley, 1984). Ponterotto and Zander (1984) have applied the approach to counselor supervision, Greenburg (1982) found multimodal methods especially helpful in counselor education, Edwards and Kleine (1986) used it as a model for working with gifted adolescents, and Ponterotto found it "a culturally sensitive and relevant therapeutic framework for nonminority and minority counselors working with clients of Mexican-American heritage" (1987, p. 308). Eimer (1988) described the application of multimodal assessment and therapy to the patient with chronic pain. Brunell (1990) devised multimodal strategies for overcoming the "strenuous lethargy" of depression. Books, chapters, and articles on multimodal therapy have been written by therapists abroad—such as in Japan, Argentina, and Holland. Translations in many different languages have appeared (e.g., Dutch, Spanish, Portuguese, Chinese, German, Italian, and Polish), and correspondence with colleagues from these countries has shown that the multimodal orientation blends in well across many different cultures.

Two distinct questions may be posed regarding the types of individuals and the variety of problems that may be dealt with: (1) Who can be helped by a multimodal practitioner? and (2) Who can be helped by multimodal therapy?

Multimodal therapists are drawn from the full range of health service providers. Psychiatrists, psychologists, social workers, psychiatric nurses, pastoral counselors, and other mental health workers each have members within their disciplines who employ multimodal methods. The therapist's professional background and personal qualities will equip him or her with special skills, talents, and knowledge to handle certain problems and particular individuals, and to function in specific settings. Thus, some multimodal therapists are highly skilled at using biofeedback, others have a strong background in behavioral medicine, and some are especially gifted and clinically adept with substance-abuse disorders, sexual offenders, school-related problems, and so forth. A multimodal psychiatrist, when prescribing medication to control psychotic behaviors (addressing the D modality), is not practicing multimodal therapy. However, when the psychotic symptoms are in remission, a multimodal psychiatrist will systematically deal with the other six modalities (the BASIC I.). When specific clients require services that lie outside the realm of the given multimodal therapist's skills, referral to an individual or agency better equipped to deal with the situation is a standard procedure.

Multimodal practitioners constantly inquire, *Who or what is best for this individual (or couple, or family, or group)?* Referral to appropriate personnel is considered a most important technique. Thus, if the therapist is not equipped to manage the client's problems, the multimodal practitioner will not continue seeing the client. Nor is it sufficient for a multimodal therapist simply to inform the client that he or she needs to see someone with skills that the therapist does not possess—it is the clinician's duty to try to make a referral. Multimodal therapists are eager to apply "treatments of choice" whenever feasible. They are well aware that a body of evidence-based, empirically supported therapy has been identified for specific conditions, and they endeavor to apply these methods when called for (or refer the client to someone who has that particular expertise).

All therapists encounter clients who require long-term supportive therapy—the development of a stable relationship with a caring person. A well-trained multimodal therapist will do more than offer concern and empathy. Within the context of a supportive therapeutic relationship, specific attention to critical BASIC I.D. excesses and deficits can transform a holding pattern into a framework where constructive learning takes place. Thus, when the mesh and artistry between client and therapist are such that thorough coverage of the BASIC I.D. is accomplished, successful outcomes are obtained even with psychotic individuals, substance abusers, and depressed persons who have failed to respond to years of drug therapy and other medical interventions. Nevertheless, it is obviously easier to achieve noteworthy gains with clients whose excesses and deficits across the BASIC I.D. are not especially rigid, encrusted, or pervasive.

Colleagues at the various Multimodal Therapy Institutes report consistent positive outcomes and follow-ups with marriage and family problems, sexual difficulties, childhood disorders, inadequate social skills, smoking, stress-related difficulties, fears and phobias, anxiety states, psychosomatic complaints, and depression. Some colleagues report positive results with certain obsessive-compulsive problems.

The multimodal orientation calls for continuous input from various sources so that subtle refinements and amplifications are tested and added. These probably hold greater interest for practitioners who employ the BASIC I.D. format with their clients and who have mastered the nuances of the various tactics that are unique to the multimodal approach—for example, bridging, tracking, structural profiles, and second-order BASIC I.D. assessments. Six recent publications address these extensions, and the curious reader may wish to peruse one or more of them (Lazarus, 2001a, 2001b, 2002a, 2002b; Lazarus & Lazarus, 2002; Palmer & Lazarus, 2001). Readers interested in a succinct update of the multimodal orientation are directed to a chapter by Lazarus (2003).

## Evaluation

In multimodal therapy, the evaluation of treatment outcomes is usually straightforward. Since modality profiles (i.e., lists of specific excesses and deficits throughout the client's BASIC I.D.) are routinely constructed, ongoing treatment evaluations are an integral part of the client-therapist interaction. Thus, instead of assuming that some ill-defined entity such as "emotional maturity" has evolved, the multimodal therapist specifies particular gains and achievements in each modality:

| | |
|---|---|
| Behavior: | Less withdrawn; less compulsive; more outspoken |
| Affect: | More warm, less hostile; less depressed |
| Sensation: | Enjoys more pleasures; less tense, more relaxed |
| Imagery: | Fewer nightmares; better self-image |
| Cognition: | Less self-downing; more positive self-statements |
| Interpersonal: | Goes out on dates; expresses wishes and desires |
| Drugs/Biology: | Has stopped smoking; sleeps well; exercises regularly |

Structural profiles, before and after multimodal therapy, tend to reflect only minor changes in most instances; that is, doers are still doers and thinkers are still thinkers. People who are active, tuned into sensory pleasures, imaginative, and social before therapy will usually show the same tendencies after therapy. If a high score on the interpersonal scale reflected an overly dependent penchant, this may decrease a few points after therapy. Conversely, if a low score on the interpersonal scale before treatment was a function of shyness and withdrawal, the post-therapeutic score will usually show an increase of several points. Depressed people are inclined to show the greatest pre- and post-treatment differences. While depressed, they usually show a low activity level, few or no feelings apart from sadness, a conspicuous absence of sensory pleasures, and decreased social participation. They may rate themselves fairly high on imagery and cognition because of visions of doom, loneliness, illness, and failure, and because of high self-blame and pervasive ideas of self-worthlessness (Fay & Lazarus, 1981). When therapy is successful for those with depression, structural profiles tend to depict significant changes in terms of greater activity, sensory joys, and social participation (Lazarus, 1992b).

In evaluating marital therapy, the use of a 16-item marital satisfaction questionnaire (Lazarus, 1997) has proven useful. The questionnaire pinpoints important areas of personal and familial distress, and quantitative changes in this pencil-and-paper test usually reflect significant improvements in marital happiness. Herman (1991a) showed that an earlier version of the Marital Satisfaction Questionnaire had high levels of validity and reliability.

A three-year follow-up evaluation of 20 complex cases who had completed a course of multimodal therapy (e.g., people suffering from obsessive-compulsive rituals, extreme agoraphobia, pervasive anxiety and panic, depression, alcohol addiction, or enmeshed family and marital problems) showed that 14 maintained their gains or had made additional progress without further therapy; two felt the need for medication from time to time; and three other cases had failed to maintain their initial gains.

In a carefully controlled outcome study, Williams (1988) compared multimodal assessment and therapy with other treatments in helping children with learning disabilities. Clear data demonstrated to the efficacy of the multimodal interventions.

Over the past 20 years, treatment goals were achieved with more than 75 percent of the people who consulted us. Follow-ups reveal a relapse rate of less than 5 percent.

Kwee (1984) conducted a controlled outcome study using multimodal therapy with 44 obsessive-compulsive patients and 40 phobic individuals in a general psychiatric hospital. Ninety percent of these patients had previously undergone treatment without success, and 70 percent had suffered from their disorders for more than four years. Various process measures were administered at intake, on admission, after 12 weeks, at discharge, and at follow-up nine months later. The follow-up data showed that 64 percent of the obsessive-compulsive individuals remained significantly improved. Among the phobic individuals, 55 percent had maintained or had proceeded beyond their treatment gains.

Eimer and his associates (Eimer & Allen, 1998; Eimer & Freeman, 1998) have presented extensive work on pain management, incorporating the multimodal therapy framework.

## Treatment

The average duration of a complete course of multimodal therapy is approximately 50 hours (about a year of therapy at weekly intervals). Brief multimodal therapy can be accomplished in 10 to 12 sessions (Lazarus, 1989b, 1997; Lazarus & Fay, 1990). Acutely disturbed people or those with special problems may require more frequent sessions, but once a week is often the best frequency to give people sufficient time to do the recommended homework. Fewer than 30 percent of the clients seen at the various Multimodal Therapy Institutes seem to require, or are willing to undergo, as much as 50 hours of therapy. While some clients may require extended support and trust building and therefore remain in therapy for several years, the majority favor short-term therapy (15 to 20 sessions). Multimodal therapy also lends itself well to crisis intervention. When clients learn to monitor each area of the BASIC I.D., self-management seems to be enhanced (Eskapa, 1992).

Various MMT treatment formats have been applied. Outpatient individual psychotherapy is perhaps most frequently used, although when the interpersonal modality becomes the focus of attention, spouses and other family members are usually seen as well. Thus, what often starts out as one-to-one psychotherapy may shift to couples therapy or family therapy, or the client may be invited to join a group. These decisions are based on the therapist's assessment of who or what appears most likely to benefit the client, and their implementation depends on the concurrence of the client and the willingness of significant others to participate. Thus, the multimodal therapist treats individuals, couples, families, and groups.

Regardless of the specific treatment format, multimodal therapy encompasses (1) specification of goals and problems, (2) specification of treatment techniques to achieve these goals and remedy these problems, and (3) systematic measurement of the relative success of these techniques. In essence, this boils down to eliminating distressing and unwanted responses throughout the BASIC I.D. and also overcoming deficits that exist in any of these modalities.

It is worth reiterating the main procedural sequences followed in multimodal therapy.

1. Information from the initial interviews and the life history inventory results in a modality profile (i.e., a systematic list of problems and proposed treatments in each area of the client's BASIC I.D.).

2. The therapist, usually in concert with the client, selects specific strategies to deal with each problem area. If treatment impasses arise, *a second-order BASIC I.D.* is carried out (i.e., the unresponsive problem is reexamined in each of the seven modalities).

3. Generalized complaints, such as anxiety and panic attacks, are usually dissected into modality firing orders. Appropriate techniques are selected to deal with each distressing element in turn.

In multimodal therapy, attention to what is traditionally called transference and countertransference phenomena takes place only when there is reason to suspect that therapeutic progress will thereby ensue. Sometimes treatment impasses are caused by specific client-therapist interactions that need to be addressed, but when therapy is proceeding well, why bother to examine the therapeutic relationship?

In multimodal marriage therapy, the couple is usually seen together for the initial interview, and the main presenting complaints are discussed. Each partner is given the life history inventory to take home and fill out independently. An individual session is then arranged with each one for the purpose of examining the completed questionnaire and constructing an initial modality profile. Thereafter, the treatment processes are tailored to the individuals and their unique dyadic requirements (see Brunell, 1985; Lazarus, 1989a). C. N. Lazarus developed an Expanded Structural Profile that is particularly useful in couples therapy. It appears as Appendix 3 in Lazarus (1997).

Participants in multimodal groups construct their own modality profiles, which serve as a blueprint for the specific gains they wish to derive. Groups can be particularly helpful in dispelling various myths (consensual validation tends to carry more weight than the views of one person, even if that person is a highly respected authority). When interpersonal deficiencies are present, group therapy can provide a more accurate training milieu. Groups lend the opportunity for vicarious or observational learning and offer a rich variety of modeling opportunities. Role-playing, behavior rehearsal, and other enactments are enhanced by psychodramatic nuances that groups provide. Lonely and isolated individuals particularly tend to benefit from group therapy, especially when the group provides a springboard for the development of friendships. Extremely hostile, paranoid, deluded, or severely depressed individuals are excluded from multimodal groups because they are usually too disruptive. Similarly, people who are locked into pervasive obsessive-compulsive rituals have responded poorly in multimodal groups. These people are better treated individually or, preferably, in marital or family contexts.

The use of psychological tests is not a standard procedure, but certain problems may necessitate their application. Intelligence tests (especially with children) may augment the appreciation of specific cognitive abilities and deficits. Neuropsychological assessment may shed light on matters of organicity, and tests of aptitude and special abilities may also be used to good effect with certain clients. The most frequently used test is a structured, interactive, projective procedure called the *deserted island fantasy* technique (Lazarus, 1971, 1989a). In essence, the client is asked to describe what might transpire if he or she were on a deserted island for six months in the company of a congenial person unknown to the client. As clients describe their fantasies about their island sojourn, the therapist is usually able to discern several important facets. The presence or absence of the ordinary give-and-take of personal interaction emerges quite clearly. Some clients are unable to picture themselves suspending their hostility, aggression, or depression. One easily detects those instances where people are especially afraid of close contact. Evidence of autistic thinking may emerge. Direct questions concerning the evolution of friendship on the island can provide important clues about the way in which the therapeutic relationship should be structured. Many additional insights tend to be gained. Elsewhere, an entire chapter has been devoted to this technique (Lazarus, 1989a).

The application of multimodal therapy to inpatient settings is beyond the scope of this chapter. The interested reader is referred to the book edited by Brunell and Young (1982), which contains information about designing, planning, and implementing multimodal treatment programs with hospitalized psychiatric patients.

While the majority of sessions are held in the therapist's office, the flexibility of multimodal procedures leaves open a variety of other settings. In dealing with certain clients who do not show some improvement in a short period of time, Fay and Lazarus (1982) emphasized that it may be helpful to shift the locus of therapy outside the office, such as outdoor walking sessions or a session in the park, or, under certain circumstances, a home visit by the therapist. The use of ancillary personnel is also often found to facilitate extensive in vivo work. Thus, nurses, psychiatric aides, teachers, parents, and other paraprofessional volunteers may expedite desensitization, provide reinforcement of adaptive responses, and contribute to other helpful modeling experiences.

*Relationships*

In keeping with individuals' needs and expectancies, multimodal therapists see relationships with clients on a continuum. Some clients thrive when the relationship is formal, rather distant, and businesslike. At the other extreme, some clients require close, warm, and empathic bonding (see Lazarus, 1993). The multimodal therapist is not likely to foster dependent, romantic, or other deep attachments because much of the therapy remains task oriented.

It is widely held that people enter therapy with implicit (if not explicit) expectations and that the effectiveness of therapy is often linked with these expectations. If the therapist's personality and approach are very much at variance with the client's image of an effective practitioner, a therapeutic impasse is likely to result. This, however, should not be construed as a passive and inevitable process. Clients' expectations can be modified by the therapist. Many clients, for instance, expect the therapist to "cure them" and seem unprepared to take responsibility for the treatment process and outcome. In these instances, considerable therapeutic skill and artistry may be required to elicit the client's active cooperation. The most elegant outcomes often depend on a reasonable degree of congruence between the client's BASIC I.D. and the therapist's BASIC I.D. (Herman, 1991b, 1994). When inappropriate matching results in an absence of rapport, it is often advisable to effect referral to a more compatible resource instead of insisting that the client-therapist difficulties can or should be worked through.

Multimodal therapists make extensive use of bibliotherapy. When a book is recommended, the readings are discussed during the session so that the therapist can ascertain the book's impact and clarify any ambiguities. Similarly, audiotherapy (the use of cassette recordings) is also a most useful therapeutic adjunct.

## CASE EXAMPLE

### Background

A 33-year-old woman was afraid of becoming pregnant. She was hypochondriacal and suffered from several somatic symptoms—headaches, chest pains, and gastrointestinal distress. A medical evaluation disclosed no organic pathology. She also suffered from premenstrual tension—becoming irritable, bloated, and anxious.

She had majored in mathematics at college and was working as a computer programmer. Her husband, a successful company president, had expressed a strong desire for children over the previous three years. "For the first five or six years of our marriage, neither of us wanted to have kids, but when Bill became very successful at work he wanted to start a family. That's when I realized that pregnancy, childbirth, and the whole scene terrified me."

For the past two and a half years she had been in therapy with a psychologist. "We explored my relationship with my mother, my father, my brother, and we also looked into my general home atmosphere. . . . We spoke a lot about attachment and separation. . . . it was very interesting." The client realized that what was interesting was not necessarily effective, and after reading a newspaper article, she consulted a behavior therapist who unsuccessfully attempted to desensitize her fears of pregnancy. "I think he hypnotized me and I was to see myself going through the whole pregnancy, including the labor and delivery." She acknowledged having fewer negative anticipations, but her overall clinical status remained essentially unchanged. Her brother advised her to try multimodal therapy because his senior partner's wife had mentioned that their son and daughter had both benefited from multimodal therapy after failing with other treatment approaches.

## Main Problem Areas

The foregoing information was obtained during the initial interview. The Multimodal Life History Inventory (Lazarus & Lazarus, 1991) was completed and returned before her second visit. The following modality profile was drawn up:

Behavior:              Excessive cigarette smoking; insufficient exercise

Affect:                Anger/resentment/hostility (seldom directly expressed); fear (of pregnancy)

Sensation:             Headaches; palpitations; stomach pains; tremors; chest pains; menstrual pain

Imagery:               Death images; not coping; failing

Cognition:             Perfectionistic; false romantic ideas; overly concerned about parental approval

Interpersonal:         Resorts to passive-aggressive tactics (spiteful), especially with husband

Drugs/Biology:         May require medical intervention for menstrual dysfunction

During the second session, the modality profile was discussed, and the client indicated that her most distressing problems were numerous sensory discomforts that she feared were symptoms of organic disease (despite reassurances from physicians). Exploration of her death images resulted in graphic pictures of her succumbing to a heart attack. Thus, "fears heart attack" was added to her profile under *Affect*.

## Treatment

It became clear immediately that the client's modality firing order almost invariably followed an SICA sequence (Sensation-Imagery-Cognition-Affect). First, she would observe sensory discomforts, whereupon she would dwell on them, thereby intensifying untoward pains and bodily tensions. Unpleasant and frightening images would then become intrusive. For example, she would recall vivid scenes of her maternal grandmother suffering a fatal heart attack when the client was 15 years old. Her negative imagery would lead her to label herself organically ill: "Instead of ignoring it and going about my business, I start thinking of all the things that could be wrong with me." Her unpleasant images and negative cognition culminated in severe bouts of anxiety. In keeping with her modality firing order, the following treatments were applied:

1.   Biofeedback was administered by means of an electromyography (EMG) apparatus attached to her frontalis muscles. She was given relaxation training cassettes for home use.

2.   Associated imagery was employed. She was asked to relax, close her eyes, and picture her grandmother's heart attack. When the image was vivid and clear, she was asked to focus on any other images that emerged. As each image was attended to, a pattern began to take shape. She appeared to have overidentified with her grandmother, but on an accelerated time frame. Thus, many of her physical complaints and infirmities paralleled those that her grandmother had suffered and finally succumbed to in her late 70s. Time projection was employed wherein she imagined herself going forward in time, remaining free from organic disease until she reached her late 70s. She was advised to practice the time projection exercise at least twice daily for five to ten minutes each time.

3.   Positive self-statements were implemented: "If I do take after my granny, I too will enjoy good health until I'm about 75. So I'll start worrying 40 years from now." These

positive self-statements were to be practiced in conjunction with the time projection images.

The foregoing procedures were administered in two sessions. She arrived for her next session feeling "weepy and depressed" although she was not premenstrual. Exploration of her feelings was unproductive and it seemed appropriate to carry out the deserted island fantasy. Five distinct themes emerged:

1.   She would inevitably be disappointed with her island companion: "I just know that I would feel let down."

2.   She felt that someone would have to be in charge. (Strong, overcompetitive tendencies became evident.)

3.   Boredom would lead her to engage in compulsive projects.

4.   She would withhold information from her island companion—she would not disclose all relevant aspects of her life. (This led the therapist to speculate about important matters that were being kept from him.)

5.   She would never initiate any acts of affection but would always wait for the companion to do so. (She attributed her inhibitions in this area to her father, who showed affection "only when he was good and ready." She claimed that, as a young child, she learned that spontaneous acts of affection had punitive consequences when her father happened to be in a bad mood.)

The relevance of her island fantasies to ongoing life situations was clear-cut. She felt let down by her husband, who was less affectionate and less nurturing than she desired. She was inclined to compete with him and tried, unsuccessfully, to take charge of his life. She never initiated sex or engaged in acts of spontaneous affection, although she craved greater warmth and caring. She frequently felt a childlike rage toward her husband, much of which was expressed in passive-aggressive and essentially indirect ways. Yet she felt a desire to achieve a close and loving relationship with him. Further clarification of her wishes indicated that her reluctance to have children was not due to phobic anxiety about the childbirth process: "I think my real hang-up is that kids will take Bill away from me even further than he is already." She had come to realize that before feeling able to make an emotional investment in a child, she would have to feel more secure within herself and in the marriage.

Therapy then focused on assertiveness training with special attention to (1) the direct expression of anger and resentment (instead of indirect, spiteful, manipulative responses), and (2) making requests, particularly asking for attention and affection. Role-playing and coping imagery (in which she pictured herself withstanding rejection and behaving rationally) were helpful facilitators of overt action.

Approximately two and a half months after her initial consultation (eight sessions), some progress was evident. Her gains across the BASIC I.D. were as follows:

B:   She had stopped smoking.

A:   She expressed feelings more openly and more frequently.

S:   She reported feeling more relaxed and was less bothered with physical discomforts.

I:   She was obtaining clear coping images of herself living a long and healthy life.

C:   She was somewhat less perfectionistic.

I:   She was taking emotional risks with her husband (e.g., asking for his affection).

D:   She had seen her physician again and this time had agreed to take medication for her menstrual difficulties.

A week later, the client mentioned that the physician had prescribed a diuretic to be taken five or six days prior to menstruation together with oxazepam (15 mg twice a day). On the first day of menstruation she was to take zomepirac sodium tablets for pain, as needed. (This combination of drugs proved highly effective.)

At the start of the ninth session she suggested going for a walk instead of meeting inside the office. "I feel like walking today," she said, "I'm not in the mood for hypnosis, or imagery, or stuff like that. The Herrontown Woods are less than five minutes away. Can we spend about half an hour on one of the trails?" Whereas traditional therapists would probably be disinclined to leave the professional confines of their offices, multimodal therapists tend to be more flexible in such matters (Lazarus, 1994). Initially, client and therapist admired the scenery, and then the client asked the therapist for his views on extramarital relationships. Was this a proposition? The therapist very much doubted it. He explained that he had no fixed rules, that he was neither blindly for nor universally opposed to extramarital sex. The client then revealed that she had been having an affair for the past year and a half. She had taken courses in computer science and had become sexually involved with her instructor, with whom she enjoyed "coffee and sex" once a week. She derived a good deal of flattery and attention from this clandestine relationship. The therapist inquired if this was having an adverse impact on her marriage, whereupon she insisted that one had nothing to do with the other. The therapist's insinuation that her affair was perhaps partly based on her wish to get even with her husband for his lack of emotional support and nurturance met with denial. She appeared eager to drop the subject. The topic switched to her use of coping imagery. Additional material from the deserted island fantasy test was also discussed.

At this juncture, therapy sessions were scheduled every two weeks, so that she had time to practice her imagery exercises and other homework assignments. She continued to make progress for a month and then began having palpitations, chest pains, and tension headaches. After some evasive comments, she admitted having stopped using the relaxation cassettes, the time projection images, and the cognitive self-statements, and she had also reverted to her unassertive (but aggressive) stance vis-à-vis her husband. The following dialogue ensued (C = Client; T = Therapist):

C: If you're mad at me and want to yell at me, I won't blame you. Go ahead.

T: It's your life. You've got the tools to make it better. I can't force you to use them. Do you want me to yell at you? What good will that do?

C: You're angry with me. I can tell.

T: It sounds like you want me to get angry with you. What's happening? Did you decide to have a relapse in order to spite me? Is this some kind of test to see if I care? Or are you annoyed with me and you don't want to give me the satisfaction of having helped you?

C: I've never seen you like this. You sound like Bill.

T: That's a good observation. I feel you set me up the way you tend to set him up. It seems like some kind of test. But whatever is going on, it is not direct, honest, frank, or positive.

C: Okay. I'll do the relaxation and all the rest of it.

T: Not for my sake, I hope. Stop looking for my approval, or your father's approval, or anybody's approval. Do what's best for you.

C: Arguing with you is like arguing with Bill. I can't win. You're both too smart, too well educated. You both think very fast on your feet.

T: It's interesting that you feel we are arguing, and I am intrigued by the way you have bracketed me with your husband.

C: I think I've always felt that Bill is too good for me. He is intellectually superior, his earning power is astronomical compared to mine.

T:  This brings us back to your overcompetitive feelings and it also shows me something else that was not apparent—you have a terrible self-concept.

C:  It took you this long to *realize* that?

T:  I never appreciated its full extent. We really need to do something to raise your self-esteem. [Pause.] I wonder if it would be a good idea one of these days for me to meet with you and Bill.

C:  What for?

T:  To upgrade the marriage.

C:  I would prefer you to meet with Bill alone so that you can get to know him first before seeing us together.

There were no further setbacks. In each dimension of her BASIC I.D. the client diligently addressed the relevant issues and carried out the prescribed exercises. Therapy reverted to weekly sessions and dwelled heavily on the false cognition that led to her self-abnegation. The husband was seen only once. The therapist impressed upon him that the client desired a much more intense level of intimacy and emotional support and reassurance. The husband was under the false impression that his wife's disinclination to have children was due to her own career aspirations. A brief discussion cleared up this misconception. The therapist explained the client's competitive reactions as a cover-up for her feelings of insecurity and advised the husband to perceive them as cries for love and support from him.

Eight months after the initial interview, therapy was discontinued by mutual consent. The client casually mentioned that she had terminated her affair.

## Resolution and Follow-Up

About four weeks after therapy had ended, the client called to say that she was pregnant and felt "very pleased" about it. During the brief telephone conversation the client added that she felt "infinitely more relaxed and self-confident" and said, "I'm so assertive these days that I even put my father in his place."

Approximately a year later she called for an appointment. Her baby boy was about four months old and she was delighted with motherhood. She had maintained all of her gains and added that since the birth of her son, her menstrual pains had cleared up, although she still took oxazepam a few days before her period. The reason she had made the appointment was to discuss the pros and cons of returning to work. As a result of the session, she decided to take a year's leave of absence and to take evening courses to maintain viability in the job market and ward off boredom.

## SUMMARY

Multimodal therapy is a comprehensive, systematic, and holistic approach to psychotherapy that seeks to effect durable change in an efficient and humane way. It is an open system in which the principle of technical eclecticism encourages the constant introduction of new techniques and the refinement or elimination of existing ones, but never in a random or shotgun manner. The major emphasis is on flexibility. There are virtues in using not only a variety of techniques but even a variety of therapists. The client always comes first, even if it means referring him or her to someone else. Multimodal therapists subscribe to no dogma other than the principles of theoretical parsimony and therapeutic effectiveness.

Assessments and interventions are structured around seven modalities summarized by the acronym BASIC I.D. (*b*ehavior, *a*ffect, *s*ensation, *i*magery, *c*ognition, *i*nterpersonal relationships, and *d*rugs/biological factors). This framework allows the therapist to take into account the uniqueness of each individual and to tailor treatment accordingly. The emphasis is constantly on who or what is best for this individual (couple, family, or group). By assessing significant deficits and excesses across the client's BASIC I.D., thorough coverage of diverse interactive problems is facilitated.

The therapist's role and the cadence of client-therapist interaction differ from person to person and even from session to session. Some clients respond best to somewhat austere, formal, businesslike transactions; others require gentle, tender, supportive encouragement. Two specific procedures that seem to enhance treatment effects are bridging and tracking. (*Bridging* is a procedure in which the therapist deliberately tunes into the client's preferred modality before branching off into other dimensions that seem likely to be more productive. *Tracking* is a careful examination of the firing order of the different modalities.)

The BASIC I.D. framework facilitates the roles of artistry and science in clinical intervention. For example, a recursive application of the BASIC I.D. to itself (a second-order assessment) often helps to shed new diagnostic light and helps to overcome some seemingly recalcitrant problems. A graphic representation of the BASIC I.D. in terms of a *structural profile* is most illuminating, especially in couples therapy. Examination of each specific modality and its interactive effect on the other six readily enables the therapist to shift the focus of attention between the individual and his or her parts to the person in his or her social setting.

In general, the trend in current psychotherapy is toward multidimensional, multidisciplinary, and multifaceted interventions. Rigid adherents to particular schools seem to be receding into a minority. Multiform and multifactorial assessment and treatment procedures have become widespread. The multimodal (BASIC I.D.) framework permits the clinician to identify idiosyncratic variables and thereby avoid fitting clients to preconceived treatments. It also offers an operational means for speaking the client's language. Apart from its heuristic virtues, the multimodal structure readily permits an examination of its own efficacy. While all multimodal therapists are eclectic, all eclectic therapists are not multimodal therapists.

# ANNOTATED BIBLIOGRAPHY

Brunell, L. F., & Young, W. T. (Eds.). (1982). *Multimodal handbook for a mental hospital.* New York: Springer.
This book is a practical guide to the use of multimodal therapy in mental hospitals, residential facilities, day hospitals, and other complete care centers. The book includes comprehensive details on goals and procedures for various treatment modules, from art and occupational therapy to social and problem skills training. Discussions focus on essential phases of patient assessment, program design, treatment, and evaluation of patient progress and the hospital system. Specific chapters transcend clinical, case-oriented considerations and address large-scale applications of multimodal procedures. The eight authors have pointed the way to more efficient and effective therapeutic interventions with people who are often given little more than custodial care.

Dryden, W. (1991). *A dialogue with Arnold Lazarus: "It depends."* Philadelphia: Open Universities Press.
The introduction and eight chapters in this book are the outcome of an intensive series of interviews conducted by Professor Dryden. It provides a clear picture of the origins of the multimodal concept and the factors that led to its refinement. The book covers the range from theories to practical applications, training, and supervision, and it has a particularly interesting chapter on "Dos and don'ts and sacred cows."

Keat, D. B. (1990). *Child multimodal therapy.* Norwood, NJ: Ablex Publishing Corporation.
The artistry and technical repertoire of an effective child-therapist involves special skills that are not required by a clinician who is gifted with adults. To reach certain children, the therapist must be equipped with numerous techniques, including games, stories, and songs, and have a flair for communicating in special ways. This book shows how an imaginative clinician applies the BASIC I.D. to many problems and disorders of children.

Lazarus, A. A. (1989). *The practice of multimodal therapy.* Baltimore: Johns Hopkins University Press.
This book is pragmatic and focuses on the common clinical situations confronting most psychotherapists. It spells out exactly how to conduct a thorough and

comprehensive assessment. An attempt is made to integrate knowledge from diverse orientations into a coherent approach. The book is essentially a condensation of the author's own experience, the recorded experience of others, and scientific data. Transcripts from actual sessions and vignettes of typical transactions provide rich clinical material. The book also contains a glossary of 37 separate therapeutic techniques.

Lazarus, A. A. (1997). *Brief but comprehensive psychotherapy: The multimodal way.* New York: Springer.

Is it possible to conduct brief, time-limited, and focused psychotherapy, and yet not cut corners? How can one be *brief* and also comprehensive? Is this not a contradiction in terms? As this book clearly demonstrates, the multimodal approach lends itself to broad-based yet short-term therapy. As Cyril Franks points out in the foreword, this book presents an "efficient, effective, teachable, demonstrably valid and comprehensive approach without being rigid."

## CASE READINGS

Breunlin, D. C. (1980). Multimodal behavioral treatment of a child's eliminative disturbance. *Psychotherapy: Theory, Research and Practice, 17,* 17–23.

> This case shows how even with highly targeted treatment goals, a multimodal approach can prove most advantageous.

Keat, D. B. (1976). Multimodal therapy with children: Two case histories. In A. A. Lazarus (Ed.), *Multimodal behavior therapy* (pp. 116–132). New York: Springer.

> When working with children, the multimodal framework offers a comprehensive and systematic context, but special expertise is required above and beyond the BASIC I.D.

Lazarus, A. A. (Ed.). (1985). *Casebook of multimodal therapy.* New York: Guilford.

> This book describes 14 different case studies in a variety of settings and situations.

Lazarus, A. A. (2002). Client readiness for change, cultural concerns, and risk taking: A multimodal case presentation. *Clinical Case Studies, 1,* 39–48.

> This case illustrates the manner in which multimodal assessment and therapy draw on several interrelated components. Matters pertaining to racial discrimination, cultural limits, and readiness for change had to be factored into the treatment trajectory. The anxiety, depression and self-denigrating tendencies that had brought the client to therapy called for careful training, some audacious advice, and several standard cognitive-behavioral procedures.

Lazarus, A. A. (2005). The case of George. In D. Wedding & R. J. Corsini (Eds.), *Case studies in psychotherapy* (4th ed.). Belmont, CA: Wadsworth.

> This case shows multimodal therapy in action and illustrates the treatment of a client who had been unresponsive to many different types of treatment.

Lazarus, A. A., Hasson, C., & Glat, M. (1991). Multimodal therapy. In K. N. Anchor (Ed.), *Handbook of medical psychotherapy* (pp. 123–140). Toronto: Hogrefe & Huber.

> This chapter provides a clear-cut example of the multimodal assessment and treatment of a case of panic, anxiety, and social phobia, and a marital therapy case compounded by depression.

Lazarus, A. A., & Whipple, A. G. (2000). Multimodal therapy. In F. Dumont & R. J. Corsini (Eds.), *Six therapists and one client.* New York: Springer.

> In response to a hypothetical case study, this chapter provides a step-by-step account of MMT, followed by an incisive commentary by Dr. Whipple. The reader can compare MMT to five other approaches to the same case.

Popler, K. (1977). Agoraphobia: Indications for the application of the multimodal conceptualization. *The Journal of Nervous and Mental Disease, 164,* 97–101.

> One of several cases that demonstrates how multimodal assessment is crucial if treatment outcomes are to be long lasting.

## REFERENCES

Ackerman, D. (1995). *A natural history of the senses.* New York: Vintage Books.

Aigen, B. P. (1980). The BASIC I.D. obsessive-compulsive profile. Doctoral dissertation, Graduate School of Applied and Professional Psychology, Rutgers University.

Anchor, K. N. (Ed.). (1991). *Handbook of medical psychotherapy.* Toronto: Hogrefe & Huber.

Bandura, A. (1969). *Principles of behavior modification.* New York: Holt, Rinehart & Winston.

Bandura, A. (1977). *Social learning theory.* Englewood Cliffs, NJ: Prentice-Hall.

Bandura, A. (1978). The self-system in reciprocal determinism. *American Psychologist, 33,* 344–358.

Bandura, A. (1986). *Social foundations of thought and action: A social cognitive theory.* Englewood Cliffs, NJ: Prentice-Hall.

Bertalanffy, L. von (1974). General systems theory and psychiatry. In S. Arieti (Ed.), *American handbook of psychiatry* (Vol. 1) (pp. 1095–1117). New York: Basic Books.

Brentano, F. (1972). *Psychology from an empirical standpoint.* New York: Humanities Press. (Originally published in 1874.)

Brunell, L. F. (1985). Multimodal marital therapy. In D. C. Goldberg (Ed.), *Contemporary marriage* (pp. 354–373). Homewood, IL: Dorsey.

Brunell, L. F. (1990). Multimodal treatment of depression: A strategy to break through the "strenuous lethargy" of depression. *Psychotherapy in Private Practice, 8,* 13–22.

Brunell, L. F., & Young, W. T. (Eds.). (1982). *Multimodal handbook for a mental hospital.* New York: Springer.

Buckley, W. (1967). *Modern systems research for the behavioral scientist.* Chicago: Aldine.

Burnham, W. H. (1924). *The normal mind.* New York: Appleton.

Clark, D. M. (1986). A cognitive approach to panic. *Behaviour Research and Therapy, 24,* 461–470.

Corsini, R. J. (Ed.). (2000). *Handbook of innovative therapy* (2nd ed.). New York: Wiley.

Dryden, W. (Ed.). (1992). *Integrative and eclectic therapy.* Philadelphia: Open University Press.

Dryden, W., & Golden, W. (Eds.). (1986). *Cognitive behavioral approaches to psychotherapy.* London: Harper & Row.

Edwards, S. S., & Kleine, P. A. (1986). Multimodal consultation: A model for working with gifted adolescents. *Journal of Counseling and Development, 64,* 598–601.

Eimer, B. N. (1988). The chronic pain patient: Multimodal assessment and psychotherapy. *Medical Psychotherapy, 1,* 23–40.

Eimer, B. N., & Allen, L. M. (1998). *The pain assessment battery.* Durham, NC: CogniSyst Inc.

Eimer, B. N., & Freeman, A. (1998). *Pain management psychotherapy: A practical guide.* New York: Wiley.

Ellis, A. (1962). *Reason and emotion in psychotherapy.* New York: Lyle Stuart.

Eskapa, R. (1992). Multimodal therapy. In W. Dryden (Ed.), *Integrative and eclectic therapy* (pp. 109–129). Philadelphia: Open University Press.

Fay, A., & Lazarus, A. A. (1981). Multimodal therapy and the problems of depression. In J. F. Clarkin & H. Glazer (Eds.), *Depression: Behavioral and directive treatment strategies* (pp. 169–178). New York: Garland Press.

Fay, A., & Lazarus, A. A. (1982). Psychoanalytic resistance and behavioral nonresponsiveness: A dialectical impasse. In P. L. Wachtel (Ed.), *Resistance: Psychodynamic and behavioral approaches* (pp. 115–132). New York: Plenum.

Ferrise, F. R. (1978). The BASIC I.D. in clinical assessment. Doctoral dissertation, Graduate School of Applied and Professional Psychology, Rutgers University.

Gerler, E. R. (1979). Preventing the delusion of uniqueness: Multimodal education in mainstreamed classrooms. *The Elementary School Journal, 80,* 35–40.

Greenburg, S. L. (1982). Using the multimodal approach as a framework for eclectic counselor education. *Counselor Education and Supervision, 22,* 132–137.

Haley, J. (1976). *Problem solving therapy.* San Francisco: Jossey-Bass.

Herink, R. (1980). *The psychotherapy handbook.* New York: Meridian.

Herman, S. M. (1991a). A psychometric evaluation of the Marital Satisfaction Questionnaire: A demonstration of reliability and validity. *Psychotherapy in Private Practice, 9,* 85–94.

Herman, S. M. (1991b). Client-therapist similarity on the Multimodal Structural Profile Inventory as predictive of psychotherapy outcome. *Psychotherapy Bulletin, 26,* 26–27.

Herman, S. M. (1992). Client-therapist similarity on the Multimodal Structural Profile Inventory as predictive of psychotherapy outcome. Doctoral dissertation, Department of Psychology, Rutgers University.

Herman, S. M. (1993a). Predicting psychotherapists' treatment theories by Multimodal Structural Profile Inventory responses: An exploratory study. *Psychotherapy in Private Practice, 11,* 85–100.

Herman, S. M. (1993b). A demonstration of the validity of the Multimodal Structural Profile Inventory through a correlation with the Vocational Preference Inventory. *Psychotherapy in Private Practice, 11,* 71–80.

Herman, S. M. (1994). The diagnostic utility of the Multimodal Structural Profile Inventory. *Psychotherapy in Private Practice, 13,* 55–62.

Herman, S. M. (1998a). Multimodal marital assessment: An exploration of the practice of multimodal marital therapy. *Journal of Couples Therapy, 7,* 103–115.

Herman, S. M. (1998b). The relationship between therapist-client modality similarity and psychotherapy outcome. *Journal of Psychotherapy Practice and Research, 7,* 56–64.

Howard, G. S., Nance, D. W, & Myers, P. (1987). *Adaptive counseling and therapy: A systematic approach to selecting effective treatments.* San Francisco: Jossey-Bass.

Jacobson, N. S. (1987). *Psychotherapists in clinical practice: Cognitive and behavioral perspectives.* New York: Guilford Press.

James, W. (1890). *Principles of psychology.* New York: Macmillan.

Judah, R. D. (1978). Multimodal parent training. *Elementary School Guidance and Counseling, 13,* 46–54.

Karasu, T. B. (1986). The specificity versus nonspecificity dilemma: Toward identifying therapeutic change agents. *American Journal of Psychiatry, 143,* 687–695.

Keat, D. B. (1979). *Multimodal therapy with children.* New York: Pergamon Press.

Keat, D. B. (1990). *Child multimodal therapy.* Norwood, NJ: Ablex Publishing.

Koocher, G. P., Norcross, J. C., & Hill, S. S. (1998). *Psychologists' desk reference.* New York: Oxford University Press.

Kwee, M. G. T. (1978). *Gedragstherapie en neurotische depressie.* In J. W. Orlemans, W. Brinkman, W. P. Haaijam, & E. J. Zwaan (Eds.). *Handboek voor gedragstherapie* (pp. 182–202). Deventer: Van Loghum.

Kwee, M. G. T. (1979). Over de ontwikkeling van een multimodale strategie van assessment en therapie. *Tijdschrift voor Psychotherapie, 5,* 172–188.

Kwee, M. G. T. (1981). Towards the clinical art and science of multimodal psychotherapy. *Current Psychological Reviews, 1,* 55–68.

Kwee, M. G. T. (1984). *Klinische multimodale gedragstherapie.* Lisse, Holland: Swets and Zeitlinger.

Kwee, M. G. T. (1990). *Denken and doen in psychotherapie.* Den Haag: East-West Publications.

Kwee, M. G. T., & Ellis, A. (1997). Can multimodal and rational emotive behavior therapy be reconciled? *Journal of Rational-Emotive and Cognitive-Behavior Therapy, 15,* 95–132.

Kwee, M. G. T., & Kwee-Taams, M. K. (1994). *Klinishe gedragstherapie in Nederland & Vlaanderen.* Delft, Holland: Eubron.

Kwee, M. G. T., & Roborgh, M. (1987). *Multimodale therapie: Praktijk, theorie, en onderzoek.* Lisse, Holland: Swets and Zeitlinger.

Landes, A. A. (1988). Assessment of the reliability and validity of the Multimodal Structural Profile Inventory. Doctoral dissertation, Graduate School of Applied and Professional Psychology, Rutgers University.

Landes, A. A. (1991). Development of the Structural Profile Inventory. *Psychotherapy in Private Practice, 9,* 123–141.

Lawler, B. B. (1985). An interrater reliability study of the BASIC I.D. (multimodal assessment). Doctoral dissertation, Graduate School of Applied and Professional Psychology, Rutgers University.

Lazarus, A. A. (1956). A psychological approach to alcoholism. *South African Medical Journal, 30,* 707–710.

Lazarus, A. A. (1958). New methods in psychotherapy: A case study. *South African Medical Journal, 32,* 660–664.

Lazarus, A. A. (1965). Towards the understanding and effective treatment of alcoholism. *South African Medical Journal, 39,* 736–741.

Lazarus, A. A. (1966). Broad spectrum behavior therapy and the treatment of agoraphobia. *Behaviour Research and Therapy, 4,* 95–97.

Lazarus, A. A. (1971). *Behavior therapy and beyond.* New York: McGraw-Hill.

Lazarus, A. A. (1973). Multimodal behavior therapy: Treating the BASIC I.D. *Journal of Nervous and Mental Disease, 156,* 404–411.

Lazarus, A. A. (1976). *Multimodal behavior therapy.* New York: Springer.

Lazarus, A. A. (1978). *In the mind's eye: The power of imagery for personal enrichment.* New York: Rawson. (Reprinted 1984, Guilford.)

Lazarus, A. A. (1981). *The practice of multimodal therapy.* New York: McGraw-Hill. (Updated paperback edition, 1989, Johns Hopkins University Press.)

Lazarus, A. A. (1982). *Personal enrichment through imagery.* New York: BMA Audiocassettes.

Lazarus, A. A. (Ed.). (1985). *Casebook of multimodal therapy.* New York: Guilford.

Lazarus, A. A. (1988). The practice of rational-emotive therapy. In M. E. Bernard & R. DiGiuseppe (Eds.), *Inside rational-emotive therapy.* New York: Academic Press.

Lazarus, A. A. (1989a). *The practice of multimodal therapy.* (Updated ed.). Baltimore: Johns Hopkins University Press.

Lazarus, A. A. (1989b). Brief psychotherapy: The multimodal model. *Psychology, 26,* 6–10.

Lazarus, A. A. (1992a). Multimodal therapy: Technical eclecticism with minimal integration. In J. C. Norcross & M. R. Goldfried (Eds.), *Handbook of psychotherapy integration* (pp. 231–263). New York: Basic Books.

Lazarus, A. A. (1992b). The multimodal approach to the treatment of minor depression. *American Journal of Psychotherapy, 46,* 50–57.

Lazarus, A. A. (1993). Tailoring the therapeutic relationship, or being an authentic chameleon. *Psychotherapy, 30,* 404–407.

Lazarus, A. A. (1994). How certain boundaries and ethics diminish therapeutic effectiveness. *Ethics & Behavior, 4,* 255–261.

Lazarus, A. A. (1996). The utility and futility of combining treatments in psychotherapy. *Clinical Psychology: Science and Practice, 3,* 59–68.

Lazarus, A. A. (1997). *Brief but comprehensive psychotherapy: The multimodal way.* New York: Springer.

Lazarus, A. A. (1999). A multimodal framework for clinical hypnosis. In I. Kirsch, A. Capafons, E. Cardena-Buelna, & S. Amigo (Eds.), *Clinical hypnosis and self-regulation: Cognitive-behavioral perspectives* (pp. 181–210). Washington, DC: APA Books.

Lazarus, A. A. (2001a). From insight and reflection to action and clinical breadth. In M. R. Goldfried (Ed.), *How therapists change* (pp. 163–181). Washington, DC: American Psychological Association.

Lazarus, A. A. (2001b). Multimodal therapy in clinical psychology. In N. J. Smelser & P. B. Baltes (Eds.), *Encyclopedia of the social and behavioral sciences* (pp. 10, 193–10,197). Oxford: Elsevier Press.

Lazarus, A. A. (2002a). Client readiness for change, cultural concerns, and risk taking: A multimodal case presentation. *Clinical Case Studies, 1,* 39–48.

Lazarus, A. A. (2002b). The multimodal assessment-therapy approach. In F. Kaslow (Series Ed.) and J. Lebow (Vol. Ed.), *Comprehensive handbook of psychotherapy* (pp. 241–254). New York: Wiley.

Lazarus, A. A. (2003). Multimodal behavior therapy. In W. O'Donohue, J. E. Fisher, & S. C. Hayes (Eds.), *Cognitive behavior therapy* (pp. 261–265). Hoboken, NJ: Wiley.

Lazarus, A. A., & Fay, A. (1990). Brief psychotherapy: Tautology or oxymoron? In J. K. Zeig & S. Gilligan (Eds.), *Brief therapy: Myths, methods & metaphors* (pp. 36–51). New York: Brunner/Mazel.

Lazarus, A. A., & Lazarus, C. N. (1991). Multimodal life history inventory. Champaign, IL: Research Press.

Lazarus, A. A., & Whipple, A. G. (2000). Multimodal therapy. In F. Dumont & R. J. Corsini (Eds.), *Six therapists and one client.* New York: Springer.

Lazarus, C. N. (1998). Biological foundations of clinical psychology. In S. Cullari (Ed.), *Foundations of clinical psychology* (pp. 272–296). Boston: Allyn & Bacon.

Lazarus, C. N., & Lazarus, A. A. (2002). EMDR: An elegantly concentrated multimodal procedure? In F. Shapiro (Ed.), *EMDR as an integrative psychotherapy approach* (pp. 209–223). Washington, DC: American Psychological Association.

Leiblum, S. R., & Rosen, R. C. (Eds.). (1988). *Sexual desire disorders.* New York: Guilford Press.

Mann, J. P. (1985). A study of the interrater agreement of therapists using the BASIC I.D. profile as an assessment tool. Doctoral dissertation, Department of Psychology, Western Kentucky University.

Margraf, J., Ehlers, A., & Roth, W. T. (1986). Panic attacks: Theoretical models and empirical evidence. In I. Hand & H. U. Wittchen (Eds.), *Panic and phobias.* Berlin: Springer-Verlag.

Meichenbaum, D. (1977). *Cognitive behavior modification.* New York: Plenum.

Nathan, P. E., & Harris, S. L. (1980). *Psychopathology and society* (2nd ed.). New York: McGraw-Hill.

Nieves, L. (1978a). *The minority college student experience: A case for the use of self-control.* Princeton, NJ: Educational Testing Service.

Nieves, L. (1978b). *College achievement through self-help.* Princeton, NJ: Educational Testing Service.

Norcross, J. C. (1986). *Handbook of eclectic psychotherapy.* New York: Brunner/Mazel.

Norcross, J. C., & Goldfried, M. R. (Eds.). (1992). *Handbook of psychotherapy integration.* New York: Basic Books.

O'Keefe, E. J., & Castaldo, C. (1980). A multimodal approach to treatment in a child care agency. *Psychological Reports, 47,* 250.

O'Keefe, E. J., & Castaldo, C. (1981a). Multimodal management: A systematic and holistic approach for the 80s. *Proceedings of the Marist College Symposium on Local Government Productivity.* Poughkeepsie, NY.

O'Keefe, E. J., & Castaldo, C. (1981b). A multimodal approach to treatment in a child care agency. *Child Care Quarterly, 10,* 103–112.

Olson, S. C. (1979). A multimodal treatment of obesity using Lazarus' BASIC I.D. Doctoral dissertation, Department of Psychology, University of South Dakota.

Palmer, S., & Dryden, W. (1995). *Counselling for stress problems.* London: Sage Publications.

Palmer, S., & Lazarus, A. A. (2001). In the counselor's chair: Multimodal therapy. In P. Milner & S. Palmer (Eds.), *Counseling: The BACP counseling reader* (pp. 94–98). London: Sage.

Paul, G. L. (1967). Strategy of outcome research in psychotherapy. *Journal of Consulting Psychology, 31,* 109–118.

Pearl, C., & Guarnaccia, V. (1976). Multimodal therapy and mental retardation. In A. A. Lazarus (Ed.), *Multimodal behavior therapy* (pp. 189–204). New York: Springer.

Ponterotto, J. G. (1987). Counseling Mexican-Americans: A multimodal approach. *Journal of Counseling and Development, 65,* 308–312.

Ponterotto, J. G., & Zander, T. A. (1984). A multimodal approach to counselor supervision. *Counselor Education and Supervision, 24,* 40–50.

Ridley, C. R. (1984). Clinical treatment of the nondisclosing black client: A therapeutic paradox. *American Psychologist, 39,* 1234–1244.

Roberts, T. K., Jackson, L. J., & Phelps, R. (1980). Lazarus' multimodal therapy model applied in an institutional setting. *Professional Psychology, 11,* 150–156.

Rosen, R. D. (1977). *Psychobabble.* New York: Atheneum.

Rosenblad, L. V. (1985). A multimodal assessment of perception and communication in distressed and non-distressed married couples. Doctoral dissertation, Department of Psychology, Rutgers University.

Rotter, J. B. (1954). *Social learning and clinical psychology.* Englewood Cliffs, NJ: Prentice-Hall.

Salter, A. (1949). *Conditioned reflex therapy.* New York: Farrar, Strauss.

Sank, L. I. (1979). Community disasters: Primary prevention and treatment in a health maintenance organization. *American Psychologist, 34,* 334–338.

Shevrin, H., & Dickman, S. (1980). The psychological unconscious: A necessary assumption for all psychological theory? *American Psychologist, 35,* 421–434.

Tyrer, P. J. (1982). Anxiety states. In E. S. Paykel (Ed.), *Handbook of affective disorders.* New York: Guilford Press.

Watzlawick, P., Weakland, J., & Fisch, R. (1974). *Change: Principles of problem formation and problem resolution.* New York: Norton.

Williams, T. A. (1988). A multimodal approach to assessment and intervention with children with learning disabilities. Unpublished doctoral dissertation, Department of Psychology, University of Glasgow.

Woody, R. H. (1971). *Psychobehavioral counseling and therapy: Integrating behavioral and insight techniques.* New York: Appleton-Century-Crofts.

Zilbergeld, B. (1982). Bespoke therapy. *Psychology Today, 16,* 85–86.

Zilbergeld, B., & Lazarus, A. A. (1988). *Mind power: Getting what you want through mental training.* New York: Ivy Books.

**Murray Bowen**
**(1913–1990)**
Courtesy of Dr. Murray Bowen

**Nathan Ackerman**
**(1908–1971)**
Courtesy of Nathan Ackerman

**Carl Whitaker**
**(1912–1995)**
Courtesy of Professor Carl Whitaker

**Salvador Minuchin**
Courtesy of Dr. Salvador Minuchin,
The Minuchin Center

# 12  FAMILY THERAPY

*Irene Goldenberg and Herbert Goldenberg*

Family therapy is both a theory and a treatment method. It offers a way to
view clinical problems within the context of a family's transactional patterns.
Family therapy also represents a form of intervention in which members of
a family are assisted to identify and change problematic, maladaptive, self-
defeating, repetitive relationship patterns. Unlike individually focused therapies, in family therapy the *identified patient* (the family member considered
to be the problem in the family) is viewed as a symptom bearer, expressing
the family's disequilibrium or current dysfunction. The family system itself is
the primary unit of treatment and not the identified patient. Helping families
change leads to improved functioning of individuals as well as families.

## OVERVIEW

### Basic Concepts

When a single attitude, philosophy, point of view, procedure, or methodology dominates scientific thinking (known as a *paradigm*), solutions to problems are sought within the perspectives of that school of thought. If serious
problems arise that do not appear to be explained by the prevailing paradigm, however, efforts are made to expand or replace the existing system.
Once the old belief system changes, perspectives shift and previous events
may take on entirely new meanings. The resulting transition to a new paradigm, according to Kuhn (1970), is a scientific revolution.

In the field of psychotherapy, such a dramatic shift in perspective occurred in the mid-1950s as some clinicians, dissatisfied with slow progress when working with individual patients, or frustrated when change in their patients was often undermined by other family members, began to look at the family as the locus of pathology. Breaking away from the traditional concern and investigation of individual personality characteristics and behavior patterns, they adopted a new perspective—a family frame of reference—that provided a new way of conceptualizing human problems, especially the development of symptoms and their alleviation. As is the case with all paradigm shifts, this new viewpoint called for a new set of premises about the nature of psychopathology and stimulated a series of new family-focused methods for collecting data and understanding individual functioning.

When the unit of analysis is the individual, clinical theories inevitably look to internal events, psychic organization, and the patient's intrapsychic problems to explain that person's problems. Based on a heritage dating back to Freud, such efforts turn to the reconstruction of the past to seek out root causes of current difficulties, producing hypotheses or explanations for *why* something happened to this person. With the conceptual leap to a family framework, attention is directed to the family context in which individual behavior occurs, to behavioral sequences between individuals, and to *what* is now taking place and *how* each participant influences and in turn is influenced by other family members.

This view of *reciprocal causality* provides an opportunity to observe repetitive ways in which family members interact, and to use such data to initiate therapeutic interventions. Family therapists therefore direct their attention to the dysfunctional or impaired family unit rather than to a symptomatic person, who is only one part of that family system and by his or her behavior is seen as expressing the family's dysfunction.

## The Family as a System

By adopting a relationship frame of reference, family therapists pay simultaneous attention to the family's *structure* (how it arranges, organizes, and maintains itself at a particular cross section of time) and also its *processes* (the way it evolves, adapts, or changes over time). They view the family as an ongoing, living system, a complexly organized, durable, causal network of related parts that together constitute an entity larger than the simple sum of its individual members.

A system, according to Buckley (1967), involves a "complex of elements or components directly or indirectly related in a causal network such that each component is related to at least some other parts in a more or less stable way within a particular period of time" (p. 41). This broad view directs attention to the relationship between interacting parts within a larger context, emphasizing the system's unity and organizational hierarchy.

Several key concepts are central to understanding how systems operate. *Organization* and *wholeness* are especially important. Systems are composed of units that stand in some consistent relationship to one another, and thus we can infer that they are organized around those relationships. In a similar way, units or elements, once combined, produce an entity—a whole—that is greater than the sum of its parts. A change in one part causes a change in the other parts and thus in the entire system. If this is indeed the case, argue systems theorists, then adequate understanding of a system requires study of the whole, rather than separate examination of each part. No element within the system can ever be understood in isolation, since elements never function separately. The implications for understanding family functioning are clear: A family is a system in which members organize into a group, forming a whole that transcends the sum of its individual parts.

The original interest in viewing a family as a system stems in part from the work of Gregory Bateson, an anthropologist who led an early study in which he and his colleagues hypothesized that schizophrenia might be the result of pathological family interaction (Bateson, Jackson, Haley, & Weakland, 1956). Although not a family therapist himself, Bateson (1972) deserves special credit for first seeing how a family might operate as a *cybernetic system*. While current views of the origins of schizophrenia emphasize genetic predispositions exacerbated by environmental stresses, Bateson's team should be recognized for first focusing attention on the flow of information and the back-and-forth communication patterns that exist within families. Rather than study the content of what transpires, family therapists were directed to attend to family processes, the interactive patterns among family members that define a family's functioning as a unit.

## A Cybernetic Epistemology

A number of significant shifts in clinical outlook occur with the adoption of a cybernetic epistemology. For example, the locus of pathology changes from the identified patient to the social context, and the interaction between individuals is analyzed rather than the troubled person. Instead of assuming that one individual causes another's behavior ("You started it. I just reacted to what you did"), family therapists believe both participants are caught up in a circular interaction, a chain reaction that feeds back on itself, because each family member has defined the situation differently. Each argues that the other person is the cause; both are correct, but it is pointless to search for a starting point in any conflict between people, because a complex, repetitive interaction is occurring, not a simple, linear, cause-and-effect situation with a clear beginning and end.

The simple, nonreciprocal view that one event leads to another, in stimulus-response fashion, represents *linear causality*. Family therapists prefer to think in terms of *circular causality:* Reciprocal actions occur within a relationship network by means of a network of interacting loops. From this perspective, any cause is seen as an effect of a previous cause, and in turn becomes the cause of a later event. Thus, the attitudes and behavior of system members, as in a family, are tied to one another in powerful, durable, reciprocal ways, and in a never-ending cycle.

*Cybernetics,* based on a Greek word for steersman, was coined by mathematician Norbert Wiener (1948) to describe regulatory systems that operate by means of *feedback loops*. The most familiar example of such a mechanism is the thermostat in a home heating system; set to a desired temperature, the furnace will turn on when the heat drops below that setting, and it will shut off when the desired temperature is reached. The system is balanced around a set point, and relies on information fed back into it about the temperature of the room. Thus, it maintains a dynamic equilibrium and undertakes operations to restore that equilibrium whenever the balance is upset or threatened.

So, too, with a family. When a crisis or other disruption occurs, family members try to maintain or regain a stable environment—*family homeostasis*—by activating family-learned mechanisms to decrease the stress and restore internal balance.

Families rely on the exchange of information—a word, a look, a gesture, or a glance that acts as a feedback mechanism, signaling that disequilibrium has been created and that some corrective steps are needed to help the relationship return to its previous balanced state. In effect, information about a system's output is fed back into its input, to alter, correct, or govern the system's functioning. *Negative feedback* has an attenuating effect, restoring equilibrium, while *positive feedback* leads to further change by accelerating the deviation. In negative feedback, a couple may exchange information during a quarrel that says, in effect, "It is time to pull back or we will regret it later." In positive feedback, the escalation may reach dangerous, runaway proportions; the quarreling couple may escalate an argument to the point when neither one cares about the consequences. In some situations, however, positive feedback, while temporarily destabilizing, may be beneficial if it does not get out of control and helps the couple reassess a dysfunctional transactional pattern, reexamine their methods of engagement, and change the system's rules. That is, a system need not go back to its previous level, but may, as a result of positive feedback, change and function more smoothly at a higher homeostatic level (Goldenberg & Goldenberg, 2004).

## Subsystems, Boundaries, and Larger Systems

Following largely from the work of Minuchin (1974), family therapists view families as comprising a number of coexisting subsystems, in which members group together to carry out certain family functions or processes. Subsystems are organized components within the overall system, and may be determined by generation, sex, or family function. Each family member is likely to belong to several subsystems at the same time. A wife may also be a mother, daughter, younger sister, and so on, thus entering into different complementary relationships with other members at various times and playing different roles in each. In certain dysfunctional situations, families may split into separate long-term coalitions: males opposed to females, parents against children, father and daughter in conflict with mother and son.

While family members may engage in temporary alliances, three key subsystems will always endure: the spousal, parental, and sibling subsystems (Minuchin, Rosman, & Baker, 1978). The first is especially important to the family: Any dysfunction in the spousal subsystem is bound to reverberate throughout the family, resulting in the scapegoating of children or co-opting them into alliances with one parent against the other. Effective spousal subsystems provide security and teach children about commitment by presenting a positive model of marital interaction. The parental subsystem, when effective, provides child care, nurturance, guidance, limit setting, and discipline; problems here frequently take the form of intergenerational conflicts with adolescents, often reflecting underlying family disharmony and instability. Sibling subsystems help members learn to negotiate, cooperate, compete, and eventually attach to others.

*Boundaries* are invisible lines that separate a system, a subsystem, or an individual from outside surroundings. In effect, they protect the system's integrity, distinguishing between those considered to be insiders and those viewed as outsiders. Boundaries within a family vary from being rigid (overly restrictive, permitting little contact with one another) to being diffuse (overly blurred, so that roles are interchangeable and members are overinvolved in each other's lives). Thus, the clarity of the boundary between subsystems and its permeability are more important than the subsystem's membership. Excessively rigid boundaries characterize *disengaged families* in which members feel isolated from one another, while diffuse boundaries identify *enmeshed families* in which members are intertwined in one another's lives.

Boundaries between the family and the outside world need to be sufficiently clear to allow information to flow to and from the environment. In systems terms, the more flexible the boundaries, the better the information flow; the family is open to new experiences, is able to alter and discard unworkable or obsolete interactive patterns, and is operating as an *open system*. When boundaries are not easily crossed, the family is insular, not open to what is happening around it, suspicious of the outside world, and is said to be operating as a *closed system*. In reality, no family system is either completely open or completely closed, but exists along a continuum.

All family systems also interact with, and thus are influenced by, one or more of society's larger systems—the courts, the health care system, schools, welfare, probation, and so forth. While such contact may be time-limited and generally free of long-term conflict, numerous families become entangled with such systems, impeding the development of family members. Family therapists today pay close attention to such interactions, looking beyond the dysfunctional family itself and coordinating the recommendations of the various agencies in order to provide a broad, coordinated set of interventions to achieve maximum effectiveness.

## Gender Awareness and Culture Sensitivity

Challenged by postmodern inquires into the diversity of perspectives for viewing life, as well as by the feminist movement, family therapists have begun to look beyond observable interactive patterns within a family, and today examine how gender, culture, and ethnicity shape the perspectives and behavior patterns of family members. Indoctrinated early into gender-role behavior in a family, men and women have different socialization experiences and as a result develop distinct behavioral expectations, are granted disparate opportunities, and have differing life experiences. In a similar way, cultural, ethnic, and social class considerations influence how families function.

Gender, cultural background, ethnicity membership, and social class are interactive; one cannot be considered without the others. As Kliman (1994) notes, the experience of being male or female shapes and in turn is shaped by being poor or middle class or wealthy, by being African American, Chinese, or Armenian. Contemporary views of family therapy emphasize taking a *gender-sensitive outlook* in working with families, being careful not to reinforce (as therapists sometimes did in the past) stereotyped sexist or patriarchal attitudes. Today, family therapists pay attention to differences in power, status, and position within families and in society in general.

Similarly, family therapists today believe a comprehensive picture of family functioning at the minimum requires an understanding of the cultural context (race, ethnic group membership, social class, religion, sexual orientation) and the form of family organization (stepfamily, single parent–led family, gay couples, etc.) seeking help. Adopting a broad, multicultural framework leads to a pluralistic outlook, one that recognizes that attitudes and behavior patterns are often deeply rooted in the family's cultural background. That pluralistic viewpoint also enables therapists to better understand the unique problems inherent in the multitude of families today that do not fit the historical intact family model.

Developing a *culturally sensitive therapy* (Prochaska & Norcross, 1999) calls for moving beyond the white middle-class outlook from which many therapists operate (prizing self-sufficiency, independence, and individual development) and recognizing that such values are not necessarily embraced by all ethnic groups. For example, many clients from traditional Asian backgrounds are socialized to subordinate their individual needs to those of their families or society in general. In developing a multicultural framework, the family therapist must recognize that acculturation is an ongoing process that occurs over generations, and that ethnic values continue to influence a client family's child-rearing practices, intergenerational relationships, family boundaries, and so forth.

A culturally competent family therapist remains alert to the fact that how he or she accesses or counsels a family is influenced not only by professional knowledge, but also by his or her own "cultural filters"—values, attitudes, customs, religious beliefs and practices, and especially, beliefs regarding what constitutes normal behavior that stem largely from the therapist's own cultural background (Giordano & Carini-Giordano, 1995). To ignore such built-in standards is to run the risk of misdiagnosing or mislabeling an unfamiliar family pattern as abnormal, when it might be appropriate to that family's cultural heritage (McGoldrick, 1998). Similarly, the culturally sensitive therapist must be careful not to overlook or minimize deviant behavior by simply attributing it to cultural differences. According to Falicov (1998), the family therapy encounter is really an engagement between a therapist's and family's cultural and personal constructions about family life.

Therapeutic intervention with all families requires the therapist to help family members understand any restrictions imposed on them as a result of such factors as gender, race, religion, social class, or sexual orientation. Cultural narratives (White, 1995), specifying the customary or preferred ways of being in a society, are sometimes toxic (racism, sexism, ageism, class bias) and thus inhibiting and subjugating to the individual, family, and group. Here the therapist must provide help in addressing the limitations imposed by the majority culture if the family is to overcome societal restrictions.

## Other Systems

Differences between family therapy and other therapeutic approaches are less clear-cut than in the past, as systems ideas have permeated other forms of psychotherapy. While therapists may focus on the individual patient, many have begun to view that person's problems within a broader context, of which the family is inevitably a part, and have adapted family systems methods to individual psychotherapy (Wachtel & Wachtel, 1986). For example, *object relations theory* has emphasized the search for satisfactory "objects" (persons) in our lives, beginning in infancy. Practitioners of psychoanalytically based object relations family therapy, such as Scharff and Scharff (1997), help family members uncover how each has internalized objects from the past, usually as a result of an unresolved relationship with one's parents, and how these imprints from the past—called *introjects*—continue to impose themselves on current relationships, particularly with one's spouse or children. Object relations family therapists search for unconscious relationship-seeking from the past as the primary determinant of adult personality formation, while most family therapists deal with current interpersonal issues to improve overall family functioning.

Conceptually, Adlerian psychotherapy is compatible with family therapy formulations. Far less reliant on biological or instinctual constructs than psychoanalysis, Adlerian theory emphasizes the social context of behavior, the embeddedness of the individual in his or her interpersonal relationships, and the importance of present circumstances and future goals, rather than unresolved issues from childhood. Both Adlerian psychotherapy and family therapy take a holistic view of the person and emphasize intent and conscious choices. Adler's efforts to establish a child guidance movement, as well as his concern with improving parenting practices, reflect his interest beyond the individual to family functioning. However, the individual focus of his therapeutic efforts fails to change the dysfunctional family relationships that underlie individual problems.

The person-centered approach developed by Carl Rogers is concerned with the client's here-and-now issues, is growth-oriented, and is applicable to helping families move in the direction of self-actualization. Its humanistic outlook was particularly appealing to experiential family therapists such as Virginia Satir (1972) and Carl Whitaker (Whitaker & Bumberry, 1988), who believed families were stunted in their growth and would find solutions if provided with a growth-facilitating therapeutic experience. Experiential family therapists are usually more directive than Rogerians, and in some cases act as teachers to help families open up their communication processes (e.g., using methods developed by Virginia Satir).

Existential psychotherapies are phenomenological in nature, emphasizing awareness and the here and now of the client's existence. Considered by most family therapists to be too concerned with the organized wholeness of the single person, this viewpoint nevertheless has found a home among some family therapists, such as Walter Kempler (1981), who argues that people define themselves and their relationships with one another through their current choices and decisions and what they choose to become in the future, rather than through their reflections on the past.

Behavior therapists traditionally take a more linear view of causality regarding family interactions than do most systems theory advocates. A child's tantrums, for example, are viewed by behaviorists as maintained and reinforced by parental responses. Systems theorists view the tantrum as an interaction, including an exchange of feedback information, occurring within a family system.

Most behaviorists now acknowledge that cognitive factors (attitudes, thoughts, beliefs, expectations) influence behavior, and cognitive behavior therapy has become a part of mainstream psychotherapy (Dattilio, Epstein, & Baucom, 1998). However, rational emotive behavior therapy's view that problems stem from maladaptive thought processes seems too individually focused for most family therapists.

# HISTORY

## Precursors

### Freud, Adler, Sullivan

Family therapy can trace its ancestry to efforts begun early in the last century, led largely by Sigmund Freud, to discover intervention procedures for uncovering and mitigating symptomatic behavior in neurotic individuals. However, while Freud acknowledged in theory the often powerful impact of individual fantasy and family conflict and alliances (e.g., the Oedipus conflict) on the development of such symptoms, he steered clear of involving the family in treatment, choosing instead to help the symptomatic person resolve personal or intrapsychic conflicts.

Adler went further than Freud in emphasizing the family context for neurotic behavior, stressing the importance of the family constellation (e.g., birth order, sibling rivalry) on individual personality formation. He drew attention to the central role of the family in the formative years, contending that family interactive patterns provide the key for understanding a person's current relationships both within and outside the family.

Harry Stack Sullivan, beginning in the 1920s, adopted an interpersonal relations view in working with hospitalized schizophrenics. Sullivan (1953) argued that people were the product of their "relatively enduring patterns of recurrent interpersonal situations" (p. 10). While not working directly with families, Sullivan speculated on the role family played in the transitional period of adolescence, thought to be the typical time for the onset of schizophrenia. Sullivan's influence on Don Jackson and Murray Bowen, two pioneers in family therapy who trained under Sullivan, as well as on his colleague Frieda Fromm-Reichmann, is apparent both in their adoption of Sullivan's early notion of redundant family interactive patterns and in their active therapeutic interventions with families.

### General Systems Theory

Beginning in the 1940s, Ludwig von Bertalanffy (1968) and others began to develop a comprehensive theoretical model embracing all living systems. General systems theory challenged the traditional reductionistic view in science that complex phenomena could be understood by carefully breaking them down into a series of less complex cause-and-effect reactions, then analyzing in linear fashion how A causes B, B causes C, and so forth. Instead, this new theory argued for a systems focus, in which the interrelations between parts assume far greater significance: A may cause B, but B affects A, which in turn affects B, and so on in a *circular causality*. General systems theory ideas can be seen in such family systems concepts as circular causality and the belief that symptoms in one family member signal family dysfunction rather than individual psychopathology.

### Group Therapy

John Bell (1961) developed a therapeutic approach called *family group therapy,* applying some of the social psychological theories of small group behavior to the natural group that is the family. Adopting group therapy's holistic outlook, family therapists involve entire families in the therapeutic process, believing that kinship groups are more real situations and provide a greater opportunity for powerful and longer lasting systems changes as a result of family-level interventions.

# Beginnings

## Research on Schizophrenia

A number of researchers, working independently, began in the 1950s to zero in on schizophrenia as a possible area where family influences might be related to the development of psychotic symptoms. Taking a linear viewpoint at first, and seeking causes of the schizophrenic condition in early family child-rearing practices, the researchers ultimately branched out into a broader systems point of view. Early efforts by the following are particularly noteworthy: Bateson's group in Palo Alto, Theodore Lidz's project at Yale, and the efforts at the National Institute of Mental Health (NIMH) of Murray Bowen and Lyman Wynne. The idea of seeing family members together for therapeutic purposes came later, as a result of research discoveries and subsequent theorizing.

A landmark paper by Bateson, Jackson, Haley, and Weakland (1956) speculated that *double-bind* communication patterns within a family may account for the onset of schizophrenia in one of its members. Double-bind situations exist when an individual, usually a child, habitually receives contradictory messages from the same important person, typically a parent (verbally, "I'm interested in what you are telling me" but nonverbally by gesture or glance signaling "Go away, you are bothering me, I don't care about you"), who forbids comment on the contradiction. Compelled to respond, but doomed to failure whatever the response, the child becomes confused and ultimately withdraws after repeated exposure to such incongruent messages, unable to understand the true meaning of his or others' communications. Schizophrenia was thus reformulated as an interpersonal phenomenon, and as a prototype of the consequences of failure in a family's communication system.

Lidz and his colleagues (Lidz, Cornelison, Fleck, & Terry, 1957) hypothesized that schizophrenics did not receive the necessary nurturance as children and thus failed to achieve autonomy as adults. According to this premise, one or both parents' own arrested development was responsible, especially because the parents were likely to have a conflict-ridden marriage, providing poor role models for children. These researchers distinguished two patterns of chronic marital discord common in schizophrenic families. In one, labeled *marital skew,* extreme domination by one emotionally disturbed partner is accepted by the other, who implies to the children that the situation is normal. In the *marital schism* scenario, parents undermine their spouses, threats of divorce are common, and each parent vies for the loyalty and affection of the children.

Bowen was especially interested in the symbiotic mother-child bonds that he hypothesized might lead to schizophrenia. Hospitalizing entire families on the research wards for months at a time in order to observe ongoing family interactions, Bowen (1960) broadened his outlook, observing emotional intensity throughout these families. As a result, he moved from his previous psychoanalytic viewpoint to one that emphasized reciprocal functioning, in what he labeled the *family emotional system.*

Lyman Wynne, who succeeded Bowen at NIMH, turned his attention to the blurred, ambiguous, confused communication patterns he and his associates found in families with schizophrenic members (Wynne, Ryckoff, Day, & Hirsch, 1958). Wynne coined the term *pseudomutuality* to describe a false sense of family closeness in which the family gives the appearance of taking part in a mutual, open, and understanding relationship without really doing so. The members of these families have poorly developed personal identities and doubt their ability to accurately derive meaning from personal experiences outside the family, preferring to remain within the safe and familiar family system with its enclosed boundaries.

## Psychodynamics of Family Life

Trained in psychoanalytic work with children, Nathan Ackerman nevertheless saw the value of treating entire families as a unit in assessing and treating dysfunctional families. In his landmark book, *The Psychodynamics of Family Life,* often considered the first text to define the new field, Ackerman (1958) argued for family sessions aimed at untangling interlocking pathologies, thus endorsing the systems view that problems of any one family member cannot be understood apart from those of all other members.

By working therapeutically with nonschizophrenic families, Ackerman demonstrated the applicability of family therapy to less disturbed patients. By 1962, he in New York and Don Jackson on the West Coast founded the first journal in the field, *Family Process,* with Jay Haley as editor, enabling researchers and practitioners to exchange ideas and identify with the growing field of family therapy.

## Delinquent Families

One project combining theory and practice was led by Salvador Minuchin (Minuchin, Montalvo, Guerney, Rosman, & Schumer, 1967) at the Wiltwyck School for Boys in upper New York State, a residential setting for delinquent youngsters from urban slums. Recognizing the limitations of traditional methods for reaching these boys and their families, generally from poor, underorganized, fatherless homes, Minuchin developed a number of brief, action-oriented therapeutic procedures aimed at helping reorganize unstable family structures.

## Current Status

Eight theoretical viewpoints and corresponding approaches to family therapy can be identified, according to Goldenberg and Goldenberg (2004):

## Object Relations Family Therapy

The psychodynamic view is currently best expressed by object relations family therapists (Framo, 1982; Scharff & Scharff, 1997), who contend that the need for a satisfying relationship with some "object" (i.e., another person) is the fundamental motive of life. From the object relations perspective, we bring *introjects*—memories of loss or unfulfillment from childhood—into current dealings with others, seeking satisfaction but sometimes "contaminating" family relations in the process. Thus, they argue, people unconsciously relate to one another in the present based largely on expectations formed during childhood. Individual intrapsychic issues and family interpersonal difficulties are examined in a therapeutic setting. Helping family members gain insight into how they internalized objects from the past, and how these objects continue to intrude on current relationships, is the central therapeutic effort, providing understanding and instigating change. Treatment is aimed at helping members become aware of those unresolved objects from their families of origin, increasing their understanding of the interlocking pathologies that have blocked both individual development and fulfillment from family relationships.

## Experiential Family Therapy

Experiential family therapists such as Satir and Whitaker believe troubled families need a "growth experience" derived from an intimate interpersonal experience with an involved therapist. By being real or authentic themselves, and often self-disclosing, experiential therapists contend that they can help families learn to be more honest, more expressive of their feelings and needs, and better able to use their potential for self-awareness to achieve personal and interpersonal growth.

## Narrative Therapy

Narrative therapists such as
nized and maintained throu
selves and the outside wor
themselves typically feel ove
Their self-narratives conced
change. The dominant cultu
is expected of them. Therap
of problem-saturated storie:
gated stories where they wei
one story with another, but
options and possibilities.

Narrative therapists are
lem, but rather how the pro
narrative therapists, is to he
laborating with them in expl
selves, and opening them u
ization (viewing the proble
of their identity) helps then
stories.

White is especially inte:
formed the basis for how the
while deShazer helps client:
directed at finding new and

## PERSONALITY

Family therapists as a grouj
although all view individua
panding on Sullivan's (1953
sonality development, famil
ships with others. Symptom
that person's current situati
the family.

### Theory of Personal:

Clinicians who adopt a fam:
personality is not overlooke
family. Nevertheless, family
behavior is related to and c
individual family members i
vate hopes, ambitions, outl
ily therapists try to remain
gularity of the individual. T
family.

How a therapist views ,
tial theoretical framework.
theorists (Scharff & Scharf
lieving that if one's relation
the characteristics of the los

For Virginia Satir, building self-esteem and learning to communicate adequately and openly were essential therapeutic goals. Calling his approach *symbolic-experiential family therapy,* Carl Whitaker gave voice to his own impulses and fantasies and depathologized human experiences as he helped family members probe their own covert world of symbolic meanings, freeing them to activate their innate growth processes. Currently, experiential family therapy is best represented by *Emotionally-Focused Couple Therapy* (Greenberg, 2002), an experiential approach based upon humanistic and systemic foundations that attempts to change a couple's negative interactions while helping them cement their emotional connection to each other.

## Transgenerational Family Therapy

Murray Bowen argued that family members are tied in thinking, feeling, and behavior to the family system, and thus individual problems arise and are maintained by relationship connections with fellow members. Those persons with the strongest affective connections (or *fusion*) with the family are most vulnerable to personal emotional reactions to family stress. The degree to which an individualized, separate sense of self independent from the family (or *differentiation of self*) occurs is correlated with the ability to resist being overwhelmed by emotional reactivity in the family; the greater the differentiation, the less likely the individual is to experience personal dysfunction.

Bowen (1978) believed that the child most vulnerable to dysfunction is the one most easily drawn into family conflict. He maintained that the most attached child will have the lowest level of differentiation, will be the least mature and thus have the hardest time separating from the family, and will likely select as a marital partner someone who is also poorly differentiated in his or her family. The least differentiated of their offspring will marry someone equally undifferentiated, and so forth. In this formulation, problems are passed along to succeeding generations by a multigenerational transmission process.

Bowen maintained that schizophrenia could result after several generations of increased fusion and vulnerability.

Another transgenerational family therapist, Ivan Boszormenyi-Nagy (1987), emphasizes the ethical dimension (trust, loyalty, entitlements, and indebtedness) in family relationships, extending over generations. He focuses on the relational ethics within a family, aimed at preserving fairness and ensuring fulfillment of each member's subjective sense of claims, rights, and obligations in relation to one another. To *contextual therapists* such as Boszormenyi-Nagy, the patterns of relating within a family that are passed down from generation to generation are the keys to understanding both individual and family functioning.

## Structural Family Therapy

Minuchin's (1974) structural view focuses on how families are organized and what rules govern their transactions. He pays particular attention to family rules, roles, alignments, and coalitions, as well as the boundaries and subsystems that make up the overall family system. Symptoms are viewed as conflict defusers, diverting attention from more basic family conflicts. Therapeutically, structuralists challenge rigid, repetitive transactions within a family, helping to "unfreeze" them to allow family reorganization.

## Strategic Family Therapy

This approach involves designing novel strategies for eliminating undesired behavior. Strategists such as Jay Haley (1996) are not too interested in providing insight to family members, preferring assignment of tasks to get families to change those aspects of the system that maintain the problematic behavior. Sometimes indirect tasks, in the form

of *paradoxical inter*
pists at the Mental
"solutions" to pro
pists have evolved
aimed at changing
Fisch, 1974).

In Milan, Italy
Cecchin, & Prata,
therapy that has fo
Palazzoli (1986) b
which parents and
their symptoms to
(Boscolo, Cecchin
terviewing techniq
family belief syster
tive of making nev
mology based on so
to describe the fam
served and treated
ticular perspective

## Cognitive–Beho

The behavioral pe
extinguished as th
been expanded in
2005; Ellis, 2005).
restructuring is de
pectations, and to
tive self-statement
torted beliefs, clier

## Social Construc

Influenced primar
thinking, especiall
They argue that ea
rather a point of v
The view of reality
termined through
sumptions (Gerger
tural consideratior
determining a fam
Family therap
pist and family me
family or how a pa
together examine
events, then jointly
low them to consid
this view include S
(1997) (*collaborati*

loss. The resulting unresolved unconscious conflict develops into frustration and self-defeating habits in the adult.

Behaviorally oriented family therapists believe all behavior, normal and abnormal, is learned as a result of a process involving the acquisition of knowledge, information, experiences, and habits. Classical conditioning, operant conditioning, and modeling concepts are used to explain how personality is learned. Following the early lead of B. F. Skinner, some strict behaviorists question whether an inner personality exists, maintaining that what we refer to as "personality" is nothing more than the sum of the environmental experiences in one's life. Rejecting explanations that infer the development of internal traits, they search instead for relationships between observable behavior and observable variations in the person's environment. In their view, situations determine behavior.

Those therapists who adopt a more cognitive orientation believe people do develop personality traits and that their behavior is based at least in part on those traits and not simply in response to situations. These family therapists contend that certain types of cognitions are learned, become ingrained as traits, and mediate a person's behavior. Perceptions of events, attitudes, beliefs, expectations of outcomes, and attributions are examples of such cognitions. Especially when negative or rigid, these cognitions can contribute to negative behavior exchanges within a family. Intervention is an attempt to change maladaptive cognitions.

Many family therapists view personality from a *family life cycle* perspective (Carter & McGoldrick, 1999). This developmental outlook notes that certain predictable marker events or phases (marriage, birth of first child, children leaving home, and so on) occur in all families, regardless of structure or composition, compelling each family to deal in some manner with these events. Because there is an ever-changing family context in which individual members grow up, there are many chances for maladaptive responses. Situational family crises (such as the death of a parent during childhood, or the birth of a handicapped child) and certain key transition points are periods of special vulnerability.

Both continuity and change characterize family systems as they progress through the life cycle. Ordinarily, such changes are gradual and the family is able to reorganize as a system and adapt successfully. Certain discontinuous changes, however, may be disruptive, transforming a family system so that it will never return to its previous way of functioning. Divorce, becoming part of a stepfamily, serious financial reverses, and chronic illness in a family member are examples of sudden, disruptive changes that cause upheaval and disequilibrium in the family system. Symptoms in family members are especially likely to appear during these critical periods of change, as the family struggles to reorganize while negotiating the transition. Family therapists may seize the crisis period as an opportunity to help families develop higher levels of functioning.

## Variety of Concepts

### Family Rules

A family is a rule-governed system in which the interactions of its members follow organized, established patterns. Growing up in a family, members all learn what is expected or permitted in family transactions. Parents, children, relatives, males, females, and older and younger siblings all have prescribed rules for the boundaries of permissible behavior, which may not be verbalized but which are understood by all. Such rules regulate and help stabilize the family system.

Family therapists are especially interested in persistent, repetitive behavioral sequences that characterize much of everyday family life, because of what these patterns reveal about the family's typical interactive patterns. Labeled the *redundancy principle,* the concept describes a family's usually restricted range of options for dealing with one another. Attending to a family's rules represents an interactive way of understanding behavior, rather than attributing that individual behavior to some inferred inner set of motives. Don Jackson (1965), an early observer of family behavioral patterns, believed that family dysfunction was due to a family's lack of rules for accommodating to changing conditions.

## Family Paradigms

All families develop paradigms about the world (i.e., make enduring assumptions that are shared by family members). Studying families in a laboratory situation in which they were given problems to solve as a family, Reiss (1981) found that the various ways different families perceived the laboratory setting and developed strategies for coping with the situation were telling. For example, families with schizophrenic adolescents frequently perceived danger and threat, while those with delinquent adolescents viewed the task as an occasion to demonstrate distance and independence from one another. By way of contrast, families with normal adolescents viewed such tasks as an opportunity to explore and master the challenging situation together.

Based on these and related findings, Reiss (1981) suggested that families develop family paradigms (ways of perceiving, interpreting, and interacting with their social world) in one of three ways. *Consensus-sensitive* families are composed of enmeshed members who see the world as chaotic and confusing, so that they must maintain agreement in all matters in order to protect themselves from danger. *Interpersonal-distance-sensitive* families are made up of disengaged members who strive for autonomy from one another, believing that closeness represents a display of weakness. *Environmentally sensitive* families typically operate as open systems and are apt to be most problem-free. They see the world as knowable and orderly, with each member expected to contribute to its understanding and mastery.

## Pseudomutuality and Pseudohostility

One result of Wynne's NIMH studies of families with schizophrenic members (Wynne, et al., 1958) was his observation of their recurrent fragmented and irrational style of communication. He discovered an unreal quality about how they expressed both positive and negative emotion to one another, a process he labeled *pseudomutuality*. Wynne reported that members in these families were absorbed with fitting together, at the expense of developing their separate identities. Rather than encourage a balance between separateness and togetherness, as occurs in well-functioning families, members in Wynne's group seemed concerned with the latter only, apparently dreading expressions of individuality as a threat to the family as a whole. By presenting a facade of togetherness, they learned to maintain a homeostatic balance, but at the expense of not allowing either disagreements or expressions of affection. The tactic kept them from dealing with any underlying conflict, and at the same time the surface togetherness prevented them from experiencing deeper intimacy with one another.

Wynne's research also identified *pseudohostility,* a similar collusion in which apparent quarreling or bickering between family members is in reality merely a superficial tactic for avoiding deeper and more genuine feelings. Members may appear alienated and split from one another, and their antagonism may even appear intense, but the turmoil is merely a way of maintaining a connection without becoming either deeply affectionate or deeply hostile to one another. Like pseudomutuality, it represents a distorted way of communicating and fosters irrational thinking about relationships.

## Mystification

Another masking effort to obscure the real nature of family conflict and thus maintain the status quo is called *mystification*. First described by R. D. Laing (1965) in analyzing the family's role in a child's development of psychopathology, the concept refers to parental efforts to distort a child's experience by denying what the child believes is occurring. Instead of telling the child, "It's your bedtime," or explaining that they are tired and want to be left alone, parents say, "You must be tired. Go to bed." In effect, they have distorted what the child is experiencing ("I'm not tired"), especially if they add that they know better than the child what he or she is feeling.

Mystification, then, refers to the fact that some families deal with conflict by befuddling, obscuring, or masking whatever is going on between members. This device does not deter conflict but rather clouds the meaning of conflict and is called into play when a family member threatens the status quo, perhaps by expressing feelings. A husband who says, in response to his wife's query about why he appears angry, "I'm not angry. Where do you dream up these things?" when he actually is angry, is attempting to mystify her. His apparent intent to avoid conflict and return matters to their previous balance only leads to greater conflict within her, because if she believes him then she feels she must be "crazy" to imagine his anger, and if she trusts her own senses, then she must deal with a deteriorating marital relationship. Mystification contradicts one person's perceptions, and in extreme or repeated cases leads that person to question his or her grip on reality.

## Scapegoating

Within some families, a particular individual is held responsible for whatever goes wrong with the family. *Scapegoating* directed at a particular child often has the effect of redirecting parental conflict, making it unnecessary for the family to look at the impaired father/mother relationship, something that would be far more threatening to the family. By conveniently picking out a scapegoat who becomes the identified patient, other family members can avoid dealing with one another or probing more deeply into what is really taking place.

Scapegoated family members are themselves often active participants in the family scapegoating process. Not only do they assume the role assigned them, but they may become so entrenched in that role that they are unable to act otherwise. Particularly in dysfunctional families, individuals may be repeatedly labeled as the "bad child"— incorrigible, destructive, unmanageable, troublesome—and they proceed to act accordingly. Scapegoated children are inducted into specific family roles, which over time become fixed and serve as the basis for chronic behavioral disturbance. Because the family retains a vested interest in maintaining the scapegoated person in that role, blaming all their problems on one member, changes in family interactive patterns must occur before scapegoating will cease. Otherwise, the scapegoated person, usually symptomatic, will continue to carry the pathology for the family.

# PSYCHOTHERAPY

## Theory of Psychotherapy

There is no single theory of psychotherapy for family therapists, although all would probably agree with the following basic premises:

1. People are products of their social connections, and attempts to help them must take family relationships into account.

2. Symptomatic behavior in an individual arises from a context of relationships, and interventions to help that person are most effective when those faulty interactive patterns are altered.

3. Individual symptoms are maintained externally in current family system transactions.

4. Conjoint sessions in which the family is the therapeutic unit and the focus is on family interaction are more effective in producing change than attempts to uncover intrapsychic problems in individuals by therapy via individual sessions.

5. Assessing family subsystems and the permeability of boundaries within the family and between the family and the outside world offers important clues regarding family organization and susceptibility to change.

6. Traditional psychiatric diagnostic labels based upon individual psychopathology fail to provide an understanding of family dysfunctions and tend to pathologize individuals.

7. The goal of family therapy is to change maladaptive or dysfunctional family interactive patterns.

Systems thinking most often provides the underpinnings for therapeutic interventions with the family. By viewing causality in circular rather than linear terms, the focus is on family transactional patterns, especially redundant maladaptive patterns that help maintain symptomatic behavior. By emphasizing family interrelationships over individual needs and drives, explanations shift from a *monadic* (based on the characteristics of a single person) to a *dyadic* (based on a two-person interaction) or *triadic* (based on interactions between three or more persons) model.

In a monadic outlook, a husband fails to pay attention to his wife because he is a cold and uncaring person. Adopting a dyadic mode, people are viewed in terms of their interlocking relationships and impact on one another. Here the therapist looks beyond the separate individuals who make up the couple, focusing instead on how these two individuals organize their lives together, and, more specifically, how each helps define the other. From a dyadic viewpoint, a husband's indifference arouses his wife's emotional pursuit, and she demands attention. Her insistence arouses the fear of intimacy that led to his withdrawal to begin with, and he retreats further. She becomes more insistent, he increasingly less available as their conflict escalates. A family therapist helping such a couple will direct attention to their interactive effect, thus making the dyad (and not each participant) the unit of treatment. Seeing the couple conjointly rather than separately underscores the therapist's view that the problem arises from both partners, and that both are responsible for finding solutions.

In a triadic model, the family therapist assumes the symptoms or presenting problems result from the dyad's inability to resolve the conflict, resulting in other family members being drawn into the conflict. A preteenage son who frustrates his father by refusing to do his homework and thus is performing badly at school may be doing so in alliance with his mother against his father, indirectly expressing her resentment at her husband's authoritarian behavior. The couple's original dyadic conflict has become a triadic one in which multiple interactions occur. To merely develop a behavioral plan or contract for the boy to receive money or special television privileges for school assignments completed would miss the complex family interaction involved. Family therapists would look at the overall impact of the symptomatic behavior in context; the youngster may or may not be included in the entire treatment, which certainly would deal with the unspoken and unresolved husband/wife conflicts and the recruitment of their child to express or act out their tensions.

In the example just presented, the child's symptom (the school problem) maintains the family homeostasis but obscures the underlying and unexpressed set of family conflicts. Symptoms often serve a function in maintaining family homeostasis; in this case, attention to the school problem keeps the parents from quarreling with each other and upsetting the family balance. If the school problem did not at some level sustain the family organization, it would not be maintained. Thus, the systems-oriented therapist might wonder: (1) Is the family member expressing feelings through symptoms that the other members are denying or not permitting themselves to experience? and (2) What would happen to other family members if the identified patient were to become symptom-free? (Wachtel & Wachtel, 1986). Symptoms thus have a protective function or are stabilizing devices used in families. Although they may not do so consciously, families may be invested in the maintenance of the symptom for homeostatic purposes.

While the idea of the symptom's purpose in helping maintain family stability has been a mainstay of family therapy theory, critics argue that it suggests families need a "sick" member and are willing to sacrifice that person for the sake of family well-being. *Narrative therapists* such as White (1995) reject the notion that a child's problems necessarily reflect more serious underlying family conflict. In White's view, families may be oppressed rather than protected by the symptomatic behavior. White's efforts are directed at getting all family members to unite in gaining control of their lives from the oppressive set of symptoms.

Family therapists usually are active participants with families and concentrate on current family functioning. They attempt to help members achieve lasting changes in the functioning of the family system, not merely superficial changes that will allow the system to return to its former tenuous balance. Watzlawick, Weakland, and Fisch (1974) distinguish between *first-order changes* (changes within the system that do not alter the organization of the system itself) and *second-order changes* (fundamental changes in a system's organization and function). The former refers to specific differences that take place within the system, while the latter involves rule changes in the system—in effect, changing the system itself.

For example, the following is a first-order change: The Ryan parents were concerned with the repeated school absences of their son Billy, and in an attempt to correct his behavior they told him that any time they learned he was truant from school he would be "grounded" the following Saturday.

The following is a second-order change: The Ryan parents were concerned with the repeated school absences of their son Billy. After consulting with a family therapist for several sessions, they realized that by struggling with Billy, they only encouraged his rebelliousness and thus were involved in sustaining the truant behavior. They also came to recognize that Billy's relationship with the school was truly his own, and that they should back off from intruding. Attempting to change the rules and pull themselves out of the struggle, they told Billy that from now on whether or not he went to school was between him and the school, and that henceforth he would be responsible for his education.

As in these examples, a problematic family on their own may try first-order changes by attempting to impose what appear to be logical solutions to their problems. Assuming the problem to be monadic—the result of Billy's rebelliousness—they are employing negative feedback, attempting to do the opposite of what has been occurring. The family actually may make some changes in behavior for a brief period, but they are still governed by the same rules, the cease-fire is not likely to hold, and Billy will probably return to his school absences sooner or later.

Second-order changes, based on positive feedback, call for a change in the way the family organizes itself. Here the rules of the game must change, viewpoints must be altered, old situations seen in a new light, providing a revised context in which new behavior patterns may emerge. Most people attempt to solve everyday problems by attempting first-order changes and repeating the same solutions in a self-perpetuating cycle, which only makes things worse. Especially with seriously troubled families, fundamental second-order changes in the system are necessary, so that the family members can give different meanings to old feelings and old experiences.

## Process of Psychotherapy

### The Initial Contact

Family therapy begins when the client asks for help. One family member, or a coalition of members, begins the process by seeking help outside the family, thus acknowledging that a problem exists and that the family has been unsuccessful in its attempts to resolve it by themselves. While the caller is assessing whether the right person has been contacted, the therapist is forming tentative hypotheses about the family. How self-aware is the caller? What sort of impression is he or she trying to make? What other members are involved? Are they all willing to attend the initial session?

Initial contact, whether in person or by telephone, provides an opportunity for a mini-evaluation, and also represents the therapist's first opportunity to enter into the family system. If the therapist is careful not to get entangled into taking sides, or become engulfed by family anxiety, or become excessively sympathetic or angry with any member based on what the caller is reporting, then he or she can establish the "rules of the game" for further family sessions.

### The Initial Session

The family therapist usually encourages as many family members as possible to attend the first session. Entering the room, members are encouraged to sit where they wish; their chosen seating arrangement (mother and child close together, father sitting apart) offers the therapist an early clue about possible family alliances and coalitions. Welcoming each member separately as equally important participants, the therapist becomes aware that some members may need extra support and encouragement to participate.

Each person's view of the problem must be heard, as well as the first-order solutions the family has attempted. Observing family interactive patterns, particularly repetitive behavioral sequences that occur around a problem, the therapist tentatively begins to redefine the identified patient's symptoms as a family problem in which each member has a stake. Together, therapist and family explore whether they wish to continue working together and who will attend; if they choose to discontinue, outside referrals to other therapists are in order. If they agree to stay, treatment goals are defined.

### Engaging the Family

Beginning with the initial session, the therapist tries to build a working alliance with the family, accommodating to their transactional style as well as assimilating their language patterns and manner of affective expression. The therapist tries to create an atmosphere where each member feels supported and safe to voice previously unexpressed or unexplored problems. By "joining" them, the therapist is letting them know they are understood and cared about, and that in such a safe climate they can begin to confront divisive family issues.

### Assessing Family Functioning

As is the case with all forms of psychotherapy, family therapy involves some form of assessment, formal or informal, as the clinician attempts to learn more about the family in order to make more informed treatment decisions. Early on, the therapist tries to determine: (1) Is treatment for the entire family needed? (2) Who are the appropriate family members with whom to work? (3) What underlying interactive patterns fuel the family disturbance and lead to symptoms in one or more of its members? and (4) What specific interventions will most effectively help this family? In later sessions, the therapist continues to revise hypotheses, basing subsequent interventions on assessments of the success of previous attempts to alter dysfunctional repetitive family patterns.

Cognitive-behavior family therapists are apt to make a careful, systematic behavioral analysis of the family's maladaptive behavioral patterns, often using questionnaires, pinpointing precisely which behaviors need to be altered and which events typically precede and follow that behavioral sequence. What exactly does the family mean by their child's "temper tantrums"? How often do they occur, under what circumstances, how long do they last, what specific reactions does each family member have, and what antecedent and subsequent events are associated with the outburst? The therapist tries to gauge the extent of the problem, the environmental cues that trigger the behavior, and the behaviors of various family members that maintain the problem. The assessment, continuously updated, helps the therapist plan interventions to reduce undesired or problematic behaviors.

Experiential family therapists such as Virginia Satir spend less time on a formal family history. They work more in the here and now, helping families examine current interactive patterns with little regard for historical antecedents. Assessment is an informal, ongoing process indistinguishable from the therapeutic process itself. Such therapists attempt to provide families with an experience, using themselves as models to explore their own feelings and give voice to their own impulses. Carl Whitaker, an experiential therapist, insists on controlling the structure of the therapy at the start of treatment, making certain that the family is not successful in imposing its own definition of the upcoming therapeutic relationship and how it should proceed. Later, he believes, the family members must be encouraged to take responsibility for changing the nature of their relationships.

Many family therapists agree with Salvador Minuchin (1974) that they get a better sense of how families function by interacting with them over a period of time than from any formal assessment process. Therapists observe how subsystems carry out family tasks, how alliances and coalitions operate within the family, how flexible are family rules in the face of changing conditions, and how permeable are the boundaries within the family and between the family and the outside world. These observations help family therapists modify and discard hypotheses and adjust intervention strategies based upon refined appraisals of family functioning.

## History-Taking

Consistent with their theoretical leanings, object relations family therapists such as Scharff and Scharff (1997) contend that an examination of family history is essential to understanding current family functioning. Because they believe people carry attachments of their parental introjects (memories from childhood) into their current relationships, these therapists are especially interested in such matters as how and why marital partners chose each other. That choice is seen as seeking to rediscover, through the other person, the lost aspects of primary object attachments that had split off earlier in life. Similarly, contextual family therapists (Boszormenyi-Nagy, 1987) examine with their patients those interconnections from the past that bind families together, in an effort to help them discover new ways of making fresh inputs into stagnant relationships.

Bowen (1978) began with a set of evaluation interviews aimed at clarifying the history of the presenting problem, especially trying to understand how the symptoms affect family functioning. He tried to assess the family's pattern of emotional functioning as well as the intensity of the emotional process of the symptomatic person. What is this family's relationship system like? How well differentiated are the various members? What are the current sources of stress, and how adaptive is the family?

Because Bowen believed dysfunction may result from family fusion extending back over generations, he probed for signs of poor differentiation from families of origin. To aid in the process, Bowen constructed a family *genogram,* a schematic diagram in the form of a family tree, usually including at least three generations, to trace recurring family behavior patterns. Hypotheses developed from the genogram, such as fusion/differentiation issues or emotional cutoffs from family, are used to better understand the underlying emotional processes connecting generations. Careful not to become drawn into the family's emotional system, Bowen used this information to coach family members to modify their relationships and especially to differentiate themselves from their families of origin.

Satir (1972) attempted to get families to think about the relevant concepts that formed the basis of their developing relationships by compiling a family life chronology for each family member. More than simply gathering historical facts, this represented an effort to help people understand how family ideology, values, and commitments had emerged in the family and influenced current family functioning. Later, she used the therapeutic technique of family reconstruction, guiding family members back through stages of their lives in an attempt to discover and unlock dysfunctional patterns from the past.

Structural and strategic family therapists pay less attention to family or individual histories, preferring to focus on the current family organization, coalitions, hierarchies, and so on. They are concerned with developing ways to change ongoing dysfunctional family patterns, and typically show less concern for how these patterns historically emerged.

Social constructionists pay particular attention to how the various family members view their world, rather than attempting to act as outside observers evaluating client responses to preconceived test categories (Neimeyer, 1993).

## Facilitating Change

Family therapists use a number of therapeutic techniques to alter family functioning. Among these are the following:

1. *Reframing.* This technique involves relabeling problematic behavior by putting it into a new, more positive perspective that emphasizes its good intention. (To an adolescent angry because he believes his mother is invading his privacy: "Your mother is concerned about your welfare and hasn't yet found the best way to help.") Labeling her as wishing to do well for her son, rather than agreeing with his perception that she does not trust him, alters the context in which he perceives her behavior, thus inviting new responses from him to the same behavior.

Reframing changes the meaning attributed to a behavior without changing the "facts" of the behavior itself. Strategic family therapists are most apt to use this technique, because it allows them to help clients change the basis for their perceptions or interpretation of events. This altered perspective leads to a change in the family system, as the problematic behavior becomes understood in a new light. Reframing, then, is a method for bringing about second-order changes in the family system.

2. *Therapeutic Double-Binds.* Another technique favored by strategic and systemic family therapists is putting the family in a *therapeutic double-bind* by directing families to continue to manifest their presenting symptoms: Obsessive people are asked to think about their problem for a specific period of time each day; quarreling husbands and wives are

instructed to indulge in and even exaggerate their fighting. By instructing family members to enact symptomatic behavior, the therapist is demanding that the presentation of the symptom, claimed to be "involuntary" and thus out of their control, be done voluntarily. Such paradoxical interventions are designed to evoke one of two reactions, either of which is sought by the therapist. If the patient complies, continuing to be symptomatic, there is the admission that the symptomatology is under voluntary control, not involuntary as claimed, and thus can be stopped. On the other hand, if the directive to continue the symptom is resisted, the symptom will be given up.

3.   *Enactment.* Most likely to be used by structural family therapists, *enactments* are role-playing efforts to bring the outside family conflict into the session, so that family members can demonstrate how they deal with it and the therapist can start to devise an intervention procedure for modifying their interaction and creating structural changes in the family. Encouraged by the therapist, the family members act out their dysfunctional transactions rather than talk about them. This allows the therapist an opportunity for direct observation of the process instead of relying on family members' reports of what occurs at home. Because of the immediacy of this approach, the therapist can intervene on the spot and witness the results of such interventions as they occur.

Helping "unfreeze" family members from repetitive family interactions that end in conflict, the therapist has a chance to guide them in modifying the interactions. By introducing alternative solutions calling for structural changes in the family, the therapist can help the family create options for new behavior sequences. Treating the family of an anorectic adolescent, Minuchin (Minuchin et al., 1978) might arrange to meet the family for the first session and bring in lunch, thus deliberately provoking an enactment around eating. Observing their struggles over their daughter's refusal to eat, Minuchin can demonstrate that the parental subsystem is not working effectively. If parents begin to cooperate with one another in making their daughter eat, they form a stronger union. At the same time, the daughter is relieved of the too-powerful and destructive position she has been maintaining. The enactment impels the family to look at the system they have created together and to literally change the dysfunctional behavior displayed in the session.

4.   *Family Sculpting.* Rather than put their feelings or attitudes toward one another into words, which may be difficult or threatening, family members each take a turn at being a "director," placing each of the other members in a physical arrangement in space. The result is often revealing of how the "director" perceives his or her place in the family and that person's perception of what is being done to whom, by whom, and in what manner. Individual perceptions of family boundaries, alliances, roles, subsystems, and so on are typically revealed, even if the "director" cannot, or will not, verbalize such perceptions. The resulting graphic picture of individual views of family life provides active, nonverbal depictions for other members to grasp. Because of its nonintellectualized way of putting feelings into action, family sculpting is especially suited to the experiential approach of Satir.

5.   *Circular Questioning.* This technique is often used by systemic family therapists (Boscolo et al., 1987) to focus attention on family connections rather than individual symptomatology. Each question posed to the family by the therapist addresses differences in perception by different members about the same events or relationships. By asking several members the same question regarding their attitudes toward those situations, the therapist is able to probe more deeply without being confrontational or interrogating the participants in the relationship. In this nonconfrontational therapeutic situation, the family is able to examine the origin of the underlying conflict. Advocates of this technique believe questioning is a therapeutic process that allows the family to untangle family problems by changing the ways they view their shared difficulties.

6. *Cognitive Restructuring.* This technique of cognitive-behavior therapists, based on the idea that problematic behavior stems from maladaptive thought processes, tries to modify a client's perceptions of events in order to bring about behavioral change. Thus, a partner may have unrealistic expectations about a relationship and catastrophize a commonplace disagreement ("I am worthless"). As Ellis (2005) suggests, it is the interpretation that causes havoc, not the quarrel itself. Cognitive restructuring can significantly modify perceptions ("It's upsetting that we're arguing, but that doesn't mean I'm a failure or our marriage is doomed").

7. *Miracle Question.* In this solution-focused technique (deShazer, 1991), clients are asked to consider what would occur if a miracle took place and upon awakening in the morning they found the problem they brought to therapy solved. Each family member is encouraged to speculate on how things would be different, how each would change his or her behavior, and what each would notice in the others. In this way, goals are identified and potential solutions revealed.

8. *Externalization.* In an effort to liberate a family from its dominating, problem-saturated story, narrative therapists employ the technique of externalization, designed to help families separate the symptomatic member's identity from the problem for which they sought help. The problem is recast as residing outside the family (rather than implying an internal family deficiency or individual pathological condition), and as having a restraining influence over the lives of each member of the family. Instead of focusing on what's wrong with the family or one of its members, they are called upon to unite to deal with this external and unwelcome story with a will of its own that dominates their lives. Thus, rather than "Mother is depressed" and therefore creating problems for the family, the symptom is personified as a separate, external, burdensome entity ("Depression is trying to control Mother's life"). By viewing the problem as outside themselves, the family is better able to collaborate in altering their way of thinking about developing new options for dealing with the problem, rather than merely being mired in it.

## Mechanisms of Psychotherapy

Family therapists generally take an active, problem-solving approach with families. Typically, they are more interested in dealing with current dysfunctional interactive issues within the family than in uncovering or helping resolve individual intrapsychic problems from the past. While past family transactional patterns may be explored, this is done to home in on ongoing behavioral sequences that need changing rather than to reconstruct the past.

Depending on their specific emphases, family therapists may try to help clients achieve one or more of the following changes:

1. *Structural Change.* Having assessed the effectiveness of a family's organizational structure and its ongoing transactional patterns, family therapists may actively challenge rigid, repetitive patterns that handicap optimum functioning of family members. Minuchin, for example, assumes the family is experiencing sufficient stress to overload the system's adaptive mechanisms, a situation that may be temporary due to failure to modify family rules to cope successfully with the demands of transitions. Helping families modify unworkable patterns creates an opportunity to adopt new rules and achieve realignments, clearer boundaries, and more flexible family interactions. Through restructuring, the family is helped to get back on track, so that it will function more harmoniously and the growth potential of each member will be maximized.

2. *Behavioral Change.* All family therapists try to help clients achieve desired behavioral changes, although they may go about it in differing ways. Strategic therapists focus treatment on the family's presenting problems: what they came in to have changed. Careful

not to allow families to manipulate or subdue the therapist and therefore control the treatment, strategic therapy is highly directive, and practitioners devise strategies for alleviating the presenting problem rather than explore its roots or hidden meanings. Through directives such as paradoxical interventions, they try to force the symptom-bearer to abandon old dysfunctional behavior. Similarly, *systemic therapists* (the Milan approach of Selvini-Palazzoli and her colleagues) may assign tasks or rituals for the family to carry out between sessions. These typically are offered in paradoxical form and call for the performance of a task that challenges an outdated or rigid family rule. Behavioral change follows from the emotional experience gained by the family through enactment of the directive.

3.  *Experiential Change.* Therapists such as Satir, Whitaker, and Kempler believe families need to feel and experience what previously was locked up. Their efforts are directed at growth-producing transactions in which therapists act as models of open communication, willing to explore and disclose their own feelings. Satir is especially intent on helping families learn more effective ways of communicating with one another, teaching them to express what they are experiencing. Kempler also tries to help family members learn to ask for what they want from one another, thus facilitating self-exploration, risk-taking, and spontaneity. Whitaker champions family members giving voice to underlying impulses and symbols. Because he sees all behavior as human experience and not as pathological, clients are challenged to establish new and more honest relationships, simultaneously maintaining healthy separation and personal autonomy. Emotionally focused couples therapists, too, help clients recognize how they have hidden their primary emotions or real feelings (say, fear of rejection) and instead have displayed defensive or coercive secondary emotions (anger or blaming when afraid). Their therapeutic efforts are directed at accessing and reprocessing the emotions underlying the clients' negative interactional sequences.

4.  *Cognitive Change.* Psychodynamically oriented family therapists are interested in providing client families with insight and understanding. Boszormenyi-Nagy stresses intergenerational issues, particularly how relationship patterns are passed on from generation to generation, influencing current individual and family functioning. By gaining awareness of one's *"family ledger,"* a multigenerational accounting system of who, psychologically speaking, owes what to whom, clients can examine and correct old unsettled or unredressed accounts. J. L. Framo also helps clients gain insight into introjects reprojected onto current family members to compensate for unsatisfactory early object relations. He has clients meet with members of their families of origin for several sessions to discover what issues from the past they may have projected onto current members, and also to have a corrective experience with parents and siblings. Narrative therapists, such as White, open up conversations about client values, beliefs, and purposes, so that they have an opportunity to consider a wide range of choices and attach new meanings to their experiences.

## APPLICATIONS

### Problems

*Individual Problems*

Therapists who adopt a family frame of reference attend primarily to client relationships. Even if they work with single individuals, they look for the context of problematic behavior in planning and executing their clinical interventions. So, for example, they might see a college student, far away from family, for individual sessions, but continue to view his or her problems within a larger context in which faulty relations with others have helped create and are still maintaining the presenting troublesome behavior. Should the parents arrive for a visit, they might join their child for a counseling session or two, to provide clues regarding relationship difficulties within the family system and assist in their amelioration.

## Intergenerational Problems

Family therapists frequently deal with parent/child issues, such as adolescents in conflict with their parents. Minuchin's structural approach might be adopted to help families, particularly at transition points in the family life cycle, adapt to changes and modify outdated rules. Here they are likely to try to strengthen the parental subsystem, more clearly define generational boundaries, and help the family carve out new and more flexible rules to account for changing conditions as adolescence is reached. To cite an increasingly common example, families in which the children are raised in this country by foreign-born parents often present intergenerational conflicts that reflect differing values and attitudes, requiring intervention at the family level if changes in the family system are to be achieved.

## Marital Problems

Troubled marriages are common today, and many of the problems involving symptomatic behavior in a family member can be traced to efforts by the family to deal with parents in conflict. In addition to personal problems of one or both spouses that contribute to their unhappiness, certain key interpersonal difficulties are frequently present: ineffective communication patterns; sexual incompatibilities; anxiety over making or maintaining a long-term commitment; conflicts over money, in-laws, or children; physical abuse; or conflicts over power and control. These issues, repeated without resolution over a period of time, escalate the marital dissatisfaction of one or both partners, placing the marriage in jeopardy. Couples who enter therapy conjointly, before one or both conclude that the costs of staying together outweigh the benefits, may be better able to salvage their relationship than if either or both seek individual psychotherapy.

# Evaluation

Family researchers are particularly interested in two aspects of family therapy: the therapeutic process itself (What mechanisms bring about client change?) and the efficacy of the procedure (How effective are the outcomes?). Usually referred to as, respectively, process research and outcome research, both are concerned with family therapy as a treatment modality rather than as a conceptual framework.

## Process Research

Still in its infancy because of the inherent difficulty of developing measuring instruments for the family as a whole, process research seeks to identify the specific conditions that facilitate or impede therapeutic change. Are there certain therapist characteristics, or perhaps family characteristics, that influence outcomes? What kinds of therapist relationships, communicative or empathic skills, or intervention techniques facilitate positive change? Can the presence or absence of well-defined therapeutic interactions help determine outcomes? If so, what precisely are those therapist/family interactions, and with what set of family problems is it best to use which set of techniques?

Process research therefore focuses attention on the interaction between the family and therapist, looking for what contributes to the process of change (Greenberg & Pinsof, 1986). Beyond what actually transpires within the session, information is also sought about out-of-session events occurring during the course of therapy. Experiences reported by the family members, as well as their accompanying thoughts and feelings, are given as much credence as their overt and observable behavior. All are considered to be part of the therapeutic process and to contribute to therapeutic movement.

Client self-reports and direct observations of behavior constitute the major sources of process research data. Of the two, direct observation appears to be more promising, particularly when it differentiates specific kinds of therapist interventions and measures their effectiveness. Efforts by Pinsof (1986) to devise a family therapist coding system to study the verbal behavior of therapists within sessions have been particularly noteworthy in linking specific interventions with specific therapeutic outcomes.

## Outcome Research

Gordon Paul (1967, p. 111) posed the following challenge to individual therapy outcome researchers: "What therapy is most effective for what problems, treated by what therapists, according to what criteria, in what setting?" Outcome research in family therapy must deal with the same problems that hinder such research in individual therapy, with the additional burden of gauging and measuring the various interactions taking place within a large and complex unit (the family) that is in a continuous state of change. Some family members may change more than others, different members may change in different ways, and the researcher must take into account intrapsychic, relationship, communication, and ordinary group variables in measuring therapeutic effectiveness. Some family therapists (Colapinto, 1979; Keeney & Sprenkle, 1982) argue that traditional research methods measuring therapy outcomes are actually of little use in untangling the complexities of systemic phenomena or in establishing a causal connection between a method of treatment and its effect on a family.

In recent years, qualitative research methods, discovery-oriented and open to multiple perspectives, have gained in popularity. Unlike more traditional quantitative research methodology, qualitative analyses are apt to rely on narrative reports in which the researcher makes subjective judgments regarding the meaning of outcome data. Qualitative research (based on case studies, in-depth interviewing, and document analysis) is especially useful for exploratory purposes, while quantitative techniques are more likely to be used in evaluating or justifying a set of experimental hypotheses (Sprenkle & Moon, 1996).

Published outcome research today is likely to take one of two forms: *efficacy studies* or *effectiveness studies* (Pinsof & Wynne, 1995). The former, more common, attempt to determine whether a particular treatment works under ideal conditions such as those in a university or medical center. Interview methodology is standardized, treatment manuals are followed, clients are randomly assigned to treatment or no-treatment groups, independent evaluators measure outcomes, and so on. Effectiveness studies seek to determine whether the therapy works under normal, real-life situations, as in a clinic, social agency, or private practice setting. Most research to date is of the efficacy kind and is encouraging, but it is not always translatable into specific recommendations for therapy under more real-world, consultation room conditions. Overall results from recent surveys (Shadash, Ragsdale, Glaser, & Montgomery, 1995), based mainly on efficacy studies, indicate that clients receiving family therapy did significantly better than untreated control group clients. In certain cases, as with severely dysfunctional clients, a combination of therapeutic modalities (psychoeducation, medication, individual therapy, group therapy) may be the treatment of choice (Pinsof, Wynne, & Hambright, 1996). The current thrust of outcome research continues to explore the relative advantages (in terms of costs, length of treatment, extent of change) of alternate treatment interventions for clients with different specific psychological or behavioral difficulties.

## Treatment

### The Family Therapy Perspective

Family therapy represents an outlook regarding the origin and maintenance of symptomatic or problematic behavior, as well as a form of clinical intervention directed at changing dysfunctional aspects of the family system. Adopting such an outlook, the therapist may see the entire family together, or various dyads, triads, or subsystems may be seen, depending on what aspects of the overall problem are being confronted by the therapist. Methods of treatment may vary, depending largely on the nature of the presenting problem, the therapist's theoretical outlook, and his or her personal style.

However, family therapy involves more than seeing distressed families as a unit or group. Simply gathering members together and continuing to treat the individuals separately, but in a group setting, fails to make the paradigm shift called for in treating relationships. Nor is it enough to perceive individual psychopathology as the therapist's central concern while acknowledging the importance of the family context in which such psychopathology developed. Rather, family therapy calls for viewing the amelioration of individual intrapsychic conflicts as secondary to improving overall family functioning.

To work in a family systems mode, the therapist must give up the passive, neutral, nonjudgmental stance developed with so much care in conventional individual psychotherapy. To effectively help change family functioning, the therapist must become involved in the family's interpersonal processes (without losing balance or independence); be supportive and nurturing at some points and challenging and demanding at others; attend to (but not overidentify with) members of different ages; and move swiftly in and out of emotional involvements without losing track of family interactions and transactional patterns (Goldenberg & Goldenberg, 2004).

The *social constructionist family therapies,* currently gaining in popularity, place particular emphasis on the egalitarian, collaborative nature of therapist-family relationships. Family members are encouraged to examine the "stories" about themselves that they have lived by, as together the therapist-family system searches for new and empowering ways to view and resolve client problems.

### Indications and Contraindications

Family therapy is not a panacea for all psychological disturbances but is a valuable option in a therapist's repertoire of interventions. However, it is clearly the treatment of choice for certain problems within the family. Wynne (1965) suggests that family therapy is particularly applicable to resolving relationship difficulties (e.g., parent/children; husband/wife), especially those to which all family members contribute, collusively or openly, consciously or unconsciously. Many family therapists go beyond Wynne's position, arguing that all psychological problems of individuals and of groups such as families ultimately are tied to systems issues and thus amenable to intervention at the family level.

Under what circumstances is family therapy contraindicated? In some cases, it may be too late to reverse the forces of fragmentation, or perhaps too difficult to establish or maintain a therapeutic working relationship with the family because key members are unavailable or refuse to attend. Sometimes one seriously emotionally disturbed member may so dominate the family with malignant and destructive motives and behavior, or be so violent or abusive or filled with paranoid ideation, that working with the entire family becomes impossible, although some members of the family may continue to benefit from the family therapy perspective.

## Length of Treatment

Family therapy may be brief or extended, depending on the nature and complexities of the problem, family resistance to its amelioration, and the goals of treatment. Changes that most benefit the entire family may not in every case be in the best interest of each family member, and some may cling to old and familiar ways of dealing with one another. In general, however, family therapy tends to be relatively short-term compared to most individual therapy approaches. In some cases, as few as 10 sessions may eliminate symptomatic behavior; others may require 20 sessions or more for symptoms to subside. Strategic therapy quickly focuses on what problems require attention; the therapist then devises a plan of action to change the family's dysfunctional patterns in order to eliminate the presenting problem. Structural approaches tend to be brief, as the therapist joins the family, learns of its transactional patterns, and initiates changes in its structure leading to changes in behavior and symptom reduction in the identified patient. The object relations approach, on the other hand, consistent with its psychoanalytic foundations, tends to be longer and to deal with material from earlier in clients' lives.

## Settings and Practitioners

Outpatient offices, school counselor settings, and inpatient hospital wards all provide places where family therapy may be carried out. No longer out of the mainstream of psychotherapy, where it dwelt in its earlier years, family therapy has been accepted by almost all psychotherapists. Marital therapy, now considered a part of the family therapy movement, has grown at an astonishing rate since the 1970s.

Psychiatrists, psychologists, social workers, marriage and family counselors, and pastoral counselors practice family therapy, although their training and emphases may be different. Three basic kinds of training settings exist today: degree-granting programs in family therapy, freestanding family therapy institutes, and university-affiliated programs.

## Stages of Treatment

Most family therapists want to see the entire family for the initial session, since overall family transactional patterns are most apparent when all participants are together. (Young children, attending the first session, are usually not expected to attend subsequent meetings unless they are an integral part of the problem.) After establishing contact with each member present and assessing their suitability for family sessions, therapists interested in family history, such as Bowen, may begin to construct a family genogram. Others, like Haley, may proceed to negotiate with the family about precisely what problem they wish to eliminate. Minuchin's opening move is to "join the family" by adopting an egalitarian role within it, making suggestions rather than issuing orders. He accommodates to the family's style of communicating, assesses problems, and prepares a treatment plan. Solution-focused therapists, such as deShazer, discourage clients from the start from speculating on the origin of a particular problem, preferring instead to engage in collaborative "solution talk," discussing solutions they want to construct together.

The middle phase of family therapy is usually directed at helping the family members redefine the presenting problem or symptomatic behavior in the identified patient as a relationship problem to be viewed within the family context. Here the family becomes the "patient" and together they begin to recognize that all have contributed to the problem and all must participate in changing ingrained family patterns. If therapy is successful, families, guided by the therapist, typically begin to make relationship changes.

In the final stage of family therapy, families learn more effective coping skills and learn better ways to ask for what they want from one another. Although they are unlikely to leave problem-free, they have learned problem-solving techniques for resolving relationship issues together. Termination is easier in family therapy than in individual therapy because the family has developed an internal support system and has not become overdependent on an outsider, the therapist. The presenting complaint or symptom has usually disappeared, and it is time for disengagement.

## CASE EXAMPLE

### Background

While the appearance of troublesome symptoms in a family member typically brings the concerned family to seek help, it is becoming increasingly common for couples or entire families to recognize they are having relationship problems that require amelioration at the family level. Sometimes therapy is seen as a preventive measure. For example, adults with children from previous marriages who are planning to marry may become concerned enough about the potential problems involved in forming a stepfamily that they will consult a family therapist before marriage.

Frank, 38, and Michelle, 36, about to marry within a week, referred themselves because they worried about whether they were prepared, or had prepared their children, sufficiently for stepfamily life. The therapist saw them for two sessions, largely devoted to discussing common problems they had anticipated along with suggestions for their amelioration. Neither Frank's two children, Ann, 13, and Lance, 12, nor Michelle's daughter, Jessica, 16, attended these sessions.

Michelle and Frank had known each other since childhood, although she later moved to a large city and he settled in a small rural community. Their families had been friends in the past, and Frank and Michelle had visited and corresponded with each other over the years. When they were in their early 20s, before Frank went away to graduate school, a romance blossomed between Frank and Michelle and they agreed to meet again as soon as feasible. When her father died unexpectedly, Michelle wrote to Frank, and when he did not respond, she was hurt and angry. On the rebound, she married Alex, who turned out to be a drug user, verbally abusive to Michelle, and chronically unemployed. They divorced after two years, and Michelle, now a single mother, began working to support herself and her daughter, Jessica. Mother and daughter became unusually close in the 12 years before Michelle and Frank met again.

Frank also had been married. Several years after his two children were born, his wife developed cancer and lingered for five years before dying. The children, although looked after by neighbors, were alone much of the time, with Ann, Frank's older child, assuming the parenting role for her younger brother, Lance. When Frank met Michelle again, their unfinished romance was rekindled, and in a high state of emotional intensity they decided to marry.

### Problem

Approximately three months after their marriage, Frank and Michelle contacted the therapist again, describing increasing tension between their children. Needing a safe place to be heard (apparently no one was talking to anyone else), the children, Ann and Lance (Frank's) and Jessica (Michelle's), eagerly agreed to attend family sessions. What emerged were a set of individual problems compounded by the stresses inherent in becoming an "instant family."

Frank, never able to earn much money and burdened by debts accumulated during his wife's long illness, was frustrated and guilty over his feeling that he was not an adequate provider for his family. Michelle was jealous over Frank's frequent business trips, in large part because she felt unattractive (the reason for her not marrying for 12 years). She feared Frank would find someone else and abandon her again, as she felt he had done earlier, at the time of her father's death. Highly stressed, she withdrew from her daughter, Jessica, for the first time. Losing her closeness to her mother, Jessica remained detached from her stepsiblings and became resentful of any attention Michelle paid to Frank. In an attempt to regain a sense of closeness, she turned to a surrogate family— a gang—and became a "tagger" at school (a graffiti writer involved in pregang activities). Ann and Lance, who had not had time or a place to grieve over the loss of their mother, found Michelle unwilling to take over mothering them. Ann became bossy, quarrelsome, and demanding; Lance at age 12 began to wet his bed.

In addition to these individual problems, they were having the usual stepfamily problems: stepsibling rivalries, difficulties of stepparents assuming parental roles, and boundary ambiguities.

## Treatment

From a systems view, the family therapist is able to work with the entire family or see different combinations of people as needed. Everyone need not attend every session. However, retaining a consistent conceptual framework of the system is essential.

The therapist had "joined" the couple in the two initial sessions, and they felt comfortable returning after they married and were in trouble. While constructing a genogram, the therapist was careful to establish contact with each of the children, focusing attention whenever she could on their evolving relationships. Recognizing that parent-child attachments preceded the marriage relationship, she tried to help them as a group develop loyalties to the new family. Boundary issues were especially important, as they lived in a small house with little privacy, and the children often intruded on the parental dyad.

When seeing the couple together without the children present, the therapist tried to strengthen their parental subsystem by helping them to learn how to support one another and share child-rearing tasks. (Each had continued to take primary responsibility for his or her own offspring in the early months of the marriage.) Jealousy issues were discussed, and the therapist suggested they needed a "honeymoon" period that they had never had. With the therapist's encouragement, the children stayed with relatives while their parents spent time alone with each other.

After they returned for counseling, Frank's concerns over not being a better provider were discussed. He and Michelle considered alternate strategies for increasing his income and helping more around the house. Michelle, still working, felt less exhausted and thus better able to give more of herself to the children. Frank and Lance agreed to participate in a self-help behavioral program aimed at eliminating bedwetting, thus strengthening their closeness to one another. As Lance's problem subsided, the entire family felt relieved of the mess and smell associated with the bedwetting problem.

The therapist decided to see Ann by herself for one session, giving her the feeling she was special. Allowed to be a young girl in therapy, and temporarily relieved of her job as a parent to Lance, she became more agreeable and reached outside the family to make friends. She and Lance had one additional session (with their father) grieving over the loss of their mother. Michelle and Jessica needed two sessions together to work out their mother/daughter adolescent issues as well as Jessica's school problems.

## Follow-Up

Approximately 12 sessions were held. At first the sessions took place weekly, later bi-weekly, and then they were spread over three-month periods. By the end of a year, the family had become better integrated and more functional. Frank had been promoted at work, and the family had rented a larger house, easing the problems brought about by space limitations. Lance's bedwetting had stopped, and he and Ann felt closer to Michelle and Jessica. Ann, relieved of the burden of acting older than her years, enjoyed being an adolescent and became involved in school plays. Jessica still had some academic problems but had broken away from the gang and was preparing to go to a neighboring city to attend a junior college.

The family contacted the therapist five times over the next three years. Each time they were able to identify the dyad or triad stuck in a dysfunctional sequence for which they needed help, and each time a single session seemed to get them back on track.

## SUMMARY

Family therapy, beginning in the 1950s, turned attention away from individual intrapsychic problems and placed the locus of pathology on dysfunctional transactional patterns within a family. Within this new perspective, families are viewed as systems, with members operating within a relationship network and by means of feedback loops aimed at maintaining homeostasis. Growing out of research aimed at understanding communication patterns in the families of schizophrenics, family therapy later broadened its focus to include therapeutic interventions with a variety of family problems. These therapeutic endeavors are directed at changing repetitive maladaptive or problematic sequences within the system.

Symptomatic behavior in the identified patient is viewed as signaling family disequilibrium. Symptoms arise from, and are maintained by, current, ongoing family transactions. Viewing causality in circular rather than linear terms, the family therapist focuses on repetitive behavioral sequences between members that are self-perpetuating and self-defeating. Therapeutic intervention may take a number of forms, including approaches assessing the impact of the past on current family functioning (object relations, contextual), those largely concerned with individual family member growth (experiential), those that focus on family structure and processes (structural) or transgenerational issues, those heavily influenced by cognitive-behavioral perspectives (strategic, behavioral), and those that emphasize dialogue in which clients examine the meaning and organization they bring to their life experiences (social constructionist and narrative therapies). All attend particularly to the context of people's lives in which dysfunction originates and can be ameliorated.

Interest in family systems theory and concomitant interventions will probably continue to grow in the coming years. The stress on families precipitated by the lack of models or strategies for dealing with divorce, remarriage, alternative lifestyles, or acculturation in immigrant families will likely increase demand for professional help at a family level.

Consumers and cost-containment managers will utilize family therapy with even greater frequency in the future because it is a relatively short-term procedure, solution-oriented, dealing with real and immediate problems. Moreover, it feels accessible to families with relationship problems who don't wish to be perceived as pathological. Its preventive quality, helping people learn more effective communication and problem-solving skills to head off future crises, is attractive not only to families, but also to practitioners of family medicine, pediatrics, or other primary care physicians to whom troubled people turn. As the field develops in both its research and clinical endeavors, it will better identify specific techniques for treating different types of families at significant points in their life cycles.

## ANNOTATED BIBLIOGRAPHY

Gergen, K. J. (1999). *An invitation to social construction.* Thousand Oaks, CA: Sage.

One of the leading figures in the increasingly influential social construction movement offers a tour of the philosophy, issues, and future directions of this postmodern phenomenon. Diversity is valued, collaborative dialogue is urged, and the traditional ideas of truth, reality, and objectivity are challenged.

Goldenberg, I., & Goldenberg, H. (2004). *Family therapy: An overview* (6th ed.). Pacific Grove, CA: Brooks/Cole.

This text describes the major theories and the assessment and intervention techniques of family therapy. Systems theory and family life cycle issues are outlined, a historical discussion of the field's development is included, and research, training, and professional issues are considered.

McGoldrick, M., Giordana, J., & Pearce, J. K. (Eds.). (1996). *Ethnicity and family therapy* (2nd ed.). New York: Guilford Press.

These authors have brought together several dozen experts to provide detailed knowledge about a wide variety of racial and ethnic groupings. Common family patterns are delineated for each group, and suggestions are offered for effective family interventions tied to the unique aspects of each set.

Minuchin, S. (1974). *Families and family therapy.* Cambridge, MA: Harvard University Press.

This widely used and influential book by the major architect of structural family therapy offers the best description of the fundamental concepts for understanding family formation and organization. Written in a lively and compelling style, and featuring specific techniques for restructuring families, Minuchin's book offers numerous detailed accounts of his work with families.

## CASE READINGS

Family therapy trainers commonly make use of videotapes of master therapists demonstrating their techniques with real families, since tapes provide a richer and greater dimensional sense of the emotional intensity of family sessions than what is available from case readings alone. Tapes are available to rent or purchase from the Ackerman Institute in New York, the Philadelphia Child Guidance Center, the Georgetown University Family Center, the Family Institute of Washington, D.C., and many other training establishments.

Three texts deal largely with descriptions and analyses of family therapy from the vantage point of leading practitioners:

Grove, D. R., & Haley, J. (1993). *Conversations on therapy: Popular problems and uncommon solutions.* New York: W. W. Norton.

Grove and Haley, apprentice and master therapist, respectively, offer a question-and-answer conversation regarding specific cases seen at the Family Therapy Institute of Washington, D.C., and together they devise strategies for intervening effectively in problematic situations.

Napier, A. Y., & Whitaker, C. A. (1978). *The family crucible.* New York: Harper & Row.

This text gives a full account of cotherapy with one family, including both parents; a suicidal, runaway, teenage daughter; an adolescent son; and a six-year-old daughter.

Satir, V. M., & Baldwin, M. (1983). *Satir step by step: A guide to creative change in families.* Palo Alto, CA: Science and Behavior Books.

Using double columns, Satir presents a transcript of a session accompanied by an explanation for each intervention.

Two recent casebooks contain descriptions offered by family therapists with a variety of viewpoints. Both effectively convey what transpires as family therapists attempt to put theory into practice.

Dattilio, F. (Ed.). (1998). *Case studies in couple and family therapy: Systemic and cognitive perspectives.* New York: Guilford Press.

Leading figures from each school of family therapy briefly summarize their theoretical positions, followed by detailed case studies of actual sessions. The editor offers comments throughout, in an attempt to integrate cognitive-behavior therapy with a variety of current family therapy systems.

Lawson, D. M., & Prevatt, F. F. (Eds.). (1999). *Casebook in family therapy.* Pacific Grove, CA: Brooks/Cole Wadsworth.

Over a dozen contemporary ways of treating families are described by various advocates, each of whom offers brief theoretical positions and elaborated case study examples of therapeutic interventions. A final chapter deals with current issues and trends in family therapy.

Other valuable works include the following.

Oxford, L. K., & Wiener, D. J. (2003). Rescripting family dramas using psychodramatic methods. In D. J. Wiener & L. K. Oxford (Eds.), *Action therapy with families and groups: Using creative arts improvisation in clinical practice* (pp. 45–74). Washington, DC: American Psychological Association. [Reprinted in D. Wedding & R. J. Corsini (Eds.). (2005). *Case Studies in Psychotherapy* (4th ed.). Belmont, CA: Wadsworth.]

This recent case illustrates how the techniques of psychodrama can be applied in a family therapy context.

Papp, P. (1983). The daughter who said no. *The process of change* (pp. 67–120). New York: Guilford. [Reprinted in D. Wedding & R. J. Corsini (Eds.). (2005). *Case studies in psychotherapy* (4th ed.). Belmont, CA: Wadsworth.]

This is a classic case that illustrates the way a master family therapist treats a young woman with anorexia nervosa.

# REFERENCES

Ackerman, N. W. (1958). *The psychodynamics of family life.* New York: Basic Books.

Anderson, C. M., Reiss, D., & Hogarty, B. (1986). *Schizophrenia and the family: A practitioner's guide to psychoeducation and management.* New York: Guilford Press.

Anderson, H. D. (1997). *Conversation, language, and possibilities: A postmodern approach to therapy.* New York: Harper Collins.

Bateson, G. (1972). *Steps to an ecology of mind.* New York: E. P. Dutton.

Bateson, G., Jackson, D. D., Haley J., & Weakland, J. (1956). Towards a theory of schizophrenia. *Behavioral Science, 1,* 251–264.

Beck, A. T., & Weishaar, M. (2005). Cognitive therapy. In R. J. Corsini & D.Wedding (Eds.), *Current psychotherapies* (7th ed., pp. 238–268). Belmont, CA: Wadsworth.

Bell, J. E. (1961). *Family group therapy.* Public Health Monograph No. 64. Washington, DC: U.S. Government Printing Office.

Bertalanffy, L. von (1968). *General systems theory: Foundation, development, applications.* New York: Braziller.

Boscolo, L., Cecchin, G., Hoffman, L., & Penn, P. (1987). *Milan systemic family therapy: Conversations in theory and practice.* New York: Basic Books.

Boszormenyi-Nagy, I. (1987). *Foundations of contextual therapy: Collected papers of Ivan Boszormenyi-Nagy.* New York: Brunner/Mazel.

Bowen, M. (1960). A family concept of schizophrenia. In D. D. Jackson (Ed.), *The etiology of schizophrenia.* New York: Basic Books.

Bowen, M. (1978). *Family therapy in clinical practice.* New York: Jason Aronson.

Buckley, W. Q. (1967). *Sociology and modern systems theory.* Englewood Cliffs, NJ: Prentice-Hall.

Carter, B., & McGoldrick, M. (Eds.). (1999). *The expanded family life cycle: Individual, family, and social perspectives* (3rd ed.). Boston: Allyn & Bacon.

Colapinto, J. (1979). The relative value of empirical evidence. *Family Process, 18,* 427–441.

Dattilio, F. M., Epstein, N. B., & Baucom, D. H. (1998). An introduction to cognitive-behavioral therapy with couples and families. In F. M. Dattilio (Ed.), *Case studies in couple and family therapy: Systemic and cognitive perspectives.* New York: Guilford Press.

deShazer, S. (1991). *Putting differences to work.* New York: Norton.

Ellis, A. (2005). Rational emotive behavior therapy. In R. J. Corsini & D. Wedding (Eds.), *Current Psychotherapies* (7th ed., pp. 166–201). Belmont, CA: Wadsworth.

Falicov, C. J. (1998). *Latino families in therapy: A guide to multicultural practice.* New York: Guilford.

Framo, J. L. (1982). *Explorations in marital and family therapy: Selected papers of James L. Framo.* New York: Springer.

Gergen, K. J. (1985). The social construction movement in modern psychology. *American Psychologist, 40,* 266–275.

Gergen, K. J. (1999). *An invitation to social construction.* Thousand Oaks, CA: Sage.

Giordano, J., & Carini-Giordano, M. A. (1995). Ethnic dimensions in family treatment. In R. H. Mikesell, D. D. Lusterman, & S. H. McDaniel (Eds.), *Integrating family therapy: Handbook of family psychology and systems theory.* Washington, DC: American Psychological Association.

Goldenberg, I., & Goldenberg, H. (2004). *Family therapy: An overview* (6th ed.). Pacific Grove, CA: Brooks/Cole.

Greenberg, L. S. (2002). *Emotion-focused therapy: Coaching clients to work through their feelings.* Washington, DC: American Psychological Association.

Greenberg, L. S., & Pinsof, W. M. (Eds.). (1986). *The psychotherapeutic process: A research handbook.* New York: Guilford Press.

Haley, J. (1996). *Learning and teaching therapy.* New York: Guilford.

Jackson, D. D. (1965). Family rules: Marital quid pro quo. *Archives of General Psychiatry, 12,* 589–594.

Keeney, B. P., & Sprenkle, D. H. (1982). Ecosystemic foundations of family therapy: Critical implications for the aesthetics and pragmatics of family therapy. *Family Process, 21,* 1–19.

Kempler, W. (1981). *Experiential psychotherapy with families.* New York: Brunner/Mazel.

Kliman, J. (1994). The interweaving of gender, class, and race in family therapy. In M. P. Mirkin (Ed.), *Women in context: Toward a feminist reconstruction of psychotherapy.* New York: Guilford.

Kuhn, T. (1970). *The structure of scientific revolutions.* Chicago: The University of Chicago Press.

Laing, R. D. (1965). Mystification, confusion, and conflict. In I. Boszormenyi-Nagy & J. L. Framo (Eds.), *Intensive family therapy: Theoretical and practical aspects* (pp. 343–362). New York: Harper & Row.

Lidz, T., Cornelison, A., Fleck, S., & Terry, D. (1957). The intrafamilial environment of schizophrenic patients: II. Marital schism and marital skew. *American Journal of Psychiatry, 114,* 241–248.

McDaniel, S. H., Hepworth, J., & Doherty, W. J. (1992). *Medical family therapy: A biopsychosocial approach to families with health problems.* New York: Basic Books.

McGoldrick, M. (1998). *Re-visioning family therapy: Race, culture, and gender in clinical practice.* New York: Guilford.

Minuchin, S. (1974). *Families and family therapy.* Cambridge, MA: Harvard University Press.

Minuchin, S., Montalvo, B., Guerney, B. G., Jr., Rosman, B. L., & Schumer, F. (1967). *Families of the slums: An exploration of their structure and treatment.* New York: Basic Books.

Minuchin, S., Rosman, B. L., & Baker, L. (1978). *Psychosomatic families: Anorexia nervosa in context.* Cambridge, MA: Harvard University Press.

Neimeyer, G. J. (Ed.). (1993). *Constructivist assessment: A casebook.* Thousand Oaks, CA: Sage.

Nichols, M. P. (1987). *The self in the system: Expanding the limits of family therapy.* New York: Brunner/Mazel.

Paul, G. L. (1967). Outcome research in psychotherapy. *Journal of Consulting Psychology, 31,* 109–188.

Pinsof, W. M. (1986). The process of family therapy: The development of the Family Therapist Coding System. In L. S. Greenberg & W. M. Pinsof (Eds.), *The psychotherapeutic process: A research handbook.* New York: Guilford Press.

Pinsof, W. M., & Wynne, L. C. (1995). The effectiveness and efficacy of marital and family therapy: Introduction to the special issue. *Journal of Marital and Family Therapy, 21,* 341–343.

Pinsof, W. M., Wynne, L. C., & Hambright, A. B. (1996). The outcomes of couple and family therapy: Findings, conclusions, and recommendations. *Psychotherapy, 33,* 321–331.

Prochaska, J. O., & Norcross, J. C. (1999). *Systems of psychotherapy: A transtheoretical analysis* (4th ed.). Pacific Grove, CA: Brooks/Cole.

Reiss, D. (1981). *The family's construction of reality.* Cambridge, MA: Harvard University Press.

Satir, V. (1972). *Peoplemaking.* Palo Alto, CA: Science and Behavior Books.

Scharff, J. S., & Scharff, D. E. (1997). Object relation couple therapy. *American Journal of Psychotherapy, 51,* 141–173.

Selvini-Palazzoli, M. (1986). Towards a general model of psychotic games. *Journal of Marital and Family Therapy, 12,* 339–349.

Selvini-Palazzoli, M., Boscolo, L., Cecchin, G. F., & Prata, G. (1978). *Paradox and counterparadox: A new model in the therapy of the family schizophrenic transaction.* New York: Jason Aronson.

Shadash, W. R., Ragsdale, K., Glaser, R. R., & Montgomery, L. M. (1995). The efficacy and effectiveness of marital and family therapy: A perspective from meta-analysis. *Journal of Marital and Family Therapy, 21,* 345–360.

Sprenkle, D. H., & Moon, S. (Eds.). (1996). *Research methods in family therapy.* New York: Guilford Press.

Sullivan, H. S. (1953). *The interpersonal theory of psychiatry.* New York: W. W. Norton.

Wachtel, E. E., & Wachtel, P. L. (1986). *Family dynamics in individual psychotherapy: A guide to clinical strategies.* New York: Guilford Press.

Watzlawick, P., Weakland, J. H., & Fisch, R. (1974). *Change: Principles of problem formation and problem resolution.* New York: W. W. Norton.

Whitaker, C. A., & Bumberry, W. M. (1988). *Dancing with a family: A symbolic-experiential approach.* New York: Brunner/Mazel.

White, M. (1995). *Re-authoring lives: Interviews and essays.* Adelaide, South Australia: Dulwich Centre Publications.

Wiener, N. (1948). Cybernetics. *Scientific American, 179*(5), 14–18.

Wynne, L. C. (1965). Some indications and contraindications for exploratory family therapy. In I. Boszormenyi-Nagy & J. L. Framo (Eds.), *Intensive family therapy: Theoretical and practical aspects.* New York: Harper & Row.

Wynne, L. C., Ryckoff, I. M., Day, J., & Hirsch, S. I. (1958). Pseudomutuality in the family relationships of schizophrenics. *Psychiatry, 21,* 205–220.

Courtesy of Stanford University News and Publications Service

Jacob Moreno (1889–1974)

# 13 PSYCHODRAMA

*Adam Blatner*

## OVERVIEW

Psychodrama is a method of psychotherapy developed in the mid-1930s by
J. L. Moreno (1889–1974). It is applicable mainly in groups, but with modifications can also be used in family therapy and with individuals. The therapist invites a client to role-play some aspect of the client's problem, and the
therapist then uses psychodramatic techniques to draw the client out. If the
method is used in a group setting, other group members may be asked to play
the roles of the other people in the situation. The enactment is then followed
by sharing and discussion.

Psychodrama draws on the natural capacity for imaginative, make-believe
play that is evident in childhood. In adulthood, this capacity is used in more
focused, task-oriented ways, for example, by candidates for political office in
rehearsing for a debate. Many techniques derived from psychodrama, such as
action methods, experiential exercises, or role playing, can be integrated with
other approaches. This is because there are times in therapy when just talking about a situation is far less helpful than staging the problem in action, discovering the underlying issues, and working out more effective responses.

### Basic Concepts

As well as investigating issues in clients' lives, psychodramatic methods may
be used to clarify the dynamics of relationships in group therapy. In exploring aspects of clients' problems, events in the past, present, or even the future

may be enacted. Psychodramatic methods can be to psychotherapy what electric power tools have been to carpentry: They can extend and vastly ease the work, whether the task (in carpentry) is building a house, a chair, or a jewel box, or, in therapy, clarifying confusion, helping to envision new possibilities, strengthening the capacity for creative adaptation, or reintegrating a previously disowned complex of feelings and attitudes.

Psychodrama in its classical form, in a group setting with an extended process of enacted exploration, is an elegant and complex process that requires a good deal of training. Using another analogy, it may be likened to surgery. More elaborate procedures require an operating room and specialists, but there is also "minor surgery," procedures performed in the offices of general practitioners, such as draining an abscess or suturing a deep cut. Any psychotherapist, with study and supervised practice, can learn to integrate some action techniques in his or her clinical work. Also, just as general medical practice has integrated certain principles of surgery, such as keeping wounds clean and using sterile instruments, so also a number of psychodramatic principles can be integrated into mainstream therapy. The theoretical principles introduced and emphasized by psychodrama complement all the other approaches, and these principles are applicable even if the clinician never uses action techniques. Psychodrama has made notable contributions to our thinking about creativity, spontaneity, social psychology, play, imagination, catharsis, self-expression, experiential learning, and the power of action as a way of deepening insight and healing.

Indeed, psychodramatic methods have already been absorbed into a variety of contemporary systems, most notably gestalt therapy, behavior therapy, family therapy, as well as many other less well-known approaches. Clinicians familiar with such approaches are invited to discover and adapt even more from the incredibly rich resource that is psychodrama.

Those who might want to pursue training in classical psychodrama deserve encouragement, because this method in its fullest expression may be one of the richest and most exciting approaches in the applied behavioral sciences. Skill in psychodrama must be learned by doing and from feedback—one can't just read about it in a book or master it in a few workshops. Training in this subspecialty involves several years of supervised training and experience. Because it is powerful, when misused it can be dangerous; in fact, many people with inadequate training have presumed to conduct psychodramas and generated casualties rather than cures.

## Other Systems

### Group Psychotherapy

Moreno was one of the earliest pioneers of group psychotherapy and continued to promote all the many variations of this general approach, including working with couples or families conjointly, throughout his career. He foresaw many of the benefits of group work at a time when clinical practice was almost entirely one on one.

### Gestalt Therapy

This approach offers many original ideas and also utilizes certain techniques taken from psychodrama—especially the technique called shuttling, which is really a mixture of what Moreno called the *empty chair technique* and *role reversal.* Historically, when Fritz Perls immigrated to the United States from South Africa in the late 1940s, he attended Moreno's open sessions in New York City. Perls found certain methods, such as those previously mentioned, as well as the personification of parts of self and dream figures, amenable to his own perspectives. Other principles, such as emphasis on the "here and now," are found in both approaches.

## Imagery Therapies

Therapists who use guided fantasy techniques can also deepen their practice by integrating psychodramatic methods. Implicit in psychodrama is the practice of imagining in very specific terms, the exact words, the facial expression, the sound of the voice, the gestures or posture of the one speaking. For example, this idea becomes a way to amplify the technique of *active imagination* as used by analytical psychologists (Jungians). Many insights can arise when not only living figures, but also parts of the body or even the inanimate objects in dreams or fantasies are personified and encouraged to speak about themselves and their message. This technique goes beyond merely verbally analyzing and interpreting these images.

## Inner Dialogue

This procedure has become a part of a number of different therapies. The underlying theory of personality posits that the psyche involves different roles, also called parts, subpersonalities, complexes, voices, selves, archetypal images, characters, ego states, and so forth, and some of the therapy then involves a process of having these roles dialogue with each other, mediated by an observing ego function. In psychodrama, this process is called the *multiple ego* technique, and it involves the principle of encounter.

## Drama Therapy

This is a parallel field, one of the Creative Arts therapies. During the middle of the twentieth century, there were many small theater groups in psychiatric hospitals around the world, and patients would actually put on plays in many of these programs. Around the early 1970s, professionals with theatrical backgrounds began to connect with each other; by the time the National Association for Drama Therapy in the United States was formed in 1979, the mainstream practice had come to incorporate a fair amount of psychodrama (Johnson, 2000). In return, some techniques from drama therapy have become more widely used by psychodramatists, such as the inclusion of some ritual-like closing activities.

## Play Therapy

This is a broad and rich field that naturally overlaps with drama therapy and psychodrama, and it is often used in a mixed format by therapists working with children and younger adolescents (Bannister, 1997). Some of the principles and techniques of play therapy can also be applied with adults. There are now many board games and books about structured activities and relatively noncompetitive games that can be played in the office or on the field, and some of these overlap with the *warm-ups* invented by psychodramatists over the years. The sand-tray technique, in which small figures are used to represent significant elements or people in a child's fantasy, is similar to the action sociometry techniques such as Raimundo's "play of life" (Raimundo, 2002).

## Body Therapies

These approaches share with psychodrama the awareness that activation of the kinesthetic modes of experiencing offer major channels to both insight and healing. Among the various approaches, the most well known has been the post-Reichian method of *Bioenergetic Analysis,* developed primarily by Alexander Lowen and his followers. There are a number of practitioners who comfortably mix this and/or other physical activation approaches with psychodramatic methods.

Another combination of drama and movement derived from dance-movement therapy is the Pesso-Boyden System Psychomotor (PBSP), which shares some insights with psychodrama, especially regarding the production of scenes in which clients can have reparative experiences involving all modalities (Pesso, 1997). Developed in 1961, it has been used widely internationally.

## Creative Arts Therapies

These have also emerged as professional fields, with their own organizations: Psychodrama, though technically not a creative arts therapy, has found it useful to affiliate with dance movement therapy, art therapy, poetry therapy, music therapy, and the aforementioned drama therapy in the National Coalition of Arts Therapies Associations. There is also a field called expressive arts therapy that tends to emphasize a multi-arts-modality approach, whereas the other arts therapies mentioned tend to stick to their own medium. Psychodramatic methods, working as good warm-ups for further explorations, may be used in conjunction with any of these approaches. In turn, some of these preverbal approaches sometimes help to work through some of the insights or feelings that are brought up in the course of a psychodrama (J. J. Moreno, 1999; Wiener, 1999).

## Transpersonal Psychology

The integration of a spiritual dimension in psychotherapy seems to be gaining increasing sympathy among practitioners. Moreno's work recognized the relevance of religious imagery and belief and worked with it from the outset. Moreno himself felt that all his methods derived from a literally mystical sense of the immanence of the Divine in the creative process, however it may be manifested in the Cosmos (Moreno, 1971). In practical terms, psychodramatic methods may be useful in exploring clients' experiences with religion, their sense of meaning and purpose, and their sources of solace.

## Cognitive Therapy, Cognitive-Behavior Therapy, and Rational Emotive Behavior Therapy

Each of these therapies uses role playing to identify maladaptive beliefs, and each requires rehearsing and individualizing the integration of new attitudes and response patterns. Behavior therapy has long used role playing, rehearsing, modeling, and other methods without specifically noting their origins with Moreno in the 1930s.

## Family Therapy

Like group work, family therapy evolved from a more psychoanalytic or counseling approach to a more dynamic, multimodal process. Virginia Satir learned about psychodrama while she was a resident scholar at Esalen in the late 1960s and began to apply it in the form of family sculpture and other more dynamic interventions. More recently, Farmer (1995) has written about psychodrama's usefulness within the framework of systemic family therapy.

## Narrative Therapy and Constructive Therapies

Fashionable in recent decades, these postmodern approaches address treatment as a process of retelling the client's life story, reinterpreting its events and phenomena in a more positive and useful fashion. This invites creativity and breaking away from tendencies to describe life's challenges only in negative and pathological terms. Since both drama and narrative relate to the more fundamental storylike nature of psychological functioning, in contrast to expository descriptions, they offer natural areas of potential synergy.

## Other Psychotherapies

Alfred Adler's Individual Psychology was promoted in the United States primarily by Rudolf Dreikurs, and he in turn employed Adeline Starr as a psychodramatist—an example of another important theory that used Moreno's procedures. Jung's analytical psychology has been integrated with psychodrama, as has Berne's Transactional Analysis and other approaches (Gass, 1997; Scategni, 2002).

# HISTORY

## Precursors

Dramatic enactment has been part of healing rituals for thousands of years and can trace its origins to shamanistic reenactments of traumatic events. In Western medicine during the seventeenth and eighteenth centuries, occasional references were made to the utility of drama as an element in healing, and in the nineteenth century, a few psychiatric hospitals engaged their patients in the activity of putting on plays. Psychodrama itself, though, was invented by J. L. Moreno. (A few others in the early twentieth century explored the interface of theatre and therapy, but these efforts were not developed and lapsed into obscurity—and there's nothing to suggest that Moreno ever heard of them.)

Another predecessor was Henri Bergson, the French philosopher, whose ideas about creativity were well known in intellectual circles in the early years of the twentieth century. Moreno acknowledged Bergson's influence. Certainly there was an intellectual ferment in many areas, including literature, art, and sociology. Novel ideas refreshed these fields, and Vienna during Moreno's youth was one of the liveliest centers of Western cultural renewal.

## Beginnings

The beginnings of psychodrama may be discerned in themes in Moreno's youth and young adulthood. He was born Jacob Levy in Bucharest, Romania, in 1889, into a Sephardic Jewish family. (He added the last name, Moreno—meaning "teacher"—in his young adulthood.) His family moved to Vienna when he was around five, and as a teenager, he read philosophy and delved into religious literatures (Marineau, 1989). As part of his interest in creativity, he engaged in storytelling and improvisational dramatics with the children in the city's parks, and was impressed with the vitality they brought to the process. While he was in medical school, one of Moreno's avocational interests was theater, which for him was a natural vehicle for the imagination. However, he felt that the theater of his time was burdened by rigid traditions; as a result, it was decadent and lacked the vitality of truth.

Moreno's interest in applied sociology was stimulated during the First World War when he was assigned as a medical consultant to one of the camps for Tyrolean refugees on the outskirts of Vienna. He noticed the plight of different types of people thrown together. Moreno envisioned social arrangements in which people could be helped to find and live with those with whom they affiliated, rather than with those who were arbitrarily assigned by administrators. (This was the precursor to his developing the method he called *sociometry*—to be described later in this chapter.)

Following WWI and his graduation from medical school, Moreno became a general practitioner in Vienna's suburbs. He traveled into the city, participated in its intellectual and literary activities, and even edited a small literary journal, *Daimon.* Addressing his interest in theatre, Moreno organized what was probably the first improvisational troupe, calling it the *Theater of Spontaneity.* This group played events reported in the daily news, but the players spoke out loud what their characters might be thinking in these situations, thus bringing out imagined depths. These enactments were held "in the round"—another of Moreno's innovations. During this time, Moreno began to see a therapeutic potential in improvisational drama, because the enactments also began to positively affect the members of the troupe's personal lives. However, the economics of postwar Europe were so distressed that Moreno immigrated to the United States in 1925.

Moreno gradually established himself as a consultant in the greater New York area, working at Sing Sing prison and in other settings. In 1931, he attended one of the early annual meetings of the American Psychiatric Association and presented a paper there, coining the term "group psychotherapy," relating to how prison inmates might best be grouped (Moreno, 1931). In subsequent years, Moreno became a tireless pioneer and promoter of group psychotherapy of all types, believing in the power of people to be therapeutic agents for each other (Hare & Hare, 1996).

In the early 1930s, as a consultant to a girls' training school in upstate New York, Moreno was able to test out some of his emerging theories of sociometry, a method that promoted psychological harmony by supporting more open choices for the girls at the school (e.g., the choice of whom to live or work with). He wrote about these ideas and methods in his first book, *Who Shall Survive?* (1934). This book also offered the beginnings of role theory and role playing, the roots of psychodrama. Soon thereafter, Moreno opened a sanitarium in Beacon, New York, about 60 miles north of Manhattan on the eastern bank of the Hudson River. Here he built a specially designed psychodrama stage and theater. At this time, there were few who dared to treat psychotic patients with psychological treatments. Moreno sought to help such patients relieve their delusions and hallucinations by symbolically "living them out," expressing their underlying needs in role playing, and thereby neutralizing their compelling influence. It was what now might be called a kind of mental *jujitsu,* going with the flow. Reportedly, he had a number of remarkable responses.

Unfortunately, the idea of acting out problems sharply contrasted with the strictly verbal method of the then dominant school of psychoanalysis. (The acting that is done consciously in psychodrama is almost the opposite of what is called acting-out in analysis—and so psychodramatic enactment might better be called "acting-in" [Blatner, 1996].) It was feared that Moreno's method might stir patients up rather than quiet them down, and, of course, it did. Qualified staff, however, who could then work with the evoked material, keep the enactment going to its natural conclusion, and process the ensuing catharsis would achieve a longer-term positive outcome. Training the staff to set up a psychodramatic environment, however, would be the equivalent of training a whole community of therapists. In retrospect, Moreno created a sort of therapeutic milieu at his sanitarium that required ongoing training and close supervision of nurses and aides and therefore didn't transfer easily to most other hospital settings in the 1940s. More than a decade later, Maxwell Jones incorporated some aspects of psychodrama in his pioneering experiments with therapeutic communities in Great Britain.

Moreno, in addition to teaching, treating, and administering, began to write and publish. He published his own professional journals, (*Sociometry, Sociatry, Group Psychotherapy, The International Journal of Sociometry and Sociatry*) and in 1942, founded the first professional association devoted to group psychotherapy, the American Society for Group Psychotherapy and Psychodrama (ASGPP). The more psychoanalytically oriented American Group Psychotherapy Association (AGPA) was founded a few months later by Moreno's rival, Samuel Slavson.

In addition to the difficulties faced by any approach competing with psychoanalysis in the 1940s through the 1960s, Moreno hindered his own success by writing in an obscure style and conducting his professional relationships in a mercurial and grandiose fashion. However, by virtue of the method's basic soundness, Moreno was able to attract and maintain a few followers who were inspired by his vitality, spontaneity, warmth, and brilliance, and gradually his enterprise grew. His third wife, Zerka Toeman Moreno (1917– ), was invaluable to him in these endeavors.

From the late 1940s through the early 1970s, the Morenos traveled widely, published prolifically (Fox, 1987), organized national and international meetings, and offered training at his sanitarium in Beacon. Jacob Moreno held open sessions in Manhattan, traveled around the country and in Europe, and attracted increasing numbers of professionals who found in psychodrama positive elements that were missing in the main approaches then currently available. His work on role theory was influential in social psychology and his method of sociometry influential in sociology. Moreno helped found the International Association of Group Psychotherapy (www.iagp.com), which involves many psychodramatists, group analysts, and practitioners of other approaches. However, in the mid-1960s, as he was growing older, Moreno's wife, Zerka, increasingly took on the role of major trainer at the Beacon Institute. She also coauthored his later books. Moreno died peacefully in May 1974. His tombstone reads, "Here lies the man who brought laughter and joy back into psychiatry."

## Current Status

Zerka Toeman Moreno has continued to teach, travel internationally, and write, and there have been increasing numbers of other psychodrama trainers and practitioners. The ASGPP (www.asgpp.org) has continued to hold annual conferences, and the peer-reviewed *Journal of Group Psychotherapy, Psychodrama, & Sociometry* has enhanced its professional status. (The journal, which has been renamed a few times, was named *The International Journal of Action Methods* from 1997 to 2003, but has returned to its previous name.) In the late 1970s, an official certification board was established, apart from but in cooperation with the ASGPP. Two levels of training are now recognized: Certified Practitioner (CP) and, with further training and supervision, Trainer, Educator and Practitioner (TEP). The latter designation is for those who are qualified to train others. At present, there are approximately 200 CPs and 200 TEPs in the United States. Psychodrama has continued to evolve, with many practitioners integrating techniques and theoretical principles from other approaches and in turn influencing therapists in those other fields. Modifications have been developed for using psychodrama more effectively with problems such as addiction or trauma, and these changes will be described in a later section on applications.

Psychodrama is expanding significantly, and more than 12,000 professionals around the world identify with this practice. At present, there are over 20 psychodrama organizations in different countries, and a number of these publish their own journals. In addition to translating books written by Moreno and his students, there are also scores of books written by authors from other countries in their own languages. International networks and organizations of trainers, Web sites and Internet listservs, in English, Spanish, and other languages all keep the field advancing. At least one international psychodrama conference has been held almost every year in various sites, in addition to regional and national conferences.

In spite of the fact that a number of established textbooks ignore current writings on psychodrama and refer only to Moreno's own books—if they mention psychodrama at all—it should be noted that publications on psychodrama, many of which are far more understandable than Moreno's own difficult-to-read books and monographs, have continued to multiply. These more current books address the many ways that psychodramatic methods continue to be refined and developed (Kellermann, 1992; Z. T. Moreno, Blomkvist, & Rützel, 2000; Røine, 1997).

# PERSONALITY

## Theory of Personality

Although elements of a theory of personality may be discerned among the pages of Moreno's writings, none have been accepted as dogma by psychodramatists. This chapter will attempt to present in more coherent form some of Moreno's key ideas, but it should be noted that many psychodramatists utilize mainstream personality theories deriving from such traditions as psychoanalysis, transactional analysis, analytical psychology, and so forth. Other practitioners have elaborated their own theories for how the process is effective in psychotherapy (Kipper, 1986, 2001; Verhofstadt-Denève, 1999). Psychodrama shouldn't be considered just a technique, though, because many of Moreno's ideas about psychology deserve to be integrated at the theoretical level. As in all psychotherapies, psychodrama has an underpinning theory of personality and a conception of human nature, with its panoply of needs, interests, drives, and creative impulses.

### Role Dynamics

Moreno was one of the pioneers of social role theory. While most role theorists focused more academically on ways of describing or analyzing phenomena, Moreno's emphasis was on practical application. His point was that by becoming more conscious of the roles we play, we could play them more creatively. Analyzing the components or definitions of a role allows one to renegotiate these definitions, to bring new interpretations to the attitudes involved. Also, new roles may be added to the role repertoire and old roles relinquished.

The word *role* derives from the rolled-up scrolls that were the scripts for early actors, and has broadened in its meaning so the word now refers to any function in a complex system. Although there are numerous definitions in the sociological literature, the simplest and most practical definition is that a role involves any stance or position that could be dramatically enacted. Roles thus imply a dramaturgical way of thinking, as expressed in Shakespeare's lines, "All the world's a stage, and all the men and women merely players" (*As You Like It,* act 2, scene vii.). Most human problems and interactions, as well as most psychological dynamics, can be expressed more understandably by describing the roles being played in a given situation, how they are defined, and how these definitions may be subject to challenge, negotiation, and revision.

Thus, a significant contribution of psychodrama is its development of role theory as a "user-friendly language" for psychology. Role theory offers a *lingua franca,* a common language that can be used by professionals of many disciplines and theoretical backgrounds. The role concept and its associated dramaturgical viewpoint is a particularly evocative metaphor. It invites people to think of themselves as creative artists and actors, not just puppets.

The term, "role dynamics," refers to a more systematic organization of applied role theory (Blatner, 2000a). More than just a language, role dynamics offers a theoretical framework that allows for the integration of the best insights of all the other approaches in psychology and psychotherapy. This is achieved by noting the essential dynamic of the interplay of two levels of mind: (1) the various roles or parts played and (2) the meta-role, the role beyond the roles, that special part that determines *how* those roles will be played. Most therapies implicitly if not explicitly address the gradual empowerment of the meta-role. Both role dynamics and psychodrama more explicitly name and emphasize the interaction of the two levels.

With all due respect to Shakespeare, "all the men and women" are *not* "merely players"! Using psychodrama, the major players shift their viewpoints, and even at times join the director in creating a different scene. As the actors move from playing the role to the meta-role position, they become codirectors and coplaywrights, exercising creativity in improvising alternative responses, either to explore new facets of the problem or to experiment with new behavioral responses. This meta-role, the inner director-playwright, has been called in other theories the "observing ego" or "witness self." However, in psychodrama the definition of the term *meta-role* is expanded, suggesting not only an analytical function but also an *executive* one, deciding, choosing, interviewing the various parts, mediating, balancing, judging, reviewing, and so on. It can be trained and developed, helped to open to intuition and spiritual resources, sensitized to more subtle interpersonal dynamics, and broadened in terms of imagination and circle of caring. In this sense, the dynamic of developing the meta-role function, when mixed with the sheer usefulness of role dynamics as a language, offers a unifying meta-theory for psychology and psychotherapy. Some of these dynamics will be noted in the following theory of psychopathology.

In role dynamics there is no need to reduce the number of motivations to any single or small set of themes. While the various sources of motivation articulated by the more traditional approaches are acknowledged, a few others are given a little more recognition: self-expression, drama, playfulness, physical exuberance, creativity, and spontaneity are also important for optimal health. These deserve to be integrated into a holistic approach to psychology.

## Variety of Concepts

### Creativity

Anticipating the ideas of humanistic psychology, Moreno felt that the human capacity for creativity was a key component of the personality. As people are helped to become more creative, they also feel more vital and experience their lives as more meaningful. In addition, from a general philosophical and socio-historical perspective, the world needs all the creativity we can give it. However, Moreno also noted an opposite inclination in personality dynamics, a tendency to avoid the responsibility of engagement and instead to rely on what has already been created (a category he called the "cultural conserve"). This was the root of automatic thoughts and rigid attitudes. Actual adaptation involves meeting the unfolding circumstances of the present moment, and this requires a continual exertion of responsibility. This is the core from which many of the other principles derive logically.

### Spontaneity

This is the innate capacity to respond adequately to the novel elements in the present, the source of creativity. While some breakthroughs arise in quiet contemplation, most require an activity of exploration, experimentation, improvisation—and this is how young children learn most naturally. One of Moreno's most important insights was that spontaneity was the best attitude and activity for generating creatively.

### Warming-Up

This is a corollary dynamic, a recognition that spontaneity is the kind of process that cannot simply be willed. It involves interplay of activity and receptivity to intuition or subconscious inspiration and must unfold gradually. These dynamics apply to the way children learn through play and also to the ways groups develop cohesion.

## Playfulness

Anxiety must be minimized, and one way to do that is to generate a context in which the consequences of making mistakes are limited: In normal development, this is one of the main functions of play. The essence of the context of play is that it is relatively fail-safe. It is also the basis of many kinds of scientific experiments, and one way to think of a laboratory is as a place in which experiments can be safely conducted. In this sense, psychodrama should be thought of as a kind of laboratory for psychosocial experimentation.

In addition to its functionality, play is recognized in psychodrama as a valid need, a part of health, so that people can enjoy a far broader range of experiences than can be actually manifested in the ordinary course of life. It's a way for imagination, spontaneity, and self-expression to be channeled, and needs to be recognized as an important dimension of normal psychology (Blatner & Blatner, 1997).

## Physical Action

The theory of psychodrama recognizes the widely appreciated principle of learning that one learns best by actually *doing*. The power of the body's internal cues as a person actually faces someone—even an imagined someone—and speaks directly to that person, stands, moves around, and feels the fullness of his or her own voice is an important component of holistic healing. In this sense, psychodrama integrates many of the benefits of the "body therapies." The power of touch, pulling, being pulled, and other physical engagements is also powerfully catalytic.

## Self-Expression

When thoughts and feelings are retained and not expressed openly, defense mechanisms come into play: "This doesn't really matter, what are you being so fussy for?" "This didn't count." "It's too hard." "It's not really happening." "It wasn't the real me who was involved." This constant undermining self-talk is countered and somewhat dissolved when a person expresses a feeling or idea openly, knowing it is heard by others. (If several people hear, the self-expressive process is even more effective—one of the reasons why group work has extra value.) When ideas are thus expressed, brought into the interpersonal context, they are also able to be reexamined in light of present awareness. The exercise of self-expression thus develops the role of the observer—the client begins to listen to what she said. (See "The Mirror" under "Applications.")

This expressiveness goes beyond the cognitive level. There is also a kind of emotional expressiveness, a deep drive to act, to do, to counter deep fears, getting past passivity and "stuckness." Sometimes talking it out does the job, but often more is needed, such as ritual and an expressive process. The deeper the stress or trauma, the more this paraverbal dimension is triggered and needs to be expressed. Moreno called this dynamic "act hunger." Therapists need to recognize the need for more than just talk, and to offer channels for more multileveled bodily expression—singing, moving, pounding, and especially the dramatization of self-affirmation. People need to experience the confrontations with their opponents, they need to hear themselves argue with a judge, confront God, and challenge their own inner persecutor. They need to feel the volume of their own voice, and the power it can channel. People can talk all they want, but if one can only talk in a whisper, it's a kind of "self-strangling" as the body muscles participate in a deeper process of psychophysical "armoring," as Wilhelm Reich described it. Self-expression breaks free of this tendency toward emotional imprisonment.

## Encounter

Indirectness is a variation of the avoidance of direct engagement and the responsibility it evokes. Therapists use psychodrama to get people to encounter others directly, talking to them instead of talking about them. This produces a sense of immediacy, intimacy, and authenticity in both parties. If the actual other person isn't available, talking to that other person imagined sitting in an empty chair is still more meaningful than explaining what one might say, or could say, to a third party. That explaining serves as a massive filter of experience. In addition, for Moreno, the idea of encounter entailed openness to a more authentic meeting in which both parties would open their minds to the viewpoints of the other—anticipating his development of the technique of role reversal.

## The Group

Moreno's personality theory was as much of a social psychology as an individual psychology, and he noted the obvious: People are embedded in relationships, groups, and networks. He was talking about interpersonal relations and family triangles a decade or more before analysts began to use such terms. The audience function mentioned in the section on self-expression is intensified when several people are present, and there is a corresponding extension of the power for validation, support, and new ideas.

## Drama

The natural social vehicle for combining the various principles of psychology previously mentioned—creativity, spontaneity, warming up, play, action, imagination, self-expression, and the like—is, of course, drama. Children naturally play make-believe, and adults organize this complex multimodal format as theater. Psychodrama further modifies the process, making it the source of a more natural way to learn and to heal.

## The Social Dimension

Role dynamics also bridges individual psychology and social psychology more than any other approach because the role concept is so innately multileveled in nature. Multiple levels of life can be integrated: cultural, group, interpersonal, intrapsychic, and even psychosomatic. Our roles are conditioned by forces operating at all these levels, and they can be best illuminated in the examination of how clients define their roles—how they view the "appropriate" expectations involved—or how they challenge these definitions. Various techniques can highlight the way clients experience their relations in their social networks.

## Rapport

Moreno was especially interested in the psychology of rapport (which he called *tele*), that subtle sense of attraction or repulsion, and sometimes indifference or neutrality or mixed feelings that exists, often reciprocally, between and among people (Blatner, 1994b). Numerous interpersonal problems arise because these issues are allowed to operate unconsciously, but attending to these dynamics can help to deal with them.

## Sociometry

Moreno developed a method for measuring tele; he called it *sociometry,* and it became a significant complex of techniques used by sociologists and social psychologists in the 1950s and 1960s, and, to a lesser extent, today. Certain sociometric techniques also are remarkably effective in bringing important individual and group dynamics to the surface. Their central focus is the investigation of who is preferred for which roles and why. The roots of our interpersonal preferences are manifold, deeply meaningful, and often subconscious or preconscious. If dreams are, as Freud (and earlier nineteenth century theoreticians) suggested, the "royal road" to the unconscious, sociometry might be the "jet stream."

## Theory of Psychopathology

Psychological problems can arise from conflict, as is noted in other theories, but also frequently involve the phenomenon of simply not having mastered the requisite role components or skills needed for effective adaptation. In other words, people are sometimes less competent than they think they are, and this is rarely questioned in therapy. Another way to think about health and illness is in terms of the way roles are balanced or distributed. Is the person's role repertoire broad enough? Furthermore, the coordinating functions of the meta-role are often crude in a surprisingly large number of people, and problems may be viewed in terms of the need for refinement in the skills of self-management. For example, what is known as a "harsh superego" may be translated as a rather crude inner disciplinarian. Just as modern managers now attend management training, so too can the inner manager use therapy to be more discerning, gentle, and effective.

Role dynamics attends not only to past events, but equally to the present predicament and anticipated future. Problems in these here-and-now dimensions may be quite sufficient to generate a maladjustment. Role dynamics also recognizes that individuals can be relatively healthy but disturbed because they are enmeshed in dysfunctional systems—perhaps a single relationship, a family, or one's workplace or neighborhood. (Historically, this view anticipated the systems-oriented thinking that arose in family therapy and other approaches.)

Another aspect of role dynamics is the idea that just as some roles can be overdeveloped, as in addictions, others can be underdeveloped. Some roles that might carry vitality remain neglected, often invalidated by family or the culture. This is one of the points of feminist psychotherapy, and psychodrama is one approach that has been noted to be particularly compatible with this orientation (Worrell & Remer, 1992). Another dimension that tends to be neglected is a noncompetitive approach to recreation, and the recognition of a number of more accessible and simple dimensions of pleasure and fun (other than intoxication, sex, and other commercially touted images). Indeed, those with addictions often suffer from a relative deficit in knowing other modes of play.

In summary, the fields of creativity research, spontaneity, "flow," play, group dynamics, and the like all converge in appreciating how psychodrama can operate to enlarge our view of personality. The role concept helps to bring these dynamics more to the fore, and also builds a bridge with social psychology, emphasizing the way the understanding of human experience must be viewed also from its relational and cultural field.

# PSYCHOTHERAPY

## Theory of Psychotherapy

Psychodramatic methods are best appreciated as being a complex of principles and procedures that are embedded within a larger, eclectic approach to psychotherapy, and not as a stand-alone system capable of managing all the phases of diagnosis and treatment. Indeed, it is arguable that no single approach to psychotherapy has such a scope. What is needed is an eclectic, integrative, or multimodal approach, and this does seem to be the emerging trend. Those who use psychodramatic methods still need to just talk with clients, engage them in therapy, generate a treatment alliance, evaluate problems, and address other issues meaningfully. There is a place for education, and for orientation of clients to the nature of the process involved. Different components need to be interwoven. There are occasions for direct instruction, and other occasions in which listening or abiding may be more helpful. Many of these components involve more conventional discussion modalities. Having a language for describing psychosocial phenomena—i.e., role talk—is one way that psychodrama is useful, even without recourse to action methods. A great deal of analytic work can be achieved simply in the process of naming and defining intrapsychic and interpersonal roles. Furthermore, a great deal of therapeutic work can be achieved by considering how those role definitions can be creatively redefined and renegotiated.

Many therapies seek to promote the client's capacity for self-reflection. Talking about problems as if they were scenes in a play, though, brings this dynamic into sharper awareness for the client, because any actor needs to exercise role distance, the capacity to shift from playing "in role" to rethinking *how that performance can be improved.* An actor as a creative artist is open to guidance from the director. Also, to avoid burn-out actors need to "de-role" between performances, and to be open to a number of other roles besides that of the character being played. Psychodrama uses these ideas to help clients to develop their capacity for observing their own behavior and underlying attitudes.

The therapist similarly needs to be open to a remarkably broad range of possible helping behaviors, which are conceptualized in psychodrama as role components. In addition to having strategies for figuring out what might be troubling the client, the therapist needs a capacity for communicating empathy, an ability to understand group dynamics, and a willingness to offer support.

A key theoretical principle in psychodrama is that two or more processes or modalities can function synergistically, each intensifying the effectiveness of each other. Psychodrama is unique in its integration of action, imagery, improvisation, creativity, the dramaturgical model, role talk, playfulness, rapport (i.e., "tele"), and direct encounter. Any one of these elements adds to the effectiveness of psychotherapy; combined, they act to profoundly deepen and broaden the therapeutic process. In addition, they are compatible and synergistic with the verbal modes of interaction described in the other chapters of this book.

## Process of Psychotherapy

Although the emphasis of this chapter is on the use of psychodramatic methods along with other approaches, a thorough acquaintance with the key elements of psychodrama is necessary for remaining oriented to the shifting roles in the process. The reason is that at one moment, the client might be in the role of himself; the next moment he may be the other person in the scene, or his own inner, ordinarily unexpressed voice. Thus, some specialized terms are needed that are drawn from the metaphor of drama: protagonist, director, auxiliary, audience, and stage.

### Basic Elements of Psychodrama

The *protagonist,* or main player, is the one whose life situation is being explored. In a group, everyone may at some point play the role of protagonist for a dramatic enactment, which can go on for anywhere from five minutes to a couple of hours. (Most play out within 40 minutes or so.) In a therapy group, two or more people might engage together as coprotagonists, using psychodramatic techniques to work through conflicts or experience something new. On occasion, the director or therapist will take on a coprotagonist role to explore certain transference dynamics or deal with a challenge.

The *director* is the one who facilitates the dramatic enactment, suggests when the protagonist might change parts or try on a different role, brings up the supporting players (auxiliaries), and in general orchestrates the process. In spite of all this directiveness, a good director can still be remarkably "person-centered," serving the needs of the protagonist in the moment rather than imposing any assumptions or frames of reference on the client-protagonist. In some groups, a director who is not a regular group member is brought in to lead the psychodrama, while the therapist participates primarily as an observer. Alternatively, the therapist might refer the whole group or individuals to a local psychodrama director for a more intensive workshop. The director and the client's primary therapist would then discuss the activities in order to provide a coordinated treatment experience.

The *auxiliary* is the third basic element in psychodrama. Originally called "auxiliary ego," this term refers to a supporting player, one who takes the role of the someone else in an enactment. Usually, the auxiliary portrays a family member, friend, supervisor, or some other person, but he or she might also portray different parts within the protagonist's own mind—the inner bully and the inner vulnerable child, for instance. Other auxiliary roles, such as the *double,* will be described further on in the text.

Gestalt therapy uses psychodrama in the form of monodrama, without the use of auxiliaries. The client plays all the parts, and dialogue is with what in psychodrama is called "the empty chair." While this more clearly exposes the client's own projections, it lacks the evocative power that can be experienced by having a living person spontaneously and vitally *be* the other and the dynamism that comes in a more vivid encounter with an actual physical person. If the auxiliary isn't playing the role properly, the director can review and correct the performance. Auxiliaries also often come up with very intuitive and insightful points that might never have occurred to the director. This supports Moreno's contention that in group therapy every person becomes the agent of healing for the others.

Auxiliaries can be directed to employ touch and physical contact, which can evoke complex feelings. This could be a tug on the sleeve, a squeeze of the hand, or a hand on the shoulder. Additional auxiliaries may play roles of other figures in the scene, so there may be several people on the stage at a time. The auxiliary in the role of the significant other also becomes the focus of the protagonist's transferences, instead of them being wholly directed toward the director or one of the group members. In most group settings, other group members can be called on to play these roles. For more complex problems, sometimes one or even a team of trained auxiliaries are used. Psychodramatists-in-training sometimes serve as auxiliaries, because the more experience one has with the method, the more sensitive one is to the nuances of the process and can serve the protagonist in a more refined way.

The *audience* generally is the therapy group itself. Psychodrama should not be thought of as a process played to a larger audience for entertainment. The protagonist's awareness that the scenes being enacted are being witnessed brings in a sense of intensified reality. The more people who have seen and heard the client's expressive behavior, the less they can retreat behind habitual verbal defenses.

The audience also functions as the source of auxiliaries. As the warming up of the protagonist commences, the question is asked, "Who here is in the scene with you?" If the protagonist—call him Alex—talks about his family, he answers, "Well, there's my dad." The director says, "Pick someone to be dad." The protagonist looks around, and intuitively picks Bill. Other group members may also go onto the stage and play Alex's mother, sister, or other roles.

In the witnessing role, the group is available for feedback, so that the transference to the therapist is diluted. The question "How did you see that interaction?" may evoke a response that has more impact than the more easily discounted observation of a therapist. The question "How would you handle that differently?" can lead to group members coming up for a brief enactment in which they take the protagonist's role and show how they would have dealt with the other person in the scene. Alex can then take his own role again and replay the scene, perhaps using the cues suggested by the audience. This process of behavioral rehearsal originated with psychodrama and was called *role training.*

The *stage* is the fifth major instrument. In classical psychodrama, sometimes there is an actual slightly raised platform area about 12 feet across, but for most groups, it suffices to simply designate a special place in the room where enactments take place. In this "stage" area, actions are understood as exploratory. It's special in that group members don't walk across it on the way to the bathroom, or for other ordinary-life actions. To sustain the even temporary suspension of disbelief, and to promote a measure of imaginative vividness, some respect must be given to the space that is to represent the protagonist's phenomenological world.

## Phases of an Enactment

Even if it is a brief facilitative intervention, therapists should be aware that there are three phases implicit in any psychodramatic process: warming-up, the action, and sharing.

*Warming-Up*    This involves a number of activities that get people involved. It can be just a bit of explanation by the director, or her getting out of her chair and starting to walk around. It might be a structured experience, though as Yalom (2002) noted, these should not be used excessively when the group dynamic has its own momentum.

*Action*    This is the second phase, and, like the middle part of a game of chess, its variations seem endless. The various techniques are orchestrated according to the needs of the client. Psychodrama is a person-centered process in many ways. Modifications are freely invited to fit the tenor of the group, the abilities of the client, and other aspects of readiness. In classical psychodrama, the process tends to follow a curve of emotional intensity and focus, increasing with the warm up, culminating with the action, and cooling down as a working-through of insights are pursued, heading toward the sharing phase. However, before sharing, the director should make sure that the protagonist and auxiliaries are "de-roled." Those who play a mother, employer, the double (the role of the protagonist's inner self) or even a dream figure, should be helped to explicitly divest those roles and become themselves as fellow group members. Some directors have these people say something like, "I'm not your sister, my real name is Sarah."

*Sharing*    After a protagonist has risked and explored, respecting this unusual degree of self-disclosure, the director invites not analysis, not criticism, but simply a counterdisclosure of what the enactment has meant in terms of the lives of the others in the group, including the auxiliaries.

Psychodrama should not be thought of as merely a hodgepodge of techniques. Rather, the techniques and principles work synergistically with each other and with other approaches, so the whole is greater than the sum of its parts. Consider this analogy: Adding anesthesia and asepsis (keeping instruments and the wound sterile) were more than just "other tools" for a surgeon; they were the conditions that made for much more successful surgery. Similarly, adding a user-friendly language, a measure of exploratory playfulness, attention to body language and physical action, the power of speaking directly, or speaking in specific imagery, and so on, all make for a far more dynamic therapeutic process.

Psychodramatic methods can be integrated with ordinary talk therapy. They simply shift the activity toward a more explicit use of the "observing ego," as therapists call it, the capacity to reflect on what is happening here and now, in the interaction with the therapist, and in the feelings in the body. Most therapies seek to heighten this capacity, but the dramaturgical context—treating life itself as a play that can be refined and improved, made more creative and effective—offers a familiar metaphor and context for achieving this goal.

## Mechanisms of Psychotherapy

Therapy is an enormously complex enterprise, and hundreds of theories have been put forward regarding what is therapeutic. Now more attention is being devoted to underlying factors that all the different approaches seem to have in common, from arousal of hope to relationship with the therapist. Psychodrama makes use of many of the various factors that are part of therapy and even uses specific techniques to emphasize these processes. Getting up with a director and entering a stage area represents a type of commitment to a process of exploration, which implies a corresponding mixture of trust in the relationship with the director and group, an expectation of a helpful outcome, and an increased sense of one's own active participation.

There is a logical development in noting the principles that follow: The best way to achieve a higher level of creativity is to develop the capacity for spontaneity and improvisation—this insight is one of Moreno's key contributions to psychotherapy. To feel free to explore spontaneity, a measure of playfulness is needed. Drama provides a natural vehicle for improvised play in older youth and adults.

### Engaging a Creative Attitude

Psychodrama generates a process that engages the curious and playful child within. Being a creative artist is a respected role in Western culture, so there's a measure of pride in daring to explore life's depths. In addition, the metaphor of life as a work of art leads the client away from the tendency to seek "answers" and allows for the generation of novel and individualized responses. Sometimes there are no solutions in any purely rational sense, but the mere expression of the predicament in an aesthetic fashion can satisfy one's emotional needs. For example, one of the ways to cope with a significant loss is simply to talk about it, draw a picture, write a poem, or role play some typical interactions. In this sense, psychodrama resonates with some of the ideas of the early psychoanalyst Otto Rank, who was an artist in his youth. Rank wrote about life as a work of art that one can engage in more or less creatively, and he recognized that creativity requires courage. Psychodrama brings this metaphor alive, and is novel, varied, and dynamic enough to remain challenging.

### Warming-Up

In addition to its being the first phase in classical psychodrama, warming-up is also a fundamental psychological dynamic. The key to authentic work in psychodrama is spontaneity, which develops gradually; *warming-up* is the psychological, physical, and interactive process that produces increased spontaneity. Even during the action, there needs to be an ongoing process of warming-up to each scene or change of role. The director uses a tone of playfulness or reminders of safety to "lubricate" the role shifts. Frictions within a group, transferential complications with the director, and confrontation of new areas that had been previously avoided are all issues that require shifts of pace, a re-grounding of the process in the healing contract, and a renewed warming-up. Psycho-dramatic methods may be used for exploring and resolving these tensions, but deeper work should not be pursued if the relationships in the group aren't harmonious.

Psychodrama sessions involving deeper experiences require more time than is typi-cally allocated to a conventional therapeutic session, so that the group members can warm up to the level of trust, group cohesion, and involvement in the relevant issues needed for overcoming the layers of subtle inner defensiveness.

There are numerous structured experiences that can be used as "warm-up tech-niques;" however, there are pitfalls associated with using them mindlessly. Different kinds of warm-ups are more appropriate for different age groups and levels of psycho-logical sophistication. The warm-up should be suited to the ostensible task of the group. Warm-ups generally are used to promote group cohesion and to motivate people to think about deeper issues. Once the group process has been galvanized, techniques often become superfluous—the interpersonal interactions suffice as continued stimuli for involvement.

The importance of warming-up needs also to be recognized as a basic principle of ordinary talk therapy. Certainly, simply waiting silently functions in one way as a warm-up, the ambiguity of the "empty" space prodding a kind of anxiety reaction that then may be analyzed. However, silence also "cools down," by removing the expected natural in-terchange that is part of ordinary relationships. Psychodrama supports a bit of introduc-tory talking, orienting the clients to the process, and other gentle warming-up suggestions that promote symmetrical and gradual self-disclosure.

## Catharsis

Psychodrama is often thought of as a method that hinges on the production of emotional catharsis. This is only indirectly true: The actual underlying dynamic is that of integration of aspects of the psyche that had been previously separated and dissociated. As these are brought back together, there is a relief and release of feelings that were associated with fear and tension. Therefore, while the display of strong emotions may be associated with certain effective interventions, simply promoting emotionality should *not* in itself be the goal of therapy. Indeed, there are many clients who are already too inclined to emote, and for them therapy should target the development of a capacity for containment. There are times in many types of expressive therapy that clients are encouraged to bring a half-stifled feeling more into full awareness. However, good psychodramatists seek to pro-mote the underlying dynamic of healing rather than the mere show of emotionality, and the image of the psychodramatist pushing clients to emote is only a caricature of the ac-tual therapeutic process.

## Insight

As clients explore dimensions of their lives that they hadn't previously considered, there are opportunities to become more explicitly conscious of overly rigid attitudes and be-liefs. These can be reevaluated, new distinctions can be drawn, and new approaches generated. However, there are degrees of insight. Occasionally, insights may come with the simple reexperiencing of a situation, accompanied by a more authentic emotional ex-pressiveness. The catharsis suffices, and no great cognitive working-through is necessary. More often, though, the emotional scenes need to be followed by a more systematic ex-ploration of the ideas and attitudes involved, because these basic beliefs may well require revision. Moreno maintained that every catharsis of abreaction should be followed by a catharsis of integration, which means that there is a more subtle release at the level of the "aha!" experience as clients are able to discover how their authentic emotions may be realistically worked with in their own lives.

A number of different scenes can address such cognitive integration. Enacting a scene that may have happened earlier in life, for example, may help offer some understanding about the context and associated beliefs that affected the way a person constructed the reactive pattern. On the other hand, scenes in related roles in the very recent past or anticipated future might be helpful for clients who are still in denial or are unclear about how they are continuing to engage in dysfunctional reactions.

Another type of insight comes with discovering that there may be alternative ways to react to a given predicament. Sometimes, simply asking other group members to share their coping strategies helps a protagonist break out of an impasse. In addition, watching or participating in another group member's psychodrama often triggers thoughts of salient themes in one's own life, and in the course of sharing, insights emerge for audience (other group members) as well as for protagonist.

## Empathy

People need to feel that they are heard, seen, and understood. The "mirroring" dynamic, an important component of Self Psychology (Kohut's school of psychoanalytic thought), is very similar to Moreno's developmental theory that children need parents to "double" for them—and people never outgrow this need. The experience of having a double is healing for the protagonist. Hearing someone else express inner feelings reduces the sense of "being the only one who thinks this way." In addition, being asked to empathize with others counters the protagonist's egocentricity and develops a more mature capability.

## Cognitive Orientation

All therapies require that clients develop new schema for understanding the world and their place in it. Role dynamics and role talk are meaningful schema that are relatively easy to understand. They have the additional advantage of not subtly suggesting pathology or promoting stigma. Anyone can admit to having an imbalance of roles, and the challenge is then simply to identify how this is so. It's not the same as having to take on some "label" that suggests sickness, weakness, or moral turpitude.

## A Corrective Experience

One of the more important therapeutic factors in psychodrama is the restorative drama, constructing what the analyst Franz Alexander called a "corrective emotional experience." Experiences of feeling helpless and shamed can be replayed so that the individual experiences a sense of mastery. This reprogramming, which involves imagery, kinesthetic experience, and the flow of a storylike process, operates at a deep level, not just in the psyche, but also in the nervous system. Experiences of being understood, validated, and supported can replace memories of feeling misunderstood, ignored, and rejected. Recent research has demonstrated the importance of this dynamic, especially in the treatment of fixations, blocks, and traumatic memories that simply aren't reached by ordinary verbal modes of therapy.

The technique of the "reformed auxiliary" involves a scene being replayed in a different way: Now the parent, sibling, teacher, or other significant person in the client's past behaves in a positive manner, and in a way that is very different from the behavior stored in the protagonist's memory. However, this replay should only happen after the protagonist has had a chance to fully own and appreciate the depth of feelings involved in that original negative experience, because the acceptance of one's own reality—in contrast to continuing to live with layers of overt or subtle denial—is a necessary precursor to the healing process. (An analogy can be made to physical wounds; infected tissue needs to be cleaned out before the healthy tissues can begin their restorative processes.)

## Transference

Tendencies to project on others expectations based on past relationships may be explored in psychodrama. After presenting a given scene, the director may casually ask, "With whom in the past have you had similar feelings?" If the transference is with the therapist, an auxiliary will be called up to stand in for the therapist, and the client as protagonist will be invited to confront the therapist. A double may be used for support and to facilitate bringing out withheld feelings. At a later point, the protagonist may be asked to change parts and play the therapist. (The actual director-therapist stands to the side.) However, the possibility that the group member is reacting to a real behavior on the part of the director should not be overlooked. In psychodrama, the therapist-director may also become a coprotagonist and the two parties can encounter each other in a spirit of equality, in front of the group, with doubles for both parties, and a cotherapist who directs the encounter.

## Simulation

Complex phenomena cannot be fully comprehended or predicted, but rather require multimodal experimentation. This is why astronauts practice simulated landings and armies go through military maneuvers. Variables that may have been overlooked can thus be noticed. It's the principle of the laboratory, and psychodrama offers such a complex of tools and environments for simulating the complexities of human interaction. No matter how much discussion is given to self-assertion in therapy, there's a different kind of challenge involved when the client is actually facing another person and asserting himself. This is why role playing is diagnostic: It reveals where weaknesses may exist, but it is also corrective, in that clients are allowed to practice, get feedback, try again, and begin to feel more confident at skill mastery. Psychodrama recognizes the need for kinesthetic-emotional "learning by doing." In the therapeutic process, as a part of working through, actual practice in implementing new attitudes as expressed in new behaviors can be crucial (Kipper, 1986).

## Spirituality

Addressing issues regarding clients' highest values, their underlying belief systems about where they belong in the universe and what they should do with their lives, offers a particularly useful framework for healing. In addition, spiritual conflicts are frequent elements in people's broader emotional development. In fact, God, Jesus, Buddha, and other significant figures also become internalized, and they play their roles in the inner psychic system. By externalizing these dialogues, participants can be subjected to the light of consciousness and the best awareness of the present moment, rather than continuing to parrot what was taught and ingrained in childhood.

Moreno was one of the first innovators to write and talk about the spiritual dimension of life and was in this sense a precursor to the later-emerging field of transpersonal psychology. In addition, since the 1980s, psychodramatists have paid increasing attention to clients' values and belief systems and have integrated Jungian, Asian, and Native American concepts into their practice.

*Learning Skills*

Clients use psychodramatic techniques in therapy, and they also learn to think as if these approaches were part of their lives. They become more capable of accessing and disclosing a greater breadth of emotional responses, and they learn to empathize with others.

In summary, psychotherapy may be thought of as a process that modifies emotional patterns, changes cognitions, and alters behaviors. Psychodramatic methods facilitate all these processes and anchor them in physical activity.

# APPLICATIONS

## Problems

Psychodramatic methods are so adaptable they can be used for almost every type of problem. More complex psychodramas generally shouldn't be used with clients whose anxiety levels are exceptionally high, such as those in a still-acute stage of psychotic disorganization, withdrawal from alcohol or drugs, or those with other brittle conditions. With people whose cognitive capacity is diminished, much simpler forms of imagery work, role playing, and role training must be used. Classical psychodrama can be modified extensively, and simplified techniques can be used with good results. For example, Tomasulo (1998) describes work with developmentally disabled clients who live in group homes and/or work in sheltered workshops. Simple role plays can help to develop skills for self-assertion, effective communication, and conflict resolution. (A case worker can learn enough about this approach to act as mediator in cases of conflict resolution.)

Therapists treating children can integrate psychodramatic techniques with other techniques derived from creative and educational drama, drama therapy, play therapy, and the other creative arts therapies (Bannister, 1997; Hoey, 1997). For example, the technique of the aside can be used with hand puppets, with the protagonist puppet turning to the audience (i.e., the therapist) and saying something he normally wouldn't directly admit to the other puppets playing counter-roles in the enactment.

Classical psychodrama is a powerful method that requires a good deal of special training on the part of the director, sufficient time for preparation and follow-up, the establishment of group support, and clients who are appropriate for this type of intervention. These sessions generally require at least two to three hours and are sometimes conducted in day-long or weekend workshop settings. Such workshops can serve as powerful adjuncts to more conventional therapies. Clients in medium- or longer-term talk therapy who have good ego strength can generate a great deal of material for later discussion and integrate some of the work they had been doing. Used judiciously, then, classical psychodrama is an especially beneficial approach. Nevertheless, it is hoped that learning about the principles and techniques of psychodrama will encourage therapists to integrate them in their own work.

*Psychodrama as an Adjunct to Individual or Group Therapy*

Clients in individual or group counseling or therapy, or even an entire therapy group, might contract to do a day-long or weekend psychodrama workshop with a trained psychodramatist. In the case of a therapy group, the group's therapist also attends and acts as a kind of cotherapist but does not function as the psychodrama director. If the workshop includes individual clients, there should be some opportunities for preworkshop and postworkshop liaison between therapist and director. For most relatively healthy clients, it would be probably enough that they report the highlights of their experience with their therapists, maintaining confidentiality regarding the identities or details of any of the work done by other group members during the psychodrama.

The day or weekend experience results in a degree of group cohesion and trust that enables a greater degree of self-disclosure among the group members. The disclosure that occurs during enactments is typically revealing and intense, and it motivates symmetrical involvements by others. Therefore, the warm-up builds on itself in a way that can't happen in more traditional and briefer (one- or one-and-a-half-hour) group sessions.

Many types of group psychotherapy can be enhanced by the integration of psychodramatic methods (Corey, 2004; Young, 2001). The main purpose of this chapter is to encourage this kind of utilization of techniques and principles. The use of role language facilitates the group dynamic, and more specific enactment techniques may be used when appropriate. Yalom (2002) calls action techniques "accelerating devices" and notes their usefulness in therapy.

## Family Therapy

Blatner (1994a) has described a number of applications of psychodramatic methods in working with families. One of these techniques, "family sculpture," expresses perceived relationships in concrete form and has been used extensively, often by those who never realized its origins in psychodrama. Other action techniques may be added to family sculpture work to make it even more effective. In working with couples, a wide range of other techniques may catalyze the process (Hayden-Seman, 1998).

## Therapeutic Milieu

This approach was an important aspect of psychiatric hospital treatment in the later twentieth century, and it became part of many residential treatment center approaches. It involves a quasi-group therapy approach and is used in outdoor-life challenge programs and many other settings. The interactions and frictions accompanying the events of everyday life in such settings (e.g., flagging morale and acting-out behaviors) can be immediately addressed using the technique of replay, followed by exploration of alternative responses.

## The Treatment of Addictions

A number of recognized leaders in *addictionology,* a new and growing subfield in the last 25 years, use psychodramatic methods to support a more comprehensive approach to recovery (Dayton, 2000). The *12-Step* methods that were developed first in the treatment of alcoholism, then in the treatment of drug abuse and many other types of addictions, codependencies, and related problems, all draw on the healing function of a "higher power" and use group dynamics and personal therapy–like interventions to reinforce this reorientation.

## Trauma

The treatment of post-traumatic stress disorders has become increasingly important because of international events in the past decade. Because many of those who suffer from post-traumatic stress disorders (PTSD) also tend to abuse drugs to alleviate their symptoms, the treatment of addictions and the treatment of PTSD overlap somewhat. Therapists who work with Vietnam veterans, victims of ethnic strife, those who were physically and sexually abused in their childhood, and those who have had other kinds of trauma have noted that these individuals share a number of common dynamics that resist verbal approaches. Psychodrama has been one of the more powerful approaches used with traumatized patients; combined with other methods, it effectively addresses the multilayered and often comorbid dimensions of PTSD. Kellermann and Hudgins (2000) published an anthology of psychodramatic approaches to trauma, and Kate Hudgins (2002) has gone further and developed ideas and techniques that build on psychodrama, adding her own original contributions. Hudgins's "Therapeutic Spiral Model" combines the provision of an orienting framework, a team approach, and other techniques to make it possible for people suffering from PTSD to benefit from psychodrama without being retraumatized in the process. As demonstrated by Hudgins's work, the powerful techniques of psychodrama can be adjusted to the tolerance levels of the client, and help the patient not only heal but become stronger and more resilient in the face of future stresses. Again, some of these techniques can be adopted and used by nonpsychodramatists, but a great deal of professional judgment is required. Working with trauma is the group psychotherapeutic equivalent of open-heart surgery—it is complicated and potentially dangerous.

## Grief Work

This process often is a component of working with trauma, and at other times stands on its own. Parents of children with life-threatening illnesses, caregivers to relatives with Alzheimer's disease, and others in situations in which loss is a significant part of the distress may be helped by an experiential approach (Blatner, 2000b).

## Cross-Cultural Dynamics

Psychodrama is used internationally and applied in many kinds of settings, with slight modifications of style as needed for the types of people attending. The quality of warming-up is different for people who are naturally more expressive, such as those who live in Latin America. In Japan, once the process has started, the subtle group influence leads to a more prolonged sharing. People who are reluctant to talk about their own problems may warm up gradually by engaging in enactments about figures in fairy tales or some other common cultural story.

## Beyond the Clinical Context

As a group of tools for exploring both individual and social psychological dynamics, psychodramatic methods can be applied for many purposes aside from therapy—in self-help groups, personal development groups, business and industry, community building, education, religious education and spiritual retreats, and just for recreation. For many of these purposes, Moreno created a modified form of psychodrama, "sociodrama," which addresses general role definitions and intergroup tensions, and which operates in a less individual-centered fashion. Indeed, sociodrama may have more of a socially constructive impact than psychodrama, just as public health measures often prevent more illness than doctors ever treat (Blatner, 1995; Sternberg & Garcia, 2000).

## Evaluation

There is an extensive literature that documents the use of psychodrama, and over 4,800 articles, books, or chapters in books have been written about the technique (Sacks, Bilaniuk, & Gendron, 2003). This continuing—indeed, growing—use of psychodramatic approaches offers compelling face validity, suggesting thousands of therapists have found these methods efficacious and useful. Nevertheless, a number of therapists and psychotherapy researchers continue to insist on evidence-based support for the effectiveness of this method. However, psychodrama, because of its multifaceted nature, does not constitute a method that can be described in a manual-like format, nor can sessions be replicated—thus, *ipso facto,* it is resistant to traditional "hard science" modes of evaluation. Instead, its work may be appreciated more in terms of the case-review approach—a well-established mode adapted for the complexity of human affairs. (A number of writers have noted the difference between the "nomothetic," statistical approach that has come to dominate academic journals and the more humanistic, "idiographic," or case-study approach.) Many question the trend for demanding evidence that can only be produced by a certain kind of research that by definition requires a limited scope. The "lens" of practical scientific technology should not limit the vision of inquiry. Nevertheless, the approach does have a number of ways of evaluating its effectiveness in any given situation.

A recent report by Dougherty (2002) notes that patients on a special psychiatric unit for the treatment of post-traumatic stress disorder included psychodrama as one of the most highly rated approaches

A scholarly meta-analysis of research on psychodrama was recently conducted by Kipper and Ritchie (2003). This analysis of 25 experimentally designed studies documented an improvement effect similar to or better than that commonly reported for group psychotherapy. The techniques of role reversal and doubling emerged as the most effective interventions. Because there are many other psychodramatic methods, and they operate in combination with other approaches, it is difficult to tease out the effect of any particular technique. As stated earlier, these methods are best thought of as being facilitating agents for other psychotherapy methods. Some psychodramatic methods have already been incorporated into various psychotherapies; still others may similarly and rationally be more fully applied.

## Treatment

Examination of the major psychodramatic techniques suggests how these approaches may be used in treatment. After warming-up clients and establishing the therapeutic contract, scores of techniques are available. Most therapists benefit from using some of the following techniques to amplify the effectiveness of the therapeutic process.

### Enactment

A typical psychodramatic instruction is "Don't tell us, show us." With this phrase, the patient is encouraged to plunge into the situation at a more intense and committed level of experience, acting "as if" instead of talking "about." "Show us what happened with your family"; "Show us the conflict you're having within yourself"; "Show us what you'd like to be doing in 10 years." Scenes from the past, present, or future may be set up, and this kind of concretizing of issues has the benefit of cutting through defensive tendencies toward vagueness and circumstantiality.

### Cut the Action

In the midst of the process, the director might call "cut," using the same term as someone directing a movie. Upon hearing this command, the protagonist and auxiliaries (or group members, if this technique is used to evaluate group dynamics apart from any explicit enactment in the stage area) are to pause and listen, awaiting the next direction—perhaps an invitation to reflect on what was just said or a recommendation to try some other technique to heighten awareness.

## Replay

The behavior just enacted is consciously repeated, thus bringing it into sharper awareness and offering the opportunity to do it differently. Each time an action is *consciously* repeated, it becomes a bit less dominated by automatic thinking. Moreno said, "Every second time is a liberation from the first." When clients are given a chance to replay their behavior, they learn that the environment is supportive and exploratory, and they learn that saying "the wrong thing" does not necessarily result in an irreversible mistake.

## Asides

This technique is used in old-time melodramas, when the villain turns to the audience, putting a hand beside his mouth, and says something like, "Little does she know that I have taken the spark plugs out of John Strongheart's car!" It's a dramatic device, a variation of what in cinema or television is the "voiceover," a way to disclose to the audience what would not ordinarily be known to the others in the scene.

## The Mirror

When the mirror technique is used, the client steps out of the scene and an auxiliary replays how the client-protagonist was just behaving. The mirror functions like video playback without the technology. The client can stand aside and observe how his style of reacting may have been counterproductive or perhaps learn that his reaction had been entirely satisfactory. (A different use of the term "mirror" in reference to psychoanalytic self psychology refers to the reflecting role of the parent.)

## Nonverbal Communications

The mirror technique also serves to bring into sharper focus the importance of nonverbal communications. Nonverbal behaviors can also serve as inner cues that subtly reinforce various attitudes. Pulling back one's shoulders, thrusting the jaw a bit forward, and making direct eye contact, for example, can shift the whole tone of an interaction, and the interpretation of the event (Blatner, 2002).

## Multiple Parts of Self

Here the client names the different inner roles, brings them to the stage, has each one stand or sit in a different chair, and then in turn, presents the concerns of each role. One way to reframe the experience of confusion is to view it as a situation in which many roles are arguing, but interrupting each other so loudly (inside) that one can't hear one's own thoughts. This technique teases these various aspects of self out and makes them take turns. The choosing self cooperates with the director to interview, mediate, and negotiate compromises, instead of allowing one role to dominate and repress all the others. This and other techniques may be modified so that they are used mainly in imagination, especially for clients who are reluctant to get out of their chairs. Alternately, they may be used just with one other empty chair.

## The Empty Chair

The client imagines someone sitting across from him in an empty chair. The "other" might be a family member or friend with whom the client needs to encounter, or it could be the client when he was younger or older; an inner role or role component, such as his "inner child," a dream figure, or a spiritual entity.

## Role Reversal

Role reversal invites the client to relinquish her egocentricity for a time and imagine what it's like to be in the role of another person. This technique is an invitation to cultivate empathy, and there is inherent value in the expectation that a patient will learn and exercise this skill. If the other person is not present, there is still an opportunity to imagine what it is like to look at the world from a different frame of reference. In the early parts of the process, what emerges first is simply the client's projections, but even this process helps people become aware of their biases and subconscious assumptions.

The art of role reversal lies in the therapist-director's ability to gently warm the protagonist up to the experience of the other's role, through interviewing the protagonist as if he or she were the other person. This technique may be used to portray the behavior of that other person, with an emphasis on such components as voice tone, pacing, intensity, posture, facial expression, and gesture. At a deeper level, role reversal can be used to help patients understand the feelings or attitudes of the other people in their lives.

It's helpful for clients to learn to imagine what it might be like to be the other person, even if the client doesn't get out of his or her chair. Practicing this is the best way to develop empathy. The key is to think more like an actor who's trying to get the feel of a character during rehearsal, and less like a student who has read a lot about psychology. In this sense, imagining "what's it like to be" embodies the ideals of phenomenology and existential psychotherapy.

## The Double

An auxiliary plays the role of the protagonist's inner self, helping to express and clarify one's unspoken thoughts. The double usually plays a supportive role for the protagonist; however, once a sense of alliance is developed between the two, the director may coach the double to include some mild provocation or confrontation to facilitate the clarification process. The double technique offers interpretation phrased in terms of "I messages" and in words consistent with the patient's self-system. The protagonist is explicitly instructed to correct any statements by the double that feel inaccurate. This creates a mutuality in which the double helps the protagonist express in an enactment what might never be spoken in the course of an ordinary exchange (Leveton, 2001).

## Surplus Reality

This is Moreno's term for that dimension of psychological experience that transcends the boundaries of physical reality by giving more respect to the potentials of fantasy and imagination. Psychologically, people can and do have relationships with others who are deceased, children who have never been born, God, hallucinatory figures, religious personages, and the like. These are often as important in a patient's psychodynamics as relations with actual people. In psychodrama, encounters with these significant psychological figures can be externalized and enacted. In this sense, as Moreno noted, psychodrama is the "theater of truth," because the full truth of a person often encompasses not only what has actually happened, but, equally importantly, what has never happened and perhaps could never happen in reality.

Surplus reality can be utilized in several ways: One example is the technique of *act fulfillment,* in which the protagonist is helped to experience a corrective emotional experience. Many patients suffer from acute or chronic trauma, which left them with residual feelings of powerlessness, shame, and a secret sense that "this is the way life has to be." Reenactment of the traumatic situation breaks through layers of denial, allowing for a catharsis of "owning" the experience, replaying the scene with a more satisfactory conclusion may help heal the client. The victim of abuse, for example, is helped to protest, to become empowered to seek effective protection, and then, using the technique of "the reformed auxiliary," is given a chance to create a more benign relationship with the aggressor.

Moreno actively used surplus reality as a vital resource in healing. He once said to Freud, "You *analyze* people's dreams. I try to give them the *courage to dream again.*" (Moreno, 1946). In this sense, psychodrama offers patients an opportunity to envision life with more faith, to reinvest emotionally in the future. (Clients who are demoralized frequently repress their hopes for a pleasant future as much as they repress desires/thoughts in the present and the past.) Moreno developed the *future projection technique* as a way to encourage patients to become more explicit in their goal-setting. It involves portraying scenes that are hoped for or anticipated. A variation of this is *role training,* a type of behavioral rehearsal, used to help a patient prepare for an event such as a date, an employment interview, or an encounter with a relative. Using coaching, modeling, videotaped or verbal feedback, and other techniques, the patient repeats the enactment until satisfactory options are developed.

## Encounter

People often talk about others and their feelings, but a great deal of insight and experiential learning can come from the experience of facing and speaking to the imagined other directly. "Tell them, not us," the director says. Dialogues in the present moment are experienced more vividly. Encounters between different roles or parts of the client's own psyche can be equally productive. This is especially helpful for clients who complain of confusion. Often this experience can be productively reframed as a conflict in which the different parts of themselves interrupt each other too much. By externalizing internal dialogues and separating voices, the client can better appreciate competing internal demands. Sometimes a client can play both parts in an encounter, using the technique of *monodrama,* employing an empty chair as the locus of his or her imagined other.

## Concretization

Psychodrama can portray even abstract ideas in more concrete form, so that, for example, if a protagonist complains of feeling "torn apart," the director might have two auxiliaries come up and each one pull on one of the protagonist's arms. These kinesthetic cues often help clients get in touch with the deeper feelings involved. Concretization also cuts through clients' tendencies to avoid their feelings by talking about them, explaining, and using generalities as a defensive maneuver.

Props of various kinds also help to express feelings, alternative identities, and attitudes—pieces of fabric are especially useful in this regard. Chairs, cloth dolls, hand puppets, and other elements also are evocative.

Even if a therapist doesn't use actual physical enactment, it can be helpful to redirect the client toward more specific images. For example, in doing grief work, the memories brought out should be linked to time, space, and the details in the event. Often these details are emotionally charged, and a single word spoken, a gesture, the color of a shawl, or the smell of the kitchen can be tremendously powerful. Konstantin Stanislavsky, the dramatic producer and trainer of actors, wrote and spoke of sense memory, and encouraged actors to use these specific details in their overall construction of their roles. There are scores of other techniques used in psychodrama that can be modified and adapted for use with diverse populations and in a variety of contexts. However, all psychodramatic approaches aim to involve patients in their ability to imagine, think, and behave in an *as-if* context and to engage in dramatic play as a resource for insight, behavioral practice, the expansion of consciousness, and healing.

# CASE EXAMPLE

## Background

Carl was a 50-year-old married engineer who came for therapy because of symptoms of low-grade depression. Tina, the therapist, began the evaluation by reviewing Carl's symptoms, which included insomnia, lack of interest in sex, irritability, and a feeling of vague sadness and emptiness in his life. In the first session, Tina asked about Carl's general health and encouraged him to make an appointment soon with his family physician to rule out possible organic causes of his symptoms.

One technique that tends to develop a treatment alliance is that of using pencil and paper to diagram the client's social network, because an exploration of relationships communicates a concern for feelings more than many other questionnaire-style approaches. Tina had Carl draw a kind of map of himself in relationship with others. She noted the number of people, their sex (indicated by little circles for females or triangles for males), how distant or close they were placed compared to the figure for Carl himself, and what he said about the quality of the relationship. Tina asked what he thought the others felt about him, as well as asking how he felt toward them, keeping in mind that a client's attributions of intentions and feelings to those around him or her are often important reflections of the client's own state of mind.

Two relationships were especially problematic for Carl: He had a sense of growing apart from his wife, and also from his only child, Stu. Carl agreed to have his wife join him in an evaluation session, and she complained about his avoidance of emotional connections. Carl also related a history of relative shallowness of emotion shown by his parents when he was growing up. Finally, Tina found a formulation that Carl felt was helpful: Carl's depression was most likely due to a lack of social skills, and this diminished his sense of belonging. Because Carl was able to express his yearning for more closeness, Tina suggested that he join an ongoing therapy group that addressed the dynamics of interpersonal relationships. Over the next year, Carl was able to discover the patterns of avoidance that led to his alienation, and psychodramatic methods served as catalysts for his healing.

## Treatment

In addition to Tina as the group therapist, and Carl, there were six other group members: Al, Ben, Deb, Eric, Fay, and Gail. Of course, their issues were also discussed, but the following vignettes focus on how psychodramatic methods were useful in Carl's treatment, in catalyzing insight and helping Carl learn new strategies. He is the "protagonist" in the following vignettes and Tina, the group therapist, is using the psychodramatic techniques as facilitating devices.

### Doubling

Shortly after joining the group, Carl finds himself the object of one member's anger.

Ben:    I think you don't care about what's happening here. You just sit there and look smug while we spill our guts out!

Carl:    I just don't have anything to say.

Ben:    Then why the hell are you here?
        (*Carl starts to stammer, his face reddens, and he looks down at the floor.*)

Tina:    When friction comes up in a group, nobody has to be left without support. I don't believe in putting people on the "hot seat." So, who in the group can imagine what it's like right now to be in Carl's shoes? You don't have to agree with him, but this is an opportunity to learn empathy.

Deb:        (*Raises hand*) I think I do.
Tina:       Okay, come and sit in this chair next to Carl. As Carl's double, will you tell us what you think Carl may be feeling, but is not able to say? (*Deb nods.*)

[Explanation of role notation: In psychodrama people can assume various roles; thus if Ben plays the role of Carl, we indicate this as Ben-Carl.]

Tina:       Carl, you can correct anything that Deb says that isn't accurate.
Carl:       (*Nods. To Deb*) Go ahead.
Deb-Carl:   If I were Carl I'd want . . .
Tina:       As a double you *are* Carl, so say, "I want to . . ."
Deb-Carl:   (*Warms up again*) I want to jump up and scream at everyone. I'm depressed. I don't know why the hell I'm depressed. You guys are making me feel like shit!
            (*Carl sits with head down and nods, then glances at Deb with weak smile. Tina puts her hand on Carl's shoulder.*)
Carl:       (*Mumbles*) It hurts.
Ben:        I hurt, too, dammit!
Fay:        (*Gently*) Carl, we're all hurting, but at least we talk about it.
Tina:       Sometimes it's really hard to find the words, particularly if they are deep inside you. So that's how we can help each other talk. Moreno said, in group therapy, everyone is a healer to the others.


## The Mirror

In the next session, Carl is accused of being "intimidating."

Carl:       Now, what the hell does *that* mean? Intimidating?
Gail:       (*Fumbling to explain*) I don't know . . . you just make me feel . . .
Tina:       Wait, let's do the mirror technique. (*Stands up and addresses Carl, who becomes the protagonist.*) Carl, come stand beside me and we'll watch as if it's a video replay. Could someone play how Carl was responding to Gail? (*Eric raises his hand.*) Carl, could Eric be you and replay that last interaction with Gail?
Carl:       Yes. (*Eric-Carl sits in Carl's chair and assumes a glowering look.*)
Tina:       Eric, please repeat Carl's last line, "What the hell does that mean?"
Eric-Carl:  What the hell does that mean?
Tina:       (*To the group*) Is Eric playing Carl's behavior accurately or exaggerating it?
Group:      That's Carl. Yep. That's the way he looks.
Tina:       (*To Carl*) What do you see on "Carl's" face? (*Pointing to Eric-Carl*).
Carl:       He looks mean.
Tina:       Right. That's a nonverbal communication. It's not what you say but maybe the look on your face.
Carl:       That's just the way I look.
Tina:       No, that's just a habitual facial expression, and people can change their habits.


## Coaching

The following is a continuing of the psychodramatic exploration just described.

Tina:       Let's analyze, break down, this facial communication. Eric, will you put on that face again?
Eric-Carl:  Sure! (*Having fun with this role, he exaggerates a mean look.*)

| | |
|---|---|
| Tina: | Notice the dropped head, and how he looks out from under his eyebrows. |
| Carl: | (*Trying to see what the therapist is getting at*) Yeah . . . So? |
| Tina: | (*To Eric-Carl*) Lift your head slightly up to face straight ahead. It's only a little change. Good. Now go back down. |
| Carl: | I don't frown that way. |
| Gail: | He's right, it's just the angle of the eyes. |
| Tina: | Okay, Eric, relax your face out of the frown, but keep the angle of the eyes. (*To group*) Is that closer? |
| Group: | Yes. |
| Tina: | Thanks, Eric. Now let's have Carl come back to his chair and assume the face. Try saying, "What the hell do you mean I'm intimidating?" but raise your face so the angle of your eyes is straight on. |
| Carl: | (*With face level, to Gail in the other chair*) What the hell do you mean I'm intimidating? |
| Gail: | (*Speechless for a moment, then laughs*) Well, now you're not! (*Carl and group laugh.*) |

## Role Reversal

A few sessions later, several group members are working on their relationships with their adult children. Carl has by now become comfortable bringing up an issue with his own son, Stu.

| | |
|---|---|
| Carl: | Boy, if I could get my son to say two words about his work, I'd already be happy. |
| Tina: | Carl, would you like to have an encounter with your son? |
| Carl: | Hell, yes. |
| Tina: | Pick someone to be your son. What's his name, again? |
| Carl: | Stu. Al, would you be Stu? |
| Tina: | Al, come on up here. (*To Carl*) Where does this encounter happen? |
| Carl: | My living room. |
| Tina: | Okay, where are you? |
| Carl: | I'm in my chair. |
| Tina: | Pull the chair up into where it would be in the room. (*Walking around with Carl*) Now where's Stu? |
| Carl: | Over here on the couch. |
| Tina: | (*To the group*) Let's put several chairs together for the couch. Now, Carl, help Al to play his role as Stu by coming here and showing how Stu is positioned on the couch. (*Carl lies down on the chairs.*) |
| Tina: | Al, you got it? Carl, go back to your chair. Al is "Stu." Let's begin the action. |
| Carl: | So, how's your work going? |
| Al-Stu: | 'Bout the same. |
| Carl: | Any more layoffs? |
| Al-Stu: | A couple. |
| Carl: | Well, hell, is it gettin' close to you or not? |
| Al-Stu: | Get off my case, willya! |
| Carl: | (*Drops out of role, turns to Tina*) That's what happens. |
| Tina: | (*To group*) What do you see going on here? |
| Gail: | He's using that intimidating face again. |
| Tina: | Carl, this is one of those stressful situations in which you tend to revert to dropping your head a little, so that's one thing you can change. |
| Carl: | Okay, but what does he want from me? |

| Tina: | That's a good question. Let's find out by using role reversal. Come over here and be Stu on the couch. Al, you stand behind these chairs and listen. Carl, you're Stu, and I'll warm you up by asking you some questions. |
|---|---|
| Tina: | So, you and your dad are at an impasse. Just between you and me, Stu, and your dad doesn't have to hear this, what is going on at work? |
| Carl-Stu: | Some tough times. It's a dotcom business. |
| Tina: | What does that mean? |
| Carl-Stu: | Downsizing. I'm not fired yet, but I've had to do the work of some of the guys who were. |
| Tina: | If I were you I'd be a little scared. |
| Carl-Stu: | Yeah, it's gettin' too close to home. |
| Tina: | Would you like to talk with your dad about this? |
| Carl-Stu: | He wouldn't understand. He's a success. He went to work for one company and he's been there for 30 years. He doesn't know about this start-up business. |
| Tina: | If he could admit that, would that open things up a bit between you? |
| Carl-Stu: | Maybe, 'cause he always wants to tell me how I should come to work for his company. |
| Tina: | But I guess you are part of a different generation? |
| Carl-Stu: | Oh, yeah, I'm not going to be married to one company all my life. |
| Tina: | So if you could tell him about the new business world without his trying to get you to come to work with him, do you think you would want to tell him things? |
| Carl-Stu: | Probably so. |
| Tina: | Come out of the action, now. Become yourself. Carl, how is this sounding to you? |
| Carl: | This is already more than Stu has said to me in a year. |
| Tina: | How does it feel? |
| Carl: | Well . . . It's almost a relationship. That's what I want with him. Just talking. |

## Future Projection

[Continuing the interaction from the previous section.]

| Tina: | Now that we're getting clearer about what is important to have happen with your son, let's move on and rehearse how it might go successfully in the future. This next scene is like the old way of talking, at least at the beginning, but Carl, you can use the insight from role reversing to try something new. Al, will you come around, get on the couch, and you're Stu again. Carl, this time you can try again, and it will be a different approach. You won't be frowning. (*Carl nods in agreement.*) And because you've empathized with your son through role reversal, you maybe have a hint to what might work between you. So, this is the scene that could happen in the future. And Al-Stu, your line, instead of saying "Get off my case," is to tell the truth, say instead, "They've just added another guy's workload to mine." Go. |
|---|---|
| Al-Stu: | They've just added another guy's workload to mine. |
| Tina: | (*Turns to Carl*) Okay, and your response . . . |
| Carl: | (*Turns to Tina, dropping out of the role*) I want to tell him to get out of the business. (*Takes a deep breath, then turns back to Al-Stu*) Shit. What are you going to do? |
| Al-Stu: | Ride it out as long as I can. |
| Carl: | (*Turns to Tina in exasperation*) I gotta tell him to get out while he can. |

| | |
|---|---|
| Tina: | (*Moves into the coach role*) Try saying, "Tell me more" and don't frown. |
| Carl: | (*Relaxes face*) Tell me more. |
| Al-Stu: | Well, I've got to work longer hours and appear to be able to handle it all. |
| Carl: | How are you going to do that? |
| Al-Stu: | At least I'm not married. I'll work all weekend. |
| Carl: | Sure is a lot harder than when I was your age. |
| Al-Stu: | Yeah, I guess 8 to 5 would be pretty easy right now. But this company could really take off. |
| Carl: | You know, I'm proud you work so hard for something you like. It shows character. |
| Tina: | Change parts. (*Al goes to Carl's chair, and Carl goes to the couch and takes the role of Stu.*) |
| Tina: | (*To Al-Carl*) Give him that last line. |
| Al-Carl: | I'm proud of your working so hard. You've got character. |
| Carl-Stu: | (*Pauses, lets it in*) Seems natural to work hard. I guess I got it from you. |

## *Follow-Up*

Over the next year, Carl practiced these lessons and, in acquiring a broader repertoire of skills in self-awareness, communications, and problem-solving, he was reinforced not only by his therapy group, but also by his wife and son, with whom he began to experience more rewarding interactions. His symptoms of depression were relieved as he felt more competent and alive.

## SUMMARY

Classical psychodrama requires extra training, but many psychodramatic methods and principles can be easily integrated into individual, family, and group psychotherapy. Simply using the dramaturgical metaphor, talking about problems in terms of the roles being played and identifying how they are defined and renegotiated, makes therapy a more accessible process for most clients, and it's also a practical language for psychotherapists and counselors of various types. In addition, the skills of role taking, role shifting, and other component activities develop clients' overall mental flexibility and capacity for empathy. Clients become more resilient and can apply their skills in everyday life. Psychodrama more systematically applies the natural dual-level operating ability to shift between involvement in role (as actor) and then the observing and negotiating, adjusting, investigating, and executive functions of the "meta-role" position (as director-playwright). As a result, the individual can bring more vitality, consciousness, and creativity to life.

The field of psychotherapy continues to grow by incorporating new approaches. Furthermore, the full potential of some of the oldest approaches has only begun to be recognized and utilized—especially hypnosis, imagery, body work, and spirituality. Psychopharmacology also can be used as an important adjunct to therapy, when used with good judgment and not treated as a panacea. Psychodrama has been used in conjunction with all of these treatments and is itself an early example of eclectic therapy. Controversies will continue and new dialectical processes will unfold—this is a vital part of the creative evolution of our art and practice.

Whether or not role dynamics is accepted as a user-friendly *lingua franca* for this endeavor, it at least stands as a challenge for other candidates. Developing a language that clients can easily understand is critical to the field's progress. Similarly, the values of the other elements of psychodrama's associated personality theory and therapy offer significant additions to our thinking about psychology.

Psychodrama offers an experiential method for learning how to integrate the best insights of psychology into life. There's a mental flexibility that comes with the ability to take roles, shift roles, and more consciously create ongoing role relationships. Once people learn to recognize and respond to a greater range of possibilities, they evolve to a new type and level of consciousness. It was the vision of this potential that motivated Moreno to say at the beginning of *Who Shall Survive?* "A truly therapeutic procedure should have as its objective nothing less than the whole of mankind."

# ANNOTATED BIBLIOGRAPHY

Blatner, A. (1996). *Acting-in: Practical applications of psychodramatic methods* (3rd ed.). New York: Springer.
This is the easiest-to-read introduction to psychodrama. The book, which has extensive references, is aimed at the beginning student, but it is also useful for anyone wanting to learn psychodrama. This book provides the "nuts-and-bolts" instructions not found in Moreno's books. It also addresses common pitfalls, areas of application, and training as well as technique. Because of its clarity, *Acting-in* has been revised and updated twice and translated into many languages. The subtitle emphasizes the idea that the methods themselves can be applied, and that one need not feel that only classical psychodramas may be conducted. This fits with the point, repeatedly made in this chapter, that these approaches are meant to be integrated with other methods in an eclectic practice.

Blatner, A. (2000). *Foundations of psychodrama: History, theory, and practice* (Revised 4th ed.). New York: Springer.
This book explains how and why psychodramatic methods are effective in psychotherapy. Many of the principles discussed are applicable in therapy even if the reader doesn't use action techniques. Perspectives on psychological theory are backed up by chapters on philosophy. The book addresses psychodrama's history, the dynamics of catharsis, and the place of skill-building, self-expression, and other general principles in treatment. The book contains many references and an extensive bibliography.

Blatner, A., & Blatner, A. R. (1997). *The art of play: Helping adults reclaim imagination and spontaneity* (Revised 2nd ed.). New York: Brunner-Routledge/Taylor & Francis.
This book includes the best introduction to role taking, explaining how to develop the capacity to move into and among different roles—a basic skill for not only psychodramatic work but for empathy itself. The book also explores the need for play, imaginativeness,

and spontaneity in life and considers the cultural factors that inhibit these elements, thus addressing a generally underestimated if not overlooked but highly relevant factor in psychology. An actual method for practicing role taking is presented along with the idea that these activities constitute a valid form of recreation. Finally, a number of areas of application are noted, including an especially important chapter on using these approaches in education.

Dayton, T. (2004). *The living stage: A step by step guide to psychodrama, sociometry and group psychotherapy.* Deerfield Beach, FL: Health Communications.
This user-friendly guide decodes the experiential process of psychodrama. The middle parts emphasize applications in working with trauma, grief, anger, and other special issues. The third part offers a psychoeducational approach to treating addictions. This book includes many warm-up techniques and sociometric procedures.

Fox, J. (Ed.). (1987). *The essential Moreno: Writings on psychodrama, group method, and spontaneity, by J. L. Moreno.* New York: Springer.
This book offers a selection of Moreno's writings, including some early, hard-to-find articles from his journals as well as his books. These selections will provide a sense of his writing style and the scope of his interests, as well as a number of transcripts of sessions. A chronology and supplementary bibliography enhance the value of this volume.

Leveton, E. (2001). *A clinician's guide to psychodrama.* New York: Springer.
This little book introduces the subject nicely and elaborates on a number of techniques, such as doubling, the magic shop, and the use of masks. It is rich in other specific suggestions for using the various techniques and addresses the important problem of dealing with resistance.

# CASE READINGS

Blatner, A. (1999). Psychodrama. In D. Wiener (Ed.), *Beyond talk therapy* (pp. 125–143). Washington, DC: American Psychological Association.

Psychodramatic methods are used to help a client work out inner conflicts and do some grief work.

Blatner, A. (2001). Psychodrama. In R. J. Corsini (Ed.), *Handbook of innovative therapy* (2nd ed., pp. 535–545). New York: Wiley.

Includes an example of an extended psychodramatic work with a woman who is exploring the roots of her timidness, and illustrates the "reformed auxiliary" technique used to provide a corrective emotional experience.

Blatner, A. (2003). Psychodrama. In C. E. Schaefer (Ed.), *Play therapy with adults* (pp. 34–61). Hoboken, NJ: John Wiley & Sons.

Presents a client in psychodramatic group therapy who discovers the roots of her lack of self-assertion.

Karp, M., Holmes, P., & Bradshaw-Tauvon, K. (Eds.). (1998). *Handbook of psychodrama.* London: Routledge–Taylor & Francis.

This anthology is rich in brief vignettes that illustrate many of the phases and aspects of psychodrama. The authors, who are mainly British, have all been trained in classical psychodrama by the first editor.

Oxford, L. K., & Wiener, D. J. (2003). Rescripting family dramas using psychodramatic methods. In D. J. Wiener & L. K. Oxford (Eds.), *Action therapy with families and groups* (pp. 45–74). Washington, DC: American Psychological Association. [Reprinted in D. Wedding & R. J. Corsini (Eds.). (2005). *Case studies in psychotherapy.* Belmont, CA: Wadsworth.]

This chapter shows how action methods can be integrated with a narrative-constructivist approach in family therapy, with an extended example.

# REFERENCES

Bannister, A. (1997). *The healing drama: Psychodrama and dramatherapy with abused children.* London: Free Association Books.

Blatner, A. (1994a). Psychodramatic methods in family therapy. In C. E. Schaefer & L. J. Carey (Eds.), *Family play therapy* (pp. 235–246). Northvale, NJ: Jason Aronson.

Blatner, A. (1994b). Tele: The dynamics of interpersonal preference. In P. Holmes, M. Karp, & M. Watson (Eds.), *Psychodrama since Moreno: Innovations in theory and practice* (pp. 281–300). London: Routledge.

Blatner, A. (1995). Drama in education as mental hygiene: A child psychiatrist's perspective. *Youth Theatre Journal, 9,* 92–96.

Blatner, A. (1996). *Acting-in: Practical applications of psychodramatic methods* (3rd ed.). Springer.

Blatner, A. (2000a). *Foundations of psychodrama: History, theory, and practice* (4th ed.). New York: Springer.

Blatner, A. (2000b). Psychodramatic methods for facilitating bereavement. In P. F. Kellermann & M. K. Hudgins (Eds.). *Psychodrama with trauma survivors: Acting out your pain* (pp. 42–51). London: Jessica Kingsley–Taylor & Francis.

Blatner, A. (2002). Nonverbal communications. Retrieved from: http://www.blatner.com/adam/papers.html

Blatner, A. (2003). Applications in everyday life. In J. Gershoni (Ed.), *Psychodrama in the 21st century* (pp. 103–115). New York: Springer.

Blatner, A., & Blatner, A. (1997). *The art of play: Helping adults reclaim imagination and spontaneity* (Revised 2nd ed.). New York: Brunner/Routledge–Taylor & Francis.

Corey, G. (2004). Psychodrama. In *Theory and practice of group counseling* (6th ed., pp. 204–237). Belmont, CA: Brooks/Cole.

Dayton, T. (2000). *Trauma and addiction: Ending the cycle of pain through emotional literacy.* Deerfield Beach, FL: Health Communications.

Dougherty, M. J. (2002). Client satisfaction survey of inpatient trauma and dissociative disorders program. *Journal of Trauma & Dissociation, 3,* 91–103.

Farmer, C. (1995). *Psychodrama and systemic therapy.* London: Karnac Books.

Fox, J. (Ed.). (1987). *The essential Moreno: Writings on psychodrama, group method, and spontaneity by J. L. Moreno.* New York: Springer.

Gass, M. (1997). *Rebuilding therapy: Overcoming the past for a more effective future.* Westport, CT: Praeger.

Hare, A. P., & Hare, J. R. (1996). *J. L. Moreno.* London: Sage.

Hayden-Seman, J. (1998). *Action modality couples therapy: Using psychodramatic techniques in helping troubled relationships.* Dunmore, PA: Jason Aronson.

Hoey, B. (1997). *Who calls the tune? A psychodramatic approach to child therapy.* New York: Routledge–Taylor & Francis.

Hudgins, M. K. (2002). *Experiential treatment for PTSD: The therapeutic spiral model.* New York: Springer.

Johnson, D. R. (2000). History of drama therapy. In P. Lewis & D. R. Johnson (Eds.), *Current approaches in drama therapy* (pp. 5–15). Springfield, IL: Charles C. Thomas.

Kellermann, P. F. (1992). *Focus on psychodrama: The therapeutic aspects of psychodrama.* London: Jessica Kingsley–Taylor & Francis.

Kellermann, P. F., & Hudgins, M. K. (Eds.). (2000). *Psychodrama with trauma survivors: Acting out your pain.* London: Jessica Kingsley.

Kipper, D. A. (1986). *Psychotherapy through clinical role playing.* New York: Brunner/Routledge–Taylor & Francis.

Kipper, D. A. (2001). Surplus reality and the experiential reintegration model in psychodrama. *International Journal of Action Methods: Psychodrama, Skill Training and Role Playing, 53,* 137–152.

Kipper, D. A., & Ritchie, T. D. (2003). The effectiveness of psychodramatic techniques: A meta-analysis.

*Group Dynamics: Theory Research and Practice, 7*(1), 13–25.

Leveton, E. (2001). *A clinician's guide to psychodrama* (3rd ed.). New York: Springer.

Marineau, R. F. (1989). *Jacob Levy Moreno, 1889–1974. (A biography).* London: Routledge.

Moreno, J. J. (1999). *Acting your inner music: Music therapy & psychodrama.* St. Louis: MMB Music.

Moreno, J. L. (1931). *Group method and group psychotherapy* (Sociometric Monograph No. 5). Beacon, NY: Beacon House.

Moreno, J. L. (1934). *Who shall survive? A new approach to the problem of human interrelations.* Washington, DC: Nervous & Mental Disease Publishing.

Moreno, J. L. (1946–1969). *Psychodrama* (3 vols; last two with Z. T. Moreno). Beacon, NY: Beacon House.

Moreno, J. L. (1971). *The words of the Father.* Beacon, NY: Beacon House.

Moreno, Z. T., Blomkvist, L. D., & Rützel, T. (2000). *Psychodrama, surplus reality, and the art of healing.* London: Routledge–Taylor & Francis.

Pesso, A. (1997). Pesso System/Psychomotor Therapy. In C. Caldwell (Ed.), *Getting in touch: A guide to body-centered therapies* (pp. 117–152). Wheaton, IL: Theosophical Publishing House.

Raimundo, C. (2002). *Relationship capital: True success through coaching and managing relationships in business and life.* Australia: Pearson Education.

Røine, E. (1997). *Psychodrama: Group psychotherapy as experimental theatre.* London: Jessica Kingsley–Taylor & Francis.

Sacks, J. M., Bilaniuk, M., & Gendron, J. M. (2003 June 3). *Bibliography of psychodrama: Inception to date.* Retrieved from http://asgpp.org/02ref/index.htm.

Scategni, W. (2002). *Psychodrama, group processes and dreams: Archetypal images of individuation.* (Translated from Italian). New York: Brunner-Routledge/ Taylor & Francis.

Sternberg, P., & Garcia, A. (2000). *Sociodrama: Who's in your shoes?* (2nd ed.). Westport, CT: Greenwood.

Tomasulo, D. J. (1998). *Action methods in group psychotherapy: Practical aspects.* Philadelphia: Accelerated Development.

Verhofstadt-Denève, L. (1999). *Theory and practice of action and drama techniques: Developmental psychotherapy from an existential-dialectical viewpoint.* London : Jessica Kingsley–Taylor & Francis.

Wiener, D. (1999). *Beyond talk therapy: Using movement and expressive techniques in clinical practice.* Washington, DC: American Psychological Association.

Worrell, J., & Remer, P. (1992). *Feminist perspectives in therapy.* New York: Wiley.

Yalom, I. (2002). *The gift of therapy.* New York: Harper & Row.

Young, M. E. (2001). *Learning the art of helping: Building blocks and techniques* (2nd ed.). Upper Saddle River, NJ: Prentice-Hall.

Courtesy of Professor Al Mahrer

Alvin R. Mahrer

# 14 EXPERIENTIAL PSYCHOTHERAPY

*Alvin R. Mahrer*

## OVERVIEW

Experiential psychotherapy can be regarded as a relatively new addition to the field of psychotherapy. It evolved rather recently, mainly from the writings of Alvin Mahrer.[1] Based largely upon philosophy of science and existential philosophy, its conceptual system, aims, and goals can be thought of as a substantial departure from previous thought in both the field of psychology and the field of psychotherapy. One of its unabashedly ambitious aims is to enable the person to undergo a radical, deep-seated, transformational change, into becoming the person that he or she is capable of becoming. A related companion aim is for the person to become essentially free of whatever painful feelings and situations are front and center for the person in the session. These two goals are present in every session.

### Basic Concepts

1.   The conceptual system is a *model of usefulness* rather than a *theory of truth* (Mahrer, 2004b). Some theories of truth postulate the reality of such things as egos and superegos, cognitions and metacognitions, basic needs and

[1] Although a number of approaches are called experiential, this chapter focuses on the experiential psychology and psychotherapy developed in the writings of Alvin Mahrer.

drives, archetypes and repressed affects, schizophrenia, addictive personalities, borderline conditions, and pathological depression.

In contrast, models of usefulness are rare in the field of psychotherapy. They differ from theories of truth in at least two main ways. (a) Theories of truth generally presume that their basic concepts are real and true; whereas the basic concepts of models of usefulness are merely convenient fictions and pictorialized representations that are invented because they are useful (Chalmers, 1982; Einstein, 1923; Mahrer, 1989a, 1996/2004, 2004b; Rorty, 1991; Skinner, 1938; Whitehead, 1929). Such things as schizophrenia, metacognitions, basic needs, and pathological depression are pictured as neither real nor true but merely convenient fictions. (b) Whereas theories of truth emphasize greater and greater approximation to truth, models of usefulness put a premium on usefulness in helping to achieve designated ends, tasks, and uses. The question is, "Is the model useful?" rather than, "Is this theory true?"

2.    Personality is pictured as made up of *potentials for experiencing in relationship with one another.* The experiential model of a person is relatively simple, made up of potentials for experiencing and their relationships. Each client is pictured as a relatively unique system of possibilities or potentialities for experiencing that the person is capable of undergoing. For example, a given person may be described as comprised of potentials for experiencing tenderness, gentleness, softness; playfulness, silliness, whimsicalness; strength, firmness, toughness; wickedness, devilishness, adventurousness; docility, compliance, giving in; ripeness, fruition, creativity; rebelliousness, defiance, opposition; domination, power, control, and many other potentials.

Some potentials for experiencing are relatively close to the surface. They help determine the way a person acts and interacts, thinks and feels, lives and exists in his or her personal world, as well as how the person functions and operates. These are called *operating potentials for experiencing.* There is also a domain of potentials for experiencing that are much further from the surface, deeper inside the person, essentially unconscious to and sealed off from the person. These are called *deeper potentials for experiencing.*

In addition to operating and deeper potentials for experiencing, there are *relationships between potentials for experiencing.* These relationships may be friendly, accepting, welcoming, harmonious, positive, or integrative, or they may be hateful, rejecting, distancing, disjunctive, negative, or disintegrative.

3.    The client is pictured as thoroughly engaged in building, creating, fashioning, and organizing his or her own *constructed personal world* and in determining the nature, content, structure, and meaning of that world (Mahrer, 1989a). The personal world is constructed to include situational contexts that are fitting and appropriate for the person to experience what is important for the person to experience, for better or for worse. In addition, the personal world is constructed to include externalizations of the deeper potentials for experiencing, also to enable the person to experience what is important for the person to experience, for better or for worse.

People use a number of methods to construct their personal worlds (Mahrer, 1989a, 1995). In some cases, the real external world presents itself to the person, and the person then receives it, uses it, and gives it sense and meaning, in whatever way that is important for the person. Sometimes, the external world is merely available, a rich marketplace or warehouse for the person to select from and to use in whatever way is important for the person. In other instances, the person and the external world work together, cooperating with one another, to construct the kind of personal world it is important for the person to construct. In still other instances, the person actively and creatively fashions and brings to life whatever real or unreal world it is important for the person to fashion and bring to life.

In each of these ways of constructing one's external world, the person can use building blocks that are exceedingly real or that are utterly unreal, or that are a creative combination of both real and unreal building blocks.

These principles apply to the construction of a personal external world. They also apply to the construction of a personal internal world of bodily phenomena, functions, states, and conditions. If it is important for one's world to include a cold merciless killer, one's external world can include a deadly terrorist, or one's internal world can include a deadly cancer.

These principles also apply to the ways in which a group, community, or society can be understood as creating their own collective social worlds out of their own collective potentials for experiencing and their relationships. In this picture, the constructed social worlds are created to enable the kinds of experiencing it is important for the collective people to experience. The social world thus created may include powerful forces or alien outsiders, peace and harmony or war and suffering, order and stability or lawlessness and chaos.

4.   The *origins of the infant* lie in the parents who create and construct the infant (Mahrer, 1989a). There are two ways that the parents are the origins. (a) When a parent experiences loss, abandonment, and rejection, a deeper potential for experiencing loss, abandonment, and rejection develops concomitantly in the infant. In other words, the parent both creates and is the infant or child. (b) The origin of the infant also lies in the nature of or role for the infant that the parents create. For example, if the same parent described in (a) creates an external world that includes the infant as the close confidante/best friend/ally, then the infant originates with a potential for experiencing loss, abandonment, rejection, as well as a potential for experiencing being a close confidante/best friend/ally.

The bottom line is that a skeletal framework of who and what the infant is, of the infant's personality, is already present in the parents who create and construct the infant-child and in the nature of the infant-child whom the parents create and construct.

5.   *Personality development* is mainly the function of the original framework of deeper potentials for experiencing and their relationships, which tend to remain essentially stable and unchanged over the course of the person's life. This underlying framework can give rise to (a) a working set of *operating potentials for experiencing,* which in turn can give rise to (b) the person's explicit ways of being and behaving, and also to (c) the creation of a fitting and appropriate personal external world. Once the operating potentials for experiencing, the concrete ways of being and behaving, and the personal external world are established, the course of the person's life typically consists of their maintenance and continuation, with occasional refinement or modification.

For example, if the infant-child's original deeper potentials for experiencing include the experiencing of dominance and control, childhood development may involve the initial development of an operating potential for experiencing meanness, maliciousness, and hurtfulness; ways of being and behaving that include physical aggressiveness, malicious lying, stealing, and destruction; a family of people who judge and reject; and a neighborhood of hateful victims. In adolescence, the same underlying deeper potential for experiencing dominance and control may give rise to an operating potential for experiencing sexual attractiveness, appeal, and seductiveness; ways of being and behaving that include natural sexual forwardness and a physically attractive body; and a personal external world of sexual playmates and admiring and manipulated sexual partners.

6.   *Pain, unhappiness, and suffering* are mainly the result of hateful, negative, antagonistic, disintegrative relationships between potentials for experiencing. Regardless of what potential is being experienced, other potentials relate negatively, and the accompanying feelings are painful, unhappy, hurtful, and bad. When relationships between potentials are disintegrative, potentials for experiencing tend to occur in a form that is painful, twisted, and hurtful. For example, when relationships are disintegrative, a potential for experiencing leadership, command, and strength can become a painful experiencing of pushiness, aggressiveness, and domineering control; a potential for experiencing inde-

pendence and autonomy can become an experiencing of painful aloneness, rejection, and isolation.

When relationships between potentials for experiencing are disintegrative, the person is inclined to use (a) painful ways of being and behaving in constructing (b) a painful external world with which the person relates (c) in pain and unhappiness, and in which the person undergoes (d) painful potentials for experiencing accompanied by (e) feelings that are painful, hurtful, and bad.

7.    Deep-seated *personality change* can come about in two related ways, each of which calls for genuinely hard work rather than occurring naturally or normally over the course of life. One consists of achieving a major qualitative change in the relationships between potentials for experiencing, from negative to positive, from hateful to loving, from disintegrative to integrative. This way of achieving deep-seated personality change is referred to as *integration.*

The second way is the achievement of a landmark radical shift in which deeper potentials become operating potentials for experiencing. What had been deeper inside the person becomes an integral new operating potential, and this literally transforms the person into a radically new person. This avenue is referred to as *actualization.*

## Other Systems

The experiential system is similar to other systems in some ways.

1.    The experiential system includes a domain of deeper potentials for experiencing which are pictured as beyond the conscious awareness of the person. This deeper domain bears some resemblance to the unconscious proposed by some dynamic systems although, on closer inspection, there are some substantial differences. (a) In psychoanalytic and analytic therapies,[2] the unconscious is made up of its own distinctive material such as primitive impulses and drives, repressed memories, and (in Jungian analysis) the collective unconscious. In the experiential model, the deeper potentials for experiencing and the more on-the-surface operating potentials are both made of the same material, namely sheer potentials or possibilities for experiencing. (b) In psychoanalytic and analytic therapies, much of the content of the unconscious is thought of as universal, as basic and fundamental in most people. In the experiential system, each person's deeper or more basic potentials for experiencing are likely to be unique. This uniqueness usually becomes evident when the potentials are carefully examined and described. Accordingly, discovering each client's world of deeper potentials can be an exciting, individualized adventure. (c) In psychoanalytic therapies, the unconscious can be accessed by a client in the conscious state. That is, the conscious person can find and discover what lies in the unconscious, especially if the person uses the right methods with the right therapist. In the experiential system, the deeper potentials for experiencing are beyond reach of the conscious person in the conscious state, regardless of the methods used by the person or by the psychoanalytic therapist. Instead, the client must be able to leave the ordinary conscious state and enter into a new state in which the person can touch and be touched by the deeper potentials for experiencing. (d) In psychoanalytic therapies, the emphasis is on preserving and enhancing the person, including the person's defenses against an encroaching unconscious. In the experiential system, the scenario is essentially reversed. Instead of building adequate defenses against the unconscious, the deeper potential for experiencing is welcomed and invited into becoming an integral new component of the qualitatively new person. Instead of preserving and enhancing the client, the person is

[2]The term "analytic" is used here to refer to Jungian analytic psychology and psychotherapy.

invited to undergo radical transformation into becoming the qualitatively new person, and this includes the risk of extinction of the old client.

2. A number of the basic concepts of the experiential system emerged from the writings of existential and Eastern philosophers, although these philosophers may not recognize what their conceptual offspring have become in the experiential system. In any case, this body of writings was the primordial soup for basic experiential concepts such as potentials for experiencing, ways of constructing a personal external world, the possibility of becoming the qualitatively new person that the person can become, and the therapeutic power of a radical shift out of, a disengagement from, one's continuing person, and the cataclysmic plunge into being the utterly new person.

3. Some therapies are looser and more flexible, with rather general principles and guidelines, whereas other therapies, such as rational emotive behavior therapy, behavior therapy, and cognitive therapy, are more structured and systematic. Experiential therapy is likewise more structured, systematic, and organized in that each session is to follow a given sequence of relatively identifiable steps.

4. Some therapies, especially rational emotive behavior therapy, behavior therapy, multimodal therapy, and cognitive therapy, emphasize the importance of postsession homework assignments. Going even further, each experiential session culminates in the qualitatively new person leaving the session and continuing as the new person after the session ends (Mahrer, 1996/2004, 1998a).

Here are some ways in which experiential therapy differs and departs from many other therapies:

1. *The goals of each session.* Each experiential session offers the client an opportunity to undergo two changes that may be distinctive enough to qualify as a new departure. One involves experiencing deep-seated change in becoming the qualitatively new person that the client is capable of becoming. This can be a radical shift, a transformation, a metamorphosis—the magnificent opportunity and the risk is letting go of virtually everything of who and what the client is and hurling him- or herself into the qualitatively new person that the client is capable of becoming. When the session is successful, the person who leaves the session is an integrated and actualized new evolution out of the old person who entered the session. The qualitatively new client has his or her own sense of self, personal world, qualities and characteristics, thoughts and feelings, and ways of being and behaving.

The other, related change occurs when the new person is essentially free of painful, hurtful feelings and the painful scenes and situations in which they occurred. The new client is free of the old person's painful and hurtful feelings, and the new person's world is free of the painful scenes and situations in which those bad feelings occurred. The focus of change is not the bad feelings nor the painful scene or situation; rather, the focus of change is the very person who has the bad feelings and the painful scene or situation.

These two goals are, in many respects, a distinctive departure from the goals of most therapies. Each experiential session is designed to free the client from remaining imprisoned in the person he or she is, becoming the whole new person that can be. Where many therapies aim at making the person's personal world better, reducing bad feelings, or returning to a state of normal functioning, experiential therapy's directions of change offer a letting go of all this in becoming the qualitatively new person, living and being in the qualitatively new personal world.

2. *Concepts as "convenient fictions."* The concepts, constructs, and components of the experiential system are "convenient fictions," invented unrealities that are created because they are useful (Mahrer, 1989a, 2004b). They are not real things; they do not signify or refer to real things. For example, a "potential for experiencing" is a convenient

fiction, not a real thing. It cannot be located in the brain. It has no structure that can be identified by research. It cannot be reduced to underlying neurological, physiological, or biochemical processes or events. There are no measures or tests or scales of its height, weight, color, density, speed, volume, or intensity. It cannot be confirmed or refuted by controlled experimentation. None of the experiential concepts or constructs are real. They are all "convenient fictions," invented because they are useful in experiential work.

Accordingly, because they are presumed by their proponents to be real things, or because they are not useful for achieving the goals of experiential therapy, virtually all of the concepts, constructs, and personality components of most other therapies are rejected and have no place in the experiential system. This includes concepts such as the anal stage of development, the collective unconscious, the ego, transference neurosis, sexual drives, dependency needs, irrational beliefs, cognitive schemas, cognitive maps, the inferiority complex, actualizing tendencies, the growth force, the entire diagnostic system of mental disorders, cognitive mediational processes, introversion-extraversion, conditioned stimuli, negative reinforcements, cognitive processing systems, and defense mechanisms (Mahrer, 2000b).

3.  *Different family ties.* The phrase "experiential psychotherapy" was perhaps first coined to designate the approach of Carl Whitaker, John Warkentin, Thomas Malone, and Richard Felder (Malone, Whitaker, Warkentin, & Felder, 1961; Whitaker, Felder, Malone, & Warkentin, 1962; Whitaker & Malone, 1953). Carl Rogers' approach was a parallel but rather separate stream, initially called nondirective therapy, then client-centered therapy, and currently referred to as person-centered therapy or, more generally, experiential therapy, in appreciation and acknowledgment of the work of Eugene Gendlin in the person-centered framework (Gendlin, 1973, 1996).

From these two separate streams, a booming experiential family has grown. In 1993 there were well over four dozen therapies (Mahrer & Fairweather, 1993) identified as "experiential psychotherapies," or with "experiential" in their title (e.g., experiential-feminist therapy, experiential-cognitive therapy), or accepting the existence of an experiential family of which it considered itself an integral member (e.g., gestalt therapy, psychodrama, existential therapy, humanistic therapy).

It is likely that the experiential family is now substantially larger than four or five dozen therapies, especially as the word "experiential" is increasingly stretched and melded into the words "feeling" and "emotion" so that the experiential family includes virtually any therapies that highlight the role of feeling and emotion.

Although Mahrer acknowledges borrowing the phrase "experiential psychotherapy" from Whitaker, Malone, Warkentin, and Felder, and also from Gendlin, Mahrer's experiential therapy cannot easily be included in the experiential family for several reasons. One reason is that there seems to be little or no substantial basis for a claim that such a family exists. The defining characteristics are either nonexistent or so loosely inclusive that many disparate therapies can easily claim membership. Also, a careful appraisal of basic concepts, theories of personality, and theories of psychotherapy seems to reveal greater differences within the so-called experiential family than between the experiential family and other families. Despite the use of the word "experiential," Mahrer's experiential psychotherapy has little if anything in common with any of the therapies in the experiential family in terms of their conceptual meanings of "experiencing," basic concepts, theories of personality, and theories and processes of psychotherapy, as discussed in Mahrer and Fairweather (1993).

4.  *The purpose and use of research.* What later evolved into a distinctive discovery-oriented approach to psychotherapy research began in informal meetings of a small number of newly graduated psychologists and psychiatrists, including Mahrer, at a large military training hospital in the mid-1950s. The impetus for the meetings was twofold:

(a) These inexperienced professionals were assigned to be in charge of establishing psychotherapeutic services for military personnel and their families from a large army training center and a much larger air force base. (b) They were to develop psychotherapy training programs for a large number of military psychologists, psychiatrists, and social workers. This was a task of almost comical proportions, because no one in the small group was trained to do more than assessments and evaluations of patients, none of them intended to specialize in psychotherapy, and none of them had studied the actual in-session work of experienced practitioners in their doctoral programs, internships, or residencies.

Their fortuitous solution was to jump-start their own training by pleading for audiotapes of actual in-session work of experienced psychotherapists from anywhere in the country, including both well-known psychotherapists and psychotherapists esteemed in their local communities but not especially well known from high offices or publications. In particular, this group solicited audiotapes of sessions that experienced practitioners considered outstanding, unusual or noteworthy, and sessions with impressive in-session changes. The group sought these tapes to learn what could be achieved by psychotherapy and how to achieve these impressive psychotherapeutic changes. They used these precious audiotapes to try to learn what they were supposed to know, to do, and to teach. This was not research; it was intensive, self-directed, on-the-job training.

Over the past 50 years, the library has steadily grown and now contains about 500 audiotapes. The small group of inexperienced, neophyte, military psychotherapists evolved into a large research team in a university setting, still studying the precious audiotapes but using much more sophisticated, rigorous, careful means and methods of analyzing them. Indeed, the research team developed what is called a "discovery-oriented" approach to psychotherapy research (Mahrer, 1985, 1988, 1996a, 1996b, 2004a; Mahrer & Boulet, 1999a).

From the very beginning, the guiding mission for doing psychotherapy research has remained essentially the same: (a) to discover more of the kinds of impressive, valued, significant, magnificent in-session and postsession changes that psychotherapy can help achieve, and (b) to discover better ways of helping to achieve these impressive changes. This mission departs from most of the commonly accepted reasons for doing psychotherapy research. These reasons can range from confirming a theory of psychotherapy to confirming that a therapy is effective in treating a given mental disorder, from comparing a therapy with its rivals to contributing to a supposedly cumulative body of psychotherapeutic knowledge, from looking for common elements of successful psychotherapies to questioning or supporting psychotherapy dictums, canons, and basic principles (Mahrer, 2004a).

# HISTORY

## Precursors

The years from 1949 to 1954 were exceedingly important for the clinical psychology program at Ohio State University. Alvin Mahrer happened to be one of many students in the doctoral program during this period. He entered the program with a middling interest in the field of psychology, but he had no interesting background in psychological matters and no passionate drive for either a doctorate or a career in psychotherapy and little appreciation for the conceptual issues associated with psychotherapy.

On the other hand, 1949 to 1954 was the center of a golden decade of creativity for the clinical psychology program at Ohio State University. Just before Mahrer's arrival at OSU as a doctoral student, Carl Rogers had left for the University of Chicago after developing client-centered therapy, Julian Rotter was writing the bible of social learning theory (Rotter, 1954), and George Kelly was creating his classical personal construct psychology (Kelly, 1955).

This trio created movements that revolutionized clinical psychology, including client-centered theory and therapy, social learning theory and therapy, personal construct theory, postmodern theory, and constructivist theory and therapy. For the doctoral students in the program at Ohio State, it was as if this trio of teachers quietly chanted in unison a message with at least three refrains: (a) Be bold. Break new ground. Dare to be as creative as you can be. (b) Think big. Think in broad strokes. Dare to revolutionize the field. Dare to violate what is taken for granted. (c) Go beyond the field of psychology. Know the works of the great philosophers and the sages of the ages. Know the underground issues that constitute the foundations of psychology and psychotherapy.

The atmosphere was electrifying, challenging, inspiring, and galvanizing. Students were invited and compelled to join this grand trio, and doctoral students in the program were encouraged to integrate their ideas in some fashion, or to go forth and create their own—or else be consigned to march lockstep to the uniform cadence of the drums of what was then the traditional field of psychology and psychotherapy. For Mahrer, this atmosphere was a major precursor of what would emerge as the experiential system, experiential psychology, and experiential therapy.

## Beginnings

Mahrer created his experiential therapy based on four streams of investigation that gradually interconnected with one another and grew from the late 1950s to the late 1990s.

1. *Existential philosophy.* For Mahrer, as for some others, truly understanding the field of psychotherapy meant devoting himself to lifetime study of the world of existential philosophical thought.

Studying the work of existential philosophers provided two precious gifts. One was an exciting introduction to the truly basic issues and questions that underlie the field of psychotherapy, basic issues and questions that existential philosophers probed, dissected, analyzed, but which the field of psychotherapy seldom acknowledged and rarely addressed (Mahrer, 1997c, 1999b, 2000a, 2003a). The other gift was learning that these existential philosophers offered their own positions on these basic issues and their own answers to the basic questions.

The beginnings of experiential therapy lay in the fundamental issues and questions, and the positions and answers, given in the writings of existential philosophers such as Binswanger, Buber, Buytendijk, Camus, Ellenberger, Gebsattel, Gendlin, Goethe, Gurdjieff, Habermas, Hegel, Heidegger, Husserl, Jaspers, Kant, Kierkegaard, Laing, Leibniz, Merleau-Ponty, Minkowski, Needleman, Nietzsche, Ouspensky, Sartre, Scheler, Schiller, Schlick, Schopenhauer, Spinoza, Strauss, Tillich, von Uexkull, and others.

2. *Philosophy of science.* Largely because the subject matter did not especially feature the field of psychotherapy, Mahrer's ventures into that field were mainly in the spirit of trying to see if philosophers of science might provide the foundation for a distinctive psychology and psychotherapy. Mahrer's aim was to try to extract or to create a psychotherapy out of these writings.

Accordingly, what later became experiential psychology and therapy grew out of a careful study of the writings of philosophers of science on such topics as

- relationships between psychological events and variables and neurology, physiology, and chemistry
- theories of truth and models of usefulness

- foundational beliefs, dictums, and canons
- the construction, refinement, and advancement of conceptual systems
- the role of research in the supposed cumulative body of psychotherapeutic knowledge
- the testing of hypotheses, including falsification and refutation of hypotheses, and feasible research alternatives
- the criteria of a genuine science of psychotherapy
- the meaning and trustworthiness of psychotherapeutic data
- the meaning and modification of categories of mental illness and disorders
- the meaning and determination of causal relationships
- criteria of adequacy and inadequacy of explanatory systems
- resources and contributors to psychotherapeutic knowledge
- determinants of the origins of personality
- presumptions in the analysis of person-world relationships
- the role of relativity in psychotherapeutic change
- change as quantum, transformational, qualitative shifts

In addition to their writings on these topics, other philosophers of science such as Barteley, Bergmann, Bertalanffy, Bridgman, Campbell, Carnap, Churchland, Cohen, Derrida, Dewey, Duhem, Einstein, Feibleman, Feigl, Feyerabend, Fodor, van Fraassen, Gadamer, Grunbaum, Heisenberg, Hempel, Kantor, Koch, Kuhn, Lakatos, Mach, Maturana, Nagel, Oppenheim, Peirce, Polanyi, Popper, Quine, Reichenbach, Russell, and Schroedinger were important to the development of experiential psychotherapy.

3. *Four decades of study of approximately 500 audiotapes of actual sessions of over 80 psychotherapists.* Hundreds of psychotherapists representing the spectrum of therapeutic approaches were gracious and helpful enough to contribute audiotapes of sessions they considered deserving of special study because the in-session changes were extraordinary. These changes were impressive, significant, compelling, magnificent, surprising, unexpected, bewildering, inexplicable—almost miraculous.

This library of audiotaped sessions was studied by Mahrer and his coworkers to see if they could uncover the secrets of psychotherapy and reveal what psychotherapy might be capable of helping to achieve. For more than four decades, their quest was to learn what a psychotherapy might look like if it were custom designed to accomplish what was accomplished in these sessions, and did so by using the methods used in these sessions. Little by little, a picture emerged of a psychotherapy in which each session offered a bold opportunity to achieve exciting changes, changes that seemed to qualify as a new departure from what was ordinarily achieved in most sessions of most therapies. Furthermore, the actual methods used in these extraordinary sessions also seemed to depart from the range of methods normally used in therapeutic approaches.

The birth of experiential psychotherapy was unusual in that it was born in part out of the clinical research of these unusual sessions. In contrast, the beginnings of most therapies lie in the ideas of gifted theoreticians and clinicians, the modification or splitting off of already established popular psychotherapies. Indeed, the beginnings of experiential therapy were relatively unique in that they included the clinical research of actual in-session changes and the ideas of philosophers.

4. *Mahrer's quest for personal growth and self-transformation.* Mahrer continued to look for what psychotherapy could provide and for ways the practitioner could undergo a journey of personal change using the means and methods of psychotherapy. In this sense,

Mahrer joined with others who followed in the initial footsteps of those such as Freud, Jung, Horney, and others in a quest to use psychotherapeutic methods in their own self-analysis, self-discovery, self-change, and self-evolution—becoming whatever they were capable of becoming.

One world consisted of being a professional psychotherapist, working with patients and clients, applying useful and effective means and methods. Appealing and attractive as this world may be, an equally or perhaps more appealing and attractive world consisted of using these means and methods for and with himself (Mahrer, 2002a). From the beginning of doctoral training, and throughout his career, Mahrer has pursued his own self-therapy. In the beginning, he included everything from free association to dream interpretation; he studied his earliest memories and talked to empty chairs. Other techniques included rewarding and punishing behaviors, dissecting irrational cognitions, undergoing birth experience, revising personal constructs, analyzing early childhood events, abreaction, and catharsis. Gradually the self-sessions evolved into using experiential methods to help achieve what experiential sessions were designed to achieve, either in working with another person or in working with oneself.

These four streams, individually and collectively, constitute the beginnings of experiential psychotherapy.

## Current Status

The current identity of experiential psychology and psychotherapy has emerged in a number of volumes. One volume (Mahrer, 1989a) provided the experiential model or conceptualization with its underlying philosophy and philosophy of science, the origins of personality, the development of personality, personality structure, the creation of personal and social worlds, the human body, pleasure and pain, human behavior, personal and social change, and optimal states of being. A second (Mahrer, 1989b) offered an experiential conceptualization and use of dreams. The conceptualization and methods of experiential psychotherapy were provided in a third volume (Mahrer, 1996/2004), and a fourth volume was written for people who want to have their experiential sessions by themselves (Mahrer, 2002a).

Experiential therapy is still evolving, ready and able to grow in new and better ways—it's not locked into place. In the future, experiential therapy may fade away, become integrated into other approaches, spawn further and better approaches, or undergo its own waves of exciting new developments. In any case, the current status invites others to make experiential therapy their own, help it improve, and develop its further implications for the field of psychotherapy. This spirit is preferred to institutionalizing experiential therapy, locking it into place with its own training centers, standards, programs, certifications and diplomas, its own organizations and societies, newsletters and journals, meetings and conferences, central office and public relations, leaders and followers, teachers and students, gurus and disciples.

Currently, there are very few dedicated practitioners of experiential psychotherapy, and they are dispersed over approximately 30 countries. This is partly because experiential therapy is a recent addition to the family of therapies. After some initial stirrings in the mid-1950s, and after a series of preliminary "dress rehearsals" in the 1970s and 1980s, experiential therapy arrived on the therapeutic "stage" in 1996. Experiential therapy would perhaps have an easier time qualifying as a significant new departure rather than as a mere addition to the large family of therapies. The more one learns about this therapy, the more a case can be made that this therapy violates, threatens, endangers, and antagonizes what most therapies hold dear (Mahrer, 2003a).

Another reason that the field of experiential therapy remains very small is that to be able to do experiential therapy, it is virtually essential that the practitioner hold the basic framework, outlook, and deep-seated way of thinking. At present, only a tiny proportion of psychotherapists think this way. Finally, experiential therapy welcomes like-minded practitioners with basically congruent outlooks, conceptualization, and therapeutic aims and goals. The respectful appreciation of the practitioner's own deep-seated way of thinking leaves little or no room for attempts to proselytize or popularize—to get large numbers of psychotherapists to adopt experiential therapy and its fundamental way of thinking.

# PERSONALITY

## Theory of Personality

The experiential system of psychology rests on a philosophy of science in which the conceptualization of personality is mainly a model or pictorialization made up of convenient fictions, rather than the much more common notion of theories as approximations of what is assumed to be true (Mahrer, 2004b). Accordingly, the experiential concepts and principles having to do with personality are to be seen as nothing more than convenient fictions, invented mainly because they are useful, rather than because they are real or true.

1.   *The origins of personality* lie in what may be pictured as a primitive field consisting of the parental figures and the physical infant (Mahrer, 1989a). Picture a circle around the parental figures and the physical infant, and think of that circle as defining the original personality of the infant. Think of the infant (a) as including the potentials for experiencing the parental figures and (b) as being created, organized, and defined by the parental figures. That is, the infant's original personality consists of the potentials for experiencing in the parental figures as well as the infant created by the parental figures.

If, for example, the potentials for experiencing in the parental figures include an experiencing of defiance/rebelliousness/opposition, and an experiencing of closeness/fusion/oneness, then these can also serve as the basic personality of the infant. In addition, parental figures can create and define the infant as components of the parents' own personal external worlds, can construct and define the basic nature of the infant and endow the infant with meaning. If, for example, the infant is created and defined as the special one/elevated one/chosen one, then this potential for experiencing comes into existence as part of the original personality of the infant. In other words, the infant's primitive personality already exists as the primitive field in which the physical infant exists.

2.   *Personality development* consists mainly of the emergence of additional potentials for experiencing and the relationships between those potentials. Together, these additional potentials for experiencing and the relationships between them constitute and define what is ordinarily thought of as the structure of personality—who and what the emerging person is, how the conscious and aware person thinks, feels, acts, interacts, and relates with him- or herself and functions and operates in the world. These additional potentials are the *operating potentials for experiencing.*

Born out of the more basic *deeper potentials for experiencing,* the operating potentials for experiencing are created (a) to constitute the conscious, aware person who functions and operates, thinks and feels, has a personality, and creates his or her own personal world; and (b) to keep the person distanced from the sealed-off, inner world of the deeper and basic potentials for experiencing.

3.   *The construction of a personal external world* is another component of personality development. Once there is a person, once a set of operating potentials for experiencing and the relationships between those potentials have been established, the person constructs and builds a personal external world. Beginning in early or middle childhood, the

operating potentials for experiencing make it possible for individuals to create and construct their own personal external worlds for at least two main purposes.

One purpose is for the external world to provide appropriate situational contexts for the person to experience the operating potentials for experiencing that are important for the person to experience. In other words, an external world is created by operating potentials to enable experiencing of the operating potentials.

For example, if the operating potential is the experiencing of dedication and devotion, this operating potential can help to create and construct an external world that supports a lifelong dedication to prayer and subservience to God; or a medical career passionately devoted to discovering the cure for cancer; or an external world that supports a musician trying to write a perfect symphony. One's own external world is created and constructed to serve as situational contexts for the experiencing of one's own operating potentials for experiencing.

Second, the person creates a personal external world to contain and to constitute one's own deeper potentials for experiencing. Because the person's relationship to the deeper potentials for experiencing is exceedingly hateful, terrifying, and disintegrative, these deeper potentials for experiencing tend to fill the external world in a form that is twisted, grotesque, awful, and monstrous, and the person's relationship with these externalized parts of the external world are typically laced with hate, terror, pain, and dread. In essence, the person creates an external world to house and to be the hissing, snarling externalization of the person's own awful relationship with the person's own awful form of the deeper potentials for experiencing. That is, the person creates a tormenting, hurtful external world out of his or her own hated, dreaded, tormenting, hurtful deeper potentials.

If, for example, a person's deeper potential is the experiencing of defiance, rebelliousness, and opposition, he or she can construct an external world consisting of a willful, defiant son, an opposing group of coworkers, an unforgiving arctic storm, or an enemy nation that hates, resists, defies, opposes, and strikes back. A person's constructed external world is the essence of his or her own hated and dreaded defiance, rebelliousness, and opposition, in exceedingly painful relationships with the person who created and constructed that personal external world in the first place.

4.  *The course of human life* is seen as persons being and doing what it is important for them to be and do in order for them to undergo the potentials for experiencing that it is important for them to experience. A person's system of potentials for experiencing and the relationships between these potentials, once established, are inclined to remain relatively stable throughout the course of life. However, there can be room for change in the person's ways of being and behaving, and in the person's constructed personal world, all in the continuing service of enabling the person to undergo and experience the relatively stable system of potentials for experiencing and their relationships.

In the experiential model, the relatively stable system of potentials for experiencing and the relationships between these potentials steers the course of the client's life. There is little or no place for things such as basic needs and drives, built-in growth or developmental forces with their stages of human growth and development, or pushes and pulls toward human maturity, adjustment, or normal functioning.

5.  *The roots of pain and unhappiness* lie mainly in relationships between potentials for experiencing, relationships that are hateful, disjunctive, antagonistic, destructive, frightening, and disintegrative. These disintegrative relationships can be between any potentials for experiencing, and they are almost uniformly present between the person who is the operating potentials for experiencing and the inner world of deeper potentials for experiencing.

When relationships are disintegrative, virtually any potential for experiencing can be feared and hated by its neighbors. An experiencing of loving closeness, warmth, and intimacy can be bathed in pain and unhappiness by neighboring potentials for experiencing whose relationships poison it.

When relationships are disintegrative, potentials for experiencing can be altered, forced out of their intrinsic, natural form and into a form that is monstrous, painful, and hurtful. An experiencing of determination, strength, and leadership can be twisted into a painful hurtful experiencing of messianic control, arrogant superiority, and uncaring dominance. A potential for experiencing loving closeness, warmth, and intimacy can be twisted into a painful experiencing of losing one's identity in fusing with another, of sacrificing one's integrity and independence, of being dangerously vulnerable.

When relationships between potentials are disintegrative, the personal external world can be populated with painful agencies and forces that jab and attack, threaten and abuse, inflict pain and suffering, constrain and control. The person creates and lives in a world of demons and devils, monsters and gargoyles, a world of pain and suffering, agony and anguish.

When deeper potentials for experiencing are stirred, roused, touched, enlivened, the person's own exceedingly disintegrative relationships toward these deeper potentials can fill the person with jolts of terror and dread that can leave the person in a state of disorganization, disharmony, disorder, disintegration, deadness, numbness, agitation, saturnine depression, vulnerability, or fragility.

6.  *Deep-seated, radical personality change* is understood as the consequence of two related changes. One is that relationships between potentials for experiencing shift from being fearful, hateful, and disintegrative, to being loving, welcoming, and integrative. This applies especially to relationships between the operating potentials who are the person and the deeper potentials that are kept sealed off and hidden. This first change is called *integration*. A second change is that the deeper potentials for experiencing become integral parts of the person, the operating potentials for experiencing. That is, deeper potentials become operating potentials. This second change is called *actualization*.

These two changes can occur as qualitative shifts, radical and transformational shifts from one state to a different state, rather than being changes that are more gradual or cumulative. In much the same way, deep-seated, radical personality change depends on one's readiness and ability to wholly sacrifice and extinguish oneself, to fully hurl oneself into being the inner deeper self, of letting go completely of the very essence and core of who and what one is. It can be appreciated that the experiential meaning of deep-seated, radical personality change is not an especially common occurrence.

## Variety of Concepts

1.  A number of other theories distinguish between a part of personality that is thought of as more superficial, in contact with the external world, and a part of personality that is thought of as deeper, removed, and internal. On this issue, the experiential model joins with other systems, even though there are varying conceptions of what is superficial and what is deep in the psychoanalytic, Adlerian, analytic, person-centered, rational-emotional-behavioral, behavioral, cognitive, existential, psychoanalytic, and gestalt theories of personality. Most theories of personality distinguish between what is superficial and what is deep. These two parts of the personality may be called the ego and the unconscious, the persona and the shadow, the social self and the personal self, the self and the primary or real self, beliefs and core beliefs, behavior and a capacity for self-directed behavior change, information and an agency that processes the information, or cognitions and primal cognitive schemata, conflicts and core conflicts.

2.  Most theories acknowledge the importance of a sense of self, a sense of consciousness and awareness, a sense of "I-ness." The experiential system accepts how crucial it is for the person to preserve, protect, and maintain this sense of self and to undergo sheer

terror and dread at the imminence of loss of self, the extinguishing and death of this sense of conscious being.

However, most other systems accept the mission of helping to change distal and surface aspects of the person's thoughts and behaviors, symptoms and pathologies, problems and mental disorders, while leaving safely intact the continuing core sense of self, the person who has the thoughts and behaviors, problems and mental disorders.

In contrast, in the experiential system, personality development and change invite the client to plunge headlong into the total extinguishing of the core sense of self, into penetrating the terror and dread of ending the precious existence of the core sense of self, of wholly surrendering the essential sense of "I-ness." In the experiential system, preservation and maintenance of the removed sense of conscious awareness is a final barrier to genuinely deep-seated and wholesale, radical, transformative personality change.

3.    The experiential system includes potentials for experiencing and their relationships. In this relatively simple model, there is little or no place for a great deal of what comprises personality in many other systems (basic instincts, needs, drives, pathological processes, traits, cognitive schemas, defense mechanisms, mental disorders, etc.).

# PSYCHOTHERAPY

## Theory of Psychotherapy

1.    *Theory of psychotherapeutic goals.* In most psychotherapies, the goals emphasize treatment of mental disorders or of presenting symptoms, complaints, and pathological problems related to mental disorders. In contrast, the experiential session is designed to enable a client (a) to undergo a radical transformation and become the qualitatively new person that the person can become, and (b) thereby to become free of his or her painful scene or situation and the painful feelings in that scene or situation.

In the experiential model, there are deeper potentials for experiencing that can become integral parts of a radically new, transformed person. This can be a magnificent, extraordinary achievement that has at least two profound consequences. One is that the client is a radically new and qualitatively different person, with new and different thoughts and feelings, ways of being and behaving, outlooks and perspectives, living and being in a new and different external world. The other side of this consequence is the risk of significant change, loss, or extinction of the ordinary, continuing former person and that person's thoughts and feelings, ways of being and behaving, outlook and perspective, and external world.

The second profound consequence is that the qualitatively new person no longer creates and lives in the former person's personal world, with its painful feelings in its painful scenes and situations. The experiential solution is to become a qualitatively new person who is free of the former person's pains and hurts in the former person's painful and hurtful personal world, and this can include what many other therapists refer to as presenting complaints, psychological problems, symptoms, and mental disorders.

2.    *The theory of problem identification.* In most therapies, there is typically something referred to as "the problem"—the diagnosed mental illness, the thing that psychotherapy is to treat. In most therapies, it is identified by giving it a name or label, for example poor impulse control, a pathological grief reaction, lack of assertiveness, sexual dysfunction, ego diffusion, post-traumatic stress disorder, premature ejaculation, chronic fatigue, hypomania, dissociation, identity disorder, fear of intimacy, hallucinations and delusions, depressive disorder, panic disorder, borderline personality disorder, or an abusive personality.

In the experiential conceptual system, what is commonly referred to by other therapists as a problem is set aside, and the preference is for careful identification of the painful scene of strong painful feeling. There are at least three reasons for this. (a) From the experiential viewpoint, the genuine difficulty or trouble or concern, the real focus of therapy, is the painful feeling in a painful scene or situation. Saying that the genuine focus of therapy is some sort of name or label, e.g., hypomania or fear of intimacy or abusive personality, would simply be inaccurate, a mistake, at least in the experiential perspective, mainly because these labels do not refer to or include the actual anguish and pain, or the scene in which the painful feeling occurs. (b) Experiential work means finding the precise instant when the painful feeling peaks, and this can be discovered by first carefully identifying and then fully living and being in the painful scene or situation of painful feeling. Identifying the scene of painful feeling is crucial in experiential work. (c) Identifying the painful scene of painful feeling can be exceedingly scary and threatening, bothersome and unpleasant. After all, the work consists of living and being in the painful scene of painful feeling. An effective way of staying away from the painful scene of painful feelings is instead to give it a name or label. Call it a marital problem, an anger management problem, a fear of intimacy, or hypomania. Merely naming and labeling it effectively keeps the person from ever carefully identifying the painful scene of painful feeling, from ever living and being in it, and certainly from ever discovering the instant of peak painful feelings. In other psychotherapies, the patient may talk about it and try to understand it. However, one does not willingly hurl oneself back into it.

3.  *The theory of access to the inner deeper world.* Many theories emphasize deeper material of which the person is essentially unaware. According to many of these theories, the person in the conscious state is nevertheless able to gain access to this unconscious material by such means as the careful study of the client's case history, symptoms, dreams, psychological tests, pathological behavior, cognitions, and thought patterns, especially under the guidance of a psychotherapist. In other words, much of the common meaning of unconscious is presumed to be accessible to discovery, insight, and understanding by the conscious person in the conscious state.

The experiential model depicts a further or deeper internal world that is essentially outside of and beyond accessibility by the person in the ordinary conscious state. Access to this other deeper world of deeper potentials for experiencing requires that the person must exit from the ordinary state of conscious awareness, must disengage from the ordinary state of consciousness, and instead must enter into an extraordinary state beyond and outside of the ordinary state of consciousness (Mahrer, 1999a).

4.  *The theory of the target of therapeutic change.* In most therapies, when the target is thought of as the outcome, the target is the client's presenting complaints, symptoms, psychological problem, or mental disorder. When the target is what is to be treated to have a successful outcome, aspects of the client, for example, the client's irrational belief, poor defense mechanisms, or inadequate insight and understanding, are the target.

In contrast, the experiential conceptualization holds that the target of change is the client who has the complaint, symptom, or mental disorder, who has the irrational belief, poor defense mechanisms, or inadequate insight and understanding. The target of change is the very person who is the "I" saying, "I have a problem . . . I am depressed . . . I feel frightened." The target is the core person oneself, rather than something about the client.

5.  *The theory of psychotherapeutic change.* The experiential model of psychotherapeutic change consists of four steps. In the first step, the client disengages from the ordinary state of conscious awareness and enters the inner deeper world of the essentially unknown and unexplored deeper potentials for experiencing. The first step culminates in the client discovering a deeper potential for experiencing, coming face to face with the deeper potential, touching and being touched by the deeper potential.

The conceptual foundation of the second step is that the client's relationships with deeper potentials are typically so negative and disintegrative that the client does not know of the existence of the deeper potentials and does not know that he or she does not know. The deeper potentials are utterly terrifying and grotesque, dreadful and twisted. The experiential model allows for the magnificent possibility of converting the awful and disintegrative relationship into a relationship of welcoming and accepting, of embracing and enjoying, of trusting and playful joyfulness. The deeper potential that had been discovered in the first step is loved and befriended in the second step, and this paves the way for the third step.

The purpose of the third step is for individuals to give up their identity, to let go of everything that they are, to surrender themselves, and instead to be the deeper potential for experiencing. They undergo the radical transformation into the utterly new person who is the deeper potential. In this conceptual picture, the person exits the old person, leaving him or her behind, and emerges as the whole new person who is the deeper potential for experiencing. The shift is to be all at once, rather than gradual; complete, rather than partial; and exuberantly vibrant, rather than muted.

The fourth and final step occurs when the formerly deeper potential becomes an integral new operating potential in the qualitatively changed system of operating potentials, and when this radically new person exists and lives in the qualitatively new world of the qualitatively new person. In this conceptualization, when a deeper potential for experiencing becomes an integral part of the former system of operating potentials, a wholesale transformation has occurred and a qualitatively new person has emerged. This whole new person is born in this session, and it is this whole new person who can leave the session and live and be in the new person's new world (Mahrer, 1998a).

6.    *The requisites of psychotherapeutic change.* Perhaps the main requisite for the client is that, in this session, there is sufficient readiness and willingness to undergo the changes of proceeding through the steps and substeps of the session.

For the therapist, there are two main requisites. (a) The therapist's own model, picture, conceptualization, and foundational beliefs should have a friendly goodness-of-fit with those of the experiential system The therapist must, for example, see the session as an opportunity for the client to become the qualitatively new person that the person can become and to be essentially free of the painful scene of painful feeling that was front and center in the session. (b) The therapist should have a sufficient measure of proficiency and competency in the working operations, methods, and skills needed to conduct the experiential session. Ordinarily, this calls for progressive and continuing training in explicit skill development.

## Process of Psychotherapy

### Logistics

The office should be soundproofed because there can be loud outbursts. The seating arrangement should enable the person and the therapist to sit in large chairs in which they can lean back with their feet on large hassocks. The chairs are almost touching one another, both pointing in the same direction. The therapist and the client are elbow to elbow. They keep their eyes closed throughout the session. The session is typically over when the following sequence of steps is completed. Generally this takes one to two hours.

### The Session as Mini-Therapy

*Each session is its own mini-therapy* in at least three ways: (a) Each session proceeds through the same four steps by starting with the scene of strong feeling that is central for the client in this session, and ending with the qualitatively new person who is ready to enter the postsession new real world. (b) The actual working goals for this session are identified in the course of this session. That is, each session opens by identifying a scene of strong feeling. If the scene is a painful scene of painful feeling, then becoming free of this session's painful scene of painful feelings is one of this session's working goals. Second, only by penetrating through the instant of peak feeling is the deeper potential for experiencing accessed so that a picture can emerge of the qualitatively new person the client can become. In other words, the first step of each session allows the client and the therapist to identify the goals for this particular session. (c) The end of each session gives both the therapist and the client an opportunity to determine if they want a subsequent session, and when it is to occur. Making these arrangements at the end of each session helps to acknowledge the mini-therapy character of each session.

## The Initial Sessions

The purposes of the initial sessions are the same as the purposes of subsequent sessions, namely to enable the client to become the person that the client can become, and to enable the client to be free of the painful scenes and the painful feelings that were front and center in the session. Each session is its own mini-therapy, and this includes the initial sessions.

Accordingly, the initial sessions go through the same steps as the subsequent sessions. Perhaps, in an initial session, there may be somewhat more explanation of each of the baby steps, but this is not necessarily so. In other words, it might be hard to distinguish tapes of initial sessions from tapes of subsequent sessions.

In many therapies, initial sessions often include a case history, family history, problem assessment, psychological testing, diagnostic evaluation, groundwork for a therapist-client relationship, discussion of treatment rationale, or formal arrangements for a program of therapeutic sessions. There are at least four reasons why all of this is typically missing from initial experiential sessions: (a) None of these topics contribute to having a successful experiential session; (b) Getting this information interferes with and blocks having a successful experiential session; (c) Each experiential session is its own mini-therapy, and there is little value in thinking in terms of an extended program of initial sessions, intermediate sessions, and terminating sessions; (d) It is better to decide whether the therapist and the person want to have a subsequent session based on what actually happens in the session than on the aforementioned kinds of information.

Using initial sessions in this way is generally natural, sensible, comfortable, and useful for experiential therapists and also for most clients. However, many therapists are reluctant to use initial sessions in this way.

## The Relationship Between the Present Session, Preceding Sessions, and Subsequent Sessions

In one sense, each session can be shown to be essentially independent of the preceding and subsequent sessions. In the beginning of each session, the client selects a scene of strong feeling. The client is free to select any scene that is front and center for the client at the moment, regardless of whatever scenes of strong feeling were found in the previous session or sessions.

In another sense, the present session relates to preceding and subsequent sessions in certain specific, useful ways. In the beginning of each session, it can be seen if the qualitatively new person who was there at the end of the preceding session is or is not present in the beginning of the present session. Second, if the preceding session selected and concentrated on a particular scene of strong painful, hurtful feeling, that scene can be included in the menu of scenes of strong feeling for the present session. Thereby it may be seen if the previous painful scene and painful feelings are or are no longer front and center for the person in this immediate session.

## Number of Sessions

How many sessions a person has is a function of a least two related determinants. One consideration is whether or not this session and recent sessions successfully proceeded through all four steps. A second consideration is whether, at the end of the session, the therapist and the client want to have another session.

There are several common patterns: (a) If a number of initial sessions fail to proceed through all of the four steps, the therapist and the client may decide that this therapy is not appropriate, at least for now. (b) Most clients have somewhat regular sessions for a period ranging from under a year to a year or so; some continue for several years. (c) Most clients are seen on a flexible schedule—some have a few sessions a week, some have a session every week or every other week, and so on. (d) Many clients move toward having a spurt of three to five sessions once or twice a year over the course of many years. (e) Some clients "graduate" to having their own experiential sessions by themselves, without a therapist (Mahrer, 2002a).

In many therapies, the question is: How and when is treatment to be terminated? In experiential therapy, the question is more inclined to be: At the close of the session, do the therapist and client want to have another session, and, if so, when is the next session to be?

## Mechanisms of Psychotherapy

### The Relationship

Throughout the session, the client's eyes are closed, and the client's attention is mainly directed "out there," on whatever is front and center for the client. The person is living in some scene and is attending to what is important in that scene, for example, to the look on her brother's face, the oranges and apples rolling on the pavement when she dropped the bag, the cancer in her left lung.

To a large extent, the client talks to or talks about what is out there, with most of the person's attention on the scene. Even when the client says words to the therapist, it is with the client's attention mainly out there, on that third thing, not on the therapist. The person is relating mainly to that third thing out there.

The therapist sits alongside the client, close to the client, facing in the same direction, and likewise has his or her eyes closed throughout the session. Furthermore, the therapist's attention is almost exclusively on what the client is attending to. Even when the therapist says words to the client, virtually all of the therapist's attention is on that third thing, rather than mainly on the client.

With both the client and the therapist attending to the client's center of attention, the therapist is positioned so that what the person says, and how the person says it, are as if they are also coming in and through the therapist. In effect, both the client and the therapist are saying these words together. The net result is that the therapist is able to feel and experience the feeling and the experiencing that are occurring in the client, both at the ongoing, manifest level and perhaps even deeper inside. It is as if the therapist is a part inside the larger encompassing client. It is as if the therapist is a part of the client, speaking with the voice of this part of the client.

In the experiential approach, the therapist is a teacher guide who shows the client what to do, who accompanies the client in going through the steps of the session, who is skilled in the methods and the steps, and who is literally being the voice of the client or part of the client (Mahrer, 1996/2004, 1997b, 2001a, 2002b; Mahrer, Boulet, & Fairweather, 1994; Mahrer & Johnston, 2002).

## The Agent of Change

In many therapies, the agent of change is the therapist who creates and uses the relationship with the client and who applies the treatment methods to the client. In the experiential approach, the agent of change is the client in at least two ways. One is that it is the client who carries out the methods and techniques, doing what needs to be done in moving from one baby step to the next. The therapist shows the client what to do and how to do it, but the client is the one who does what has to be done.

Second, the client's own immediate level of readiness and willingness are prime determinants of the pace of proceeding through the session. They determine whether or not the therapy will proceed to the next baby step. If the client is not sufficiently ready or willing, work pauses, beginning again if and when the client is sufficiently ready and willing. One of the apparent bonuses of ceding virtually all power to the client's own level of readiness and willingness is the extinction of most of the basis for what is ordinarily called *resistance*. The decision to move ahead, pause, or stop is in the hands of the client, and the therapist essentially has no agenda or program that the client can resist.

## Leaping into the Abyss

*The main mechanism of change* is the radical and qualitative shift into becoming the radical and qualitatively new person. In each session, the client comes to the critical ledge or cusp of transformative change. The client can see the qualitatively whole new person that he or she can become and the scene or situation in which he or she can be the qualitatively new person. Now it is up to the client to hurl himself into being the whole new person, to leap into the abyss of change—the main mechanism of experiential change.

One of the consequences of this shift is that the qualitatively new person has an altogether new outlook and perspective, a radical new way of making sense of him- or herself and others, new understandings and insights into him- or herself and others, and new thoughts and cognitions. Instead of these perhaps being the causes of change, the story is reversed, and these are among the consequences of the quantum shift into being the qualitatively new person.

## Getting into the Right State to Begin the Session

Each session begins with the therapist and the client spending the first minute or so unlocking the usual controls and going directly into a state that is almost essential for the mechanisms of change to work. There are at least four reasons why it is so important for both the therapist and the client to first get into the right state: (a) Being in this state frees them of their typical restraints, constraints, and controls. (b) It enables the client to disengage from the ordinary, common state and to enter a state that is far more friendly to carrying out the mechanisms of change and achieving the aims and goals of the session. (c) If the client can enter into the right state, the session can be successful; if he or she cannot, it is unlikely that the session will be successful. (d) Being ready and able to enter into the right state is an indication that the client is ready to have a session. If the client does not enter into the right state, the session is not ready to begin.

The therapist shows the client how to enter into the right state and models entrance. One way is to repeatedly inhale deeply and to blast out the exhalations with unrestrained power, volume, and force. Another way is simply to give up all controls and to pour out the loudest possible noises, shrieks, yelps, screeches, blasts, and roars. A third way is to ratchet up whatever feeling state one is in until the level is as high as possible. Still an-other way is to give up bodily control, and to hurl the body into having fits and seizures, clenching and unclenching, twisting and thrashing, kicking, stamping, and throwing about the arms, legs, and torso.

Experiential therapists are ready to get into the right state, and therefore so too are most people who have sessions. For nonexperiential therapists, it is often surprising how easy it is for experiential therapists and clients to get into this state.

## Finding the Scene of Strong Feeling

The therapist shows the client how to find a time, circumstance, situation, or scene satu-rated with a strong, intense feeling. The feeling may be of any kind, good and pleasant or bad and painful. The scene of strong feeling may be relatively new and distinctive, or it may be part of a familiar, recurrent theme.

The scene may be from real life or from a dream. It may have been dramatic or quite mundane. The scene may be directly front and center for the client, or it can take some searching around to find it. The scene is usually from the last few days, but it may be from some time in the past, even the remote past. The feeling may have been a brief burst, or it may have lasted for some time. The feeling may have been manifest and public, or it may have been private and kept inside. In any case, each session's identified scene of strong feeling is rarely found by, and is distinctly different from, the traditional pretreat-ment assessment of a presenting complaint, psychological problem, diagnosed mental disorder, or symptoms of mental disorders.

## Mechanisms for Discovering the Deeper Potentialities

In the experiential system, deep-seated psychotherapeutic change begins by discovering a deeper potential for experiencing. Discovery starts by identifying a scene of strong feel-ing. Then, by actually living and being in the scene of strong feeling, the client is shown how to discover the precise instant or moment when the strong feeling peaks. Discover-ing the actual moment of peak feeling is precious because it is so rarely even sought after and even more rarely discovered, either inside or outside the world of psychotherapy, and, perhaps more importantly, because the deeper potential for experiencing lies inside the moment of peak feeling.

Once the therapist and the client are inside the moment of peak feeling, there are a number of uncommon ways of discovering the deeper potential for experiencing (Mahrer, 1996/2004, 1999a, 2002a). These include (a) filling in the final missing critical detail of the circumstances comprising the moment of peak feeling, thereby discovering the deeper potential for experiencing; (b) progressively intensifying the experiencing until the deeper potential for experiencing bursts forth; (c) penetrating deeper and deeper into the inner core of the awful painful feeling, until the deeper potential for experiencing is released; (d) undergoing a radical shift into literally being the other person or thing, in the moment of peak feeling, at which point the deeper potential for experiencing fills the client; or (e) replacing the painful, bad feeling state with a state of thorough pleasure and buoyant en-joyment of what had been so painful and unpleasant, until the deeper potential for ex-periencing appears. The deeper potential for experiencing is accessed and discovered by proper use of the appropriate method in the precise moment of strong feeling.

The steps and substeps of change in each session are shown in Figure 14.1. Each ses-sion proceeds through the same four steps of change. These steps and substeps are the on-the-job, working mechanisms of change in each session.

Once the therapist is proficient and seasoned in proceeding through the sequence of steps, there is a kind of naturalness and flow across the session, a smooth seamlessness in moving from one step to the next.

**FIGURE 14.1     The Steps Taken in Each Session of Experiential Psychotherapy**

**Step 1**
**Discover the Deeper Potential**
**for Experiencing**

- Get into a state of readiness for change.
- Find a scene of strong feeling.
- Live and be in scene of strong feeling.
- Discover the moment of peak feeling in scene of strong feeling.
- Discover the deeper potential for experiencing in the moment of peak feeling.

**Step 2**
**Welcome and Accept Deeper Potential**
**for Experiencing**

- Name and describe the deeper potential.
- React positively and negatively to the deeper potential for experiencing.
- Use other methods of welcoming and accepting the deeper potential.

**Step 3**
**Being the Deeper Potential**
**for Experiencing in Past Scenes**

- Find past scenes.
- Be the deeper potential for experiencing in past scenes.

**Step 4**
**Being the Qualitatively New Person**
**in New World**

- Find unrealistic new postsession scenes.
- Be the qualitatively new person in these unrealistic postsession scenes, including the initial scene of painful feeling.
- Find realistic new postsession scenes.
- Be the qualitatively new person in these realistic postsession scenes.
- Rehearse being the qualitatively new person in postsession scenes, modifying scenes and behavior if necessary.
- Establish readiness and commitment to continue being the qualitatively new person in the new postsession world.
- Be the qualitatively new person in the rehearsed postsession scene.

Accordingly, the picture of change starts with discovering something that is deeper inside (Step 1), then welcoming and accepting it (Step 2), and then actually becoming and being what is deeper inside (Step 3), and finally integrating the formerly deeper part so that one becomes a qualitatively new person (Step 4). The net result is a qualitatively new person who exists in a qualitatively new world, free of the former person's painful scenes and the painful feelings in those scenes.

The four steps provide the overall program for the session, the general mechanisms of change. The more operational, working mechanisms of change are the substeps under each step. As indicated in Figure 14.1, it is the substeps that provide the actual, in-session, working operations. The steps and substeps constitute the mechanisms of change in each session.

## The Feeling State in the Session

Occasionally the client locates a scene of strong feeling that is pleasant and happy, but usually the selected scene is a painful scene. When this happens, the initial step of probing down inside the scene can intensify the painful feelings so that they are even more torturous, dreadful, anguished, and painful.

However, once the first step culminates in discovering the deeper potential, the balance of the session is almost always accompanied with a feeling state that is happy and pleasant, whimsical and silly, vibrant and full of energy. The client welcomes and embraces what is deeper (Step 2), dives into being the deeper potential (Step 3), and emerges as the qualitatively new person (Step 4). These steps are helped to occur when the therapist can encourage a state of deliberate playfulness, absurdity, zaniness, silliness, outrageousness, unconstrained unreality, joyful freedom, and bubbling spontaneity.

Sessions of such momentous change can be and are, for both the client and therapist, sessions of exceptionally wonderful feelings, rather than sessions that are relatively neutral, constrained, ordinarily conversational, serious, controlled, and without emotional flares and outbursts.

# APPLICATIONS

## Problems

In general, this therapy is for virtually any kind of painful unhappy feeling in any kind of painful unhappy scene or situation. That is, this therapy is for virtually any kind of concern, worry, trouble, bother, or painful or unhappy feeling. This includes feelings, scenes, and states that are painful but not necessarily extreme and shattering, and feelings, scenes, and states that are extreme, shattering, dreadful, and terrifying. It is for both events, scenes, and situations located in the external world, and also bodily phenomena commonly referred to as ulcers, headaches, and cancers. It is for people who think of themselves as more or less ordinary and normal, and also for people who think of themselves as plagued with something seriously wrong, as out of their minds, deranged, psychotic, or crazy (Mahrer, 2001e; Mahrer & Boulet, 2001b).

Is this therapy appropriate for treatment of what are commonly called presenting complaints, psychological problems, symptoms, and mental disorders? Yes. Becoming a qualitatively new person, free of the painful scenes of painful feeling, usually has the positive "side effect" of "washing away" what are ordinarily called presenting complaints, psychological problems, symptoms, and mental disorders (Mahrer, 1996/2004, 1997a, 2002a).

However, experiential therapy may not necessarily be helpful to those presenting with symptoms or diagnosed with disorders. Although the opening scene of strong feeling can be either painful or joyous, joyous opening scenes are not especially helpful in treating presenting complaints, psychological problems, symptoms, and mental disorders. In addition, the opening scene of strong feeling and the discovered deeper potential are free to shift from session to session, and therefore the aims and goals can and do shift from session to session. Experiential therapy would close down if the therapist imposed a continuing goal of trying to treat the client's alcoholism, infertility, eating disorder, drug addiction, pain management, inadequate grief reaction, gambling problems, lack of impulse control, abusive personality, depression, or seasonal affective disorder. In other words, this therapy works with an exceedingly broad range of opening scenes and feelings.

### Limitations and Restrictions

Experiential psychotherapy relies on the client's immediate readiness and willingness to proceed through the steps and substeps of a session. While the degree of readiness and willingness can fluctuate from session to session, if it falls below the necessary threshold, work comes to a halt, perhaps for a few moments or so, or perhaps for the session.

Experiential psychotherapy is inappropriate and inadequate for people for whom the underlying strong attraction is being and continuing with a therapist who fulfills some important role in the client's current world, such as the client's nurturing caregiver, solid and trustworthy friend, seductive charmer, organizer and manager, wise sage, or "rock"—one on whom the client can be safely dependent.

Experiential sessions can be useful for most people, but its availability is sharply limited and its use is restricted to those therapists whose ways of thinking fit the experiential conceptual system. This is a major limitation and restriction. However, interested parties may be able to learn to conduct their own experiential psychotherapy sessions. They may even be able to teach themselves, without any help from a practitioner. (See the section on "Having One's Own Experiential Sessions," below.)

## Managed Care Systems

Experiential psychotherapy is poorly suited to both the spirit and the letter of some managed care systems. Here are two conspicuous ways in which experiential psychotherapy fails to fit the managed care model:

1.  Experiential psychotherapy is neither designed for nor can it be trusted as useful for treatment of mental disorders, their symptoms, and related problems and complaints. Although some sessions may include the "washing away" of what are traditionally regarded as mental disorders, this is not the express aim or goal of the sessions..

2.  Each experiential session is a unique and separate mini-therapy. Instead of a target of treating a specific mental disorder in every session, each session produces its own painful scene of painful feeling (or its own scene of strong happy, pleasant feelings). In addition, each session enables the person to become whatever that session discovers the person can become. Such a lofty goal is perhaps beyond the scope of managed care.

## Multicultural Differences

Experiential therapy seems to be relatively free of the common problems associated with differences between the client and the therapist. These include such dimensions as gender, age, body size, skin color, physical state, sexual preferences, religious beliefs, and cultural background. "Physical state" may include health conditions such as paraplegia, being blind, being in a wheelchair, or having cancer.

The relative lack of such problems may be illustrated in regard to the dimension of *multicultural differences*. Experiential therapy minimizes these common problems in at least two ways: (a) Experiential therapy offers the client a way of becoming the person that the person can become, free of the client's painful scenes of painful feelings. If, for whatever reason, including cultural reasons, the client is not especially interested in achieving this goal, then experiential sessions can be declined. In other words, multicultural differences can determine whether what experiential therapy offers is of value to the person, rather than multicultural differences being issues to be resolved or addressed by the therapy. In addition, the person's own culture, not experiential therapy, may determine whether, and concretely how, the client is to be the concretely new person the person can become, and what takes the place of the former painful scenes of painful feeling. (b) The experiential therapist can essentially disengage from his or her own cultural background and values and can enter into the client, melding and fusing with the person, becoming and being the person, undergoing the person's feelings and experiencings. The skilled experiential therapist is literally able to take on the person's culture, background, and values. Far-fetched as this may seem, this skill helps to minimize cultural differences between the person and the therapist.

## Having One's Own Experiential Sessions

Experiential psychotherapists may work with people who want to be able to have experiential sessions by themselves (Firestone, 2001; Mahrer, 2000c, 2002a). In either case, the steps and substeps are the same. What is different is the role of the experiential psychotherapist. One can learn by oneself how to have one's own experiential sessions, and in this case the experiential psychotherapist plays no role at all (Mahrer, 2002a). It is also common for the experiential psychotherapist to help by teaching "practitioners" or "students" to hold their own experiential sessions.

## Evaluation

### Evaluation of Each Session

In many therapies, it is common to evaluate the success or failure of a program of sessions, starting with a pretreatment evaluation of the problem or mental disorder, and ending with a post-treatment evaluation of the outcome of the program of sessions. In contrast, each experiential session is its own mini-therapy, and success or failure is only judged in terms of each immediate session. Because each session is its own mini-therapy, evaluation refers to seeing if each session is successful or unsuccessful.

There are two ways to evaluate the nature and degree of success of each experiential session:

(a) To what degree did the session achieve each of the steps of the session? For each of the four steps, evaluation can focus on whether or not the step was achieved, and on how well the step was achieved. These determinations are typically evident to the therapist and the person in the session. If a researcher has observed the session, it is typically evident to him or her as well.

(b) To what degree did the session achieve the two goals of each session? Was the client successful in undergoing the qualitative shift into becoming the qualitatively new person, and if so, to what degree? This can be determined carefully and objectively in the session itself, and it can be determined by whether the qualitatively new person is present in the opening of the subsequent session. The second question is whether the person is free of the painful scene of painful feeling. This can be determined both in the session itself and by whether or not the painful scene of painful feelings is still present or is essentially gone in the subsequent session when the person identifies the scene of strong feeling that is front and center in the session.

### Evaluation of Initial Sessions

Initial sessions are used to evaluate the goodness-of-fit between the client and experiential psychotherapy. Most people can and do achieve successful and effective initial sessions, and they proceed through all four steps. Most people can at least go through the opening substeps. On the other hand, some clients may have low goodness-of-fit, at least for the present, and this is typically clear from the very beginning of the initial sessions, and especially after an initial session or two. Even after several initial sessions, there are clients who do not get into the appropriate state of strong feeling, do not find a scene of strong feeling, and do not achieve the first step of discovering the deeper potential for experiencing.

It can be quite clear, both to the person and to the therapist, that there is little or no goodness-of-fit, at least for now. It can also be clear that goodness-of-fit is quite high. Evaluation of goodness-of-fit can be an important part of both the therapist's and the client's decision, at the end of an initial session, whether to have a subsequent session. Initial sessions can show that this may not be the most appropriate therapy for some clients or therapists.

### Evaluation of the Psychotherapist

Achieving a successful session requires that the psychotherapist have a sufficiently high degree of competency in the skills of each substep and step. Evaluation by a competent teacher can either confirm the psychotherapist's competency or identify the skills in need of further development. In other words, a successful session requires that the therapist be truly competent, and evaluation can spot the actual skills that require further development.

Examination of tapes of the session can help identify which skills are well developed and which can benefit from further training and competency development.

## Evaluation and Research

In many therapies, research is used to test, check out, or confirm (a) that the therapy is effective, especially in relation to rival therapies, in treating identified problems and mental disorders; (b) that selected components of therapies are related to successful and effective outcome; (c) that the theory is efficacious or superior to its rivals; (d) that there are research-supported truths that belong in the cumulative body of psychotherapeutic knowledge.

Experiential therapy rejects these goals and favors research that is "discovery oriented" (Mahrer, 1985, 1988, 1996a, 1996b, 1998a, 2004a; Mahrer & Boulet, 1999a). Experiential research seeks to discover the secrets of psychotherapy and explore the unknown world of what psychotherapy can become. Compared to most traditional research, discovery-oriented research has its own distinctive mission, purposes, and uses.

## Treatment

### Practice Management

Since each session is its own mini-therapy, sessions are open-ended. Accordingly, appointments are made for the session to begin at an agreed upon time, and they end when they end, usually after one to two hours.

At the end of each session, both the person and the therapist agree on when the next session is to be. Sessions may be only a few days apart, or a week or more may pass between sessions. It is common for sessions to fall into a somewhat regular schedule, but there is always room for flexibility.

Many therapies consist of a program or an extended series of sessions, and it is understandable that a candidate may want to know something about the therapy before committing to an extended series of sessions. This may be handled by a pretreatment interview, by conducting a preliminary series of initial sessions, by providing written information to prospective clients, or by an initial session or so in which the therapist explains the nature of the therapy. Since each experiential session is its own mini-therapy, and the person is free to end the session at any point, most of these issues are taken care of by undergoing a session firsthand.

### Contexts and Settings

Experiential therapy is designed for one person and one therapist who work together in at least two kinds of settings or contexts. The most common context includes the person and the therapist in a soundproofed room. Nevertheless, the context can be enlarged to couples therapy, family therapy, or small group therapy. Largely because experiential therapy accepts virtually any kind of opening scene of strong feeling, and because each session is its own mini-therapy, these sessions can be carried out in virtually any setting or context.

### Experiential Sessions by Oneself

The proportion of people interested in providing their own self-help may be high, but the proportion of those taking the self-help route to undergo deep-seated transformational change is exceedingly low. Even more surprising, professional psychotherapists are among those most reluctant to undergo their own transformational change and become the qualitatively new person they can become. In general, treatment of oneself seems to be appealing to only a small proportion of people, especially when treatment means serious and significant change in one's core self (Mahrer, 2002a).

Nevertheless, experiential therapists can train those who are interested in having their own experiential sessions in a number of ways. They can hold tutorials for a single student or a small group of students learning to have their own sessions. A second way is for the teacher to conduct larger classes. In both formats, the teacher can rely on the study of exemplars' tapes of their own experiential sessions and on careful study of the students' own tapes of their sessions. It is likely that increasing numbers of people will have their own experiential sessions in the future (Mahrer, 2001b, 2002a).

## Training and the Optimal State

In the experiential approach, the aim is not only to identify an ideal or optimal state (Mahrer, 1989a, 1996/2004, 2003b), but to take a next step and to try to clarify the specific, concrete ways of being and behaving that actually identify the experiential version of an optimal state. Accordingly, experiential training includes groups in which participants are free to select whichever concretely optimal ways of being and behaving are of interest to them, to gain as much proficiency and skills as they wish in each, and to incorporate these new ways of being and behaving either in a limited fashion or more generally, thereby undergoing as little or as much change as they wish in achieving the experiential version of an optimal state.

These training groups can enable ready and willing participants to attain as much of the optimal state as they wish, and to do so with or without experiential psychotherapy or having their own experiential sessions. This is another step in the evolution of experiential psychotherapy.

## The Experiential System and Social Change

When a group of people become integrated and actualized, when they become the people they are capable of becoming, when they attain an optimal state, their world can become a better world. If a group of 2 or 20 or 2 million people can have their own experiential sessions and can move toward becoming the people they are capable of becoming, then there can be consequent changes in their mutually and collectively constructed interpersonal and social worlds (Mahrer, 1989a). Their interactions, their communities, and their social worlds can become more integrated, peaceful, harmonious, welcoming, and characterized by good feelings, and less characterized by painful, hateful, and agonizing scenes and feelings. In other words, having one's own experiential sessions and training toward an optimal state can help bring about the kinds of deep-seated personal changes that can have consequent and collective social changes (Mahrer, 2002a). However, we are now in what is perhaps the early phase of the evolution of experiential psychotherapy.

## Professional Training

Experiential therapy and having one's own experiential sessions rest on the principle of the importance of discovering what lies deeper in the person. When the spirit of this principle is applied to professional training, it can add a useful component to the education and supervision of psychotherapists (Mahrer, 1998b; Mahrer & Boulet, 1997, 1999b). The principle also suggests that training can enable the student to discover, develop, and use his or her own deeper framework for psychotherapy, and that this added component can enhance the trainee's functioning as a professional psychotherapist.

# CASE EXAMPLE

This case presents a representative example of clients who (a) are ready to enter into experiential change; and (b) are ready to allow in-session changes to carry over into post-session personal and life changes.

This case also provides an example of therapists who (a) can be ready and willing to consider a somewhat new departure in what a session of psychotherapy can be; (b) are ready to use each session as an opportunity for the client to become the person the client can become, including being free of a painful situation that was front and center in the session; and (c) are proficient in guiding clients through the in-session steps and substeps at the client's own pace and readiness.

## Background

Melanie, a woman in her early fifties, grew up and still lives in a small town. She gave birth to twins in high school and dropped out of school to take care of them. At 19, she married Frank and had another child. The children are now grown; two of them live in town. Frank owned a gas station where Melanie worked occasionally. A few months ago, Frank died of a sudden heart attack while fishing with a friend. Melanie visits his grave often and misses him terribly. She was getting on rather well with her grief until a worrisome incident left her agitated and frightened. Melanie went to her physician, who gave her the name and telephone number of a psychotherapist. She called and made an appointment with the therapist shortly after seeing her physician.

## Logistics

The two chairs are identical, both large and comfortable, almost touching each other, both facing in the same direction. The therapist invites Melanie to sit in one chair, saying, "You can lean back and put your feet up on the large footrest." He then sits back in the other, putting his feet up (T = Therapist; P = Patient).

T:  I'm ready to begin. Can we begin? Are you ready?
P:  Sure. I like the chairs.
T:  Yeah, me too . . . We will keep going till we're done, that's usually an hour or so, maybe even two hours. Is this all right?
P:  Sure thing.
T:  Okay. Now here's the next weird thing. I'll describe it, see if it is all right with you . . . I am going to shut my eyes . . . There . . . and I'm going to keep them shut the whole time.
P:  Okay. Should I shut mine too?
T:  I hope so, but see how you feel. It's up to you. I keep them shut cause . . . well, I find that I can concentrate better on what you're saying. And I can actually see things better with my eyes closed. When I listen and you talk, I can see better . . . So I'd like you to close your eyes and keep them closed, if that seems all right with you. Or you can open your eyes if you want.

## Step 1. Discover What Is Deeper Inside

The purpose of the first step is to discover what is deeper inside Melanie in this session, a deeper potentiality for experiencing. Getting ready for this inner probing means getting into the right state:

T:  Okay, my eyes are closed . . . Now, I want to try and listen to you as carefully as I can, and I want to be able to go with you into the thoughts and feelings inside. It helps if

I can do my best to be as open as I can to whatever you're thinking and feeling. So I am not only going to keep my eyes closed, I'm going to spend about 30 seconds or so taking some deep breaths, and then exhaling as hard as I can and as loud as I can. That helps clear things so I can listen better. Is this all right with you?

P: (*Laughing*) Sure! What do I do?

T: You can join me if you want to. It's up to you. But it helps me to get ready.

P: (*Pleasantly disbelieving*) You're going to make a lot of noise? This is weird! You're going to scream and yell? This is really weird!

T: Loud as I can. That's why the room's soundproofed. But I won't yell if it seems too weird to you. And you don't have to unless you want to.

P: (*Laughing*) Well, this is something! Sure, go ahead. You do this every time?

T: Every time . . . Okay, here I go . . . It's going to be loud . . . And you can join me if you want.

Inhaling deeply, the therapist blasts out the exhalations with explosive outbursts of sheer volume. He starts with a few bellows and roars. After five seconds or so, Melanie joins in with some high volume shrieks. In a kind of duet, they move on to yelps and whelps, growls and snarls, screeches and howls. After about 30 seconds or so, the therapist is in a kind of pleasant free state, and he says, "That's enough for me. I think I'm ready to begin." Melanie is giggling and talking loudly. "I wish I had a room like this!" she exclaims.

The next substep is for Melanie to find some time when her feelings were strong, a scene of strong feeling. The therapist shows her how to do this:

T: Good! Now we look for some time that is maybe on your mind, a time when something happened, some time when the feeling in you is kind of strong. It could be a good feeling or a bad one, any kind of feeling at all. Maybe the feeling showed, so others could see it. Or maybe it was just inside you, and you're by yourself. Is this all right? Am I clear? No?

P: Oh yes! I got one . . . It's sure been on my mind . . . I don't sleep . . . something's wrong!

The therapist shows her how to describe the scene in careful detail, both what is happening outside and inside, her thoughts and feelings. "See it as if it is happening right now. You are actually in the scene. Put all your attention on what you see and what is happening inside. Is this all right? Are you clear on what to do and how to do it?"

From this point on, both Melanie and the therapist mainly attend to what is "out there," to whatever she is seeing and talking about. They rarely attend to one another from here to the end of the session. Even if they address one another, most of their attention is still directed "out there," on whatever they are looking at, on the scene they are living in.

Melanie chooses a recent scene in which she is weeding in the garden at the back of the house. She is on her hands and knees about 20 or 30 feet from the back porch.

P: (*Shaky, frightened, on edge*) I know that Frank is gone, and I'm not even thinking about Frank. It's early in the morning and here I am weeding . . . It's quiet. Mostly I hear the birds . . . (*She pauses, takes a few deep breaths, and carefully accentuates the following words.*) And I hear Frank call out to me from the porch. "You want some coffee?" Like that!

T: I hear it! Just normal! It's his voice! Clear as a bell. I hear it!

P: I know it can't be Frank . . . But it sounds so clear, so real!

T: "You want some coffee?" It sure is clear . . . This is strange! How can this be? . . . Oh oh . . .

Melanie is crying lightly, almost whimpering, as she describes turning to the back porch where Frank's voice is coming from, staring wide-eyed at the back porch. She is confused, frozen, and numb. She sees nothing on the porch. She is trembling, on her hands and knees, and she is so frightened. "What's happening to me! What's wrong with me! Something's wrong with me!" She is quietly sobbing. This is the scene of strong feeling. Melanie is living in it.

With both the therapist and Melanie living and being in the scene of strong feeling, the next substep is to search for the precise instant when the feeling peaks. Remaining in the scene, the therapist shows Melanie how to slow things down, to see the scene in slow motion, and to look around for exactly when the feeling reaches its peak. This usually takes a fair amount of searching. Almost always, finding the exact moment is a new discovery. Melanie searches for a while and then finds the exact instant.

P: I'm staring at the porch . . . No . . . I'm so scared . . . Closer . . . Something's happening in my head . . . I'm so scared that I'm losing my mind. Something's really wrong . . . and then . . . (*she gasps*) I know! That's when it happened! I remember! Yes! I remember now! For a second! That's when it happened! . . . Like a flash! I'm in the air! I'm in the air and . . . this is weird . . . I actually see myself on the ground! It's like everything stops. It just stops! I remember! That's what happened! That's it! That was so . . . strange . . .

The final substep is to discover the deeper potential for experiencing. It is here, somewhere, in this brief moment of peak feeling. With both of them living and being in this brief moment, both hovering in the air, looking down at Melanie on the ground, the therapist shows Melanie how to freeze this instant, hold it still, and to inch her way closer to the nearby deeper potential for experiencing. When she is close enough, Melanie will be touched by the deeper experiencing. She will undergo something new and different. This shift is the presence of the discovered deeper potential for experiencing.

One way of moving closer to the deeper potential for experiencing is to fill in the missing details of what is happening in the peak moment. If there is a critical missing detail, identifying that final piece can fill Melanie with the deeper experiencing. This is one way of discovering the deeper potential for experiencing. It is the way selected by the therapist and used by Melanie.

T: Stay here! Hold it still. I'm up here . . . I see Melanie down there. What is going on?
P: I see myself! That's the thing! I'm up here, and I'm just in the air here.
T: Mainly seeing Melanie down there? Mainly?
P: Yeah, I see myself, but that's not it . . . No . . . But there's something else.
T: Something else. Mainly something else. Something you see? I can't tell.
P: No . . . I am just floating here . . . And . . . And . . . I'm . . . I don't know . . . Oh! Oh! I'm thinking . . . Yeah.
T: Something's happening to me . . . What? . . . What? . . . A thought? Here's the thought . . .
P: (*Her voice is hushed, peaceful, yet so alive and vital. She says each word slowly. She does not sound like Melanie. She fills in the critical missing piece.*) I know what I'm thinking. This is it! Yes . . . I'm thinking that I know all about this . . . I understand what's happening to Melanie down there . . . I understand everything . . . It all seems so clear . . . I know things . . . I understand poor old sweet Melanie, how she's such a nice person, and I understand her hearing Frank's voice . . . I just . . . I know things . . .
T: (*Laughing*) Who are you? This is a switch!
P: (*She is Melanie again.*) It was that up in the air thing! . . . And I felt so different. I never felt that before. Like I understood . . . everything . . . Hey, that's not me! That's

really not me! But I sure felt it all of a sudden. It just came over me. I knew everything. That's a hoot!

## Step 2. Welcome and Accept the Deeper Potential for Experiencing

The purpose of this step is to enable the client to welcome and accept, to feel good about, to love and embrace what had been deeper inside, what had been sealed off, hidden, without her even being aware of it. The first step enabled her to be in its immediate presence. Now she can welcome and accept what had been discovered.

One way is for therapist and client to provide a description of it, to say what it is. The therapist begins:

T:  I'm still feeling it, and I want to describe what just happened. What did Melanie say it was like? Understanding what's happening, knowing about everything . . .

P:  That's it . . . It's funny, like being really wise, understanding what's going on, the world. Like I know . . . everything.

They arrive at this description of what had touched her from deep inside: being really wise, having infinite wisdom, knowing everything, fully understanding the world.

One way to welcome and accept the discovered deeper potential for experiencing is to openly admit your positive and negative feelings about it: "Actually, it was kind of cool! I like it—I think!" Look for people you know who exemplify that particular quality: "No one where I live, that's for sure!" Look for times when you actually felt it, or something close: "Once I taught the other kids how to play this game. I was just a kid. But really? I never felt that. Never!" Among the other ways, one is to show how this particular deeper quality is not you, you are not like this, you may even be quite different.

T:  So if I go around town, to people who know Melanie, and ask them who I'm talking about. She's really wise, infinite wisdom, knowing everything, infinite knowing, fully understanding the world, they'd all say that's Melanie!

P:  (*A sudden explosive outburst*) Ha! Never! Not one person! I barely finished tenth grade! And I was the dummy in my family at doing anything practical. Well, I'm not dumb. Grades don't mean much anyhow. I've got common sense.

T:  I see Melanie with a T-shirt saying, "I am infinite wisdom, all-knowing, fully understanding". . .

P:  And on the back it says, "That's a lie!" They'd lock me up! No way I'm like that. I'm a good mother, and a loyal friend, and I don't talk behind someone's back, and I miss Frank, and I smoke too much and maybe drink too much beer sometimes, but that all-knowing stuff—no way. Not even close. If there's something like that in me it's really . . . been hidden all these years. No one could tell.

After a while, using some of the methods for this step, Melanie seems to be drawn toward this quality, welcoming and accepting this quality in itself, but not especially something that might be in her. That strikes her as pleasantly unrealistic, a fantasy, some way she could never be, delightful as it might be.

## Step 3. Being the Deeper Potential for Experiencing in Past Scenes

In Step 1, Melanie found something hidden deep inside, a quality for experiencing infinite knowing, infinite wisdom, fully understanding the world. Although this seemed to be so unlike her, such an alien quality, in Step 2 she was able to welcome and accept it to some extent, to befriend this quality, to let it stay around for awhile. She even could like it.

Step 3 begins by looking for times in the past when she came close to having that same deeper experiencing, or where such a deeper experiencing was painfully absent. She recollects a time, many years ago, when her son asked her what an eclipse was, and she was so befuddled, so pitifully ignorant, that her son took pity on her and hugged her. Step 3 also starts by finding past incidents that might be associated with the sense of surprised shock at hearing Frank's voice. Melanie quickly remembers secretly smoking with her best friend. They were both young adolescents, and she was almost frozen with shock when her best friend confessed to being a lesbian. Melanie is appalled and disgusted. "How could you do something like that?" she asked.

In Step 3, the past scene can be used as a context in which Melanie has a magnificent opportunity to detach from the person she is, to let go of and disengage from being Melanie, and instead to plunge headlong into being the deeper experiencing of infinite knowing, infinite wisdom, fully understanding the world. The shift is radical and qualitative, and involves transformation into a whole new person.

With both of them living and being in the scene with the girlfriend, the therapist explains what Melanie is to do, provided she is quite ready and willing. (a) She is to remain living and being here with the girlfriend. (b) She is to be replaced by a whole new person, perhaps an actor. Melanie is gone, off to the side. What happens from now on is not coming from Melanie, but from the whole new person who is infinite knowing, infinite wisdom, all-understanding. Is Melanie clear on who she is to be? Does she have a clear picture of her role? "Yeah, that's a great part! Sure thing. This is going to be fun!" (c) This actor is to live and be in the scene with the girlfriend, and to do so in sheer silliness, slapstick playfulness, enjoyment, fun, and pleasure. The context is wholesale unreality, with no reality constraints or restraints whatsoever. (d) This radical shift is to occur only if Melanie is truly eager; any hesitancies or misgivings stop the shift. "No! I mean yes! I want to do this! I know what to do!" (e) This shift is to occur all of a sudden, in a flash:

T:  So Sandy just said, "I wanted to tell you. I had sex with girls. I'm a lesbian . . ." And now, the big switch! The actor is ready! Three! Two! One! Go!

P:  (*In a theatrical voice, oozing with knowingness, understanding, wisdom.*) You are about to explore the wonderful and scary world of sexuality, my child. And I know you. I know you have the courage of risking the whole new world of tabooed sexuality. And I will tell you what the world can be like for you because I am gifted with knowledge. I know . . . everything . . . I can foresee the future. I have unlimited wisdom, as you well know. Ask me all your questions because I know . . . And you know that I know. I am blessed with such infinite understanding . . . Yeah verily, verily, and that is the truth. Bless you my child, and go forth . . .

The therapist invites this qualitatively new person to carry forth in past scene after past scene, and to remain being this new person from now on. Melanie luxuriates in undergoing and acting out the role of this whole new person, and the therapist guides her into the final step of the session.

## Step 4. Being the Qualitatively New Person in the New World

The final step gives Melanie an opportunity to taste and sample what it can be like to be a qualitatively new Melanie in the real world outside the office. The emphasis is on full and complete freedom of choice to go ahead or to decline, to make slight or significant changes, to make changes that are safe and limited or broader and more comprehensive, to weigh and consider any imminent changes, to do what is right and proper, appropriate and fitting, sensible and responsible, including doing nothing at all.

Step 4 begins with Melanie remaining the one who is all-knowing, all-understanding, the wise one. And the context remains that of sheer silliness, play, whimsy, wholesale un-reality, full fantasy. The difference is that the scenes are from today, tomorrow, and the next few days or so. The therapist explains all this and then asks:

T:  Is this all right?
P:  Oh yes! I love this!
T:  And keep things silly and unrealistic?
P:  Yeah yeah!
T:  I'm looking for some times, places, like right after the session, and the door opens, and I see you walking to your truck, and where are you? Driving back home?
P:  The town council is tonight, and I am in the audience. What are we going to do about the wells and the drainage, Melanie? (*In a lowered voice, brimming with playful excitement.*) I stand up and my arms are stretched up, and my eyes half closed, and the congregation punctuates my sentences.
T:  They punctuate? Well!
P:  As I talk and they chant . . . I know the answer.
T:  She knows, she knows.
P:  You all depend on me. Trust me.
T:  We trust, we trust.
P:  I will take care of the drainage.
T:  And the wells, don't forget the wells.
P:  Entrust yourselves to me. I have the knowledge of the ages . . . The wisdom of the sages. I know, I know. I see by the looks on your faces that you all know that I know, I know. I do understand the world.

Melanie stays in character, being this qualitatively new personality as she moves from one playfully unrealistic scene to another, each one occurring later in the day or tomorrow or soon. She is this whole new person with her sister, whom she calls tonight, and with Roger the butcher, whom she has known all her life. Melanie seems to be thoroughly delighting in being all-knowing, all-understanding, and all-wise in imminent postsession scenes that are pure whimsy and silliness, fantasy and make-believe, without any reality restraints or constraints.

The final phase of this step offers Melanie an opportunity to undergo this new experiencing as much or as little as she wishes in the exceedingly real world right after the session. The make-believe context of unreality is replaced with the real world. Melanie can continue being this whole new person. She can decline being this person and return to the Melanie who entered the session. She can compromise by finding some token safe way to enjoy this newly discovered experiencing in some token safe situation in the next day or so.

T:  Well, this is fun. But now what? I mean, are you really going to be this way? You don't have to, you know. I am seeing you after the session. And you go to your truck, and what? What do I see now? I mean for real?
P:  I'm not going to the town council tonight.
T:  She stays home. I see her at home.
P:  I'm going to write.
T:  She's at the dining room table, writing.
P:  With the old typewriter. I'm going to write. I used to write in a diary. My sister and I did. I am going to write a diary, every day. I start tonight.

The therapist invites Melanie to rehearse this, to see what it feels like, especially if she can have this new experiencing as she writes a page or so. Melanie is typing her thoughts about her sister and her garden and missing Frank. "I understand everything. I am all-knowing . . . I have wise thoughts . . . I know what the world is like . . . And this is so much fun!"

T: I do believe she is going to do it.

P: I sure am. Tonight! I sure feel different. (*Practicing*) I understand. I know what the world is like . . .

The session comes to a close with the therapist and Melanie letting parts of Melanie give voice to their reactions, for better and for worse.

T: Okay! Now I am hearing from other parts of Melanie . . . Maybe you do too. It goes like this. Hey, Melanie, who do you think you are? You never even finished high school! Just write a few thoughts and stop. That'll be enough. And keep it to yourself. Remember, you're still Melanie.

P: I am writing my thoughts on sheets of paper, with the old typewriter, and I am writing details, everything I see, everything I do.

T: This is not the real you! People will think you lost your mind. Your son will have you locked up. Think of your family! Besides, you never did anything like this. You can't even spell!

P: (*Laughing*) I'm just writing my thoughts, and my observations.

T: Listen to her. "Observations." Ha! So what's going to happen when you're in the garden and you hear Frank's voice again? Maybe it's going to happen tomorrow, soon. You'll flip out again. No more sleep. You'll fall apart. "I'm losing my mind!" Right?

P: (*In an exaggeratedly tolerant tone*) That is the way the world is. Frank is dead. His memory lingers on. A person carries the loved one's voice inside. It can happen. Accept it. Enjoy it. I know this happens. It is so understandable. I will describe it all in my writings. T: My writings? I thought loose notes in a diary!

P: My writings.

T: You're kidding, right?

P: Just a wee bit . . . I am going to type out my thoughts and see what it's like.

## Follow-Up

Melanie entered the session agitated and disturbed about a recent incident that left her sleepless and worried about falling apart. She left the session, after almost two hours, as a substantially new person with an integral new quality that had not been part of the person she had been.

From that session on, Melanie was free of her sleepless nights and her disturbing worries about something being seriously wrong with her. She had a number of further sessions, returned every year or so for three to five sessions.

Melanie did her homework after the session, typing her thoughts and having a new-found sense of knowing herself and the world, being all-wise and all-understanding. That was the beginning of a remarkable change in Melanie and her life. Over the ensuing 18 years, what started with a half hour of typed notes became three hours a night of serious writing. Melanie began with a notebook of essays, some short stories published in the town newspaper, and a few articles in magazines with small circulations. Her work galvanized into renown as she won a number of literary prizes, published several plays, numerous essays and articles, and eight novels. Melanie, the mother who left high school to take care of her twins, has recently been the recipient of a national award in literature, a number of visiting lectureships at universities, and two honorary doctorates.

Melanie still has a home in the same small town, and, in her early seventies, she radiates a sense of knowing herself and her world, a sense of wisdom and understanding. It may be that she first discovered this quality in a session many years ago, and helped bring it to life at the dining room table, typing some of her thoughts, after she drove her truck home after the session.

## SUMMARY

Experiential psychotherapy rests on a model of potentials for experiencing in relationship with one another. The key to experiential sessions is a scene of strong feeling as a doorway into the inner world of deeper potentials for experiencing. The gift offered by experiential sessions is the opportunity to undergo a magnificent shift into becoming the qualitatively new person that the person is capable of becoming, a new person who can be free of the old person's painful scenes of painful feelings.

It is rather likely that the future of experiential psychotherapy includes (a) further adoption by a relatively small constituency of psychotherapists whose way of thinking is friendly to the experiential way of thinking; and (b) progressive evolution and development so that experiential psychotherapy becomes more and more the psychotherapy it is capable of becoming.

Further glimpses into the future seem to suggest at least three ways in which the psychotherapies of today may be essentially unrecognizable a hundred years or so from now (Mahrer, 1997c, 1999b, 2001b; Mahrer & Boulet, 2001a, 2001b). (a) Future technologies will likely provide far better ways of creating, offering, providing virtual reality people and contexts that psychotherapists currently provide for clients, e.g., the good listener, the one who can be counted upon, the attractive confidante. (b) The methods of self-change are likely to undergo a powerful evolution, both in sheer effectiveness and in popular adoption by people in general. (c) Today's experiential psychotherapy will likely be replaced by methods and programs enabling people to achieve higher and higher levels of optimal being and behaving.

## ANNOTATED BIBLIOGRAPHY

Mahrer, A. R. (1978/1989). *Experiencing: A humanistic theory of psychology and psychiatry.* Ottawa, Canada: University of Ottawa Press. (Original work published in 1978.)

This volume sets forth experiential philosophy, philosophy of science, and experiential psychology. It provides the experiential perspective on the origins of personality, human development, the structure of personality, the human body, construction and functions of the external world, human behavior, painful feelings and states, personal and social change, and optimal states of integration and actualization.

Mahrer, A. R. (1989). *Dream work: In psychotherapy and self-change.* New York: Norton.

This volume provides the experiential conceptualization of dreams and describes how to use dreams in experiential psychotherapy and self-change.

Mahrer, A. R. (1996/2004). *The complete guide to experiential psychotherapy.* Boulder, CO: Bull.

This volume provides the conceptual foundation and the practical in-session methods of experiential psychotherapy. It is the comprehensive and complete enunciation of this approach for the experiential practitioner and for those interested in what experiential psychotherapy is, how it works, why it works, and its conceptual foundations.

Mahrer, A. R. (2002). *Becoming the person you can become: The complete guide to self-transformation.* Boulder, CO: Bull.

This volume is both a conceptual and practical guide for anyone who is ready and willing to learn how to undergo his or her own experiential session.

## CASE READINGS

Mahrer, A. R. (1996). Existential-humanistic psychotherapy and the religious person. In E. P. Shafranske (Ed.), *Religion and the clinical practice of psychology* (pp. 433–460). Washington, DC: American Psychological Association.

The therapist works with a person in a session starting with a scene of compellingly morbid fascination with religious texts on death.

Mahrer, A. R. (2005). Experiential psychotherapy with a troubled physician. In D. Wedding & R. J. Corsini (Eds.), *Case studies in psychotherapy* (4th ed.). Belmont, CA: Wadsworth.

Mahrer provides a description of a session with a physician who is agonizing over his bizarre and frightening behavior.

Mahrer, A. R., & Boulet, D. B. (2001a). How can experiential psychotherapy help transform the field of sex therapy? In P. J. Kleinplatz (Ed.), *New directions in sex therapy: Innovations and alternatives* (pp. 234–256). Philadelphia: Brunner-Routledge.

> This session opens with a scene in which the husband is on the bed with his wife, racked with agonizing pain. He is sex dead, numb, suffering, and torn apart.

Mahrer, A. R., & Roberge, M. (1993). Single-session experiential therapy with any person whatsoever. In R. Wells & V. J. Giannetti (Eds.), *Case book of the brief psychotherapies* (pp. 179–196). New York: Plenum.

> The session starts with the person in a state of utter panic, screeching chaos, and falling apart, and follows the steps throughout a dramatic session of significant change.

# REFERENCES

Chalmers, A. F. (1982). *What is this thing called science?* Queensland, Australia: University of Queensland Press.

Einstein, A. (1923). *Sidelights of relativity.* New York: Dutton.

Firestone, A. D. (2001). What it was like to go through three awe-full moments in my own experiential session. In R. B. Marchesani & E. M. Stern (Eds.), *Frightful stages: From the primitive to the therapeutic* (pp. 141–147). Binghamton, NY: Haworth.

Gendlin, E. T. (1973). Experiential psychotherapy. In R. J. Corsini (Ed.), *Current psychotherapies* (pp. 317–352). Itasca, IL: F. E. Peacock.

Gendlin, E. T. (1996). *Focusing-oriented psychotherapy.* New York: Guilford.

Kelly, G. (1955). *The psychology of personal constructs.* New York: Norton.

Mahrer, A. R. (1985). *Psychotherapeutic change: An alternative approach to meaning and measurement.* New York: Norton.

Mahrer, A. R. (1988). Discovery-oriented psychotherapy research: Rationale, aims, and methods. *American Psychologist, 43,* 694–703.

Mahrer, A. R. (1989a). *Experiencing: A humanistic theory of psychology and psychiatry.* Ottawa, Canada: University of Ottawa Press. (Original work published in 1978.)

Mahrer, A. R. (1989b). *Dream work: In psychotherapy and self-change.* New York: Norton.

Mahrer, A. R. (1995). A solution to an illusory problem: Clients construct their worlds versus there really is a reality. *Journal of Constructivist Psychology, 8,* 327–338.

Mahrer, A. R. (1996a). Discovery-oriented research on how to do psychotherapy. In W. Dryden (Ed.), *Research in counseling and psychotherapy: Practical applications* (pp. 232–258). London: Sage.

Mahrer, A. R. (1996b). Studying distinguished practitioners: A humanistic approach to discovering how to do psychotherapy. *Journal of Humanistic Psychology, 36,* 31–48.

Mahrer, A. R. (1996/2004). *The complete guide to experiential psychotherapy.* Boulder, CO: Bull.

Mahrer, A. R. (1997a). Experiential psychotherapy: An unabashedly biased comparison with some other psychotherapies. In C. Feltham (Ed.), *Which psychotherapy? Leading exponents explain their differences* (pp. 119–148). London: Sage.

Mahrer, A. R. (1997b). Empathy as therapist-client alignment. In A. C. Bohart & L. S. Greenberg (Eds.), *Empathy reconsidered: New directions in psychotherapy* (pp. 187–213). Washington, DC: American Psychological Association.

Mahrer, A. R. (1997c). What are the "breakthrough problems" in the field of psychotherapy? *Psychotherapy, 34,* 81–85.

Mahrer, A. R. (1998a). How can impressive in-session changes become impressive post-session changes? In L. Greenberg, J. Watson, & G. Lietaer (Eds.), *Handbook of experiential psychotherapy* (pp. 201–223). New York: Guilford.

Mahrer, A. R. (1998b). A new departure in experiential supervision: Discovering the trainee's deeper personal approach to psychotherapy. *The Clinical Supervisor, 17,* 125–133.

Mahrer, A. R. (1999a). The doorway into the inner world is the instant of peak feeling in the scene of strong feeling. In J. Rowan & M. Cooper (Eds.), *The plural self* (pp. 213–237). London: Sage.

Mahrer, A. R. (1999b). Embarrassing problems for the field of psychotherapy. *Journal of Clinical Psychology, 55,* 1142–1156.

Mahrer, A. R. (2000a). Philosophy of science and the foundations of psychotherapy. *American Psychologist, 55,* 1117–1125.

Mahrer, A. R. (2000b). So many researchers are sincerely scientific about factitious fictions: Some comments on the DSM classification of personality disorders. *Journal of Clinical Psychology, 56,* 623–627.

Mahrer, A. R. (2000c). How to use psychotherapy on, for, and by oneself. *Professional Psychology: Research and Practice, 31,* 226–229.

Mahrer, A. R. (2001a). What can the clinician trust—Research? Theory? Clinical knowledge? Introduction to a serious problem and preview of some solutions. *American Journal of Psychotherapy, 55,* 323–335.

Mahrer, A. R. (2001b). An historical review of the field of psychotherapy—from the year 2199. *Psychotherapy Bulletin, 36,* 9–14.

Mahrer, A. R. (2001c). An experiential alternative to counter transference. *Journal of Clinical Psychology, 57,* 1021–1028.

Mahrer, A. R. (2001d). Experiential psychotherapy. In R. J. Corsini (Ed.), *Handbook of innovative therapy* (pp. 218–229). New York: Wiley.

Mahrer, A. R. (2001e). If you want to do something about your own craziness, have your own psychotherapy session. *Journal of Contemporary Psychology, 31,* 41–49.

Mahrer, A. R. (2002a). *Becoming the person you can become: The complete guide to self-transformation.* Boulder, CO: Bull.

Mahrer, A. R. (2002b). In experiential sessions, there is no therapist or client: There is a "teacher" and a "practitioner." *Journal of Contemporary Psychotherapy, 32,* 71–82.

Mahrer, A. R. (2003a). What are the foundational beliefs in the field of psychotherapy? *Psychology: Journal of the Hellenic Psychological Society, 10,* 1–19.

Mahrer, A. R. (2003b, August). Beyond positive: The optimal state. Symposium address, annual meeting of the American Psychological Association, Toronto, Canada.

Mahrer, A. R. (2004a). *Why do research on psychotherapy? Introduction to a revolution.* London: Whurr.

Mahrer, A. R. (2004b). *Theories of truth, models of usefulness: Toward a revolution in the field of psychotherapy.* London: Whurr.

Mahrer, A. R., & Boulet, D. B. (1997). The experiential model of on-the-job teaching. In C. E. Watkins (Ed.), *Handbook of psychotherapy supervision* (pp. 164–183). New York: Wiley.

Mahrer, A. R., & Boulet, D. B. (1999a). How to do discovery-oriented psychotherapy research. *Journal of Clinical Psychology, 55,* 1481–1493.

Mahrer, A. R., & Boulet, D. B. (1999b). An unabashedly unrealistic wish list for the education and training of psychotherapists. *Journal of Clinical Psychology, 55,* 393–398.

Mahrer, A. R., & Boulet, D. B. (2001a). How can experiential psychotherapy help transform the field of sex therapy? In P. J. Kleinplatz (Ed.), *New directions in sex therapy: Innovations and alternatives* (pp. 234–257). Philadelphia: Brunner Routledge.

Mahrer, A. R., & Boulet, D. B. (2001b). What are some promising developments in psychotherapy with "psychosis"? Introduction and preview. *Journal of Contemporary Psychotherapy, 31,* 5–14.

Mahrer, A. R., Boulet, D. B., & Fairweather, D. R. (1994). Beyond empathy: Advances in the clinical theory and methods of empathy. *Clinical Psychology Review, 14,* 183–198.

Mahrer, A. R., & Fairweather, D. R. (1993). What is "experiencing"? A critical review of meanings and applications in psychotherapy. *The Humanistic Psychologist, 21,* 2–25.

Mahrer, A. R., & Johnston, C. (2002). Promising new developments in the therapist-client relationship: A philosophy of science review and preview. *Journal of Contemporary Psychotherapy, 32,* 3–24.

Malone, T. P., Whitaker, C. A., Warkentin, J., & Felder, R. E. (1961). Rational and nonrational psychotherapy. *American Journal of Psychotherapy, 15,* 212–220.

Rorty, R. (1991). *Philosophy and the mirror of nature.* Princeton, NJ: Princeton University Press.

Rotter, J. B. (1954). *Social learning and clinical psychology.* Englewood Cliffs, NJ: Prentice Hall.

Skinner, B. F. (1938). *The behavior of organisms.* New York: Appleton-Century-Crofts.

Wedding, D., & Corsini, R. J. (Eds.). (2004). *Case studies in psychotherapy* (4th ed). Belmont, CA: Wadsworth.

Whitaker, C. A., Felder, R. E., Malone, T. P., & Warkentin, J. (1962). First-stage techniques in the experiential psychotherapy of chronic schizophrenic patients. In J. H. Masserman (Ed.), *Current psychiatric therapies,* Vol. 2 (pp. 157–174). New York: Grune and Stratton.

Whitaker, C. A., & Malone, T. P. (1953). Experiential or nonrational psychotherapy. In W. Sahakian (Ed.), *Psychotherapy and counseling* (pp. 416–431). Chicago: Rand McNally.

Whitehead, A. N. (1929). *Process and reality: An essay in cosmology.* Cambridge: Cambridge University Press.

# 15 CONTEMPORARY ISSUES IN PSYCHOTHERAPY

*Danny Wedding*

## THE PROFESSIONS

During the eighteenth and nineteenth centuries, responsibility for people with emotional disorders and disorganized thinking passed gradually from clerics to physicians, and psychiatry became the dominant mental health profession. Since World War II, other disciplines have emerged to address mental health care and collectively they now dominate the field in terms of number of practitioners and number of clients served. The U.S. Substance Abuse and Mental Health Services Administration (SAMHSA) currently collects and reports human resources data for the four core mental health disciplines (psychiatry, psychology, social work, and psychiatric nursing) as well as for five other disciplines in which practitioners provide mental health services: mental health counseling, marriage and family therapy, psychosocial rehabilitation, school psychology, and sociology.

It is notoriously difficult to define the mental health workforce with any precision, and the problem is compounded by the facts that many therapists work part-time and a given individual may identify with more than one mental health profession at the same time (e.g., a therapist may be both a social worker *and* a marriage and family therapist). However, we know that at the beginning of the twenty-first century there were approximately 41,000 clinically active psychiatrists practicing in the United States. In contrast, there were about 77,000 clinically trained psychologists and 193,000 clinically trained social workers. These numbers stand in marked contrast to a far smaller number of psychiatric nurses, and only about 7,000 psychiatric nurses are currently providing clinical services. There are approximately 45,000 marriage and family therapists providing clinical services in the United States, but this number is growing rapidly, and an increasing number of these providers hold doctorates. There are currently 108,000 credentialed professional counselors practicing in the United States, and almost all states now regulate the practice of counseling. Psychotherapy and counseling services may also be provided by professionals who identify themselves as rehabilitation counselors, guidance counselors, school psychologists, or clinical sociologists. Whatever their professional identification, the majority of these individuals practice *technical eclecticism* (described by Arnold Lazarus in Chapter 11) and use a variety of methods derived from the therapies described in *Current Psychotherapies.*

In recent years, psychologists and social workers have come closer to achieving the status of medical therapists, especially in the areas of insurance reimbursement, participation in federal health programs, and admission to psychoanalytic training. Psychologists also have gained hospital admitting privileges in many states. Other groups that practice counseling or psychotherapy are making rapid strides toward achieving the privileges now available to psychologists and social workers.

The accreditation standards of the Joint Commission on Accreditation of Healthcare Organizations (JCAHO) influence the hiring practices and staffing decisions made by administrators of hospitals, community mental health centers, and other settings where psychotherapy services are delivered. These administrators, confronted with fiscal limitations and budget constraints, are acutely aware that there is tremendous variation in the core salaries expected by therapists who may have different professional backgrounds, but who deliver essentially comparable services. Almost all states classify psychotherapy as a legitimate part of medical practice, without any requirement that its use be restricted to psychiatrists. However, psychiatrists now devote the majority of their time to medication management, and far fewer psychiatrists are being trained to provide psychotherapy to their patients (Luhrmann, 2000). This trend results in part from the fact that approximately half of new psychiatrists licensed in the United States are International Medical Graduates (IMGs) who are more likely to be trained in biological psychiatry. Bernard Beitman and other psychiatrists have decried the abdication of psychotherapy training by psychiatry residency programs and have developed time-limited, modular approaches to training that can be adapted to fit psychiatry residency curricula (Beitman & Yue, 1999).

## Licensing and Credentialing

In 2004, psychologists, psychiatric nurse practitioners, and social workers were licensed or certified in all 50 states, and professional counselors were licensed or certified in almost all states. A growing number of states also require marriage/family and substance abuse counselors to be licensed or certified.

Licensing is more meaningful than certification, because *licensure* restricts the practice of a profession, whereas *certification* restricts the use of a profession's name. These distinctions are difficult to apply to psychotherapy because it is virtually impossible to restrict the practice of a profession that includes such a varied range of activities. Certain professional activities may be state-regulated, however. Psychological testing may be restricted to psychologists, for example, while the authority to prescribe medication may be granted only to physicians, dentists, and other health care practitioners such as advanced practice nurses, physicians' assistants, optometrists, and podiatrists. Regulatory authority is usually invested in a state board appointed by the governor and composed of professionals and members of the public. Frequently, state boards will use *reciprocity* to license professionals who hold a license to practice in other states.

Licensing boards regulate the professional activities of practitioners and revoke the licenses of those believed unfit to practice. Loss of a license may result from a felony conviction or from misrepresentation, unprofessional conduct, practicing beyond one's area of competence, abandoning patients, maintaining inadequate records, and breaching patients' confidentiality (Stromberg et al., 1988). In one study (Pope & Vasquez, 1998), the most frequent reasons for loss of license were dual relationships (including sexual intimacy), unprofessional conduct, conviction for a felony, failure to comply with a board order, improper billing practices, and incompetent practice. Other reasons included mental incompetence, falsification of Medicaid claims, fraud in application for license, misrepresentation of competence, and failure to report child abuse.

It is difficult to decide who should have the right to practice psychotherapy because there are few unambiguous practice guidelines to define what is appropriate professional care for patients with mental and emotional disorders. A psychoanalyst and a behavior therapist may provide dramatically different treatment for a patient with an anxiety disorder, for example. Yet both will claim—and genuinely believe—that their mode of treatment is appropriate, and both will expect payment for their services. This problem is not limited to the mental health professions; the absence of clear guidelines characterizes much of medical practice. The United States government has attempted to deal with this lack of uniform standards by establishing the Agency for Healthcare Research and Quality (AHRQ). This agency and a number of professional organizations have developed explicit treatment guidelines for behavioral problems such as depression and anxiety, but the use of practice guidelines and critical pathways in mental health remains controversial. Proponents of practice guidelines argue that they bring much-needed standardization to a field that has suffered greatly from extensive but unnecessary variance in practice (largely as the result of a lack of standardized training in the mental health professions), whereas critics of the guidelines argue that every clinical case is unique and adamantly reject any attempt to apply standardized treatment protocols, algorithms, or "cookbooks." Students interested in reviewing the large number of existing guidelines for treating behavioral disorders should visit the *AHRQ Guideline Clearinghouse* on the World Wide Web (www.guideline.gov). In addition, Nathan and Gorman (2002) have edited an excellent review of evidence-based approaches to the treatment of behavioral health disorders.

# ETHICAL ISSUES

## Dual Relationships

*John Schafer had been working hard to establish a private practice in social work. One of his clients was Keith Twiehaus, the chief executive officer for a biotechnology company. One day in therapy, Mr. Twiehaus mentioned that he was worried about his decision to purchase Symatec, a promising but badly managed smaller company. The purchase was a sound business decision, and it was likely that Symatec stock would double in value as soon as word got out. The client was worried, however, because the purchase of the smaller company would eliminate the jobs of hundreds of Symatec's employees.*

*John devoted several therapy sessions to analyzing the options available to Mr. Twiehaus, who eventually decided his primary obligation was to his shareholders. In one of his therapy sessions Twiehaus made a decision to go ahead and purchase Symatec the following week. John slept fitfully that night, wondering if he could ethically buy Symatec stock. He was in a dual relationship, because he had let Mr. Twiehaus become his investment advisor as well as his client.*

It is often awkward for both the therapist and the client when interactions occur outside the psychotherapeutic relationship. Some relationships, such as those that include sexual or financial involvement, clearly violate the ethical codes of almost all professional organizations and are often illegal. Others, such as allowing a client to buy the therapist a cup of coffee after a chance meeting in a restaurant, appear to be quite harmless. Most decisions are not this straightforward, however, and deciding whether to accept a holiday gift or flowers for the waiting room can become a vexing dilemma.

Social interaction with clients may be unavoidable, especially in rural areas, and contact with clients outside therapy will not necessarily impede therapeutic work if dual relationships are acknowledged and dealt with in therapy. For example, a police officer who stops a speeding motorist who turns out to be his therapist may decide not to write a ticket, and the therapist would be grateful. However, it is important in such circumstances that both parties acknowledge the special features of their relationship and the unique nature of their encounter.

Psychotherapists Alfred Adler and Rudolf Dreikurs maintained that counseling and psychotherapy are essentially *educational,* and therefore therapeutic work with friends and even relatives is entirely appropriate. At the other end of the spectrum, there are therapists who argue that transference and countertransference are powerful responses that will inevitably influence therapy in every dual relationship; consequently, dual relationships should almost always be avoided. Arnold Lazarus and Ofen Zur (2002) edited a provocative book challenging the rigidity of many of the professional restrictions on out-of-office, nonsexual interactions with psychotherapy clients.

## Sexual Attraction to Clients

*Nancy Tharp was given the diagnosis of borderline personality disorder after numerous suicide attempts. After her last attempt, she was hospitalized and assigned to a first-year psychiatry resident, Bill Wilson. The supervising psychiatrist felt it was important for this patient to work with a male therapist because of her propensity to use her sexuality to manipulate men.*

*Ms. Tharp was an extremely attractive 23-year-old woman. Her prior history included childhood sexual abuse and a seemingly endless series of short, casual sexual relationships. She generally held men in contempt and had never been able to sustain a relationship for more than a few months.*

*During the first therapy session, Ms. Tharp wore a short skirt and shifted positions in her chair indiscreetly. Dr. Wilson averted his eyes, but he began to suspect that his patient was using her sexuality to establish dominance in the relationship. He knew he probably should say something about his patient's immodesty, but he felt quite uncomfortable talking about sexual issues. He also believed her inappropriate behavior might be unconscious, and he wanted to avoid sexualizing the relationship. However, he felt manipulated each time he was forced to avert his gaze to avoid looking at his patient's panties. He realized he was both angry and sexually aroused, and he began having frequent fantasies about this patient.*

It is not surprising that psychotherapy can result in sexual arousal and fantasies for both patients and therapists. Psychotherapy is a unique encounter in which the most intimate topics are discussed in a quiet and private setting, and clients are likely to be emotionally vulnerable. The feelings of intimacy and shared commitment that emerge during a therapeutic relationship are often strikingly similar to the emotions associated with the early stages of courtship.

Sexual attraction between psychotherapists and clients is commonplace and predictable, and learning to deal with these feelings appropriately is an important part of the training of all mental health professionals. In two national surveys, four out of five psychologists and social workers report experiencing sexual attraction to at least one client, and a majority in both professions reported feeling guilty, anxious, or confused about this attraction. Only about 10 percent of both psychologists and social workers responding to

TABLE 15.1 **Ten Common Scenarios**

| Scenario | Description |
| --- | --- |
| Role Trading | Therapist becomes the "patient," and the wants and needs of the therapist become the focus. |
| Sex Therapy | Therapist fraudulently presents therapist-patient sexual intimacy as a valid treatment for sexual or other kinds of problems. |
| As If . . . | Therapist treats positive transference as if it were not the result of the therapeutic situation. |
| Svengali | Therapist creates and exploits an exaggerated dependence on the part of the patient. |
| Drugs | Therapist uses cocaine, alcohol, or other drugs as part of the seduction. |
| Rape | Therapist uses physical force, threats, and/or intimidation. |
| True Love | Therapist uses rationalizations that attempt to discount the clinical/professional nature of the relationship with its attendant responsibilities. |
| It Just Got Out of Hand | Therapist fails to treat the emotional closeness that develops in therapy with sufficient attention, care, and respect. |
| Time Out | Therapist fails to acknowledge and take account of the fact that the therapeutic relationship does not cease to exist between scheduled sessions or outside the therapist's office. |
| Hold Me | Therapist exploits the patient's desire for nonerotic physical contact and possible confusion between erotic and nonerotic contact. |

these surveys felt their training in graduate school, practica, and internships had adequately prepared them to deal with these feelings (Pope, 1998).

Feeling sexually attracted to a client is usually quite harmless. However, some therapists cross ethical boundaries and become sexually involved with their patients. This can result in tremendous harm for both parties (Edelwich & Brodsky, 1991; Pope, 1994; Pope, Sonne, & Holroyd, 1993). The prototypical pattern of exploitation in both psychotherapy and clinical training is for an older, high-status man to become sexually involved with a younger, subordinate woman.

Pope and Bouhoutsos (1986) present 10 common scenarios in which therapists cross professional boundaries and become sexually involved with their patients. These are listed in Table 15.1.

Professional associations have long recognized the potential for sexual exploitation in therapy. The Hippocratic oath includes the pledge to "abstain . . . from the seduction of females or males, of freemen and slaves." The American Psychological Association's ethical principles (2002) explicitly prohibit sexual involvement with current clients or acceptance of former lovers as patients. Psychologists are also advised to avoid sexual intimacy with former clients for at least two years after termination of therapy. Even then, the practice is discouraged, and psychologists bear the burden for proving that a sexual relationship with a former client is not exploitative. Similar injunctions against having sex with clients are found in the ethical principles of almost all mental health organizations. As noted by Edelwich and Brodsky (1991),

> The guidelines are clear. Although some doctors have been sleeping with their patients since the days of Hippocrates (and some teachers with their students since the

days of Socrates), a consensus has developed with the helping professions (and the courts) that there is no place for sex or other forms of personal intimacy in a professional helping relationship with a vulnerable person. (p. xxi)

Despite these injunctions and the potential for serious harm to clients, a surprising number of therapists engage in sexual misconduct. Incidence rates are similar across professional groups, and rates of sexual involvement are always much higher for male therapists (Pope, 1994). Gartrell, Herman, Olarte, Feldstein, and Localio (1989) surveyed 5,574 psychiatrists and found that 7 percent of the male respondents and 3 percent of the female respondents admitted having had sexual contact with a patient on at least one occasion. A third of these psychiatrists had had intercourse with more than one patient. Surveys of social workers and psychologists assessing therapist-client intimacy have produced similar results, documenting that sexual misbehavior is found with both male and female therapists, but with lower rates consistently noted for female therapists (Pope, 1994). These data suggest that inappropriate sexual contact with clients is a serious problem for all mental health professionals.

## Third-Party Payers

*Tom Jeffords, a counseling psychologist who limited his practice to marital therapy, had just completed his initial interview with Jim and Mary Daschle. The Daschles were a committed and articulate couple who were hoping to salvage a strained marriage. Dr. Jeffords was encouraged by the couple's insight into their marital difficulties, and he thought he could help. He outlined a therapeutic plan, discussed his fees, and recommended that the Daschles return in a week. However, as he was walking the couple to the door, Mr. Daschle took him aside and remarked, "Look, Doctor, I think your fees are reasonable, but I simply can't afford them. I've got great insurance as long as you can give me or my wife a diagnosis my insurance company will accept. But if you can't do that for us, we can't come back." Dr. Jeffords had come across the problem before, and he was ready with his response. "Well, your wife's fairly discouraged because of all the marital problems, and she has low self-esteem and is having trouble sleeping. I suspect she's depressed, and that would qualify. Don't worry about it. We'll work something out."*

Mental health providers have been frustrated by the myriad difficulties involved in working with dozens of insurance companies, and sometimes they have responded in ways that range from passive-aggressive to illegal. Some providers restrict their practices to clients who can pay for services "up front," and refuse to deal with insurance companies altogether. This eliminates the headaches associated with dealing with third-party payers, but it also creates a considerable financial barrier for those seeking help, and restricts access for those with limited financial resources. Other clinicians lower their rates or provide *pro bono* care for such clients rather than deal with the paperwork involved in submitting insurance claims.

Mental health providers occasionally manipulate the insurance system to serve their own needs. For example, some providers favor reimbursable diagnoses over those that don't get reimbursed, submit bills in the name of high status providers for services performed by lower status (and often nonreimbursable) employees, or bill for services that are reimbursable rather than for those procedures that are actually performed but not covered by insurance companies (e.g., biofeedback sessions may be billed under psychotherapy codes with the rationalization that some counseling occurs before and after each session). Finally, there are both overt and covert pressures to "stretch out" therapy with well-insured clients, to drop clients once their insurance benefits have run out, and to limit services to indigent clients and those unlikely to pay their bills. New therapists can find themselves under considerable pressure, from both colleagues and clients, to accept dubious or illegal billing practices and to base treatment decisions on economic rather than therapeutic criteria.

# LEGAL ISSUES

Therapists often have multiple obligations that may overlap or conflict. Legal issues arise from competing responsibilities, such as those to clients, spouses, children, potential victims, and society.

## Duty to Warn

*Sarah Brown enjoyed her new job as a social worker in an inner-city mental health clinic, but she was troubled by the fact that she knew one of her clients was HIV positive and yet claimed that he continued to have unprotected sex. Sarah had given the client a diagnosis of antisocial personality, and it seemed to be justified. No amount of persuasion on her part could convince him that what he was doing was wrong. The client seemed to revel in the fact that he might be infecting his partners. Because his HIV status had been revealed in confidence, Sarah felt paralyzed by the need to balance her professional responsibility to her client against her responsibility to protect the public, and she found herself wishing she had discussed the limits of confidentiality early in therapy.*

Deciding when to break a client's confidence is difficult, and some therapists believe it is unethical to break a client's confidentiality under any circumstances. However, confidentiality is routinely broken when professionals consult with colleagues, participate in treatment team meetings, or provide diagnostic and treatment information to insurance companies. In these cases, sharing of information is assumed to be in the patient's best interest. In other situations, the needs of society may take precedence over one's obligations to a client, even when the client is harmed by disclosure.

Every therapist should be familiar with the case of *Tarasoff v. the Regents of the University of California,* in which the California Supreme Court held that a psychologist working in a university counseling center had a duty to break his client's confidence once the client declared his intent to murder his girlfriend. Furthermore, the psychologist, who had told the campus police that his client was dangerous and should be hospitalized, was found negligent in not attempting to notify the potential victim. In the words of the court, ". . . protective privilege ends where the public peril begins." In a related case, *Hedlund v. Superior Court of Orange County,* the court stated it was the therapist's duty to warn family members potentially at risk. This case extends the Tarasoff decision by explicitly stating that negligent failure to *diagnose* dangerousness is a basis for liability (Meyers, 1986). Later cases involving the duty to warn include one in which a patient killed someone through reckless driving and another in which a client committed suicide by driving a car into a tree, also killing her daughter, who was a passenger (Beck, 1990).

Under the legal doctrine of *respondent superior* ("let the master respond"), supervisors of psychotherapy trainees may also be legally responsible for failure to warn. It is unlikely that once-a-week or once-a-month supervision of therapists in training is sufficient to absolve the supervisor of responsibility for tragic outcomes (Cohen, 1986).

Along with the duty to warn others of potential harm, all states have laws mandating immediate reporting of known or suspected cases of child abuse. In most states, reportable circumstances include physical abuse, sexual abuse, neglect, and mental or emotional maltreatment (Heyman, 1986). Therapists sometimes ignore these reporting requirements, which may appear to place an insurmountable obstacle between the therapist and a client seeking to control anger and abusive tendencies. However, therapists who put client welfare ahead of public law do so at their own peril.

## Privileged Communication

*When a man angry about his ex-wife's decision to remarry held a busload of schoolchildren hostage at gunpoint, the police consulted a psychologist. After about 15 hours of negotiation, the psychologist persuaded the man to turn himself in. Later, the psychologist testified in court that the gunman did not appear to be mentally ill when he held the children hostage. Much to his surprise, the psychologist was sued by the gunman some months later for violating doctor/patient confidentiality.*

*Privilege* refers to the special status extended to particular types of communication that are recognized by the legal system as unique, important, and worthy of protection. Traditionally, privilege has been extended to the interactions of attorneys and their clients, husbands and wives, physicians and patients, and priests and penitents. There is extensive case law establishing the right of privileged communication between clients and therapists, although state laws vary widely and it is incumbent on all mental health professionals to be familiar with the laws governing privilege in the state in which they practice (Koocher, 1998). The United States Supreme Court affirmed the right of privileged communication between social workers and their clients in the 1996 case of *Jaffe v. Redmond.*

Privileged communication is a right *vested in the client,* and it can be waived only by the client. When a client waives the right to privileged communication, a therapist must testify as any other witness, and a therapist will be held in contempt of court for failure to do so (Knapp & VandeCreek, 1987).

The concept of privileged communication is an extension of the right to privacy established by the fifth amendment to the U.S. constitution. Without the protection of privileged communication, clients who had committed illegal acts would be unlikely to be fully candid and forthcoming, and the work of therapy would be seriously impeded.

Even the most superficial communication between a client and provider may be privileged. For example, a telephone call to a psychiatrist from a person seeking treatment was deemed confidential by the courts, even though the man who called did not know the psychiatrist and never became a patient at the state hospital where the psychiatrist worked (Knapp & VandeCreek, 1987).

## Prediction of Dangerousness

*Cynthia Johnson, a psychologist employed by a rural mental health clinic, was increasingly worried about Dave Mason, a rugged Appalachian "mountain man" who was coming in for weekly therapy. It had been difficult to establish rapport with Dave, but Cynthia was pleased they had established a meaningful therapeutic alliance and Dave was beginning to confide in her. In their last session, Dave admitted frequent sexual fantasies about some children who played near his cabin. He denied any history of pedophilia and had not been abused as a child. Dave was confident he could control his fantasies, but he certainly looked dangerous, and Cynthia wondered about her moral and legal obligation to warn Dave's neighbors about his fantasy life.*

Therapists routinely see patients who seem potentially dangerous. There is no evidence, however, that therapists have superior ability to predict violent behavior. In fact, there is evidence that therapists *overpredict* violence, having accuracy rates somewhat lower than the average person (Stromberg et al., 1988). Although it is far more serious to make a false negative diagnosis of potential homicide than a false positive one, there are serious problems with curtailing the civil liberties of clients because of a small potential for dangerous behavior. Livermore, Malmquist, and Meehl (1968) described this conundrum:

> Assume that one person out of a thousand would kill. Assume also an exceptionally accurate test is created which differentiates with 95% effectiveness those who will kill from those who will not. If 100,000 people were tested, out of the 100 who would

kill, 95 would be isolated. Unfortunately, out of the 99,900 who would not kill, 4,995 people also would be isolated as potential killers. (p. 84)

Predicting violence is like predicting the weather—it is easier in the short term. Some short-term predictors that correlate positively with violence include male gender, youth, unemployment, and addiction to alcohol or drugs. A history of violence is the most powerful predictor. Other variables associated with violence include low intelligence, impulsivity, paranoid ideation, and the stated desire to hurt or kill someone. Head injuries, being abused as a child, witnessing a family member abuse another, and a history of family psychosis are other predictors (Beck, 1990). Despite these correlations, it remains extraordinarily difficult for a therapist to predict which patients will become violent in stressful situations. Professional training in a mental health specialty appears to contribute little to this ability (Ziskin & Faust, 1988).

## Informed Consent

*Margaret McCulskey had grown increasingly despondent since her oldest daughter left for college. Now all three of her children were out on their own, and her husband was totally preoccupied with his work. She felt listless and bored and found little pleasure in her household routine. Hoping to gain some focus in her life, she sought advice from a minister at the church she attended, someone who had been recruited to provide pastoral counseling for the congregation. After three helpful sessions, she decided to return to college. Mrs. McCulskey was shocked when she received a bill from the church. She could easily afford to pay, but it seemed wrong that she had not been informed about the fee.*

Clients are entitled to know about all matters that affect their care and treatment. They deserve to know the likelihood of harm (physical or mental) that could result from treatment, the possibility of side effects, the probability of success for treatment, the limits of confidentiality, whether student counselors will be involved, and the likely duration and cost of treatment. Should the therapist doubt that he or she is the right person to treat the client, or that the proposed approach is the proper one, the therapist has an ethical obligation to inform the client and perhaps suggest alternative treatment by other providers. For example, while depressed patients often can be treated exclusively with psychotherapy (Rush & Hollon, 1991), antidepressant medication or electroconvulsive therapy may be the treatment of choice for some markedly depressed patients. Patients should be informed of the availability and efficacy of alternative treatments and providers.

One way to assure that clients understand the limits of confidentiality and their financial obligations is to have them sign a therapeutic contract before therapy begins. These contracts typically list clients' rights (e.g., terminating therapy at any time, reviewing their records) and specify conditions under which the therapist must reveal information without clients' permission (e.g., after a threat of harm to self or others, or when the therapist is required to respond to a court subpoena). See Pinckney (1994) for an example of such a contract. This approach seems cold and mechanical to many therapists. Others maintain that the contract demonstrates respect for clients by making them active participants in treatment planning.

## Health Insurance Portability and Accountability Act

The Health Insurance Portability and Accountability Act (HIPAA) grew out of legislation sponsored by Senators Nancy Kassebaum and Ted Kennedy. The Kassebaum/Kennedy bill was signed into law in 1996 but did not become fully implemented until April 2003. This new law codifies privacy and confidentiality for any information transmitted electronically, referred to as *protected health information (PHI)*. Although HIPAA affects only those providers who elect to transmit information electronically, it is hard to imagine patient billing or interaction with third parties that does not involve the use of computers and fax machines to bill or verify treatment eligibility. In effect, all health practitioners accepting payment from insurance companies will be bound to meet HIPAA standards.

HIPAA legislation makes it very clear that in the United States, information generated from patients in a health care setting belongs to the individual from whom it was obtained, and it cannot be used without his or her informed consent for any purpose extraneous to the client's personal care. Under HIPAA standards, patients have a right to review and amend their own health records and to know who else has had access to these records. However, there is a provision under the HIPAA guidelines for the protection of psychotherapy notes, and patients do *not* have a right to inspect these records (unless more permissive state laws permit access to these notes). This provision protects therapists who may have a working diagnosis that would be prejudicial if shared with the clients (e.g., concerns about malingering or a diagnosis of borderline personality disorder).

HIPAA also requires that all providers ensure that clients be notified of privacy practices. It limits use of personal medical information and prohibits the use of patient information for marketing purposes. Although many therapists have complained about the perceived burden imposed by HIPAA guidelines, these regulations underscore the importance of safeguarding client information and apply the force of law to the standards regarding confidentiality found in the code of ethics of most professional organizations in the mental health field.

## Risk Management

Managing risk in a psychotherapy practice requires strict adherence to applicable ethical standards as defined by professional organizations such as the American Psychological Association or the National Association of Social Workers. In addition, general principles of risk management are applicable to almost all therapists. These include the identification of high-risk clients and situations, the development of good record-keeping practices, a willingness to seek out consultation, and an understanding that all patient complaints should be taken seriously.

High-risk patients include individuals who have an Axis II diagnosis (e.g., borderline personality disorder), dissociative identity disorders, patients who were abused as children, potentially suicidal or violent patients, patients involved in ongoing litigation, and patients who are dealing with intense positive or negative transference issues or concerns about abandonment. Contested divorce and child custody issues are also problematic for the therapist. Therapists dealing with problem patients almost always benefit from seeking out advice and guidance from other experienced therapists, and sometimes it will be necessary to consult with attorneys specializing in health law.

Record keeping is an especially critical component of risk management, and, from a legal perspective, the general rule is that "if you didn't write it down, you didn't do it." When treating patients with mental health problems, it is important to document that the need for medication and hospitalization has been evaluated and that previous records have been reviewed. An evaluation of the need for medication is especially critical when treating patients who are dysthymic or depressed and potentially suicidal. Some of the predictors of suicide that must be considered in evaluating suicide risk include age (adolescents and the elderly are at greater risk), gender (males are more likely to actually kill themselves), a history of previous suicide attempts, a clear plan and evidence of preparation, hopelessness about the future, and a history of chronic medical illness or persistent pain. Patients who are believed to be acutely suicidal should be hospitalized.

# CROSS-CULTURAL COUNSELING AND PSYCHOTHERAPY

## Ethnic Minorities

*Cindy Eichhorn, a graduate student in clinical psychology, was assigned to a juvenile court for a practicum. Cindy had been raised in an upper-class neighborhood, and her parents were affluent professionals who had given their daughter every advantage. She was unprepared for her first client, an angry 15-year-old African American male, who asked "How you going to help me, lady? You don't know shit about me or my problems." With a sinking heart, Cindy realized he was right.*

Cultural diversity poses difficulties for therapists uninformed about the cultural values of their clients, as well as therapists who respond to clients on the basis of cultural stereotypes. Striking the proper balance between cultural sensitivity and stereotyping requires clinical acumen and an understanding of and appreciation for cultural differences.

Specific strategies that have been proposed for conducting therapy with ethnic minorities include action-oriented and directive approaches for African American clients, deemphasizing the need for self-disclosure and reframing psychological problems as medical disorders with Hispanics, using highly structured therapy with Asian Americans, and adopting an authoritative as opposed to an egalitarian role with Filipino Americans (Sue & Zane, 1987). Sue and Zane note that these approaches may be incompatible with the theoretical style or values of the clinician and that they may ignore the broad range of individual differences within ethnic groups.

Fukuyama (1990) has proposed a broad definition of culture that includes gender, sexual orientation, and age. To avoid the problem of cultural stereotyping by therapists, Fukuyama argues for a global, transcultural approach to training in which students learn the dangers of stereotyping, the power of language and its significance in therapy, the importance of pride in one's own culture, and the pernicious effects of political and social oppression. Others have argued that therapists need to devote their time to learning as much as possible about the specific cultural groups likely to be encountered in day-to-day practice (e.g., African Americans in Detroit; Hispanics in San Antonio).

A variety of resources can help clinicians relate to different cultural groups (see, for example, books by Baruth & Manning, 2003, and Ramirez, 1991). Reading selected books such as Amy Tan's *The Joy Luck Club* or *The Kitchen God's Wife* will also introduce clinicians to other cultures and values. Finally, there are excellent texts that specifically address the cross-cultural issues that arise in counseling and psychotherapy in more depth than is possible in the current text (e.g., Sue, Ivey, & Pederson, 1996; Sue & Sue, 2003).

*Ms. Kim, a 24-year-old second-generation Korean American, lived at home with her parents. She initially sought counseling because she was depressed and unhappy with her lack of independence. Her father was angry about her plans to marry a non-Korean. Her therapist immediately began assertion training and role-playing to prepare Ms. Kim to deal with her father. The counselor was disappointed when Ms. Kim failed to keep her second appointment.*

Problems occur when the cultural values of clients clash with those of therapists. For example, therapists may find it difficult to understand the parenting practices of clients who use strict corporal punishment to discipline their children, as is common in many Pacific Island countries. Similarly, therapists in the United States may find it difficult to work with clients from countries where women accept secondary societal roles. The values and beliefs of both therapists and clients are class- and culture-bound, and good therapists transfer cases to other therapists when conflicting cultural values interfere with therapy.

## Working with Gay and Lesbian Clients

*Jim Kellogg retired at age 50 after a successful career as a police officer. He went back to school, received a master's degree in counseling, and obtained a position in a community mental health center. One of his first clients was Leo. Jim and Leo got along well and established good rapport in their early sessions. Jim was sympathetic with Leo's feelings of inferiority and his occasional panic attacks, and Leo felt comfortable with Jim, who played the role of a supportive, understanding, and caring older individual. The relationship changed in the fifth session, however, when Leo confided to Jim that he was gay. Jim and his fellow police officers had ridiculed homosexuals and expressed their disgust by using pejorative terms such as fags, homos, and dykes. Jim also belonged to a religious denomination that condemned homosexual behavior. He went to his supervisor and explained that he no longer wanted to work with Leo and that in the future no "sexual deviates" should be assigned to him.*

Almost all therapists will treat gay men and lesbians. In one survey of members of the American Psychological Association, 99 percent of psychotherapy providers reported they had seen at least one gay male or lesbian client in therapy, and respondents reported that 6 percent of their current clients were gay men and 7 percent were lesbians (Garnets, Hancock, Cochran, Goodchilds, & Peplau, 1991). This survey produced numerous examples of biased, inadequate, or inappropriate practice. For example, one therapist commented to a lesbian client, "If you have a uterus, don't you think you should use it?"

A lesbian psychologist has described four ways in which homophobic therapists respond to lesbian clients. These include the "You're not a lesbian" response, in which the therapist dismisses the reality of the client's feelings; "the lecture," wherein the client's sexual feelings are described as pathological; the liberal response, in which the therapist simply treats the client's lesbianism as if it were no different from any other client's sexual orientation; and the inadequate response, characterized by the therapist's avoidance of the issue (Falco, 1991).

The American Psychiatric Association removed homosexuality from its official list of mental disorders in 1973. The American Psychological Association's Council of Representatives adopted the following resolution in 1974:

> Homosexuality, per se, implies no impairment in judgment, stability, reliability, or general social or vocational capabilities. Further, the American Psychological Association urges all mental health professionals to take the lead in removing the stigma of mental illness that has long been associated with homosexual orientations (Conger, 1975, p. 633).

Therapists who feel uncomfortable working with homosexual clients need to learn more about gay and lesbian issues (see Garnets et al., 1991; Gonsiorek, 1988; Moses & Hawkins, 1982; Rothblum & Cole, 1989; Stein & Cohen, 1986). The article by Garnets et al. includes suggested readings for therapists and students who want to learn more about psychotherapy with gay males, lesbians, and same-sex couples. In addition, all therapists and counselors can benefit from reviewing the *Guidelines for Psychotherapy with Lesbian, Gay, and Bisexual Clients* published by the American Psychological Association (2000).

## FEMINIST PSYCHOTHERAPY

*Theresa Phillips, a licensed professional counselor, found herself increasingly frustrated in her work with Karen Woods, a victim of domestic violence. Theresa had been trained as a Rogerian counselor and worked hard to avoid giving direct advice to clients. However, therapy did not seem to be working for Karen, who persisted in believing that she should stay in a terribly abusive relationship because (1) she genuinely loved her husband, (2) she was convinced he would change, (3) she had never worked outside the home and questioned her ability to financially support herself and her children, and (4) she was a devout Catholic who had been taught from childhood that a woman's place was beside her husband, irrespective of his behavior. Theresa found herself wondering what would happen if she followed her instincts and simply told her client, "Damn it, Karen, you have to leave the son-of-a-bitch!"*

Some therapists whose practice is shaped by feminist theory and values have little sympathy for many of the theoretical approaches in this book, and they will often use therapy as a vehicle to examine the salience of gender issues and unequal power relationships in the lives of their clients. Such therapists focus on their client's interpersonal relationships with significant others and often frame clinical problems in terms of social roles and oppression. Much of therapy focuses on education and is directed at raising the consciousness of the client regarding the ubiquity of sexism in contemporary society and the extent to which sexist values have consciously or unconsciously shaped the client's belief system.

Cheatham et al. (1997) have described how mental health professionals grounded in feminist theory approach their role as therapists. First, feminist therapists believe in *egalitarian relationships* between therapists and clients. They are far more likely than other therapists to *self-disclose* in the therapy hour and to view sharing their personal growth experiences as an appropriate and even critical part of therapy. In particular, feminist therapists are likely to share their views about inequities in power in relationships and in society. Feminist therapists also respect *pluralism* and recognize that many factors other than sexism influence clients' attitudes and behaviors. They focus on *external issues* rather than internal conflicts, and they rely heavily on *community resources* such as women's support groups. They advocate an active, *participatory counseling style* and devote much of the therapy hour to actively *providing information*. Finally, feminist therapists focus on *personal validation* of clients and disputation of negative self-concepts that they may have acquired as a result of cultural conditioning and the acceptance of gender (and other) stereotypes. A more complete examination of the basic postulates of feminist therapy is found in Ballou (1996).

## PRESCRIPTION PRIVILEGES

*A middle-aged man who had been in therapy for almost half his life was referred by his psychologist to a psychiatrist for medication management. The psychiatrist became intrigued with this case. He offered a number of different medications but also delved into the patient's psychotherapeutic history. Dissatisfied with his psychologist, the patient began seeing the psychiatrist for therapy as well as for medication management. He described numerous therapeutic relationships in which he had first become deeply involved, had gradually become angry and disappointed, and finally had abandoned therapy. In pharmacotherapy, he went through a honeymoon period with each medication, then reported no effect. After a few months, he became angry and critical of the psychiatrist and left to find help elsewhere, repeating the same pattern.* (Adapted from Beitman, 1991.)

One of the most divisive professional questions in mental health as we begin the new millennium is whether nonmedical mental health professionals should be trained to prescribe psychotropic medications. This issue is becoming especially important as health policy leaders look for new ways to contain escalating health care costs while attempting to expand coverage to traditionally underserved groups such as Native Americans, people living in rural areas or inner cities, and the seriously mentally ill. Consumer groups such as the Public Citizen Health Research Group and the National Alliance for the Mentally Ill (NAMI) have endorsed additional training and prescriptive authority for psychologists, physician assistants, and nurse practitioners to increase access to care for these underserved populations (Torrey, Erdman, Wolfe, & Flynn, 1990).

Opponents of prescription privileges for nonphysician practitioners argue that expansion of prescriptive authority will (1) blur the distinction between psychiatry and other mental health professions, and (2) potentially endanger the public because of failure to recognize medical risks and potential drug interactions (e.g., Coleman & Shellow, 1991). Studies by the U.S. Congress, however, suggest that nonphysicians are more cautious—and therefore safer—than physicians when prescribing medicine (Office of Technology Assessment, 1986). These comparisons are confounded by the fact that nonphysician therapists tend to prescribe from a formulary, use a smaller number of medications, and treat patients who are less seriously ill.

Fox, Schwelitz, and Barclay (1992) have proposed a psychopharmacology curriculum for professional psychologists. This training would produce *limited practice prescribers* with constraints similar to those found in dentistry, podiatry, or optometry. Limited practice providers would work independently and without physician oversight, their prescriptive authority would be limited, and they would be required to consult with physicians and other health professionals when treating clients with problems outside their scope of practice. These providers would be differentiated from *physician extenders,* such as many nurses and all physicians' assistants, who can only work under direct physician supervision.

The value of prescriptive authority for nonphysician mental health practitioners is uncertain, its impact on mental health professions is unclear, and many practitioners find themselves disagreeing over this issue. However, it seems inevitable that organized psychology will continue to lobby for expanded scope of practice laws that empower appropriately trained psychologists to add psychopharmacology to their armamentarium. This movement gained momentum in 1999 when Guam passed a bill granting prescriptive authority to psychologists, and in 2002 when New Mexico became the first state to allow psychologists to prescribe medications.

The U.S. General Accounting Office (GAO) investigated a Department of Defense experiment in which psychologists were trained and authorized to prescribe medications and found that the graduates of this program had been well trained, were well integrated into the military mental health services system, worked independently, and did not require direct physician supervision. The report documented that the graduates of this program were providing high-quality, comprehensive care. However, the GAO expressed concerns about the additional costs involved in training the 10 psychologists who participated in this early experiment (GAO, 1999).

Combining psychotherapy and pharmacotherapy could have important clinical ramifications. For example, medication may reduce symptoms to such an extent that patients become less motivated to work in therapy or even prematurely discontinue therapy. Other patients may regard medication as a crutch or an admission that they have failed to develop the necessary insight to work through their problems. On the positive side, drugs may facilitate psychotherapeutic work by improving cognitive functioning, enhancing memory, promoting abreaction, or contributing to a sense of confidence and enhanced optimism (Klerman, 1991). Beitman and Klerman (1991) discuss effective integration of pharmacotherapy and psychotherapy. The most important arguments *against* prescriptive authority for psychologists are found in Hayes and Heiby (1998); the most persuasive arguments *for* legislation supporting prescriptive authority for psychologists are found in Sammons, Paige, and Levant (2003).

## THE FUTURE OF PSYCHOTHERAPY

It is difficult to distinguish between evanescent fads and genuine, durable trends in psychotherapy. It appears inevitable, however, that the field of psychotherapy will change dramatically in response to the social, political, and economic forces shaping clinical practice in the twenty-first century.

Norcross, Alford, and DeMichele (1992) used a Delphi polling technique to assess the future of psychotherapy. This method requires each participant to respond twice: first anonymously and then after feedback from other respondents. The 75 experts polled included many prominent figures conducting research and writing about psychotherapy at that time. These experts accurately predicted

> ... psychotherapy will become more directive, psychoeducational, present-centered, problem-focused, and briefer in the next decade. Concomitantly, aversive, relatively unstructured, historically oriented, and long-term approaches are predicted to decrease. . . . self-help groups, social workers, and psychiatric nurses will proliferate . . . integrative, systemic, and cognitive persuasions will thrive . . . specialization and peer review will become vital activities and pharmacotherapy will expand at the expense of psychotherapy. (Norcross et al., 1992, p. 155)

It is clear that practice guidelines and psychotherapy treatment manuals will be used more widely in the future. Practice guidelines will increasingly define optimal treatments for specific problems as determined by expert committees (e.g., the AHRQ has published practice guidelines for treating depressed patients). Therapy manuals operationally define good therapeutic practice, and some contain rating scales that can assess the quality of care provided by a therapist (Lambert & Ogles, 1988). Behavioral and cognitive-behavioral approaches to therapy can be easily adapted to fit modules and manuals, and it is likely that these approaches will be favored in the coming years. In addition, there will be an increasing emphasis on evidence-based medicine and *empirically supported treatments* (ESTs) (Nathan & Gorman, 2002).

Guidelines, manuals, and ESTs will become increasingly important as policy-makers continue to grapple with the vexing problems of (1) which diagnoses should be covered by insurance, (2) which treatments are appropriate for these conditions, (3) which providers are adequately trained to deliver services for these conditions, and (4) how many therapy sessions should be covered for any given diagnosis or problem. Each of these issues is ambiguous and contentious, and insurance companies, government programs, and other third-party payers will look to practice guidelines for assistance in promulgating rules regarding payment for psychotherapy and counseling. Widespread adoption of requirements for empirical validation may make it more difficult for new, creative, and innovative therapies like those discussed in *Handbook of Innovative Therapy* (Corsini, 2001) to be accepted in the psychotherapy marketplace.

Another clear trend is the exponential growth in the number of women practicing psychotherapy. Clinical social work and psychiatric nursing have always been predominantly female professions, whereas psychology and psychiatry have been predominantly male professions. Gender patterns in the helping professions are changing, however, and more women are becoming psychologists and psychiatrists. For example, women received approximately 66 percent of all PhDs in psychology in 1998, in contrast to 49 percent in 1985 and only 32 percent as recently as 1975 (Sanderson, Dugoni, Hoffer, & Selfa, 1999). This can be interpreted as evidence that psychiatry and psychology have succeeded in meeting affirmative action goals and eliminating gender bias from the admissions process; however, some critics have predicted that the perceived societal value of psychotherapy and counseling will diminish as increasing numbers of women enter traditionally male-dominated mental health professions.

Many individuals in affluent societies like the United States, Canada, Australia, and Great Britain have the luxury of engaging mental health providers to enhance their enjoyment of life as well as remediate their interpersonal and emotional problems. In addition, people who don't have a diagnosable mental illness will often seek out therapy to improve their ability to relate to others, enhance their capacity for intimacy, and advance their sexual competence. These individuals will not be concerned with reducing suffering or remediating clinical disorders; instead, they will be concerned about living a life that is full, abundant, and meaningful. This interest in using knowledge in the behavioral and social sciences to enhance quality of life is sometimes referred to by the general rubric of *positive psychology* (Snyder & Lopez, 2002).

Noting the decline of medical psychotherapy and the increasing political power of newer professional groups, the Group for the Advancement of Psychiatry predicted that a new mental health profession—psychotherapy, with psychoanalysis as a subspecialty—would emerge from the confusion regarding appropriate training (Rosenblatt et al., 1992). However, the events of the past decade have offered little support for this prediction.

Manderscheid and Henderson (2001) have speculated about what mental health services will look like in a hundred years, and they made the following predictions: (1) human rights will be established as fundamental in our health care system; (2) consumers and family members will seek and be given more responsibility for health and health care; (3) technology will become a primary vehicle for delivering health care; and (4) genetic treatments for biologically based disorders will become routine. The development of telemedicine, HIPAA legislation, and the mapping of the human genome all suggest these changes will come sooner rather than later. In particular, our understanding of the genetic basis of behavior has tremendous value as a way of enhancing quality of life, and mental health professionals will increasingly be expected to understand the ways in which genes influence behavior.

It is fascinating to speculate about the future of psychotherapy. It is likely to be financed in dramatically different ways in the United States and will probably involve a wider range of providers. The legal, ethical, and professional dilemmas faced by therapists in the twenty-first century are likely to be similar to those encountered by today's therapists, however, and the core skills used by therapists will continue to be those described in *Current Psychotherapies.*

# REFERENCES

American Psychological Association. (2000). Guidelines for psychotherapy with lesbian, gay, and bisexual clients. Division 44/Committee on Lesbian, Gay, and Bisexual Concerns Joint Task Force on Guidelines for Psychotherapy with Lesbian, Gay, and Bisexual Clients. *American Psychologist, 55,* 1440–1451.

American Psychological Association. (2002). *Ethical principles of psychologists and code of conduct.* Washington, DC: Author.

Ballou, M. (1996). Multicultural counseling and women. In D. Sue, A. Ivey, and P. Peterson (Eds.), *A theory of multicultural counseling and therapy.* Pacific Grove, CA: Brooks/Cole.

Baruth, L. G., & Manning, M. L. (2003). *Multicultural counseling and psychotherapy: A lifespan perspective* (3rd ed.). Upper Saddle River: Prentice Hall.

Beck, J. C. (1990). *Confidentiality versus the duty to protect: Foreseeable harm in the practice of psychiatry.* Washington, DC: American Psychiatric Press.

Beitman, B. (1991). Medications during psychotherapy: Case studies of the reciprocal relationship between psychotherapy process and medication use. In B. Beitman & G. L. Klerman (Eds.), *Integrating pharmacotherapy and psychotherapy.* Washington, DC: American Psychiatric Press.

Beitman, B., & Klerman, G. L. (1991). *Integrating pharmacotherapy and psychotherapy.* Washington, DC: American Psychiatric Press.

Beitman, B., & Yue, M. D. (1999). *Learning psychotherapy.* New York: Norton.

Cheatham, H., Ivey, A. E., Ivey, M. B., Pederson, P., Rigazio-DiGilo, S., Simek-Morgan, L., et al. (1997). Multicultural counseling and therapy II: Integrative practice. In A. E. Ivey, M. B. Ivey, and L. Simek-Morgan (Eds.), *Counseling and psychotherapy: A multicultural perspective.* Boston: Allyn & Bacon.

Cohen, R. J. (1986). The professional liability of behavioral scientists: An overview. In L. Everstine & D. S. Everstine (Eds.), *Psychotherapy and the law* (pp. 251–265). Orlando, FL: Grune & Stratton.

Coleman, P., & Shellow, R. A. (1991). Prescribing privileges for psychologists: Should only "medicine men" control the medicine cabinet? *The Journal of Psychiatry and Law, 18,* 269–318.

Conger, J. (1975). Proceedings of the American Psychological Association for the year 1974: Minutes of the annual meeting of Council of Representatives. *American Psychologist, 30,* 620–651.

Corsini, R. J. (Ed.). (2001). *Handbook of innovative therapy* (2nd ed.). New York: Wiley.

Edelwich, J., & Brodsky, A. (1991). *Sexual dilemmas for the helping professional.* New York: Brunner/Mazel.

Falco, K. L. (1991). *Psychotherapy with lesbian clients: Theory into practice.* New York: Brunner/Mazel.

Fox, R. E., Schwelitz, F. D., & Barclay, A. G. (1992). A proposed curriculum for psychopharmacology training for professional psychologists. *Professional Psychology: Research and Practice, 23,* 216–219.

Fukuyama, M. (1990). Taking a universal approach to multicultural counseling. *Counselor Education and Supervision, 30,* 6–17.

Garnets, L., Hancock, K. A., Cochran, S. D., Goodchilds, J., & Peplau, L. A. (1991). Issues in psychotherapy with lesbians and gay men. *American Psychologist, 46,* 964–972.

Gartrell, N., Herman, J., Olarte, S., Feldstein, M., & Localio, R. (1989). Prevalence of psychiatrist-patient sexual contact. In G. O. Gabbard (Ed.), *Sexual exploitation in professional relationships* (pp. 3–25). Washington, DC: American Psychiatric Press.

Gonsiorek, J. (1988). Current and future directions in gay/lesbian affirmative mental health practice. In M. Shernoff & W. Scott (Eds.), *The sourcebook on lesbian/gay affirmative health* (2nd ed., pp. 107–173). Washington, DC: National Lesbian-Gay Health Foundation.

Hayes, S., & Heiby, E. M. (1998). *Prescription privileges for psychologists: A critical appraisal.* Reno, NV: Context Press.

Heyman, G. M. (1986). Mandated child abuse reporting and the confidentiality privilege. In L. Everstine & D. S. Everstine (Eds.), *Psychotherapy and the law* (pp. 145–155). Orlando, FL: Grune & Stratton.

Klerman, G. L. (1991). Ideological conflicts in integrating pharmacotherapy and psychotherapy. In B. D. Beitman & G. L. Klerman (Eds.), *Integrating pharmacotherapy and psychotherapy* (pp. 3–20). Washington, DC: American Psychiatric Press.

Knapp, S., & VandeCreek, L. (1987). *Privileged communications in the mental health professions.* New York: Van Nostrand Reinhold.

Koocher, G. P. (1998). Privacy, confidentiality, and privilege. In G. P. Koocher, J. C. Norcross, & S. S. Hill III (Eds.), *Psychologists' desk reference.* New York: Oxford University Press.

Lambert, M. J., & Ogles, B. M. (1988). Psychotherapy treatment manuals: Problems and promise. *Journal of Integrative and Eclectic Psychotherapy, 7,* 187–204.

Lazarus, A. A., & Zur, O. (Eds.). (2002). *Dual relationships and psychotherapy.* New York: Springer.

Livermore, J. M., Malmquist, C. P., & Meehl, P. E. (1968). On the justification for civil commitment. *University of Pennsylvania Law Review, 117,* 75–96.

Luhrmann, T. M. (2000). *Of two minds: The growing disorder in American psychiatry.* New York: Knopf.

Manderscheid, R. W., & Henderson, M. J. (Eds.). (2001). *Mental Health, United States, 2000.* (DHHS Pub. No. [SMA] 01-3537. Center for Mental Health Services.) Washington, DC: U.S. Government Printing Office.

Meyers, C. J. (1986). The legal perils of psychotherapeutic practice: The farther reaches of the duty to warn. In L. Everstine and D. S. Everstine (Eds.), *Psychotherapy and the law* (pp. 223–247). Orlando, FL: Grune & Stratton.

Moses, A. E., & Hawkins, R. O. (1982). *Counseling lesbian women and gay men: A life issues approach.* St. Louis: Mosby.

Nathan, P. E., & Gorman, J. M. (Eds.). (2002). *A guide to treatments that work* (2nd ed.). New York: Oxford University Press.

Norcross, J. C., Alford, B. A., & DeMichele, J. T. (1992). The future of psychotherapy: Delphi data and concluding observations. *Psychotherapy, 29,* 150–158.

Office of Technology Assessment. (1986). *Nurse practitioners, physician assistants, and certified nurse-midwives: A policy analysis* (Health technology case study No. 37; OTA-HCS-37). Washington, DC: U.S. Government Printing Office.

Pinckney, N. (1994). Contracts for practicing psychologists. In R. J. Corsini (Ed.), *Encyclopedia of psychology,* Vol. 4 (pp. 544–546). New York: Wiley.

Pope, K. (1994). *Sexual involvement with therapists: Patient assessment, subsequent therapy, forensics.* Washington, DC: American Psychological Association.

Pope, K. S. (1998). Sexual feelings, actions, and dilemmas in psychotherapy. In G. P. Koocher, J. C. Norcross, & S. S. Hill, III (Eds.), *Psychologists' desk reference.* New York: Oxford University Press.

Pope, K. S., & Bouhoutsos, J. C. (1986). *Sexual intimacy between therapists and patients.* New York: Praeger.

Pope, K. S., Keith-Spiegel, P., & Tabachnick, G. G. (1986). Sexual attraction to clients: The human therapist and the (sometimes) inhuman training system. *American Psychologist, 41,* 147–158.

Pope, K., Sonne, J., & Holroyd, J. (1993). *Sexual feelings in psychotherapy: Explorations for therapists and therapists-in-training.* Washington, DC: American Psychological Association.

Pope, K. S., & Vasquez, M. J. T. (1998). *Ethics in psychotherapy and counseling: A practical guide* (2nd ed.). San Francisco: Jossey-Bass.

Ramirez, M. (1991). *Psychotherapy and counseling with minorities: A cognitive approach to individual and cultural differences.* New York: Pergamon.

Rosenblatt, A. D., Adler, G., Bemporad, J. R., Feigelson, E. B., Michels, R., Morrison, A. P., et al. (1992). *Psychotherapy in the future.* Washington, DC: American Psychiatric Association.

Rothblum, E. D., & Cole, E. (Eds.). (1989). Lesbianism: Affirming non-traditional roles. *Women and Therapy, 8*(Special Issue 1–2).

Rush, A. J., & Hollon, S. D. (1991). Depression. In B. D. Beitman & G. L. Klerman (Eds.), *Integrating pharmacotherapy and psychotherapy.* Washington, DC: American Psychiatric Press.

Sammons, M. T., Paige, R. U., & Levant, R. F. (Eds.). (2003). *Prescriptive authority for psychologists: A history and guide.* Washington, DC: American Psychological Association.

Sanderson, A., Dugoni, B., Hoffer, T., & Selfa, L. (1999). *Doctorate recipients from United States universities: Summary report 1998.* Chicago: National Opinion Research Center.

Snyder, C. R., & Lopez, S. J. (Eds.). (2002). *Handbook of positive psychology.* New York: Oxford University Press.

Stein, T., & Cohen, C. (Eds.). (1986). *Psychotherapy with lesbians and gay men.* New York: Plenum.

Stromberg, C. D., Haggarty, D. J., Leibenluft, R. F., McMillian, M. H., Mishkin, B., Rubin, B. L., et al. (1988). *The psychologist's legal handbook.* Washington, DC: National Register of Health Service Providers.

Sue, D. W., Ivey, A., & Pederson, P. (1996). *A theory of multicultural counseling and therapy.* Pacific Grove, CA: Brooks/Cole.

Sue, D. W., & Sue, D. (2003). *Counseling the culturally diverse: Theory and practice* (4th ed.). New York: Wiley.

Sue, S., & Zane, N. (1987). The role of culture and cultural techniques in psychotherapy. *American Psychologist, 42,* 37–45.

Torrey, E. F., Erdman, K., Wolfe, S. M., & Flynn, L. M. (1990). *Care of the seriously mentally ill. A rating of state programs* (3rd ed.). Washington, DC: Public Citizen Health Research Group.

United States General Accounting Office (1999). *Prescribing psychologists: DOD demonstration participants perform well but have little effect on readiness or costs.* Report to the Chairman and Ranking Minority Member, Committee on Armed Services, U. S. Senate.

Ziskin, J., & Faust, D. (1988). *Coping with psychiatric and psychological testimony* (4th ed.). Marina del Rey, CA: Law and Psychology Press.

# GLOSSARY

*The following abbreviations are used to indicate primary associations: (AD) Adlerian Psychotherapy; (AP) Analytical Psychotherapy; (BT) Behavior Therapy; (CT) Cognitive Therapy; (EXP) Experiential Psychotherapy; (EXT) Existential Therapy; (FT) Family Therapy; (GT) Gestalt Therapy; (MM) Multimodal Therapy; (PA) Psychoanalysis; (PC) Person-Centered Therapy; (PD) Psychodrama; (REBT) Rational Emotive Behavior Therapy.*

**Abreaction (PA).** The reliving or recovery of painful, repressed emotional experiences in psychotherapy, accompanied by a discharge of affect or intense feelings. *See also* Catharsis.

**Act Fulfillment (PD).** Reenacting a traumatic situation correctively, producing more satisfactory results.

**Active Imagination (AP).** A form of reflection through which people activate and follow their imaginative reveries in a purposive way.

**Activity Scheduling (CT, BT).** Setting up routine activity in order to offset inertia.

**Actualization (EXP).** Manifest expression of personal qualities that had not been previously evident.

**Actualizing Tendency (PC).** An innate human predisposition toward growth and fulfilling one's potential.

**Agape.** Unconditional love for humanity (literally, "love between friends").

**Aggression (GT).** The basic biological movement of energy extending out from the organism to the environment. Aggression is required for assimilation, love, assertion, creativity, hunger, humor, discrimination, warmth, etc.

**Agoraphobia.** An excessive fear of open spaces and/or leaving one's own home.

**Aha! (GT).** Awareness of a situation in which a number of separate elements come together to form a meaningful whole; sudden insight into the solution to a problem or the structure of a situation.

**Anal Phase (PA).** Freud's second phase of psychosexual development, extending roughly from 18 months to 3 years of age, in which most libidinal pleasure is derived from retaining and expelling feces.

**Anima (AP).** A feminine archetypal image that serves as a bridge to the unconscious in both men and women, but is most often expressed as the feminine part of a man. *See also* Animus.

**Animus (AP).** A masculine archetypal image that serves as a bridge to the unconscious in both men and women, but is most often expressed as the masculine part of a woman. *See also* Anima.

**Anorectic.** A person engaging in self-starving behavior.

**Antisuggestion (AD).** *See* Paradoxical Intervention.

**Aphasia.** An organic speech deficit involving difficulty understanding or using language.

**Applied Behavior Analysis (BT).** A form of behavior therapy, closely tied to Skinner's philosophy of radical behaviorism, that stresses observable behavior rather than private events and uses single-subject experimental design to determine the relationship between behavior and its antecedents and consequences.

**Arbitrary Inference (CT).** Drawing conclusions without supporting evidence or despite evidence to the contrary.

**Archetype (AP).** An innate universal pattern or organizing principle similar to an instinct. It has no specific form but can be seen through archetypal images observable in the common motifs present in myths, fairy tales, legends, and dreams across cultures and times. Examples include the Earth Mother, the Wise Old Man, the Hero's Quest, the Shadow, and the Trickster.

**Armamentarium.** The complete range of psychotherapeutic methods and techniques used by a therapist.

**Assertion Training (BT).** A treatment procedure designed to teach clients to openly and effectively express both positive and negative feelings.

**Assimilation (GT).** The process of breaking something into component parts so that these parts can be accepted and made part of the person, rejected, or modified into suitable form.

**Audience (PD).** People present during an enactment other than the therapist, protagonist, or auxiliaries.

**Autoeroticism (PA).** Obtaining gratification from self-stimulating a sensual area of the body.

**Automatic Thought (CT).** A personal notion or idea triggered by particular stimuli that lead to an emotional response.

**Autonomy.** A personality dimension based on needs to be independent, to be self-determining, and to attain one's goals.

**Auxiliary (PD).** A person who aids the therapist or client in enacting a particular scene.

**Awfulizing (REBT).** Seeing something inconvenient or obnoxious as awful, horrible, or terrible.

**Basic Encounter (PC).** One member of a group's responding with empathy to another member's being genuine and real.

493

**BASIC I.D. (MM).** An acronym that groups together the fundamental concerns of the multimodal therapist: Behaviors, Affective processes, Sensations, Images, Cognitions, Interpersonal relations, and Drugs (i.e., biological functions).

**Basic Mistake (AD).** Myth used to organize and shape one's life. Examples include overgeneralizations, a desperate need for security, misperceptions of life's demands, denial of one's worth, and faulty values.

**Behavioral Experiment (CT, REBT).** Testing distorted beliefs or fears scientifically in a real-life situation (e.g., having a shy person initiate a conversation to see what actually happens).

**Behavioral Medicine (BT).** Applying learning theory techniques to prevent or treat physical problems (e.g., pain reduction, weight loss).

**Behavioral Rehearsal (CT, BT, PD).** Practicing an emotionally charged event and one's response to it prior to its actual occurrence.

**Belonging (AD, BT).** An innate need, drive, and source of human behavior. It leads people to seek relationship and involvement with other human beings.

**Boundary (FT).** A barrier between parts of a system, as in a family in which rules establish who may participate and in what manner.

**Bridging (MM).** A procedure in which the therapist purposely tunes in to what the client wants to address, then gently channels the discussion into more productive areas.

**Broad-Spectrum Behavior Therapy (MM).** The treatment approach, based on learning theory, advocated by Arnold Lazarus prior to development of multimodal therapy.

**Catastrophizing (REBT, CT).** Exaggerating the consequences of an unfortunate event.

**Catharsis.** The expression and discharge of repressed emotions; sometimes used as a synonym for *abreaction*.

**Cathexis (PA).** Investment of mental or emotional (libidinal) energy into a person, object, or idea.

**Circular Causality (FT).** The feedback model of a network of interacting loops that views any causal event as the effect of a prior cause, as in family interactions.

**Circular Questioning (FT).** An interviewing technique directed at eliciting differences in perceptions about events or relationships from different family members, especially regarding those points in the family life cycle when significant coalition shifts occur.

**Classical Conditioning (BT).** A form of learning in which existing responses are attached to new stimuli by pairing those stimuli with those that naturally elicit the response; also referred to as *respondent conditioning*.

**Closed System (FT).** A self-contained system that has impermeable boundaries and thus is resistant to new information and change.

**Cognitive Behavior Modification (BT).** A recent extension of behavior therapy that treats thoughts and cognition as behaviors amenable to behavioral procedures. Cognitive behavior modification is most closely associated with the work of Aaron Beck, Albert Ellis, and Donald Meichenbaum.

**Cognitive Distortion (CT).** Pervasive and systematic errors in reasoning.

**Cognitive Restructuring (AD, BT, REBT).** An active attempt to alter maladaptive thought patterns and replace them with more adaptive cognitions.

**Cognitive Shift (CT).** A systematic and biased interpretation of life experiences.

**Cognitive Triad (CT).** Negative views of the self, the world, and the future that characterize depression.

**Cognitive Vulnerability (CT).** Individual ways of thinking that predispose one to particular psychological distress.

**Collaborative Empiricism (CT).** A strategy of seeing the patient as a scientist capable of objective interpretation.

**Collective Unconscious (AP).** The part of the unconscious that is universal in humans, in contrast to the personal unconscious belonging to individual experience. The contents of the collective unconscious come into consciousness through archetypal images or basic motifs common to all people. *See also* Personal Unconscious.

**Complex (AP).** An energy-filled cluster of emotions and ideas circling a specific subject. A complex has an archetypal core but expresses aspects of the personal unconscious. Jung's discovery and explanation of the complex lent validity to Freud's belief in the personal unconscious.

**Conditional Assumption (CT).** An erroneous "if-then" interpretation of events that leads to an erroneous conclusion (e.g., "*If* one person dislikes me, *then* I am not likable").

**Confluence (GT).** A state in which the contact boundary becomes so thin, flexible, and permeable that the distinction between self and environment is lost. In confluence, one does not experience self as distinct but merges self into the beliefs, attitudes, and feelings of others. Confluence can be healthy or unhealthy.

**Congruence (PC).** Agreement between the feelings and attitudes a therapist is experiencing and his or her professional demeanor; one of Rogers's necessary and sufficient conditions for therapeutic change. *See also* Genuineness.

**Conjoint Session (FT).** Psychotherapy in which two or more patients are treated together.

**Constructivism (FT).** The view that emphasizes the subjective ways in which each individual creates a perception of reality.

**Contact (GT).** Basic unit of relationship involving an experience of the boundary between "me" and "not-me"; feeling a connection with the "not-me" while maintaining a separation from it.

**Convenient Fiction (EXP).** A philosophy of science phase signifying concepts that are imaginary and unreal, but that may be helpful in conceptualization.

**Conviction.** Conclusion based on personal experience and perceptions, usually biased because each person's perspective is unique.

**Coping Imagery (MM).** A technique that pairs relaxation with images of successful self-control in situations that previously elicited anxiety.

**Counterconditioning (BT).** Replacing a particular behavior by conditioning a new response incompatible with the maladaptive behavior. Counterconditioning is one of the explanations for the effectiveness of systematic desensitization.

**Countertransference (PA, AP).** The activation of unconscious wishes and fantasies on the part of the therapist toward the patient. It can either be elicited by and indicative of the patient's projections or come from the therapist's tendency to respond to patients as though they were significant others in the life, history, or fantasy of the therapist.

**Courage (AD).** Willingness to take risks without being sure of the consequences; necessary for effective living.

**Cybernetic Epistemology (FT).** A framework for conceptualizing and analyzing what is being observed in terms of the flow of information through a system.

**Cybernetic System (FT).** The study of methods of feedback control within a system.

**Decatastrophizing (CT, REBT).** A "what if" technique designed to explore actual, rather than feared, events and consequences.

**Decentering (CT).** Moving the supposed focus of attention away from oneself.

**Decision (EXP).** The bridge between wishing for something and taking action to see that it happens; often difficult to make because every "yes" choice means saying "no" to another possibility.

**Deconstructionism.** A theory of literary criticism that challenges many of the prevailing assumptions of psychotherapy. Therapists influenced by deconstructionism attempt to "deconstruct" the ideological biases and traditional assumptions that shape the practice of psychotherapy. Like postmodernism, deconstructionism rejects all claims of ultimate truth.

**Deeper Potentials (EXP).** Personality qualities and possibilities for experiencing that have little connection with manifest behavior.

**Defense Mechanism (PA).** Method mobilized by the ego in response to its danger signal of anxiety as protection from inner and outer threat. Examples include repression, denial, and projection.

**Deflection (GT).** A means of blunting the impact of contact and awareness by not giving or receiving feelings or thoughts directly. Vagueness, verbosity, and understatement are forms of deflection.

**Dementia Praecox.** An obsolete term for schizophrenia.

**Denial (PA).** A basic defense through which aspects of experienced reality are treated as if they did not exist; often directed against personal existential death anxieties.

**Determinism.** The assumption that every mental event is causally tied to earlier psychological experience.

**Dialogue (EXT, GT).** Genuine, equal, and honest communication between two people; the "I-Thou" relationship.

**Dichotomous Thinking (CT, REBT).** Categorizing experiences or people in black-and-white or extreme terms only (e.g., all good vs. all bad), with no middle ground.

**Dichotomy (GT).** A split in which a field is experienced as comprising competing and unrelated forces that cannot be meaningfully integrated into a whole.

**Differentiation of Self (FT).** Psychological separation by a family member, increasing resistance to being overwhelmed by the emotional reactivity of the family.

**Director (PD).** The person who manages a psychodrama scene, usually the therapist.

**Discriminative Stimulus (BT).** A stimulus signifying that reinforcement will (or will not) occur.

**Disengaged Family (FT).** A family whose members are psychologically isolated from one another because of overly rigid boundaries between the participants.

**Disorientation.** Inability to correctly identify time and place (e.g., dates and locations).

**Double (PD).** The auxiliary role that involves playing the protagonist's inner self or what the protagonist might be feeling or thinking but not expressing outwardly. *See also* Auxiliary.

**Double Bind (FT).** Conflict created in a person who receives contradictory messages in an important relationship, but is forbidden to leave or escape from the relationship or to comment on the discrepancy.

**Drama Therapy (PD).** Use of theater techniques to gain self-awareness or increase self-expression in groups.

**Dramaturgical Metaphor (PD).** Framing situations as if they were like scenes in a play, which helps to include and more effectively describe vividly the range of psychosocial phenomena that are difficult to describe in more prosaic or abstract terms.

**Dual-Instinct Theory (PA).** The notion that humans operate primarily in terms of pervasive and innate drives toward both love and aggression. *See also* Eros, Thanatos.

**Dyadic (FT).** Pertaining to a relationship between two persons.

**Dynamics (PA).** Interactions, usually conflicted, between one's basic drives or id and the ego's defenses. *See also* Psychodynamics.

**Dysarthria.** Speech deficit involving difficulty with the mechanical production of language.

**Early Recollection (AD).** Salient memory of a single incident from childhood; used as a projective technique by Adlerian therapists.

**Eclecticism.** The practice of drawing from multiple and diverse sources in formulating client problems and devising treatment plans. Multimodal therapists are technical eclectics (e.g., they employ multiple methods without necessarily endorsing the theoretical positions from which they were derived).

**Ego (PA).** The central controlling core of the personality mediating between the *id* (primitive, instinctive needs) and the *superego* (civilized, moralistic elements of the mind).

**Eigenwelt (EXT).** One level of the way each individual relates to the world. *Eigenwelt* literally means "own world" and refers to the way each of us relates to self.

**Electra Complex (PA).** Erotic attraction of the female child for her father, with accompanying hostility for her mother; the female equivalent of the Oedipus complex. *See also* Oedipus Complex.

**Elegant Solution (REBT).** Solution that helps clients make a profound philosophical change that goes beyond mere symptom removal.

**Emotional Cognition (PA).** The means by which, both consciously and unconsciously, we perceive and process emotionally charged information and meaning in the service of adaptation.

**Emotive Techniques (REBT).** Therapy techniques that are vigorous, vivid, and dramatic.

**Empathic Understanding (PC).** The ability to appreciate a person's phenomenological position and to accompany the person's progress in therapy; one of the necessary conditions for therapeutic change.

**Empathy (PC).** Accurately and deeply feeling someone else's expressed emotions, concerns, or situation.

**Empty Chair (PD).** A chair whose inhabitant is imagined by a client, with all the client's projected attitudes. The imaginary occupant might be a significant person in the client's life, a figure from a dream, a part of the client's body or mind, or even the therapist. The chair is usually used along with role reversal, and the term "shuttling" is used to describe the client's moving back and forth between the chairs as the two parts engage in an encounter. *See also* Encounter, Role Reversal.

**Enactment (PD).** Showing (rather than verbalizing) a situation that deserves to be explored.

**Encounter (PD).** A dialogue between two persons, or two aspects of the same person, either in reality or with one part played by someone else.

**Encounter Group.** A small number of people who meet (sometimes only once, sometimes on a weekly basis for a specified time) to truly know and accept themselves and others.

**Enmeshed Family (FT).** Family in which individual members are overly involved in each other's lives, making individual autonomy impossible.

**Eros (PA).** The life instinct, fueled by libidinal energy and opposed by Thanatos, the death instinct. *See also* Libido, Thanatos.

**Existential Isolation (EXT).** Fundamental and inevitable separation of each individual from others and the world; it can be reduced but never completely eliminated.

**Existentialism (EXT).** A philosophical movement that stresses the importance of actual existence, one's responsibility for and determination of one's own psychological existence, authenticity in human relations, the primacy of the here and now, and the use of experience in the search for knowledge.

**Existential Neurosis (EXT).** Feelings of emptiness, worthlessness, despair, and anxiety resulting from inauthenticity, abdication of responsibility, failure to make choices, and a lack of direction or purpose in life.

**Experiencing (PC).** Sensing or awareness of self and the world, whether narrowly and rigidly or openly and flexibly. Experience is unique for each person.

**Experiential Actualization (EXP).** Manifest expression of personality qualities, characteristics, and potentialities that are deeper in the structure of personality.

**Experiential Change (EXP).** A method of therapeutic change emphasizing heightened intensity and fullness of feeling.

**Experiential Family Therapist (FT).** A therapist who reveals himself or herself as a real person and uses that self in interacting with families.

**Extinction (BT).** In classical conditioning, the result of repeated presentation of a conditioned stimulus without the unconditioned stimulus and the resulting gradual diminution of the conditioned response. In operant conditioning, extinction (no response) occurs when reinforcement is withheld following performance of a previously reinforced response.

**Facilitator.** An individual who aids a group in going the direction they choose and accomplishing their chosen goals without doing harm to any member.

**Family Constellation (AD).** The number, sequencing, and characteristics of the members of a family. The family constellation is an important determinant of life-style.

**Family Sculpting (FT, PD).** A nonverbal technique to be used by individual family members for physically arranging other family members in space to represent the arranger's symbolic view of family relationships.

**Feedback.** The process by which a system makes adjustments in itself; can be negative (reestablishing equilibrium) or positive (leading to change).

**Field Theory (GT).** A theory about the nature of reality and our relationship to reality, in which our experiences are understood within a specific context. A field is composed of mutually interdependent elements, and changes in the field influence how a person experiences reality. No one can transcend embeddedness in a field, and therefore no one can have an objective perspective on reality.

**First-Order Change (FT).** Change within a system that does not alter the basic organization of the system itself.

**Formative Tendency (PC).** An overall inclination toward greater order, complexity, and interrelatedness common to all nature, including human beings.

**Free Association (PA).** A basic technique of psychoanalysis in which analysands are asked to report, without structure or censure, whatever thoughts come to mind.

**Fusion (EXT, FT).** In existential therapy, the giving up of oneself to become part of another person or a group; a particular attempt to reduce one's sense of isolation. In family therapy, a blurring of boundaries between family members with the resultant loss of a separate sense of self by each member.

**Future Projection (PD).** Demonstration of what one sees going on in life at some specified time in the future.

**Gemeinschaftsgefühl (AD).** A combination of concern for others and appreciation of one's role in a larger social order; usually translated as "social interest."

**Generalization (BT).** The occurrence of behavior in situations that resemble but are different from the stimulus environment in which the behavior was learned.

**Genital Stage (PA).** The final stage in psychosexual development, also termed the oedipal phase, in which heterosexual relations are achieved. Its roots are formed at ages five to six, and it is said to be the basis for the mature personality.

**Genogram (FT).** A schematic diagram of a family's relationship system, used to trace recurring family patterns over generations.

**Genuineness (PC).** The characteristic of being real and true to oneself; lack of pretense, social facade, or refusal to allow certain aspects of one's self into awareness.

**Gestalt (GT).** A word with no literal English translation, referring to a perceptual whole or a unified configuration of experience.

**Graded-Task Assignment (CT, BT).** Starting with a simple activity and increasing the level of complexity or difficulty in a step-by-step fashion.

**Hidden Agenda.** The actual goal of an interaction between people (as in a game), which is different from what superficially appears to be the goal.

**Holism (AD).** Studying individuals in their entirety, including how they proceed through life, rather than trying to separate out certain aspects or parts, such as studying the mind apart from the body.

**Homeostasis.** A balanced and steady state of equilibrium.

**Homework (REBT, BT).** Specific activities to be done between therapy sessions.

**Hot Cognition (CT).** A powerful and highly meaningful idea that produces strong emotional reactions.

**Hysteria.** An early term for conversion reaction, a disorder in which psychological disturbance takes a physical form (e.g., paralysis in the absence of organic disturbance). Many of Freud's theories grew out of his experience in treating hysterical patients.

**Id (PA).** The reservoir of the biological, instinctual drives with innate and developmental components. *See also* Ego, Superego.

**Identification (PA).** A mental mechanism, used unconsciously in normal interactions and as a psychic defense, through which one person absorbs and takes on the traits, values, and defenses of another person.

**Identified Patient (FT).** The person who seeks treatment or for whom treatment is sought.

**Imagery Reactor (MM).** An individual who responds to the environment predominantly in terms of images, usually auditory or visual.

**Inclusion (GT).** Putting oneself as completely as possible into another's experience without judging or evaluating, while still maintaining a separate sense of self.

**Individual Psychology (AD).** An approach to understanding human behavior that sees each person as a unique, whole entity who is constantly becoming rather than being and one whose development can only be understood within a social context.

**Individuation (AP).** The process by which an individual becomes an indivisible and integrated whole person responsibly embodying his or her individual strengths and limitations.

**Inferiority Complex (AD).** An exaggeration of feelings of inadequacy and insecurity resulting in defensiveness and neurotic behavior. It is usually, but not always, abnormal.

**Inferiority Feeling (AD).** Seeing oneself as inadequate or incompetent in comparison with others, with one's ideal self, or with personal values; considered universal and normal. *Contrast with* Inferiority Complex.

**Integration (EXP).** Organized and harmonious relationships among personality components.

**Intensive Group (PC).** A small number of people who come together for a brief but condensed period (e.g., a weekend) to engage in special interpersonal experiences that are designed to expand awareness of self and others.

**Interlocking Pathologies (FT).** Multiple forms of dysfunction within a family that are interdependent in the way they are expressed and maintained.

**Interlocking Triangles (FT).** Basic units of family relationships consisting of a series of three-person sets of interactions (e.g., father-mother-child; grandparent-parent-child).

**Internal Frame of Reference (PC).** A view or perception of both the world and self as seen by the individual, as distinguished from the viewpoint of an observer, psychotherapist, or other person.

**Intrapsychic.** Within the mind or psyche of the individual.

**Introject (FT).** Internalized object from one's past that affects current relationships.

**Introjection (PA, GT).** In psychoanalysis, an unconscious process of identifying with other persons, real or imagined, by incorporating attributes of these others into oneself. In gestalt therapy, accepting information or values from the outside without evaluation; not necessarily psychologically unhealthy.

**Irrational Belief (REBT).** Unreasonable conviction that produces emotional upset (for example, insisting that the world should or must be different from what it actually is).

**Isolation (GT).** A state in which the contact boundary is so thick, rigid, and impermeable that the psychological connection between self and environment is lost, and the person does not allow access from or to the outside. Isolation can be healthy or unhealthy. *Contrast with* Withdrawal.

**Latency Period (PA).** A relatively inactive period of psychosexual development said to begin around age six and end around age 11.

**Leaning Tower of Pisa Approach (FT).** A variation of paradoxical intention in which a therapist intentionally makes a problem worse until it falls of its own weight and is thereby resolved.

**Libido (PA).** The basic driving force of personality in Freud's system. It includes sexual energy but is not restricted to it.

**Life-style (AD).** One's characteristic way of living and pursuing long-term goals.

**Life Tasks (AD).** The basic challenges and obligations of life: society, work, and sex. The additional tasks of spiritual growth and self-identity are included by Rudolf Dreikurs and Harold Mosak.

**Linear Causality (FT).** The view that one event causes the other, not vice versa.

**Locus of Evaluation (PC).** The place of a judgment's origin, its source; whether the appraisal of an experience comes more from within the individual (internal) or from outside sources (external).

**Logotherapy (EXT).** A therapeutic approach developed by Viktor Frankl emphasizing value and meaning as prerequisites for mental health and personal growth.

**Magnification (CT).** Exaggerating something's significance.

**Marital Schism (FT).** A disturbed family arrangement characterized by disharmony, undermining of the spouse, and frequent threats of divorce. *See also* Marital Skew.

**Marital Skew (FT).** A disturbed family arrangement in which one person dominates to an extreme degree, and in which the marriage is maintained through the distortion of reality. *See also* Marital Schism.

**Mediational Stimulus-Response Model (BT).** A behavioral model that posits internal events, such as thoughts and images, as links between perceiving a stimulus and making a response.

**Meta-role (PD).** The functional role that chooses which social roles are most appropriate to play in a given situation and decides how to play them. It is a dynamic mixture of self-observation and investigation, as well as other mature self-management functions. Also known by other terms such as "choosing self" or "executive ego." Part of Role Dynamics, a systematized form of applied role theory, with its roots in Moreno's psychodrama.

**Minimization (CT).** Making an event far less important than it actually is.

**Mirror (PD).** Person who imitates a client's behavior and demeanor so that the client can more clearly see him- or herself in action.

**Mitwelt (EXT).** The way in which each individual relates to the world, socially and through being with others; the age we live in, our age, our own times, the present generation, our contemporaries.

**Modality Profile (MM).** A specific list of problems and proposed treatments across the client's BASIC I.D.

**Mode (CT).** Network of cognitive, affective, motivational, and behavioral schema that composes personality and interprets ongoing situations.

**Monadic (FT).** Based on the characteristics or traits of a single person.

**Monodrama (PD, GT).** One client's playing both parts in a scene by alternating between them.

**Multigenerational Transmission Process (FT).** The passing on of psychological problems over generations as a result of immature persons marrying others with similar low levels of separateness from their families.

**Multiple Ego (PD).** A technique in which several different roles within the client encounter each other.

**Multiple Psychotherapy (AD).** A technique in which several therapists simultaneously treat a single patient.

**Musturbation (REBT).** A term coined by Albert Ellis to characterize the behavior of clients who are absolutistic and inflexible in their thinking, maintaining that they *must* not fail, *must* be exceptional, *must* be successful, and so on.

**Mystification (FT).** The deliberate distortion of another person's experience by misinterpreting or mislabeling it.

**Narcissism (PA).** Self-absorption, self-concern, and self-love arising from psychic energy directed at the self; the term currently is used to include tension regulation, self-image, and self-esteem.

**Negative Feedback (FT).** The flow of output information back into a system to correct too great a deviation from normal and return the system to its steady state.

**Negative Reinforcement (BT).** Any behavior that increases the probability of a response by terminating or withdrawing an unpleasant stimulus. Negative reinforcement increases the likelihood of future occurrence of the behavior it follows.

**Neurosis (PA).** A term first used by Freud to include all but the most severe psychological syndromes; currently narrowly defined as an emotional disorder in which psychic functioning is relatively intact and contact with reality is sound.

**Neurotic Anxiety (EXT).** A state of fear or apprehension out of proportion to an actual threat. Neurotic anxiety is destructive or paralyzing and cannot be used constructively. *Compare with* Normal Anxiety.

**Normal Anxiety (EXT).** A sense of apprehension appropriate to a given threatening situation, which can be faced, dealt with, and used creatively. *Compare with* Neurotic Anxiety.

**Object Relations Theory (PA, FT).** The view that the basic human motive is the search for satisfying object (person) relationships.

**Oedipus Complex (PA).** Erotic attraction of the male child for his mother, accompanied by hostility toward the father. *See also* Electra Complex.

**Ontological (EXT).** Concerned with the science of being or existence.

**Open System (FT).** A system with relatively permeable boundaries permitting the exchange of information with its environment.

**Operant Conditioning (BT).** A type of learning in which responses are modified by their consequences. Reinforcement increases the likelihood of future occurrences of the reinforced response; punishment and extinction decrease the likelihood of future occurrences of the responses they follow.

**Operating Potentials for Experiencing (EXP).** Personality qualities that have direct connections with manifest behavior.

**Oral Phase (PA).** The earliest phase of psychosexual development, extending from birth to approximately 18 months, in which most libidinal gratification occurs through biting, sucking, and oral contact.

**Organ Inferiority (AD).** Perceived or actual congenital defects in organ systems believed by Alfred Adler to result in compensatory striving to overcome these deficits.

**Organismic Valuing Process (PC).** Making individual judgments or assessments of the desirability of an action or choice on the basis of one's own sensory evidence and life experience.

**Overgeneralization (CT, REBT).** Constructing a general rule from isolated incidents and applying it too broadly.

**Panacea.** A remedy for all diseases and difficulties; a cure-all.

**Paradigm.** A set of assumptions limiting an area to be investigated scientifically and specifying the methods used to collect and interpret the forthcoming data.

**Paradigm Shift.** A significant and widespread change in the concepts, values, perceptions, and practices that define a community or a structured activity (e.g., psychotherapy).

**Paradoxical Intervention (FT).** A therapeutic technique whereby the patient is directed to continue the symptomatic behavior. To comply is to admit voluntary control over the symptom; to rebel is to give up the symptom.

**Paradoxical Theory of Change. (GT).** A theory of change that is based on a paradox: The more one tries to be who one is not, the more one stays the same; the more one tries to stay the same in a changing world, the more one changes relative to the world. When a person knows and accepts himself or herself, maximum growth can occur. When one rejects oneself, e.g., by forcing oneself beyond one's support, growth is hindered by internal conflict.

**Paraphilias.** Unusual or atypical sexual behaviors that are thought to have clinical relevance. The major paraphilias include exhibitionism, fetishism, frotteurism, pedophilia, sexual masochism, sexual sadism, transvestic fetishism, and voyeurism.

**Persona (AP).** A mask or way of appearing that is appropriate to a specific role or social setting. It both shields an individual and reveals suitable aspects of the personality, but is often at variance with the personality as a whole.

**Personal Unconscious (AP).** An individual unconscious layer of the personality containing undeveloped parts of the personality, repressed ideas, experiences, emotions, and subliminal perceptions. *See also* Collective Unconscious.

**Personalization (CT).** Taking personal responsibility for negative events without supporting evidence of personal involvement.

**Phallic Phase (PA).** A psychosexual phase in boys of ages three to five in which penile experiences and fantasies of thrusting and exhibiting are predominant. The comparable phase in girls is termed the vaginal phase. *See also* Vaginal Phase.

**Phenomenology (AD, EXT, GT).** A method of exploration that primarily uses human experience as the source of data and attempts to include all human experience without bias (external observation, emotions, thoughts, and so on). Subjects are taught to distinguish between current experience and the biases brought to the situation. Phenomenology is the basic method of most existentialists.

**Placebo.** In medicine, placebos are inert substances given to patients in place of bona fide medications. In psychotherapy, placebos are most often sham treatments used in research to control for the nonspecific effects of attention.

**Pleasure Principle (PA).** The basic human tendency to avoid pain and seek pleasure, especially salient in the first years of life. *Contrast with* Reality Principle.

**Positive Feedback (FT).** The flow of output information back into the system in order to amplify deviation from a steady state, thus leading to instability and change.

**Positive Reinforcement (BT).** Any stimulus that follows a behavior and increases the likelihood of the occurrence of the behavior that it follows.

**Postmodern Therapies (GT).** Any approach to therapy that recognizes the validity and assumptions of multiple realities while rejecting the primacy of the worldview of the therapist. Postmodern therapies stress the importance of culture in determining reality and emphasize the influence of language and power relationships in shaping and defining psychopathology.

**Projection (PA, AP).** Attributing to others unacceptable personal thoughts, feelings, or behaviors.

**Projective Identification (PA).** An interactional form of projection, used both normally and as a defense, through which one person places into another person his or her inner state and defenses.

**Protagonist (PD).** In psychodrama, the term used for the client whose situation is being explored, who is also usually the main player in the role-playing process.

**Pseudohostility (FT).** Superficial bickering that allows one to avoid dealing with deeper, more genuine, and more intimate feelings.

**Pseudomutuality (FT).** A facade of family harmony that gives the appearance of an open and satisfying relationship that does not truly exist.

**Psychodrama (PD).** A method of psychotherapy developed by J. L. Moreno in the mid-1930s, in which clients role-play their problems.

**Psychodramatic Methods (PD).** Also called action techniques, experiential exercises, or role-playing techniques, these are specific techniques derived from psychodrama that can be integrated with other therapeutic approaches, whether in group, family, couples, or individual therapy.

**Psychodynamics (PA).** A term similar to dynamics, which refers to mental interactions and conflict, usually formulated in terms of ego, id, and superego. *See also* Dynamics.

**Psychological Masquerade.** Apparent psychological symptoms actually caused by physical or organic conditions.

**Punishment (BT).** An aversive event likely to terminate any behavior that it follows.

**Reality.** An individual's private world, but more generally, a group of perceptions or "facts" with substantial consensus about their meaning.

**Reality Principle (PA).** The guiding principle of the ego, which permits postponement of gratification to meet the demands of the environment or secure greater pleasure at a later time. *Contrast with* Pleasure Principle.

**Reattribution (CT).** Assigning alternative causes to events; reinterpreting one's symptoms.

**Redundancy Principle (FT).** Repetitive behavioral sequences between participants, as within a family.

**Reframing (FT).** Relabeling behavior by putting it into a new, more positive perspective.

**Regression (PA).** Variously defined as an active or passive slipping back to more immature levels of defense or functioning, or seeking gratification from earlier phases of development.

**Reinforcement (BT).** The presentation of a reward or the removal of an aversive stimulus following a response. Reinforcement always increases the future probability of the reinforced response.

**Replay (PD, BT).** A psychodramatic technique, often used in behavior therapy and other approaches, in which the client repeats a previous scene. It is often applied in the mastery of interpersonal skills.

**Repression (PA).** A major defense mechanism in which distressing thoughts are barred from conscious expression.

**Resistance (PA, GT).** In psychoanalysis, any obstacle, pathological or nonpathological, to the progress of an analysis or therapy, usually involving a modification of a ground rule of treatment and based on unconscious sources within both patient and analyst (i.e., interactionally determined). In gestalt therapy, the reluctance of people to know, show, or own aspects of themselves. Resistance can be healthy or unhealthy.

**Respondent Conditioning (BT).** *See* Classical Conditioning.

**Retroflection (GT).** A contact boundary disturbance in which a person substitutes self for the environment and does to self what he or she originally did or tried to do to others. Retroflection is the chief mechanism of isolation and is not necessarily unhealthy.

**Role Playing (PD).** Acting the part of oneself or someone else under therapeutic guidance. Also used to describe a process equivalent to psychodrama. (The term has now come to be used also as a way of problem exploration in many other therapies, as well as in education and business.)

**Role Reversal (PD).** In psychodrama, the dropping of the point of view of one's own role and taking on the attitudes and physical position and perspective of the other person in an interaction. A plays B and B plays A. Or sometimes, if the actual other person isn't present, A takes the role of whoever he imagines B to be, using an empty chair, thus opening his mind to a deeper level of empathy. *See also* Empty Chair.

**Scapegoating (FT).** Casting a person in a role that unfairly exposes him or her to criticism, blame, or punishment.

**Schema (CT).** Strategy or way of thinking comprising core beliefs and basic assumptions about how the world operates.

**Second-Order BASIC I.D. (MM).** Focusing on a particular aspect of the BASIC I.D. to get more detailed information; useful for diagnosis and for breaking impasses in therapy.

**Second-Order Change (FT).** Fundamental change in a system's organization and function.

**Selection Abstraction (CT).** Basing a conclusion on a detail taken out of context and ignoring other information.

**Self-Actualization.** A basic human drive toward growth, completeness, and fulfillment.

**Self-Concept.** One's own definition of who one is, including one's attributes, emotions, abilities, character, faults, and so on.

**Self-Instructional Training (BT).** A technique, described most completely by Donald Meichenbaum, for replacing self-defeating thoughts with self-enhancing cognitions.

**Self-Regard (PC).** That aspect of the self-concept that develops from the esteem or respect accorded oneself.

**Sensate Focus (BT).** A series of exercises used in sex therapy designed to reintroduce clients to receiving and giving sensual pleasure.

**Sensory Reactor (MM).** An individual who interacts with the world primarily in terms of the five basic senses.

**Shadow (AP).** Unconscious, unaccepted, or unrecognized parts of the personality that are most often, but not always, negative.

**Sharing (PD).** The third phase of a psychodramatic enactment in which other group members in the audience and even auxiliaries share how that role playing may have touched on similar or related events in their own lives—in contrast to giving advice, interpretations, or analysis.

**Social Interest (AD).** The feeling of being part of a social whole; the need and willingness to contribute to the general social good. *See also* Gemeinschaftsgefühl.

**Social Learning Theory (BT).** A system that combines operant and classical conditioning with cognitive mediational processes (e.g., vicarious learning and symbolic activity) to account for the development, maintenance, and modification of behavior.

**Sociometry (PD).** A method in which groups give feedback about their interpersonal preferences (e.g., attraction or repulsion).

**Sociotrophy (CT).** A personality dimension characterized by dependency on interpersonal relationships and needs for closeness and nurturance.

**Socratic Dialogue (CT).** A series of questions designed to arrive at logical answers to and conclusions about a hypothesis.

**Splitting (PA, GT).** In psychoanalysis, a primitive defense through which persons are classified as all-good or all-bad individuals, making it impossible to have a full and balanced picture of other people. In gestalt therapy, a situation in which a person splits off part of him- or herself as a polar opposite. The individual is aware of one pole and oblivious to the other. For example, an individual may split into competent and incompetent selves and vacillate between these roles. A split is one form of a dichotomy.

**Spontaneity.** A frame of mind enabling one to address situations afresh, often with a significant measure of improvisation.

**Stimulus Control (BT).** Arranging the environment in such a way that a given response is either more likely or less likely to occur (e.g., buying only one pack of cigarettes per day in order to decrease the likelihood of smoking).

**Strategic Intervention Therapy (FT).** An approach to family therapy employing specific strategies, plans, and tactics to force changes in behavior.

**Structuralism (FT).** An approach to family therapy, associated with Salvador Minuchin, that emphasizes the importance of the nuclear family and seeks to change pathological alliances and splits in the family.

**Structuralist (FT).** A therapist who emphasizes changing or realigning a family's organizational structure to improve its transactional patterns.

**Structural Profiles (MM).** A quantitative assessment of the relative involvement of each of the elements of the BASIC I.D.

**Structural Theory or Hypothesis (PA).** Freud's second model of the mind. The model postulates three agencies of the mind—ego, superego, and id—each with conscious and unconscious components. *See also* Id, Ego, *and* Superego.

**Stuck-Togetherness (FT).** A situation observed in schizophrenic families in which roles and boundaries are blurred and no family member has an identity distinct from the family.

**Subjective Reasoning (CT).** Believing that feelings are the same as, or equivalent to, facts.

**Subsystem (FT).** An organized component within an overall system, such as a family.

**Superego (PA).** A structure of the mind, developed from innate tendencies and early parental interactions and identifications, that embraces moral and other standards and regulates psychic tensions, self-image, self-esteem, and drive-discharge. *See also* Ego, Id.

**Support (GT).** To provide the psychological, physiological, social, or material aid needed to initiate, terminate, regulate, and maintain contact or withdrawal as needed by the person or the environment. People are self-supporting to the degree that they are the chief agents in initiating, terminating, regulating, and maintaining contact/withdrawal and do so based on self-identification. For example, knowing what one wants and being able to ask for it appropriately is self-supporting.

**Surplus Reality (PD).** Psychological experiences involving other than physical reality (e.g., spiritual events, a relationship with a significant deceased other).

**Survival.** An innate need, drive, and source of human behavior. It leads human beings to seek health, nutrition, and protection from physical danger.

**Symbiosis (FT).** A relationship in which two people, often a mother and her child, become so intertwined that it is impossible to find a boundary between them.

**Symbolization (PC).** A process of allowing a life event or experience into one's consciousness or awareness and interpreting it in terms of the self-concept; it may be straightforward, distorted, or prohibited altogether.

**Synthesis.** Making a whole from elements or parts; constructing the overall meaning of a situation from many different aspects of it.

**System.** A complete unit made up of interconnected and interdependent parts operating in a stable way over time.

**Systematic Desensitization (BT).** A step-by-step procedure for replacing anxiety with relaxation while gradually increasing exposure to an anxiety-producing situation or object.

**Tele (PD).** Moreno's term for dynamic of rapport or interpersonal preference. It is what is measured by the social psychological or group method called sociometry. *See also* Sociometry.

**Thanatos (PA).** An instinct toward death and self-destruction, posited by Freud to oppose and balance Eros, the life instinct.

**Third-Party Payer.** Financial intermediary that controls payment to therapists. In therapy, third-party payers are usually insurance companies or government agencies.

**Token Economy (BT).** A program that provides people with short-term reinforcement for specific behaviors by allotting tokens (poker chips or points) that are accumulated and later exchanged for privileges or desired objects.

**Topographic Theory (PA).** Freud's first model of the mind in which access to awareness of contents and functions was the defining criterion. The model had interactional elements, but was eventually replaced by Freud's structural model. *See also* Unconscious.

**Tracking (MM).** A careful examination of the firing order of the BASIC I.D. modalities to facilitate more effective sequencing of the treatment procedures.

**Trait Theory.** The belief in stable and enduring personality characteristics.

**Transference (PA, AP).** The therapy situation in which the patient responds to the therapist as though he or she were a significant figure in the patient's past, usually a parent. *See also* Countertransference.

**Triadic (FT).** Pertaining to a relationship involving the interaction of three or more persons.

**Trust (PC).** Basic faith in oneself and others as being growth-directed and positively oriented.

**Two-chair Technique (GT).** An affective, experiential procedure in which the client engages in dialogue with another person (or with another part of the self) symbolically represented by an empty chair. The client may assume different roles by switching from one chair to the other.

**Umwelt (EXT).** A way of relating to the world through its biological and physical aspects; one's relationship with nature and the surrounding world.

**Unconditional Positive Regard (PC).** A nonpossessive caring and acceptance of the client as a human being, irrespective of the therapist's own values. One of Rogers's necessary and sufficient conditions for therapeutic change.

**Unconscious (PA, AP).** A division of the psyche; the repository of psychological material of which the individual is unaware.

**Vaginal Phase (PA).** The phase in girls that corresponds to boys' phallic phase, ages three to five, during which vaginal sensations and incorporative imagery predominate.

**Vicarious Learning (BT).** Learning through observation and imitation; a synonym for modeling.

**Warming-Up (PD).** The process of becoming more spontaneous, often associated with a relaxation of self-consciousness, anxiety, a higher level of trust, and an increasing degree of involvement in the task at hand.

**Warmth (PC).** Positive and real feelings of acceptance toward another person.

**Will to Power (AD).** Individual striving for superiority and dominance in order to overcome feelings of inadequacy and inferiority.

**Withdrawal (GT).** Temporary withdrawing from contact while maintaining a permeable contact boundary. Withdrawal can be healthy or unhealthy. *Contrast with* Isolation.

**Work (GT).** The process of exploring by phenomenological focusing in order to increase awareness. One can work in any setting and can focus on any theme (here and now contact, life problems, developmental themes, spiritual concerns, creativity and emotional expansion, dreams, belief systems, etc.)

**Zeitgeist.** The spirit of the times; the prevailing cultural climate.

# CREDITS

This page constitutes an extension of the copyright page. We have made every effort to trace the ownership of all copyrighted material and to secure permission from copyright holders. In the event of any question arising as to the use of any material, we will be pleased to make the necessary corrections in future printings. Thanks are due to the following authors, publishers, and agents for permission to use the material indicated.

Chapter 2.  15: © Bettmann/CORBIS
Chapter 3.  52: © Bettmann/CORBIS
Chapter 4.  96: © Bettmann/CORBIS 108: © Werner Forman/CORBIS
Chapter 5.  130: © Bettmann/CORBIS
Chapter 6.  166: Courtesy of Dr. Albert Ellis, Albert Ellis Institute
Chapter 7.  202: far left, © Bettmann/CORBIS 202: center left, © Bettmann/CORBIS 202: center right, Courtesy of Professor Joseph Wolpe 202: far right, The Psychology Archives, University of Akron.
Chapter 8.  238: Courtesy of Aaron T. Beck, PhD, University of Pennsylvania
Chapter 9.  269: left, Courtesy of Professor Rollo May 269: right, Courtesy of Professor Irvin Yalom
Chapter 10.  299: Courtesy The Gestalt Journal Press
Chapter 11.  337: Courtesy of Dr. Arnold A. Lazarus
Chapter 12.  372: far left, Courtesy of Dr. Murray Bowen 372: center left, Courtesy of Nathan Ackerman 372: center right, Courtesy of Professor Carl Whitaker 372: far right, Courtesy of Dr. Salvador Minuchin, The Minuchin Center
Chapter 13.  405: Courtesy of Stanford University News and Publications Service
Chapter 14.  439: Courtesy of Professor Al Mahrer

# NAME INDEX

] Family Therapy

# SUBJECT INDEX

TO THE OWNER OF THIS BOOK:

I hope that you have found *Current Psychotherapies*, Seventh Edition, useful. So that this book can be improved in a future edition, would you take the time to complete this sheet and return it? Thank you.

School and address:_____

Department:_____

Instructor's name:_____

1.  What I like most about this book is:_____

_____

_____

2.  What I like least about this book is:

_____

_____

3.  My general reaction to this book is:

_____

_____

4.  The name of the course in which I used this book is:

_____

5.  Were all of the chapters of the book assigned for you to read?_____

    If not, which ones weren't?_____

6.  In the space below, or on a separate sheet of paper, please write specific suggestions for improving this book and anything else you'd care to share about your experience in using this book.

_____

_____

_____

_____

**THOMSON**

**BROOKS/COLE** ™

## BUSINESS REPLY MAIL

FIRST-CLASS MAIL     PERMIT NO. 34     BELMONT CA

POSTAGE WILL BE PAID BY ADDRESSEE

Attn: Counseling/Amy Lam

BrooksCole/Thomson Learning
10 Davis Dr
Belmont CA  94002-9801

OPTIONAL:

Your name: _____     Date: _____

May we quote you, either in promotion for *Current Psychotherapies*, Seventh Edition, or in future publishing ventures?

Yes: _____     No: _____

Sincerely yours,

Raymond Corsini

Danny Wedding